Cape Cod
and the Islands

AN EXPLORER'S GUIDE

Chappaquiddick

Cape Cod
and the Islands

AN EXPLORER'S GUIDE
SECOND EDITION

KIMBERLY GRANT
with photographs by the author

The Countryman Press
Woodstock, Vermont

Dedication

For travel writing mentors
Tom Brosnahan and Christina Tree

Library of Congress Cataloging-in-Publication Data
Grant, Kimberly.
Cape Cod and the islands: an explorer's guide/Kimberly Grant;
photographs by the author.—2nd ed.
p.   cm.
Includes indexes.
ISBN 0-88150-392-4 (alk. paper)
1. Cape Cod (Mass.)—Guidebooks. 2. Nantucket Island (Mass.)—Guidebooks.
3. Martha's Vineyard (Mass.)—Guidebooks.   I. Title.
F72.C3G72 1997
917.44'90443—dc21
96–48305
CIP

Maps by Paul Woodward, © 1995, 1997
The Countryman Press.
Book design by Glenn Suokko
Cover photograph and all interior photographs
by Kimberly Grant
Published by The Countryman Press
PO Box 748, Woodstock, Vermont 05091
Distributed by W.W. Norton & Company, Inc.,
500 Fifth Avenue, New York, New York
10110
Printed in the United States of America
10 9 8 7 6 5 4 3 2 1

Explore With Us!

Welcome to the second edition of the most comprehensive travel guide to Cape Cod, Martha's Vineyard, and Nantucket. In choosing places to lodge, dine, and visit on the Cape and the islands, I have been highly selective but broadly inclusive, based on years of repeated visits, cumulative research, and ongoing conversations with locals. All entries—attractions, inns, and restaurants—are chosen on the basis of personal experience, not paid advertising.

I hope you find the organization of this guide easy to read and use. The layout has been kept simple; the following pointers will help you get started.

WHAT'S WHERE

In the beginning of the book you'll find an alphabetical listing of special highlights and important information that you may want to reference quickly. You'll find advice on everything from where to find the best art galleries to where to hop onto bicycle trails to where to take a whale-watching excursion.

LODGING

Prices: Please don't hold us or the respective innkeepers responsible for the rates listed as of press time in 1997. Changes are inevitable. At the time of this writing, the state and local room tax was 9.7 percent. Please also see *Lodging* under "What's Where on Cape Cod and the Islands."

RESTAURANTS

In most sections, note the distinction between Dining Out and Eating Out. Restaurants listed under Eating Out are generally inexpensive and more casual; reservations are often suggested for restaurants in Dining Out. A range of prices for à la carte menu items is included with each entry.

GREEN SPACE

In addition to trains and walks, "green space" also includes white and blue spaces, that is, beaches and ponds.

KEY TO SYMBOLS

❋ The "off-season" symbol appears next to activities that are appealing in the off-season or are open year-round.

☞ The "value" symbol appears next to lodging entries, restaurants, and activities that combine exceptional quality with moderate prices.

✐ The "child and family interest" appears next to lodging entries, restaurants, activities, and shops of special appeal to youngsters and families.

I would appreciate your comments and corrections about places you discover or know well. Please address your correspondence to Explorer's Guide Editor, The Countryman Press, PO Box 748, Woodstock, VT 05091.

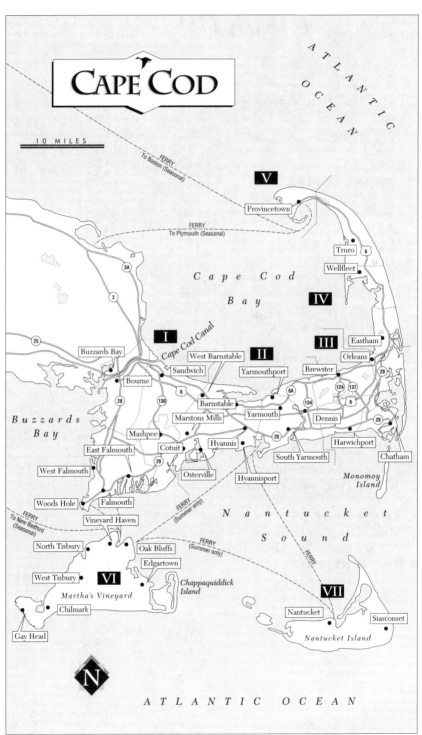

CAPE COD

10 MILES

Contents

Introduction

Welcome to the second edition of *Cape Cod and the Islands: An Explorer's Guide.* Those of you familiar with the first edition will notice in this edition: information on where to rent houses; more shops, galleries, and artisans; and a greatly expanded Martha's Vineyard chapter. This edition benefits from the accumulated knowledge that fellow explorers have shared with me, through letters and over breakfast at B&Bs.

More than 80,000 cars cross the Cape Cod Canal every day in July and August, and the ferries to Martha's Vineyard and Nantucket transport more than 2.4 million people each summer. So it would be a stretch of the imagination to say that these fragile parcels of prized real estate are undiscovered or unexplored. In fact, sometimes it seems there isn't a grain of sand that hasn't been written about or walked on by someone.

But just when I think I've seen it all, a ray of bright, clear sunlight will hit the dune shacks in Provincetown or the Gay Head cliffs on the Vineyard in such a way as to make it all seem new again. I'll strike up a conversation with Mary Hallet Clark at Hallet's in Yarmouthport, and she'll regale me with stories about her grandfather's role in town affairs at the turn of the century. I'll be walking down a trail in October that I previously walked in May and hear different birds and see different plants. Or I'll take a van tour with Gail in Nantucket, and she'll find just the right anecdote to make history jump off a ship captain's logbook.

I don't claim to "know" Cape Cod and the islands—never will. What I do claim is an ability to sift through thousands of pieces of information and present them to you in a way that will help you make confident decisions about how to spend your time and money. I hope you will agree.

In one sense, there is no lack of printed information about Cape Cod and the Islands. But the way I see it, there are a few big problems with the material. Some stem from its abundance, and many of the compilations are overwhelming and undiscriminating. (You could fill shopping bags with the stuff—trust me, I have!) Much of what passes for editorial recommendation is actually just paid advertising copy written by the establishments themselves. And finally, many of the special-interest brochures—for antiquing or kids' activities, for instance—cover the entire area. So, if you're just visiting one town or concentrating on one region, you must wade through a lot of unneeded information.

This guidebook is intended to be many things to many people. The publishers and I have set our sights to include a wide audience. This book is written for people who live close enough, or are fortunate enough, to be able to make many short trips to the Cape throughout the year—people who know that the region takes on a whole different character from Labor Day weekend to Memorial Day weekend. (It is a common misconception that the region closes down from September to May.) It will prove valuable, as well, to year-rounders who must give advice to a steady stream of summer guests. It's for Cape residents who may live in the upper Cape, but don't know much about the lower Cape. It's for people whose only trip to the Cape or the islands is their annual summer holiday—people who have always vacationed in Dennis, let's say, but are ready to explore other places. My highest hope, though, is to introduce the "other Cape and islands" to that segment of the traveling public who thinks traffic jams, crowded beaches, and tacky souvenir shops define the region.

This book is the result of years of research, conversation, observation, pleasure reading, and personal exploration. I am a Bostonian who spent youthful summer vacations on Cape Cod, bicycling at the Cape Cod National Seashore, eating saltwater taffy in Provincetown, and camping on Martha's Vineyard. My introduction to Nantucket came later, in the mid-1980s; by then I was old enough to appreciate the island's sophisticated culinary treats and rich history all the more.

Since I am also a professional photographer, I have taken all the photographs for the book. Personally, I am pleased to be able to share this visual portrait of the area in addition to my observations and recommendations. I have intentionally emphasized scenes without people; conventional wisdom already associates the Cape with masses of humanity. But the photos are proof, really, that there are beaches where you can walk alone on a sunny September day.

Traveling, and writing about it, is a nice lifestyle; there's no doubt about that and I'm grateful for the opportunity to do it. But it is work (as my friends and family, temporarily abandoned in favor of my laptop computer, will attest). The book wouldn't have been possible without the encouragement, guidance, and firsthand experience of many people who appreciate the Cape and the islands from many different perspectives.

As much as I love both four-star dining and a bucket of fried clams from a shack on the pier, I just can't eat every dish on every menu. I have called upon my innkeeper friends who benefit from the collective opinions of dozens of guests who eat in dozens of places night after night and then discuss their experiences the next morning over breakfast. Likewise, it is impossible to sleep in every room in every B&B, but I can assure you that I have personally visited and inspected every establishment in this guide.

The folks at The Countryman Press (which recently became a W.W. Norton division) epitomize everything that's good about the publishing industry. I appreciate their responsiveness to and respect for writers, as well as their commitment to providing a quality guidebook to the book-buying public. Special thanks are reserved for editor-in-chief Helen Whybrow. And thanks to Norton, for its decision to allow these *Explorer's Guides* to carry on in their great tradition.

For their local expertise and willingness to share it with me, thanks go out to Frank Schaefer in Provincetown, Jane Peters in Truro, Nan Aitchison in Eastham, the Vessellas and Johnsons in Orleans, Marie Brophy in Dennis, Valerie Butler in Yarmouth, Carol and Tom Edmondson in Brewster, Lois Nelson in Hyannis, Bill DeSouza and Glenn Faria at Destinnations in Osterville, Caroline and Jim Lloyd in Falmouth, Phil Williams Jr. in Woods Hole, Steve and Kathy Catania in Sandwich, Rusty Scheuer on Martha's Vineyard, and Sandy Knox-Johnston on Nantucket. I also appreciate the input, enthusiasm, and fact-checking provided by each town's chamber of commerce staff, as well as the Cape Cod chamber's Michael Frucci and Elaine Perry. Thanks, too, to Janice Hewins at Cape Air and Gina Barboza at the Steamship Authority.

I welcome readers' thoughtful comments, criticisms, and suggestions for the next edition of *Cape Cod and the Islands: An Explorer's Guide.*

What's Where on Cape Cod and the Islands

AIRPORTS AND AIRLINES

There is regularly scheduled air service from Boston to Provincetown. Hyannis (Barnstable County Municipal Airport) is reached by air from Boston and New York. Nantucket and Martha's Vineyard enjoy regularly scheduled year-round service; Cape Air (228-7695, 1-800-352-0714) offers the most flights. Sight-seeing by air is best done in Chatham and Provincetown.

ANTIQUARIAN BOOKS

Among the many shops on Route 6A, two are great: **Titcomb's Book Shop** in Sandwich and **Parnassus Book Service** in Yarmouthport. I also recommend **Isaiah Thomas Books & Prints** in Cotuit.

ANTIQUES

Antiques shops are located all along Route 6A, on the 32-mile stretch from Sandwich to Orleans, but there is an especially dense concentration in Brewster, often called An-

tique Alley. You'll also find fine antiques shops in Sandwich Center, Barnstable, Chatham, and Nantucket. Look for the complete supplement "Arts & Antiques" in the *Cape Cod Times.*

AQUARIUMS

The **Aquarium of the National Marine Fisheries** in Woods Hole is small but it is an excellent introduction to marine life. There is also the small **Maria Mitchell Association's Aquarium** on Nantucket.

AREA CODE

The area code for the entire region of Cape Cod, Martha's Vineyard, and Nantucket is 508.

ART GALLERIES

Wellfleet and Provincetown are the Cape's fine-art centers. Both established and emerging artists are well represented in dozens of diverse galleries. Artists began flocking to Provincetown at the turn of the century, and the vibrant community continues to nurture creativity. The islands also attract large numbers of artists, some of whom stayed to open their own studios and galleries.

Pick up a copy of "Arts & Antiques," a very complete supplement published by the *Cape Cod Times.* A directory of the **Cape Cod Antique Dealers' Association** (c/o Thomas Slaman, 625 Route 6A, West Barnstable 02668) is available free with a business-sized, self-addressed, stamped envelope.

ATTIRE

The Cape and the islands are casual for the most part; a jacket and tie are rarely required. At the other end of the spectrum, you'll always need shoes and shirts at beachfront restaurants.

AUCTIONS

Estate auctions are held throughout the year; check the newspapers. Among the venues are: **Sandwich Auction House; Eldred's Auctions** in East Dennis; **Merlyn Auctions** in North Harwich; and **Rafael Osona** in Nantucket. Just a few of the benefit auctions include: the **Fine Arts Work Center Annual Benefit Silent Auction** and the **AIDS Support Group Auction** in Provincetown; an auction held by the **Truro Center for the Arts at Castle Hill;** and the celebrity-studded **Possible Dreams Auction** on Martha's Vineyard.

BASEBALL

The 10-team **Cape Cod Baseball League** was established in 1946. Only players with at least one year of collegiate experience are allowed to participate. Wooden bats are supplied by the major leagues. In exchange for the opportunity to play, team members work part time in the community, live with a community host, and pay rent. Carlton Fisk and the late Thurman Munson are just two alumni of the Cape Cod League who succeeded in the majors. Currently, about 100 major league players are former league players. Games are free and played from mid-June to mid-August; it's great fun. Baseball is listed under *Entertainment.*

BEACHES

Cape Cod National Seashore (CCNS) beaches are the stuff of dreams: long expanses of dune-backed sand. In fact, you could walk with only one or two natural interruptions (breaks in the beach), as Henry David Thoreau did, from Chatham to the tip of Provincetown. My favorites on the Cape include **Sandy Neck Beach** in West Barnstable; **Nauset Beach** in Orleans; **Old Silver Beach** in North Falmouth; **Chapin Memorial Beach** in Dennis; **West Dennis Beach; Craigville Beach** near Hyannis; and all the **Outer Cape** ocean beaches. Practically all of Nantucket's beaches are public, and although the same cannot be said for Martha's Vineyard, there are plenty of places to lay your towel.

A daily parking fee is enforced from mid-June to early September; many of the smaller beaches are open only to residents and weekly cottage renters. CCNS offers a seasonal parking pass for its beaches. There is no overnight parking at beaches. Four-wheel-drive vehicles require a permit and their use is limited. Open beach fires require a permit. Greenhead biting flies plague non–Outer Cape beaches in mid- to late July; they disappear with the first high tide at the new or full moon in August, when the water level rises, killing the eggs.

Generally, beaches on Nantucket Sound have warmer waters than the Outer Cape Atlantic Ocean beaches, which are also pounded by surf. Cape Cod Bay beaches are shallower and the water a bit cooler than Nantucket Sound beaches. Because of the proximity of the warm Gulf Stream, you can swim in Nantucket Sound waters well into September.

BICYCLING

The Cape is generally flat and there are many paved, off-road bike trails. The 28-mile **Cape Cod Rail Trail** runs along the bed of the Old Colony Railroad from Route 134 in Dennis to Wellfleet; bike trails can be found along both sides of the **Cape Cod Canal;** the **Shining Sea Trail** runs from Falmouth to Woods Hole; and bike trails can be found within the **Cape Cod National Seashore (CCNS)** in Provincetown and Truro. Nantucket is ideal for cycling, with six routes emanating from the center of town and then circling the island. Bicycling is also great on the Vineyard, but stamina is required for a trip up-island to Gay Head. For more information, consult *25 Bicycle Tours on Cape Cod and the Islands* by Susan Milton and Nan and Kevin Jeffrey.

BIRD-WATCHING

The **Bird Watcher's General Store** in Orleans is on every birder's list of stops. Natural areas that are known for bird-watching include: **Monomoy National Wildlife Refuge** off the coast of Chatham; **Wellfleet Bay Wildlife Sanctuary; Felix Neck Wildlife Sanctuary** in Vineyard Haven; **Ashumet Holly and Wildlife Sanctuary** in East Falmouth; and on Nantucket, **Coatue–Coskata–Great Point.** The **Maria Mitchell Association** and **Birding Adventures,** both in Nantucket, offer bird-watching expeditions, as do **Wellfleet Bay Wildlife Sanctuary** and **Monomoy National Wildlife Refuge.** Scheduled bird walks are also offered from both Cape Cod National Seashore (CCNS) visitors centers: **Salt Pond Visitor Center** in Eastham and **Province Lands Visitor Center** in Provincetown.

BUS SERVICE

The **Plymouth & Brockton** bus line (775-5524) serves points along Route 6A and the Outer Cape from Boston; **Bonanza** (1-800-556-3815) serves Bourne, Falmouth, Woods Hole, and Hyannis from Boston, Providence, and New York City.

CAMPING

There is no camping permitted on Nantucket, but there are a few campgrounds on Martha's Vineyard. The Cape offers dozens of private campgrounds, but only those in natural areas are listed; the best camping is in **Nickerson State Park** in Brewster and in Truro. For the complete Massachusetts Campground Directory, write to the Massachusetts Department of Travel and Tourism, 100 Cambridge Street, Boston 02202 (617-727-3201, 1-800-447-6277).

CAPE COD NATIONAL SEASHORE

Established on August 7, 1961, through the efforts of President John F. Kennedy, the Cape Cod National Seashore (CCNS) stretches over 40 miles through Eastham, Wellfleet, Truro, and Provincetown. It encompasses more than 43,500 acres of land and seashore. Sites within the CCNS have been identified with "CCNS" at the beginning of the entry. The **Salt Pond Visitor Center** in Eastham and **Province Lands Visitor Center** in Provincetown are excellent resources and offer a variety of exhibits,

16

films, and ranger-led walks and talks. The CCNS is accessible every day of the year, although you must pay to park at the beaches in summer.

CHAMBER MUSIC

Cape & Islands Chamber Music Festival (255-9509), PO Box 2721, Orleans 02653. Founded by a New York City pianist in 1980, the festival includes master classes and top-notch performances the first three weeks in August, at various venues across the Cape. Write for a schedule.

CHILDREN, ESPECIALLY FOR

Within this guide a number of activities and sites that have special "child appeal" are identified by the symbol "✐." When you're on the Cape, look for the free "Kids on the Cape" booklet, which gives a great overview of things to do.

CINEMAS

The **Cape Cinema** in Dennis is a special venue, but you can also find art films at the **Gaslight Theatre** in Nantucket. In addition to the standard multiplex cinemas located across the Cape, the **Wellfleet Drive-In** remains a much-loved institution.

COAST GUARD

The US Coast Guard has operations in Woods Hole (548-5151), Chatham (945-3830), Provincetown (487-0070), and on the Cape Cod Canal (888-0020).

COUNTRY STORES

Old-fashioned country stores still exist on Cape Cod and the islands. Aficionados can seek out **Bournedale Country Store** in Bournedale; the **Country Store** in Osterville; **The Brewster Store;** and **Alley's General Store** in West Tisbury on the Vineyard.

CRAFTS

Craftspeople have made a living on the Cape and the islands since they began making baskets, ships, and furniture 300 years ago. The tradition continues with artists emphasizing the aesthetic as well as the functional. Today's craftspeople are potters, jewelers, scrimshaw- and bird-carvers, weavers, glassblowers, clothing designers, and barrel makers. Look for the highly coveted (and pricey) lightship baskets in Nantucket, glass objects in Sandwich, and barrels (yes, barrels) at the **Cape Cod Cooperage** in Chatham. The **Artisan's Guild of Cape Cod** (PO Box 1, East Sandwich 02537) publishes a small pamphlet, as does **Cape Cod Potters** (PO Box 76, Chatham 02633).

CRANBERRIES

The cranberry is one of only three native North American fruits (the other two are Concord grapes and blueberries). Harvesting began in Dennis in 1816 and evolved into a lucrative industry in Harwichport. Harvesting generally runs from mid-September to mid-October, when the bogs are flooded and ripe red berries float to the water's surface. Before the berries are ripe, the bogs look like a dense green carpet, separated by 2- to 3-foot dikes. Nantucket, which has more than 200 acres of bogs, and Harwich, which lays claim to having the first commercial cranberry bog, celebrate with a **Cranberry Harvest Festival** in October. Most on-Cape bogs are located on the mid- and lower Cape. Off-Cape, the **Cranberry World Visitors' Center** in Plymouth (747-1000), operated by Ocean Spray, offers tours and demonstrations about the history of cranberry cultivation and modern processing techniques.

DINING

Many fine restaurants stay open through the winter. During the off-season, many chefs experiment with creative, new dishes and offer them at moderate prices. With the exception of July and August (when practically all places are open nightly), restaurants are rarely open every night of the week. The major problem for a travel writer (and a reader relying on the book) is that restaurants close depending on such unpredictable factors as weather and how many people are around. To avoid disappointment, it's best to phone ahead before setting out for a much anticipated meal.

Expect to wait for a table in July and August, and make reservations whenever possible. Remember that many restaurants are staffed by college students who are just learning the ropes in June and who may depart before Labor Day weekend, leaving the owners shorthanded. Smaller seasonal establishments don't take credit cards.

ECOSYSTEM

This narrow peninsula and these isolated islands have a delicate ecosystem. Remember that dunes are fragile, and beaches serve as nesting grounds for the endangered piping plovers; avoid the nesting areas when you see signs directing you to do so. Residents conserve water and recycle, and they hope you will do likewise.

EMERGENCIES

Call 911 from anywhere on Cape Cod.

EVENTS

The largest annual events are listed within each chapter of this book. Call the local radio station, WCOD (790-1061), for up-to-the-minute event information. Or invest $.50 in the *Cape Cod Times,* which features a special section about the day's events, and on Friday a calendar supplement for the following week. Two Cape-wide events are worth noting here: **Cape Heritage Week** (mid-June) celebrates the cultural, historical, and environmental heritage of Cape Cod; and **Cape Cod Maritime Week** (mid-May) focuses on the region's long commercial and cultural association with the sea.

FISHING

Cape Cod Outdoors, published four times annually, features articles on fresh- and salt-water fishing. Find it in tackle shops, or write to Little Pond Publishing, PO Box 904, Orleans 02653 (240-0077). The cover price is $2.95, and a yearly subscription is $8.95. The Cape Cod Chamber of Commerce (362-3225) publishes a large foldout "Fishing Guide to Cape Cod," which details where and when to find certain fish; write to PO Box 16, Hyannis 02601. You don't need a license for saltwater fishing, but you do for freshwater. Get a state license at any of the various town halls.

Charter boats generally take up to six

people on 4- or 8-hour trips. Boats leave from the following harbors on Cape Cod Bay: Barnstable Harbor in West Barnstable; Sesuit Harbor in Dennis; Rock Harbor in Orleans; Wellfleet Harbor; and Provincetown. On Nantucket Sound, head to Hyannis Harbor, Saquatucket Harbor in Harwichport, and Chatham. You can also fish from the banks of the Cape Cod Canal and surf-fish on the Outer Cape.

FLEA MARKETS

The two biggies are the **Wellfleet Drive-In Flea Market** and **Dick and Ellie's Flea Market** in Mashpee.

GOLF

There are about 50 courses on the Cape and the islands, and because of relatively mild winters, many stay open all year (although perhaps not every day). **Cape Cod Golf Holidays** (790-7823, 1-800-833-2255), PO Box 37, South Yarmouth 02664, specializes in custom golf packages.

HIGHWAYS

This guide identifies state highways by using "Route" instead of "MA." Route 6, also called the Mid-Cape Highway, is a speedy, four-lane, divided highway until exit 9½, when it becomes an undivided two-laner. After the Orleans rotary (exit 13), it becomes an undivided four-lane highway most of the way to Provincetown.

Scenic Route 6A, also known as Old King's Highway and Main Street, runs from the Sagamore Bridge to Orleans. It is lined with sea captains' houses, antiques shops, bed & breakfasts, and huge old trees. Development along Route 6A is strictly regulated by the Historical Commission. Route 6A links up with Route 6 in Orleans. Without stopping, it takes an extra 30 minutes or so to take Route 6A instead of Route 6 from Sandwich to Orleans.

Route 28 can be confusing. It is an elongated, U-shaped highway that runs from the Bourne Bridge south to Falmouth, then east to Hyannis and Chatham, then north to Orleans. The problem lies with the Route 28 directional signs. Although you're actually heading north when you travel from Chatham to Orleans, the signs will say: Route 28 South. When you drive from Hyannis to Falmouth, you're actually heading west, but the signs will say: Route 28 North. Ignore the north and south indicators, and look for towns that are in the direction you want to go.

HIGH SEASON

Memorial Day weekend in late May kicks things off, then there is a lull until school lets out in late June. From then on, the Cape is in full swing through Labor Day (early September). Innkeepers tell me there are often last-minute lodging vacancies for the week after the July 4 weekend. As a rule, however, traveling to the Cape or the islands without reservations in high season is not recommended. Accommodations—especially cottages, efficiencies, and apartments—are often booked by January for the upcoming summer.

HISTORIC HOUSES

Every town has its own historical museum/house, but some are more interesting than others. Among the best are **Hoxie House** in Sandwich; **Centerville Historical Society Museum** and **Osterville Historical Society Museum,** both in Barnstable; **Winslow**

Crocker House in Yarmouthport, operated by the Society for the Preservation of New England Antiquities (SPNEA); **Truro Historical Museum;** and the **Provincetown Heritage Museum.** The center of Nantucket has been designated a Historic District, so there are notable houses everywhere you turn; the oldest is the **Jethro Coffin House.** The **Nantucket Historical Association** publishes a walking guide to its 14 properties. Don't miss the **Vineyard Museum and Dukes County Historical Society** on Martha's Vineyard.

HORSEBACK RIDING

There are a surprising number of riding facilities and trails on the Cape. Look for them in Buzzards Bay (Bourne), West Falmouth, Barnstable, East Harwich, Brewster, Provincetown, and on Martha's Vineyard.

INFORMATION

Cape-wide information can be picked up off-Cape on Route 3 (exit 5) south of Boston.

There are also **Cape Cod Chamber of Commerce** information booths at the Bourne Bridge rotary (759-3814), at the Sagamore Bridge rotary (888-2438), and at exit 6 off Route 6. Or write to the **Cape Cod Chamber of Commerce,** PO Box 16, Hyannis 02601 (362-3225).

LIBRARIES

The Cape and the islands boast a few libraries with world-class maritime collections and works pertaining to the history of the area: **Sturgis Library** in Barnstable; **William Brewster Nickerson Memorial Room** at Cape Cod Community College in West Barnstable; the **Atheneum** and the **Edouard A. Stackpole Library and Research Center,** both in Nantucket; and the **Vineyard Museum and Dukes County Historical Society** in Edgartown on Martha's Vineyard.

LIGHTHOUSES

The most picturesque lighthouse is perhaps **Nobska Light** in Woods Hole, but there are also working lighthouses in Chatham, Eastham, Truro, and Provincetown. Nantucket and Martha's Vineyard, too, have their share of working lighthouses.

LODGING

There are many choices—from inns and bed & breakfasts to cottages, apartments, and efficiencies. Rates quoted are for two people sharing one room. Cottages are rented from Saturday to Saturday. Most inns and bed & breakfasts don't accept children under 10 or 12 years of age. All accept credit cards unless otherwise noted. Pets are not accepted unless otherwise noted. Many smaller establishments restrict smoking to outdoors. Many places require a 2-night minimum stay during the high season; holiday weekends often require a 3-night minimum stay.

MUSEUMS

People who have never uttered the words "museum" and "Cape Cod" in the same breath don't know what they're missing. Don't skip the **Sandwich Glass Museum** and **Heritage Plantation of Sandwich,** both in Sandwich; **Aptucxet Trading Post and Museum** in Bourne Village; **Cahoon Museum of American Art** in Cotuit; **John F. Kennedy Museum** in Hyannis; **Cape**

Museum of Fine Arts in Dennis; **Cape Cod Museum of Natural History** in Brewster; **Provincetown Art Association & Museum,** the **Pilgrim Monument & Provincetown Museum,** and the **Old Harbor Lifesaving Museum,** all in Provincetown; **Vineyard Museum and Dukes County Historical Society** in Edgartown on Martha's Vineyard; and the **Museum of Nantucket History, Nantucket Whaling Museum, Peter Foulger Museum,** and **Nantucket Lifesaving Museum,** all on Nantucket.

Children will particularly enjoy the **Railroad Museum** in Chatham and the **Thornton W. Burgess Museum** in Sandwich.

MUSIC

Outdoor summertime band concerts are now offered by most towns, but the biggest and oldest is held in Chatham at **Kate Gould Park. Heritage Plantation** of Sandwich offers a variety of outdoor summer concerts.

There are a few venues for folk music, including: **Woods Hole Folk Music Society** in Woods Hole; **Benefit Coffeehouse** in Marstons Mills; **First Encounter Coffee House** in Eastham; and the **Wintertide Coffeehouse** in Vineyard Haven on Martha's Vineyard.

NATURE PRESERVES

There are walking trails—around salt marshes, across beaches, through ancient swamps and hardwood stands—in every town on the Cape and the islands, but some traverse larger areas and are more "developed" than others. For a complete guide, look for the excellent *Walks & Rambles on Cape Cod and the Islands* by Ned Friary and Glenda Bendure. Watch for poison ivy and deer ticks; the latter cause Lyme disease.

To find some upper Cape green space, head to: **Green Briar Nature Center &**

Jam Kitchen in Sandwich; **Lowell Holly Reservation** in Mashpee; and **Ashumet Holly and Wildlife Sanctuary** and **Waquoit Bay National Estuarine Research Reserve,** both in East Falmouth. In the mid-Cape area, you'll find **Sandy Neck Great Salt Marsh Conservation Area** in West Barnstable. The lower Cape offers **Nickerson State Park** in Brewster and **Monomoy National Wildlife Refuge** off the coast of Chatham. The **Cape Cod National Seashore** (CCNS) has a number of short interpretive trails on the outer Cape, while Wellfleet has the **Wellfleet Bay Wildlife Sanctuary** and **Great Island Trail**.

On Martha's Vineyard you can escape the crowds at **Felix Neck Wildlife Sanctuary** in Vineyard Haven; **Cedar Tree Neck Sanctuary** and **Long Point Wildlife Refuge,** both in West Tisbury; and **Cape Pogue Wildlife Refuge** and **Wasque Reservation** on Chappaquiddick.

Nantucket boasts conservation initiatives that have protected one-third of the land from development, including the areas of **Coatue–Coskata–Great Point, Eel Point, Sanford Farm, Ram Pasture,** and **The Woods**.

NEWSPAPERS AND PERIODICALS

The *Cape Cod Times,* with Cape- and island-wide coverage, is published daily. The *Cape Codder* is published Tuesday and Friday and focuses on the lower and outer Cape. Their "What's on Cape" section is published on Tuesday and the "Weekend" section on Friday. Provincetown's weekly *Advocate* is noteworthy, as are the *Vineyard Gazette* (627-4311), the *Nantucket Beacon* (228-8455), and the Vineyard's *Inquirer and Mirror* (228-0001). Some local papers include the supplement "A-Plus," a guide to arts, artists, antiques, authors, architecture, and so on.

The bimonthly *Cape Cod Life* (444-4466) publishes annual "Best of the Cape & Islands" and "Leisure Time Planner" editions. The cover price is $3.75; a 12-month subscription costs $19.75. *Boston Magazine* (617-262-9700) publishes its list of the "Best of Cape Cod and the Islands" in June.

OFF-SEASON

In an attempt to get people thinking about visiting the Cape and the islands off-season, I have put the "❋" symbol next to activities, lodging, and restaurants that are open and appealing in the off-season.

PERFORMING ARTS

The regional performing arts scene has been rich since the turn of the century. In 1998 the **Boch Center for Performing Arts** will open in Mashpee. It promises to be an exciting venue. Currently, the largest multiple-use venue is the **Cape Cod Melody Tent** in Hyannis, which brings big-name performers to the Cape. See also *Music* and *Theater.*

PONDS

Supposedly there are 365 freshwater ponds on Cape Cod, one for every day of the year. As glaciers retreated 150,000 years ago and left huge chunks of ice behind, depressions in the earth were created. When the ice melted, "kettle ponds" were born. The ponds are a refreshing treat, especially in August when salty winds kick up beach sand.

POPULATION

More than 180,000 people live year-round on the Cape and the islands. No one *really* has an accurate idea of how many people visit in summer, but it's in the multiple millions.

RECOMMENDED READING ABOUT CAPE COD

Henry David Thoreau's naturalist classic *Cape Cod* details his mid-1800s walking tours. Henry Beston's equally classic *The Outermost House: A Year of Life on the Great Beach of Cape Cod* recounts his solitary year in a cabin on the ocean's edge. Josef Berger's 1937 Works Project Administration (WPA) guide, *Cape Cod Pilot*, is filled with good stories and still-useful information. Pick up anything by modern-day naturalists Robert Finch and John Hay. Finch also edited a volume of writings by others about the Cape, *A Place Apart.* Another collection of writings about Cape Cod is *Sand in Their Shoes,* compiled by Frank and Edith Shay. Look for *Cape Cod, Its People & Their History* by Henry Kittredge (alias Jeremiah Digges) and *The Wampanoags of Mashpee* by Russell Peters. Mary Heaton Vorse, a founder of the Provincetown Players, describes life in Provincetown from the 1900s to the 1950s in *Time and the Town: A Provincetown Chronicle.* And for children, Brian Shortsleeve has written an illustrated history book, *The Story of Cape Cod.* Look for Admont Clark's *Lighthouses of Cape Cod, Martha's Vineyard, and Nantucket: Their History and Lore* and photographer Joel Meyerowitz's *A Summer's Day* and *Cape Light.*

RECOMMENDED READING ABOUT MARTHA'S VINEYARD

On the Vineyard II contains essays by celebrity island residents, including Walter Cronkite, William Styron, and Carly Simon, and photographs by Peter Simon (Carly's brother). *Martha's Vineyard* and *Martha's Vineyard, Summer Resort* are both by Henry Beetle Hough, Pulitzer Prize–winning editor of the *Vineyard Gazette.* Photographer Alfred Eisenstadt, a longtime summer resident of the Vineyard, photographed the island for years. Contemporary *Vineyard Gazette* photographer Alison Shaw has two Vineyard books to her credit: the black-and-white *Remembrance and Light* and the color collection *Vineyard Summer.*

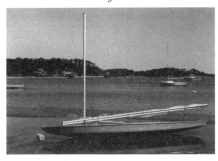

RECOMMENDED READING ABOUT NANTUCKET

Edwin P. Hoyt's *Nantucket: The Life of an Island* is a popular history, and Robert Gambee's *Nantucket* is just plain popular. Architecture buffs will want to take a gander at *Nantucket Style* by Leslie Linsley and Jon Aron and the classic *Early Nantucket and Its Whale Houses* by Henry Chandler Forman.

ROTARIES

When you're approaching a rotary, cars already within the rotary have the right of way.

SHELLFISHING

Permits, obtained from local town halls, are required for the taking of shellfish. Sometimes certain areas are closed to shellfishing due to contamination; it's always best to ask.

SHOPPING

Main Streets in Chatham, Falmouth, and Hyannis are well suited to walking and shopping. Provincetown has the trendiest shops. Shopping on the Vineyard and Nantucket is a prime activity.

SUMMER CAMPS

Since the 1930s, programs all over the Cape give children opportunities to enjoy the Cape's natural environment. Contact the **Cape Cod Association for Children's Camps,** PO Box 38, Brewster 02631.

SURFING AND WINDSURFING

Surfers should head to **Nauset Beach** in Orleans, **Coast Guard** and **Nauset Light Beaches** in Eastham, and **Marconi Beach** in Wellfleet. Windsurfers flock to Falmouth. The Vineyard beaches are also good for windsurfing.

SWIMMING POOLS

For a small fee you can swim at the **Norseman Athletic Club** in Eastham, **Provincetown Inn** in Provincetown, and the **Nantucket Community Pool.**

THEATER

Among the summer-stock and performing arts venues are **Cape Playhouse** in Dennis; **Cape Rep Outdoor Theatre** in Brewster; **Monomoy Theatre** in Chatham; **Academy Playhouse** in Orleans; **Wellfleet Harbor Actors' Theater; Provincetown Theater Company; College Light Opera Company** in Falmouth; **Barnstable Comedy Club** in Barnstable; **Harwich Junior Theater;** the **Actors Theatre of Nantucket** and **Theatre Workshop** on Nantucket; and the **Vineyard Playhouse** on Martha's Vineyard.

TIDES

Tides come in and out twice daily; times differ from day to day and from town to town. At low tide the sandy shore is hard and easier to walk on; at high tide, what little sand is visible is more difficult to walk on. Call 771-

5522 or 255-8500 for up-to-the-minute tide information.

TRAFFIC

It's bad in July and August no matter how you cut it. It's bumper to bumper on Friday afternoon and evening when cars arrive for the weekend. It's grueling on Sunday afternoon and evening when they return home. And there's no respite on Saturday when all the weekly cottage renters have to vacate their units and a new set of renters arrives to take their places. Call **Smart Traveler** (617-374-1234, °1 on your cellular phone) for up-to-the-minute information on traffic. This service uses remote cameras and airplanes to report current traffic conditions.

TRAINS

The tourist trail to Cape Cod was blazed by the railroad. **Amtrak's** (1-800-872-7245) Cape Codder, with connections along the eastern seaboard, stops in Buzzards Bay, Sandwich, West Barnstable, and Hyannis on Friday afternoon from mid-May to mid-September. It makes the return trip on Sunday. The **Cape Cod Scenic Railroad** runs between Sandwich and Hyannis.

VALUE

The "☞" symbol appears next to entries that represent an exceptional value.

WEATHER

Call the **Weather Line** (790-1061) 24 hours a day. Or call either of two radio stations: WCOD (790-1061) and WQRC (771-5522.)

WHALE-WATCHING

Whale-watches leave from Provincetown Harbor, including the excellent **Dolphin Fleet Whale Watch** (349-1900, 1-800-826-9300), but you can also catch the **Hyannis Whale Watcher Cruises** (362-6088, 1-800-287-0374) out of Barnstable Harbor and the **Nantucket Whalewatch** (283-0313, 1-800-322-0013) from Nantucket.

YOUTH HOSTELS

Youth hostels are located on Martha's Vineyard, Nantucket, Provincetown, Eastham, and Truro.

I. THE UPPER CAPE

Pocasset River Estuary, Bourne

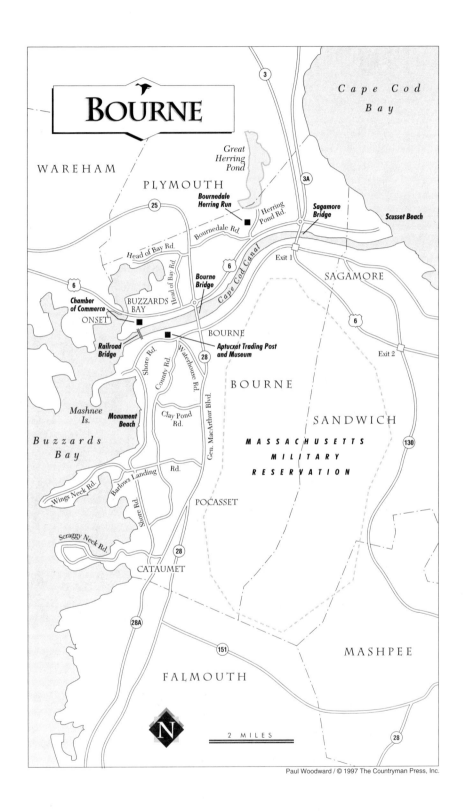

BOURNE

Cape Cod Bay

WAREHAM

PLYMOUTH

Great
Herring
Pond

Bournedale
Herring Run

Bournedale Rd.

Herring
Pond Rd.

Sagamore
Bridge

Scusset Beach

Head of Bay Rd.

Head of Bay Rd.

Cape Cod Canal

Exit 1

SAGAMORE

Bourne
Bridge

Chamber
of Commerce

BUZZARDS
BAY

ONSET

Railroad
Bridge

BOURNE

Aptucxet Trading Post
and Museum

Shore Rd.

County Rd.

Waterhouse Rd.

Gen. MacArthur Blvd.

BOURNE

Exit 2

SANDWICH

Mashnee
Is.

Monument
Beach

Clay Pond
Rd.

MASSACHUSETTS
MILITARY
RESERVATION

Buzzards
Bay

Barlows Landing

Rd.

Wings Neck Rd.

Shore Rd.

POCASSET

Scraggy Neck Rd.

CATAUMET

MASHPEE

28A

151

FALMOUTH

N

2 MILES

Bourne

Unless you arrive by plane or boat, you must pass through Bourne, over the Cape Cod Canal via the Sagamore or Bourne Bridge (5 miles apart). There's something magical about the first glimpse of these bridges, a sure sign you're entering a place separate from where you've been.

Bourne straddles the canal, nips at the heels of Sandwich on the Cape Cod Bay side, and follows the coastline south toward Falmouth along Route 28. (All the land to the immediate east of Route 28 belongs to the Massachusetts Military Reservation.) Bourne is often completely bypassed as travelers head south to catch the Vineyard ferry from Falmouth or Woods Hole. Indeed, there is some justification in not spending a monthlong holiday here. Bourne is predominantly inhabited by year-rounders who enjoy a quiet, rural, unharried existence tending their gardens and their lives. But perhaps of the entire Cape, Bourne remains the most unexplored. The back roads off County and Shore Roads are lovely for bicycling, as are the peninsulas reached by Scraggy Neck Road and Wings Neck Road. Fishing, walking, and bicycling are prime activities along the Cape Cod Canal.

When Sandwich refused to grant Bourne its independence, an act of the state legislature incorporated it in 1884. Originally known for its fishing wharves, shipbuilding, and factories, Bourne quickly attracted prominent vacationers to its sandy shores. Named for an affluent resident who made his fortune during the whaling heyday, Bourne encompasses 40 square miles and consists of nine tiny villages.

Sagamore, on both sides of the canal and on Cape Cod Bay, has more in common with Sandwich; it even has a renowned glassmaking factory. Bournedale, on the "mainland" wedged between the two bridges, has a handsome country store, a diminutive old red schoolhouse, and a picturesque herring pond. And although Buzzards Bay, north and west of the Bourne Bridge, is the region's commercial center, it also offers some lovely glimpses of Buttermilk Bay. Buzzards Bay, by the way, was misnamed by inexperienced birdwatchers. If the original settlers had gotten it right, it would be called Osprey Bay today. On the western end of the canal, the Massachusetts Maritime Academy affords nice views of the canal as well as of handsome summer homes on the other side.

Across the 2384-foot Bourne Bridge (almost twice as long as the Sagamore Bridge), the Cape villages of Monument Beach, Bourne Village, Gray Gables, Pocasset, and Cataumet are tranquil in summer and downright sleepy in winter, although many people live there year-round. The first summer White House was in Gray Gables, where President Grover Cleveland spent his summers fishing during the 1890s. Monument Beach, Cataumet, and Pocasset are pleasant, residential seaside towns with old houses, just west of Route 28. Residents don't take much notice of visitors; they just go about their business, fishing, shopping, raising kids, and commuting to work. Cataumet Pier was the site of the nation's first labor strike, when dockworkers demanded a 100 percent pay raise in 1864, from 15¢ per hour to 30¢.

GUIDANCE

Cape Cod Canal Region Chamber of Commerce (759-6000), 70 Main Street, Buzzards Bay 02532. Open 9–5 weekdays, year-round, the chamber is housed in an old railroad station in the center of town.

U.S. Army Corps of Engineers (USACE) Field Office (759-4431), Academy Drive off Main Street, Buzzards Bay 02532. Open 8–4 weekdays, year-round. Staffed by USACE personnel, the office dispenses information about boating, fishing, camping, and other canal activities. The following 1- to 2-hour guided programs are free and offered on certain mornings from late June to early September: There are Monday walks on Bournedale Hill, Friday walks on Sagamore Hill, Saturday and Sunday biking and hiking along the canal, and Tuesday tours of the marine traffic control center.

Herring Run Visitors Center (no phone), Route 6 on the mainland side of the canal, about a mile south of the Sagamore Bridge rotary. Open 8–dusk, year-round; staffed 9:30–5 in summer. Although this is the USACE's administrative building, the staff can also provide canal-related information.

The **Cape Cod Canal Recreation Hotline** (759-5991) is a 24-hour number with up-to-date tide, weather, and recreation information provided by the USACE.

GETTING THERE

By car: To reach Sagamore, take exit 1 onto Route 6A from the Sagamore Bridge. For Bournedale and Buzzards Bay, take Route 6 west at the Sagamore Bridge rotary. To reach the other villages, take the Bourne Bridge across the canal, and at the rotary take Shore Road. You can also whiz down Route 28 and head west to Pocasset, Cataumet, and Monument Beach.

By bus: **Bonanza** (1-800-556-3815) operates from Boston to Bourne. The bus stops at the Tedeschi Food Shop at the Bourne Bridge rotary.

By train: From July to mid-September, **AMTRAK's** (1-800-872-7245) Cape Codder from New York stops in Buzzards Bay on Friday and returns to New York (and points along the eastern seaboard) on Sunday.

GETTING AROUND

Bourne is quite spread out, so you'll need a car to get around. The Cape Cod Canal has a great bicycle trail (see *To Do—Bicycling/Rentals*).

MEDICAL EMERGENCY

Call **911**.

TO SEE

❄ **Cape Cod Canal,** 7.5 miles long, separates the mainland from Cape Cod. The canal, between 480 and 700 feet wide at various points, is the world's widest ocean-level canal. In 1623 Captain Myles Standish, eager to facilitate trade between New Amsterdam (New York City) and the Plymouth colonies, was the first to consider creating a canal, which also would have eliminated the treacherous 135-nautical-mile voyage around the tip of the Cape. George Washington brought up the idea again in the late 18th century as a means to protect naval ships and commercial vessels during war, but the first serious effort at digging a canal was not attempted until 1880, by the Cape Cod Canal Company.

For a few months, the company's crew of 500 immigrants dug with hand shovels and carted away the dirt in wheelbarrows. Then, in 1899 New York financier Augustus Belmont's Boston, Cape Cod, and New York Canal Company took over the project with more resolve. They began digging in 1909, and the canal opened to shipping five years later on July 30, 1914. (It beat the Panama Canal opening by a scant 17 days.) On hand at the opening was then Assistant Secretary of the Navy Franklin D. Roosevelt. But the enterprise wasn't a financial success, because the canal was too narrow (it could only handle one-way traffic) and early drawbridges caused too many accidents. In 1928 the federal government purchased the canal, and the USACE built the canal we know today. The USACE has overseen the canal ever since. The canal provides a north–south shortcut for some 30,000 vessels each year, hundreds daily in summer. Water currents in the 32-foot-deep canal change direction every 6 hours.

Buzzards Bay Vertical Railroad Bridge is at the western end of the canal at the **Buzzards Bay Recreation Area.** At 270 feet high and 540 feet long, it's the third longest vertical railway bridge in the world. (Chicago, Illinois, and Long Island, New York, boast the other two.) The railroad bridge was completed the same year as the Sagamore and Bourne Bridges. When trains approach, it takes 2–3 minutes for the bridge to lower and connect with tracks on either side of it. The most reliable time to witness this event is at 5 PM and 6 PM (more or less), when trains haul trash off-Cape. Free parking. This is a good place to start the bicycle trail on this side of the canal.

❄ **Massachusetts Maritime Academy** (830-5000), Taylors Point, off Main Street, Buzzards Bay. Open year-round. The academy's presence explains why you'll see so many young men with close-cropped hair jogging along the canal bicycle trail. Although tours of the 55-acre campus are no longer conducted for the general public, you can arrange to tag along on a tour for prospective merchant-marine cadets. Not only will you see the oldest maritime academy in the country (established in 1891) from an insider's perspective, but you'll also tour the 547-foot *Patriot State,* the cadets' training ship. At the end of August, freshmen learn basic skills in huge dories up on stilts on the expansive front lawn; it's quite a sight. Free.

Aptucxet Trading Post and Museum (759-9487), Bourne Village. From the Cape-side Bourne Bridge rotary, follow signs for Mashnee Village, then Shore Road and Aptucxet Road; follow the signs. Open 10–5 daily in July and August; open 10–5 Tuesday through Saturday and 1–5 Sunday, May through June and September to mid-October. Since two rivers converged here before the canal was built, English settlers thought the location perfect for a post to promote trade with their neighbors, the Wampanoag Indians and the Dutch from New Amsterdam. Furs, sugar and other staples, tools, glass, tobacco, and cloth were bought and sold; wampum (carved quahog shells made into beads) served as currency. Organized commerce was born.

The trading post you see today was built in 1930 by the Bourne Historical Society on the foundations of the original; a few bricks from the fireplace date to the Pilgrims. The hand-hewn beams and wide floor planks came from a 1600s house in Rochester, Massachusetts. On the grounds is the small Victorian railroad station used solely by President Grover Cleveland when he summered at his Gray Gables mansion in Monument Beach. You'll also find a Dutch-style windmill (which was intended merely "to add interest and beauty to the estate"), an 18th-century saltworks, an herb garden, a gift shop, and a shaded picnic area. Curator Eleanor Hammond is a treasure. Adults $2.50, children 6–18 $1.

✎❋ **Bournedale Herring Run** (759-4431), Route 6, about a mile south of the Sagamore rotary. After the canal destroyed the natural herring run into Herring Pond, local engineers created an elaborate artificial watercourse so that the fish could reach the pond at spawning time. Each twice-daily tide brings thousands of the bony fish slithering upstream, navigating the pools created by wooden planks. These 3-year-old mature herring are returning to their birthplace. Herring season generally runs from mid-April to mid-June; the gates to the run are open 5 PM–9 AM. You can also fish with a net at Herring Pond (off Herring Pond Road from Route 6) 6 AM–9 PM during herring season. With the aid of automated fish counters, it's estimated that upwards of 400,000 herring pass through the Bournedale run annually. Kids get a kick out of this spring ritual. Free.

Massachusetts Military Reservation (Otis Air Force Base) (968-4003), off the rotary at the junction of Routes 28 and 28A. Tours for groups of

10 or more can be arranged; call well in advance. The 21,000 acres east of Route 28 are a closed installation that contains Camp Edwards Army National Guard Training Site, Otis Air National Guard Base, the US Coast Guard Air Station, the State Army Aviation complex, and the PAVE PAWS radar station, which detects nuclear missiles and tracks military satellites (it was established during the Cold War). In August, Otis holds a 2-day open house, featuring equestrian, parachute, and flying units; 30 aircraft are on static display. Tours free.

Although you won't read about it in most guidebooks, the MMR has long been designated by the Pentagon as a federal environmental "Superfund" site. Most experts agree that it will take decades to clean up the toxic Cold War–era pollutants that are contaminating an estimated 8 million gallons of groundwater a day. Other experts suggest it may be impossible to clean up the underground chemical plumes that resulted from various training exercises, landfill leaks, and oil spills. In 1996 the Air Force drew up a plan that called for pumping the pollution out of the ground, but that would have lowered pond levels and dried out marshes, creating another ecological disaster. In addition to being a top priority cleanup site, there are current plans to create a state-of-the-art environmental technology center that would develop and test new groundwater pollution cleanup technologies for use around the world.

Briggs McDermott House (759-6120), Sandwich Road, Bourne Village. Open for special events from mid-June to late September. This early 19th-century Victorian home is maintained by the Bourne Society for Historic Preservation. Docents are on hand to discuss local architecture and former neighbor Grover Cleveland.

❊ **Mashnee Island.** From the Cape-side rotary of the Bourne Bridge, take Shore Road and follow signs for Mashnee Island. From the 2-mile-long causeway, there are lovely views on either side of summer homes that dot the shoreline, sailboats on the still waters, and the railroad bridge and Bourne Bridge in the distance. Parking is nonexistent in summer, and since the island is private, you'll have to turn around at the end of the causeway. But from fall to spring, you can park at Kokomo's Island Beach Club on Mashnee Island and walk around.

Mashnee Island's celebrated, homespun Fourth of July parade consists of the current crop of island kids (and their parents) marching or riding their bikes through town.

TO DO

BICYCLING/RENTALS

Cape Cod Canal. The canal is edged by level, carefully maintained service roads perfect for biking. The mainland side has 7.7 miles of trail; the Cape side has about 6.5 miles. Clearly marked access points along the mainland side of the canal include the Scusset State Park off Scusset Beach Road; the Sagamore Recreation Area off Canal Road at the Sagamore rotary; near the Herring Brook Fishway in Bournedale; and beneath the Bourne Bridge. On the Cape side of the canal, there are access points from the US Engineering Observation Station on Freezer Road in Sandwich; from Pleasant Street in Sagamore; and from the Bourne Bridge. If you want to cross the canal with your bike, use the Sagamore—its sidewalk is safer.

P&M Cycles (759-2830), 29 Main Street, Buzzards Bay. Open daily except Monday, March through December. Across from the railroad station and the canal path, the shop rents bicycles ($10 for 2 hours or $25 per day) and offers free parking here while you tour the canal trail.

BOAT EXCURSIONS/RENTALS

Maco's (759-9836), at Routes 6 and 28, Buzzards Bay. Open daily April through October, Maco's rents 16-foot skiffs with 10-horsepower motors ($60 a day) and Boston whalers ($165–180 per day on summer weekends; 15 percent less on weekdays). If you only want to rent for a half day, pick up your boat after 11 AM.

CANAL TOURS

Cape Cod Canal Cruises (295-3883), off Routes 6 and 28 at the Onset Bay Town Pier (a few miles west of the mainland-side Bourne Bridge rotary), Onset. Two- and 3-hour tours—with running commentary—are conducted from mid-May to mid-October. This is the way the canal is meant to be experienced—by boat. $6.50–8 adults, $3.25–4 children 6–12. There are also sunset, jazz, and dance cruises offered, as well as a family discount cruise at 4 PM.

FISHING

Freshwater licenses are available from the Bourne Town Hall (759-0613) on Perry Avenue. The banks of the Cape Cod Canal provide plenty of opportunities for catching striped bass, bluefish, cod, and pollock. Just bait your hook and cast away; no permits are required if you're fishing with a rod and line from the shore. There is no fishing, lobstering, or trolling by boat permitted on the canal.

Flax Pond and **Red Brook Pond** in Pocasset offer freshwater fishing.

See also Bournedale Herring Run under *To See*.

FOR FAMILIES

Water Wizz Water Park (295-3255), Routes 6 and 28, 2 miles west of the Bourne Bridge, Wareham. Open daily mid-June to early September, and weekends only late May to mid-June. The largest water park in New England has it all: a 50-foot-high water slide with tunnels, a six-story tube ride, a river ride, and more mundane (and dry!) amusements like an arcade and mini-golf. Adults $17, children under 4 feet tall $10; reduced admission after 3:30 PM.

Thunder Mine Adventure (563-7450), Route 28A and County Road, Wareham. Open daily until 10 PM, late May through September. A revolving mill and flower gardens make this mini-golf park more attractive than most. It's not very challenging, but after battling with motorists at the rotaries and bridges, it might be just your speed.

✐ **Adventure Isle** (759-2636, 1-800-535-2787), Route 28, 2 miles south of the Bourne Bridge, Bourne. Open daily 9 AM–11 PM, late May through September. Diversions include go-carts, a bumper boat lagoon, a brand new mini-golf course, batting cages, a pirate ship in the kiddie area, a "mega-slide," basketball, a little Ferris wheel, and a café after you've worked up an appetite. All-day passes go for $9–18, depending on how much fun you want to have.

HORSEBACK RIDING

Grazing Fields Farm (759-3763), off Head of the Bay Road, Buzzards Bay. Private and semiprivate lessons are offered year-round at the farm that held up the construction of I-495 in the early 1900s.

ICE SKATING

John Gallo Ice Arena (759-8904), 231 Sandwich Road, Bourne. Public skating practically every day September through March.

SCUBA DIVING

Aquarius Diving Center (759-3483), 3239 Route 28, Buzzards Bay. Owner Norman Baron offers rental equipment, instruction, general information, and charters that head off to explore the rocky bottom of Sandwich Town Beach (where you'll see lobsters scurrying about), a wreck off Provincetown, or the Plymouth coast for $55 per person.

SPECIAL PROGRAM

✐ **US Army Corps of Engineers** (759-4431), Academy Drive off Main Street, Buzzards Bay. Junior ranger programs are offered for children 6–12, usually on Wednesday afternoons, from late June to early September. For 90 minutes, a different program each week explores canal history, water resources, environmental protection, and traffic control.

SWIMMING POOL

Bourne Scenic Park (759-7873), Route 6 on the mainland side of the canal, Buzzards Bay. Open late March to late October. For a $2 day-use fee (free for children up to 18), you can swim in a saltwater swimming hole, fed by canal tides that are controlled by a system of floodgates. Reeds grow along the edges of the swimming hole, which has a sandy bottom and is surrounded by a chain-link fence. There are also picnic tables, a playground, and camping practically underneath the pylons of the Sagamore Bridge.

TENNIS

Public courts are located at **Bourne Memorial Community Building** and **Town Hall,** Shore Road in Buzzards Bay; the **old schoolhouse** on County Road in Cataumet; **Chester Park,** across from the old railroad station, Monument Beach; and behind the fire station on Barlow's Landing Road in Pocasset Village.

GREEN SPACE

BEACHES

Due to swift currents and heavy boat traffic, swimming is prohibited in the Cape Cod Canal.

Scusset and **Sagamore Beaches,** Cape Cod Bay, Sagamore. Both beaches are located off the Sagamore Bridge rotary via Scusset Beach Road. Facilities include changing areas and rest rooms.

Monument Beach, Buzzards Bay, on Emmons Road off Shore Road, Monument Beach. Facilities at this small beach include free parking, rest rooms, and a snack bar. The warm waters of Buzzards Bay usually hover around 75 degrees in summer.

Town Beach, Buttermilk Bay off Route 28 and Head of the Bay Road, Buzzards Bay. Facilities are limited to free parking.

WALKS

Red Brook Pond, Thaxter Road off Shore Road, Cataumet. Park at the corner and walk 0.1 mile to the trailhead to explore 40 acres of wooded conservation land.

Cape Cod Canal. (See *To Do—Bicycling/Rentals.*)

LODGING

BED & BREAKFASTS

❄ **Wood Duck Inn** (564-6404), 1050 County Road, Cataumet 02534. Open year-round. This lovely bed & breakfast offers three 2-room suites that have entrances separate from the rest of the 1848 farmhouse. One suite has stenciled walls and is filled with antiques; another feels more like a cottage, furnished in wicker and rattan. Tree Tops, more contemporary with a skylight and bleached-wood floors, has a balcony overlooking a cranberry bog. Innkeeper Maureen Jason will deliver breakfast to your suite. $85. No credit cards.

CAMPGROUNDS

Bayview Campgrounds (759-7610), Route 28, 1 mile south of Bourne 02532. Open May to mid-October. There are certainly lots of facilities for RV users, but about 50 of the 430 sites are reserved for tenters.

There is also camping at Bourne Scenic Park (see *To Do—Swimming Pool*) and Scusset Beach State Park (see *Green Space* in "Sandwich"). Although there is no camping at the Midway Recreation Area (Route 6A on the Cape side of the Canal in Bourne), campfire programs led by the Cape Cod Canal Rangers (759-4431) are held Wednesdays at 8 PM.

WHERE TO EAT

Chart Room (563-5350), Shipyard Lane off Shore Road at the Cataumet Marina, Cataumet. Open for lunch and dinner daily June through September; Thursday through Sunday in May and October. This low-slung building is well positioned on the edge of picturesque Red Brook Harbor. If you have to wait for a table—and you might, since the Chart Room does a high volume of business—there are a few Adirondack chairs and tables scattered across a short lawn. For the best sunset views, get a table on the edge of the outer dining room. The Chart Room serves reliable sandwiches and seafood standards, including lobster salad, bisque, and grilled swordfish. Vinny McGuiness has been chef since the early 1980s. Reservations recommended. Entrées $9–18.

☞✐**Sagamore Inn** (888-9707), 1131 Route 6A, Sagamore. Open 11–9 daily except Tuesday, April through November. Shirley and Joseph Pagliarani have served "Yankee Italian" food since 1964. Inside the shuttered green and white building are signs of "old Cape Cod": shiny wooden floors, captain's chairs at round tables, a white tin ceiling, and wooden booths. The Yankee pot roast has been on the menu from the beginning, but homemade pies were added in 1994. Finish up with traditional Grape-Nut custard or bread pudding. There's a lot of very fresh seafood on the menu, but the scallops are always particularly fresh, fresh, fresh. Children's menu. Dishes $7.50–10.25.

✐✳ **The Bridge** (888-8144), 21 Route 6A, Sagamore. Open for lunch and dinner daily, year-round. On the Cape side of the Sagamore Bridge, this pleasant and friendly place has been in the Prete family since 1953. You can find something to suit everyone. For lunch The Bridge offers its renowned Yankee pot roast, as well as tuna melts, spaghetti with meat sauce, and burgers. At dinnertime the menu is Italian-influenced, with a few well-executed Thai dishes to spice things up. Children's menu. Lunch $4.40–8, dinner $7–16.

Anthony's (888-6040), Route 6A, Sagamore, next to the Christmas Tree Shop on the Cape side of the Sagamore Bridge. Open year-round except January. Tired of inching along in traffic? Stop here and get some ice cream or a sandwich before tackling the last leg of your journey.

ICE CREAM

Emack & Bolio's (564-5442), Route 28A and County Road, Cataumet. Open mid-May to mid-October. A local favorite, Cosmic Cataumet Crunch (vanilla ice cream with butterscotch, chocolate chips, and pralines), vies for attention with raspberry chip and coffee Heath Bar crunch frozen yogurt.

FISH MARKET

Cataumet Fish (564-5956), 1360 Route 28A, Cataumet. Open year-round.

ENTERTAINMENT

Band concerts (759-6000), Buzzards Bay Park, off Main Street, Buzzards Bay. Concerts are held July and August on Thursday at 7 PM.

SELECTIVE SHOPPING

ART & ARTISANS

Pairpoint Crystal (888-2344, 1-800-899-0953), 851 Route 6A, Sagamore. Retail shop open daily year-round; glassmaking weekdays 9–4:30 April through December. This place has existed under one name or another since 1837. Thomas Pairpoint, a glass designer in the 1880s, used techniques created by Deming Jarves. Master craftspeople still practice the art and these techniques here today. Clear or richly colored glass is hand-blown, -sculpted, or -pressed on a 19th-century press. The crystal contains 34 percent lead. Through large picture windows you can watch the master glassblowers working on faithful period reproductions and cup holders or more modern lamps, paperweights, vases, and candlesticks. (See the introduction and *To See* in "Sandwich" for more about the glass industry.)

Cataumet Arts Center (563-5434), 76 Scraggy Neck Road, Cataumet. Open year-round, this community arts center has ever-changing exhibits; an airy gallery that shows crafts, paintings, wearable art, and whimsical wooden sculptures (among other art); artist studios to rent; and a host of classes for children, printmakers, and others.

FACTORY OUTLET

☞ **Christmas Tree Shops** (888-7010), Sagamore, on the Cape side of the Sagamore Bridge, exit 1 off Route 6. This may be the first Christmas Tree Shop you see, but it won't be the last—there are a half dozen scattered around the Cape. This is the main outlet "where everyone loves a bargain" and they've gone all out to get your attention: You can't miss the revolving windmill and thatched roof. (Interestingly, the thatch, marsh grass from Canada, must be groomed every other year.) Merchandise has absolutely nothing to do with the end-of-the-year holiday. It revolves around inexpensive housewares, random gourmet food items, or miscellaneous clothing accessories—whatever the owners, Doreen and Charles Bilezikian, happen to get in close-out sales that week. Those who turn their noses up at the shops might be interested to know that the Bilezikians employ 1700 to 2200 year-round residents.

OUTLET MALLS

Cape Cod Factory Outlet Mall (888-8417), exit 1 off Route 6, Sagamore. Open daily year-round. Surrounding a food court, 20 or more stores like London Fog, Bass, Corning-Revere, Carter's Children's Wear, Bed & Bath, Oshkosh, and Bannister Shoes tempt even the most harried.

Tanger Outlet Center (1-800-727-6885), at the Bourne Bridge rotary. Open daily year-round. Liz Claiborne, Barbizon lingerie, Aldolfo II, Izod, and Levi's.

SPECIAL SHOP

Bournedale Country Store (833-0700), 26 Herring Pond Road, off Route 6, Bournedale. Open daily year-round. This classic red building with wooden floors has been here about 200 years, but the brother and sister team of Susan Teixeira and Rich Macchi has owned it only since 1993. On my last visit the aroma of baking brownies filled the store. What more could you ask for?

SPECIAL EVENTS

Mid-May: Cape Cod Canal Region **Striped Bass Fishing Tournament**.

Mid-June: **10k Roadrace, Run & Walk** along the canal from Scusset Beach to the Buzzards Bay Railroad Bridge.

Early August: Otis Air Force Base's **Cape Cod Air Show** (see Massachusetts Military Reservation under *To See*).

Mid-September: **Bourne Scallop Festival.** This weekend celebration is held in Buzzards Bay and along the shores of the canal. There are games, concerts, and lots of vendors and restaurants that create dishes that celebrate—what else—the scallop.

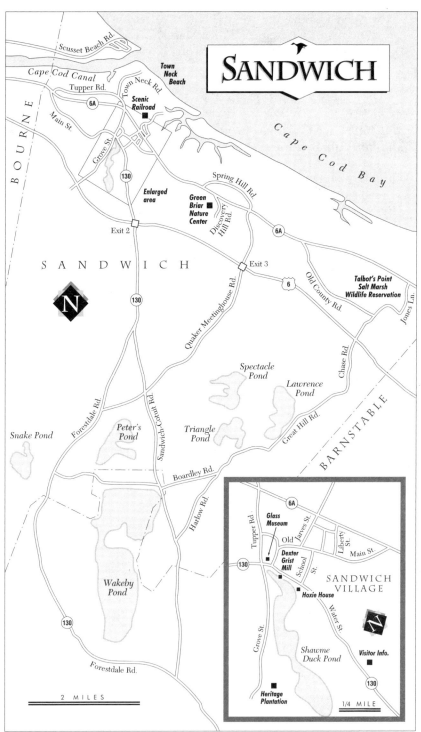

SANDWICH

Sandwich

Sandwich is calm, even in the height of summer. Many visitors whiz right by it, eager to get farther away from the "mainland." Even people who know about the delightful treasures within historic Sandwich Village often get back onto Route 6 without exploring the back roads and historic houses off the beaten path. Those who take the time to explore will find that Sandwich is a real gem.

The oldest town on the Cape, Sandwich was founded in 1637 by the Cape's first permanent group of English settlers. The governor of Plymouth Colony had given permission to "tenn men from Saugust" (now Lynn, Massachusetts) to settle the area with 60 families. Sandwich was probably chosen for its close proximity to the Manomet (now Aptucxet) Trading Post and for its abundant salt-marsh hay, which provided ready fodder for the settlers' cows. Agriculture supported the community until the 1820s, when Deming Jarves, a Boston glass merchant, decided to open a glassmaking factory. The location couldn't have been better: There was a good source of sand (although more was shipped in from New Jersey), sea salt was plentiful, salt-marsh hay provided packaging for the fragile goods, and forests were thick with scrub pines to fuel the furnaces. But by the 1880s midwestern coal-fueled glassmaking factories and a labor strike shut down Sandwich's factories. The story is told in great detail at the excellent Sandwich Glass Museum. Glassblowers work in a few studios in town.

You could spend a day wandering the half-mile radius around the village center, a virtual time capsule spanning the centuries. Antiques shops, attractive homes, and quiet, shady lanes are perfect for strolling. Shawme Duck Pond, as idyllic as they come, is surrounded by historic houses (including one of the oldest on the Cape), an old cemetery on the opposite shore, a working gristmill, swans and ducks, and plenty of vantage points from which to take it all in. Also pondside is a museum dedicated to the naturalist Thornton W. Burgess, a town resident and the creator of Peter Cottontail. Both children and adults delight in the museum and in the Green Briar Nature Center & Jam Kitchen down the road. Sandwich's greatest attraction lies just beyond the town center: Heritage Plantation of Sandwich, a 76-acre horticulturalist's delight with superb collections of Americana and antique automobiles.

Beyond the town center, the Benjamin Nye Homestead is worth a visit; have a look-see, even if it's closed, because it sits in a picturesque spot. East of town on Route 6A, past densely carpeted cranberry bogs (harvested in autumn), you'll find a few farm stands, antiques shops, and artisans' studios. At the town line with Barnstable, you'll find one of the Cape's best beaches and protected areas: Sandy Neck Beach (see *Green Space—Beaches* in "Barnstable") and Sandy Neck Great Salt Marsh Conservation Area (see *Green Space—Walks* in "Barnstable"). The marina, off Tupper Road, borders the Cape Cod Canal with a recreation area. The often overlooked town beach is nothing to sneeze at, and there are numerous conservation areas and ponds for walking and swimming.

Although a considerable number of Sandwich's 18,000 year-round residents commute to Boston every morning, their community dedication isn't diminished. Pick up a copy of the daily *Sandwich Broadsider* to glimpse the spirit that drives this town. A perfect example took place after fierce storms in August and October 1991 destroyed the town boardwalk, which had served the community since 1875. To replace it, townspeople purchased more than 1700 individual boards, each personally inscribed, and a new boardwalk was built within 8 months.

Sandwich was named, by the way, after the English town, not after the sandwich creator Earl, as many think. (*That* Earl of Sandwich was born 81 years after the town was founded.)

GUIDANCE

Cape Cod Canal Region Chamber of Commerce (759-6000), 70 Main Street, Buzzards Bay 02532. Open 9–5 weekdays, year-round. This office covers Sandwich, but you can find a walking guide of Sandwich Village at many shops in town. A **seasonal information booth** is located on Route 130 as you head into Sandwich from Route 6.

GETTING THERE

By car: Take the Sagamore Bridge to Route 6 east to exit 2 (Route 130 north), and travel 2 miles to Main Street. From exit 1 and Route 6A, you can take Tupper Road or Main Street into the village center.

By bus: There is no bus service to Sandwich, but **Plymouth & Brockton** (775-5524) and **Bonanza** (1-800-556-3815) buses stop nearby in Bourne.

By train: In summer, **AMTRAK** (1-800-872-7245) has Friday-evening service to Sandwich from New York City and points south.

GETTING AROUND

Although Sandwich Village is perfect for strolling, some attractions are a bit farther away. Daily in summer, 9–5, the **Glasstown Trolley** makes a 1-hour circuit among the Dan'l Webster Inn, Heritage Plantation of Sandwich, Pairpoint Glass Works (see *Selective Shopping* in "Bourne"), and the railroad station where you can board the scenic train (see *To Do—Scenic Railroad*). The fare is good all day, allowing you to hop on and off. Adults $5, children 4–12 $3, age 3 and under free.

MEDICAL EMERGENCY
Call **911.**

TO SEE

In Sandwich Village

☞ **Sandwich Glass Museum** (888-0251), 129 Main Street. Open 9:30–4:30 daily, April through October; 9:30–4 Wednesday through Sunday, November through March (except closed in January). During the 19th century, Sandwich glassmaking flourished at Deming Jarves's Boston & Sandwich Glass Company (1825–1888) and the Cape Cod Glass Works (1859–1869). Operated by the Sandwich Historical Society, this internationally known museum chronologically displays thousands of decorative and functional glass objects, which became increasingly more elaborate and richly colored as the years progressed. The displays are dramatically backlit by natural light streaming through banks of windows. A video describes the rise and crash of the local glass industry, and a diorama displays how the glass was made. If you're in the habit of skipping town historical museums, break the habit this time; you won't be disappointed. Adults $3.50, children 6–16 $1.

✐ **Yesteryears Doll Museum** (888-1711), at Main and River Streets. Open 10–4 Monday through Saturday, mid-May to mid-October. Housed in an 1833 Gothic Revival church (that has seen better days), this museum showcases three centuries of antique dolls, dollhouses (including a four-story Victorian one), and miniatures from around the world. Balinese shadow puppets, Barbie, Eloise, Betty Boop, German and French bisque dolls . . . they're all here. The church's stained-glass windows were made in town. Adults $3.50, children under 12 $1.50.

First Church of Christ, 136 Main Street. This Christopher Wren–inspired church with a tall white spire was built in 1847, but its brass bell, cast in 1675, is thought to be the oldest in the country.

Town Hall (888-5144), Main Street. Sandwich has certainly gotten its money's worth out of this Greek Revival building, which was constructed at a cost of little more than $4000 in 1834 and still serves as the center for town government.

Dexter Grist Mill (888-1173), on Shawme Pond. Open 10–4:45 Monday through Saturday and 1–4:45 Sunday, mid-June to mid-September; 10–4:45 Saturday and 1–4:45 Sunday, mid-May to mid-June and mid-September to mid-October. The circa-1640 mill has had a multiuse past, and the site wasn't always as quaint as it is now. The mill was turbine powered during Sandwich's glassmaking heyday; it then sat idle until 1920, when it was converted into a tearoom. After the mills around it were torn down in the late 1950s, it was opened to tourists in 1961, with the cypress waterwheel you see today. On-site miller and local schoolteacher Leo Manning describes the intricacies of the milling process.

You can purchase cornmeal—great for muffins, Indian pudding, and polenta—but keep in mind that it's best used within 24 hours. Adults $1.50, children 6–12 $.75.

Artesian fountain, between the gristmill and Town Hall. You can join residents filling water jugs with what some consider the Cape's best water.

Old Town Cemetery, Grove Street, on the shore opposite the Hoxie House and Thornton W. Burgess Museum. You'll recognize the names on many gravestones (including those of Burgess, Bodfish, and Bourne) from historic houses and street signs around town. Although the oldest marker dates to 1683, most are from the 1700s; many are marked with a winged skull, a common Puritan design.

✐✷ **Thornton W. Burgess Museum** (888-4668, 888-6870), 4 Water Street. Open 10–4 Monday through Saturday and 1–4 Sunday, mid-April to late December; open 10–4 Tuesday through Saturday the rest of the year. This Sandwich native and renowned children's author and naturalist wrote more than 15,000 stories and 170 books, featuring the escapades of Jimmy Skunk, Grandfather Frog, and the beloved Peter Cottontail (not to be confused with Beatrix Potter's Peter Rabbit.) The house is crammed with Burgess's books, original Harrison Cady illustrations, a "see-and-touch room," and exhibits honoring Burgess's life and work as a naturalist. Don't miss story time, which takes place on Monday, Wednesday, and Saturday mornings at 10:30 on the lawn in July and August; $1 per person. The Thornton Burgess Society was begun by local bookseller Nancy Titcomb in 1974 to celebrate the centennial of Burgess's birth. Donation of $1 requested. (See also Green Briar Nature Center & Jam Kitchen under *Green Space.*)

☞ **Hoxie House** (888-1173), 18 Water Street. Open 10–5 Monday through Saturday and 1–5 Sunday, mid-June to mid-October. For a long time this circa-1675 structure was thought to be the oldest on Cape Cod. Although it's impossible to know definitively, since the Barnstable County Courthouse deeds were lost in a fire, that claim is now generally thought to be inaccurate. Nonetheless, the house has a rare saltbox roofline, small diamond-shaped leaded windows, and a fine vantage above Shawme Duck Pond. Thanks to loaner furniture from Boston's Museum of Fine Arts, the restored interior looks much as it did during colonial times. One of the most remarkable facts about this house is that it was occupied without electricity or indoor plumbing until the 1950s. The house was named for Abraham Hoxie, who purchased it in 1860 for $400. Reverend John Smith lived here in 1675 when he came to be minister of the First Parish Church. Adults $1.50, children 12–16 $.75, under 12 free. Combination admission ticket with the Dexter Grist Mill: adults $2.50, children 12–16 $1, under 12 free.

Elsewhere around town

Heritage Plantation of Sandwich (888-3300), Pine and Grove Streets, Sandwich. Open 10–5 daily, early May to late October (last tickets sold at 4:15). Established in 1969 by Josiah Lilly III, descendant of the Eli

A cruise ship passes through the canal at the Sandwich Marina.

Lilly Pharmaceutical Company, Heritage Plantation is an oasis for garden lovers, antiques and vintage-car buffs, and Americana enthusiasts. These 76 acres are planted with outstanding collections of rhododendrons, including the famous Dexter variety, which bloom from mid-May to mid-June. (Charles O. Dexter was the estate's original owner, and he experimented with hybridizing here.) There are also impressive collections of holly bushes, heathers, hostas, and almost 1000 daylilies, which bloom from mid-July to early August. The estate is equally pleasant for an autumnal walk.

The **Military Museum** features a collection of 2000 hand-painted miniatures, while the replica **Shaker Round Barn** houses the museum's outstanding vintage-car collection. A 1981 DeLorean, a 1930 Duesenberg built for Gary Cooper, and President Taft's White Steamer (the first official auto of the White House) are a few mint-condition classics.

The **Art Museum** features folk art, scrimshaw, cigar-store figures, weather vanes, carvings by Elmer Crowell, and Currier & Ives lithographs. Also on the grounds: an 1800 windmill, an operational Coney Island–style 1912 carousel, and the **Carousel Café**. The alfresco café has a limited but more-than-adequate menu of overstuffed sandwiches, salads, and desserts. A trolley transports people around the grounds, but it is not intended for sight-seeing. Keep your eyes peeled for numerous special events hosted by the museum, including plant sales and concerts (see also *Entertainment*). Adults $8, youths 6–18 $4, children 5 and under free.

Benjamin Nye Homestead (888-2368), 85 Old County Road, East Sandwich. Open noon–4 weekdays, mid-June to mid-October. Off Route 6A, this 1685 homestead belonged to one of Sandwich's first settlers and has undergone many structural changes over the years. It began as a small peaked room with a central chimney; an addition turned it into a saltbox, and an added second floor created the full Colonial you see today. Although the interior is hardly a purist restoration, you'll see original paneling, 18th-century wallpaper, a spinning wheel, and handwoven sheets. Adults $3, children 12 and under $1.

1641 Wing Fort House (833-1540), 69 Spring Hill Road (off Route 6A), East Sandwich. Open 10–4 Tuesday through Saturday, mid-June to mid-September. The Wing house is the country's oldest home continuously inhabited by the same family. This circa-1646 house began as a one-room cottage when Stephen Wing, descendant of Reverend John Wing, arrived with his new bride. In the mid-1800s a second house was added to it, to create the current three-quarter Colonial. Guided tours are given by the caretaker. Admission $2 adults, $1 children 12 and under.

Friends Meeting House (888-4181), Quaker Road, off Spring Hill Road (off Route 6A), East Sandwich. Services Sunday at 10 AM and Thursday at 6 PM. The building standing today was built in 1810, the third Quaker meetinghouse to be built on this site. The congregation has been meeting since 1657, which makes it the oldest continuous meeting in North America. The interior is simple, with pews and a wood-burning stove that is stoked for the 25 or so congregants in winter. The meetinghouse is flanked by carriage barns.

✐ **Sandwich Fish Hatchery** (888-0008), Route 6A, Sandwich. Open 9–3 daily year-round. More than 200,000 trout at various stages of development are raised to stock the state's ponds. Throw in pellets of food (bring quarters for the vending machines) and watch 'em swarm.

☞✐❀ **Boardwalk,** Harbor Street off Factory Street, Sandwich. The boardwalk crosses marshland, Mill Creek, and low dunes to connect to Town Neck Beach (see *Green Space—Beaches*). Depending on the season, you might see kids jumping into the creek or blue heron poking around the tidal pools and tall grasses. There are expansive views at the end of the 1350-foot walkway.

TO DO

BICYCLING/RENTALS

Cape Cod Bike Rentals/Sandwich Cycles (833-2453), 40 Route 6A. David and Kim Buldini rent bicycles and in-line skates, and they'll do emergency repairs to your own bicycle, on-road if needed. On multiday rentals, Sandwich Cycles offers delivery to and pickup from your cottage or room. The shop is located between Sandwich's shady back roads and the Cape Cod Canal bike path (see *To Do* in "Bourne").

BLUEBERRY PICKING

The Blueberry Bog, Spring Hill off Route 6A. In the 1940s this former cranberry bog was turned into a blueberry farm. Today there are about 400 bushes on more than 4 acres. The fruit matures from early to mid-

July through August; pick your own by the quart or pound.

Sandwich Conservation Blueberry Patch, Route 6A at Jones Lane, East Sandwich. Pull off to the side of the road and help yourself.

CANOEING

Shawme Duck Pond, Water Street (Route 130), is actually linked to two other ponds, so you can do a lot of canoeing here.

Scorton Creek. Heading east on Route 6A, take a right just after the Sears Auto store (which is on your left), and go down beyond the culvert, where you'll be able to park. This is a good place for picnics, too.

Wakeby Pond, off Cotuit Road, South Sandwich.

FISHING/SHELLFISHING

Licenses and regulations are acquired at Town Hall (888-5144), Main Street. **Sandcastle Recreation Area** (at the Sandwich Marina) and **Scusset Beach Reservation Pier** (off Scusset Beach Road from the rotary on the mainland side of the canal) are good places to cast a line into the Cape Cod Canal.

FITNESS CLUB

Sportsite Health & Racquet Club (888-7900), 315 Cotuit Road. Open daily year-round. Two weight rooms, a cardiovascular area, aerobics classes, a sauna, a steam room, basketball and racquetball courts, and baby-sitting services while you work out. $40 for eight visits, $10 per day, or $20 per week.

GOLF

Holly Ridge (428-5577), off Route 130, South Sandwich. Open year-round; 18 holes, 3000 yards, par 54.

Round Hill Country Club (888-3384), exit 3 (Service Road) off Route 6, East Sandwich. Open year-round; 18 holes, 6288 yards, par 72.

MINI-GOLF

Sandwich Minigolf (888-1579), 159 Route 6A. Open daily in summer; weekends only, mid-May to mid-June and from mid-September to mid-October. Built on his family's cranberry bog, Maurice Burke has designed an upscale mini-golf course that boasts a floating raft for a green! An honest-to-goodness stream winds around many of the 27 holes.

SCENIC RAILROAD

Cape Cod Scenic Railroad (771-3788), Jarves Street, off Route 6A. Operates weekends in May, November, and December; Tuesday through Sunday, June through October; additional Christmas trains are added on weekends, mid-November to mid-December. The 42-mile round-trip journey departs at 11:10 AM and 1:40 PM and takes 2 hours. Trains travel alongside cranberry bogs, salt marshes, and little villages between Hyannis and just south of the Sagamore Bridge. Adults $11.50, children $7.50.

TENNIS

Public courts are at **Wing Elementary School** on Route 130, **Oak Ridge School** off Quaker Meetinghouse Road, and **Forestdale School** off Route 130.

GREEN SPACE

✐✳ **Green Briar Nature Center & Jam Kitchen** (888-6870), 6 Discovery Hill
Road off Route 6A, East Sandwich. Trails open year-round; Jam Kitchen
open same hours as the Thornton W. Burgess Museum (see *To See*). Even
in an area with so many tranquil spots, Green Briar rises to the top.
Perhaps that's because it's run by the Thornton W. Burgess Society "to re-
establish and maintain nature's fine balance among all living things and to
hold as a sacred trust the obligation to make only the best use of natural
resources." Located on Smiling Pond and adjacent to the famous Briar
Patch of Burgess's stories, these 57 acres of conservation land have many
short, interpretive nature trails (less than a mile long) and a lovely
wildflower garden. The society hosts natural-history classes, lectures, and
nature walks, as well as other wonderful programs for children, adults,
and families, throughout the year. Young children enjoy creeping along
a marsh creek in search of hermit crabs, while older children can take
canoeing expeditions and learn Native American crafts and lore. Fees
vary. Write or call for a schedule.

The Jam Kitchen was established in 1903 by Ida Putnam, who used
her friend Fanny Farmer's recipes to make jams, jellies, and fruit preserves. Step inside the old-fashioned, aromatic, and homey place to see
mason jars filled with apricots and strawberries and watch fruit simmer-
ing on vintage 1920 Glenwood gas stoves. Pick up a jar of beach plum
jam or take home some of the original recipes and try them in your own
kitchen. Two-hour workshops on the art of preserving fruit and making
jams and jellies are also held. About this sweet and aromatic place, Burgess said to Putnam in 1939, "It is a wonderful thing to sweeten the
world which is in a jam and needs preserving."

✐ **Shawme Duck Pond,** Water Street (Route 130), Sandwich Village. Flocks
of ducks, geese, and swans know a good thing when they find it. And even
though this idyllic spot is one of the most easily accessible on the Cape, it
remains a tranquil place for humans and waterfowl alike. Formerly a
marshy brook, the willow-lined pond was dammed prior to the gristmill
operating in the 1640s. It's a nice spot for canoeing.

Shawme-Crowell State Forest (888-0351), Route 130. You can walk, bicycle, and camp ($6 nightly) at 280 sites on 742 acres. Often when the
popular Nickerson State Park (see *Campground* in "Brewster") is full
of campers, there are dozens of good sites still available here.

Scusset Beach Reservation (888-0859), on Cape Cod Bay, off Scusset
Beach Road from the rotary on the mainland side of the canal. The
reservation has 450 acres, some of which are set aside for camping,
bicycling, picnicking, and walking. Campfire programs are held Thursday evenings by Cape Cod Canal Rangers (see US Army Corps of Engineers (USACE) Field Office under *Guidance* in "Bourne"). Facilities
include in-season lifeguard, rest rooms, changing rooms, and a snack
bar. Parking $2.

Tranquil Shawme Pond and the gristmill in Sandwich village

BEACHES

Town Neck Beach, on Cape Cod Bay, off Town Neck Road and Route 6A. This pebble beach extends a mile and a half from the Cape Cod Canal to Dock Creek. Visit at high tide if you want to swim; otherwise it's great for walking at low tide. Facilities include changing rooms and rest rooms. Parking $5.

Sandy Neck Beach, off Route 6A on the Sandwich/Barnstable line (see *Green Space—Beaches* in "Barnstable").

See also Scusset Beach Reservation.

PONDS

Wakeby Pond (off Cotuit Road), South Sandwich, offers freshwater swimming.

WALKS

Talbot's Point Salt Marsh Wildlife Reservation, off Old County Road from Route 6A. This little-used, 1½-mile (round-trip) hiking trail winds past red pines, beeches, and a large salt marsh.

See also Green Briar Nature Center & Jam Kitchen and Shawme-Crowell State Forest.

LODGING

RESORT MOTOR INN

❋ **Dan'l Webster Inn** (888-3622, 1-800-444-3566, http://www.media3.com/dan'lwebsterinn/), 149 Main Street, Sandwich 02563. Open year-round. The present building was modeled after the original 18th-century hostelry, which, before it was destroyed by fire, was a meeting place for Revolutionary patriots. The Catania family purchased the property in

1980 and vigilantly maintains its Colonial charm. A full-time staff horti-culturist has created pleasant courtyards and an attractive pool area behind the inn. Most of the 46 rooms and suites are of the top-notch motel/hotel variety; modern amenities include telephone, cable TV, turn-down service, room service, and a daily newspaper at your door. Rooms in the Fessenden Wing overlook gardens. A few rooms are more innlike, more distinctive; these are in two separate older houses. There are three highly regarded dining rooms on the premises (see *Dining Out*). Guests have privileges at the nearby Sportsite Health Club (see *To Do—Fitness Club*). Late May to mid-October $120–195; mid-October to late May $89–169. Numerous off-season packages .

BED & BREAKFASTS

❊ **Wingscorton Farm Inn** (888-0534), 11 Wing Boulevard, East Sandwich 02537. Open year-round. The circa-1758 working farm, on 13 acres of orchards and lawns, is worlds away from the often congested commercial byways of Cape Cod. Dick Loring opened this peaceful, gracious place, nestled between Route 6A and Cape Cod Bay, in 1980. The tranquil surroundings make for a welcome retreat in the height of summer. Once a stop on the Underground Railroad, the house has low ceilings, wainscot-ing, wide-plank floors, rich paneling, and wood-burning fireplaces in the guest rooms. Two living rooms—one with the largest hearth in New England—provide plenty of common space for guests. Accommodations include three suites (each with private bath, refrigerator, period antiques, and canopy bed) and a two-story carriage house with a private deck and patio, full kitchen, and woodstove. A multicourse breakfast is served at a long harvest table in front of a working fireplace. Dogs and cats roam around the property, which is also home to pygmy goats, horses, and sheep. You can bring your own well-behaved pets. Free-range chickens and fresh eggs are sold from the barn. As if all this weren't enough, you can walk to the inn's private bay beach. $115–150.

❊ **Captain Ezra Nye House** (888-6142, 1-800-388-2278, e-mail: captnye-@aol.com), 152 Main Street, Sandwich 02563. Open year-round. Elaine and Harry Dickson have run this 1829 Federal-style bed & breakfast since 1986. The five rooms and one suite (all with private bath; one with a working fireplace; all carpeted) are decorated with an eclectic assort-ment of antiques and things the Dicksons have collected from around the world. The common front parlor is a bit formal, but there's a small TV room off the dining room that's more casual. There are two breakfast seatings for the full meal. June through October $95–100; $65–85 off-season; service charge added.

❊ **Inn at Sandwich Center** (833-6958, 1-800-249-6949), 118 Tupper Road, Sandwich 02563. Open year-round. This 18th-century saltbox (expanded during the Federal period) sits atop a little rise in the center of town. Completely renovated and elegantly appointed, most of the five guest rooms have a working fireplace and four-poster bed. Innkeepers Elaine and Al Thomas, recent transplants from California, have combined French country and English aesthetics in the common and guest rooms. (Elaine was born in France and is multilingual.) The dining room, where a full breakfast is served, boasts a beehive oven and fireplace. Mid-May through October $85–95; $10 less off-season.

☞ **Summer House** (888-4991), 158 Main Street, Sandwich 02563. Open year-round. This 1835 Greek Revival Cape has five rooms (all with private bath), furnished simply with antiques and quilts; many feature fireplaces, original hardware, and painted hardwood floors. A bountiful breakfast is served in the fanciful living/dining room with Chinese-red walls and a black-and-white checkerboard floor. Take your afternoon tea in the sun room, in the English-style garden, or (very carefully) in the hammock. Marjorie and Kevin Huelsman, longtime Nantucket and Cape residents, began innkeeping in 1996. Late May to mid-October $75–85.

Belfry Inne & Bistro (888-8550), 8 Jarves Street, Sandwich 02563. Open year-round. In the center of town, the circa-1879 Victorian Belfry Inne has eight newly renovated guest rooms, all with private bath. Some of the rooms have a private balcony, gas fireplace, or an antique bathtub. Common space includes a formal parlor, front porch, and a two-person treetop cupola. The small pub, where you can have an after-dinner drink and dessert, is also open to the public. A full breakfast, of perhaps chocolate hazelnut French toast, is served in winter, but summertime guests get an expanded continental. $85–135.

Village Inn at Sandwich (833-0363, 1-800-922-9989), 4 Jarves Street, Sandwich 02563. Open April through October. Surrounded by a white picket fence in the middle of town, this 1830s Federal house has a wrap-around porch (decked with rocking chairs) and two living rooms for guests to enjoy. Innkeeper Patricia Platz renovated it from top to bottom in 1986. Six of eight guest rooms have private baths; third-floor rooms share a bath. All rooms have hardwood floors (some bleached) and down comforters. A full breakfast is served at individual tables. Mid-June through October $95–125; $85–105 otherwise; 10 percent service charge added.

☞ **Dillingham House** (833-0065), 71 Main Street, Sandwich 02563. Open June through October; in winter by appointment. This circa-1650 three-quarter Cape, built by one of Sandwich's founders, is about a mile from the village center on Route 130. If you enjoy old, historic homes, this place is for you. One guest room is across the hall from the front door; another, on the first floor, has a working fireplace; an upstairs guest room gets good afternoon sun. Both living rooms are comfortable—one has a large working hearth and the other (a former tack room now done in blue barn board) is filled with books, games, a grand piano, and a potbellied stove. A continental breakfast is served at one long table. Pets are occasionally accepted. $70–80.

The beloved boardwalk, rebuilt by townspeople after a fierce storm destroyed it, leads over a picturesque marsh to the town beach.

Bay Beach (888-8813, 1-800-475-6398), 1–3 Bay Beach Lane, Sandwich 02653. Open mid-May through October. Right on the water and dunes, with a view of the Cape Cod Canal's east entrance, this modern house is more evocative of Florida, perhaps, than of New England. Room amenities include air-conditioning, refrigerators, telephones, and outdoor decks. The six rooms (all with private baths, some with a Jacuzzi) are furnished with wicker, and the living/dining room with rattan and glass pieces. Bay Beach also has many windows and sliding glass doors to let in the expansive views. Rooms $150–195, including an ample continental breakfast.

Dunbar House (833-2485), 1 Water St. Open year-round. Across from Shawme Pond, this 18th century house is run by Mike and Mary Bell, who hail from England. They offer three simple, English-style B&B rooms with full breakfast. $85–95 April through October; $65–75 off-season.

COTTAGES

Pine Grove Cottages (888-8179), 348 Route 6A, East Sandwich 02537. Open May through October. These 10 tidy cottages with kitchens come in various sizes: tiny one-room, small one-bedroom, larger one-bedroom, and "deluxe" two-bedroom cottages. (Sandwich bylaws require two-bedroom units to measure 20 feet by 24 feet.) The cottages have been in Kathy Bumstead's family for three generations, and she keeps them freshly painted white. Although guests spend most of their time at the beach, there is also an aboveground pool and play area in the pine grove.

Pets are accepted. Mid-June to early September $285–495 weekly for two to four people.

MOTELS

☞ **Spring Garden Motel** (888-0710, 1-800-303-1751), 578 Route 6A, East Sandwich 02537. Open mid-April to mid-November. The Gluckmans have presided over this, one of the best motels on Route 6A, since 1984. Reserve early if you can. Although modest-looking from the front, from the back the motel has two levels of rooms that overlook a salt marsh and Scorton River, particularly beautiful at sunset. The backyard is dotted with lawn chairs, grills, and picnic tables. Each of the eight carpeted rooms has knotty-pine paneling, with two double beds, TV, air-conditioning, refrigerator, and telephone. In addition there are two efficiencies and a two-room suite with a private deck. An enclosed pool is shielded from Route 6A. Sandy Neck Beach is a 10-minute walk from here. July and August $71; $45–53 off-season.

❉ **Shadynook Inn & Motel** (888-0409, 1-800-338-5208, e-mail: thenook-@capecod.net), 14 Route 6A, Sandwich 02563. Open year-round. Sharon and Jim Rinaldi take well-deserved pride in their spiffy, shaded motel with lush landscaping. The large rooms are typically appointed as far as motel rooms go, only a bit nicer. You'll also have a choice of two- and three-room suites, some of which are efficiencies. Mid-June to early September $89–140 for two to four people; $65–120 otherwise.

CAMPGROUNDS

Peter's Pond Park (477-1775), 185 Cotuit Road, Sandwich. Open mid-April to mid-October. The park consists of 480 well-groomed camp-sites, walking trails, and a popular spring-fed lake for trout and bass fishing, boating, and swimming. There are organized children's activi-ties at the playground in summer. On-site tepee rentals.

See also Shawme-Crowell State Forest and Scusset Beach Reservation un-der *Green Space*.

WHERE TO EAT

DINING OUT

❉ **Dan'l Webster Inn** (888-3622), 149 Main Street, Sandwich. Open for lunch and dinner daily year-round; open for breakfast daily mid-April to mid-November and on weekends mid-November to mid-April. Even though Dan'l Webster is the only fine dining in town, it doesn't rest on this singular privileged position. Instead, the inn serves reliable, classic American dishes. The dress code is neat but informal. The sunlit conservatory is an indoor oasis, especially for lunch and brunch, while the main interior dining room is more traditional. The tavern, an authentic replica of the one frequented by patriot Daniel Webster, is reserved for lighter fare and drinks. In a nod to the ecologically minded and health-conscious, the inn raises fish in a state-of-the-art, enclosed aquafarm, and has installed an excellent water-filtration system. The inn's water is perhaps the best tasting on the Cape. Children's menu; early-bird specials. Lunch $5.75–12, dinner $16–25.

EATING OUT

❋ **Bee-Hive Tavern** (833-1184), 406 Route 6A, East Sandwich. Open for lunch and dinner daily and for breakfast on weekends, year-round. There are benches in front for a reason—there is often a wait at this popular restaurant. Low ceilings, barn board, and booths make this dark, Colonial-style tavern a comfortable choice year-round. If you're tired of eating at picnic tables or in "quaint" clam shacks, try this place. Standard fare includes pasta, sandwiches (including the "roll-up" variety), and burgers. Full-fledged dinner entrées are more substantial: chicken teriyaki, baked scrod, and lobster pie. Lunch $4.75–9, dinner $8–15.

❋ **Dunbar Tea Shop** (833-2485), 1 Water Street, Sandwich. Open 10 AM–5 PM daily, year-round. This tiny tearoom has been bustling since it opened, proof positive that good news travels fast on the Upper Cape. Come for a ploughman's lunch, or specials of the day like seafood quiche (which sells out fast), or sweets like pies, cakes, and Scottish shortbread. An authentic English tea ($6), with two scones, cream, and raspberry preserves, is offered 11–4:30 in the American-style country setting. A fancy high tea is served Sundays in the off-season. In summer, garden tables are an oasis; in winter, the woodstove makes it cozy indoors. Lunch $6–10.

☞❋ **Marshland Restaurant** (888-9824), 109 Route 6A, Sandwich. Open for breakfast and lunch on Monday, all three meals Tuesday through Saturday, and breakfast on Sunday, year-round. Locals primarily frequent this small, informal roadside place for coffee and breakfast muffins, lunch specials like meat loaf, quiche, or baked stuffed shells, and take-out sandwiches and roll-ups. Eat at one of the Formica booths or on a swiveling seat at the U-shaped counter.

☞❋ **Captain Scott's** (888-1675), 71 Tupper Road, Sandwich. Open 11:30–8:30 daily year-round. This casual, inexpensive place is hopping with locals who come for the no-frills Italian dishes, fried seafood dinners, and baked or broiled fish. Early-bird specials. Entrées $4–15.

☞✐ **Seafood Sam's** (888-4629), Coast Guard Road, Sandwich. Open for lunch and dinner daily, mid-March to mid-November. This casual spot near the marina serves fried seafood, seafood sandwiches, and seafood salad plates. Children's menu $2.75. Dishes $4.75–16.

Horizons on Cape Cod Bay (888-6166), Town Neck Beach, Sandwich. Open April to late October. Horizons is the only place in town right on the beach. Although the food isn't noteworthy, it's a nice place for an afternoon drink on the deck. Views are spectacular.

See also The Bridge and Sagamore Inn in "Bourne."

ENTERTAINMENT

As you enter Sandwich, there are a couple of well-placed marquees that will tell you what's happening that day or week.

Opera New England of Cape Cod (775-3858), PO Box 9, East Sandwich 02537, a touring company from New York City, performs two operas for adults and children at Sandwich High School on Quaker Meeting-house Road (East Sandwich) each spring and fall.

Heritage Plantation of Sandwich (888-3300), Pine and Grove Streets, sponsors outdoor concerts—from big band to jazz, from chamber singers to ethnic ensembles. June to late August. (See also *To See*.)

Band concerts, at the Wing School off Route 130, are given by the Sandwich Town Band on Thursday evenings at 7:30 in July and August.

SELECTIVE SHOPPING

ANTIQUES

H. Richard Strand Antiques (888-3230), Grove and Main Streets. Open daily year-round. Located in an impressive 1800 house, Strand sells an outstanding collection of Queen Anne and Chippendale furniture, glass, Oriental china, paintings, and lamps. Browsing here feels more like a self-guided "house beautiful" tour.

Brown Jug Antiques (833-1088), Main and Jarves Streets. Open daily May through October. Antique glass (including Sandwich glass, of course, as well as Tiffany and Steuben), Staffordshire china, and English cameos are the specialty of this shop.

ARTISANS

See also *Selective Shopping—Artisans* in "Bourne."

Glass Studio (888-6681), 470 Route 6A, East Sandwich. Open Wednesday through Monday year-round. Michael Magyar offers a wide selection of glass made with modern and century-old techniques. He's been plying his trade since 1980, and you can watch him work on Wednesday, Friday, Saturday, and Sunday. Choose from graceful Venetian goblets, bud vases, handblown ornaments (some of which are sold during the Christmas in Sandwich celebration; see *Special Events*), and "sea bubbles" glassware, which is influenced by the water around him.

AUCTIONS

Sandwich Auction House (888-1926), 15 Tupper Road. Consignment estate sales are held Wednesdays in summer and Saturdays off-season.

BOOKSTORE

Titcomb's Book Shop (888-2331), 432 Route 6A, East Sandwich. Open daily year-round. Owner Nancy Titcomb helped resurrect interest in Thornton W. Burgess, and, as you might imagine, she offers a great selection of his work. Three floors of this old barn are filled with new, used, and rare books for adults and children, as well as a good selection of Cape and maritime books.

SPECIAL SHOPS

Madden & Company (888-3663), 16 Jarves Street. Open Monday through Saturday, May through December; less regular hours the rest of the year. Set up to resemble a country store (albeit an upscale one), Paul Madden's shop offers antiques, lots of cookbooks, decorative country-style household gifts, and a few specialty foods.

The Weather Store (888-1200), 146 Main Street. Open Monday through Saturday, Sunday by chance or appointment, April through December. Owned by Paul Madden (of Madden & Company) with his son Parke, this shop's got it if it relates to weather: weather vanes, sundials, nautical gauges for yachts, umbrellas, "weather sticks" to indicate when a storm is headed your way, even whirligigs (weather instruments are broadly defined here).

Home for the Holidays (888-4388), 154 Main Street. Open daily from late May through December; Friday through Sunday the rest of the year. Within this 1850 house, each room is filled with decorations and gifts geared to specific holidays or special occasions. Items in one room are changed every month, so there's always a room devoted to the current holiday.

Maypop Lane (888-1230), Route 6A at Main Street. Open daily year-round. With many dealers under one roof, you'll find a broad selection: decoys, dolls, quilts, clothing, jewelry, glass, furniture, and other collectibles and antiques.

Horsefeathers (888-5298), 454 Route 6A, East Sandwich. Open year-round; call ahead in the off-season. Stop in for linens, lace, Victoriana, teacups, and vintage christening gowns.

Giving Tree Gallery (888-5446), 550 Route 6A, East Sandwich. Open May through December. Outdoor sculpture is situated on 4 acres of marshland, but don't overlook the indoor gallery.

See also Green Briar Nature Center & Jam Kitchen under *Green Space*.

SPECIAL EVENTS

Late April: **Daffodil Festival** pays homage to over 500,000 daffodils that were planted in the village center.

July 4: **Independence Day** festivities include a charming children's Boat Parade on Shawme Duck Pond.

Mid-September: **Boardwalk celebration** includes a road race/walk, a kite festival, and a beachgoers parade.

Early December: **Christmas in Sandwich** is a 3-week festival that includes caroling, hot cider at the Dan'l Webster Inn (see *Lodging—Resort Motor Inn*), open houses, trolley tours, and crafts sales.

Falmouth, Woods Hole, and Mashpee

The second largest town on the Cape, Falmouth has more shore and coastline than any other town, with 14 harbors, four public beaches with facilities, and more than 30 ponds. Saltwater inlets reach deep into the southern coastline, like fjords—only without the mountains. Buzzards Bay waters lap the western shores of quiet North and West Falmouth and bustling Woods Hole. The town's eight distinctive villages accommodate about 100,000 summer people, more than triple Falmouth's year-round population. Just east of Falmouth, Mashpee, with a fast-growing town center, is home to about 500 members of the Wampanoag tribe.

The villages differ widely in character. Quiet, restful lanes and residents who keep to themselves characterize Sippewissett and both North and West Falmouth. The West Falmouth Harbor (off wooded, scenic Route 28A) is tranquil and placid, particularly at sunset. Although Falmouth Heights is known for its opulent, turn-of-the-century shingled houses on Vineyard Sound, its beach is a popular gathering spot for New England–area college students. You'll see them everywhere—playing volleyball, sunbathing, flying kites, and enjoying the warm water and comfortable, relatively inexpensive seaside apartments that line Grand Avenue and Menauhant Road. Falmouth Heights has early ties to the Kennedys: Rose Fitzgerald was vacationing here with her family when Joe Kennedy came calling.

East Falmouth is a largely residential area, where many Portuguese and Cape Verdean fishermen and workers live. There are several inexpensive motels and summer homes lining the inlets of Green Pond, Bourne's Pond, and Waquoit Bay.

The center of Falmouth, with plentiful shops and eateries, is busy year-round. And the village common, picture-perfect with historic houses (converted to beautiful bed & breakfasts) encircling the tidy green space, is well worth a stroll. Falmouth's Inner Harbor is awash with restaurants, boatyards, a colorful marina, and moderate nightlife.

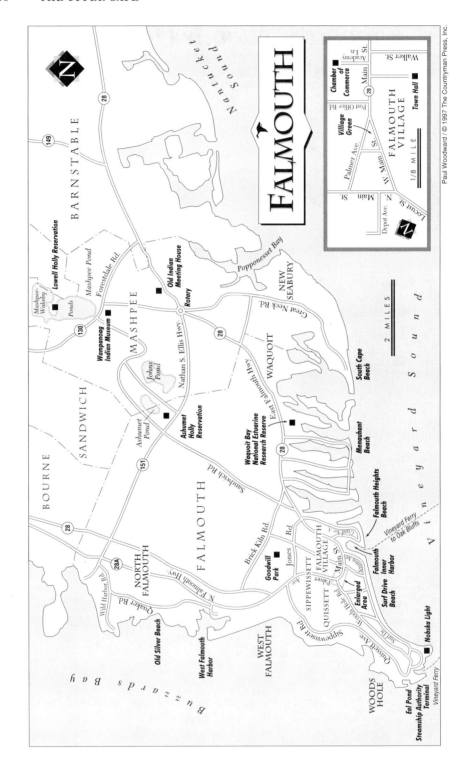

Two passenger ferries to Martha's Vineyard operate from here.

Four miles south of Falmouth, Woods Hole is more than just a terminus for the Steamship Authority auto and passenger ferries to the Vineyard. It is also home to three major scientific institutions: the National Marine Fisheries Service ("the Fisheries"), Woods Hole Oceanographic Institution (or WHOI, pronounced *hooey* by locals and scientists alike), and the Marine Biological Laboratory (MBL).

Woods Hole, named for the "hole" or passage between Penzance Point and Nonamessett Island, was the site of the first documented European landing in the New World. Bartholomew Gosnold arrived here from Falmouth, England, in 1602. For a thousand years prior to the colonists' arrival, the native Wampanoag Indians had established summer camps in this area of the Cape, but with the settlement of Plymouth Colony, they saw larger and larger pieces of their homeland taken away from them and their numbers decimated by a plague. In 1617, three years after Captain John Smith explored the area, six Native Americans were kidnapped and forced into slavery. In 1665 the missionary Reverend Richard Bourne appealed to the Massachusetts legislature to reserve about 25 square miles for the Native Americans. The area was called Mashpee (or Massapee or Massipee, depending on who's doing the translating) Plantation, in essence the first Native American reservation in the United States. In 1870 the plantation was incorporated as the town of Mashpee. When the *Mayflower* arrived at Plymouth, the Wampanoag population had been an estimated 30,000; there are a scant 500 Wampanoags in Mashpee today. Mashpee (which means "land near the great cove") is one of two Massachusetts towns to be administered by Native Americans (the other is Gay Head on Martha's Vineyard).

Mashpee wasn't popular with wealthy 19th-century settlers, so there are few stately old homes there. The Wampanoags maintain a museum and church, both staffed by knowledgeable tribespeople who can tell you more about their people's history. In the 1930s classic *Cape Cod Ahoy!*, Wilson Tarbel observed something about Mashpee that could still be said today: It's "retiring, elusive, scattered, a thing hidden among the trees."

The largest developed area of Mashpee is New Seabury, a 2300-acre resort of modern homes, cottages, condos, several restaurants, golf courses, shops, and beaches. When developers won their lengthy legal battle with the Wampanoags, the tribe—and the town—lost much of its prettiest oceanfront property. The only remaining beach of note is South Cape Beach, a relatively pristine barrier beach with several miles of marked nature trails and steady winds that attract windsurfers. Compared with its neighbors, Mashpee is a quiet place.

GUIDANCE

Falmouth Chamber of Commerce (548-8500, 548-4724 for 24-hour information that can be faxed back to you, 1-800-526-8532), Box 582, 20

Academy Lane, Falmouth 02541. Open 9–5 weekdays year-round; 9–5 weekends mid-May to mid-October. There is also a small, seasonal satellite office but at press time the location had yet to be determined. The offices also have plenty of information on Woods Hole; pick up the good foldout map. Look for the Historical Society's walking tour brochure.

Mashpee Chamber of Commerce (477-0792, 1-800-423-6274), in the Cape Cod Five Cents Savings Bank off the Mashpee rotary (Routes 28 and 151). Mailing address: PO Box 1245, Mashpee 02649. Open weekdays 9:30–4:30 year-round; weekends 9–3 in summer. Across the street in the Mashpee Commons mall, in summer a booth is open 6 PM– 9 PM on Fridays, 11–8 on Saturdays, and 11–4 on Sundays.

PUBLIC REST ROOMS

In Falmouth, public rest rooms are located at the Chamber of Commerce office, Academy Street; Town Hall, Main Street; the Harbormaster's Office at Marina Park, Scranton Avenue. In Woods Hole, head to the Steamship Authority.

In Mashpee public rest rooms are available at South Cape Beach (at the end of Great Oak Road) and at John's Pond, a town park off Hoophole Road.

GETTING THERE

By car: Via Route 28 south, Falmouth is 15 miles from the Bourne Bridge and 20 miles from the Sagamore Bridge. Route 28 turns into Main Street. In northern Falmouth, Route 28A parallels Route 28 and is much more scenic. Route 28 leads directly to Locust Street and Woods Hole Road for Woods Hole.

The directional signposts for Route 28 are a tad confusing from this point on. Although Hyannis and Chatham are east of Falmouth, the signpost from Falmouth to Chatham says ROUTE 28 SOUTH. This is because Route 28 originates in Bourne and does indeed head south to Falmouth before jogging east.

To reach Mashpee from the Sagamore Bridge, take Route 6 east to Route 130 south to North Great Neck Road to the Routes 151 and 28 Mashpee rotary. Although there's no Mashpee town center per se, Mashpee Commons shopping area at the rotary acts as its hub.

By bus: **Bonanza** (1-800-556-3815) has service to Falmouth (stopping at the Depot Avenue terminal) and Woods Hole (stopping at the Steamship Authority) from New York, Providence, and Boston. There is direct service to Boston's Logan Airport. Some buses are intended to connect with ferries to Martha's Vineyard, although the ferry won't wait for a late bus. The round-trip fare from Boston to Woods Hole is $21.95.

GETTING AROUND

The **Whoosh** trolley travels on a fixed route between and through Falmouth and Woods Hole. It stops at about 14 major points of interest. Tourists can hop on and off at both "downtown" areas and at shops and beaches. Whoosh ($.50 fare) operates 10–9 daily, late May to mid-

October. Pick up a schedule at the Falmouth Chamber of Commerce (see *Guidance*) or at any stop along the route. Parking is extremely limited in tiny Woods Hole, and roads can be quite congested with ferry traffic, so take the Whoosh if you're just visiting for the afternoon.

Getting to Martha's Vineyard: There is year-round automobile and passenger ferry service to Martha's Vineyard from Woods Hole; there are two seasonal passenger ferry services to the Vineyard from Falmouth Harbor. For complete information, see *Getting There* in "Martha's Vineyard."

MEDICAL EMERGENCY

Falmouth Hospital (548-5300), 100 Ter Heun Drive (off Route 28), Falmouth. Open 24 hours a day.

Falmouth Walk-In Medical Center (540-6790) at 309 Route 28 in Teaticket takes walk-ins weekday mornings 8–11.

Mashpee Family Medicine (477-4282) on Route 28 in Mashpee takes walk-ins on weekdays and Saturday mornings.

TO SEE

In Falmouth

Village green. Falmouth's village green is bordered by Colonial, Federal, Italianate, and Greek Revival homes, many of which were built for wealthy ship captains and have been turned into inns and bed & breakfasts. Designated as public land in 1749 and recently placed on the National Historic Register, this large triangle of grass is enclosed by a white picket fence, surely as pastoral a sight today as it was more than 200 years ago. With these historic buildings surrounding you, it's not difficult to imagine local militiamen practicing their marches and drills and townspeople grazing their horses. In fact, a reenactment of local militia maneuvers takes place on July 4.

First Congregational Church, at 68 Main Street, on the village green. This quintessential New England church—with its high steeple and crisp white lines—is graced by a bell (which still rings) commissioned by Paul Revere. The receipt for the bell—from 1796—is on display; the inscription on the bell reads: "The living to the church I call, and to the grave I summon all." The church standing today was built on the foundation of the one erected in 1796.

Conant House (548-4857), 55–65 Palmer Avenue. Open 2–5 weekdays, mid-June to mid-September; the office and archives are open 9–noon Wednesday and 9–4 Friday year-round. Operated by the Falmouth Historical Society, this 1794 half-Cape just off the village green contains sailors' valentines, scrimshaw, rare glass and china, and old tools. One room is set aside to honor Katherine Lee Bates, a Wellesley College professor and composer of "America the Beautiful," who was born nearby in 1859 at 16 Main Street (not open to the public). Most Falmouth residents would lend support to the grassroots movement in the United States to change the national anthem from "The Star-Spangled Banner" to Bates's easier-to-sing, less militaristic song. Adults $2, children $.50. (A tour guide takes you around; admission also includes a tour of the Julia Wood House.)

Julia Wood House (548-4857), next to the Conant House, Palmer Avenue. Open 2–5 weekdays, mid-June to mid-September. Also maintained by the Falmouth Historical Society, this early-19th-century house was home to Dr. Francis Wicks, who is known for his work with smallpox inoculations. One room of the house is set up as the physician's office; note the selection of dental tools. (Doctors in those days performed dental work; that is, they pulled teeth.) Behind the main house, the **Dudley Hallett Barn** contains tools, a 19th-century sleigh, a carriage, and an old town pump (all the things that would normally end up in a barn). There is also a lovely garden. Admission: adults $2, children $.50.

Bourne Farm (548-0711), Route 28A, North Falmouth. Open by appointment year-round. Owned by the nonprofit Salt Pond Area Bird Sanctuary, this 1775 historic landmark includes a restored farmhouse, a bunkhouse, and a barn (all unfurnished but open for touring), as well as 40 acres of orchards, fields, and wooded trails. It's a perfectly tranquil spot overlooking Crockers Pond, complete with a picnic area under a grape arbor. The effort to reclaim this property in 1980 was spearheaded by Ermine Lovell. Trail fees: adults $2, children $1.

In Woods Hole

☞✐❋ **Aquarium of the National Marine Fisheries** (548-7684), Albatross Street. Open 10–4 weekdays, mid-September to mid-June; 10–4 daily, mid-June to mid-September. When it opened in 1871, it was the first aquarium in the country. Today it's a fun place to learn a little about a lot of slippery fish, living shellfish (rather than the empty shells we're all accustomed to seeing), and other lesser-known creatures of the deep. Kids are encouraged to use the microscopes and to interact with the dozen or so tanks and shallow pools of icy-cold bubbling seawater inhabited by lobsters, hermit crabs, and other crawling sea critters. Free.

☞ **Woods Hole Oceanographic Institution (WHOI) Exhibit Center** (457-2100), 15 School Street. Open 10–4:30 Tuesday through Saturday and Sunday noon–4:30, May through October; also open Monday 10–4:30 in July and August. Closed January through March; weekend hours in the off-season. A Rockefeller grant of $25 million got WHOI off the ground in 1930, and since then its budget has grown to about $87 million annually. It is the largest independent oceanography lab in the country; about 1000 students and researchers from all over the world are employed year-round. In summer the place swells with elite scientists who work day and night. Relatively unpolluted waters and a naturally deep harbor make Woods Hole an ideal location for their work.

Considering that WHOI buildings cover 200 acres in Woods Hole, the institution is strangely inhospitable to visitors (perhaps the scientists are too busy doing their research). WHOI's concession to interested visitors is a small exhibit center that features several excellent videos that run throughout the day, exhibits of some odd-looking preserved sea creatures, and a fascinating display of the *Alvin,* the tiny submarine that allowed WHOI researchers to locate and photograph the *Titanic* in 1986. During World War II, the institute worked on underwater explosives and submarine detection. Visitors over 10, $2.

Marine Biological Laboratory (MBL) (548-3705; 289-7623 for tour reservations), Water Street. Open weekdays, June through August; tours at 1, 2, and 3 PM only. Founded in 1888 as "a non-profit institution devoted to research and education in basic biology," the MBL studies more than fish. It studies life at its most basic level, with an eye toward the question "What is life?" And marine creatures tend to be some of the most useful animals in the quest for that answer. Scientists (including 35 Nobel laureates over the years) study the problems of infertility, hypertension, Alzheimer's, AIDS, and other diseases. It's not hyperbole to say there's no other institution or academy like it in the world. Former researchers lead excellent tours that include a slide program about what goes on at the MBL. Tours are restricted in size and are very popular, so try to make reservations a week in advance. History buffs will be interested to note that one of the MBL's granite buildings was a former factory that made candles with spermaceti from whale oil. Free. Not appropriate for children under 10.

Waterfront Park, on Water Street near the MBL overlooking the *Ocean Quest* (see *Boat Excursions/Rentals*). There are shaded benches and a Yalde sundial, from which you can tell time to within 30 seconds.

Eel Pond, off Water Street. The harborlike pond has a drawbridge that grants access to Great Harbor for the myriad fishing boats, yachts, and research vessels moored here. (The walk around the shore is lovely.) The little bridge goes up and down on the hour and half hour; in summer you can see boats lining up waiting to pass through.

St. Joseph's Bell Tower, Millfield Street (on the north shore of Eel Pond). To encourage his colleagues not to become too caught up in the earthly details of their work and lose their faith in the divine, a student at the MBL designed this pink-granite Romanesque bell tower in 1929. He arranged for its two bells to ring twice a day to remind the scientists and townspeople of a higher power. (One bell is named for Gregor Mendel, the 19th-century botanist, the other for Louis Pasteur.) Nowadays, the bells ring three times, at 7 AM, noon, and 6 PM. The meticulously maintained **St. Mary's Garden** surrounds the tower with flowers, herbs, a bench, and a few chairs. Right on the harbor, this is one of the most relaxing places in the entire area.

Church of the Messiah, Church Street. Nine Nobel Prize winners are buried in the churchyard. This 1888 stone Episcopal church is admired by visiting scientists, tourists, and townsfolk alike, and the herb meditation garden is a treasure.

☞✐**Woods Hole Historical Museum and Collection** (548-7270), 573 Woods Hole Road. Open 10–4 Tuesday through Saturday from mid-June through September. Archives are open year-round. A treasure. Near the top of the Steamship Authority parking lot (stop in even if you're not waiting for the boat), the **Bradley House** historical museum maintains a good library on maritime subjects, more than 200 oral histories recorded by local townsfolk, and a diorama of Woods Hole in the late 1800s. There is also an exhibit on summer life in the 1890s, featuring the Yale family of Quissett. Small historic boats that plied local waters are exhibited in the adjacent **Swift Barn.** There is a lovely view of Little Harbor from here, and staff give a free 90-minute walking tour around Eel Pond on Tuesdays at 4 during July and August. Donations.

❋ **Nobska Light,** Church Street, off Woods Hole Road. Built in 1828 and rebuilt in 1876, the fixed beacon (automated in 1985) commands a high vantage point on a bluff, visible from 17 miles out at sea. The breezy bluff is a particularly good place to get a view of the "hole" (after which Woods Hole was named), the Elizabeth Islands, and the north shore of Martha's Vineyard, and to watch the sunset. More than 30,000 vessels—ferries, fully rigged sailing ships, and pleasure boats—pass by annually. Not surprisingly, the internationally regarded Falmouth Road Race also runs by the picturesque lighthouse. During **Cape Heritage Week** in mid-May, the Coast Guard opens many Cape lighthouses, including Nobska.

❋ **Spohr's Garden,** Fells Road off Oyster Pond Road. Open year-round. Thanks to the generosity of Charles and Margaret Spohr (Charles won the citizen-of-the-year award in 1993), this spectacular 3-acre private garden is yours for the touring. Park on Fells Road, or tie up at the dock on Oyster Pond. Come in spring when more than 700,000 daffodils do their magic. Throughout the remainder of the blooming season, you'll revel in lilies, azaleas, magnolias, hydrangeas, and other colorful flora. (You'll share the wide paths with geese and ducks.)

See also The Dome under *Entertainment.*

In Mashpee

Old Indian Meetinghouse (477-0208, Wampanoag Tribal Council), on Meetinghouse Way off Route 28. Hours uncertain at press time. Located on the edge of what was once a Wampanoag-only cemetery ("They even took our burial ground away from us and made it theirs," laments a volunteer guide), this is the oldest surviving meetinghouse on the Cape. It was built in 1684 and moved to its present location in 1717. Take the short tour of the small, simple church and you'll see quilts commemorating the "glorious dead" tribe members. Climb up the narrow stairs into the choir loft to see accomplished carvings of multimasted ships that were whittled during lengthy Baptist sermons in the 19th century. Donations.

✐✷ **Mashpee Wampanoag Indian Museum** (477-1536), on Route 130 across from Lake Avenue. Open 10–2 Monday through Saturday year-round. This small, early-19th-century house was built by Richard Bourne, minister and missionary to the Mashpee Wampanoags. Exhibits include tools, baskets, traditional clothing, arrowheads, a reconstructed wigwam, and a model of a pre-European-invasion tribal village. Although the displays aren't particularly enlightening, explanatory literature is available and the Wampanoag staff are happy to answer questions. They appreciate interest in their modest museum. (There is a herring run at the end of the parking lot.) Donations.

SCENIC DRIVE

Take Route 28A to Old Dock Road to reach placid **West Falmouth Harbor.** Double back and take Route 28A to Palmer Avenue, to Sippewissett Road, to hilly and winding Quissett Avenue, to equally tranquil **Quissett Harbor.** At the far edge of the harbor you'll see a path that goes up over the hill of **The Knob,** an outcrop that's one-half wooded bird sanctuary and one-half rocky beach. Walk out to The Knob along the water and back through the woods. It's a great place for a picnic or to take in the sunset. Sippewissett Road takes you to Eel Pond and Woods Hole the back way.

TO DO

BICYCLING/RENTALS

Shining Sea Bike Path. The easygoing and level 3.3-mile (one way) trail is one of Falmouth's most popular attractions. Following the old Penn Central Railroad line between Falmouth and Woods Hole, the path parallels unspoiled beaches, marshes, and bird sanctuaries. It was named in honor of Katherine Lee Bates (see Conant House under *To See*), composer of "America the Beautiful." The last line of her song— "from sea to shining sea"—is a fitting description of the trail, which offers lovely views of Vineyard Sound, Martha's Vineyard, and Naushon Island. The trail connects with several others: from Falmouth to Menauhant Beach in East Falmouth; from Woods Hole to Old Silver Beach in North Falmouth; and from Woods Hole to Quissett and Sippewissett. There is a trailhead and parking lot on Locust Street (at Mill Road) in Falmouth, as well as access points at Elm Road and Oyster Pond Road. Park here; it's very difficult to park in Woods Hole.

Holiday Cycles (540-3549), 465 Grand Avenue, Falmouth Heights. Along with a wide variety of bikes (including tandems and surreys) and equipment (from child seats to locks), Holiday Cycles offers free parking. Ask for details about the 23-mile route through Sippewissett.

Corner Cycle (540-4195), 115 Palmer Avenue, Falmouth, also rents bicycles.

Nobska Light, Woods Hole

BOAT EXCURSIONS/RENTALS

Ocean Quest (385-7656, 1-800-376-2326), Water Street, Woods Hole. Since 1993, from mid-May to mid-October, founder and director Kathy Mullin has offered a hands-on marine education for the entire family. A science teacher and naturalist, Kathy gives a brief overview of oceanography. The 90-minute trip costs $14 for adults, $10 for children 3–12. The boat departs four times daily.

Patriot Party Boats (548-2626), 227 Clinton Avenue, Falmouth. July to early September. This outfit operates 2- and 3-hour sails on the *Liberté,* a 1750s schooner replica; adults $20, children 12 and under $14. Sightseeing trips, including sunset and moonlight cruises, are $10 adults, children 12 and under $6. Owner Bud Tietje has been chartering boats since the mid-1950s and knows the ins and outs of this shoreline better than most. Bud's son Jim now runs the business, but Bud is often on board. Patriot also has ferry service to the Vineyard. And although they primarily service commuters and island workers, you can catch a ride with them daily year-round.

Maco's at Green Pond (457-4155), 366 Menauhant road, Green Pond, East Falmouth. Open for boat rentals daily May through September.

CANOEING

Edward's Boatyard (548-2216), 1209 East Falmouth Highway, on Waquoit Bay, East Falmouth. From May to mid-October rent a canoe ($35 daily) to paddle around Waquoit Bay and over to Washburn Island.

See also Waquoit Bay National Estuarine Research Reserve and Mashpee River Woodlands under *Green Space.*

FISHING/SHELLFISHING

Contact Town Hall (548-7611) on Main Street in Falmouth for fishing and shellfishing licenses and regulations. In Mashpee head to the town clerk's office (539-1416) at Town Hall, 16 Great Neck Road North.

Fish for trout, smallmouth bass, chain pickerel, and white perch at **Ashumet Pond, John's Pond, Quashnet River, Mashpee-Wakeby Pond, the Mashpee River** (access from Quinnaquissett Road), and at the town landing on **Santuit Pond.** See Massachusetts Military Reservation in "Bourne" for information about water quality at Ashumet and John's Pond. Surf casting is great at **South Cape Beach State Park** in Mashpee (see *Green Space*) and on **Surf Drive** in Falmouth.

Patriot Party Boats (548-2626), 227 Clinton Avenue, Falmouth. The Goliath of boat tours in Falmouth also offers sport- and bottom fishing from late May to mid-October. Bottom fishing aboard the enclosed *Patriot II* is $20 adults, $12 children 6–12, free age 5 and under. Sportfishing is $50 per person aboard the custom-outfitted *Minuteman*.

Susan Jean (548-6901), Eel Pond, off Water Street, Woods Hole. From late May to mid-October, Captain John Christian's 22-foot Aquasport searches for trophy-sized striped bass. This trip is for the serious angler—John departs in the middle of the night (well, more like 4 AM), which he thinks will give him the best chance of finding the fish. All tackle and live eels for bait are included. $375 for an 8-hour trip for one to three people. Reservations necessary.

Other boats available for fishing charters include Captain William Kidd's *Antigua* (540-5955, 1-800-652-5955) and Captain Dan Junker's *Relentless* (457-9445). **Cygnet Sport Fishing** (548-6274) also offers full- and half-day trips.

Eastman's Sport & Tackle (548-6900), 150 Main Street, Falmouth. A good source for local fishing information and rental equipment.

FITNESS CLUB

Falmouth Sports Center (548-7433), Highfield Drive, Falmouth. Open year-round. Pay $6 per day for access to racquetball courts, as well as aerobics classes and a full array of body-building equipment. Tennis courts are available for $10 per person.

FOR FAMILIES

✐❋ **Cape Cod Children's Museum** (457-4667), Falmouth Mall, Route 28, Falmouth. Open 10–5 Monday through Saturday, noon–5 Sunday year-round. The most popular regularly scheduled activities include an enormous range of arts and crafts. Toddlers love the sand room, castle, puppet theater, and the pirate ship. Admission: $3 age 5 and over, $2 age 1–4. Membership, providing unlimited visits: $40 first person in a family, $5 each additional person. (On Fridays 3–5, admission is $1.)

GOLF

Quashnet Valley Country Club (477-4412, 1-800-433-8633), 309 Old Barnstable Road, Mashpee. Open year-round. This semiprivate course winds around cranberry bogs and groves of trees, and requires some skill if you don't want to lose your ball in the ponds and marshes that surround 12 of the course's holes. 18 holes, 6000 yards, par 72.

Falmouth Country Club (548-3211), 630 Carriage Shop Road, East Falmouth. Open year-round. A good mix of easy and difficult pars. 18 holes, 6535 yards, par 72.

Ballymeade Country Club (540-4005), 125 Falmouth Woods Road, North Falmouth. Open year-round. 18 holes, 6358 yards, par 72. Marked with boulders and several deep pits, this tough semiprivate course requires some precision.

Cape Cod Country Club (563-9842), off Route 151 and Ranch Road, North Falmouth. Open year-round. 18 holes, 6400 yards, par 71. This scenic course has great variety.

Paul Harney Golf Club (563-3454), 74 Club Valley Drive off Route 151, East Falmouth. Open year-round. 18 holes, 3500 yards, par 59. This course has somewhat narrow fairways but is generally within the ability of weekend golfers.

Woodbriar (540-1600), 339 Gifford Street, Falmouth. Open year-round. This nine-hole, 1285-yard, par-27 course is quite forgiving.

New Seabury Country Club (477-9110), Shore Drive, New Seabury. Open to the general public weekdays September to May. This semiprivate club has two excellent 18-hole courses: the blue course is 7200 yards, par 72; the green course is 5986 yards, par 72.

HORSEBACK RIDING

Haland Stables (540-2552), 878 Route 28A, West Falmouth. Open 9–5 Monday through Saturday year-round; reservations absolutely necessary. Haland offers excellent English instruction and guided trail rides through pine woods and marshland.

Fieldcrest Farms (540-0626), 774 Palmer Avenue, Sippewissett. Open year-round for English lessons; indoor riding ring. No trails available if you're not taking lessons.

ICE SKATING

Falmouth Ice Arena (548-9083, 548-0275 for recorded information on public skating and the day's activities), Palmer Avenue, Falmouth. Open mid-September to mid-March for public skating.

KAYAKING

Cape Cod Kayak (548-1695), North Falmouth. Open late May to mid-October. Exploring salt marshes, tidal inlets, freshwater ponds, and the ocean shoreline from the vantage point and speed of a kayak is a great way to experience the Cape. For $55 (half day), $80 (full day), or $100 (weekend), Cape Cod Kayak will deliver to you and pick up a two-seater kayak. Rates are $25, $35, and $70 (respectively) for a one-seater and rates are slightly less in autumn. If you want to go kayaking and don't know where to go, owner Kim Fernandes will recommend her favorite spots or locations suited to your interests and level of ability. She also has organized tours with about five people per guide.

SEAL CRUISES

Patriot Party Boats (563-6390), Scranton Avenue, Falmouth. Seal cruises led by the Massachusetts Audubon Society depart on weekends from late March through April and in late December and early January. Tickets cost $25 adults, $20 children. Onboard naturalists will tell you about local sights in between pointing out seals and waterfowl.

STRAWBERRY PICKING

Tony Andrew's Farm Stand (548-5257), 398 Old Meeting House Road, East Falmouth. Open daily, mid-June through October, since 1927. Strawberries, strawberries everywhere, and other produce, too, all reasonably priced (especially if you pick your own). From the looks of it, East Falmouth was once the strawberry center of the world! Strawberry season runs from mid-June to early July, more or less. And from late June to late August, you can also pick your own tomatoes, green beans, and peas. Children welcome.

TENNIS

The following courts are public: at the **elementary school,** Davisville Road, East Falmouth; **Lawrence School,** Lakeview Avenue, Falmouth; the **high school,** Gifford Street Extension (reservations required: 457-2567), Falmouth; **Nye Park,** North Falmouth; Blacksmith Shop Road, behind the fire station, West Falmouth; **Taft's Playground,** Bell Tower Lane, Woods Hole; the **middle school,** Old Barnstable Road, Mashpee.

Ballymeade Country Club (540-4005), 125 Falmouth Woods Road, North Falmouth. Six Har-Tru and four hard courts; lessons and clinics.

Falmouth Sports Center (548-7433), 33 Highfield Drive, Falmouth. Six indoor and three outdoor courts.

Falmouth Tennis Club (548-4370), Dillingham Avenue, off Route 28 heading toward Hyannis. Open late May to early September. Three clay and three Har-Tru outdoor courts.

WINDSURFING

Cape Sailboards (540-8800, e-mail capesailbd@aol.com), 661 Main Street, Falmouth. Often closed in February. Although this surf shop doesn't rent equipment, it sells all the requisite gear and clothing. If you're at all interested in windsurfing on these waters, the staff are quite knowledgeable and expert. Falmouth is the unofficial Cape capital of windsurfing. And although nearly all of Falmouth's public beaches are well suited to the sport, Old Silver Beach (a long beach) is particularly popular. The less populated Trunk River (at the west end of Surf Drive Beach) is another favorite, but you can only windsurf from 9 to 4:30 late June to mid-August, when lifeguards are on duty.

New England Windsurfing Academy (540-8106), in front of the Sea Crest Hotel, Old Silver Beach, off Route 28A, North Falmouth. Open May through September. Western-facing Old Silver Beach gets a good, predominantly southwestern wind and the academy is well positioned to take advantage of it. Lessons are offered daily, preferably by appointment, in summer. By the end of the 3-hour lesson ($60) you'll be on your way to trouble-free sailboarding. Lessons are professional, friendly, and relaxed.

GREEN SPACE

❋ **Ashumet Holly and Wildlife Sanctuary** (563-6390), 286 Ashumet Road (off Route 151), East Falmouth. Open daily sunrise to sunset year-round. Local philanthropist Josiah K. Lilly III (of Heritage Plantation of Sandwich fame; see *To See* in "Sandwich") purchased and donated the land in 1961, after the death of Wilfred Wheeler, who cultivated most of these plants. Wheeler had been very concerned about holiday overharvesting of holly. Crisscrossed with eight self-guided nature trails, this 45-acre Massachusetts Audubon Society sanctuary overflows with holly: There are more than eight species, 65 varieties, and 1000 trees (from America, Europe, and Asia). More than 130 bird species have been sighted here: Since 1935 nesting barn swallows have made their home in the rafters of the barn from mid-April to late August. Other flora and fauna thrive as well. Rhododendrons and dogwoods bloom in spring. Large white franklinia flowers (named for Benjamin Franklin) make a show in autumn, and in summer Grassy Pond is filled with the blossoms of lotus plants. The sanctuary offers nature trips to Cuttyhunk Island, guided bird walks, and a holly bush sale in December. Classes are offered throughout the year. Pick up the informative trail map before setting out. Adults $3, children $2. See Massachusetts Military Reservation under *To See*, "Bourne," for information regarding water quality near Ashumet Pond.

❋ **Waquoit Bay National Estuarine Research Reserve** (457-0495), off Route 28, East Falmouth. Reserve open year-round except during autumn and winter hunting seasons. Headquarters open 10–4 Monday through Saturday in summer; off-season hours vary. There are three components to the reserve: South Cape Beach (see also Beaches), Washburn Island, and the headquarters (which houses temporary exhibits during summer). More than 2500 acres of delicate, protected estuary and barrier beaches surround lovely Waquoit Bay. Stop in at the headquarters for a trail map. In July and August a guided "Head of the Bay" walk is given on Saturday mornings. On Tuesday evenings look for the "Evenings on the Bluff" talk. Within the South Cape Beach State Park is the little-used, mile-long Great Flat Pond Trail. It winds past salt marshes, bogs, and wetlands and along coastal pine forests. Guided walks are offered Friday mornings in July and August. The 330-acre, pine-filled Washburn Island is accessible year-round if you have a boat. The 10 primitive island campsites require a permit.

❋ **South Cape Beach State Park** (457-0495), on Vineyard Sound, at the end of Great Neck Road, Mashpee. The 432-acre state park boasts a lovely 2-mile-long, dune-backed barrier beach and nature trails. Facilities include a concession stand, rest rooms, handicap ramp onto the beach, and lifeguards. Parking is $2 during summer.

See also Spohr's Garden and Bourne Farm under *To See,* as well as The Knob under *Scenic Drives.*

BEACHES

Along Buzzards Bay and Vineyard Sound, Falmouth's 68-mile shoreline boasts nine saltwater beaches (only four of which are open to nonresidents). Visitors renting a cottage for a week or more qualify to purchase a beach sticker, obtainable at the Surf Drive Beach bathhouse 9–4 daily in summer. The permit costs $40 for one week, $50 for two weeks. Some innkeepers provide beach stickers as a courtesy to their guests. Otherwise, you may pay a daily fee to park at the following beaches. (The Town Beach Committee, 548-8623, has further details.)

Old Silver Beach, on Buzzards Bay, off Route 28A and Quaker Road, North Falmouth. One of the longest and sandiest beaches in town, this is a good one for children, since an offshore sandbar creates shallow tidal pools. Facilities include a bathhouse, a lifeguard, and a snack bar. Parking is $10.

Menauhant Beach, on Vineyard Sound, off Route 28 and Central Avenue, East Falmouth. Waters are less choppy on Vineyard Sound than they are off the Atlantic. Parking is $5 weekdays, $8 weekends and holidays.

Surf Drive Beach, on Vineyard Sound. On Surf Drive, off Main and Shore Streets, Falmouth. Surf Drive Beach attracts sea kayakers, walkers, and swimmers who want to escape the crowds on the beaches of "downtown" Falmouth. Surf Drive Beach is accessible via the Shining Sea Trail (see *To Do—Bicycling*); by foot it's 30 minutes from the middle of Falmouth. Facilities include a bathhouse. Parking is $5 weekdays, $8 weekends and holidays.

Falmouth Heights Beach, on Vineyard Sound. On Grand Avenue, Falmouth Heights. Although there is no public parking, the beach is public and popular. Facilities include lots of snack bars.

See also South Cape Beach State Park.

PONDS

Mashpee and **Wakeby Ponds,** off Route 130, Mashpee. Combined, these ponds create the Cape's largest freshwater body, wonderful for swimming, fishing, and boating. This area was a favorite fishing spot of both patriot Daniel Webster and President Grover Cleveland.

John's Pond, off Hoophole Road from Route 151, Mashpee. Facilities include rest rooms, a snack bar, a picnic table, and grills. See Massachusetts Military Reservation under *To See* in "Bourne" for information regarding water conditions.

Grews Pond, off Gifford Street at **Goodwill Park,** West Falmouth. Lifeguard in-season, as well as picnic and barbecue facilities and a playground. There are also hiking trails all around the pond.

WALKS

Lowell Holly Reservation (921-1944, 617-740-7233), off Sandwich Road from Route 130, Mashpee. Open 8 AM–sunset daily, May through October. Donated by Harvard University president Abbott Lawrence Lowell to the Trustees of the Reservation in 1943, this 130-acre preserve is a tranquil oasis. It contains an untouched forest of native American beeches and more than 500 hollies, as well as white pines, rhododendrons, and wildflowers. The Wheeler Trail circles the peninsula that separates Wakeby and Mashpee Ponds. A small bathing beach (no lifeguard) and picnic tables invite you to linger in this peaceful place. Admission to the park is $5 on summer weekends.

Mashpee River Woodlands/South Mashpee Pine Barrens, Mashpee. Open year-round. Parking available on Quinnaquissett Avenue (off Route 28 just east of the rotary) and at the end of River Road off Great Neck Road South. The 8-mile hiking trail winds along the Mashpee River, through a quiet forest, and along marshes and cranberry bogs. Put in your canoe at the public landing on Mashpee Neck Road. Free.

Beebe Woods, access from Ter Heun Drive off Route 28 or Highfield Drive off Depot Avenue, Falmouth. The Beebes, a wealthy family originally from Boston, lived in Falmouth from the late 1870s to the early 1930s. Generous town benefactors, they were among the first elite to purchase land in Falmouth. Highfield Hall, built in 1878, was the centerpiece of the property, but it now stands in disrepair. (Friends of Highfield are working to save and restore the building.) The 387 acres around it contain miles of public trails for walking, mountain biking, and bird-watching. Free.

See also Ashumet Holly and Wildlife Sanctuary, Grews Pond, and Waquoit Bay National Estuarine Research Reserve.

LODGING

Lodging options and prices in Falmouth vary as much as the villages do: There are full-scale resorts, romantic 19th-century bed & breakfasts, and funky bohemian apartments by the beach.

RESORT

✐❋ **New Seabury Resort** (477-9111, 1-800-999-9033), Great Oak Road, New Seabury 02649. Open late March through October. New Seabury is more of a development unto itself than a part of Mashpee. Scattered across 2300 acres of property fronting Nantucket Sound, the 13 "villages" of small, gray-shingled buildings offer a variety of rental accommodations. One- and two-bedroom units are available in town houses (Sea Quarters), condominium-style, or stand-alone buildings. Maushop Village resembles Nantucket with its lanes of crushed shells and weathered buildings; Tidewatch is a 1960s-style hotel near the golf course; Mews consists of contemporary California-influenced units. All apartments and condos have fully equipped kitchens. Some overlook golf courses; some are oceanfront; others have more distant water views. Facilities include two restaurants (see Popponessett Inn under *Dining Out*), 16 tennis courts, two golf courses, a well-equipped health club, two outdoor pools, a 3½-mile private beach on Nantucket Sound, bike rentals and trails, a small shopping mall, mini-golf, and a full schedule of activities for children. If it sounds like you don't have to leave this enclave to have a full vacation, you're right. That's the idea. Prices are $210–375 per night in July and August, $90–260 in the off-season.

INN

✎❅ **Coonamessett Inn** (548-2300), Jones Road and Gifford Street, Falmouth 02540. Open year-round. The Coonamessett, popular with an older crowd, had the feel of a traditional 1950s inn. But it has new owners since mid-1996, and it remains to be seen what changes will be instituted. Although it's billed as an inn, the 25 informally decorated rooms are furnished more like pine and paisley motel units. Most rooms have outside entrances; two rooms can be connected by an adjoining entryway (good for family reunions). Ask for a suite overlooking picturesque Jones Pond. With 7 acres of meticulously landscaped lawns, the Coonamessett hosts its share of weddings (two to three in-season), conferences, and other events. The inn is filled with the late Cotuit artist Ralph Cahoon's whimsical, neoprimitive paintings of outdoor scenes. Along with attentive service, you have a choice of four dining rooms, all with very good food (see *Dining Out* and *Eating Out*). July to early September $95–145; late October to mid-May $55–95.

BED & BREAKFASTS

In Falmouth

❅ **Mostly Hall** (548-3786, 1-800-682-0565), 27 Main Street, Falmouth 02540. Closed January. In the heart of the historic district and set well back from the road, this B&B acquired its name after an observant child aptly commented, "Why Mama, it's mostly hall!" All of the six rooms—corner rooms with air-conditioning—are large enough not to be overwhelmed by enormous queen-sized canopy beds or tall, shuttered casement windows. Upstairs, a cupola now serves as a TV and VCR room. Longtime innkeepers Caroline and Jim Lloyd have green thumbs as well as talent for cooking—the parklike gardens, landscaping, and gazebo are visible from the wraparound porch, where you will enjoy a delicious full breakfast. Mostly Hall has loaner bicycles. Late May through October $110–125; otherwise $85–105.

❅ **Inn at West Falmouth** (540-6503, 1-800-397-7696), 66 Frazar Road (off Route 28A), West Falmouth 02574. Open year-round. Well hidden on a side road, this turn-of-the-century, shingle-style house features six exquisitely decorated rooms. Furnished with English, Oriental, and Continental antiques, most of innkeeper Karen Calvacca's rooms have a private deck and fireplace. All have Italian marble baths. There are quiet nooks and luxurious common spaces aplenty, including a lushly landscaped deck overlooking the pool and a tennis court. The beach is a 10-minute walk. May through October $150–250; off-season $125–215.

❅ **Inn on the Sound** (457-9666, 1-800-564-9668), 313 Grand Avenue, Falmouth Heights 02540. Open year-round. The brother and sister innkeeping team of Renee and David Ross (former interior designer and theatrical lighting expert, respectively) have transformed this shingle-style, turn-of-the-century inn into an elegantly upscale yet casual oceanfront B&B. Nine of the 10 bedrooms, each with private bath, have a great view of the long Falmouth Heights Beach. The living room features a large stone fireplace, with couches perfectly situated to take advantage of the ocean view. Full breakfast. Mid-June to mid-September $95–140; otherwise $60–115; $30 additional for a third person.

❋ **Beach House** (457-0310, 1-800-351-3426), 10 Worcester Court, Falmouth Heights 02540. Open year-round. This unusually fanciful B&B has seven guest rooms. Each is handpainted with a different beach-inspired motif: Perhaps you'll get a room covered with fish and sea horses, or stars and moons, or a wave, or a lighthouse mural. The cottage furniture has been painted, too, but in solid colors. Down comforters and new bathrooms are the norm. There is also an adjacent bright and airy cottage. You can eat the continental breakfast in the open kitchen or by the pool. May through October $115–125 for the rooms, $135–150 for the cottage.

❋ **Village Green Inn** (548-5621, 1-800-237-1119), 40 Main Street, Falmouth 02540. Open year-round. Overlooking the village green, as the name suggests, this pleasant B&B has five Victorian-style guest rooms, each with a unique feature. For instance, one has a pressed tin ceiling, another has a parquet floor. Innkeepers Diane and Don Crosby provide loaner bikes. Common space includes a small formal parlor and two open porches. A full breakfast, with blueberry puff pancakes perhaps, is served at 8:30. June through October $115–135 double, $25 for an additional person; off-season $85–120.

❋ **Inn at One Main** (540-7469, 1-888-281-6246), 1 Main Street, Falmouth 02540. Open year-round. When Karen Hart and Mari Zylinski took over this shingled and turreted bed & breakfast in 1993, they spiffed up the Queen Anne–style building with new upholstery and prints and furnished it with antiques. Even on dark days the rooms are airy and bright, and the bathrooms are unusually large for a house of this period. (All six air-conditioned guest rooms have private baths, although one is detached.) Just steps from the town green and on the corner of a busy road, the house was built in 1892 by the Swift family, prosperous local merchants. Rates include a full breakfast. June through October $90–110; $10 less off-season.

☞✎**Elm Arch Inn** (548-0133), Elm Arch Way, Falmouth 02540. Open April through October. This classic, old-fashioned hostelry is less than a block from Main Street, but it might as well be worlds away. Built in 1810 and bombed by the British in 1814 (there are still cannonball "scars" in the former dining room), the friendly inn has several common rooms downstairs and is chock-full of Colonial touches, braided rugs, and easy chairs. A large, screened-in flagstone porch overlooks a small pool surrounded by lawn chairs. Half of the 24 guest rooms have private baths; others have a sink in the room; many can accommodate three people. In the main house, some of the Colonial-style guest rooms have four-poster canopy

Garden at St. Joseph's Bell Tower with a view across Eel Pond, Woods Hole

beds, but beyond that they're quite modestly furnished. Across the street, rooms in the Richardson House are more modern. The inn has been in the Richardson family since 1926. $60–80 double, $55–80 single, coffee included. Inquire about the cottage. No credit cards.

☞❀ **Sjöholm Bed and Breakfast** (540-5706, 1-800-498-5706), 17 Chase Road (off Route 28A), West Falmouth 02574. Open year-round. Innkeepers Bob and Barbara White's reasonable prices belie Sjöholm's simple charms. The laid-back 19th-century farmhouse sits on a quiet back road and the feeling within is one of old-fashioned hospitality and shared experience. Fifteen rooms in the main inn are simply furnished, while those in the adjacent Sail Loft are decidedly summer-camp rustic. On my last visit, the innkeepers were organizing weekend retreats for artists and writers. You may wish to inquire. A private cottage sleeps five or six, while the "sleeping porch" is convenient for families. Mid-June to mid-September $55 in the Sail Loft, $85–90 for a private bath in the main inn, $70 shared, $55 single, including a full breakfast; cottage $550 per week.

Grafton Inn (540-8688, 1-800-642-4069), 261 Grand Avenue South, Falmouth Heights 02540. Open mid-February to mid-December. The Grafton Inn is a comfortable Victorian seaside B&B. It boasts five rooms with full views of the ocean and another five that have decent oblique views. Amenities include televisions, bathrobes, and telephones in every room. Since it can be a bit noisy at this end of town, innkeeper Liz Cvitan (who has owned the B&B with her husband, Rudy, since 1983) puts "white noise machines" in each room. Since Falmouth Heights

Beach is across the street, the inn provides beach towels and chairs. $95–149 in-season, including a full, self-serve breakfast on the glassed-in front porch. $75–115 off-season.

In Woods Hole 02540

❊ **Woods Hole Passage** (548-9575), 186 Woods Hole Road. Open year-round. On the road that connects Woods Hole and Falmouth, this quiet B&B has a welcoming feel thanks to Robin and Todd Norman, who purchased the inn in 1996. Since the Normans hail from Arizona, you might enjoy residual southwestern influences at breakfast: On my last visit I had a wonderful green chili frittata soufflé with sour cream and avocado. The attached barn has four completely renovated guest rooms; second-floor rooms are more spacious with vaulted ceilings and exposed beams. Decor is crisp country modern, and each room has a bold splash of color. Mid-May to mid-September $95–105; otherwise $75–95.

MOTELS

Sands of Time (548-6300, 1-800-841-0114), 549 Woods Hole Road, Woods Hole 02543. Open April through October. Some of the guests here missed the last ferry; others know that this is a convenient place to stay if you want to walk or bike around Woods Hole. There are 20 air-conditioned motel rooms (most with a delightful view of Little Harbor), an apartment with a kitchen, and 12 lovely and large innlike rooms in an adjacent 1870s Victorian house (many with a harbor view and working fireplace.) Fresh flowers and a morning newspaper set this place apart. There is also a small pool. $102–125 in summer; otherwise $50–100.

EFFICIENCIES

✐❊ **Shore Haven Inn** (548-1765, 1-800-828-3255), 321 Shore Street, Falmouth 02540. Open year-round. Steps from Surf Drive Beach and a 10-minute walk to the center of town along one of Falmouth's prettiest residential streets, Shore Haven is a good place for a barefoot seaside vacation. And I do mean seaside—the waves break less than 100 yards away. This place is neither showy nor quaint, just comfortable, relaxed, and unfussy. Most rooms have a TV and refrigerator; many are poolside. Room 6 in the main house can comfortably sleep a family of four. Mary and Art Manarite have improved and presided over the place since 1990. In-season $69–159 for motel rooms, $109 for studios ($595 weekly), $159–169 for one- and two-bedroom apartments ($695–795 weekly); children 12 and under free.

❊ **Ideal Spot Motel** (548-2257), Route 28A at Old Dock Road, West Falmouth 02540. Open year-round. In a quiet part of town, this nicely landscaped motel has two simple rooms (that can accommodate four people) and 12 efficiencies. There is a barbecue and picnic area. Mid-June to mid-September $99–105; $58–75 in spring and fall; weekly rates.

Mariner's Point Resort (457-0300), 425 Grand Avenue, Falmouth 02540. Open mid-March to late November. This bi-level time-share offers 37 efficiency studios and apartments within a short stroll of Falmouth Heights Beach. Most units overlook the pool area; a few have an unobstructed view of Vineyard Sound and a town-owned park popular with kite enthusiasts. Each sleeps up to six people, provided they're all very good friends. In-season $85–95 for a two- to four-person studio, $135–160 for four to six people; off-season $55–85.

RENTALS

Real Estate Associates, with four offices, has the local market covered. Depending on where you want to be, call the office in North Falmouth (563-7173), West Falmouth (540-3005), Falmouth (540-1500), or Poccassett (563-5266). Although first priority is given to monthly and seasonal rentals, if you're interested in weekly or two-week rentals, call them and they'll get back to you in April or early May to fill the holes in their schedule. There are 100 or so listings.

Century 21 Regan Realty (539-2121), Mashpee. Weekly rentals.

CAMPGROUNDS

Sippewissett Campground and Cabins (548-2542, 548-1971, 1-800-957-2267, e-mail: CampCapeCd@aol.com), 836 Palmer Avenue, Falmouth 02540. Open mid-May to mid-October. This is a well-run, private campground with 11 cabins and 100 large campsites for tents, trailers, and RVs; clean, large bathrooms and showers; and free shuttles to Chapoquoit Beach, the ferry to Martha's Vineyard, and other Falmouth-area locations. In-season, $27 per day for camping, $290–550 per week in a cabin; off-season $20 per day for camping and $190–450 per week in a cabin.

See Waquoit Bay National Estuarine Research Reserve under *Green Space*.

WHERE TO EAT

DINING OUT

The Regatta of Falmouth (548-5400), 217 Scranton Avenue, Falmouth. Open for dinner mid-May to mid-September (first dinner seating at 4:30). The Regatta is always at or near the top of the list for best Cape restaurants. Interesting combinations of creative French and global cuisines are the general rule here. Try a combination of two fish and two sauces or a grilled seafood selection served with a three-mustard sauce. Leave room to indulge in the signature dessert: chocolate seduction. The contemporary restaurant, accented in pink, mauve, and white, commands a great view of Inner Harbor and Vineyard Sound. Co-owner Wendy Bryan, by the way, designed the Limoges china pattern on which your food is served. Chef Heather Allen, who has worked in the kitchen since 1991, enjoyed her first year as chef in 1994. Reservations suggested for dinner. A three-course special for $20 is available 4:30–5:45. Otherwise, entrées $17–27.

Popponessett Inn (477-8258), Shore Drive, New Seabury, Mashpee. Open for lunch and dinner daily in summer; dinner Wednesday through Sunday mid-April to mid-June and early September to mid-October. Head chef David Schneider's traditional New England seaside cuisine is served in airy blue and white dining rooms at the Cape's largest resort village. In good weather, dine outside under a beachfront tent. Reservations advised. Entrées $15–20.

✳ **Coonamessett Inn** (548-2300), Jones Road and Gifford Street, Falmouth. Open for lunch and dinner year-round. This restaurant features traditional regional American fare with an emphasis on seafood—baked stuffed lobster, seafood Newburg, and an especially tasty lobster bisque. Each of the three dining rooms has something to recommend it: hot-air-balloon paintings of the late Ralph Cahoon, a view of secluded Jones Pond, and vines and tiny grapelike lights in the Vineyard Room. Self-taught chef David Kelley has presided over the kitchen since 1990. Reservations recommended. Entrées $15–22.

✳ **Chapoquoit Grill** (540-7794), 410 Route 28A, West Falmouth. Open for dinner daily at 5 PM, year-round. From the moment this New American bistro opened in mid-1994, it was a success. No longer did locals have to drive 45 minutes to get innovative cooking in a low-key atmosphere that didn't cost an arm and a leg. You can spot the regulars: They only order from the nightly special menu. On my last visit, we had pan-seared salmon topped with spinach and roasted pine-nut sauce ($13) and sautéed scallops over a saffron risotto ($13). The popular wood-fired, thin-crust pizzas are excellent. No reservations are taken, so get there when it opens or be prepared for a lengthy wait in the convivial bar. Entrées $9–16.

✳ **Flying Bridge** (548-2700), 220 Scranton Avenue (on the west side of Inner Harbor), Falmouth. Open 11:30-11 daily, April through December. This enormous 600-seat restaurant overlooks the busiest area of Falmouth's Inner Harbor, including the *Island Queen* dock. Absolutely ask for a table on the deck for the best view at lunchtime. (The view is the main attraction.) The menu emphasizes seafood, shellfish, steak, and pasta, but you may just want a few appetizers. Check the blackboard specials, and if nothing strikes your fancy, there are always sandwiches and burgers. Lunch and dinner $6–20.

✳ **Eli's** (548-2300), at the Coonamessett Inn, Jones Road and Gifford Street, Falmouth. Open for lunch and dinner daily year-round. Eli's is known for good service and conventional and conservative New England fare. Deep green trim, brass pieces, and light woods create a taverny atmosphere. Look for the day's specials (on Mondays it's chicken Parmesan); otherwise, scallop dishes are usually quite good. Entrées $10–14.

EATING OUT

All listings are in Falmouth unless otherwise noted.

☞✎✳ **The Quarterdeck** (548-9900), 164 Main Street. Open for lunch and dinner daily year-round. It's no wonder this place has a loyal local following. With hand-hewn beams, barn-board walls, and a fire in the woodstove in winter, it has a warm, pubby feel. The service is also quite friendly. You could be happy with a number of dishes here: chowder, kale soup, seafood scampi, a half order of pasta, or a baked scrod platter. Children's menu. Lunch $6–9.50, dinner entrées $9.50–18.50.

☞✐**Clam Shack** (540-7758), 227 Clinton Avenue. Open late May to mid-September. One of the Cape's best clam shacks, this really tiny, busy place rarely has enough room inside. It's just as well—you'll do better at one of the picnic tables on the back deck, watching the pleasure boats and fishermen coming and going from Falmouth's Inner Harbor. Look for the little weathered gray shack next to The Regatta restaurant (see *Dining Out*).

✳ **Laureen's** (540-9104), 170 Main Street. Open 8:30–6 daily year-round. Even without taking into consideration its prime downtown location, Laureen's would still be a fine choice for casual lunches, homemade desserts, and good coffee. This busy catering operation was purchased in 1995 by Elizabeth and John Marderosian. John is Armenian, so the Middle East sampler plate ($8.45) and flaky baklava ($.75) are authentic. Otherwise, the eclectic lunch menu includes a vegetarian burrito plate, pasta of the day, a few fancy feta pizzas, and sandwiches. There's table service as well as takeout.

☞✳ **Peach Tree Circle Farm** (548-4006), 881 Old Palmer Avenue, West Falmouth. Open daily year-round. On a quiet country road surrounded by gardens, you can dine alfresco or at a few tables inside. Light lunches of quiche, sandwiches, excellent soups (including a great chowder), and seafood salads are the order of the day. Or just come for tea and something sweet from the bakery.

☞✐✳ **Moonakis Cafe** (457-9630), 460 Route 28, Waquoit. Open for breakfast and lunch daily, year-round (closed Monday and Tuesday from mid-October through April). With the possible exception of one or two B&Bs, Paul Rifkin and Ellen Mycock run the best breakfast joint in town. Specialties include homemade sausage, corn beef hash, and chowder, as well as fresh fruit waffles, crabcakes, and Reubens. Ellen is family-friendly: She'll make simple, small dishes for kids, depending on what they'll eat. Dishes $3–8.

☞ **Pat's Pushcart** (548-5090), 339 Main Street (Route 28), East Falmouth. Open for dinner April through December; nightly in summer, flexible in the off-season. Pat's has been in this small, brick-fronted cottage since 1986, and in Boston's Italian North End since 1970. Pat's is known for a fabulous red sauce that tops pasta dishes, enormous portions, and no-nonsense, authentic homestyle cooking. Dishes $7.50–16.

The Wharf (548-2772, 548-0777), 281 Grand Avenue, Falmouth Heights. Open for lunch and dinner May through October. This rustic restaurant overlooks Falmouth Heights Beach, crowded with college kids playing volleyball. And it tends to be popular with those volleyball players when they're ready to take a breather. Have a drink at the **Dry Dock Bar** or settle down on the wide, double-decker back porch for some fish-and-chips, burgers, a fisherman's platter, or the daily catch. The motto: "If our fish were any fresher you'd have to slap it." It's really true. Lunch and dinner $5.75–22.

Food for Thought (548-4498), 37 North Main Street. Open daily except Monday year-round; also closed Tuesday in the off-season. Locals are partial to this small and casual eatery with an exposed kitchen. If you're not staying at an inn that serves breakfast, come on over here. Otherwise, stop in at lunch for a sandwich or something more interesting like tempeh veggie stir fry or spinach lasagna (both $5.50).

☞✐✾ **Betsy's Diner** (540-4446), Route 28, East Falmouth. Open daily, year-round. Falmouth has an unusually wide array of dining options, including this old-fashioned 1957 Mountain View Diner that was transported in 1992 by truck from Pennsylvania to Main Street, on the former site of another diner. The boxy addition is not historic in the least, just functional. Although the cigarette smoke may bother some, the place is packed with locals and families who come for the inexpensive fare: club sandwiches for $4.95, breakfast specials (including homemade doughnuts) for $3–4, or perhaps a turkey dinner for $6.25. Children's menu.

☞✾ **Peking Palace** (540-8204), 452 Main Street. Open 11:30 AM–midnight daily, year-round (until 2 AM in summer). If you're tired of fried seafood platters or grilled fish, and wishing for takeout from your favorite Chinese restaurant at home, the Peking Palace won't disappoint you. If anything, it will make you think twice about your Chinese back home. There must be a hundred Mandarin, Szechuan, and Cantonese dishes on the menu, at $8.50–12.50 per dish.

West Falmouth Market (548-1139), 623 Route 28, West Falmouth. Open daily year-round. This old-fashioned neighborhood market carries deli meats for sandwiches and hearty, Cape-famous Pain d'Avignon bread. You haven't tasted bread until you've tasted Pain d'Avignon.

In Woods Hole

☞✐ **Fishmonger Cafe** (548-9148), 56 Water Street. Open for all three meals daily, mid-February to early December, except closed Tuesdays prior to mid-May and after Labor Day; no breakfast is served on Tuesdays in summer. The Monger has been the most consistent place in town since chef-owner Frances Buehler opened it in 1974. The eclectic, international menu features natural foods like Thai spring rolls and tofu and veggies, as well as clam chowder, Cajun-fried fish-and-chips, and sirloin steak. Specials change not only throughout the day but sometimes during a meal as well; keep an eye on the blackboard. The location couldn't be better, overlooking the Eel Pond bridge. And even though the Monger is always bustling, the friendly staff keep it comfortable. The evenings sparkle, thanks to candlelight, shiny wooden tables, and lots of little windowpanes. Lunch $4.75–7, dinner $8–22.

✐ **Landfall** (548-1758), Luscombe Avenue. Open 11–10 daily, mid-April through October. Another survivor of Hurricane Bob, the Landfall is one of the Upper Cape's best places to soak up local atmosphere: Take note of the preppies and weather-beaten fishermen, both regulars here. Bedecked with seafaring paraphernalia and built with salvaged materials, the large dining room is made cozy in the evening with hurricane lamps. The

Old Indian Meetinghouse, Mashpee

waterfront location is excellent: Try for a table overlooking the ferry dock. As you might have guessed, the fare tends toward Cape Cod traditional: lobster and seafood. Landfall has been in the Estes family since 1946. Children's menu. Lunch $4.50–12, dinner $17.50–23.

❈ **Captain Kidd** (548-8563), 77 Water Street. Open for lunch and dinner daily, year-round. The fancier waterfront portion of the restaurant overlooking Eel Pond is open for dinner daily, mid-June to early September. The Kidd, as it's affectionately called, offers specialty pizzas, teriyaki chicken, mussels, kabobs, and blackboard fish specials. The glassed-in patio with a woodstove is a cozy place to be in winter. This local watering hole is named for the pirate who supposedly spent a short time in the environs of Woods Hole on the way to his execution in England. A playful pirate mural lines the walls above barrel-style tables across from the long, hand-carved mahogany bar. The primary drawback here: the staff are often more attentive to the TV at the bar than to the patrons. Lunch and dinner in the tavern $5–12, dinner entrées in the formal dining room $8.50–25.

☞⌀**Swope** (289-7589), MBL Street. Open for all three meals in summer. Overlooking Eel Pond, this is one of the most picturesque and least expensive places to eat in Woods Hole. You don't have to be a student or researcher to eat here. All you can eat: $5 breakfast, $6 lunch, $7 dinner.

❈ **Pie in the Sky** (540-5475), 10 Water Street. Open 6:30 AM–10 PM Monday through Saturday (until 5 PM in the off-season), year-round, and on Sundays in summer. Strong coffee, good pastries and deli sandwiches, too. There are a few tables inside and outside.

In Mashpee

☞❈ **Gone Tomatoes** (477-8100), Mashpee Commons. Open for lunch and dinner daily, year-round. This contemporary Italian grill, suffused with the heady aroma of garlic, is an all-around pleasant surprise. The crowd is a mix of old and young, locals and tourists. And the atmosphere is simultaneously hip and handsome, with high ceilings and wood floors. Specialties include grilled focaccia pizza, a hearty Tuscan vegetable roast, and the requisite pasta dishes. Look for the special: dinner for two with tickets to movie next door for $28. Otherwise, lunch $5, dinner $8–15.

The Flume (477-1456), Lake Avenue, off Route 130 near the Mashpee Wampanoag Indian Museum (see *To See*). Open 5–9 Monday through Saturday and noon–8 Sunday, April through November. Wampanoag and Mashpee native chef-owner Earl Mills trained at the Popponessett and Coonamessett Inns before opening his own restaurant 20 years ago. His creative rendering of traditional recipes attracts food lovers from across New England to this small, casual restaurant built right over a herring run. Fish figures prominently on the menu. Dishes include salt codfish cakes; marinated herring garnished with sour cream, red onion, and apple; and chowder. In spring, when the herring are running (along with Brewster, this is one of the oldest herring runs in the state), try the herring roe and bacon. Oysters are always a great choice. For dessert, you'll have the chance to try genuine Indian pudding, made with corn-meal, molasses, and ginger. Dishes $9–20. Few reservations accepted.

Bobby Week's Raw Bar (477-9400, ext. 0, then ext. 1572), Popponessett Marketplace, New Seabury. Open mid-May to mid-October (weekends only in the off-season). You know this tiny place has something going for it when regulars outnumber tourists. Part Cape Cod, part Carib-bean, the raw bar boasts a loyal staff, incredibly fresh seafood, and an owner who's known for his charity work.

COFFEE

✳ **Coffee Obsession** (540-2233), 110 Palmer Avenue, Falmouth. Open at least 7 AM–9 PM daily year-round. This bohemian place opened in 1992, and caffeine addicts flocked to it immediately. Stop for a bracing espresso, a slice of coffee cake, and a smidgen of counterculture à la Falmouth.

ENTERTAINMENT

Baseball, Fuller Field, just off Main Street, Falmouth. The Commodores, one of 10 teams in the Cape Cod Baseball League, play in July and August. The Falmouth Chamber of Commerce has a schedule (see *Guidance*).

Falmouth Town Band, at the Harbor Band Shell, Marina Park, on the west side of the Inner Harbor. Thursday evenings at 7:30 or 8 in July and August; bring a chair or a blanket and watch the kids dance to simple marches and big-band numbers. Or wander around and look at the boats moored in the Inner Harbor. There are also free Friday-evening concerts at 7 at the Margaret Noonan Park on Main Street in July and August.

College Light Opera Company (548-0668), Depot Avenue next to Highfield Hall, Falmouth. Open late June through August. Performances Tuesday through Sunday at 8:30 and Thursday at 2:30. Founded in 1969, the energetic collegiate company, which includes 32 singers and a 17-piece orchestra, has risen to the challenge of providing the only live musical and theatrical entertainment for area visitors. Music majors and theater-arts students from across the country perform nine shows in nine weeks.

Woods Hole Folk Music Society (540-0320), Community Hall, Water Street, Woods Hole. Well-known folkies play on the first and third Sundays of each month, October through May.

NIGHTLIFE

Flying Bridge (548-2700), 220 Scranton Avenue (west side of Inner Harbor), Falmouth. Open daily year-round. Sit on the deck overlooking Inner Harbor and watch the boats go by. Live acoustic entertainment on weekends.

Boathouse (548-7800), 88 Scranton Avenue, Falmouth. Open late May to mid-October. An attractive and popular restaurant by day, the Boathouse jumps with live music and lively crowds at night.

The Dome (548-0800), Woods Hole Road, Woods Hole. When Buckminster Fuller was teaching at MIT, he designed this geodesic dome, a 1950s-style lookout just north of town. It's definitely worth a look—and a listen. On Sunday nights in July and August, there's Dixieland jazz. On Friday and Saturday nights from early April to mid-October, the beat changes considerably—to contemporary piano music.

SELECTIVE SHOPPING

ANTIQUES AND CURIOS

Enseki Antiques (548-7744), 43 North Main Street, Falmouth. Open Friday through Sunday year-round. Gary Enseki runs the place by himself, so when he's delivering a prized item or visiting a carefully guarded source, he closes up shop—even if it's in the middle of the day on a busy holiday weekend. Enseki opened this shop in 1992 after a successful antiquing career in England, so he really knows his stuff: maps, furniture, curios, and advice.

Sophisticated Junk (548-1250), 108 King Street, Falmouth. Open Thursday through Sunday, late May to mid-October. This is one of the largest "one-person's-junk-is-another-person's-treasure" shops on the Cape. Pick up a set of kitchen chairs for $20, a vintage steamer trunk for $25, or flip through a stack of old records. The Grandma's-dusty-attic smell is classic.

ART GALLERIES

Gallery 333 (564-4467), 333 Old Main Road, North Falmouth. Open Wednesday through Sunday, June to mid-September. Arlene Hecht's gallery is housed in a wonderful 19th-century house that's been added onto many times over the last 200 years. Once the site of a former asparagus farm, the house showcases a medley of work by 40 local, regional, and national artists who work in a full range of media. Don't miss the sculpture garden. On many Saturdays in summer, the gallery holds meet-the-artists receptions.

Woods Hole Gallery (548-4329), 14 School Street, Woods Hole. Open late June through September. Owner, curator, and all-around arbiter of fine art Edith Bruce has operated this gallery since 1963. You can trust her good taste in area artists.

Market Barn Gallery (540-0480), 15 Depot Avenue, Falmouth. Open late June to mid-September. Behind the namesake bookshop, this bright barn makes a wonderful gallery for local and regional artists.

Falmouth Artists' Guild (540-3304), 774 Main Street, Falmouth. Open 10–3 Monday through Saturday and noon–5 Sunday, year-round. This nonprofit guild (active since the 1950s) holds 10 to 12 exhibitions a year, half of which are juried. There's a fund-raising auction in July and a holiday sale.

BOOKSTORES

Market Bookshop (548-5636), 15 Depot Avenue, Falmouth (also at 22 Water Street in Woods Hole, 540-0851). Open daily in summer; nonsummer hours vary, but the shop is open year-round. Independent bookstores rarely rise to this level. This place is a fixture in the community, and the fire in the fireplace in winter isn't the only reason. Tables and chairs make it hospitable to browsers.

Eight Cousins Children's Books (548-5548), 189 Main Street, Falmouth. Open year-round. Named for one of *Little Women* author Louisa May Alcott's lesser-known works, Eight Cousins is a great resource, whether you're looking for a gift or entertaining a child on a rainy afternoon.

CLOTHING

Europa Imports (540-7814), 628 Route 28A, West Falmouth. Open year-round. Don't miss this off-the-beaten-path shop that offers clothing and accessories from around the world.

Liberty House (548-7568), 89 Water Street, Woods Hole. Open daily, mid-April through December. It's tough to find a women's clothing store on the Cape or the Islands that combines good taste and reasonable prices. But that's what you'll find here—comfy linen shorts and slacks, sundresses, and stacks of cotton T-shirts. Look for the big postholiday sale.

FLEA MARKET

Dick & Ellie's Flea Market (477-3550), on Route 28 across from Deer Crossing Shopping Center, Falmouth. Open Wednesday through Sunday in summer; weekends only in the off-season, mid-April through June and September through October. More than 100 antiques and collectibles dealers peddle their wares here; other diversions include mini-golf and Four Seas ice cream.

MALLS

Falmouth Mall (540-8329), Route 28, Falmouth. Open daily year-round. A smaller version of the nearby Cape Cod Mall in Hyannis.

Mashpee Commons (477-5400), at the rotary at Routes 151 and 28, Mashpee. Open daily year-round. If you're familiar with Seaside, the planned community of architectural note in Florida, you may recognize elements of this 30-acre shopping mall–cum–new town center. The buildings are pleasant and the layout is better than at most malls, but it still looks a bit contrived. (Developers went so far as to measure the sidewalk widths in an old, quintessential Vermont town and duplicated the dimensions here.) Having said that, it's won numerous awards for renovating a strip mall into a downtown commercial district. It's one of the most concentrated shopping venues on the Cape, boasting several good clothing stores, specialty boutiques, a movie theater, restaurants, cafés, and free outdoor entertainment in summer.

SPECIAL SHOPS

Woods Hole Handworks (540-5291), 68 Water Street, Woods Hole. Open daily mid-June to early September and weekends only in May and September through December. This tiny artisans cooperative, hanging over the water near the drawbridge to Eel Pond, has a selection of fine handmade jewelry, scarves, weaving, beadwork, and tiles.

Signature Gallery (539-0029), Mashpee Commons, Routes 151 and 28. Open year-round. This gallery carries an eclectic selection of work by fine Cape Cod artists, including glassware by craftsman William Salas, clay sculptures and objets de whimsy by Al Davis, paper collages by Kim Victoria, and woven scarves, vests, and jackets by Randall Darwall.

Falmouth Hospital Auxiliary Thrift Shop (457-3992, 548-5300), 702 Palmer Avenue (visible from Route 28), Falmouth. Open daily, year-round. If you forgot your sweater and you don't want to shell out a lot of money at a pricey shop in the middle of town, this is a great place to pick up a slightly worn addition to your vacation wardrobe. It seems like every Cape town has a thrift shop like this one.

Ben & Bill's Chocolate Emporium (548-7878), 209 Main Street, Falmouth. Open daily year-round, 9 AM–11 PM in summer. In this old-fashioned sweet shop, you'll be surrounded by walls of candy, some of it made on the premises. The store-made ice cream is tasty, cheap, and served in abundant quantities.

SPECIAL EVENTS

July 4: **Blessing of the Fleet** off the Falmouth Heights Beach; 11:30 AM. Spectacular evening **fireworks** are displayed over Vineyard Sound.

Early July: **Mashpee Powwow** (477-0208, Wampanoag Tribal Council) at Heritage Ballfield on Route 130, Mashpee. The People of the First Light's Mashpee Wampanoag powwow has been open to the public since 1924; the Mashpee Wampanoag Tribal Council has sponsored it since 1974. The powwow attracts Native Americans in full regalia from nearly every state as well as from Canada, Mexico, and some Central and South American countries. These traditional gatherings provide an opportunity for tribes to exchange stories and to discuss common problems and goals. Dancing, crafts demonstrations, and vendor booths occupy the grounds of Heritage Park ballfield. Kids love it, and they're encouraged to join in the dancing and nearly constant percussive music. Adults $6, children under 12 $3.

Mid-July: **Arts and Crafts Street Fair,** Main Street, Falmouth. Beginning at 10 AM, Main Street is blocked off to autos, and it's filled with crafts, artisans, and food stalls.

Late July: **Barnstable County Fair** (563-3200), Route 151, East Falmouth. Local and national musical acts, midway, livestock shows (including horse, ox, and pony pulls), horticulture, cooking, and crafts exhibits and contests have made this annual event a popular tradition since 1866. Adults $5, children ages 6–12 $1.

Mid-August: **Falmouth Road Race** (540-7000). This internationally renowned 7-mile race, limited to 8000 participants, is the event of the year in Falmouth. Register before March 31 (Falmouth Road Race, Box 732, Falmouth 02541). Reserve your lodging before May; places usually fill up by then.

Early December: **Christmas by the Sea** (548-8500). The weekend festivities, including tree lighting and caroling at the lighthouse and on the town green, culminate with a Christmas parade.

II. MID-CAPE

Exploring the curves of Swan Pond River in Dennis from paddleboats

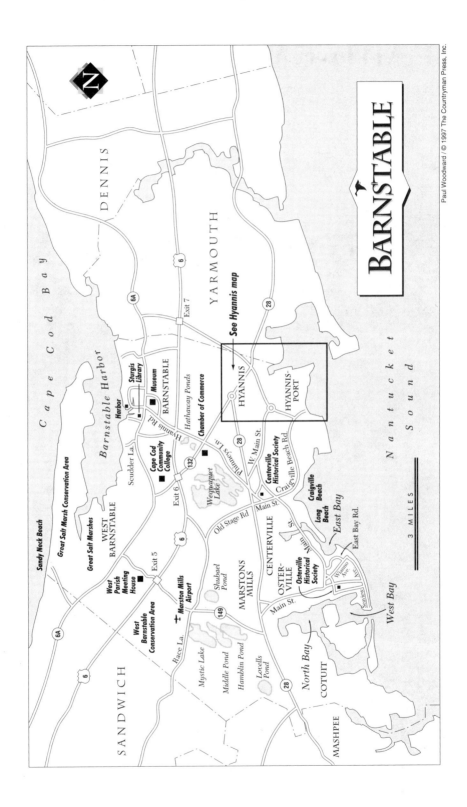

BARNSTABLE

Paul Woodward / © 1997 The Countryman Press, Inc.

Barnstable

The Cape's largest town, which covers 60 square miles and is home to 41,000 year-round souls, is also the Cape's second oldest, incorporated in 1639 (just 2 years after Sandwich). Barnstable actually comprises seven distinct villages—Cotuit, Marstons Mills, Osterville, Centerville, and Hyannis along Route 28 and West Barnstable and Barnstable along Route 6A. (Barnstable is sometimes referred to as Barnstable Village to distinguish it from Barnstable County, which embraces the whole of the Cape.)

On the Cape Cod Bay side, Route 6A (also called Old Kings Highway and Main Street) winds through West Barnstable and Barnstable Village. Development—or lack of it—is rigidly controlled by the Kings Highway Historical Commission, which regulates signage and does not allow gas stations, chain stores, or unconventional restorations anywhere within sight of the highway. Sandy Neck, a haven for naturalists and beachgoers, is located off Route 6A, as are many stately homes that have been turned into B&Bs.

Centerville, Osterville, and Cotuit—parts of which front Nantucket Sound—are off Route 28. Centerville's Main Street is full of handsome old homes built during the 19th century by affluent sea captains and businessmen. Its proximity to Hyannis has made it something of a suburb in recent years, but shopping centers are strictly limited to Route 28, the commercial district of Centerville. Osterville boasts some of the Cape's largest summer mansions, all with Nantucket Sound as their front yard. Osterville's Main Street is lined with upscale shops. At the turn of the century, Cotuit was dubbed Little Harvard, since it was home to many academicians. Cotuit's Main Street is lined with impressive Federal, Greek Revival, and Queen Anne houses, with flags flapping in the sea breeze and Adirondack chairs dotting the lawns. In terms of public beaches, the popular Craigville Beach dominates this side of Barnstable.

Landlocked and wedged between Routes 28 and 6, Marstons Mills is tiny, quiet, and residentially developed. It was founded by the Marston family, who built and ran the mills driven by the Goodspeed River.

Barnstable was founded by English Congregationalist minister John Lothrop and a small band of religious renegades who felt that

Plymouth Colony was a bit too settled for them. Oysterville, as it was called, was purchased from the Native Americans in 1648 for "two copper kettles and some fencing." The area then was called Mattakeese, which translates as "plowed fields"—indeed, the land had already been cleared—but the settlers eventually named it after a similar harbor in Barnstaple, England.

GUIDANCE

Hyannis Area Chamber of Commerce (775-2201, 1-800-449-6647 for 24-hour information, http://www.hyannischamber.com), 1481 Route 132, Hyannis 02601. Open 9–5 Monday through Saturday year-round; open Sunday, late May to early September. A mile south of Route 6 on Route 132, the chamber has information about all Barnstable villages.

GETTING THERE

By car: Barnstable is 15 miles from the Sagamore Bridge. Take Route 6 to exit 5 for West Barnstable (Route 149 north) and Marstons Mills, Cotuit, and Osterville (Route 149 south). Take exit 6 for Barnstable Village (Route 132 west) and Centerville (Route 132 east).

By bus: The **Plymouth & Brockton** bus line (775-5524) connects Barnstable with other Cape towns and Boston's Logan Airport.

GETTING AROUND

The Villager (1-800-352-7155) connects Barnstable's villages with two bus routes along Routes 132 and 149. Pick up a complete schedule of stops at the chamber of commerce (see *Guidance*). Fares: $.50 adults, children under 5 free.

MEDICAL EMERGENCY

Cape Cod Hospital (771-1800), 27 Park Street, Hyannis. Open 24 hours.

TO SEE

Along or near Route 6A

West Parish Meetinghouse (362-8624), Route 149 at Meetinghouse Way, West Barnstable. Open daily; Sunday services at 10. This majestic example of early Colonial architecture is the second oldest surviving meetinghouse on Cape Cod. (Its senior, the 1684 Old Indian Meetinghouse, is in Mashpee.) Its members belong to the oldest Congregationalist church fellowship in America, established in 1639 and descended from London's First Congregationalist Church. Founding pastor John Lothrop and his small band of followers erected their first meetinghouse in 1646. By 1715 the Congregational church had become so popular that Barnstable split into two parishes; the building you see today was constructed in 1717. Its bell tower, topped by a gilded rooster, holds a bell cast by Paul Revere in 1806; it still rings. Until 1834 the meetinghouse doubled as a town hall—so much for separation of church and state! In the 1950s, the meetinghouse was fully restored to its original modest neoclassical beauty. Donations.

☞✻ **William Brewster Nickerson Memorial Room at Cape Cod Community College** (362-2131), Route 132, West Barnstable. Open 8:30–3 Tuesday and 8:30–4 Monday, Wednesday, and Friday year-round. Rainy day or not, visitors with more than a passing interest in the social history, literature, institutions, and people of Cape Cod and the islands owe it to themselves to stop here. This significant collection was set up in 1966 by a vote of the students to honor the memory of the college's second president, a Vietnam War hero and *Mayflower* descendant. The classical collection contains more than 5000 documents, including religious treatises, biographies, autobiographies, oral histories, letters by dune poet Harry Kemp, scrimshaw, ship registers and logs, early diaries, US Lifesaving Service reports, telephone directories from 1886 and on, and aerial photographs—to name but some of what you'll find. Several excellent books have been written using these materials solely.

✐✻ **Sturgis Library** (362-6636), 3090 Route 6A, Barnstable Village. Open 10–2 Monday and Wednesday, 1–9 Tuesday and Thursday, 1–5 Friday, and 10–4 Saturday. William Sturgis went off to sea at age 15 when his father died and returned four years later as a captain. Although he received no formal education, the self-made Sturgis obtained reading lists from a Harvard-educated friend. Sturgis was born in the original part of the building, which he deeded to the town as a library. Researchers from all over the country (including entrepreneurs looking for shipwrecks) visit the country's oldest public library building. It boasts one of the finest collections of genealogical records, dating to the area's first European settlers; an original 1605 Lothrop Bible; more than 1500 maps and charts; and archives filled with other maritime material. $5 fee for the research collection; otherwise, free. The library has a good children's corner.

Barnstable County Courthouse (362-2511), 3195 Route 6A, Barnstable Village. This imposing, granite, Greek Revival building, built in 1831–1832, is one of few reminders that tranquil Barnstable is the county seat for the Cape. (It's been the county seat since 1685.) Original murals and a pewter codfish in the main courtroom were recently restored. On the side lawn, a bronze sculpture commemorates James Otis Jr., a West Barnstable "patriot" who wrote the famous 1761 Writs of Assistance speech. President John Adams said that Otis was the "spark by which the child of Independence was born."

Lothrop Hill Cemetery, Route 6A, just east of Barnstable Village. Slate headstones are scattered across this little hillock, where John Lothrop and other Barnstable founders rest. Near the stone wall along Route 6A, look for a large granite memorial bearing the following inscription: "In this cemetery lie the mortal remains of Capt. John Percival known as 'Mad Jack.' Born April 3, 1779. Died September 17, 1862 in command of Old Ironsides around the world 1844–1846."

Barnstable Harbor, Mill Way Road off Route 6A. Fishing charters and whale-watching trips leave from this small harbor.

✐ **Donald G. Trayser Memorial Museum Complex (Old Customs House)**
(362-2092), 3353 Route 6A, Barnstable Village. Open 1:30–4:30 Tuesday
through Saturday in July and August. Before Barnstable Harbor filled
with silt around the turn of the century, it had been the busiest port on the
Cape. In response, the Old Customs House was built in 1856 to oversee
the enormous stream of goods going through the harbor. After harbor
activity diminished, the brick Italian Renaissance Revival building served
as a post office, until the Barnstable Historical Commission made it their
headquarters in 1959. The commission restored the beautiful building,
painted it deep red, and opened this museum complex. It contains a
second-floor custom keeper's office (with a view of the harbor), Native
American arrowheads, Sandwich glass, ivory, and children's toys. Adjacent is a shed with a horse-drawn hearse, an 1869 velocipede, and a 1900
wooden frame bicycle. Also on the grounds is a circa-1690 jail cell,
complete with colonial "graffiti." Donations.

Off Route 28

✐ **Centerville Historical Society Museum** (775-0331), 507 Main Street,
Centerville. Open 1:30–4:30 Wednesday through Sunday, mid-June to
mid-September; last guided tour at 4. The 1840s Mary Lincoln House (no
relation to Abraham) was built by her father, Clark Lincoln, who was
prominent in civic affairs. Centerville folks donated many of the mid-
19th-century furnishings, but much of the museum was endowed by
Charles Ayling, a wealthy Cape businessman and philanthropist. Ayling
also assembled and donated an entire Cape Cod kitchen, complete with
a large open fireplace and dozens of iron utensils. The 14 rooms are filled
with a collection of rare Sandwich glass, more than 300 quilts, gowns and
other costumes from 1650 to 1950, children's toys and games, perfume
bottles, and A.E. Crowell's miniature duck carvings. Adults $2.50, chil-
dren 6–12 $.50.

The 1856 Country Store (775-1856), 555 Main Street, Centerville. Beyond a selection of cutesy country and perfumed things, you'll find large
pickles in a barrel of brine and wheels of cheddar cheese. The store is
more picturesque outside than inside, although the original wood floors
have been preserved.

Country Store (428-2097), 877 Main Street, Osterville. This circa-1890
building is classic: crammed with goods, including "penny candy," which
is more like 15¢ than 1¢.

Osterville Historical Society Museum (428-5861), 155 West Bay Road,
Osterville. Open 1:30–4:30 Thursday through Sunday, June through
September. The society maintains three properties: the **Captain John
Parker House,** which contains a collection of Majolica and Lowestroft
pottery and other booty from the China trade; the one-room-deep
Cammett House, built in 1728; and **Crosby Boat House.** Crosby
designed and built his famous and speedy *Crosby Cat,* the preferred
vessel of such sailors as President Kennedy. In fact, Kennedy's *Victura*

Osterville Historical Society Museum

was built here in 1931 and stored here winters. Don't miss the period gardens maintained by the Osterville Garden Club. Admission $2 adults.

Cahoon Museum of American Art (428-7581), 4676 Route 28, Cotuit. Open 10–4 Tuesday through Saturday, April through January. This magnificent 1775 Georgian Colonial farmhouse was once a stagecoach stop on the Hyannis-to-Sandwich route. Today it houses a permanent collection of paintings by neoprimitive artists Martha Cahoon and the late Ralph Cahoon, as well as a gallery where other contemporary art and Hudson River school paintings are displayed. Don't miss it. The museum also offers ever-changing classes in watercolor, bird carving, and other fine and applied arts. Donations.

Samuel B. Dottridge House (428-0461), 1148 Main Street, Cotuit. Open 2:30–5 Thursday through Sunday, mid-June to mid-September. Owned by the Sansuit and Cotuit Historical Association, this 1790 house contains historical but otherwise fairly unremarkable objects pertaining to daily 19th-century agrarian and nonagrarian life.

TO DO

AIRPLANE RIDES

Cape Cod Soaring Adventures (540-8081, 1-800-660-4563), Marstons Mills Airport, Route 149 and Race Lane, Marstons Mills. Open year-round, weather permitting. (On a sunny winter day, you can see for 40 miles, far better than on the average hazy summer day, when visibility peaks at about 5 miles.) Randy Charlton has been taking people up in his glider since 1989, but he began flying in 1974. Flying at 5000 feet and 40 mph, you'll see butteries, seagulls, hawks, and even, unfortunately, debris like airborne cardboard. The unrestricted views and the quietness are like nothing you've ever experienced. One person at a time: $60–75 for 20–35 minutes; $90 for 30–40 minutes; $100 for 25 minutes of acrobatics. Fall is perhaps the best time to fly.

Cape Cod Flying Service (428-8732, 1-888-247-5263), Marstons Mills Airport, Route 149 and Race Lane, Marstons Mills. Open year-round, weather permitting. Biplane rides, with passengers in an open cockpit while the pilot flies in back, cost $80 for two people. Sight-seeing trips, which can go virtually anywhere on the Cape, cost $60 for 30 minutes. This is the Cape's only grass strip airport.

BICYCLING

If you don't have a friend with a classy summer place in the exclusive Wianno section of town, the best way to enjoy the village of Osterville is to cycle or drive along Wianno Avenue to Seaview Avenue, then turn right onto Eel River Road to West Bay Road and back into town.

FISHING/SHELLFISHING

Fishing licenses are obtained from the town clerk's office (790-6240) in Town Hall, 367 Main Street, Hyannis. Shellfishing permits are required and may be obtained from the Department of Natural Resources (790-6272), 1189 Phinney's Lane, Centerville.

Wequaquet Lake in Centerville has plenty of largemouth bass, sunfish, and tiger muskies to go around; park along Shoot Flying Hill Road. Marstons Mills has three pretty ponds well stocked with smallmouth bass, trout, and perch: **Middle Pond,** Race Lane; **Hamblin's Pond,** Route 149; and **Schubel's Pond,** Schubel Pond Road off Race Lane.

Barnstable Harbor Charter Fleet (362-3908), 186 Mill Way, off Route 6A, Barnstable Harbor. Late May to mid-October. A fleet of seven boats take up to six passengers each for 4- to 8-hour fishing expeditions in Cape Cod Bay.

Sea Witch (776-1336, 413-283-8375), Barnstable Harbor. May through September. Captain Bob Singleton, who has been fishing these waters since 1960, uses a custom-built, 32-foot sportfishing boat. Up to six people: $375 for 6 hours, $425 for 8 hours.

FOR FAMILIES

✐ **Main Street Playground,** next to the Centerville recreation building, Centerville. Built by local volunteers in 1994, there are swings for big kids and toddlers, slides, a fancy jungle gym, sand for digging and building, climbing rings, and picnic tables.

✐✱ See also Cape Cod YMCA under *For Families* in "Hyannis."

GOLF

Cotuit Highground Country Club (428-9863), Crocker Neck Road, Cotuit. A popular 9-hole, 1500-yard, par-28 course; open year-round.

Olde Barnstable Fairgrounds Golf Course (420-1142), 1460 Route 149, Marstons Mills. Open daily year-round. An 18-hole course so close to an airport that a large sign is needed at the driving range to warn players to "Stop driving when planes approach." 6113 yards, par 70.

SPECIAL PROGRAMS

Tales of Cape Cod (362-8927), 3018 Route 6A at Rendezvous Lane, Barnstable Village. This simple, white-clapboard building served as the Barnstable County Courthouse from 1772 to 1832, when the "new" granite structure down the road was built. The secular Old Courthouse then became a Baptist church until it was purchased in 1949 by Tales of Cape Cod, a nonprofit organization that preserves Cape folklore and oral histories. The organization sponsors an excellent lecture series Tuesday evenings in July and August. Subjects range from "Inventors, Entrepreneurs, and Opportunists of Cape Cod," to "Cape Cod Attics: Antique Appraisal Evening," to "Growing Up on Cape Cod in the 1930s." Talks are delivered by knowledgeable townspeople.

TENNIS

Public courts are located in Centerville on **Bumps River Road** near the elementary school; in Cotuit at the **elementary school** on Old Oyster Road; in Osterville off West Bay Road between Eel River Road and Main Street; in West Barnstable at **Cape Cod Community College** on Route 132.

WHALE-WATCHING

Hyannis Whale Watcher Cruises (362-6088, 1-800-287-0374 within Massachusetts; http://www.capecod.net/whales), Mill Way off Route 6A, Barnstable Harbor. Daily departures, April through October. A convenient mid-Cape location and a new, fast boat make this outfit a very good choice for whale-watching. An on-board naturalist provides commentary. There are also sunset cruises in summer. Adults $18–22, children 4–12 $15.

GREEN SPACE

BEACHES

Sandy Neck Beach, on Cape Cod Bay, off Route 6A, West Barnstable. One of the Cape's most stunning beaches, this 6-mile-long barrier beach is in West Barnstable, although the entrance is in Sandwich. Sandy Neck dunes protect Barnstable Harbor from the winds and currents of Cape Cod Bay. Encompassing almost 9000 acres, the area is rich with marshes, shellfish, and bird life. Sandy Neck was the site of a summer Native American encampment before the colonists purchased it in 1644 for the sum of three axes and four coats. The settlers set about harvesting salt-marsh hay and boiling whale oil in tryworks on the beach. Today, a private summertime cottage community occupies the far eastern end of the beach. Known locally as The Neck, the former hunting and fishing camps, built in the late 19th century and early 20th, still rely on water pumps and propane lights. Facilities at the beach include rest rooms, changing rooms, and a snack bar. Parking $8; four-wheel drives allowed with permit, purchased at the gatehouse (362-8300).

Millway Beach, just beyond Barnstable Harbor. Although a resident parking sticker is needed in summer, off-season you can park and look across to Sandy Neck Beach.

Craigville Beach, on Nantucket Sound, Centerville. This crescent-shaped beach—long and wide—is popular with both college crowds and families. Facilities include rest rooms, changing rooms, and outdoor showers. Parking $8 per day, $35 per week.

Long Beach, on Nantucket Sound, Centerville. Centerville residents favor Long Beach, at the western end of Craigville Beach; walk along the water until you reach a finger of land between the Sound and the Centerville River. Long Beach is uncrowded, edged by large summer homes on the shore side and a bird sanctuary on the western end, next to East Bay. Although a resident sticker is required for parking, I mention it because it's the nicest beach around.

PONDS

Hathaway's Pond, Phinney's Lane, Barnstable Village, is a popular spot for those who prefer fresh water to salt water; bathhouse; lifeguard; parking $4. The following three freshwater locations require a resident parking sticker: **Lovell's Pond,** off Newtown Road from Route 28, Marstons Mills; **Hamblin's Pond,** off Route 149 from Route 28, Marstons Mills; and **Wequaquet Lake,** off Shoot Flying Hill Road from Route 132 (Iyanough Road), Centerville.

WALKS

Sandy Neck Great Salt Marsh Conservation Area (362-8300), West Barnstable. First things first: Hike in the off-season when it's not so hot. The trailhead is located off Sandy Neck Road at the beach parking lot. The 9-mile (round-trip) trail to Beach Point winds past pine groves, wide marshes, low blueberry bushes, and 50- to 100-foot dunes. It takes about 4 hours to do the whole circuit. This 4000-acre marsh is the East Coast's largest. Be on the lookout for the endangered piping plovers that nest in the sand and whose eggs are very difficult to see and, therefore, very easily crushed. Parking $8.

St. Mary's Church Gardens, 3005 Route 6A (across from the library), Barnstable Village. Locals come to these peaceful, old-fashioned gardens to escape the swell of summer traffic on Route 6A. In spring, it's full of crocuses, tulips, and daffodils. A small stream, crisscrossed with tiny wooden bridges, flows through the property; it's rather like an Anglicized Japanese garden.

Scudder Lane, off Route 6A, West Barnstable. From the town landing at the end of the road, you can walk onto the flats at low tide, and then almost across to the neck of Sandy Neck ahead of you.

West Barnstable Conservation Area, Popple Bottom Road, off Route 149 (near Route 6), West Barnstable. Park at the corner and take the wooded trails.

Cape Cod Horticultural Society Park, Route 28 near East Bay Road, Osterville. This park has shaded picnic tables, wooded walking trails with identified specimens, and a wetland walkway—a lovely place.

LODGING

BED & BREAKFASTS

❋ **Charles Hinckley House** (362-9924), Route 6A at Scudder Lane, Barnstable Village 02630. Open year-round. Hundreds of wildflowers, tended by Miya and Les Patrick since 1983, have overtaken the grounds of this 1809 Federal-style house. Miya, a wonderfully talented caterer, serves exquisite breakfasts (scrambled eggs with smoked salmon or poached eggs on crabcakes, for instance) in the Colonial-style dining room. A small living room has deep, soft couches and comfortable wing chairs. Each of the four guest rooms has a queen-sized four-poster bed, private bath, working fireplace, and antiques. My favorite room is the Summer Kitchen, a delightful cathedral-ceilinged haven with whitewashed walls and soft golden accents. $119–149.

Waratah House (362-1469, 1-800-215-8707), 4308 Route 6A, Cummaquid 02637. Open mid-April to early December. One of two B&Bs on Route 6A with an ocean view, this 18th-century house is well hidden. Innkeepers Nancy and Gary Hopkins offer four tastefully decorated guest rooms and a common room filled with comfortable antiques. A refurbished cottage (which feels even more like a hideaway) has two bedrooms, a living room with working fireplace, a full kitchen, and a deck. A full breakfast (perhaps featuring a Brie and herb omelet) is served on the brick patio or on the sun porch. Both houses overlook 5 acres of gardens and a deep lawn that rolls down to a private pond. Afternoon picnics and a four-course dinner can be arranged on request. Late May to mid-October $85–115; $210 for four in the cottage. The cottage can be rented weekly without breakfast at the inn.

❋ **Henry Crocker House** (362-6348), 3026 Route 6A, Barnstable 02630. Open year-round. This circa-1800 former tavern—its history is visible in scads of architectural details—once served weary visitors to the courthouse across the street. Today, it's still an unpretentious place to unwind. There is plenty of common space, including a comfortable parlor, the former keeping room with its massive hearth, a screened-in porch, and a brick terrace. All three guest rooms (each with private bath) are airy and spacious; two have an adjoining room that can accommodate an extra person or two (unusual for B&Bs.) Doubles $95, full breakfast included.

☞❋ **Crocker Tavern Bed & Breakfast** (362-5115, 1-800-773-5359), 3095 Route 6A, Barnstable Village 02630. Open year-round. This handsomely restored circa-1750 tavern and stagecoach stop also served as a meeting place for the Whigs during the American Revolution. Today it has five large guest rooms (all with private bath) elegantly furnished with period

On Nantucket Sound, Osterville's shoreline is ringed with small scalloped beaches

antiques and reproductions. Architectural details include raised paneling, window seats, ceiling beams, and working fireplaces. An expanded continental breakfast is served at the dining room harvest table. Innkeepers Jeff and Sue Carlson came on board in 1993. $85–105.

✾ **Beechwood** (362-6618), 2839 Route 6A, Barnstable Village 02630. Open year-round. Named for the copper and weeping beeches flanking the house, Beechwood offers six romantic guest rooms that are furnished with high Victorian charm. Although they are all very different from one another, they might feature a brass bed, private entrance, marble fireplace, or steeply angled walls as in the Garret Room, tucked under the eaves on the third floor. A wide veranda overlooks the beeches and the privacy hedge that separates the inn from Route 6A. The dining room—a full breakfast is included—features tongue-in-groove paneling and a pressed-tin ceiling. Innkeepers Debbie and Ken Traugot, who love talking with guests, purchased this 1853 Queen Anne–style house in 1994. May through October $120–150; off-season $90–130.

✾ **Acworth Inn** (362-3330), 4352 Route 6A, Cummaquid 02637. Open year-round. Cheryl and Jack Ferrell's B&B is distinct from all other places on Route 6A. The formal living room is contemporary, awash in light tones, handpainted furniture, and colorful fabrics. (Cheryl guesses that Martha Stewart would feel at home here.) The six guest rooms have triple sheeting, lots of pillows on the bed, and turn-down service. The nicest room is Cummaquid, decorated in shades of oatmeal and white, with a working fireplace and modern bath. The carriage house rooms are the least desirable. In warm weather the expanded continental breakfast is served on the small backyard deck. Mid-May through October $85–95;

$10 less in the off-season.

❋ **The Inn at the Mills** (428-2967), 71 Route 149 (at Route 28), Marstons Mills 02648. Open year-round. If you didn't know this circa-1780 red farmhouse and barn was a B&B, you'd note how lovely it was and drive right by. There's no sign because innkeeper Bill Henry has plenty of business with weddings and by word of mouth. On a knoll overlooking a pond, gazebo, and pool, the inn has five lovely rooms plus the "hayloft" room, which has a long sitting area and cathedral ceiling. Common rooms include a formal front living room and a wicker-filled sun room. Continental breakfast included. In-season $75–110; $10 less off-season.

❋ **Inn at Fernbrook** (775-4334, e-mail: sal@capecod.net), 481 Main Street, Centerville 02632. Open year-round. This 1881 shingled, Queen Anne–style mansion sits on 18 lush acres landscaped by Frederick Law Olmsted. Innkeepers Brian Gallo and Sal DiFlorio resurrected it from a state of disrepair in 1986. Now it's a grand and refined B&B: The rooms are furnished with antiques, Oriental carpets, and fine reproductions while the facade features a turret, porches, and dormers. Most of the luxurious rooms overlook the gardens; some have bay windows and sitting areas. The spectacular third-floor Olmsted suite has cathedral ceilings, two bedrooms (perfect for two couples traveling together), living room with fireplace, a roof deck, and a telescope. Ask about the private, airy cottage. A multicourse breakfast is served in the formal dining room. In-season $125–270; off-season $85–210.

❋ **Adam's Terrace Gardens Inn** (775-4707), 539 Main Street, Centerville 02632. Open year-round. If you're looking for a simple, unpretentious place off the beaten path, this circa-1830s sea captain's house is it. One of the eight rooms (some with private bath) has a fireplace; all have televisions and homey furnishings. Louise Pritchard serves a full breakfast. Late May to mid-September: $85–95 private bath, $20 less shared bath. Off-season $70–80 private, $55–65 shared.

MOTEL

Trade Winds Inn (775-0365), Craigville Beach, Craigville 02636. Open April through November. The raison d'être for this four-building complex is its proximity to Craigville Beach, right across the street. (The motel maintains its own private stretch of this beach.) Ocean-view rooms and efficiencies have sliding glass doors that open onto little balconies. Less expensive non–ocean view rooms, some with kitchens, are also available. This is the best in the area. Mid-June to early September $95–159; off-season $60–95. (More expensive rooms have ocean views.)

RENTALS

Craigville Realty (775-3174), Box 216, 648 Craigville Beach Road, West Hyannisport 02672. This agency specializes in two- to four-bedroom rental houses in quiet neighborhoods within a mile of Craigville Beach in Centerville. At any given time there are about 125 houses in the rental pool; $600–1000 per week in-season.

CAMPGROUND
Sandy Terraces Nudist Family Campground (428-9209), Box 98C, Marstons Mills 02648. Open mid-May to mid-October. Geared toward couples and families, you must call or write in advance of your visit. There are wooded sites and lots of activities.

WHERE TO EAT

DINING OUT
❋ **The Regatta of Cotuit** (428-5715), 4613 Route 28, Cotuit. Open for dinner year-round; usually closed Monday and Tuesday in the off-season. The tavern opens at 4, serving less expensive and lighter fare. The location may not be as picturesque as the Regatta of Falmouth, Brantz and Wendy Bryan's other superb restaurant, but this 200-year-old Federal mansion— a former stagecoach stop—is more romantic, with eight intimate dining rooms. Many think the food here is superior. And although the setting is elegant, the atmosphere is relaxed. The menu features untraditional pairings of traditional New England meats and seafood. My last gastronomic romp included two highly recommended dishes: center-cut swordfish, sesame-encrusted with a scallop and shrimp farci and wasabi ginger vinaigrette, and boneless rack of lamb *en chemise,* wrapped in puff pastry with pine nuts, spinach, chèvre, and a cabernet sauce. Dessert choices might include fresh fruit tarts, "chocolate seduction" with sauce framboise, or a classic crème brûlée with berries. The service is as outstanding as the food. A jazz pianist performs in the tavern most evenings. Reservations suggested. Dining room entrées $18–26; tavern menu $14–16.

EATING OUT
✐ **Mattakeese Wharf** (362-4511); 271 Mill Way, Barnstable Harbor. Open 11:30–9 daily, May through October. Although this quintessential harborside eatery is a bit overpriced, nobody can beat the location and million-dollar view over the water. Get a table about an hour before sunset so you can watch the fishermen and pleasure craft come and go in this quiet harbor. Entrées include almond-coated swordfish steak, large burgers, mussels with your choice of sauce—Dijon or marinara—and boiled lobster. Mattakeese has been around under the same management since 1968. Children's menu. Lunch $5.25–9; dinner entrées $11–19.

☞✐❋ **Barnstable Tavern** (362-2355), 3176 Route 6A, Barnstable Village. Open for lunch and dinner year-round. Stop in for a drink or casual meal at this handsome old tavern building in Barnstable's historic district. Recent renovations removed some of the tavern's character, but the old, low-ceilinged rooms maintain some of the former charm. Although the fare leans toward classic American (steaks and grilled fish), chef-owner Geoffrey Jamiel has introduced some exceptions from his homeland: hummus, grape leaves, spinach pie, kofta, and Lebanese entrées. Wednesday nights feature an authentic Middle Eastern feast for $14.95.

This is a good choice for predictably good food. Outside patio. Lunch $5–10; dinner entrées $11–23.

Mill Way Fish and Lobster Market (362-2760), 276 Mill Way, Barnstable Village. Culinary Institute of America–trained chef Ralph Binder puts his heart into this unordinary market. Prepared foods for vegetarians and seafood lovers, as well as take-out fried seafood and grilled fish. Open May through October.

☞❋ **Joseph's** (420-1742), 825 Main Street, Osterville. Open daily 7 AM–9 PM year-round. Chef-owner Joe Murray has run this pleasant, reasonably priced restaurant since 1990. You can get hash browns, bacon, and eggs for breakfast and light pasta dishes, salads, and sandwiches for lunch. But dinners are classic, hearty Italian-American (often accompanied by fresh pasta and/or seafood)—cherrystone clams over linguine, pasta with low-fat Alfredo sauce, a mixed platter of grilled meats, and homemade desserts to top it off. Early-dinner specials are a good value (5-6:30 PM): $9 for eggplant Parmesan or $12 for wood-grilled salmon fillet. Otherwise, dinner entrées are $10–15.

☞❋ **Cafe Centerville** (775-6023), 23 Park Avenue, off Old Stage Road, Centerville. Open for breakfast and lunch year-round. This low-key place, which the new owners brightened up considerably when they took over in 1995, is primarily frequented by locals. They come for both dessert pies and savory meat pies, all justifiably renowned. $2–10.

❋ **Osterville Cheese Shop** (428-9085, 1-800-498-9085), 29 Wianno Avenue, Osterville. Open daily year-round. Osterville residents and summer folks order cheeses and other goodies for their cocktail parties here. Enjoy a thick sandwich, a slice of chicken pie or quiche, or a pint of pasta salad, all wrapped up to take away.

❋ **Breaking Grounds** (420-1311), 791 Main Street, Osterville. Open for breakfast and lunch daily year-round. This pleasant, newly constructed place serves omelets and a limited menu of soups, salads, and hot sandwiches. Large selection of flavored coffee and espresso drinks. $2.50–5.25.

ICE CREAM

✐ **Four Seas** (775-1394), 360 South Main Street, at Centerville Four Corners. Open 9 AM–10:30 PM daily, mid-May to mid-September; sandwiches served 10–2:30. Founded in 1934, Four Seas has been owned by Dick Warren since 1960, when he bought the place from the folks who gave him a summer job as a college student. It's named for the four "seas" that surround the Cape: Buzzards Bay, Cape Cod Bay, the Atlantic Ocean, and Nantucket Sound. Ice cream is made every day, using the freshest ingredients. For instance, Dick makes beach plum ice cream only once a year—when the beach plums are ripe. The walls of this funky place, a former garage, are lined with photos of preppy summer crews, newspaper articles about Four Seas (it wins national ice cream awards every year), and poems written for Four Seas' 60th anniversary. It's also known for its lobster-salad sandwiches.

ENTERTAINMENT

Baseball. The Cotuit Kettlers play at Lowell Park in Cotuit.

Barnstable Comedy Club (362-6333), 3171 Route 6A, Barnstable Village. The oldest amateur theater group in the country performs more than comedies; the summer schedule also includes musicals, mysteries, and farces. Since 1922 its motto has been "to produce good plays and remain amateurs." (Kurt Vonnegut got his feet wet here.) "Imagine! Theater For Children" is a relatively new dramatic venture in which local kids choose the plays, build the sets, sit in the audience, and act in the plays during summer. Scaled-down versions of classics like *Tom Sawyer* and *Snow White* are adapted for the troupe. Admission $5.

Benefit Coffeehouse (775-5165, 428-1053), Liberty Hall, Main Street, Marstons Mills. These folk-rock and New Age acoustic–folk concerts have benefited kids with cancer since 1990. Musicians hail from the Cape and the Boston area. Tickets $8–10.

SELECTIVE SHOPPING

ANTIQUES

Harden Studios (362-7711), 3264 Route 6A, Barnstable Village. Open year-round. This late-17th-century house was beautifully restored by Charles M. Harden in 1993 and now functions as a two-story antique shop-cum-gallery. It's a true family affair: Harden's son Charles operates an etching press and art gallery in the adjacent shed and his son Justin researches the fine antique collection. American antiques from the early 1700s to the 1840s; Empire and Federal pieces; Oriental rugs, lamps, and chandeliers.

Sow's Ear Antiques (428-4931), Route 28 at Route 130, Cotuit. Open Thursday through Monday year-round. Laurie and Stephen Hayes sell Americana and primitive folk art from their 18th-century house.

Cotuit Antiques (420-1234), 4404 Route 28, Cotuit. Open daily except Tuesday, year-round. The exterior of the barn is so colorful, covered with vintage signs, that many passersby are compelled to stop even if they're not interested in antiques. For those of you who are, you'll find a trove of Coca-Cola items, advertising memorabilia, and vintage toys.

ART GALLERIES

Cape Cod Art Association (362-2909), 3480 Route 6A, Barnstable Village. Open February through November. The headquarters of this peer-judged, nonprofit organization, founded in 1947, displays a good mix of art and artists in a beautiful, airy building. Studio facilities on premises.

Cummaquid Fine Arts (362-2593), 4275 Route 6A, Cummaquid. Open year-round. Gallery owners Jim Hinkle and Roy Hammer prefer to highlight work by living artists rather than dead ones. You'll find a wide range of landscapes, stills, coastal scenes, and figure studies in this 18th-century house.

See also Harden Studios under *Antiques*.

ARTISANS

The Blacks Handweaving Shop (362-3955), 597 Route 6A, West Barnstable. Open year-round. The Blacks create beautiful woven pieces with a variety of textures, colors, and materials: chenille, mohair, wool, and cotton. They are quite well known for custom, one-of-a-kind Jacquard coverlets and throws, signed and dated. Bob Black—who's been weaving since he was 14 and studied at Rhode Island School of Design—and his wife, Gabrielle, have been working at their looms in this post-and-beam shop since 1954.

Oak and Ivory (428-9425), 1112 Main Street, Osterville. Open year-round. If you've always wanted a Nantucket lightship basket, but haven't made it to Nantucket, this is the off-island place for you. The baskets are expensive (from about $700 to several thousand dollars), reflecting the fine craftsmanship and 35–45 hours of work that go into each delicate piece. Basketmaker Bob Marks hails from Nantucket; he also offers scrimshaw and miniature gold baskets.

Salt & Chestnut Weathervanes (362-6085), 651 Route 6A, West Barnstable. Open year-round. Since 1978, proprietor Marilyn Strauss has sold typical New England–style vanes—roosters, ships, and crickets—as well as unusual designs like bicycles, planes, and vintage cars. She also does custom work. Past commissions have included a giant manicotti for the president of Prince Spaghetti and a swimming skeleton for Edward Gorey. Prices vary, but inventory is in the range of $85–3000. Antiques might cost as much as a small car.

BOOKSTORES

Isaiah Thomas Books & Prints (428-2752), 4632 Falmouth Road, at Routes 28 and 132, Cotuit. Open year-round (weekends only, January through March). James Visbeck offers more than 60,000 antique, first-edition, and slightly used books, as well as books for children divided by age group and interest. He also offers appraisals, search services, archival materials, restoration, and repair. This place is marvelous; a book lover could easily spend hours here.

✐ **Sign of the Owl** (428-9393), 13 Wianno Avenue, Osterville. Local books, a good children's section, and national best-sellers.

SPECIAL SHOPS

West Barnstable Tables (362-2676), Route 149, West Barnstable. Open daily year-round. Steve Whittlesey is a master craftsman. Since it's difficult (not to mention prohibitively expensive) to find antique tables anymore, Steve makes tables using 19th-century wood scavenged from houses that are about to be torn down. His creations are exquisite and worth admiring even if you don't have a couple of thousand dollars to spare. Less expensive pieces include windowpane mirrors and a chandelier made from driftwood found at Sandy Neck Beach. Furniture maker Richard Kiusalas shares the big barn; his fanciful, whimsical, primitive pieces are equally worthy.

Tern Studio (362-6077), Route 149, West Barnstable. Open year-round. Wood turner Al Barbour creates artful bowls and vases using local woods, including driftwood that washes ashore during hurricanes. His work is very organic. He's obviously doing something right; he's been in the same spot since 1976 (and it can't be chalked up to lethargy).

Pinske Gallery (362-5311), 1989 Route 6A, Barnstable Village. Open year-round. Carved with a hydraulic chain saw, wooden grizzly bears and uncut timbers guard the entrance to Barre Pinske's 6000-square-foot studio. These sculptures may look odd on historic Route 6A, but they're nothing compared to the 4-foot-high mailbox that Pinske erected to needle the Old King's Highway Historical Commission. The gallery is on the second floor of the old warehouse Pinske purchased and renovated in 1992. He carves wooden sculptures and chairs, enormous couches burrowed out of logs, and other large wooden pieces, many of which make a political statement. It's a little bit of Greenwich Village, right in dignified old Barnstable Village.

Maps of Antiquity (362-7169), 1022 Route 6A, West Barnstable. Open May to mid-October. Maps of the 19th century and earlier, from around the world. If you want to know what the Cape or a specific town looked like 200 years ago, these folks will have a reproduction map that will tell you. (The supply of originals is limited, and when they find them, they go quickly.)

Packet Landing Iron (362-9321), 1040 Route 6A, West Barnstable. Open daily except Monday, year-round. Most of the blacksmith forging—of lamps, hooks, andirons, candlesticks, plant stands, and curtain rods—is done on the premises. Commissions accepted. Look for their smithing demonstrations at the Barnstable County Fair.

Margo's Practically Unusual (428-5664), 876 Main Street, Osterville. Open mid-April to mid-January; in winter by appointment. The name dictates the buying: "unusual" picture frames, serving pieces, hand-painted furniture and home accessories, handmade lamps with "unusual" finials.

Cotuit Grocery/Cotuit Pizza Factory (428-6936, 420-1994), Main Street, Cotuit. Open year-round. This old multiuse building would go unnoticed in Vermont, but on the Cape it's an anomaly. On one hand it's simply a convenience store–cum–wine shop. But owners Steve and Jan Gould also sell Jan's jewelry, a few antiques, and pizza. It's a prime example of year-rounders doing whatever they have to do to enjoy the Cape in all seasons.

SPECIAL EVENTS

Mid-July: **Osterville Village Day** (428-9700, 428-6327). Held since 1976, this event includes a crafts and antiques fair, children's events, and parade.

Late July: **Barnstable County Fair** (563-3200), Route 151, East Falmouth. Local and national music acts, a midway, livestock shows (including horse, ox, and pony pulls), and horticulture, cooking, and crafts exhibits and contests. A popular tradition, especially for teens and families with young children. Adults $5, children 6–12 $1.

Mid-August: **Centerville Old Home Week.** Until 1994 this event hadn't been held for 90 years. Main Street open houses.

Late September: **Osterville Village Fall Festival Days.** Wine tasting, an arts and crafts show, entertainment, and food.

Early December: **Osterville Christmas Open House and Stroll** (428-6327). Since 1972, bell ringers, hayrides, magicians, wine tastings, crafts demonstrations, and more.

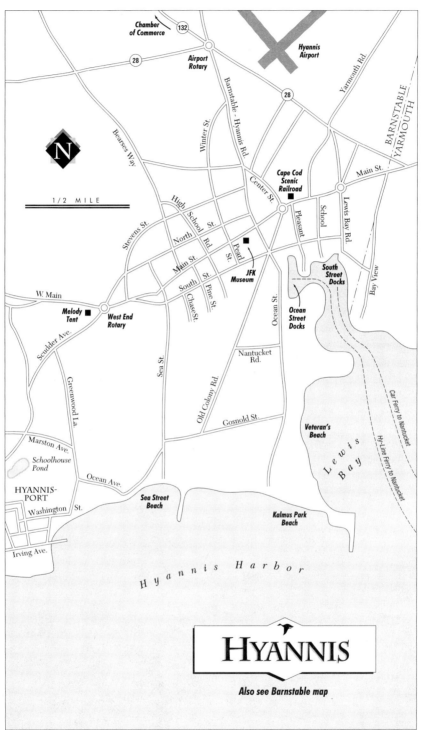

Paul Woodward / © 1997 The Countryman Press, Inc.

Hyannis

Hyannis is the Cape's commercial and transportation hub: An astonishing 1 million people take the ferry from Hyannis to Nantucket every year. Most Cape visitors end up in Hyannis at some point, whether by choice or from necessity.

Among Cape visitors, Hyannis seems to be everyone's favorite whipping boy: A sigh of sympathy is heard when one mentions he "has" to go into Hyannis in July or August. Yes, traffic is gnarly and Route 28 is overbuilt, but those same Cape residents and off-Cape visitors who moan about congestion in Hyannis couldn't live as easily without its services. They come here to buy new cars, embark to the islands, visit their doctors, shop at the malls. And so, although Hyannis is technically one of Barnstable's seven villages, I have given it its own chapter because it is so distinct from the rest of Barnstable.

Over the last few years, Hyannis's harborfront and Main Street have been revitalized, thanks in part to the encouragement of Ben Thompson, architect of Boston's Quincy Market shopping complex and other successful urban waterfront development projects. It's quite pleasant to mill around Main Street (although it still has its share of T-shirt shops) and watch the boating activity on Lewis Bay. Hyannis has a bit of everything: discount outlets, more than 60 eating establishments in the waterfront district *alone* (a number of them quite good), some quiet cottages and guest houses, plenty of motels geared to overnight visitors waiting for the morning ferry, harbor tours, and lots of lively bars and nightlife.

Then there's the mystique of the Kennedy family. Hyannisport—a neighborhood in Hyannis but quite separate from Hyannis—will forever be remembered as the place where, in the early 1960s, President John F. Kennedy and Jacqueline sailed offshore and played with children Caroline and John. Visitors who come in search of the "Kennedy compound" or in hopes of somehow experiencing the Kennedy mystique will only find a residential Yankee community of posh estates.

Hyannis's harbor area was inhabited about 1000 years ago by ancestors of the Eastern Algonquian Indians, who set up summer campsites south of what is now Ocean Street. The first European to reach Cape Cod, Bartholomew Gosnold, anchored in the harbor in 1602.

Shortly thereafter, settlers persuaded Native American Sachem Yanno to sell them what is now known as Hyannis and Centerville for £20 and two pairs of pants.

Main Street was laid out in 1750, and by the early 1800s, Hyannis was already known as the Cape's transportation hub; the harbor was bustling with two- and three-masted schooners. When the steam-train line was extended from Barnstable in 1854, land-based trade and commerce supplanted the marine-based economy. Tourists began arriving in much greater numbers by the end of the century. Pleasure-seeking yachts filled the harbor by the 1930s, until John Kennedy (who tied up at the Hyannisport Yacht Club) renewed interest in traditional local sailboats, known as Catboats, in the 1950s.

GUIDANCE

Hyannis Area Chamber of Commerce (775-2201, 1-800-449-6647 for 24-hour information, http://www.hyannischamber.com), 1481 Route 132, Hyannis 02601. Open 9–5, Monday through Saturday year-round, with slightly reduced hours on Saturday in winter; open Sunday, late May to early September. About a mile south of Route 6, the chamber has plenty of printed information and an informational booklet with discount coupons. There is also a small visitors booth at the JFK Museum (see *To See*) on Main Street, staffed in summer only.

PUBLIC REST ROOMS

Public rest rooms are located at the beaches (see *Green Space— Beaches*), the Village Green parking lot (behind the JFK Museum on Main Street), and at the Ocean Street Docks (Bismore Park).

GETTING THERE

By car: To reach Hyannis, about 30 minutes from either bridge, take exit 6 off Route 6; follow Route 132 south to the airport rotary (at the junction of Routes 28 and 132). Take the second right off the rotary onto Barnstable Road, which intersects with Main Street and Ocean and South Streets (for the harbor).

By bus: The **Plymouth & Brockton** bus line (775-5524), Center Street at Elm Street, connects Hyannis with other Cape towns and with Boston's Logan Airport.

By air: **Barnstable Municipal Airport** (775-2020), at the airport rotary, at the junction of Route 28 and Route 132, Hyannis. Small carriers flying in and out of Hyannis include **Colgan Air** (1-800-272-5488), offering year-round service between Hyannis and Newark, New Jersey, and seasonal service from La Guardia, New York. **Cape Air** and **Nantucket Air** (775-8171, 1-800-352-0714) have year-round service from Boston to Hyannis. Cape Air and Nantucket Air have grown considerably in the recent past; they currently fly over a quarter of a million people to the Cape and islands each year.

By train: **AMTRAK** (1-800-872-7245), at Main and Center Streets, at the Cape Cod Scenic Railroad Station. The Cape Codder runs on Friday,

July to mid-September, from New York (with connections along the eastern seaboard). The same train returns to New York on Sunday. The round-trip fare from New York to Hyannis is $158.

GETTING AROUND

By car: In summer Hyannis suffers from serious traffic problems. Parking on Main Street is free if you can get a space. If not, try North Street, one block north of Main Street and parallel to it. Main Street (one way) is meant for strolling, but it's a long walk from end to end.

Rental cars. Hyannis is one of the few places where it's convenient to get a rental car. Call the big agencies based at the Barnstable Municipal Airport: **Hertz** (1-800-654-3131), **National** (1-800-227-7368), **Avis** (1-800-331-1212), **Budget** (775-3832 or 1-800-527-0700), and **Thrifty** (771-0450 or 1-800-367-2277). Or try **Trek** (771-2459), two blocks from the airport and bus terminal, or **U-Save** (790-4700).

By shuttle: **Hyannis Area Trolley** (775-8743, 1-800-352-7155). The state-funded summertime shuttle has been very popular, and it's expected to continue operating, but nothing is guaranteed. One route covers shopping plazas; another makes its way along Main Street and the waterfront; a third loop covers West Main Street. Buses operate daily in summer and on weekends from late May to late June and early September to mid-October.

Yarmouth Easy Shuttle. The viability of this popular summertime shuttle also depends on the benevolence of the Statehouse; its fate remains unclear from year to year. The shuttle begins at the Plymouth & Brockton Bus Terminal (Center Street at Elm Street) and runs along Route 28 to various points (including the beaches) in Yarmouth. The route is circled seven times daily.

Sea Line (1-800-352-7155). Operating daily except Sunday, year-round except on major holidays, Sea Line connects Hyannis to Barnstable, Mashpee, Falmouth, and Woods Hole. The fare depends on the distance traveled: $.75–$4 per ride; children 5 and under ride free. Look for a schedule for complete details.

The Villager (1-800-352-7155) connects Barnstable's villages with two bus routes along Routes 132 and 149. You can pick up a complete schedule of stops at the chamber of commerce. Fares: $.50 adults, children under 5 free.

Getting to the islands: For complete information, see *Getting There* in "Martha's Vineyard" and "Nantucket."

Hy-Line Cruises (778-2600), Ocean Street Dock, takes passengers and bicycles to Nantucket and Martha's Vineyard seasonally; the company also has an in-season, interisland trip. In 1996 Hy-Line introduced a high-speed catamaran to Nantucket.

Steamship Authority (477-8600 for advance auto reservations, 771-4000 for day-of-sailing information), South Street Dock, transports autos, people, and bikes to Nantucket year-round.

Note: You can also fly to the islands on a number of carriers.
MEDICAL EMERGENCY
   Cape Cod Hospital (771-1800), 27 Park Street. Open 24 hours.

TO SEE

John F. Kennedy Hyannis Museum (790-3077), 397 Main Street in the Old Town Hall. Open 10–3:45 Monday through Saturday, 1–4 Sunday, mid-April to mid-October; 10–4 Wednesday through Saturday the rest of the year except closed completely from January to mid-February. This museum opened in 1992 to meet the demands of visitors making a pilgrimage to Hyannis in search of JFK; people wanted to see "something," so the chamber gave them a museum that focuses on JFK's time in Hyannisport and on Cape Cod. The museum features more than 100 photographs of Kennedy from 1934 to 1963, arranged in themes: JFK's friends, his family, JFK the man. JFK said, "I always go to Hyannisport to be revived, to know the power of the sea and the master who rules over it and all of us." (If you really want to learn something about the president and his administration, head to the JFK Museum in Boston.) Adults $3, free for children under 16.

JFK Memorial, Ocean Street. The fountain, behind a large presidential seal mounted on a high stone wall, is inscribed with the following: "I believe it is important that this country sail and not sit still in the harbor." There is a nice view of Lewis Bay from here.

Kennedy compound. Joe and Rose Kennedy rented the Malcolm Cottage in Hyannisport from 1926 to 1929 before purchasing and remodeling it to include 14 rooms, nine baths, and a private movie theater in the basement (the first private theater in New England). By 1932 there were nine children scampering around the house and grounds, which included a private beach, dock, tennis court, and pool. In 1956, then Senator John Kennedy purchased an adjacent house (at the corner of Scudder and Irving Avenues), which came to be known as the Summer White House. Bobby Kennedy bought the house next door, which now belongs to his widow, Ethel Kennedy. Senator Edward Kennedy's former house (it now belongs to his ex-wife, Joan) is on private Squaw Island. Eunice (Kennedy) and Sargent Shriver also purchased a nearby home on Atlantic Avenue. If you drive or walk around this stately area, you'll see nothing but high hedges and fences. For those who can't resist a look-see, you'll be far better off taking a boat tour (see *To Do—Boat Excursions/Rentals*); some boats come quite close to the shoreline and the white frame houses. It was at Malcolm Cottage that JFK learned he'd been elected president, Malcolm Cottage that Jacqueline and the president mourned the loss of their infant son, Malcolm Cottage where the family mourned the death of the president and Bobby Kennedy, Malcolm Cottage that Senator Edward Kennedy every year would present his mother with a rose for each of her years, and Malcolm Cottage that matriarch Rose Kennedy died in 1995 at the age of 104. Regardless of the fact that it's nearly impossible to get a glimpse of any Kennedy, the Kennedys are still Hyannis's number one "attraction."

St. Francis Xavier Church, South Street. When Rose Kennedy's clan was in town, they worshiped here. The pew used by JFK when he was in town is marked with a plaque. More recently, Maria Shriver and Arnold Schwarzenegger were wed here.

Village green, adjacent to the JFK Museum. Note the life-sized bronze of Sachem Ivanough, chief of the Mattakeese tribe of Cummaquid and friend to the Pilgrims, done in 1995 by Osterville sculptor David Lewis.

SCENIC RIDES

Cape Cod Scenic Railroad (771-3788), Main and Center Streets. Operates weekends only in May, November, and December; Tuesday through Sunday, June through October. The 42-mile trip departs at 10, 12:30, and 3, and takes 2 hours. It passes alongside cranberry bogs and the Sandy Neck Great Salt Marsh. You can hop off in Sandwich, take the trolley into the picturesque village, and then catch a later train back if you want. Adults $11.50, children $7.50.

Hyannisport is by far the loveliest section of Hyannis, but don't come expecting to see the Kennedys. The "compound" is wedged between Scudder and Irving Avenues. From Main Street, turn left on Sea Street, right on Ocean Avenue, left on Hyannis Avenue, left on Iyanough Avenue, right on Wachusett Avenue, and left on Scudder Avenue.

TO DO

AIRPLANE RIDES

Hyannis Air Service (775-8171), Barnstable Municipal Airport, Routes 132 and 28, Hyannis. Flights year-round; reservations advisable. Get away from the traffic in a Cessna 172 or a Piper Warrior. On the 30-minute trip (one or two people $49, three people $69), you can head east to Chatham Light or west to the Cape Cod Canal. An hour-long trip (one or two people $89, three people $129) goes to the Outer Beaches and Pilgrim Monument in Provincetown. The Grand Tour lasts 2 hours (one or two people $169, three people $209) and takes you all over the Cape and out to the islands. You can also take a colorful cranberry tour in autumn.

BICYCLING/RENTALS

Cascade Motor Lodge (775-9717), 201 Main Street. Just one block from the harbor and bus and train stations, Cascade rents mountain, 10-, and 3-speed bikes daily April to mid-November (and through winter, weather permitting).

BOAT EXCURSIONS/RENTALS

Hyannisport Harbor Cruises (778-2600), Ocean Street dock. Early April

Steamship Authority ferry from Nantucket docking in Hyannis

to late October. Lewis Bay and Hyannis Harbor are beautiful, and the best way to appreciate them is by water. Also, if you're like about 85,000 other visitors each season, and you want the best possible view of the Kennedy compound, head to Hy-Line for its hour-long excursions. The boat comes within 500-feet of the shoreline. Hy-Line also offers a special deal for families: From late June to early September, children ride free on the early-morning and late-afternoon boats. During the height of summer, there are two sunset trips, a Sunday-afternoon cruise for families with Ben & Jerry's ice cream sundaes, and a Thursday-evening jazz cruise. Adults $8–12, children 12 and under $3.50–6.

Eventide (775-0222, http://www.virtualcapecod.com/market/catboat), Ocean Street dock. Mid-April to late November. *Eventide* has a full complement of trips: a "blue-water" sail far out into Nantucket Sound; a sunset trip that goes where the wind takes you; a starlight trip often venturing no farther than the twinkling shoreline of Lewis Bay; a nature trip good for kids and birdwatchers; a trip skirting the Kennedy compound, which sails well within the mooring area of Hyannisport Harbor. For relaxed sailing, Captain Marcus Sherman uses the engines as little as possible. Look for the big cat on the sail. The galley serves appetizers, including PB&J sandwiches for the kids. (Marcus also has toys onboard, in case the kids start to get antsy.) Adults $16, children $6.

Hesperus (790-0077), Ocean Street dock. Salty sailor Neil Dauphinne skippers this 1937 John Alden sloop, a beautiful 50-foot wooden boat. There are three 2-hour trips daily from May through October. Bring your own beverages.

FISHING/SHELLFISHING

Freshwater fishing permits are obtained from the town clerk's office (790-6240) in Town Hall, 367 Main Street. Shellfishing permits are obtained from the Department of Natural Resources (790-6272), 1189 Phinney's Lane, Centerville.

Hy-Line Fishing Trips (790-0696), Ocean Street dock. Do some "bottom fishing" for black sea bass, flounder, and tautog from late April to late October. Half day, $20 adults, $12.50 children; full day, $35 adults, $20 children. Rod rental is $1. Or head out for a half-day trip to Nantucket Sound in search of blues from late June to early September: $25 adults, $15 children.

"Site-Sea-Ing" (771-7394), Ocean Street dock. Mid-May to mid-October. Hop aboard this 34-foot boat for deep-sea-fishing trips: $375 (six people max) for a 4-hour trip in search of blues, or $475 (six people max) for a 6-hour trip in search of bass.

Among the supercruisers that go in search of big fish, try **Helen-H** (790-0660), Pleasant Street dock, **Champion Line** (398-2266), Ocean Street dock, and **Navigator** (771-9500, 1-800-771-9534).

FITNESS CLUB

Fitness Club of Cape Cod (771-7734), 55 Attucks Way, Independence Park, off Route 132. Open year-round. Racquetball, basketball, aerobics classes, fitness machines, tanning booths, and day care for $10 daily.

FOR FAMILIES

Cape Cod YMCA (362-6500), Route 132 (PO Box Y), West Barnstable. Open year-round. With an emphasis on rejuvenating the mind, body, and spirit, the YMCA offers a number of programs (short-term visitors are welcome): open swims, Saturday-morning teen center for grades 5–9, "kids' night out" for ages 5–12 (drop off the kids and go out to dinner while they do arts and crafts). The Y also has two summer camps with weekly sessions. Write for a complete schedule.

Cape Cod Potato Chip Factory (775-7253), Breed's Hill Road, Independence Park, off Route 132. Open 9–5 weekdays, 10–4 Saturday. Chatham resident Steve Bernard began the company in 1980, parlayed it into a multimillion-dollar business that he sold to corporate giant Anheuser-Busch in 1986, and moved on to the business of purveying Chatham Village Croutons. But in late 1995, when Anheuser-Busch wanted to sell it or close it down, Bernard bought it back, saving 100 year-round jobs on the Cape. Take the 5-minute self-guided tour of the potato-chip-packaging assembly line, then sample the rich flavor and high crunchability resulting from all-natural ingredients cooked in small kettles. You, too, will be glad Bernard saved the company.

GOLF

Hyannis Golf Club (362-2606), Route 132, is an 18-hole, 6700-yard, par-71 course; **Tara Hyannis Golf Course** (775-7775, ext. 473), West End Circle, is an 18-hole, 2621-yard, par-54 course. Both open year-round.

ICE SKATING
Kennedy Memorial Skating Rink (790-6346), Bearses Way. Public skating mid-October through March.

MINI-GOLF
Storyland Miniature Golf (778-4339), 70 Center Street. April to mid-October. Bumper boats and a 2-acre mini-golf course. Adults might use this opportunity to teach their kids a little about regional architecture and history, as some holes are modeled after local landmarks. Adults $6, children $5.

SAILING LESSONS
Cape Cod Sailing (771-7918, 1-800-484-5091, ext. 7245, e-mail: CaptSirius-@aol.com), Hyannis. Mid-June through October. If you've always wanted to learn to sail, or if you'd like to hone your intermediate skills, this may be the place to do it. Geared toward women, couples, and "adult" families, Cape Cod Sailing offers 1- to 5-day trips that include a full curriculum, all meals, overnight on-board lodging, and, of course, the boat and captain. The boat is a new 36-foot Catalina yacht. You may wish to arrange your own group of three to five people (the maximum number on board); otherwise, people with similar skill levels will be put on the same boat. Fees are $140 per person per day, all inclusive. You can also hire the boat for fully crewed charters.

SPECIAL PROGRAMS
Eastern Mountain Sports (EMS) (775-1072), 233 Stevens Street, in the Village Marketplace (call for directions). In addition to renting kayaks (great for navigating herring rivers, creeks, and inlets), the Cape's largest purveyor of outdoor gear offers free instructional clinics every couple of weeks through the year. Topics range from outdoor cooking, to compass skills, to bike trips. Check the bulletin board for a schedule.

TENNIS
Public courts can be found at **Barnstable High School** on Route 28 and **Barnstable Middle School** on West Bay Road.
Tara Hyannis Hotel & Resort (775-7775), West End Circle. Two outdoor courts are available for a day-use fee of $10.

WILDLIFE TOURS
International Wildlife Coalition (1-800-548-8704, ext. 200), Hyannis. The coalition sponsors these daylong marine expeditions to Nantucket, the Vineyard, and Monomoy that offer an introduction to oceanography, marine biology, and coastal ecology. Each trip is limited to 18 people and costs $95 per person, including lunch. Proceeds go toward protecting whales and the coastal environment.

GREEN SPACE

BEACHES
Weekly cottage renters can purchase beach stickers 8–5 at the Recreation and Human Services Department (790-6345), 141 Basset Lane, behind

the Kennedy Memorial Skating Rink.

Kalmus Park Beach, on Nantucket Sound, at the end of Ocean Street. Facilities include a rest room and bathhouse. Parking $8. This beach is good for windsurfing. The land was owned and donated by Technicolor inventor Herbert Kalmus, who also owned the Fernbrook estate in Centerville (see *Lodging*).

✐ **Veterans Beach,** on Hyannis Harbor (Lewis Bay), off Ocean Street. The beach is good for children because the waters here are fairly shallow and calm. It's also a good place to watch harbor sailboats (the Hyannis Yacht Club is next door). Facilities include a rest room, bathhouse, snack bar, swings, grills, and a big wooded area with picnic tables. Parking $8.

Sea Street Beach, also known as Keyes Beach, on Nantucket Sound, off Sea Street. Facilities include a rest room and bathhouse. Parking $8.

LODGING

All properties are located in Hyannis unless otherwise noted. The zip code for Hyannis is 02601.

RESORT MOTOR INN

✐❋ **Tara Hyannis Hotel & Resort** (775-7775, 1-800-843-8272), West End Circle. Open year-round. These 224 standard-issue rooms, equipped with cable TV and refrigerators, are pleasant enough. Hotel facilities include a large indoor pool overlooking an 18-hole golf course, tennis courts, an exercise room, an outdoor pool, a popular nightclub, and dining facilities. Ask for a room with a view of the gardens. A complete children's program is offered during school vacations. In-season $129–169, off-season $79–119.

BED & BREAKFASTS

☞ **Inn on Sea Street** (775-8030, e-mail: 71142.322@compuserve.com), 358 Sea Street. Open May through October. When Lois Nelson and J.B. Whitehead opened this B&B in 1983, it was the first one in town; it's still the best. Sea Street has nine rooms (most with private baths). Some are furnished with Victorian antiques, including the Garden Room, which has a private entrance. The most popular rooms, completely refurbished and decorated with English country antiques and canopy beds, are in a separate building across the street. The inn also boasts one of the sweetest places to stay on the Cape—a small but airy, all-white cottage with peaked ceiling, kitchen, separate bedroom, and sitting room. Other pluses: Lois and J.B. serve a delicious full breakfast on lacy-clothed tables set with china; there's plenty of common space; it's located a 2-minute walk from the beach. The inn never has a minimum-night stay. $115 for the cottage, $78–105 for rooms.

❋ **Sea Breeze Inn** (771-7213), 397 Sea Street. Open year-round. These 14 rooms (all with private baths, some with two beds) are within a stone's throw of the beach. Although the rooms aren't fancy or filled with antiques, they are certainly comfortable, clean, and pleasant. Expanded continental breakfast included. Mid-June to mid-September $65–140; off-season $49–98.

✱ **Simmons Homestead Inn** (778-4999, 1-800-637-1649, e-mail: SimmonsInn-@aol.com), 288 Scudder Avenue. Open year-round. This is one of the more unusual places to stay on the Cape. Innkeeper Bill Putman relishes his quirkiness and has furnished the restored 1820s sea captain's home to reflect his offbeat tastes. The basics: All 10 antiques-appointed guest rooms have private baths; some have a fireplace and canopy bed; the living room measures 32 feet by 16 feet; outdoor space includes porch rockers and hammocks. But beyond that there are idiosyncrasies you can't overlook: The place has been taken over by carved, stuffed, and painted animals (each room has a different animal theme); the living room is chock-full of bric-a-brac, ceramic and papier-mâché, and plants; Datsun hoods from Bill's old racing cars stand in the hallway. A full breakfast and wine at "six-ish" are included. May through October $120–150, off-season $80–120. Non-smokers note: Bill smokes.

☞ **Mansfield House** (771-9455), 70 Gosnold Street. Open late May to mid-September. If you want a simple but nice, relatively inexpensive place to stay that's within walking distance of a beach (three beaches, actually!), the Mansfield House is a good bet. There are four comfortable guest rooms, all with private bath and television. Outdoor space includes a porch and garden patio. Innkeeper Don Patrell heads back to Manhattan when he closes for winter. $75–85 including breakfast. Pets are accepted with advance notice.

COTTAGES AND EFFICIENCIES

✎ **Harbor Village** (775-7581, e-mail: HarborVill@aol.com), Marstons Avenue, Hyannisport 02647. Open April through November. Delightfully off the beaten path, but still centrally located, these one- to four-bedroom cottages can sleep 3–10 people. Each cottage has a living room, dining area, fully equipped kitchen, individual heat, a fireplace, deck or patio with grill, and cable TV. Daily housekeeping is provided. On a private, wooded, 17-acre compound, Harbor Village is within a 2-minute walk of Quahog Beach. In-season $900–1400 weekly; off-season $90–145 nightly (with a 3-night minimum). Small service charge added; no credit cards; pets with prior approval.

✎ **The Breakwaters** (775-6831), Sea Street Beach. Open May to mid-October. Within a sandal shuffle of Sea Street Beach, these 16 well-maintained cottages accommodate two to six people. Kitchens are small but complete. All cottages have a private deck or patio, some have ocean views. Although it's on the beach, Breakwater also has a heated pool with a lifeguard; swimming lessons offered. May to mid-October $975–1700 weekly; off-season $375–600; May and October $68–98 daily (3-day minimum). No credit cards.

Rose Garden Cottage (771-7213), 256 Ocean Avenue. Open April through November. Owned by the same folks who run the Sea Breeze

Inn, this three-bedroom house (complete with a namesake rose garden) is fully equipped for longer stays. There are also two studio efficiencies, one with Jacuzzi and canopy bed. House $1200-1600 weekly, mid-June to mid-September; $850–1000 off-season. Efficiencies $690–850 weekly in-season; $600 off-season.

Capt. Gosnold Village (775-9111), 230 Gosnold Street. Open year-round. Although some of the motel rooms are a tad dull, most of the knotty-pine-paneled cottages are spacious, with a private deck. Request a newer cottage with three bedrooms, and you'll also get three bathrooms and three televisions. Daily maid service; fully equipped kitchens. Children enjoy the wooded grounds with a fenced-in pool and lifeguard, lawn games, and a play area. In a residential area near the harbor, Gosnold's is a short walk to the beach. Forty-eight units. Mid-June to early September $75 for rooms, $95 for studios, $140 for a one-bedroom cottage, $210–250 for a two- or three-bedroom cottage. Off-season $45 for rooms, $55 for studios, $90 for a one-bedroom cottage, $130–150 for a two- or three-bedroom cottage. Three-night minimum on cottages, 2 nights on other lodging. 5 percent service charge added.

TOWN HOUSES

The Yachtsman (771-5454, 1-800-695-5454), 500 Ocean Street, Hyannis 02601. Open year-round. These privately owned townhouse condominiums, with their own private stretch of beach between Kalmus and Veterans Beaches, are right on Lewis Bay. During summer, about 50 of the 125 units are available for rent. Although the decor varies from one unit to another, all must meet certain standards. Multilevel units have a full kitchen, 2½ baths, private sun deck, sunken living room, and two to four bedrooms. About half have water views; half overlook the heated pool. Late June to early September $1050–1695 weekly.

RENTALS

Harvard Realty (771-1778), 17 High School Street, Hyannis 02601. At any given time it lists six or so three-bedrooms houses to rent by the week. Call in January for the best choice among properties and dates.

WHERE TO EAT

With more than 60 eateries, most open year-round, you can find everything from fine Continental to Tex-Mex. Reservations are recommended at all the establishments under *Dining Out*. All the entries in this section are in Hyannis.

DINING OUT

Penguins Seagrille (775-2023), 331 Main Street. Open for Sunday brunch and dinner, year-round except January; closed Monday, February through May. This menu (and its winning execution) is by far the most innovative and creative in town. Dishes sail the globe, from wood-grilled meats (a specialty) to Szechuan salmon (excellent), from a vegetable quesadilla to an Italian feast of seafood stewed in marinara sauce. Your taste buds will likely be tickled; trust your instincts when ordering. There are usually a half-dozen daily fish specials; pastas and risottos make regular appearances on the menu. Chef-owners Robert and Portia Gold have been at the helm since 1980. Entrées $15–22.

✷ **Fazio's Trattoria** (771-7445), 586 Main Street. Open for dinner nightly, year-round. Tom and Eileen Fazio, chef-owners who hail from San Francisco's Italian North Beach neighborhood, have created a cozy trattoria that provides a good value. Decorated with Chianti bottles, red-and-white-checkered tablecloths, and photos of Sicily, the restaurant offers specialties from the restaurant's focal point: the wood grill. Excellent pizzas (traditional and thin-crust) and delicious homemade pasta dishes (like fettuccine rosmarino con pollo) are menu highlights. Service is somewhat relaxed, but it's well worth the wait. Dinner $10–15.

✷ **Alberto's Ristorante** (778-1770), 360 Main Street. Open for lunch and dinner year-round. Catering to a loyal following from the minute it opened in 1984, Felisberto Barreiro's popular northern Italian restaurant is elegant and romantic, all done up in pink and off-white. Alberto's offers an extensive menu: eggplant parmigiana, lobster diavolo, seafood ravioli, or veal Sienese, a mushroom lover's delight. To top it off, Alberto's offers free limo service to diners within a certain radius. Early-dinner specials ($11–16) 4–5:45 PM. Dinner entrées $13–26.

The Paddock (775-7677), West End Rotary. Open for lunch and dinner April to mid-November. If you're in the mood for traditional Continental cuisine or local seafood in a formal setting, The Paddock's Victorian airs provide the perfect backdrop. The main dining room sports dark beams, upholstered armchairs, and frosted glass. The Zartarian family has run this institution since 1970 and John Anderson has been the chef since 1973. They offer standards like Black Angus steak, farm-raised seafood, and 2-pound lobsters. Excellent wine list; children's menu $6.95; casual dress accepted; early-bird specials 30 percent off food portion. Dinner entrées $15.50–25.

✷ **Roadhouse Cafe** (775-2386), 488 South Street. Open for dinner nightly, year-round. This pleasant place—with polished floors, Oriental carpets, hanging plants, exposed beams, artwork, and a fireplace—is also quite dependable, thanks to the long tenure of owner Dave Colombo. The American and Italian seafood menu features a tender calamari marinara as well as a variety of pasta and beef dishes, and large salads (with a very good house dressing). A lighter café menu with creative, thin-crust pizzas is offered in the bistro, which has a clubby feel, thanks to dark paneling and a mahogany bar. The Back Door Bistro (see *Entertainment*) also boasts a large selection of wine by the glass and 40 brands of beer. Save $3 off your entrée by arriving from 5 to 6 PM. Dinner entrées $11–22.

Common West Garden Court shops on Main Street in Hyannis

EATING OUT

☞✐❋ **Up the Creek** (771-7866), 36 Old Colony Road. Open for dinner nightly and Sunday brunch, June through September; lunch and dinner Thursday through Monday year-round. This casual and friendly place serves hearty and large selections like baked stuffed lobster, broiled seafood platter, and seafood-filled pastry strudel. There's also a fair amount of chicken and beef. One of the best aspects: Although it's just a block from the harbor, it's worlds away from the crush of humanity that is Hyannis in summer. Owners Mary and Jim Dow have developed a loyal clientele, whom the Dows repay by offering every dish on the menu for $6.95 on Mondays in the off-season. Children's menu; early-bird specials. Lunch and dinner average $6 and $9, respectively.

✐❋ **Sweetwaters Grille & Bar** (775-3323), 644 Main Street. Open for lunch and dinner, year-round. Sure as coyotes howl and adobe is made of mud and straw, southwestern cuisine has come to Hyannis. After Steve and Colleen Jais opened in 1991, the place was so popular with locals that seating mushroomed from 40 to 140. The extensive menu certainly has its share of sizzling chicken fajitas and burritos, but there are also Thai, Caribbean, and Cuban dishes, as well as creative nightly specials. There are always lots of families here in the early evening; children's menu. Lunch $5–6, dinner entrées $9.50–16.

☞❋ **La Petite France** (771-4445), 349 Main Street. Open daily year-round, except closed Sunday from early September to late May. This informal café serves fresh salads, sandwiches, and soups. Owner Lucien Degionanni hails from the south of France, so many of the homemade offerings are distinctly French—like French onion soup; or a cold tomato, feta, and basil salad; or baguettes and pastries. But in a nod to his current home, he also makes a great clam chowder and roasts his own beef, turkey, and ham for the sandwiches. As might be expected, the café also serves a good cup of coffee. There are a half-dozen tables; otherwise, take a picnic to the park. Dishes $3–5.25.

Baxter's Boat House Club and Fish 'n Chips (775-4490), 177 Pleasant Street. Open for lunch and dinner, mid-April to mid-October. Since 1956, Baxter's has been the kind of place that can satisfy everyone in your party. Built on an old fish-packing dock near the Steamship Authority Terminal, Baxter's serves fried and broiled seafood. Order some and gobble them up harborside on the old ferryboat. There's also a raw bar, a busy lounge, an airy indoor dining room. Dishes $10–17.

Sam Diego's (771-8816), 950 Iyanough Road. Open for lunch and dinner year-round. Decorated with little white lights, colorful serapes, toucans, and sombreros, this fun place is often full of families. They come for reliable southwestern- and Mexican-inspired fare like chicken fajitas ($10), barbecue ribs, burritos, and enchiladas. In warm weather, there is outdoor patio dining. For weekday lunches (year-round), try the all-you-can eat chili, soup, and taco bar for $5.25, $2.95 for kids 8 and under. Children's menu. Dishes $5–13.

The Moorings (771-7177), 230 Ocean Street. Open daily for lunch and dinner, year-round; open for breakfast in summer. Of the many harborfront eateries with outdoor seating, The Moorings currently has the most consistent food and the best views. Lunch standards include sandwiches, burgers, and salads in the $5–10 range. Dinners are fancier and feature Italian dishes with pasta, chicken, and seafood for $9–22. Aiming to please, The Moorings also has a lighter tavern menu with lots of appetizers. Try to get a table on the lower patio or upper deck.

Starbuck's (778-6767), Route 132. Open for lunch and dinner year-round. Part bar, part family restaurant, part roomy barn–cum–bric-a-brac, Starbuck's opened in 1985 with a diverse menu: pastas, Tex-Mex, Thai hot-peppered shrimp, burgers, and chicken sandwiches. Many people come just for the frozen drinks and 20-ounce cocktails, though. Children's menu; live entertainment in the bar. Lunch $4–6, dinner $8–12.

The Prodigal Son (771-1337), 10 Ocean Street. Open from about 9:30 AM to 1 AM year-round. Billing itself as a California-style coffeehouse, The Prodigal Son features a more-than-admirable selection of microbrews, wine by the glass, and strong coffee drinks. As for the limited but selective menu, try a smoked trout sandwich or a plate of vegetarian pâté. The art is as offbeat and colorful as the Victorian couches are soft. There's a full calendar of live entertainment scheduled: acoustic folk, writer's workshops, open-mike nights on Wednesdays. Dishes $4.25–7.

Harry's (778-4188), 700 Main Street. Open for lunch and dinner daily year-round. This small, local hangout features Cajun dishes, seafood (including popular stuffed quahogs), and homemade soups. Lunch leans more heavily toward New Orleans with "hoppin' John" rice (with black-eyed peas), jambalaya rice, and blackened chicken. The joint jumps with live blues and jazz on some summer evenings. Lunch $4–7, dinner $8–16.

☞✐**The Egg & I** (771-1596), 521 Main Street. Open for breakfast 11 PM–1 PM, March through November. With night-owl hours and offerings like chicken-fried steak, it's not your run-of-the-mill breakfast joint. Chef-owner Anthony Bonelli has been dishing up create-your-own omelets, pancakes, and corned beef hash since 1971. Children's menu for $1.99. Dishes $1.95–8.

COFFEE

Spiritus (775-2955), 500 Main Street. Open daily year-round. If you can make your way past the twenty-somethings and Generation Xers hanging around out front, you'll be in for some strong coffee, hot slices of pizza decked with broccoli, eggplant, and sun-dried tomatoes if you want, and focaccia sandwiches.

See also La Petite France and The Prodigal Son under *Eating Out.*

ICE CREAM

You've got two great choices for ice cream (one local, the other regional): **Maggie's Ice Cream** (775-7540), 570 Main Street, is run by the Sweeney family and open May to mid-September; and **Ben & Jerry's** (790-0910), 352 Main Street, is from Vermont (and open year-round).

DINNER TRAIN

Cape Cod Dinner Train (771-3788), at Main and Center Streets. Trains depart Tuesday through Sunday at 6:30 in July and August; off-season schedule varies; there are no trains from mid-December to mid-February. In 1996 the cuisine made it onto the same track that the evocative atmosphere did: the right one. The 3-hour journey was timed perfectly, right down to our taking the last sip of coffee as we pulled into the station. The Victorian-style train cars, with piped-in classical music, are wonderfully nostalgic and elegant. The five-course dinner (choose among prime rib, seafood, and chicken) is served at tables for four, but you can pay a supplement of $30–40 to dine alone with your companion. By reservation only. $41.86 per person ($48.86 Saturdays in July and August). Cocktails and gratuities are additional.

ENTERTAINMENT

Cape Cod Melody Tent (775-9100 for tickets), West Main Street. Open June through September. When this big white tent was erected in 1950, entertainment was limited to Broadway musicals. Today it's the Cape's biggest and best venue for top-name comics and musicians like Joan Rivers, Tony Bennett, Julio Iglesias, and Little Feat. There are children's shows Wednesday mornings in July and August. Profits are poured into arts programs and education on the Cape and Boston's South Shore.

Baseball. The Hyannis Mets play on McKeon Field on Old Colony Boulevard, mid-June to early August.

Band concerts. Head to Bismore Park on Ocean Street most Wednesdays at 7:30 in July and August.

Soccer. The Crusaders, a professional soccer team, play at the Barnstable High School, West Main Street, from early May to mid-August.

Back Door Bistro at the Roadhouse Cafe (775-2386), 488 South Street. Open year-round. Live jazz nightly in summer. The rest of the year there's jazz on Friday, Saturday, and Monday nights, but if it's Wednesday night and Dave McKenna is playing, make an effort to get there.

Cape Cod Brew House (775-4110), 720 Main Street. Open year-round. If you consider a sampler rack of beer "entertainment," this is the place for you. The Cape's only microbrewery does an excellent job with its signature beers: Nantucket Red Ale, Cranberry Ale, Chatham Light, and Lighthouse Lager. Unfortunately, the food doesn't live up to the beverages.

See also Harry's and The Prodigal Son under *Eating Out*.

SELECTIVE SHOPPING

ART GALLERY

Guyer Barn Gallery (790-6370), 250 South Street. The Barnstable Arts and Humanities Council established this art gallery in 1986. Shows are hung from late June to mid-September.

BOOKSTORE

Barnes & Noble (771-1400), Route 132, just north of Route 28. Open year-round. Although there are a few smaller new and used bookstores on Main Street, if you want a particular book, it's probably here.

CLOTHING

Plush & Plunder (775-4467), 605 Main Street. Open year-round. Vintage, eccentric, and wacky used clothing and hats are purchased from the likes of Cyndi Lauper and Joan Baez and sold to the likes of Demi Moore and Bruce Willis (for Demi presumably). But you don't have to be in the entertainment industry to stop here. Hats hang from the rafters like bats do in the Carlsbad Caverns. This is a great place.

Europa, the Importer's Outlet (790-0877), 37 Barnstable Road. Open year-round. Loose-fitting clothes made of natural fibers from around the world, plus jewelry, scarves, shoes, among other items.

Tibetan Mandala International Imports (778-4134), 584 Main Street. Open March through December. Handcrafted objects and clothing from Nepal, Tibet, and India.

FACTORY OUTLETS

Christmas Tree Shops (778-5521), Route 132. Of the seven Christmas Tree Shops on the Cape, this Victorian-style one is the largest.

Dansk Factory Outlet (775-3118), Cape Town Mall on Route 132. Contemporary designs for the kitchen and table.

MALL

Cape Cod Mall (771-0200), Routes 132 and 28. Open daily year-round. The Cape's only "real" mall—as distinguished from the plethora of strip malls—is anchored by big retailers and supplemented by almost 100 other stores, a large food court, and four cinemas.

SPECIAL SHOPS

Hyannis Antique Co-op (778-0512), 500 Main Street. Open year-round. More a flea market than an antiques outlet, the co-op is worth a look-see. You never know what you'll find: jewelry, prints, collectibles.

Play It Again Sports (771-6979), 25 Route 28. Whether it's new or used equipment you're after, this shop has it all.

Golf Market (771-4653), 1070 Route 132. Open year-round. It carries the Cape's largest selection of equipment, sportswear, shoes, and bags.

SPECIAL EVENTS

May: **Great Race Weekend** (775-2201). The largest sailboat race in New England, the annual Figawi Boat Race goes from Hyannis to Nantucket.

Early June: **WCOD Chowder Festival** (775-6800), Cape Cod Melody Tent; $5 adults, $2 children.

Early June: **Harbor Festival/Blessing of the Fleet,** downtown and on the waterfront. Boat parade, fireworks. Free.

Early August: **Pops by the Sea** (790-2787). Boston Pops Esplanade Orchestra on the village green. In the past, guest conductors have included Mike Wallace, Julia Child, Olympia Dukakis, and Walter Cronkite. Tickets $20.

Early December: **Harbor Lighting** (775-2201). Parade of boats including the arrival of Santa and entertainment with a holiday theme.

Early December: **Christmas Shoppers Stroll** (775-2201). Shopping, entertainment, and open houses along Main Street.

December 31: **First Night,** New Year's Eve activities held around town.

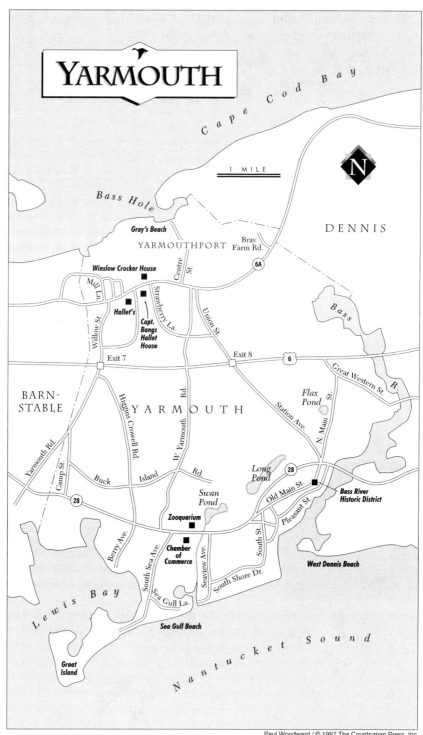

YARMOUTH

Cape Cod Bay

1 MILE

N

Bass Hole

DENNIS

Gray's Beach

YARMOUTHPORT   Bray Farm Rd.

Winslow Crocker House

6A

Centre St.

Bass

Mill Ln.

Hallet's

Strawberry La.

Union St.

Willow St.

Capt. Bangs Hallet House

Exit 7

Exit 8

6

Great Western St.

BARN-STABLE

Higgins Crowell Rd.

YARMOUTH

Flax Pond

N. Main St.

Station Ave.

W. Yarmouth Rd.

Yarmouth Rd.

Rd.

Long Pond

28

Camp St.

Buck   Island

Swan Pond

Old Main St.

Bass River Historic District

28

Berry Ave.

Zooquarium

Pleasant St.

South St.

South Sea Ave.

Chamber of Commerce

Seaview Ave.

South Shore Dr.

West Dennis Beach

Sea Gull La.

Lewis Bay

Sea Gull Beach

Nantucket Sound

Great Island

Yarmouth

Stephen Hopkins, a *Mayflower* passenger, built the first house in Yarmouth in 1638 (off Mill Lane); the town was incorporated just one year later. Yarmouth's active ports bustled in the 19th century: Packets sailed to Boston from Yarmouthport and boats sailed to New York and Newark from South Yarmouth at Bass River. Both villages (the former on Route 6A, the latter on Route 28) have lovely historic districts lined with houses built for and by rope makers, sea captains, bankers, and shipbuilders. At one time, a mile-long section of Yarmouthport was referred to as Captain's Row since it was home to almost 50 sea captains. Today, Yarmouth is the third most populous town on the Cape, with 22,000 year-round residents.

Yarmouth, like neighboring Dennis, stretches from Cape Cod Bay to Nantucket Sound; it unfolds along quiet Route 6A and congested Route 28. It's a family-oriented town, with many golf courses, tennis courts, and town-sponsored sailing lessons, as well as quite a few resorts on the southside beaches—in fact, there are almost 4000 beds to rent in Yarmouth.

Although Yarmouth's 5.3-mile section of Route 28 was planted with more than 350 trees in 1989 (on the occasion of its 350th birthday), the road is still a wall-to-wall sea of mini-golf courses, shops, fast-food places, and family-style attractions like a combination zoo-aquarium, a billiards emporium, and boating on Bass River. A larger-than-life plastic polar bear, lunging shark, and elephant bear witness to the kitschier side of the Cape. They're alternately viewed as icons and eyesores by locals. It's difficult to imagine that Route 28 was once open land dotted with small farms. The scenic Bass River and South Yarmouth historic district provide a delightful detour south of Route 28.

On the north side, Route 6A was settled in the 1600s, traveled by stagecoaches in the 1700s, and reached its height of prosperity in the 1800s. Many former sea captains' houses are now attractive bed & breakfasts. Wind your way along tranquil Route 6A and you'll find crafts and antiques shops, a former apothecary with a working soda fountain, a quiet village green, a couple of fine historic houses open to the public, walking trails, and an antiquarian bookstore. Take any of the lanes off Route 6A to the north, and you're bound to find picturesque residential areas.

GUIDANCE

Yarmouth Area Chamber of Commerce (778-1008, 1-800-732-1008), Route 28, West Yarmouth 02673. Open 9–5 Monday through Saturday and 10–3 Sunday, late May to mid-October; open 9–5 weekdays the rest of the year. The chamber booklet is filled with money-saving coupons to area attractions and restaurants, and the chamber staff are very helpful. Pick up two self-guided historical tours of Yarmouth and Old South Yarmouth here.

PUBLIC REST ROOMS

Public rest rooms are located on Route 6 between exits 6 and 7, and at Gray's Beach (open seasonally).

GETTING THERE

By car: Yarmouth is 26 miles from the Bourne Bridge; take Route 6 to exit 7 for the north side (Yarmouthport and points along Route 6A). For points along Route 28 on the south side, take exit 7 south to Higgins Crowell Road for West Yarmouth, or exit 8 south for South Yarmouth and the Bass River.

By bus: The **Plymouth & Brockton** bus line (775-5524) connects Yarmouth to Boston and points along the Cape. The bus stops at Peterson's Market on Route 6A in Yarmouth and Hallet's (see *To See*) on Route 6A in Yarmouthport.

GETTING AROUND

Yarmouth Easy Shuttle operates late June to early September. Funded by a grant from the state, the shuttle begins at the Plymouth & Brockton Bus Terminal in Hyannis and runs along Route 28 to various points (including the beaches) in Yarmouth. The route is circled seven times daily; flag down the driver, who will pull over to pick you up. The one-way fare is $.50.

MEDICAL EMERGENCY

Yarmouth Medical Center (760-2054), 23F White's Path (off South Yarmouth Road near Route 6), South Yarmouth. Open daily year-round.

TO SEE

Hallet's (362-3362), 139 Route 6A, Yarmouthport. Open March through December. Hallet's has been a fixture in the community since it was built as an apothecary in 1889 by Thacher Taylor Hallet. Mary Hallet Clark (T.T. Hallet's granddaughter) and her son Charles own and operate the store, which boasts an old-fashioned oak counter and a marble-topped soda fountain. As time stands still, sit on a swivel stool or in one of the wrought-iron, heart-shaped chairs beneath the tin ceiling, and relax over a light breakfast, soda, or lunchtime sandwich. The second floor was recently turned into something of a museum, documenting Yarmouth's history as seen through one family's annals and attic treasures. In addition to being a pharmacist (old medicine bottles are on display), T.T. Hallet was a postmaster (during his tenure, only 15 families had mail slots), selectman (the second floor was used as a meeting room from 1889 to the early 1900s), and justice of the peace. The charming displays include old posters that have been in the store over the last 100 years and historical photographs. Donations for museum.

Village pump, Route 6A near Summer Street, Yarmouthport. This wrought-iron pump has served the community since it was installed in 1886; it's located just west of the Old Yarmouth Inn, the oldest inn (and stagecoach stop) on the Cape, dating from 1696. The pump's iron frame, decorated with birds, animals, and a lantern, is supported by a stone trough from which horses drank. (Horse-drawn carriages traveling from Boston to Provincetown stopped here.)

Captain Bangs Hallet House (362-3021), 2 Strawberry Lane (park behind the post office on Route 6A), Yarmouthport. Open 1–3:30 Sunday, June through October, and 1–3:30 Thursday in July and August. The original part of this Greek Revival house was built in 1740 by Thomas Thacher, one of the town's original founders, but it was substantially enlarged by Captain Henry Thacher in 1840. Captain Hallet and his wife, Anna, lived here from 1863 until 1893. The house, maintained by the Historical Society of Old Yarmouth, is decorated in a manner befitting a prosperous sea captain who made his fortune trading with China and India; note the original 1740 kitchen. Don't miss the gracious weeping beech behind the house. Adults $3, children 12 and under $.50.

Winslow Crocker House (362-4385), 250 Route 6A, Yarmouthport. Tours on the hour between noon and 4 PM Tuesday through Thursday and on weekends, June to mid-October. Set back from Route 6A, the Crocker house is a two-story Georgian built in 1780, with 12-over-12 small-paned windows and rich interior paneling. The house was built for a wealthy 18th-century trader and land speculator and moved to its present location in 1936 by Mary Thacher. Thacher, a descendant of Yarmouth's original land grantee, was an avid collector of 17th-, 18th-, and 19th-century furniture, and she used the house as a backdrop for her magnificent collection. The Winslow Crocker House was donated to the Society for the Preservation of New England Antiquities (SPNEA) and is the only SPNEA property on Cape Cod. Sara Porter and Jim McGuinness administer the house and will regale you with stories about the house and furnishings. Adults $4, children 5–12 $2.

Baxter Mill, Route 28, West Yarmouth. Open limited hours Thursday through Sunday, mid-June to early September, and on weekends until mid-October. The original mill was built in 1710 with an exterior waterwheel, but in 1860, when water levels in Mill Pond became so low that the wheel froze, an inside water turbine was built. (This is the Cape's only mill with an inside water turbine.) Free.

Windmill Park, off River Street from Old Main Street, South Yarmouth. On the Bass River, this eight-sided windmill was built in 1791 and moved here in 1866. There are plans to restore the windmill and open it to the public. This scenic spot also has a small swimming beach.

SCENIC DRIVES

South Yarmouth and the Bass River Historic District, on and around Old Main Street (off Route 28), South Yarmouth. The Pawkannawkut Indians (a branch of the Wampanoag tribe) lived, fished, and hunted on a tract of land Yarmouth set aside for them along Long Pond and Bass River in 1713. By the 1770s, a smallpox epidemic wiped out most of the Native population. In 1790 David Kelley (a Quaker) acquired the last remaining Pawkannawkut land from the last surviving Pawkannawkut, Thomas Greenough. Quakers then settled the side streets off Old Main Street near Route 28; the streets are lined with handsome old homes. The simple traffic rotary at River and Pleasant Streets is thought to be the oldest in the country. The Historical Society of Old Yarmouth publishes a walking tour to Old South Yarmouth, which can be purchased at the Yarmouth Area Chamber of Commerce (see *Guidance*).

From Route 6A, turn onto Church Street across from the village green. Follow it around to Thacher Shore Drive and Water Street. When Water Street turns left, head right down a dirt road for a wide-open view of marshland. Continue on Water Street across Keveney Bridge, which crosses Mill Creek; Keveney Lane takes you back to Route 6A. Turn left to head east, back into Yarmouthport. This scenic loop is nice for a quiet walk, a bicycle ride, or early-morning jog.

TO DO

ARCHERY

✎ **Boone & Crockett's Archery Range & Sport Shop** (760-1900), 463 Station Avenue, South Yarmouth. Open year-round. Only one of two such places in the state, Boone & Crockett's has a 20-yard range ($5 per hour, plus $5 for bow rental) and an interactive target system ($12 for a half hour).

BICYCLING/RENTALS

All Right Bike (790-3191), 627 Route 28, West Yarmouth. Open March through December. Near Parker's River, All Right rents 3-speeds, 10-speeds, BMX, mountain bikes, tandems, and mopeds.

BILLIARDS AND BOWLING

Classical Billiards (771-5872), 657B Route 28, West Yarmouth. Open year-round. This family-oriented billiards room has 16 tables, darts, table tennis, air hockey, and table soccer.

✎ **Ryan Family Amusement Center** (394-5644), 1067 Route 28, South Yarmouth. Open daily year-round. When rain strikes, head indoors to bowl away the blues. Ten-pin, candlepin, and duckpin.

See also In-Putt, under *Golf.*

FISHING/SHELLFISHING

Shellfishing permits are required and can be obtained from the licenses department at Town Hall (398-2231), Route 28, South Yarmouth.

Truman's Bait & Tackle (771-3470), 608 Route 28, West Yarmouth. One-stop shopping for rod rentals, repairs, freshwater licenses, and local maps and charts.

Riverview Bait & Tackle (394-1036), 1273 Route 28, South Yarmouth. Among other services, the staff will direct you to local fishing spots, including the Bass River and High Bank Bridges, Seagull Beach at Parker's River, and Smugglers Beach off South Shore Drive. Riverview also has an indoor archery range.

Goose Hummock Shop (778-0877), Route 28 at Iyanough Road, Yarmouth. Open year-round. Fresh- and saltwater fishing paraphernalia, clothing, maps, and camping accessories.

FITNESS CLUBS

Mid-Cape Racquet Club (394-3511), 193 White's Path (off South Yarmouth Road), South Yarmouth. Open year-round. For a day-use fee of $10, you have access to racquetball and squash courts, basketball, Nautilus, free weights, and childcare. Additional fee for the indoor courts.

Bass River Athletic Club (398-0131), 1067 Route 28, South Yarmouth. Open daily year-round. Facilities include racquetball, wallyball, half-court basketball, free weights, cardiovascular equipment, steam, and sauna. Daily membership $10, each consecutive day $8.

FOR FAMILIES

Zooquarium of Cape Cod (775-8883), Route 28, West Yarmouth. Open 9:30–5 daily mid-February to late November and 9:30–8 daily in summer. Part zoo (with a petting area), part aquarium (with performing sea lions), this place is packed on cloudy days, but if you come at the beginning or end of a sunny beach day, you can avoid the crowds. Although the place may conjure up thoughts of the movie *Free Willy,* keep in mind that many of these animals would have died if they hadn't been brought here—for instance, some arrived injured or blind. All the land and sea creatures are native (except the farm animals); small endangered animals educate small children at the **Zoorific Theater.** Children 10 and older $7.50, children 2–9 $4.50.

Jump On Us (775-3304), Route 28, West Yarmouth. Open late May to mid-October. It costs $3.50 to jump for 10 minutes at this trampoline center.

Flax Playground, North Main Street from Route 28, South Yarmouth. Flax hosts lots of activities for children ages 6–12 on weekdays in July and August. The program is run by the Recreation Department (398-2231, ext. 284).

See also Bass River Sports World, under *Mini-Golf.*

GOLF

King's Way (362-8870), off Route 6A, Yarmouthport. Open March through November. A challenging 18-hole, 4100-yard, par-59 course designed by Cornish and Silva and opened in 1988.

Bayberry Hills (394-5597), off West Yarmouth Road, West Yarmouth. Open early April to late November. A town-owned, 18-hole, 7150-yard, par-72 course with driving range.

Bass River Golf Course (398-9079), off Highbank Road, South Yarmouth. Open year-round. Founded in 1900, this town-owned, 18-hole, 6154-yard, par-72 course offers great views of the Bass River.

Blue Rock Golf Course (398-9295), off Highbank Road, South Yarmouth. Open year-round. An 18-hole, 2760-yard, par-54 course.

In-Putt (394-5300), Stop & Shop Plaza, Route 28, South Yarmouth. Open daily except Monday, year-round. The 21st century arrived on the Cape in 1996, in the form of an intriguing, indoor, virtual-reality golf simulator. You take full swings (using real clubs and regulation balls) on recreations of seven famous courses. The indoor entertainment center also offers computer swing analysis, a 10-hole mini-golf course, practice areas, and billiards. Simulated golf costs $25 per hour for an individual, $32 for a foursome.

MINI-GOLF

Pirate's Cove Adventure Golf (394-6200), 728 Route 28, South Yarmouth. Open daily mid-April to late October. At the granddaddy of all mini-golf courses on the Cape, kids have their choice of two 18-hole courses complete with lavish landscaping, extravagant waterfalls, dark caves, and pirate-themed holes. Kids receive eye patches, flags, and tattoos.

Bass River Sports World (398-6070), 928 Route 28 at Long Pond Road, South Yarmouth. Open daily, mid-May to late September. In addition to mini-golf, Bass River lures families with baseball and softball machines, a game room, paint ball, and a driving range.

PARASAILING

Aquaray Water Sports (394-3939), at the Red Jacket Beach Resort, South Shore Drive, South Yarmouth. With the help of a parachute, boats suspend passengers 600 feet above the ocean. Departures daily, June to early September. It costs $48 for the 10–12 minutes you're up in the air, and figure about an hour in the boat.

SPECIAL PROGRAMS

Sailing lessons on Lewis Bay are offered to adults and children by the Recreation Department in July and August. Contact the department (398-2231, ext. 284) for specific schedules for the weeklong courses. This is one of the best public sailing programs on the Cape.

TENNIS

Public courts are located at **Flax Pond,** which has 4 courts (off North Main Street from Route 28 in South Yarmouth); **Sandy Pond,** which has 4 courts (from Route 28 in West Yarmouth, take Higgins Crowell Road to

Bass Hole Boardwalk at Gray's Beach in Yarmouthport

Buck Island Road); and **Dennis-Yarmouth High School,** which has 10 courts (from Route 28, take Station Avenue to Regional Avenue in South Yarmouth). Weekly classes are offered for adults and children at the high school and Sandy Pond courts; contact the Recreation Department for details (398-2231, ext. 284).

See also Mid-Cape Racquet Club under *Fitness Clubs.*

GREEN SPACE

BEACHES

Some lodging places offer discounted daily beach stickers; don't forget to ask. Weekly stickers for cottage renters are available for $30 at Town Hall (398-2231), 1146 Route 28, South Yarmouth.

Seagull Beach, off South Sea Avenue from Route 28, West Yarmouth. This is the longest, widest, and nicest of Yarmouth's southside beaches, which generally tend to be small, narrow, and often plagued by seaweed. The approach to the beach is lovely, with views of the tidal river. (The blue boxes you see, by the way, are fly traps—filled with musk oil, they attract dreaded biting greenhead flies that terrorize beaches in July.) Parking $8; facilities include a bathhouse, rest rooms, and food service.

Bass Hole (or Gray's) Beach, off Centre Street from Route 6A. The small protected beach is good for children, but the real appeal lies in the **Bass Hole Boardwalk,** which extends across a marsh and creek. From the benches at the end of the boardwalk, you can see across to Chapin Memorial Beach in Dennis; it's a great place to be at sunset, although you won't be alone. There is a 2½-mile trail from the parking lot through conservation lands to the salt marsh. As you walk out into the bay, a mile or so at low tide, keep in mind that this former harbor used to be deep enough to accommodate a schooner shipyard in the 18th century. Free parking.

POND

Flax Pond, off North Main Street, South Yarmouth. Although there's no beach (just pine needles covering the ground), there is a lifeguard and swimming here, along with a picnic area.

WALKS

Botanical Trails of the Historical Society of Old Yarmouth, behind the post office and Captain Bangs Hallet House (see *To See*), off Route 6A, Yarmouthport. This 1½-mile trail, dotted with benches and skirting 60 acres of pines, oaks, and a pond, leads past rhododendrons, holly, lady's slippers, and other delights. The trail begins at the gatehouse, which has a lovely herb garden. A spur trail leads to the profoundly simple **Kelley Chapel,** built in 1873 as a seaman's bethel by a father for his daughter, who was mourning the untimely death of her son. The interior contains a few pews, an old woodstove, and a small organ. It may be rented (362-3021) for small weddings and special events.

Bray Farm, Bray Farm Road, off Route 6A near the Dennis town line. The Bray brothers purchased this land in the late 1700s and created a successful shipyard and farm. Now owned by the town of Yarmouth, this working farm has a short walking trail and views of a tidal march. It's a nice place for a picnic.

See also Bass Hole (or Gray's) Beach under *Beaches*.

LODGING

RESORTS

✐✽ **The Cove at Yarmouth** (771-3666, 1-800-228-2968), 183 Route 28, West Yarmouth 02673. Open year-round. This full-service time-share resort boasts lots of amenities: indoor and outdoor pools, a health club with steam room and sauna, a video arcade, a barbecue area, indoor tennis, racquetball, basketball, a concierge, and a whole host of organized activities for kids. As for the accommodations, each of the 229 suites and town houses has a bedroom and separate living room (furnished with a pullout sofa), two bathrooms, a television with VCR, a refrigerator, and a coffeemaker. The most popular rooms for families are the 15 or so units around the indoor pool. Some rooms have decks and double whirlpool baths. The beach is about a mile away; a restaurant with lounge (and live entertainment) is on the premises. Late June to early September $120–145; off-season $75–110; weekly rates also available.

✐ **Red Jacket Beach Resort** (398-6941, 1-800-672-0500), South Shore Drive, South Yarmouth 02664. Open April through October. Occupying 7 acres on the western end of South Shore Drive, wedged between Nantucket

Sound and Parker's River, this large complex is filled with families each summer. Amenities include a large private beach bordered on one side by a jetty, indoor and outdoor pools, a supervised children's program, tennis, parasailing, and a putting green. A pleasant, family-style restaurant serves all three meals. All accommodations (150 rooms and 13 cottages) have their own deck or patio. Room rates vary considerably, according to view: near the hotel entrance, riverside or poolside, ocean view, and oceanfront (from least to most expensive). July to early September $155–235; off-season $80–160; first two children under age 8 are free in a room with parents; inquire about family accommodations.

BED & BREAKFASTS

❊ **Wedgewood Inn** (362-5157), 83 Route 6A, Yarmouthport 02675. Open year-round. An elegant and sophisticated 1812 B&B, the Wedgewood Inn offers six spacious rooms, all with private baths and air-conditioning. The antiques-filled rooms are furnished with pencil-post beds, quilts, and wing chairs. Most have a fireplace and hardwood floors covered with Oriental carpets or hooked rugs. Two rooms have their own screened-in porch. At press time innkeepers Milt and Gerrie Graham were in the process of renovating the barn to include three large rooms with fireplaces, decks, and canopy beds. Gerrie cooks and Milt serves a full breakfast on fine china at individual tables; both hosts are helpful without being fussy or overbearing. This inn is very appealing in the cooler months. June through October $115–160; off-season $90–135.

❊ **Captain Farris House** (760-2818, 1-800-350-9477), 308 Old Main Street, South Yarmouth 02664. Open year-round. Located within a small pocket of historic homes in South Yarmouth off Route 28, the 1845 Captain Farris House offers understated elegance and luxurious modern amenities. Contemporary decorative arts (like an abstract iron sculpture) and antiques (like a country French armoire) are soothingly combined. Other nice touches include fine linens, damask duvets, down comforters, thick white towels, and Jacuzzi tubs. Of the 10 rooms (all with private bath), four are suites and a few have private decks. A creative breakfast is served at individual tables in the courtyard, on the front porch, or at one long formal dining room table. $85–225.

Strawberry Lane (362-8631), One Strawberry Lane, Yarmouthport 02675. Open May through October. This former 1809 sea captain's house, expertly renovated in 1994, is hosted by Judy and Bo Dandison. Their low-key but refined hostelry isn't advertised; guests find the house by word of mouth. Conveniently located off Route 6A and the village green, the B&B offers one guest room, with a rich plum bedstead and light floral wallpapers, and a two-room suite, with elegant moldings and wide-plank floors; both have private baths. Guests share a comfortable common room. $95, including a full breakfast. No credit cards.

❊ **Lane's End Cottage** (362-5298), 268 Route 6A, Yarmouthport 02675. Open year-round. Down a quiet lane off Route 6A, this circa-1710 cottage is surrounded by flowers, woods, and a back patio encircled by potted geraniums. Host Valerie Butler presides over your stay, attending to your needs and whipping up a full breakfast. The three guest rooms, each with a private bath, are simply furnished; one has a fireplace and French doors leading to its own cobblestone patio (complete with private outdoor shower). The living room is "lived-in comfortable," with American, English, and country antiques and a fireplace. $95–105. No credit cards.

✳ **Blueberry Manor** (362-7620), 438 Route 6A, Yarmouthport 02675. Open year-round. Innkeepers Victoria Schuh and Gerald Rosen (a painter and jeweler, respectively) offer three airy guest rooms in their former sea captain's house. Now completely refurbished and sparingly furnished, the rooms are comfortable and refreshing, right down to the fine linens and towels. The airy living/dining room has a television and fireplace for those quiet off-season nights. An extensive continental breakfast is served on fine china to the strains of classical music. May through October $95–115; $20 less off-sesason.

☞✳ **Village Inn** (362-3182), 92 Route 6A, Yarmouthport 02675. Open year-round. This historic colonial landmark has been operated as an inn by Esther Hickey and her family since 1952. In keeping with the old-fashioned idea of providing a place for travelers to relax and interact, there are two comfortable living rooms that fit like an old shoe—they are immediately comfortable and comforting. There's also a wicker-filled, screened-in porch overlooking the backyard. The 10 guest rooms are modestly furnished and modestly priced: $60–75 for a private bath, $40–55 for a shared bath. A full breakfast, served on Cape Cod place mats, is included. They don't make them like this anymore.

☞✐ **August House** (760-0412), 175 Old Main Street, Bass River 02664. Open May through October. Delightfully off the beaten path in a neighborhood of historic homes, the August House is a mile from the beaches along Nantucket Sound. (It's a 5-minute walk to the small Windmill beach.) The late-18th-century house has three modestly furnished guest rooms that are well suited to a family or couples traveling together. Host June Augustine encourages guests to use the house as if it were their own. (That could mean, perhaps, eating takeout in front of the TV in the large living room.) $60–70, including continental breakfast.

✳ **Manor House Bed & Breakfast** (771-3433, 1-800-962-6679), 57 Maine Avenue, West Yarmouth 02673. Open year-round. In a residential neighborhood near a small, protected beach, this Dutch Colonial has six guest rooms (all with private bath, two with an ocean view). A full breakfast, beach towels, and beach chairs are included. Mid-May through October $78–98, $58–88 off-season.

COTTAGES

✐ **Seaside** (398-2533), 135 South Shore Drive, South Yarmouth 02664. Open May to mid-October. These 32 one-, two-, and three-room cottages, built in the 1930s but nicely upgraded and well maintained, are very popular for their oceanfront location. There's a reason they fill up quickly; reserve a year in advance if you can. Sheltered among pine trees, the shingled and weathered units are clustered around a sandy barbecue area and sit above a 500-foot stretch of private beach. (A playground is next door.) Kitchens are fully equipped and linens are provided. Many of the tidy units have a working fireplace. The least expensive units (without views) are decorated 1950s-style. Late June to early September $525–1095 weekly for one room, $900–1150 weekly for two and three rooms; off-season $60–120 daily for one room, $90–150 daily for two and three rooms.

See also Ocean Mist under *Motor Inns*.

MOTOR INNS

Ocean Mist (398-2633, 1-800-248-6478), 97 South Shore Drive, South Yarmouth 02664. Open mid-February through December. This shingled three-story complex fronting a 300-foot section of private beach on Nantucket Sound offers 31 rooms and 32 loft suites. Each of the contemporary rooms has a wet bar or full efficiency kitchen, two double beds, and air-conditioning. Loft suites feature an open, second-floor sitting area—some with ocean views, some with a sofa bed; many of these have skylights and two private balconies. There's a small indoor pool on premises. Late June to early September $135–250; three children up to age 15 stay free in parent's room.

Beach House at Bass River (394-6501, 1-800-345-6065), 73 South Shore Drive, Bass River (South Yarmouth) 02664. Open late March to mid-November. This tasteful bi-level motor inn sits on a 110-foot stretch of private Nantucket Sound beach. Each room is decorated differently (some with antiques). Most rooms have private balconies; all have refrigerators. Cliff Hagberg built the tidy complex in the 1970s and still operates it. July to early September $115–160; off-season $80–98; children under 10 free in parent's room. Buffet breakfast included.

TOWN HOUSES

Clipper Ship Cove (394-6044), 183 South Shore Drive, South Yarmouth 02664. Open March through October. The grounds surrounding this cluster of 10 freestanding, two-story town houses are nicely landscaped with brick walkways, green lawns, rosebushes, and privacy fences. Newly built, the town houses accommodate up to six people in two bedrooms. Each is complete with hardwood floors, a fireplace, 1½ bathrooms, cable TV, outdoor patio furniture, washer and dryer, central air-conditioning, and a modern kitchen. You provide the linens. July to early September $1400–1700 weekly; June and September $875–1295 weekly; off-season $735–875 weekly. No credit cards.

See also The Cove at Yarmouth under *Resorts*.

RENTALS

Crocker & Flinksterom (362-3953), Cranberry Court, 947 Route 6A, Yarmouthport 02675. Nancy and Charlie Flinksterom rent about 30 houses each season (by the week, month, or longer). For best pick, call in January.

Century 21–Sam Ingram Real Estate (362-1191, 1-800-697-3340), 938 Route 6A, Yarmouthport 02675. This agency rents 100 or so private homes that go for as little as $450 and as much as $3800 weekly in-season. One- to seven-bedroom units are available. Call in January or February to get the house of your choice. Rentals are shown throughout winter by appointment.

WHERE TO EAT

DINING OUT

✱ **Abbicci** (362-3501), 43 Route 6A, Yarmouthport. Open for lunch, dinner, and Sunday brunch year-round. If you've had your fill of seafood served in nautical surroundings, try this mod eatery housed in a 1775 cottage. The track lighting, sleek bar, steel chairs, and decor might feel more apropos of New York's SoHo than conservative Route 6A, so it's a fun change of pace. Sophisticated and contemporary Italian cuisine, infused with olive oil and garlic, includes such creations as a seafood stew with lobster, clams, mussels, fish, and shrimp in a saffron broth or roasted duck with sweet and sour sauce and apricots. The early, three-course dinner special costs $11–16 and is a great value. Dinner entrées $15–27.50. Reservations recommended.

✱ **Inaho** (362-5522), 157 Route 6A, Yarmouthport. Open nightly except Monday for dinner year-round. Now happily ensconced on Route 6A, Alda and Yuji Watanabe relocated their sophisticated Japanese restaurant from Hyannis in 1992 because their loyal year-round patrons tended to avoid Hyannis in the summertime. Dining areas are separated by rice-paper screens, while the sushi bar caters to a constant stream of single patrons. The traditional menu features tofu and teriyaki dishes, tempura, and miso soup, but it's hard to bypass sushi and sashimi as fresh as this. Don't miss the beautiful garden in the rear. Dishes $12–21.

EATING OUT

☞✐✱ **Jack's Outback** (362-6690), 161 Route 6A, Yarmouthport. Open for breakfast and dinner daily, year-round. Classic American down-home cooking is served from an exposed, dinerlike kitchen that revels in its no-nonsense attitude. While the tone is far from charming, this place is a local institution. Patrons help themselves to coffee, write their own orders after looking at the menu on the wall, and take their plates back to the pine-paneled dining room. Meals $2–6.

☞✐✱ **Oliver's** (362-6062), Route 6A, Yarmouthport. Open 11:30–10 year-round. This "eating and drinking establishment" opened in 1983 and serves generous portions in a cozy, tavernlike interior. In summer, the wide-ranging menu features reduced portions at reduced prices for reduced appetites. Oliver's attracts an older crowd at lunchtime, longtime Cape residents who like to keep things simple, and families who wish to satisfy everyone. Specialties include broiled seafood, but teriyaki steak and

Yarmouthport antiquarian bookshop

hearty sandwiches are also quite popular. Children's menu. Live entertainment on weekends. Dishes $5–15.

Lobster Boat (775-0486), 681 Route 28, West Yarmouth. Open 4–10:30 daily, early April to late October. Take equal parts oversized lobster boat, pirate ship, and wharf restaurant and you've got yourself a popular Cape tourist eatery. The parking lot is enormous for a reason: This place packs 'em in with enticing specials like a complete twin lobster dinner for $14.95. You've seen the menu before: fried-fish platters, swordfish steaks, broiled scrod, and scallops. The interior is cavernous, with raised rafters and lots of dark wood. Try to arrive early to claim a table overlooking the inlet and to take advantage of early-bird specials. Children's menu for $5.95. Dishes $10–20.

✐❋ **Clancy's** (775-3332), 175 Route 28, West Yarmouth. Open for lunch, dinner, and Sunday brunch. This is the kind of no-surprises place that appeals to a variety of palates and budgets: chicken fingers and peel-and-eat shrimp appetizers; Reubens and smoked turkey sandwiches; eggplant Parmesan and chicken cordon bleu for dinner. The pleasant decor is classic Victorian, with wainscoting. Dave Palmer has presided over the kitchen's generous portions since 1985. Children's menu. Lunch $5–8, dinner entrées $11–17.

See also Hallet's under *To See*.

COFFEE

Java Express (760-2010), Purity Supreme Parking Lot, Route 28, South Yarmouth. Open 7 AM–1:30 PM daily, closed on Sundays October to mid-April. Occupying a former quickie-film-processing booth, the resurrected kiosk now "processes" caffeine, in the form of gourmet coffee. Java Express even publishes a schedule of daily specialty brews.

PICNICS

Lambert's (790-5954), 320 Route 28, West Yarmouth. Open daily year-round. An enormous selection (a veritable "rainbow basket") of bread, deli items, fruit, and drinks to take to the beach.

ENTERTAINMENT

Band concerts (778-1008), Mattachesse Middle School band shell, Higgins Crowell Road, West Yarmouth. Since 1970, concerts have been held on Monday nights at 7:30 in July and August.

Cape Cod Symphony Orchestra (362-1111), Mattachesse Middle School, Higgins Crowell Road, West Yarmouth. Concerts for children and adults are presented from October through May.

☞ **Baseball.** The Yarmouth-Dennis Red Sox play at Merill Wilson Field, Dennis-Yarmouth High School, Station Avenue, South Yarmouth.

SELECTIVE SHOPPING

ANTIQUES

Town Crier Antiques (362-3138), 153 Route 6A, Yarmouthport. Open May to mid-October. A few dealers share this space, where you can find plates, glassware, collectibles, small furniture, and dolls.

Nickerson Antiques (362-6426), 162 Route 6A, Yarmouthport. Open year-round. This space is chockablock with American and English country antiques, porcelain, brass, and glass pieces; prices are quite reasonable. Since it's often difficult to find vintage pieces anymore, this shop also carries a first-class line of handcrafted antique reproductions.

Yarmouthport Antiques (362-3599), 431 Route 6A, Yarmouthport. Open April through October. Three dealers, who collect formal and country furniture, glass, decorative accessories, decoys, pewter, paintings, and folk art, share this barnlike space that's fun to wander around.

ARTISANS

Pewter Crafters of Cape Cod (362-3407), 933 Route 6A, Yarmouthport. Open daily except Sunday, year-round. Barrie Cliff and Ron Kusins have been toiling at this ancient craft, creating traditional and contemporary designs, from their studio/showroom since the late 1970s. Finishes are both satin and bright; forms are functional. This is one of only a half-dozen pewter studios in the country, so now may be the time to get an up-close view of pewter making.

BOOKSTORE

Parnassus Book Service (362-6420), 220 Route 6A, Yarmouthport. Open year-round. Don't tell proprietor Ben Muse you read about Parnassus Books in this guide; he thinks people should discover and explore on their own. The same can be said for visitors to his bookstore, which is lacking in signs and categories—Muse wants people to browse and dig around, perhaps finding a first edition of James or Melville among the stacks! Specializing in maritime, Cape Cod, and ornithology, Muse has been selling new, used, and rare books since 1960. Bookshelves line the wall outside (under a little roof), where the books are available for browsing or purchase on a 24-hour honor system. In its former incarnations, this 1840 building served as a general store and church; it was once home to the Yarmouth Society of the New Jerusalem.

SPECIAL SHOPS

Design Works (362-9698), 159 Route 6A, Yarmouthport. Open daily year-round. Festive and fanciful Mackenzie-Childs pottery, Scandinavian country antiques, home furnishings, and accessories like throws, pillows, and linens.

Peach Tree Designs (362-8317), 173 Route 6A, Yarmouthport. Open daily year-round. Homebodies will delight in this two-floor shop filled to the brim with an assortment of decorative accessories for gracious living.

Nineteenth Century Mercantile (398-1888), at Route 28 and North Main Street, South Yarmouth. Open year-round. Step inside, away from this busy 20th-century intersection, and enter Barbara Amster's re-created mercantile world. You can buy authentic reproductions of almost everything your great-great-grandmother might have used—from lotions, powders, and kerosene lamps to hardware, glassware, cookstoves, Victorian furniture, and toys for the grandkids. Only the building and shelving are vintage. Barbara dons 19th-century garb sewn from a pattern replica she sells.

SPECIAL EVENTS

Mid-May: **Maritime Days,** open houses at historic homes, demonstrations of lightship basket weaving, ship models and other maritime artifacts, and stories and historical anecdotes.

Early July: **Fireworks,** visible from any southside beach.

Mid-July: **Fiesta Shows,** behind the Lobster Boat Restaurant (681 Route 28, West Yarmouth). Carnival rides, "games of chance," and food. Free. **Cape Cod Family Fair** (1-800-732-1008), at the Dennis-Yarmouth High School. A family-style weekend with kid's games, pony rides, music, and arts and crafts.

Mid-October: **Seaside Festival** (394-0889). Begun in 1979, this festival has featured jugglers, clowns, fireworks, field games, a parade, crafts, and bicycle and road races.

Mid-December: **Yarmouthport Christmas Stroll,** includes a tree lighting on the village common, caroling, and special children's activities.

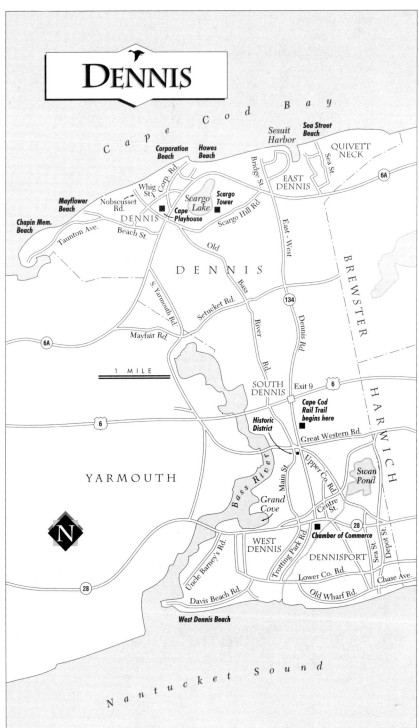

DENNIS

Cape Cod Bay

Sesuit Harbor · Sea Street Beach

Corporation Beach · Howes Beach · QUIVETT NECK

Mayflower Beach

Chapin Mem. Beach

Whig St. · Corp. Rd. · Bridge St. · EAST DENNIS

Nobscusset Rd.

Scargo Lake · Scargo Tower · Scargo Hill Rd.

DENNIS · Cape Playhouse

Taunton Ave. · Beach St.

DENNIS

Old

S. Yarmouth Rd. · Setucket Rd. · Bass · River Rd.

Mayfair Rd.

East - West

134

Dennis Rd.

BREWSTER

6A

6A

1 MILE

SOUTH DENNIS · Exit 9 · 6

Cape Cod Rail Trail begins here

Historic District · Great Western Rd.

6

HARWICH

YARMOUTH

Bass River

Upper Co. Rd. · Swan Pond

Grand Cove

Main St.

Centre St.

28

N

WEST DENNIS

Trotting Park Rd.

Chamber of Commerce · DENNISPORT

Sea St. · Depot St.

Uncle Barney's Rd.

28

Lower Co. Rd. · Chase Ave.

Davis Beach Rd. · Old Wharf Rd.

West Dennis Beach

Nantucket Sound

Dennis

Located at the Cape's geographic center, Dennis is a convenient base for day trips. Some visitors are drawn to Dennis for the fine summer theater, others come for the family-style attractions along Route 28. Indeed, to outsiders (including the 40,000 or so summer visitors), Dennis suffers from a split personality. Luckily, the 13,000 year-round residents have long since reconciled the village's conflicting natures.

On the north side of town, Route 6A continues along its scenic way, governed by a historical commission. Skirting Dennis and East Dennis, Route 6A is lined with a smattering of antiques shops, crafters, and sea captains' gracious homes. Colonial side roads off Route 6A lead to beach communities, Quivett Neck (settled in 1639), and Sesuit Marsh and Sesuit Harbor, where the fishing industry once flourished and fishing charters now depart. Note the streets in this area, named after methods of preserving fish: Cold Storage Road and Salt Works Road. The oldest cranberry bog is also off Route 6A; Dennis resident Henry Hall cultivated the first cranberries in 1807. He discovered that the berries grow much better when covered with a light layer of sand. It wasn't until the 1840s, when sugar became more readily available, that anyone could do much with these tart berries, though.

On the southern side of town, the 6-mile-long Bass River is the largest tidal river on the eastern seaboard. It serves as a natural boundary between Yarmouth and Dennis, offering numerous possibilities for exploration, fishing, and birding. Although it's never been proved, it's widely believed that Viking explorer Leif Eriksson sailed up the Bass River about 1000 years ago, built a camp, and stayed awhile. Follow Cove Road off Route 28 and Main Street for nice views of Bass River and sheltered Grand Cove. (The villages of South Dennis and West Dennis were once connected by a bridge here.) In Dennisport, kids can appreciate the smaller Swan River in a paddleboat, and parents and children will love the Cape Cod Discovery Museum, a delightful alternative to mini-golf and trampolines.

Each side of Dennis has its own nice, long beach: Chapin Memorial Beach on Cape Cod Bay and West Dennis Beach on Nantucket Sound. Head to the top of Scargo Tower for an expansive view.

GUIDANCE

Dennis Chamber of Commerce (398-3568, 1-800-243-9920), at the corner of Routes 134 and 28, West Dennis. Mailing address: PO Box 275, South Dennis 02660. Open 10–2 daily, mid-February to late June; 9:30–4 daily, late June to early September; 10–2 daily, early September to late November; 10–2 weekdays, late November to mid-February. Chamber members are knowledgeable and proud of the long hours they staff their booth. Since this booth doesn't face Route 28, you might miss it if you're not looking for it. There are lots of discount coupons in the town-sponsored information booklet. There is also a small satellite information outlet at the Irish Items shop, 821 "Rear" Route 6A, Dennis, just east of Scargo Cafe.

PUBLIC REST ROOMS

Public rest rooms are located at Sesuit Harbor in East Dennis and at Town Hall on Main Street in South Dennis.

GETTING THERE

By car: Take exit 9 off the Mid-Cape Highway (Route 6) for various points in Dennis. Head north on Route 134 to Route 6A for Dennis and East Dennis. Head south on Route 134 to Route 28 for West Dennis and Dennisport. The tiny historic district of South Dennis is just west of Route 134 as you head south. Depending on traffic, it takes 20–30 minutes to get to various points in Dennis from the canal.

By bus: The **Plymouth & Brockton** bus line (775-5524) connects Dennis with other Cape towns and with Boston's Logan Airport. The bus stops at the Dennis Post Office and at Player's Plaza in East Dennis, both on Route 6A.

GETTING AROUND

As the crow flies, Dennis is only about 7 miles long from Cape Cod Bay to Nantucket Sound; it's 2–5 miles wide. When navigating, keep a couple of things in mind: South Dennis is in the geographic center of Dennis (not the south), and Dennisport (the southeastern portion of town) doesn't have a harbor on the ocean as you might expect. In general, there isn't much to interest travelers between Routes 6A and 28. Year-rounders make their homes here, visit doctors' and lawyers' offices, and buy food and gardening supplies. Concentrate your meandering north off Route 6A and around the tiny historic district on Main Street in South Dennis.

MEDICAL EMERGENCY

Cape Cod Medical Center (394-7113), Cranberry Square, 434 Route 134, South Dennis. Walk-ins weekdays 9–6, Saturday 9–3, and, in summer only, Sunday 8–2.

TO SEE

✐❀ **Cape Museum of Fine Arts** (385-4477), Route 6A, Dennis. Open 10–5 Tuesday through Saturday, 1–5 Sunday, year-round; also 10–5 Monday in summer. On the grounds of the Cape Playhouse (see *Entertainment*), Cape Cod's important artists—both living and dead—are represented by more than 800 works on paper and canvas as well as sculpture. The museum, which opened in 1985, also sponsors trips to artists' studios, classes for adults and children, and lectures. One of the most popular events is a Secret Garden tour in late June, which features local artists painting scenes inspired by Dennis's most lovely gardens; tickets $45 (see *Special Events*). Adults $2, children under 16 free.

Scargo Tower, off Scargo Hill Road from Route 6A, Dennis. The 28-foot stone tower sits 160 feet above sea level atop the tallest hill in the area. On a clear day the panoramic view extends all the way to Provincetown. Even on a hazy day you can see the width of the Cape: from Nantucket Sound to Cape Cod Bay. Scargo Lake, a glacial kettle pond, is directly below the tower.

Josiah Dennis Manse and **Old West Schoolhouse** (385-2232), 77 Nobscusset Road at Whig Street, Dennis. Open 2–4 Tuesday through Thursday, late June through August. This 1736 saltbox was home to the town's founder, the Reverend Mr. Dennis. The house is set up much as it would have been during his time, with a keeping room, a child's room, a maritime wing, and a spinning exhibit in the attic. The 1770 one-room schoolhouse, filled with wooden and wrought-iron desks, was moved to its present location in the mid-1970s. Donations.

South Parish Congregational Church (394-5992), 234 Main Street, South Dennis. Open weekdays 9–noon, Sunday 10–noon. The chapel in this 1835 church features a chandelier made with Sandwich glass and a 1762 Snetzler pipe organ, the oldest in the country still in use. The church is also referred to as the Sea Captain's Church because 106 of its original founding members were sea captains.

Jericho House and Barn Museum (398-6736), Trotting Park Road and Old Main Street, West Dennis. Open 2–4 on Wednesday and Friday in July and August. The 1801 full-Cape contains period furnishings, and the 1810 barn is filled with a fanciful collection of folk art animals (a veritable "driftwood zoo") made in the 1950s by Sherman Woodward. Donations.

SCENIC DRIVES

The **South Dennis Historic District**, on and around Main Street from Route 134, gets very little traffic and wonderful afternoon light. Escape the crowds who bypass this little gem; it's worth a short drive or quiet walk. Note the **South Dennis Library** (circa 1858) on Main Street, a cottage-style building covered with wooden gingerbread trim. Also noteworthy is **Liberty Hall,** which was used for concerts, fairs, lectures, and balls when the second story was added in 1865. Edmond Nickerson, founder of the Old South Dennis Village Association, deserves much of the credit for initiating fund-raising drives and overseeing restoration projects.

TO DO

BICYCLING/RENTALS

Cape Cod Rail Trail is a well-maintained asphalt bikeway that follows the Old Colony Railroad tracks for 26 miles from Dennis to Wellfleet. The trail begins off Route 134 in South Dennis across from Hall Oil. Parking and bike rentals are available at the trailhead from **Barbara's Bike and Sports Equipment** (760-4723), Route 134. Bikes are $8 for 2 hours or $18 per day. The shop also rents in-line skates. The free chamber of commerce booklet available here details seven undeveloped bicycle routes through Dennis.

See also Rick's Rollers under *In-Line Skating.*

BOAT EXCURSIONS/RENTALS

The Schooner *Freya* (385-4399), Northside Marina at Sesuit Harbor, East Dennis. Take a 2-hour Cape Cod Bay sail aboard the 63-foot tall ship captained by Frank and Elaine Meigs. Adults $16, children 2–12 $10; the morning sail is $4 less. Sunset trip: $18 per person.

Water Safari's *Starfish* (362-5555), Bass River Bridge, Route 28, West Dennis. These 90-minute narrated trips of the Bass River, the largest tidal river on the East Coast, operate late May to early September. Along the shoreline you'll see windmills, sea captains' homes, and lots of birds. The flat-bottom aluminum boat (which has an awning) can accommodate almost 50 people. Adults $10, children $5.

Cape Cod Boats (394-9268), Bass River Bridge, Route 28, West Dennis. Open late June to late September. Motorboats, Sunfish, windsurfers, powerboats, and canoes ($30 per day) can be rented for use on the Bass River. The shop rents all-essential roof racks, bait, tackle, and licenses.

Cape Cod Waterway Boat Rentals (398-0080), Route 28 near Route 134, Dennisport. Open May to mid-October. The small and winding Swan River heads about 0.75 mile north to the 200-acre Swan Pond and 2 miles south to Nantucket Sound. Cape Cod Waterway rents electric and manual paddleboats, canoes, and kayaks that can accommodate two adults and one child.

FISHING/SHELLFISHING

Freshwater fishing is good at **Scargo Lake**, stocked with smallmouth bass and trout. Obtain a state fishing license at Town Hall (394-8300), Main Street, South Dennis, or at **Bass River Bait & Tackle** (394-8666), Bass River Bridge, Route 28, West Dennis. Shellfishing permits are required and can also be obtained at Town Hall, South Dennis.

Bass River Bridge, Route 28, West Dennis. Park on one side of the bridge and try your luck; or just stop and watch.

A number of competitively priced, seasonal fishing charters depart from Sesuit Harbor, off Route 6A in East Dennis. Among them: *Prime Rate* (385-4626), *Albatross* (385-3244), and the *Blue Fish* (385-7265).

FITNESS

Lifecourse, at Old Bass River and Access Roads, South Dennis, is a 1½-mile trail through the woods with 20 exercise stations along the way.

FOR FAMILIES

✐✳ **Cape Cod Discovery Museum** (398-1600, 1-800-298-1600 within Massachusetts), 444 Route 28, Dennisport. Open 9:30–7:30 daily in summer; 9:30–4:30 Wednesday through Sunday in the off-season. Special-needs teacher Kate Clemens and her husband, Jim Nowack, opened this wonderful place in 1993. Challenge your child's imagination with hands-on exhibits and activities: science and nature areas, a construction area with building blocks, story and crafts hours, theme workshops, a music room, puzzles and brainteasers. There are also live reptile shows. Educational toys to take home, too. The admission price of $4.50 adults and $4 children is good all day; $50 for an annual family membership.

GOLF

Dennis Highlands (385-8347), Old Bass River Road, Dennis. Open year-round. This 18-hole, 6500-yard, par-71 course opened in 1984 and also has a great practice range.

Dennis Pines (385-8347), Route 134, East Dennis. Open year-round. This is a tight and flat 18-hole, 7000-yard, par-72 course.

The Longest Drive (398-5555), 131 Great Western Road, South Dennis. Open year-round. This driving range with heated enclosures also offers lessons and clinics.

ICE SKATING

Tony Kent Arena (760-2400, 760-2415), 8 Gages Way, South Dennis. Off Route 134, the rink served as Olympic silver medalist Nancy Kerrigan's training ground. It's open for public skating every afternoon.

IN-LINE SKATING

Rick's Rollers (760-6747), Shad Hole Shopping Plaza, Lower County Road, Dennisport. Open daily May to early September and on weekends until mid-October for skate rentals that include full protective gear. Bikes and jet skis are also available; if you don't have a trailer hitch, there's an additional $25 fee for jet ski delivery.

See also Barbara's Bike and Sports Equipment under *Bicycling/Rentals.*

MINI-GOLF

✐ **Holiday Hill** (398-8857), Route 28, Dennisport. Open late April to mid-October. Route 28 is lined with mini-golf courses similar in quality.

TENNIS

Sesuit Tennis Centre (385-2200), 1389 Route 6A, East Dennis. Open year-round depending on the weather. The center offers three outdoor plexi-pave courts, a ball machine, open tournaments, and instruction.

Mashantum Tennis Club (385-7043), Route 6A, Dennis. Open seasonally to the general public.

GREEN SPACE

BEACHES

Cottage renters may purchase a weekly parking pass for $25 at Town Hall (394-8300), Main Street, South Dennis. Day-trippers can pay a daily fee of $8 to park at the following beaches:

West Dennis Beach (off Davis Beach Road) on Nantucket Sound, is the town's finest and longest beach (it's more than a mile long); like many Nantucket Sound beaches, it's also rather narrow. There's parking for more than 1000 cars, and the lot rarely fills. If you drive to the western end, you can usually find a few yards of beach for yourself. The eastern end is for residents only. Facilities include 10 lifeguard stations and a snack bar at the eastern end. It's difficult to imagine that fishing shanties, fish weirs, and dories once lined the shores of West Dennis Beach.

Chapin Memorial Beach, off Chapin Beach Road on Cape Cod Bay, is open to four-wheel-drive vehicles; it's a nice, long, dune-backed beach. As you drive up to Chapin, you'll probably notice an incongruous-looking building plunked down in the marshes and dunes. In fact, it is the headquarters for the Aquaculture Research Corporation (known as the Cultured Clam Corp.), the only state-certified seller of shellfish seed. Begun in 1960, the company is a pioneer in the field of aquaculture. There's no better place to study shellfish.

Corporation Beach, off Corporation Road on Cape Cod Bay, is also backed by low dunes and was once used as a packet-ship landing by a group of town residents who formed the Nobscusset Pier Corporation (hence its name). The crescent-shaped beach has concession stands.

Mayflower Beach, off Beach Street on Cape Cod Bay, has a boardwalk, rest rooms, and a concession stand; **Sea Street Beach,** off Sea Street, and **Howes Street Beach,** off Howes Street and backed by low dunes, both have boardwalks. The Sea Street parking lot fills up by noon. These three beaches are relatively small and good for families with young children because the water is shallow. As at Corporation and Chapin Memorial Beaches, at low tide you can walk a mile out into the bay.

There are about eight public beaches on Nantucket Sound, but all are small.

PONDS/LAKES

Scargo Lake, a deep, freshwater kettle hole left behind by retreating glaciers, has two beaches: Scargo Beach (off Route 6A) and Princess Beach (off Scargo Hill Road). Princess Beach has a picnic area; bathers at Scargo Beach tend to put their beach chairs in the shallow water or on the narrow tree-lined shore. There are two legends concerning the creation of the lake. One maintains that an Indian princess had the lake dug for fish that she received as a present. The other says that a giant named Maushop dug the hole as a remembrance of himself to the local Native Americans.

Tidal flats at Chapin Memorial Beach stretch into Cape Cod Bay for over a mile at low tide.

Swan Pond Overlook, off Centre Street from Searsville Road and Route 134. Beach, picnic area, and bird-watching area.

WALKS

Indian Lands Conservation Area, South Dennis. This easy, 2-mile round-trip walk skirts the banks of the upper Bass River. In winter you'll see blue herons and kingfishers; lady's slippers bloom in May. From the northern end of the Town Hall parking lot on Main Street, follow the powerline right-of-way path for ½ mile to the trailhead.

LODGING

RESORT

☞✐**Lighthouse Inn** (398-2244), off Lower County Road, West Dennis 02670. Open mid-May to mid-October. On Nantucket Sound, this old-fashioned, family-friendly resort has 61 rooms and tidy cottages set on 9 grassy acres of waterfront property. The working Bass River Lighthouse tops the center of the main inn. The inn, expertly operated by the Stone family since 1938, has all sorts of amenities: a full program of supervised children's activities, a special children's dinner, a heated pool, tennis, shuffleboard, mini-golf, volleyball, and the Sand Bar Club and Lounge. On rainy days guests gather in the common rooms of the lodge-style main building, stocked with games, books, and a television. Lunch is served on the deck or poolside; dinner is served in the large oceanside dining room (see *Dining Out*). A full breakfast is included in the rates: mid-June to early September $85–145. Children sharing a room with their parents cost an additional $35–60 per day, depending on their ages. Rates that include dinner are an additional $15 per night per person.

BED & BREAKFASTS

Isaiah Hall Bed and Breakfast Inn (385-9928, 1-800-736-0160), 152 Whig Street, Dennis 02638. Open mid-April to mid-October. On a quiet street behind the Cape Playhouse off Route 6A (see *Entertainment*), this rambling 1857 farmhouse is one of the most comfortable places mid-Cape. Innkeeper Marie Brophy's enthusiasm is infectious and her garden a delight. The main house has five rooms, comfortably furnished with country-style antiques. Six more rooms in the attached carriage house are newer, each decorated with stenciling, white wicker, and knotty-pine paneling. All air-conditioned rooms are cable-ready; just ask Marie for a TV. There is plenty of indoor and outdoor common space, including a cathedral-ceiling great room and a deep lawn that leads to the Cape's oldest cranberry bog. (Isaiah Hall's brother, Henry, cultivated the first cranberries, and cooper Isaiah patented the barrels used to transport the harvest.) An expanded continental breakfast is served at one long table. Mid-June to early September $81–112 with private bath, $61 with shared; off-season rates are slightly less.

☞ **1721 House** (760-1140), 46 Chase Avenue, Dennisport 02639. Open late May to mid-October. This restored Colonial B&B is decorated with both a modern designer's sense and a nod to history. Innkeepers Cindy Wood and Gerry Bojanowski have stripped wood paneling, polished wide floorboards, opened up fireplaces, and used feather beds to create a warm feeling. Of the five guest rooms (all with private bath), two can be made into a two-bedroom suite, perfect for a family or two couples traveling together. Ask for a complete description of the rooms; you can't go wrong in any of them. Breakfast might include fresh fruit and pastries along with a potato and onion frittata, which you can eat on the front patio in warm weather. The house sits on a high knoll across from Inman Beach. $75–95 double; $140 for a two-bedroom suite that sleeps four. No credit cards.

✐ **By The Sea** (398-8685, 1-800-447-9202), Chase Avenue at Inman Road, Dennisport 02639. Open late April through November. This old-fashioned guesthouse on Inman Beach has 12 renovated rooms, each with a newly tiled bathroom, refrigerator, and television. The large rooms are basically but pleasantly furnished with 1950s-style cottage furniture, white bedspreads, and white curtains. Some rooms have two double beds. On rainy days, head to the enclosed porch overlooking the beach or the large living room with stereo, books, television, and games. Guests have use of the heated swimming pool next door. Late June to mid-September $70–120 double, $15 each additional person. Off-season $60–85, $10 each additional person. Inquire about a two-room cottage that sleeps five.

Four Chimneys Inn (385-6317, 1-800-874-5502), 946 Route 6A, Dennis 02638. Open late April to late October. This Queen Anne Victorian house, across from Scargo Lake, offers eight nicely decorated rooms, most of which are large, light, and airy, with high ceilings, tall windows, and hardwood floors. When Kathy and Russell Tomasetti purchased the inn in 1993, they installed new bathrooms and added wicker and antique reproduction furniture. An expanded continental breakfast is included. Mid-June to early September $75–110; off-season $5–10 less.

☞✐**Captain Nickerson Inn** (398-5966, 1-800-282-1619), 333 Main Street, South Dennis 02660. Open March through December. Just off Route 28, in a lovely and tranquil part of town, innkeepers Pat and Dave York offer five comfortable rooms (three with private baths) within this Queen Anne Victorian sea captain's home. One room can accommodate parents and a young child (for no extra charge). The backyard has a play set and sandbox. Bicycles can be rented for a small fee; the Rail Trail is only a half-mile from the inn. A full breakfast of crêpes or pancakes is included. Mid-May to mid-October $60–75 for a shared bath and $80–90 for private bath; off-season $60–65.

✐ **Beach House Inn Bed & Breakfast** (398-4575), 61 Uncle Stephen's Road, West Dennis 02670. Open mid-April to mid-October (weekends only in spring and fall). Off a sandy lane in a residential area (well off Route 28), the Beach House is well suited to families who want to be right on the beach: Parents can watch their kids from the glassed-in breakfast porch or deck overlooking the private beach. Although the living room has a beach-worn appearance, the seven guest rooms with wood floors (each with a private bath, television, and private deck) are nicely decorated. Each room can accommodate two adults and two children, who sleep in sleeping bags on futons. Guests have access to the fully equipped kitchen. An expanded continental breakfast buffet is included; picnic, barbecue, and play areas on the premises. Mid-June to mid-September $85–125 nightly, $550–650 weekly; off-season $75–95.

COTTAGES

✐ **Dennis Seashores** (398-8512, 432-5465 for advance inquiries), 20 Chase Avenue, Dennisport 02639. Open May through October. These 33 housekeeping cottages, rented weekly, are some of the best on Nantucket Sound; make reservations a year in advance. The two-, three-, and four-bedroom shingled cottages, with knotty-pine paneling and fireplaces, are decorated and furnished in a "Cape Cod Colonial" style. Cottages, with fully equipped kitchens, towels, and linens, are either beachfront or nestled among pine trees; each has a grill and picnic table. The resort's private stretch of beach is well tended. Early July to early September $695–1080 per week for a two-bedroom, $695–2225 for a three-bedroom; off-season $215–480 per week for a two-bedroom. Inquire about 3-night rentals in May, September, and October. No credit cards.

Pine Cove Inn Cottages (398-8511, 508-832-4517 off-season), Old Main Street at Route 28, West Dennis 02670. Open May to mid-October. These eight cottages and one studio, while quite modest, are situated on the edge of the Bass River. That's what makes them so appealing— that and the private beach and complimentary use of boats. The Johnsons have owned the Pine Cove since 1980 and recommend reserving a year in advance. Baby-sitters are available. Pets possible with permission. $300–400 weekly in-season.

See also By The Sea under *Bed & Breakfasts.*

EFFICIENCIES

✎ **The Club of Cape Cod** (394-9290, 1-800-228-2968), 177 Lower County Road, Dennisport 02639. Open mid-February to mid-December. These 27 "minisuites" have fully equipped kitchenettes, a basic bedroom, and a living room/dining room with a pull-out couch. It's a block to the beach, but just steps from the enclosed and outdoor pools. $120–135 in-season for four people, $70–110 off-season.

RENTALS

For northside summer rentals, try **Peter McDowell Associates** (385-9114), 585 Route 6A Street in Dennis. They have about 170 houses that rent for an average of $950 weekly in summer.

On the southside, call **Rick Uppvall Associates** (398-0515, 1-800-444-8801), 60 Ocean Drive, Dennisport. Uppvall lists more than 125 one- to five-bedroom houses in his color brochure. Reservations are taken starting on the first Tuesday in January; agents are happy to show properties throughout winter. $300–1500 per week.

See also Century 21–Sam Ingram Real Estate in "Yarmouth."

WHERE TO EAT

DINING OUT

✳ **Red Pheasant Inn** (385-2133), Route 6A, Dennis. Open for dinner year-round. With attentive service to match the fine cuisine and excellent wine list, a meal here will be long remembered as one of the Cape's finest. Low ceilings, wood floors, and exposed beams set a rustic and romantic tone in the dining rooms, located in a 200-year-old renovated barn (a former ship chandlery on Corporation Beach). Local arts grace the white-linen-covered tables: glassware from Sydensticker, pieces from Scargo Pottery, and Bill Block's Victorian lighting. Among the regional American specialties are roast duckling, lamb and game dishes, and lobster May through October. Visit in winter when the fireplace is roaring and chef-owner Bill Atwood tries out new creations. Bill and his wife, Denise, have been here since 1980. Entrées $15–23. Reservations highly recommended.

☞✎✳ **Scargo Cafe** (385-8200), Route 6A, Dennis. Open for lunch and dinner year-round. This bustling, renovated former sea captain's house is awash in wood: paneling, wainscoting, and floors. The friendly staff are adept at getting patrons to the Cape Playhouse shows on time without hurrying them. Light bites and finger foods such as potato skins, escargots, and a grilled lamb sandwich are served in the pleasant bar. Always-dependable specials include wildcat chicken with Italian sausage and mushrooms, a vegetable and Brie sandwich, and a regional favorite, Grape-Nut custard, for dessert. Brothers Peter and David Troutman have presided over the extensive and well-executed menu since 1987. Early specials for those seated by 5:30; children's menu. Lunch $5–12, dinner $10–18.

Ø **Lighthouse Inn** (398-2244), on the road to West Dennis Beach. Open for breakfast, lunch, and dinner, mid-May to mid-October. The extensive dinner menu features reasonably priced seafood as well as pork chops and New York sirloin. On my last visit I had a house specialty: chicken hazelnut, a boneless breast lightly encrusted with nuts and sautéed in a Dijon sauce. Steamed lobster is always a popular choice. All the desserts, and the dinner rolls, are baked on premises. The cuisine, as well as the decor, is at once decidedly old-fashioned and surprisingly '90s. Tables are draped with white linen and the service is professional. The large and open dining room has peaked ceilings, flags hanging from the rafters, knotty-pine paneling, and a full wall of windows overlooking the ocean. Casual lunches, served on the oceanfront deck, include sandwiches, burgers, and light salads. Cocktails are served on the deck after 4 PM. The hot and cold buffets ($9 and $6, respectively) are open to the public. Children's menu. Lunch $5–10; dinner entrées $15–18.

EATING OUT

Gina's By The Sea (385-3213), 134 Taunton Street, Dennis. Open for lunch weekdays in July and August and for dinner Thursday through Sunday April through November (nightly in summer). Since Gina's is small, very popular, and doesn't take reservations, arrive early or wait until after 9 PM. Otherwise, put your name on the waiting list and take a walk on nearby Chapin Memorial Beach. Gina's is a friendly place, with a low-key bar, knotty-pine walls, a fireplace, and exposed beams. The northern Italian menu features items like garlicky shrimp scampi, lightly breaded chicken on a bed of spinach and mushrooms, and cannelloni Florentine. Gina's has been a fixture in the beachside enclave since 1938. Lunch $4–9, dinner $9–22.

☞Ø❋ **Marshside** (385-4010), 25 Bridge Street, East Dennis. Open for all three meals year-round. A local favorite, Marshside is noted for its casual atmosphere (with country-floral tablecloths, for instance), good food (shrimp scampi, lobster, salads, and veggie melts), and reasonable prices (you can get a teriyaki chicken salad for $6.50). This family-oriented restaurant provides coloring books, toys, and contests for children, along with its children's menu. Some tables overlook the namesake marsh, with a view of Sesuit Harbor. Lunch $6-11.

Ø **Swan River Seafood** (394-4466), 5 Lower County Road, Dennisport. Open for lunch and dinner, late May to late September; takeout. This casual restaurant's appeal is fresh, fresh, hook-caught fish, thanks to the attached fish market. Cynthia Ahern, chef-owner since the mid-1970s, keeps it simple with lobster, clams, oysters, and the catch of the day. Although the restaurant does a large volume of business, if you get there early, you can get a table next to the big picture windows, which look onto a river, marsh, and windmill. Skip the dessert and head straight to the cappuccino course. Children's menu. Lunch $5–10, dinner $11–16.

☞✐**Bob Briggs' "Wee Packet"** (398-2181), Depot Street, Dennisport. Open 11:30–8:30 daily, May through September; open for breakfast, late June to early September. This spick-and-span little restaurant, regarded with great affection by hordes of repeat customers, was opened in 1949 by Bob Briggs. Today Bob's son Rob and daughter Sheila carry on the tradition. An exposed kitchen, counter-style seating, and a dining room with shiny yellow tables and bright yellow walls lend the place a homespun feel. As for the food, specialties include Cape Cod bay scallops, onion rings, fried lobster, and Sheila's homemade desserts, including blueberry shortcake. Children's menu. Look for the new doughnut shop/bakery next door. Dishes $2.50–12.

☞✐**Dino's By The Sea** (398-8740), Chase Avenue and Inman Road, Dennisport. Open for breakfast and lunch, late May to late September. A neighborhood favorite by the beach, operated by Helen and Dino Kossifos since 1972, Dino's offers big platters of fried food, a take-out window, and a homey atmosphere. Popular dishes include corned beef hash, chowder, and Dino's plantation special. Breakfast is the main attraction, though, featuring Dino's Special: two eggs, bacon, sausage, homefries, and two pieces of French toast, pancakes, or Belgian waffles—all for $6.25. Children's portions are available. Breakfast $2.65–6.25; lunch $2–9.

Bass River Deli (760-1260), Bass River Marina, 140 Route 28, West Dennis. Open for breakfast and lunch, mid-April through October. The menu has standard deli fare plus specials like eggs rarebit and omelets for breakfast and roast beef with grilled mushrooms, onion, and peppers for lunch. But the real reason to come is to eat on the deck overlooking the marina. Breakfast $1.75–5, lunch $3.50–5.75.

The Mercantile (385-3877), 766 Route 6A, Dennis. Open daily year-round. Located behind the post office, this "gourmet" deli and bakery makes fancy cold salads and sandwiches. Breakfast is limited to bagels, granola, quiche of the day, and pastries. There are a couple of tables inside and on the front porch; otherwise have a picnic. Dishes $3.25–5.

☞✐**Captain Frosty's** (385-8548), 219 Route 6A, Dennis. Open 11 AM–8 or 9 PM early April to mid-September; closed Monday in the off-season. Not your average roadside clam shack, Frosty's takes pride in its hooked (not gillnetted) Chatham cod, Gulf shrimp, small sea scallops, clam fritters, and, for those in your party who've tired of fish, grilled chicken. Seafood and onion rings are deep-fried with 100 percent canola oil. There are always daily specials. Casual dining room, outdoor seating, and takeout. Dishes $2.50–13.

☞✐**McGuirl's Roadstand** (394-5882), 189 Lower County Road, Dennisport. Open for lunch and dinner early May to late October. Jill and Dan's small roadside shed specializes in hot dogs ($1.80); eat on a picnic table in the gravel parking lot (hey, at least you're off Route 28!). Chowder, chili dogs, chicken shish kebabs, and charbroiled sandwiches, too.

BAKERIES

Woolfies Home Bakery (394-3717), 279 Lower County Road, Dennisport. Open May through September. On Dennis's south side, Terri Moretti whips up raspberry nut squares, giant Danish, granola, double chocolate muffins, and honey wheat bread. The small red Cape has a shaded front lawn with a few rocking chairs and benches.

See also Bob Briggs' "Wee Packet" under *Eating Out*.

SNACKS

Ice Cream Smuggler (385-5307), 716 Route 6A, Dennis. Open late March to late October. Homemade ice cream—including a great mocha chip—and frozen yogurt.

Sundae School Ice Cream Parlor (394-9122), 387 Lower County Road, Dennisport. Open mid-April to mid-October. This old-fashioned parlor has a marble soda fountain, round marble tables, old tin signage, and a nickelodeon. Some of the confections are delightfully modern: Frozen yogurt and ice cream with two-thirds less fat are on the menu. The Endres family has been doing something right: They've been in business since 1976. Open until 11 PM in-season, for that late-night fix.

ENTERTAINMENT

☞⊘ **Cape Playhouse** (385-3838; 385-3911 box office), Route 6A, Dennis 02638. Open daily except Sunday, late June to mid-September. The Cape Playhouse was established in 1927 by Californian Raymond Moore, who initially went to Provincetown to start a theater company but found it too remote. Moore's attitude when he purchased this former 1830s Unitarian meetinghouse for $200 was, "If we fix it up they will come." The playhouse proudly claims the title of the country's oldest continuously operating summer theater and the Cape's only Equity theater. Basil Rathbone starred in the company's first production, *The Guardsman*. Over the years, the playhouse has featured the likes of Helen Hayes, Julie Harris, and Jessica Tandy, when they were already "stars," and Henry Fonda, Bette Davis, and Gregory Peck before they were "discovered." On Friday mornings during the 10-week season there is children's musical theater. If you only make it to one summer production, let it be here. Tickets $13–27; children's theater $6.

Cape Cinema (385-2503), Route 6A, Dennis. Screenings daily, mid-April through October. Built in 1930 as a movie theater, Cape Cinema has continued to bring fine art films, foreign films, and independent productions to Cape audiences. The exterior was designed after the Congregational church in Centerville, while the interior ceiling was designed by Rockwell Kent to represent his view of heaven, filled with comets and constellations. Jo Mielziner supervised the painting of the 6400-square-foot art deco mural, which was done by the Arts Students League in a New York theater and shipped by train to the Cape. Kent refused to set foot in Massachusetts because he was protesting the 1921 verdict in the Sacco and Vanzetti trial. There are about 300 seats in this theater, which was chosen to premier *The Wizard of Oz* in 1940. Tickets $6 adults, $4 children.

Band concerts, whether the music be country or American classics, are held on both town greens (in Dennis on Route 6A and in Dennisport off Route 28) on Monday or Wednesday evenings in July and August.

SELECTIVE SHOPPING

ANTIQUES

Webfoot Farm Antiques (385-2334), 1475 Route 6A, East Dennis. Open daily in summer, daily except Wednesday the rest of the year. Each of the four tasteful rooms in this 1845 captain's house is crammed with impressive Continental, American, and English decorative arts and fine antiques. (The house shows off pieces quite nicely indeed.) The collection of sterling is strong, as are the Oriental porcelains and pottery.

Gloria Swanson Antiques (385-4166), 632 Route 6A, Dennis. Open year-round. This shop is crammed with Flow Blue, Mulberry, and Staffordshire china, early glass and bottles, teapots, and tins. It's a treasure.

Old Towne Antiques (385-5202), 593 Route 6A, Dennis. Open year-round. This multidealer shop offers an eclectic selection: popular collectibles, old postcards, fishing gear, woodworking tools, and other items.

Antiques Center of Cape Cod (385-6400), 243 Route 6A, Dennis. Open daily year-round. With about 135 dealers, this two-story former building-supply store is the Cape's largest cooperative, offering items large and small. Don't miss it. Most objects sell for under $200 and are classified as "old," "vintage," or "collectible" rather than "antique."

Oxyoke Antique Shop (398-3067), Upper County Road, South Dennis. Because George Marceline has been selling antiques and used furniture since 1948, he doesn't need to advertise. Bed frames are propped up in the yard, and heaps of old hinges and hardware lie on an ironing board in the garage where George repairs and refinishes items.

Ellipse (385-8626), 427 Route 6A, Dennis. Open year-round. This shop features an enviable selection of the brilliant and highly sought after 1950s Fiestaware dinnerware, as well as 18 other lines of tableware.

Antiques 608 (385-2755), 608 Route 6A, Dennis. Open year-round. This multidealer shop deals more in what owner Marcia Cardaropoli calls "junque," but if you hunt through the stuff you'll find antiquarian books, daguerreotypes, and ephemera.

ART GALLERY

Grose Gallery (385-3434), 524 Route 6A, Dennis. Open year-round. This barn-gallery features the work of illustrator and printmaker David Grose. David created the wood engravings and pen drawings for three of John Hay's books: *The Great Beach, Nature's Year,* and *The Run.* He also has produced a series of serigraphs of Dennis landmarks.

ARTISANS

Scargo Pottery (385-3894), 30 Dr. Lord Road South, off Route 6A, Dennis. Open year-round. Down a path in the middle of the woods, potter Harry Holl, his four daughters, and one son-in-law make whimsical and eccentric birdhouses, fountains, and architectural sculptures, among other things. Harry, in fact, has been working here since 1952. It's a completely untraditional, magical world that you won't want to miss: Pieces hang from tree branches and sit on tree stumps. The work isn't cheap, but it isn't run-of-the-mill, either. There's no question that this is pottery as art.

Michael Baska (385-5733), 766 Route 6A, Dennis, and **Ross Coppelman** (385-7900), 1439 Route 6A, East Dennis, have both fashioned stunning designs as goldsmiths for more than 20 years. Both men work on the premises year-round.

AUCTIONS

Eldred's Auctions (385-3116), 1483 Route 6A, East Dennis. Open year-round. This high-end auction house, the largest on the Cape with over $5 million in sales, moves magnificent collections. In July the weekly auctions center on books, collectibles, marine items, and painting. In August, there is an Americana auction the first weekend of the month, a fine and decorative auction the second weekend. A weeklong Oriental auction takes place late in the month. In the off-season there are generally auctions once a month; call for a schedule.

BOOKSTORES

Royal Discount Bookstores (398-5659), Patriot Square, 500 Route 134, South Dennis.

Paperback Cottage (760-2101), 927 Route 28 at Route 134, next to the chamber of commerce booth, South Dennis. Open daily in summer, Thursday through Monday in spring and fall, and Saturday through Monday in winter. In addition to selling books the old-fashioned way, the Sullivan family rents books by the week.

FACTORY OUTLETS

Basketville (394-9677), Route 28, West Dennis. Open year-round. Watch basket-makers at work while you browse among wicker furniture and baskets for picnics, plants, and just about anything else you can think of.

SPECIAL SHOPS

B. Mango & bird (385-6700), 780 Route 6A, Dennis. Open May through December. Behind the post office, this eclectic shop has an ever-changing assortment of decorative items for the home. Since it opened in 1992, it seems like there hasn't been a day when UPS didn't drop off something new. Goods are reasonably priced, too.

Pizazz (760-3888), 633 Route 28, Dennisport. Giant blow-up beach toys.

The Side Door (394-7715), 103 Route 28, and **Dennisport Dollhouse** (398-9356), 497 Upper County Road, both in Dennisport, offer an amazing variety of supplies, kits, ready-made houses, furniture, and other collectibles to warm a child's or a collector's heart.

Tobey Farm, Route 6A, Dennis. This colorful farm has been in the same family since 1678 when it was given to Thomas Tobey for his service during King Phillip's War.

SPECIAL EVENTS

Late June: **Secret Garden tour,** sponsored by the Cape Museum of Fine Arts. Tour gardens around town and watch artists paint from their inspiration. Tickets $45.

Mid- to late August: **Dennis Festival Days.** Billed as the oldest festival on the Cape (since 1958), this five-day celebration includes a crafts fair, an antique auto parade, kite-flying and sand-castle-building contests, puppet shows, fireworks, and band concerts.

III. THE LOWER CAPE

Brewster
Harwich
Chatham
Orleans

Brewster's Stony Brook Grist Mill

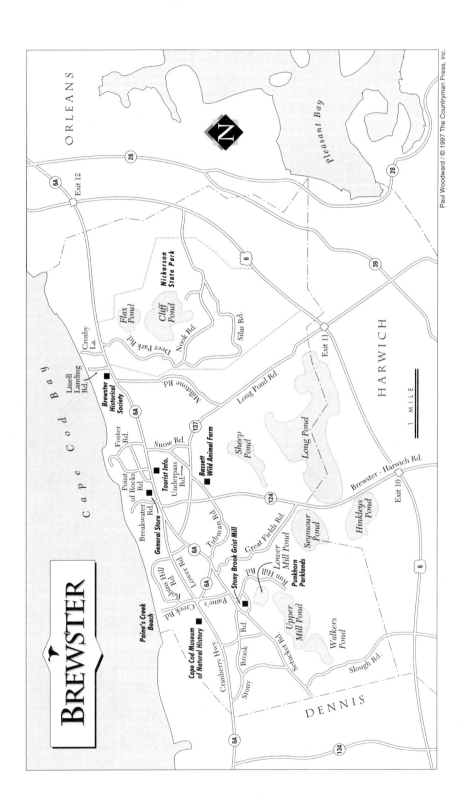

BREWSTER

Paul Woodward / © 1997 The Countryman Press, Inc.

Brewster

Brewster, settled in 1659 and named for *Mayflower* passenger Elder William Brewster, wasn't incorporated until 1803, when it split from Harwich. By then, the prosperous sea captains who had built their homes on the bay side wanted to distance themselves from their less well off neighbors to the south. Between 1780 and 1870, 99 sea captains called Brewster home (although they sailed their clipper ships out of Boston and New York), a fact that even Henry David Thoreau commented on during his 1849 trip. Many of these beautiful houses on Route 6A have been converted to bed & breakfasts and inns.

In the early 1800s, Breakwater Beach was a popular landing for packet ships, which transported salt and vegetables to Boston and New York markets and brought tourists to the area. Salt making was big business in 1837, when more than 60 saltworks dotted Brewster beaches. Windmills pumped seawater into 36-by-18-foot vats, where it was left to evaporate (this process was developed in Dennis). During the late 18th and early 19th centuries, Brewster's Factory Village sold cloth, boots, and food to people all over the Cape.

You could spend a charmed week in Brewster and still find plenty to occupy you. While the 2000-acre Nickerson State Park boasts facilities for a dozen outdoor activities, there is also Punkhorn Parkland, an undeveloped 800-acre parcel of conservation land in town. Although Brewster has only 8700 year-round residents, it has more than its share of attractions, including two good golf courses, tennis courts, horseback riding trails, an outstanding museum of natural history, a few smaller museums, and exceptional dining choices.

Brewster's section of Route 6A is a vital link in the 80-square-mile Old King's Highway Historic District. Known for its selection of fine antiques shops, Brewster also attracts contemporary artists who are drawn to a landscape more evocative of the countryside than the seaside—the land south of Route 6A is dotted by ponds, hills, and dales.

GUIDANCE

Town Hall (no phone), 2198 Route 6A, about a half-mile east of Route 124. Open 9–3 daily in summer. In the rear of Town Hall, this informal visitors center dispenses information. To receive printed materials prior to your arrival, write or call the **Brewster Board of Trade** (868-8088),

PO Box 1241, Brewster 02631, for its booklet or the **Brewster Chamber of Commerce** (255-7045), PO Box 910, Brewster 02631, for its excellent map. Neither the Board of Trade nor the chamber of commerce maintains its own drop-in center. The Board of Trade deals with social and civic issues, while the chamber deals with business.

PUBLIC REST ROOMS

Public rest rooms are located at Nickerson State Park, at Town Hall, and in the police station next to Old Town Hall.

GETTING THERE

By car: Brewster is 30 minutes from the Cape Cod Canal (take Route 6 east to exit 9, to Route 134, to Route 6A); it is 45 minutes from Provincetown at the tip of the peninsula.

By bus: The **Plymouth & Brockton** bus line (775-5524) connects Brewster to various points on Cape Cod and to downtown Boston. Buses stop at Cumberland Farms and The Brewster Store (see *To See*); both are on Route 6A.

GETTING AROUND

Brewster is very easy to get around: Most points of interest are located on or just off Route 6A.

MEDICAL EMERGENCY

Call **911.**

TO SEE

☞✐❋ **Cape Cod Museum of Natural History** (896-3867 for a listing of daily events, or 1-800-479-3867), 869 Route 6A. Open 9:30–4:30 Monday through Saturday, 12:30–4:30 Sunday, year-round. Founded by naturalist John Hay in 1954, this is one of the best resources for learning about the Cape's natural world. The museum takes its mission seriously: to "inspire and foster an understanding and appreciation of our environment through education, and a means to sustain it." There are fish tanks, whale displays, a working beehive, hands-on activities, and a natural-history library. A series of photographs documents how Chatham's barrier beach changed during one storm. Parents will appreciate the gift shop packed with fun and educational toys, books, and games. The John Wing Trail—just one trail traversing the museum's 80 acres of marshes, beaches, and hills—begins from here (see *Green Space—Walks*). Adults $4, children 6–14 $2; fee for some programs. (See *Special Programs.*)

☞ **Stony Brook Grist Mill and Museum and Herring Run,** 830 Stony Brook Road. Open 2–5 Thursday through Saturday in May and June, and 2–5 Friday in July and August. This millside pond is one of the most picturesque places on Cape Cod, especially during the spring migration, when the herring are "running," and the natural fish "ladders" are packed with the silver-backed fish. In 1663 America's first water-powered mill stood on this location. The present gristmill, constructed on the foundation of an 1873

Locals and visitors enjoy coffee and the morning paper at the 1866 Brewster Store.

woolen mill (part of the 19th-century Factory Village), contains old milling equipment and a 100-year-old loom on which age-old techniques are sometimes demonstrated. Donations.

The Brewster Store (896-3744), 1935 Route 6A at Route 124. Open daily year-round. Purveying "groceries and general merchandise" since 1866, this two-story quintessentially Cape Cod store was built in 1852 as a Universalist church. Beneath red, white, and blue bunting and small-paned windows covered by gingham curtains, locals and visitors sit on old church pews, sip coffee, read the morning newspaper, eat penny candy, and watch the world go by. There are customers whose families have relied on the store for four generations. Upstairs has been re-created with memorabilia from the mid-1800s to the mid-1900s; downstairs has a working antique nickelodeon and oft-used peanut roaster.

Higgins Farm Windmill and **Harris-Black House** (896-9521), 785 Route 6A. Open 1–4 Tuesday through Friday in July and August, and 1–4 on weekends in June and September. These two structures are operated by the Brewster Historical Society. Members are on hand to tell you that a family of 10 children was raised in the one-room house, and that the 1795 windmill is known for its octagonal design and its top that resembles a boat's hull. Donations.

New England Fire & History Museum (896-5711), 1429 Route 6A. Open 10–4 weekdays and noon–4 weekends, May to early September; open 10–3 weekends, early September to mid-October. Surrounding a 19th-century New England–style town common, the five buildings include an apothecary's shop, blacksmith shop, antique fire-fighting equipment, a diorama of the Chicago Fire of 1871, more than 30 working fire engines, and the late Boston Pops conductor Arthur Fiedler's collection of fire-fighting memorabilia. Picnic area. Adults $4.75, children 5–12 $2.50.

✍✳ **Brewster Ladies' Library** (896-3913), 1822 Route 6A. Open noon–8 Tuesday and Wednesday, 10–4 Thursday and Friday, 10–2 Saturday. In 1852 two teenage Brewster girls established this "library," which began as a shelf of books lent from one of the girls' houses. After local sea captains donated funds in 1868, the ever-expanding library moved to this yellow Victorian building. The two original front parlor rooms—each with a fireplace, stained-glass windows, and armchairs—are filled with portraits of sea captains and ships. In addition to a wonderful children's area, the library screens family movies and sponsors a story hour for preschoolers. The library doubled its size in 1996 and the modern additions have computers, videos, and best-sellers.

✍ **First Parish Church** (896-5577), 1969 Route 6A. The 1834 clapboard exterior is marked by Gothic windows and a bell tower, while pews on the interior have been marked with names of prominent Brewster sea captains. Take a few minutes to wander around the graveyard behind the church. In July and August, the Unitarian Universalist church hosts popular puppet shows for children on Thursday mornings at 10. Tickets go on sale at 8:30 and sell out quickly.

Brewster Historical Society Museum (896-9521), 3341 Route 6A. Open 1–4 on weekends in May, June, September, and October; 1–4 Tuesday through Friday in July and August. Highlighting Brewster's rich heritage, the small museum has an 1884 barbershop, an 1830s sea captain's room, dolls and toys, the old East Brewster Post Office, and antique gowns. Free. A walking trail originates from the house (see Spruce Hill Conservation Area under *Green Space—Walks*).

Crosby Mansion, Crosby Lane off Route 6A. According to the state—which owns it but cannot afford to maintain it—this 28-room mansion needs about $1.5 million in repairs. The once elegant home of Albert and Matilda Crosby, a yellow and white Colonial Revival structure, sits on 19 acres of bayside property. In fact, the state took the land (and the house by default) by eminent domain in 1986 so that the public could have access to Cape Cod Bay from Nickerson State Park (which is across from the property; see *Green Space*). A volunteer group, the Friends of Crosby Mansion, had done its best to repair the worst damage. Albert Crosby owned the Chicago Opera House and fell in love with Matilda, one of the showgirls. When she came to live in Brewster at Albert's modest house, she was so unhappy that Albert had a mansion built for her—attached to his four-room house. Matilda is said to have entertained in the mansion while Albert stayed in his boyhood home. Although the house is closed, you can peek into the oversized windows.

✍ **Tidal flats.** At low tide, you can walk about 2 miles out onto the tidal flats of Cape Cod Bay. During Prohibition, townspeople walking on the flats would often stumble onto cases of liquor that had been thrown overboard by rumrunners. Encounters are tamer these days: Kids love discovering sea life in the tidal pools, playing in the channels left by the receding water, and marveling at streaked "garnet" sand. On a clear day you can see from the Provincetown Monument to Sandwich. You can reach the flats from any of the beaches.

TO DO

BICYCLING/RENTALS

Because the **Cape Cod Rail Trail** runs through Brewster, and **Nickerson State Park** (see *Green Space*) has its own network of bicycle trails that are linked to the Cape Cod Rail Trail, there are many places to rent bicycles in town. Look for **Idle Times Bike Shop** (896-9242), Route 6A, on the edge of Nickerson State Park; **Rail Trail Bike Rentals** (896-8200), 302 Underpass Road, next to Pizza & More (see *Eating Out*); and **Brewster Bike Rental** (896-8149), 442 Underpass Road. All are open seasonally and offer plenty of parking. Rates are generally $5–8 for 2 hours, $8–12 for 4 hours, $14–18 for 24 hours.

Parking for the Rail Trail is available at the intersection of Route 137 and Underpass Road, at Nickerson State Park on Route 6A.

BOATING/RENTALS

Jack's Boat Rentals (896-8556), within Nickerson State Park, Route 6A. Open seasonally. Jack's rents canoes, kayaks, seacycles, Sunfish, pedal boats, and sailboards on Flax Pond.

FISHING/SHELLFISHING

Brewster has almost 50 freshwater ponds; required state fishing licenses may be obtained from Town Hall (896-3701, ext. 41), 2198 Route 6A. The following ponds are stocked: **Sheep Pond** and **Seymour Pond,** both off Route 124, and Cliff Pond (in Nickerson State Park).

Shellfishing permits are also obtained from Town Hall. Quahogs and sea clams are harvested June to mid-September; steamers are harvested October to mid-April. No shellfish can be taken on Friday or Saturday during July and August. Permits cost $15 weekly for nonresidents.

FOR FAMILIES

Bassett Wild Animal Farm (896-3224), 620 Tubman Road, off Route 124. Open 10–5 daily, mid-May to mid-September. This 20-acre, generally wooded area opened in the 1960s and is home to a variety of animals. In addition to a petting zoo and free-ranging goats and peacocks, there are domestic and exotic birds, porcupines, llamas, and even a lion and a cougar. Picnic areas, pony rides, and hayrides. Adults and children over 12 $5.75; children 2–11 $3.75.

Puppet shows. See the First Parish Church under *To See.*

GOLF

Captain's Golf Course (896-5100), 1000 Freeman's Way off Route 6A.

Open year-round; 18 holes. A 1990 survey by *Golf Digest* rated this one of the top 25 public courses in the country. Holes are named after Brewster sea captains.

Ocean Edge Golf Club (896-5911), Villages Drive off Route 6A. Open year-round, this 18-hole, tournament-caliber course has Scottish-style bunkers and one hole that crosses a cranberry bog. **Ocean Edge Resort** offers a golf school (1-800-343-6074), also, from mid-April to early August.

HORSEBACK RIDING

Moby Dick Farm (896-3544), Great Fields Road, between Stony Brook Road and Route 124. Open year-round for instruction with Allen Rodday and trail riding.

See also Woodsong Farm Equestrian Center under *Special Programs.*

IN-LINE SKATING

See Rail Trail Bike Rentals, under *Bicycling/Rentals.*

SAILING

Cape Sail (896-2730), out of Brewster and Harwich Harbors; call to arrange trips from late May to mid-October. Since 1983, Captain Bob Rice has offered customized sailing lessons and an overnight sailing school. The price for two people for instruction and an overnight to Nantucket (accommodations on board) is $450. Otherwise, the 6-hour basic course takes place over 3 days and costs $240 for one, $390 for two. Bob also does custom charters, and sunset and moonlight cruises. He doesn't have any set schedule, so call him to discuss your interests.

SPECIAL PROGRAMS

Cape Cod Museum of Natural History (896-3867, 1-800-479-3867), 869 Route 6A. A variety of day camps, lasting 2 hours, 2 days, or 2 weeks, is offered for children ages 3–15. Classes explore "incredible insects," "marine mania," tidal flats, an archaeology dig, and Monomoy's barrier beach. The emphasis is on fun, outdoor adventure, and education. Adults are catered to with canoe trips, excursions to Monomoy and Nauset Marsh, and the Cape Cod nature train. Classes meet for varying times and fees; call for a schedule of programs.

Woodsong Farm Equestrian Center (896-5555), 121 Lund Farm Way. Open daily, by appointment, year-round. Established in 1967, Woodsong offers riding instruction, boarding, training, coaching for the competitive rider, children's day programs, horse shows, two phase events, and an on-premises tack shop. Instruction: $30 per lesson; summertime horsemanship day programs: $235 weekly; beginners program for children 5–11: $235 weekly, $166 for 3 days, $114 for 2 days.

Baseball clinics. The Brewster Whitecaps sponsor weeklong clinics (896-9430) in July and August for boys and girls 7–14. Meet at the Community Center field in front of Town Hall on Route 6A.

Cooking School and **Innkeeping Seminars.** See The Captain Freeman Inn under *Bed & Breakfasts.*

STRAWBERRY PICKING

Namskaket Farm (896-7290), off Route 6A. Open approximately early June to early July. This 4-acre farm opens at 8 AM and closes after the last ripe berry has been picked for the day. That could be in an hour or it could extend well into the afternoon.

TENNIS

Four public courts are located behind the **Fire and Police Department** near Town Hall, off Route 6A.

Ocean Edge Resort (896-9000, 1-800-343-6074) offers a tennis school from mid- to late July.

GREEN SPACE

☞❋ **Nickerson State Park** (896-3491), 3488 Route 6A. Open daily, dawn to dusk, year-round. This former estate of Chatham native Roland Nickerson, a multimillionaire who founded the First National Bank of Chicago, covers more than 2000 acres of pine, hemlock, and spruce and includes eight kettle ponds. Nickerson and his wife, Addie, who entertained such notables as President Grover Cleveland, had a fairly self-sufficient estate, with their own electric generator, ponds teeming with fish, vegetable gardens, and game that roamed the land. The mansion that Roland's father, Samuel, built for him burned down in 1906, and a disconsolate Roland died 2 weeks later. (The "replacement" is now the Ocean Edge Conference Center.) Addie ultimately donated the land in 1934 to honor their son, who died from the 1918 influenza epidemic.

Nickerson State Park has been developed with walking trails, bicycling trails, jogging paths, picnic sites, boat launches, and sandy beaches (further details for various activities can be found under *To Do* and *Lodging—Campground*). Winter conditions usually provide for ice skating and cross-country skiing. If you're at all interested in the out-of-doors, don't bypass Nickerson, one of the Cape's treasures. Almost 300,000 people visit each year. Free admission.

BEACHES

Brewster has 8 miles of waterfront on Cape Cod Bay and eight public beaches, none of which is particularly spacious and all of which are located off Route 6A. Daily ($8), weekly ($25), and seasonal parking permits are purchased at the Town Office Building Annex (896-3701), 2198 Route 6A, 9–3 daily in-season.

Paine's Creek Beach, Paine's Creek Road off Route 6A. This is one of Brewster's most picturesque beaches because of the creek that feeds into it. Parking fee.

PONDS

Long Pond and **Sheep Pond,** both off Route 124, have freshwater swimming and sandy beaches. Long Pond has a lifeguard. Long and Sheep Ponds are among the best of Brewster's more than 50 ponds.

Flax Pond and **Cliff Pond,** within Nickerson State Park, Route 6A. Flax Pond has the best public beach in the park; it has picnic tables and a bathhouse, but no lifeguard. Cliff Pond is ringed with little beaches, but bathers share the pond with motorized boats. (You'll find it's really not a problem.)

WALKS

John Wing Trail, South Trail, and **North Trail,** at the Cape Cod Museum of Natural History, 869 Route 6A. Named for Brewster's first settler, a Quaker forced to leave Sandwich due to religious persecution, the John Wing Trail (about 1⅓ miles round-trip) meanders past a sassafras grove and salt marshes, which provide habitat for diverse plants and animals. It traverses a tidal island and ends on the dunes with a panoramic view of Cape Cod Bay. South Trail is on the opposite side of Route 6A and extends about a mile past Stony Brook, a beech grove, and the remnants of a cranberry bog. Follow the short North Trail around the museum's immediate grounds, crossing a salt marsh. Naturalist-led walks depart from the museum daily in summer and on weekends in the off-season.

Punkhorn Parklands, Run Hill Road, off Stony Brook Road. Forty-five miles of scenic trails on more than 800 acres—some overlooking kettle ponds—traverse oak and pine forests, meadows, and marshes. Trails are used by birders and mountain bikers, even coyotes and fox.

Spruce Hill Conservation Area, behind the Brewster Historical Society Museum, 3341 Route 6A. This 30-minute, round-trip trail follows a wide old carriage road—probably used for off-loading fish and lumber and rumored to have been used by bootleggers during Prohibition—that runs from the Brewster Historical Society Museum (an 1840s private homestead; see *To See*) to Cape Cod Bay and a 600-foot stretch of private sandy beach. The Conservation Commission manages the 25-acre area.

See also Nickerson State Park under *Beaches.*

LODGING

The zip code for Brewster is 02631.

RESORT

❊ **Ocean Edge Resort** (Resort and Conference Center: 896-9000, 1-800-343-6074; Atlantic Rentals: 896-4600, 1-800-896-4606), 2660 Route 6A. Open year-round. Once part of the vast Roland Nickerson estate, this 380-acre complex includes a Gothic and Renaissance Revival stucco mansion (now used as a conference center) and 17 contemporary condominium "villages." Units vary considerably, but you can choose among the following configurations: apartments, two-story town houses (with one, two, and three bedrooms), Cape cottages, and hotel rooms and suites. Some units are bayside; others overlook the golf course. Atlantic rents individually owned units that do not include linens and towels; maid service and midweek cleaning are available for an additional charge. If you rent through the resort, prices are a bit higher because you're paying for daily maid service and more uniform decor and standards. No matter who you rent through, guests enjoy complimentary use of the indoor and outdoor pools. Unless you opt for a golf or tennis package, you must pay for tennis and golf privileges. On-premises facilities include exceptional golf, a private 1000-foot bayside beach (if you rent through the resort), bicycle rentals, four restaurants, a fitness center, a playground, and organized programs for kids 4–14. The following rates quoted are for bayside condos listed with Atlantic Realty/Coldwell Banker. Summer: $995 weekly (Saturday to Saturday) for one bedroom; $1145–2195 weekly for two bedrooms; $1995–3345 weekly for three bedrooms. Off-season rates are about 30 percent lower; winter rates include meals.

INNS

High Brewster (896-3636, 1-800-203-2634), 964 Satucket Road. Open April through December. On a 3½-acre countryside setting overlooking a pond, High Brewster offers three lovely cottages and two antiques-appointed inn rooms. (An additional single can be rented when there are three people traveling together.) The 1738 homestead, in one family for more than 200 years, retains its Colonial charm, right down to the low-ceiling dining rooms (see *Dining Out*) and steep, narrow set of stairs that lead up to the guest rooms. As for the cottages, Brook House has a full kitchen, two bedrooms, and a large deck; Barn Cottage also sleeps four with a loft, full kitchen, fireplace, patio, and private yard. My favorite is the romantic Pond Cottage—bright white with a large screened-in porch and efficiency kitchen. Rooms $90–110 nightly; $50 for a third person; cottages $150–210 nightly or $900–1300 weekly. Pets permitted in cottages for additional fee.

Chillingsworth (896-3640), 2449 Route 6A. Open late May to late November. This 1689 house, which is believed to be the second oldest house in town, is renowned primarily for its restaurant (see *Dining Out*), and its three guest rooms are only rented to dinner guests. The antiques-filled Stevenson Room boasts a private entrance and four-poster bed—it's the largest and nicest of the rooms. The Foster Room has views of the back gardens and gazebo, and although the Ten Eyck Room is small and without a view, it's nonetheless charming. Room rates include afternoon wine and cheese, a full breakfast, access to the private beach at the end of the street, and privileges at a private club with an indoor/outdoor pool, tennis courts, and golf. Rates $95–135.

Bramble Inn (896-7644), 2019 Route 6A. Open mid-May through December. Innkeepers Cliff and Ruth Manchester opened the Bramble Inn in 1985 and offer eight rooms in two 18th- and 19th-century buildings. Some rooms have brass beds and wicker; others are more formal with antiques, wide sanded floorboards, and four-poster canopy beds; all have air-conditioning. Ruth Manchester, a talented chef (see *Dining*

Out), will wow you with her full buffet breakfast. Rates $95–128.

❋ **Old Sea Pines Inn** (896-6114), 2553 Route 6A. Open year-round. In 1907 the Old Sea Pines Inn was the Sea Pines School of Charm and Personality for Young Women. Today longtime hosts Michele and Steve Rowan combine nostalgia with modern comforts. All 19 rooms and two suites are pleasant, furnished with old brass or iron beds. The less-expensive "classrooms" are small and share three baths—it will be easy to imagine yourself as a young girl at boarding school. Rooms in the rear annex are handicapped accessible, more modern, and have televisions. The house is set on 3½ acres, and there's plenty of space to relax inside, too, including a large, comfy living room with fireplace that leads onto the wraparound porch set with rockers. If you've planning a family reunion or wedding, you might want to look into Old Sea Pines. June through October $75–105, $110–115 for three or four people in a family suite; $10–20 less the rest of the year.

BED & BREAKFASTS

❋ **Brewster Farmhouse Inn** (896-3910, 1-800-892-3910; e-mail: bnbinn-@capecod.net), 716 Route 6A. Open year-round. This Greek Revival farmhouse has a light-infused reception area with one large dining table and a small sitting area with a fireplace. Four stylishly decorated guest rooms and a two-bedroom suite (rented as separate rooms with shared bath in the off-season) include luxurious amenities. One room has a private deck; another has a fireplace. The back deck, where afternoon tea is served, leads to a heated pool and hot tub. A sumptuous full breakfast is included. Mid-June to mid-September $95–150; off-season $75–110.

Ruddy Turnstone (385-9871, 1-800-654-1995), 463 Route 6A. Open March through December. This is one of only two B&Bs on Route 6A with a view of Cape Cod Bay and the salt marsh. And what an expansive view it is! If the weather is good, you'll enjoy it from a chair in the garden or under the fruit trees, or from a hammock. If it's cold or rainy, a second-floor common room has a large picture window with an unobstructed view. This early-19th-century Cape house has four guest rooms and one large suite (with fireplace and a view!) appointed with antiques, Oriental carpets, and luxurious feather beds. The adjacent barn, recently restored and furnished with pencil-post canopy beds and quilts, offers a bit more privacy. Hosts Swanee and Sally Swanson offer a full breakfast. Mid-June to mid-September $95–135; off-season $75–100. No credit cards.

❋ **Captain Freeman Inn** (896-7481, 1-800-843-4664), 15 Breakwater Road. Open year-round. Next to The Brewster Store (see *To See*) on the town green, the Captain Freeman Inn has been gussied up with four-poster canopy beds, sanded hardwood floors, and designer window treatments. Of the 12 rooms, my favorites are the bright corner rooms with high ceilings and those with retiled bathrooms. Three suites—with television, VCR, minifridge, fireplace, and whirlpool bath on a private enclosed porch—are very popular. Although third-floor rooms are smaller, they are more moderately priced and have good views. Innkeepers Carol and Tom Edmondson offer a full breakfast on the screened-in porch overlooking the large pool. Carol is an expert cook who specializes in tasty low-fat creations; she holds cooking classes on many winter weekends. Carol and Tom also hold seminars for prospective innkeepers. Late May through October $90–95 for shared bath, $130–205 private; off-season $80–85 shared, $105–165 private.

❋ **Isaiah Clark House** (896-2223, 1-800-822-4001), 1187 Route 6A. Open year-round. This 1780s former sea captain's home sits right on Route 6A but the back deck looks onto lovely gardens. The seven guest rooms each have a private bath (although some of the bathrooms are outside the room). All have air-conditioning; some have a fireplace. The atmosphere is comfortable and homey, not polished. A full breakfast is served in the Colonial keeping room or, in warm weather, on the back deck. Beach transportation, towels, and chairs are provided. Mid-May to mid-October $95–115; off-season $20 less.

❋ **Pepper House Inn** (896-4389), 2062 Route 6A. Open year-round. This federal-style B&B has four comfortably elegant guest rooms. All are spacious corner rooms. Although the rooms have wide floorboards, period (decorative) fireplaces, and canopy beds, they also have modern comforts like air-conditioning and television. Guests can relax on the screened-in porch, large deck, or in the country-comfortable living room. Bill and Cheri Metters opened in spring 1996. A full breakfast is included in the rates: $109–139 late May to mid-October, $89–119 off-season.

COTTAGES AND APARTMENTS

Linger Longer By The Sea (896-3451, e-mail: Jrichar379@aol.com), 261 Linnell Landing Beach. Open April through November. Off a sandy lane and within a sandal shuffle of a private stretch of Linnell Landing Beach, this place is perfect for families who appreciate not having to get into a car or cross a busy street to get to the beach. A few of the 10 cottages have been completely remodeled, and all of the six apartments overlook Cape Cod Bay. All have decks, barbecue grills, and picnic tables. Late June to early September $700–850 for a one-bedroom unit, $800–1350 weekly for a two- or three-bedroom. In the off-season, cottages and apartments are rented by the day or week.

Ellis Landing Cottages (896-5072), Ellis Landing. Open late May to mid-October. These 15 cozy waterfront and water-view cottages have been in Gil Ellis's family since the 1930s. Most of the other simply furnished housekeeping cottages were built by Gil's father in the 1940s and 1950s, and have recently been refurbished. At the end of a quiet side road off Route 6A, the pine-paneled cottages have complete kitchens; many have fireplaces. Some are more rustic than others. Rest Easy can sleep seven comfortably in two bedrooms. Late June to early September $1400–1500 weekly for a three-bedroom waterfront cottage, $1200–

1300 weekly for a two-bedroom waterfront cottage, $750–850 weekly for a two-bedroom off-the-water cottage. In the off-season cottages can be rented for three nights; inquire about rates. No credit cards.

See also High Brewster under *Inns.*

RENTALS

Bay Village Realty (896-7004), 1990 Route 6A, Brewster 02631. This agency has about 200 listings, from two-bedroom knotty-pine cottages to more year-round-like homes with four bedrooms. Prices vary accordingly. The bulk of rentals are booked January through March, but if you wait until July, they can still probably find something for you (although it may not be exactly what you want.)

See also Ocean Edge Resort under *Resort*.

CAMPGROUND

✳ **Nickerson State Park** (896-4615 for reservations; 896-3491 for general information), 3488 Route 6A. Open mid-April to mid-October for tenters; open year-round if you have self-contained camping facilities (water and toilets). Reservations are accepted for 250 of the 418 available sites. In summer, it is first come, first served—you often have to wait 2 to 3 days before getting a campsite. This place is so popular and inexpensive that the campground has problems with people registering under phony names in order to stay longer than the 14-day limit. It's the second busiest campground in the state. $6; pets permitted. (See also *Green Space*.)

If you have to wait a night or two to get into Nickerson State Park, bide your time at **Shady Knoll Campground** (896-3002), Route 6A at Route 137, or **Sweetwater Forest** (896-3773), off Route 124, both in Brewster. See also **Shawme-Crowell State Forest** under "Sandwich."

WHERE TO EAT

DINING OUT

Chillingsworth (896-3640), 2449 Route 6A. Open daily except Monday for lunch and dinner, late May to late November; in high season, the bistro is open on Monday; in the off-season, open on weekends only. Long regarded as the Cape's best dining experience, there is nothing I can say about Chillingsworth that hasn't been said before, by *Bon Appétit, Gourmet,* and other arbiters of haute cuisine. But for those who have, heretofore, been unaware of this exceptional restaurant, here are the basics. Seven-course, prix fixe French/California-style dinners are served at two seatings (one in the off-season); choose the early seating, otherwise you'll be eating until 11:30 or midnight. The small, candlelit dining rooms, filled with antiques (some dating to Louis XV), feel rather like salons; service is well paced and discreet. There are always a dozen or so appetizers and entrées on the menu, which changes daily to take advantage of the freshest ingredients available. Pace yourself, and don't forget to save room for at least a bite of dessert! For those with less of an appetite, a bistro menu is served in the airy greenhouse. À la carte luncheons in the greenhouse are a relaxing, decadent endeavor: try scallops with leek orzo, sea beans, and tomato coulis. Nothing is ordinary at Chillingsworth: Soup and dessert du jour are called "chef's whim of the moment." Chef Robert Rabin and his wife, Nitzi, proudly preside. Lunch $8–11.50; dinner $40–52. Reservations required; jacket suggested for dinner.

Bramble Inn (896-7644), 2019 Route 6A. Open for dinner nightly, mid-May through December. The exceptional New American and internationally inspired cuisine, gracious service, and five intimate dining rooms are the result of chef-owner Ruth Manchester's talent and diligence. Place settings are mix-and-match antique china, elegantly casual. Dine by candlelight from a broad, prix fixe menu that changes every few weeks. House specialties include rack of lamb, boneless breast of chicken with lobster, and assorted seafood curries. This place is underrated; I've never talked with a diner who was less than wholly satisfied. Four-course dinners $38–48; by reservation only.

High Brewster (896-3636), 964 Satucket Road. Open for dinner April through December; closed various nights in the slow season. In a town with many notable restaurants, High Brewster ranks right up there with the best (and the Cape's best, for that matter). On my last visit, we enjoyed rack of lamb with pink peppercorn demiglaze and polenta, as well as broiled swordfish topped with tomatoes, bread crumbs, and Asiago and served with scallion fritters. Three charming dining rooms in this former farmhouse are romantic: candlelight, low ceilings, exposed beams, wood floors, antique paneling, fresh flowers, and ladderback chairs. Four-course dinners range from $30 for the vegetarian meal to $50 for the rack of lamb. Reservations recommended.

Brewster Fish House (896-7867), 2208 Route 6A. Open for lunch and dinner, daily, mid-April to mid-December. This small roadside fish house doesn't look like much from the outside, although inside it is quite pleasant with white linen on the tables, Windsor chairs, fresh flowers, and high ceilings. There is always a steady stream of customers who appreciate consistently well-prepared, very fresh seafood at reasonable prices. Fried oysters covered in cornmeal and served on a bed of spinach is a good appetizer choice, while the lobster bisque has a nice spicy kick to it. For dinner, try any of David and Vernon Smith's (chef-owners) innovative specials. Sea scallops with sun-dried tomatoes, garlic, and tarragon is a good bet. Arrive before 7 PM or expect to wait; no reservations accepted. Lunch $8–12, dinner entrées $11–22.

EATING OUT

Brewster Coffee Shop (896-8224), Route 6A. Open 7 AM–2 PM for breakfast and lunch late March to mid-December. The Brewster Coffee Shop rises to the top of its genre as an inexpensive, classic, family-style joint. It's a pleasant place. Take a seat at the old-fashioned diner-style counter, at a small Formica table, or outside at one of the few picnic tables. Order up a short stack of pancakes with bacon, a western omelet, or an egg-salad sandwich. Children's menu. Dishes $2–6.

Cobie's (896-7021), 3260 Route 6A. Open for lunch and dinner, late May to mid-September. Serving northside patrons since 1948, Cobie's is a justly renowned clam shack, with covered picnic tables near the pine trees. It's very convenient for cyclists on the Cape Cod Rail Trail.

✳ **Pizza & More** (896-8600), 302 Underpass Road. Open for lunch and dinner year-round. A wide variety of pizzas (including zucchini-topped selections), grinders, sandwiches (like steak and onions), pasta dishes, Greek salads, Greek gyros (lamb or beef with onions, tomatoes, and cucumbers wrapped up in a pita), and sticky baklava. Dishes $3–12.

PICNICS

Le Bistrot (896-3640), 2449 Route 6A. Open late May to late November. Truly gourmet picnic fixings—from pâté and focaccia to cheeses and salads, from lemon tea cakes to chocolate roulade. It's enough to make you forget the ants and bugs that normally accompany such an outing.

Satucket Farm Stand (896-5540), Route 124 just off Route 6A. Open seasonally. Farm-fresh produce, baked goods, jams, relishes, honey, and cheeses; a popular spot for local chefs.

ICE CREAM

Brewster Scoop (896-3744), Route 6A. Open mid-June to early September. Behind The Brewster Store, this small shop is purveyor of Bliss Dairy's sugar-free ice cream and nonfat frozen yogurt.

ENTERTAINMENT

Band concerts, Route 6A, about 1.5 miles west of Route 137. A new gazebo was built on the Drummer Boy property in 1994 and is a lovely forum for summertime concerts Sunday at 6 PM.

✐ **Cape Cod Repertory Outdoor Theatre** (896-1888 for schedule) 3379 Route 6A. Performances year-round. Under the directorship of Bob Troie, who has New York credits to his name, the company presents engaging productions at an open-air theater in the woods (on the former Crosby estate). In the off-season the company moves indoors to the Old Sea Pines Inn (896-6114; see *Inns*), where it also puts on a musical dinner revue on Sunday nights from June to mid-September.

Baseball. The Brewster Whitecaps, who joined the Cape Cod Baseball League in 1988 as an expansion team, play at the Cape Cod Technical High School, Route 124, Harwich. Games begin at 7 PM.

SELECTIVE SHOPPING

ANTIQUARIAN BOOKS

Punkhorn Bookshop (896-2114), 672 Route 6A. Open daily except Monday, June to mid-October; off-season by appointment. David Luebke deals in rare, quality used books from the ground floor of his house; specialties include Cape Cod, New England, natural history, fine arts, and biographies. Selections are well organized and categorized by the Dewey decimal system. Free search service.

Kings Way Books and Antiques (896-3639), 774 Route 6A. Open Thursday through Sunday, April through December (daily in summer). Proprietors Dick and Ella Socky specialize in out-of-print and rare books. The collection includes medieval and modern history, biography, architecture, archaeology, and nature books. Kings Way also does book searches at no charge. The antique cherrywood shelves were salvaged from the New Haven (Connecticut) public library. As for their select small antiques, most are book-related items.

ANTIQUES

Dozens of antiques shops line Route 6A; a sampling follows.

Homestead Antiques (896-2917), 2257 Route 6A. Open year-round. Housed in an old barn, Homestead has a fine selection of nautical items, weapons, weather vanes, scrimshaw, canes, paintings, lighting, and fireplace and garden items.

Breton House Antiques (896-3974), 1222 Stony Brook Road. Open year-round. After 20 years in business, it's no surprise that the three floors of antiques leave very little room to maneuver.

Tymeless Antiques & Art Gallery (255-9404), 3811 Route 6A. Open year-round. Watercolors by Tom Stringe and antiques collected by Jim Kostulias are paired nicely in this neat and tidy shop, which specializes in country furnishings and antique pine.

ARTISANS

Brewster Pottery (896-3587), 437 Harwich Road. Open April through December. Potter Marion Eckhardt moved to this house in 1947 and opened up her shop in 1969. Since then she's hired young apprentices from universities all over the country to learn hand-built and wheel-thrown pottery; one young man came to learn the craft when he was 15 and he's still here (and in his 40s.) Her porcelain and stoneware are lovely, made all the more so by watching Marion work.

Kemp Pottery (385-5782), 258 Route 6A. Open May through December. Fountains, garden sculpture, stained glass, and decorative and functional forms. Kemp also has a bigger shop in Orleans.

ART GALLERIES

Underground Gallery (896-6850), 673 Satucket Road. Open year-round. A working studio beneath 100 tons of soil and supported by 10 tree trunks, this gallery features the work of watercolorist Karen North Wells. Her husband, Malcolm Wells, who is also a painter, designs earth-covered solar buildings like this one. Their composting toilet is one of a handful on the Cape that don't pollute the drinking water supply. Passing bicyclists are encouraged to make use of the facilities.

Maddocks Gallery (896-6223), 1283 Route 6A. Open March through December and by appointment off-season. James Maddocks has been selling his nostalgic traditionalist and representational paintings (and limited-edition prints) of Cape Cod since 1983. His gallery, where you'll often find him painting and where he's also happy to talk with visitors, is an 1840s carriage house attached to his home.

Ruddeforth Gallery (255-1056), 3753 Route 6A. Open year-round. Watercolors, oils, and lithographs of Cape Cod scenes, florals, and still lifes by Debra Ruddeforth (a signature member of the Copley Society in Boston). Color photographs by her husband, Tom Ruddeforth.

Franny Golden (896-6353), 502 Harwich Road. The road sign proclaiming ARTIST caught my attention. Once inside Franny's home/studio, it was clear that her work defies easy interpretation. There are some portraits, some landscapes (sort of), some expressionist abstracts, many visual journals that have to do with experience. She works a lot with process. Franny teaches part time at Cape Cod Community College and does a local public TV cable show. This is not your standard Cape fare. Bigger pieces go for $2000–8000.

See also Tymeless Antiques & Art Gallery under *Antiques*.

BOOKSTORE

✐ **Brewster Book Store** (896-6543), 2648 Main Street, Brewster. A large and excellent offering of children's books. Also games, toys, story time, and book signings. Open year-round.

SPECIAL SHOPS

Eve's Place (896-4914), 564 Route 6A. Open year-round. Eve Roulier lived in Hawaii for eight years, and there she learned all about pearls. Now, from this modest little Cape house, she buys directly from growers, strings her own pearls, sells antique pearls, and can talk your ear off about rare black Tahitian pearls, pearls from Kobe, Japan, and freshwater pearls from China. She'll tell you that cultured pearls are created by injecting an irritant into an oyster's shell. About half the oysters die in reaction to the injection. Those that don't die will secrete a substance (nacre, which is the basis of the pearl) in reaction to the irritant. It then takes about three or four years for the pearl to mature. Whether you're ready to buy or just want to learn about pearls, Eve is the one to talk to.

Spectrum (385-3322), 369 Route 6A. Open year-round. This shop displays a most wonderful collection of high-quality contemporary crafts and fine art. It represents over 500 craftspeople from all over the country. I hesitate to itemize even a few of their pieces, because I don't want to limit your imagination. Two floors of beautifully designed objects (blown glass, woodworking products, handmade jewelry, textiles), plus sculpture that spills out of doors.

Sydenstricker Galleries (385-3272), 490 Route 6A. Open daily April through December; closed on Monday, January through March. Glass fusing demonstrations, using a technique developed by Brewster native Bill Sydenstricker (who died in 1994), are given 10–2 Tuesday through Saturday. Sydenstricker glass is used in two American embassies and displayed in museum collections around the country.

The Cook Shop (896-7698), Lemon Tree Village, Route 6A. Open year-round. Although you probably didn't come to the Cape with thoughts of cookware, this shop has just about everything a serious or would-be cook needs to outfit an impressive kitchen. Apparently many other people think so, too; the shop has been here since 1978.

Great Cape Cod Herb, Spice & Tea Co. (896-5900), 2628 Route 6A. Open daily year-round. With more than 170 varieties of Western and Chinese herbs in stock, this herbal apothecary may very well be the largest retailer of its kind in New England. Proprietor Stephan Brown (who opened the rustic shop in 1991) also stocks a selection of New Age literature on health and well-being.

SPECIAL EVENTS

April to early May: **Herring run.** Hundreds of thousands of alewives (herring) return from the salt water to lay their eggs in the same freshwater ponds where they were born (see Stony Brook Grist Mill and Museum and Herring Run under *To See*).

Late April: **Brewster in Bloom.** Faith Dibble proposed the idea to plant 100,000 daffodils in 1983. Today, there's an annual festival celebrating the bright yellow flowers that line the already picturesque streets. Events include an arts and crafts festival, food festival, and parade.

Mid-September: **Bird Carvers Exhibit,** at the Cape Cod Museum of Natural History (Route 6A). One of the premier exhibits of its kind in the country boasts carving and painting demonstrations and birdhouse builders. A fund-raising event since 1976 for the museum.

Early December: **Christmas Prelude.** Since 1991, this event culminates with a crafts show held at the Town Hall.

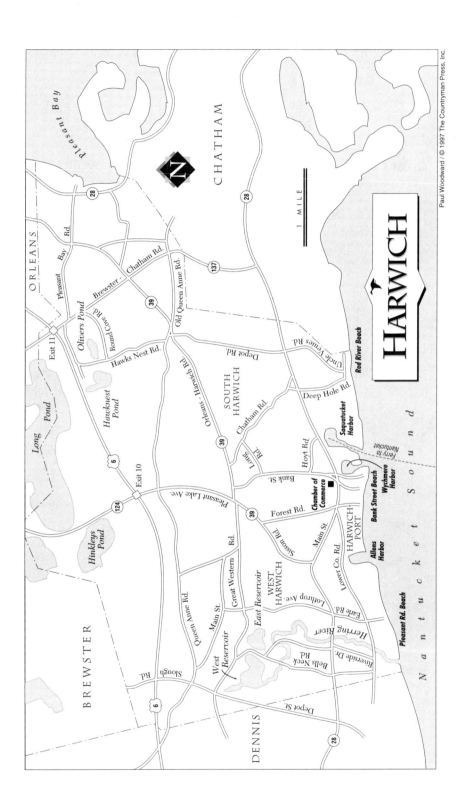

Harwich

Harwich isn't nearly as developed as its westerly neighbors, although its stretch of Route 28 does have its share of bumper boats, mini-golf courses, and go-carts. In fact, the town exudes a somewhat nonchalant air. It's as if the 11,000 year-rounders are collectively saying, "This is what we have and you're welcome to come and enjoy it with us if you wish," which is not to say that Harwich doesn't attract visitors. Harwich boasts a wide range of places to stay and eat, from the fanciest Victorian inn to the most humble B&B, from fine French cuisine to roasted chicken-on-a-spit. At the same time, although Harwich has more salt-water and freshwater beaches than any other town on the Cape, only a few have parking for visitors on a day-use basis.

Harwich, comprising seven distinct villages, is blessed with one of the most picturesque harbors on the Cape, Wychmere Harbor. Nearby Saquatucket Harbor, also lovely, is reserved for fishing charters and ferry service to Nantucket. It's worth poking around the quiet center of Harwich, which stands in marked contrast to the more developed areas just a mile or so away. Harwich, which bills its annual Cranberry Harvest Festival as "the biggest small-town celebration in the country," lays claims to cultivating the first commercial cranberry bog.

GUIDANCE

Harwich Chamber of Commerce (432-1600, 1-800-441-3199), Route 28, PO Box 34, Harwichport 02646. Open 9–5 daily, mid-June to mid-September; 9–5 on weekends, mid-May to mid-June and mid-September to mid-October. An informed chamber staff and a well-organized, townwide publication make Harwich an easy place to navigate. You can park for free in the booth's large parking lot and walk to Bank Street Beach.

PUBLIC REST ROOMS

Public rest rooms are located at the chamber parking lot and at Brooks Park on Route 39 and Oak Street.

GETTING THERE

By car: Take Route 6 from either bridge across the canal to exit 10 (Route 124 south and Route 39 south) to Route 28, or take exit 11 to Route 137 for East Harwich. It takes about 35–40 minutes to reach Harwich from the canal.

Getting to Nantucket: There is seasonal passenger ferry service to Nantucket from Harwichport. For many people, this service is more convenient than going into Hyannis to catch a boat. For complete information, see *Getting There* in "Nantucket."

GETTING AROUND

Route 28 is also called Main Street. (This is not to be confused with Main Street—aka Route 39—in the center of Harwich, which is inland.) Although most points of interest are located along or off the developed Route 28, it's worth heading inland to explore Harwich's ponds and conservation areas.

MEDICAL EMERGENCY

Medicenter Five (432-4100), Route 124, Harwich.

TO SEE AND DO

All listings are in Harwich Center unless otherwise noted.

Brooks Academy Museum (432-8089), at Routes 124 and 39 and Main Street. Open 1–4 Thursday through Sunday, mid-May to mid-October. This 1844 Greek Revival schoolhouse was home to the country's first vocational school of navigation, established by Sidney Brooks. Now operated by the Harwich Historical Society, it contains a history of cranberry harvesting, a collection of historical photographs, and displays of Native American and maritime artifacts. Also here are a gunpowder house used from 1770 to 1864 and a restored 1872 outhouse. Free.

First Congregational Church, Route 139 and Great Western Road. Built in the mid-1700s, this church is surrounded by a white picket fence and anchors the tiny town center.

BICYCLING/RENTALS

About 5 miles of the **Cape Cod Rail Trail** run through Harwich; you can pick it up near the Pleasant Lake General Store on Route 124 and off Great Western Road near Herring Run Road.

Harwichport Bike Company Inc. (430-0200), 431 Route 28, and **Sandy's Sport Shop** (432-0787), 537 Route 28, rent bicycles and in-line skates; both open year-round.

BIRD CARVINGS

Cape Cod Five Cents Savings Bank (430-0400), Route 28 in the center of Harwichport, displays a fine collection of carved miniature shore- and songbirds by hometown artist Elmer Crowell.

BOATING/CANOEING

Red River Beach, off Depot Road. Small sailboats may be launched from the east end of this beach.

Cape Water Sports (432-7079), at the junction of Routes 28 and 124. Open year-round. Herring River, which runs north to a reservoir and south to Nantucket Sound, is great for canoeing. This shop rents canoes by the day ($39) or week ($139); you can also rent Sunfish.

Saquatucket Harbor, Route 28. With 200 berths, this is the largest municipal marina on the Cape; about 10 slips are reserved for visitors.

Wychmere Harbor, Harbor Road off Route 28. A large fleet of sloops is often moored here, making it one of the most scenic (albeit man-made) harbors on the Cape. In the late 1800s, Wychmere Harbor was simply a salt pond, around which a racetrack was laid. But locals, disapproving of horse racing, convinced the town to cut an opening from the pond into Nantucket Sound. Thus the harbor was born.

Allens Harbor, on Lower County Road, is the town's other picturesque, well-protected, and man-made harbor; it has a docking ramp.

See also Herring River/Sand Pond Conservation Area under *Green Space—Walks*.

FISHING/SHELLFISHING

Shellfishing permits ($5) are obtained from the Town Offices (430-7513) on Route 39 on weekdays 8–4, and from the harbormaster (430-7532) at Saquatucket Harbor, 8–4 on weekends, June through September.

A number of charter fishing trips depart from Saquatucket Harbor, Route 28, including *Yankee* (432-2520) and *Fishtale* (432-3738, 240-9090). From Wychmere Harbor off Route 28, the *Golden Eagle* (432-5611) offers deep-sea-fishing trips and evening blues trips, $17–25 per person, mid-May to mid-October. Rod, reel, bait, and fish bag included. Try your luck casting from a jetty at Red River Beach or the Herring River Bridge in West Harwich.

Fishing the Cape (432-1200, 1-800-235-9763), Routes 137 and 39, Harwich commons. From mid-May through August, the king of fly-fishing—Orvis—offers a 3-day saltwater fly-fishing course for $395. (The price includes food for you at lunchtime and food for the fish.) Guided fishing trips are also offered, as well as a full line of Orvis supplies, flies, and tackle at the shop, which is open year-round.

FOR FAMILIES

✐❋ **Harwich Junior Theatre** (432-2002), Division and Willow Streets, West Harwich. This year-round semiprofessional theater—the country's oldest children's theater, established in 1952—produces four shows in July and August. Children age 7–15 star in kids' roles, manage the sound and lighting, and sell refreshments. (Adults from the community take the adult roles.) Classes or workshops at the theater are a prerequisite to acting; $60 for a 4-week class that meets two or three times a week for a couple of hours each class. Whether your child is considering acting in a production or being an audience member, this is an imaginative alternative to yet another round of mini-golf.

✐ **Grand Slam Entertainment** (430-1155), 322 Route 28. Open mid-April to mid-October (9 AM–11 PM daily in summer and weekends in the off-season). Batting cages with varying degrees of difficulty and bumper boats for toddlers to teens.

Wychmere Harbor in Harwichport

Trampoline Center (432-8717), 296 Route 28. Open weekends only April to late June and early September to mid-October; 9 AM–11 PM daily, late June to early September. There are no age or height restrictions; the only restriction at this outdoor center is that kids can't do flips. Ten minutes of bouncing costs $3.50. With this pricing structure, it's conceivable that three kids could each jump for a few minutes.

Bud's Go-Karts (432-4964), 364 Sisson Road, at Route 28. Open 9 AM–11 PM daily, mid-June to early September, and weekends only in April and May and early September to mid-October. Kids have to be above a certain height (54 inches) and at least 8 years old to ride without parents at this busy track. Six minutes costs $5.

Castle in the Clouds, behind the Harwich Elementary School, South Street. A fun playground. There are also picnic tables and a playground at **Brooks Park,** Route 39, Harwich.

GOLF

Cranberry Valley Golf Course (430-7560), Oak Street, off Route 39. Open March through December. This 18-hole, 6500-yard, par-72 course also has a driving range and practice putting green. Junior clinics are offered in summer only.

Harwichport Golf Club (432-0250), South and Forest Streets. Open mid-May to mid-November. A nine-hole, par-34 course.

HORSEBACK RIDING

Deer Meadow Riding Stables (432-6580), Route 137, East Harwich. Year-round riding (weather permitting) and guided trail rides.

IN-LINE SKATING

See *Bicycling/Rentals* for in-line skate rentals.

MINI-GOLF

✐ **Harbor Glen Miniature Golf** (432-8240), Route 28. Open April to mid-October. With fountains and imitation rocky waterfalls, this place packs 'em in, especially at night. Perhaps it's due to the adjacent **Weather Deck** restaurant, which offers kids' meals (chicken nuggets and fries for $3.25) and ice cream.

✐ **Club House Mini Golf** (432-4820), Route 39 near Route 137. Open daily, mid-June to early September, and weekends only during the month preceding and following.

SAILING

See Cape Sail, under "Brewster."

SPECIAL PROGRAMS

Cape Cod Naturally (432-0805), 456 Route 28. Daily, year-round. Naturalist Lee Baldwin takes groups of 4 to 15 people on guided hikes and nature walks all over the Cape. These 2- or 3-hour walks follow cart tracks, foot trails in the woods, and the shoreline of ponds, bay beaches, or the Atlantic Ocean. $5–7 per person or $120 to hire Baldwin to lead a group on an all-day hike (eight people max).

✐ **Baseball Clinics** (432-2000, 432-8515), Whitehouse Field, off Oak Street from Route 39, behind the high school in Harwich Center. From late June to mid-August, weekly clinics (9–noon) are held for kids age 6–12. The cost is $50 for the week. Sign up on Monday morning at the field.

TENNIS

Public courts are located at the **Cape Cod Technical High School** (432-4500), Route 124, and **Brooks Park** (430-7553), Route 39 and Oak Street. Call for reservations.

Wychmere Harbor Tennis Club (430-7012), 792 Route 28. Open mid-May through September. This full-service facility offers nine clay and two hard courts, private and group instruction, a pro shop, daily round-robins, and adult and junior clinics.

GREEN SPACE

BEACHES

Obtain weekly beach stickers ($25) at Town Hall (432-7638, 430-7513), Route 39. Open 9–3:30 daily, June to early September. All of Harwich's 16 public saltwater beaches are located on Nantucket Sound, but parking at most is limited to residents and weekly cottage renters with parking stickers. A free trolley service discharges passengers at Nantucket Sound beaches, making public beaches all the more public.

Red River Beach, off Depot Road or Uncle Venies Road from Route 28, is the only noteworthy beach with parking for day visitors. Parking $5 weekdays, $10 weekends. Facilities include rest rooms, concessions, and a lifeguard.

PONDS

Hinckleys Pond and **Seymour Pond,** both off Route 124, are open to nonresidents and non–cottage renters. You can swim at **Bucks Pond,** off Route 39, and **Pleasant Bay,** off Route 28.

Long Pond has two beaches: one off Long Pond Drive from Route 124 and the other off Cahoons Road from Long Pond Drive from Route 137; both require town beach stickers for parking.

Sand Pond is off Great Western Road.

WALKS

Herring River/Sand Pond Conservation Area, park off Bell's Neck Road (from Great Western Road) in West Harwich. These 23 acres (which also go by the name of Bells Neck Conservation Area) of marshland, tidal creeks, reservoir, and riverway are great for birding and canoeing. You may see cormorants, ospreys, and swans.

Thompson's Field, south of Route 39 near Chatham Road. This 93-acre preserve is full of wildflowers in springtime.

LODGING

INN

❋ **Augustus Snow House** (430-0528, 1-800-320-0528), 528 Route 28, Harwichport 02646. Open year-round. This 1901 Queen Anne Victorian mansion—complete with turrets, gabled dormers, a gazebo, and a wraparound porch—has five large guest rooms furnished in authentic Victorian style to complement the luxuriously outfitted bathrooms. Some rooms have a Jacuzzi or fireplace; all have TV. Innkeepers Joyce and Steve Roth serve a full breakfast at individual tables in the elegant breakfast room. The house is open to the public for afternoon tea (see *Dining Out*). Late May to mid-October $145–160; off-season $105–150. In the off-season, dinner for two at the inn is offered with a 3-night stay.

BED & BREAKFASTS

☞✑❋ **House on the Hill** (432-4321), 968 Route 28, South Harwich 02661. Open year-round. Although located on Route 28, this 1832 Federal-style farmhouse is set back from the road with lots of open space around it. It's been in host Allen Swanson's family since 1948, when he was 18 years old; Swanson and his wife, Carolyn, began taking guests in 1986. The house has three charmingly simple guest rooms all with private bath. The homey living room and breakfast room feature original pine wainscoting, hand-wrought door latches, a beehive oven, and fireplaces. Continental breakfast included. It's conveniently located only ½ mile from a ferry to Nantucket. $55–65; $5 additional for a child in the same room. No credit cards.

Barnaby Inn (432-6789), 36 Route 28, West Harwich 02671. Open year-round. Although this rambling farmhouse is on busy Route 28, it's set back from the road. Innkeepers Bill and Eileen Ormond purchased this formerly ramshackle place in 1995 and set about gutting and refur-

Digging for clams at low tide in Pleasant Bay

bishing it. (Bill grew up 300 yards from the inn.) The six rooms are modest, each with new carpeting and private bathroom. Breakfast is delivered to your room. Well-behaved pets are accepted. Summer $75, off-season $55–65.

✐❋ **Lion's Head Inn** (432-7766, 1-800-321-3155), 186 Belmont Road, West Harwich 02671. Open year-round. On a quiet residential street within walking distance of a beach, this modest B&B has some nice attributes. A few of the six guest rooms can accommodate three people; one room has a private deck and original pine floors; the Huntington suite is large, with a sitting area, TV, and private entrance to the pool. Nineteenth-century common rooms include two comfortable parlors, one with fireplace. The sunny breakfast room/terrace overlooks the nicely land-scaped pool. Inquire about the two moderately priced cottages; they're darkish but fully equipped for a family of five. June through September $80–120; off-season $60–100, expanded continental breakfast included.

☞❋ **Blue Heron Bed & Breakfast** (430-0219), 464 Pleasant Lake Avenue, Harwich 02645. Open year-round. The main attraction of this pleasant and homey 19th-century B&B is its proximity to the Cape's largest freshwater lake: There's a private beach across the street. Another plus is that the Cape Cod Rail Trail is also right across the street. Off the beaten path, these three simple rooms (one with private bath) rent for $50–75, including an expanded continental breakfast.

GUEST HOUSES

❋ **Beach House Inn** (432-4444, 1-800-870-4405), 4 Braddock Lane, Harwich-port 02646. Open year-round. Owners Gregg Winston and David Plunkett have transformed this formerly modest beachfront house into an upscale establishment with 14 deluxe rooms off a central hallway. All but two offer a beach view; some have a private deck. All rooms have air-conditioning, private baths (some with Jacuzzi), TV, and refrigerators. The back porch, sheltered by *Rosa rugosa,* leads to multilevel decks set with lounge chairs. There's nothing between the decks and the ocean except a private beach. Extensive continental breakfast buffet included; full breakfast available. Mid-June to mid-September $155–255; off-season $95–165.

☞ **Seadar Inn By-The-Sea** (432-0264; 842-4525 off-season), Braddock Lane at Bank Street Beach, Harwichport 02646. Open May through September. Just a short shuffle from the beach in a quiet neighborhood, the rambling and shingled Seadar Inn has 23 rooms decorated in Early American style. Bill Collins's family has proudly hosted guests at this old-fashioned hostelry since 1970; they are only the fourth family to own the Seadar since it opened in 1946. A buffet breakfast, served in the Colonial-style dining room, is included. Mid-June to early September $75–105; $15 each additional person in a room.

☞ **Cape Winds By-The-Sea** (432-1418, 1-609-597-7620 off-season), 28 Shore Road, West Harwich 02671. Open late May to mid-October. Owner Catherine Scales offers five quiet and airy rooms with views of Nantucket Sound across the street; a studio that can accommodate three people; and a two-room efficiency apartment. No breakfast is served, but you can enjoy a cup of complimentary coffee from a front-porch rocker. The beach is just a 5-minute walk away. Mid-June to mid-September $75 for rooms, $90 for the studio, $95 for the efficiency; $16 each additional person. Pets accepted on occasion. No credit cards.

COTTAGES

✑ **Tern Inn** (432-3714, 1-800-432-3718), 91 Chase Street, West Harwich 02671. Open April through October. These six nicely maintained and recently renovated cottages and efficiencies (one of which is shaped like a gazebo) are set on a 2-acre wooded lot. A pool and basketball court are on the premises. The Tern Inn also rents eight rooms in a half-Cape house; included in the room rate is a continental breakfast at the nearby Commodore Inn, a "Coastal Innkeeper" sister property (see *Motels*). The Tern is a 10-minute walk from the beach. Mid-June to mid-September $79–115 for rooms, $425–775 weekly for cottages; off-season $65–90 nightly for all accommodations. A 3-day minimum is usually required.

See also Cape Winds By-The-Sea (under *Guest Houses*) and Lion's Head Inn (under *Bed & Breakfasts*).

MOTELS

✑✱ **Harbor Breeze** (432-0337, 1-800-272-4343, e-mail: dvangeld@capecod.net), 326 Lower County Road, Harwichport 02646. Open year-round. Across from Allens Harbor, Harbor Breeze offers nine pleasant rooms (all with private entrances, a few with private decks) that are delightfully off the beaten path. Rooms are clustered around a garden courtyard, next to a hidden pool. Decorated with wicker and country florals, many rooms can accommodate a family of four; others can be connected as family suites. All have private bath, TV, and refrigerator. Expanded continental breakfast included; grills available for the picnic area; microwave in the breakfast room. Mid-June to early September $75–120; $99 for 2 nights midweek in the off-season; $12.50 for an extra person in the room.

Sandpiper Beach Inn (432-0485, 1-800-433-2234), 16 Bank Street, Harwichport 02646. Open April through October. Fronting its own private beach, this U-shaped building is constructed around a well-tended grassy courtyard. All 19 renovated and redecorated rooms have TV, refrigerator, telephone, and air-conditioning. Some can sleep three to five people; most have a private patio. The duplex cottage that opens directly onto the beach is stunning, but it's often booked a year in advance. Continental breakfast included. Mid-June to mid-September $110–150 for rooms, $225 for cottage; off-season $80–100 for rooms, $150 for cottage; $25 per additional person. A 3-day minimum is usually required.

Commodore Inn (432-1180, 1-800-368-1180), 30 Earle Road, West Harwich 02671. Open April through October. At first glance, this complex looks like just another cluster of motel rooms set around a pool. But on closer inspection, it's quite a large (heated) pool, and the 25 rooms are nicely outfitted with wicker furniture and white cotton bedspreads. Some even have Jacuzzi, gas fireplace, wet bar, and microwave. Many can sleep a family of four in two double beds. Ask for a room with a vaulted ceiling; they feel much more spacious. The rooms are just down the road from the beach. The play area has lots of activities for the kids. Mid-June to mid-September $119–150; off-season $80–125; $20 per additional person. Extensive buffet breakfast included. A 3-day minimum is usually required.

WHERE TO EAT

DINING OUT

Cape Sea Grille (432-4745), 31 Sea Street, Harwichport. Open for dinner mid-April to mid-November; closed Tuesday in the off-season. Chef-owners Jim and Beth Bryde offer well-prepared New American cuisine served by candlelight in a lovely old house by the beach. Specialties include seafood paella and a mixed grill of roasted lobster, herb-crusted salmon fillet, and swordfish wrapped in bacon. There is a special tasting menu 5–6:15, which is distinct from an early-bird special. Reservations are suggested. Entrées $13–20.

❈ **L'Alouette** (430-0405), 787 Route 28, Harwichport. Open for dinner Tuesday through Sunday, year-round except February; open for Sunday brunch year-round except in July and August. Danielle Bastres and her chef-husband, Louis, have developed a loyal clientele since they opened L'Alouette in 1986. Bastres's consistently well-prepared and -presented

Harwich cultivated the country's first commercial cranberry bog; it celebrates with a Cranberry Harvest Festival in mid-September.

French cuisine appeals to sophisticated, generally older people who don't necessarily think that more is better. Specialties include country-style pâté and sautéed escargots to start, and braised fillet of sole and bouillabaisse for entrées. If you've had a hankering for châteaubriand, this is the place to have it. Reservations suggested. Brunch $10–14; dinner $17–27.

EATING OUT

Thompson's Clam Bar (430-1239), 600 Route 28, Harwichport. Open for lunch and dinner, mid-June to early September. Just when you were lulled into thinking that certain things in life would never change, Thompson's changed. It moved from its superb location overlooking the mouth of Wychmere Harbor, where it had been since 1949, to a nice but generic Route 28 location. The same menu is offered: baked and fried seafood, clam chowder, fish-and-chips. But the new place has a self-serve feel; you order at a counter, seat yourself, and the waitstaff bring your food. There's a raw bar, and takeout, and outdoor seating along Route 28. But frankly, it just doesn't have the charm of the old place. Of course, if you didn't know the old place, this one is pleasant enough, with shellacked tables and green director's chairs. Children's menu. Lunch $8–15; dinner $15–22.

☞✐✲ **Stewed Tomato** (432-2214), 707 Main Street, Harwich Center. Open for breakfast and lunch daily, year-round. This bright and cheery neighborhood place, established in 1983, is delightfully off the beaten path. The specialties are homemade soups, baked goods (like muffins, biscuits, and turnovers), and a few sandwiches (crab roll), burgers (get the one with tomatoes and fried onions), and omelets. $2.50–5.

☞❄ **Bonatt's Restaurant & Bakery** (432-7199), 537 Route 28, Harwichport. Open for breakfast and lunch year-round. Bonatt's successfully fulfills four important missions: It offers good breakfasts from the short-order kitchen, luncheon specials like fish-and-chips and open steak sandwiches in the pleasant dining rooms, box lunches for the beach (call an hour in advance in summer), and famous "meltaway" sweet bread from the bakery. Dishes $3–9.50.

✐ **400 East** (430-1800), Route 39 and 137, East Harwich. Open for lunch and dinner year-round. 400 East is a friendly place, good for families. The menu features standards like Cajun chicken breast, charbroiled sirloin steaks, fettuccine Alfredo, hearty tavern sandwiches, and burgers. Children's menu and crayons. Many think 400 East is better than its more visible cousin, **The 400** on Route 28 in Harwichport. Dishes $4.50–15.

Seafood Sam's (432-1422), 302 Route 28, West Harwich. Open for lunch and dinner, March to mid-October. You can always count on Seafood Sam's for reliable, informally presented, reasonably priced seafood. Outdoor picnic tables, too.

AFTERNOON TEA

Augustus Snow House (430-0528, 1-800-320-0528), 528 Route 28, Harwichport. Tea served 1–5 Wednesday, Thursday, and Saturday, year-round. Few places on the Cape serve afternoon tea like this. For $12, you get a pot of brewed tea, warm scones with crème frâiche and jam, a selection of finger sandwiches, and a choice from the pastry dessert tray. Tea is served in the ground-level garden room.

SNACKS

Thompson's Farm Market (432-5415), 710 Route 28, Harwichport. Open 10–6 daily. This upscale market and deli is an appealing place to gather picnic fixings. Café seating, where you can enjoy baked goods and coffee in an air-conditioned setting, is also an option.

Nick and Dick's (430-2444), Route 28, Harwichport. Open seasonally. The place to go for homemade ice cream and yogurt.

ENTERTAINMENT

Baseball. The Harwich Mariners (432-2000, 432-8515) play ball at Whitehouse Field, off Oak Street from Route 39, behind the high school in Harwich Center. Games begin at 7 and are played from early June to early August.

Band concerts are held Tuesday evenings at 7:30 in Brooks Park, Route 39 and Oak Street.

See Harwich Junior Theatre under *To See and Do—For Families*.

SELECTIVE SHOPPING

ANTIQUES

The Barn at Windsong (432-8281), 245 Bank Street, Harwichport. Open April through October. A variety of dealers offer a variety of goods: quilts, silver, toys, linen, glassware, and furniture.

The Mews at Harwichport (432-6397), 517 Route 28, Harwichport. Open mid-May through October. A few dealers have joined forces and offer glasses, plates, stoneware, baskets, and majolica.

ART GALLERY

Just Africa (432-8098), Route 28 at Bank Street, Harwichport. Open late April to late September. Contemporary African art and sculpture.

ARTISAN

Pamela Black/Paradise Pottery (432-1713), 928 Route 28, South Harwich. Open year-round. Black creates and displays her whimsical and functional stoneware and raku (as well as hand-cut paper designs) in an old barn next to her house.

AUCTIONS

Merlyn Auctions (432-5863), 204 Main Street, North Harwich. Open March to mid-December; auctions every Saturday. Although he usually handles complete estate auctions, Merlyn will also auction anything that comes out of a house.

BOOKSTORE

Sea Street Books (430-1816), 537 Route 28, Harwichport. Open year-round.

SPECIAL SHOPS

Monahan (432-3302), 540 Route 28, Harwichport. Open year-round. Prices on Monahan's jewelry (which is purchased from estate auctions and taken on consignment) range from the double digits to six figures. The shop has been in Michael Monahan's family for generations; they claim to be the oldest family-owned jewelry store in the country.

Cape Cod Tileworks (432-7346), 705 Main Street, Harwich Center. Open year-round. This colorful new shop sells nothing but tile: ceramic, marble, limestone, and hand-painted tiles. They're lovely; custom designs and installation, too.

Cape Cod Bonsai Studio (432-8400), 1012 Route 28. Open March through December. In addition to selling more bonsai trees than you've ever (perhaps) seen under one roof, this shop also holds classes ($25) and longer workshops ($75) in juniper care (good for beginners), creating miniature landscapes, and rock planting.

Pleasant Lake General Store (432-5305), Route 124. A good old-fashioned store, perfectly situated for cyclists on the Rail Trail.

SPECIAL EVENTS

Late June to early September: **Guild of Harwich Artists** sponsors "Art in the Park" at Wheeler Park, off Lower Country Road. Artists and craftspeople sell their wares every Monday in summer. (Rain date on Wednesdays.)

Mid-August: **Sails Around Cape Cod** (432-1600). Begun in 1990, this 140-mile race circumnavigates the Cape and begins and ends off the coast of Harwichport.

Mid-September: **Cranberry Harvest Festival** (430-2811). This popular 10-day celebration includes fireworks, arts and crafts, a parade, and a country-and-western jamboree.

Mid-December: **Christmas Weekend in the Harwiches** (432-1600). Hayrides, strolling minstrels, and a choral group.

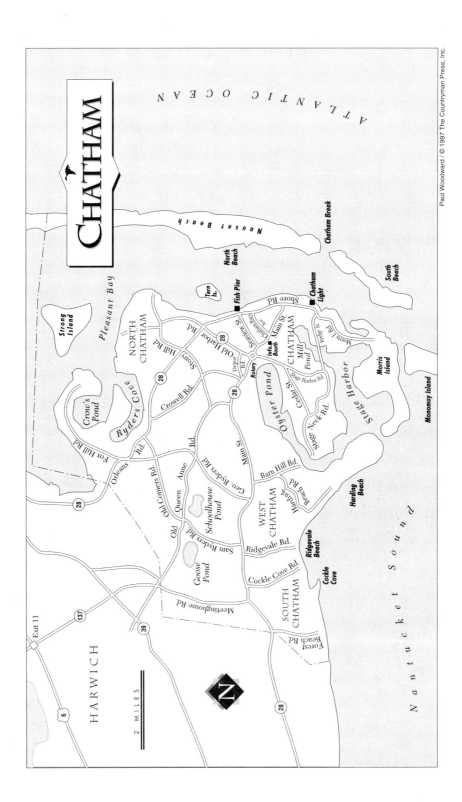

CHATHAM

ATLANTIC OCEAN

Nauset Beach

Chatham Break

North Beach

South Beach

Chatham Light

Pleasant Bay

Strong Island

Tern Is.

Fish Pier

Shore Rd.

NORTH CHATHAM

Stony Hill Rd.

Old Harbor Rd.

Seaview St.

Cockle Cove Rd.

Main St.

Bishop St.

Morris Ln.

CHATHAM

Mill Pond

Info Booth

Depot Rd.

Rotary

Cedar St.

Stage Harbor Rd.

Oyster Pond

Stage Harbor

Morris Island

Stage Neck Rd.

Monomoy Island

Crow's Pond

Ryders Cove

Crowell Rd.

Fox Hill Rd.

Orleans Rd.

Old Comers Rd.

Anne Rd.

Queen Anne Rd.

Old Queen Anne Rd.

Sam Ryders Rd.

Geo. Ryders Rd.

Main St.

Schoolhouse Pond

Goose Pond

Barn Hill Rd.

WEST CHATHAM

Harding Beach Rd.

Beach Rd.

Harding Beach

Ridgevale Rd.

Ridgevale Beach

Cockle Cove

Cockle Cove Rd.

SOUTH CHATHAM

Meetinghouse Rd.

Forest Beach Rd.

Nantucket Sound

Exit 11

HARWICH

137

39

28

6

28

28

2 MILES

N

Chatham

Although Chatham is less accessible from Route 6 and 28 than its neighbors, even the most hurried Cape visitors stop here. Occupying the tip of Cape Cod's elbow, the town offers a good mix of archetypal Cape Cod architecture, a classic Main Street, a refined sensibility, plenty of beaches and shops, and a rich seafaring history.

When Samuel de Champlain and his party tried to land at Stage Harbor in 1606, they were met with stalwart resistance from the native inhabitants. Fifty years later, though, Yarmouth's William Nickerson purchased a great deal of land from Chief Mattaquason. By 1712 the permanent "settlers" had incorporated the town.

Among Cape towns, Chatham is known for its calm, genteel, independent spirit. The town's vigilant zoning commission has kept tourist-trap activity to a minimum. Bordered on three sides by water, the town is populated by descendants of its oceangoing founders, many of whom continue in their ancestors' footsteps. Despite the difficulty in navigating the surrounding waters, Chatham sustains an active fleet of fishermen and leisure-time sailors. Sailors, fishermen, shop owners, and an increasing number of retirees live quietly in this delightfully traditional village.

Chatham, along with the spectacularly desolate Monomoy National Wildlife Refuge, boasts 65 miles of shoreline. Chatham's beaches are varied: Some are hit by pounding surf, others are sheltered by inlets; some are good for shell collecting, others are wide and sandy. A walk along the shore reveals long sandbars and beautiful seafront homes. Inland, a drive or bicycle ride takes you past elegant shingled cottages and stately white houses surrounded by picket fences, with primroses and tidy lawns.

In the center of Chatham, Main Street is chock-full of upscale and somewhat conservative shops, offering everything from tony antiques and nautically inspired gifts to jewelry, clothing, and culinary supplies. This central part of town has excellent restaurants and inns, and some of the Cape's finest bow-shaped roof houses (so named because they're shaped like the bow of a ship turned upside down). North Chatham, primarily residential, is dotted with several picturesque inlets. West and South Chatham border the beaches; you'll find lots of rental houses, summer cottages, and piney woods here.

GUIDANCE

Information booth (945-5199, 1-800-715-5567 for recorded information year-round), 533 Main Street, PO Box 793, Chatham 02633. Open 10–6 Monday through Saturday and noon–6 Sunday, late May to mid-October. The map-lined walls come in handy when you're planning an itinerary or looking for a specific place—as does the walking guide of Chatham's sites.

There is also an information booth at the intersection of Routes 137 and 28 in South Chatham.

PUBLIC REST ROOMS

Public rest rooms are located behind the town offices on Main Street and at **Kate Gould Park.**

GETTING THERE

By car: Take Route 6 east to exit 11 (Route 137 south) to Route 28 south. The center of Chatham is 3 miles from this intersection, about 45 minutes from either bridge.

By bus: There is no bus service to Chatham; you'll have to catch the **Plymouth & Brockton** bus line (775-5524) in Orleans or Barnstable.

GETTING AROUND

In July and August, Chatham is crowded, and you'll be happiest exploring Main Street on foot. It's about a 10-minute walk from mid–Main Street to the lighthouse and another 15 minutes from the light to the pier (one way). There is free parking at Town Hall (off Main Street), the Colonial Building (off Stage Harbor Road), one block west of the rotary at the elementary school, and on Chatham Bars Avenue behind the Impudent Oyster (see *Dining Out*) off Main Street.

MEDICAL EMERGENCY

Call **911.**

TO SEE

❋ **Chatham Light,** Main Street between Bridge Street and Shore Road. Built in 1828 and rebuilt in 1876, the lighthouse's beacon is visible 15 miles out to sea. The US Coast Guard–operated lighthouse is open to visitors only during Cape Heritage Week in mid-May.

❋ **Chatham Break.** Coin-operated telescopes—across from the lighthouse—allow visitors to take a closer look at the famous Chatham Break, the result of a ferocious nor'easter on January 2, 1987. Low dunes were flattened, tidal waters rose, and eventually waves and high winds forced a channel through the barrier beach (the lower portion of Nauset Beach) that had previously protected Chatham Harbor from the open ocean. Boating around the harbor's strong currents is now more difficult than ever. In a matter of hours rather than over the natural course of 50 years, the break also created circumstances that destroyed prime pieces of waterfront realty. Ocean currents have a mind of their own; in 1846 a previous break in South Beach repaired itself. Chatham Light Beach is directly below the lookout area; South and North Beaches are visible to the south.

✳ **Fish Pier,** at the corner of Shore Road and Bar Cliff Avenue. Chatham's fleet of fishing boats returns—from as far away as 100 miles—to the pier at about 2. From the pier's second-floor observation deck you can watch fishermen unloading their catch of haddock, lobster, cod, halibut, flounder, and pollock. While you're at the pier, stop at the **Fisherman's Monument.** A 1992 call for entries attracted nearly 100 applicants from around the world, but the committee chose Sig Purwin, a Woods Hole sculptor, to memorialize the town's fishermen.

In recent years, as fish stocks have begun to dwindle, fishermen have increasingly turned to shellfish harvesting. (Bay scallops harvested in the late fall are like nothing you've ever tasted.) In fact, more commercial licenses are purchased yearly in Chatham (about 500) than anywhere else on the Cape. And while Chatham has particularly rich, natural beds, many are turning to organized aquaculture farming. The harvest goes on amid a contentious debate over the regulation of this new industry.

✐ **Railroad Museum** (945-0342), 153 Depot Road. Open 10–4 Tuesday through Saturday, mid-June to mid-September. This carefully restored 1887 depot—on the National Register of Historic Places—is chock-full of Victorian details, from a turret to gingerbread trim. Inside you'll find treasures such as a 1910 New York Central train caboose and photos, models, and equipment pertaining to the Cape's railroad history. Free.

Old Atwood House (945-2493), 347 Stage Harbor Road. Open 1–4 Tuesday through Friday, mid-June through September. The gambrel-roofed Atwood house, built by a sea captain in 1752, has been maintained by the Chatham Historical Society since 1926. (Note the low doorways and how much we've grown by eating our vegetables over the last two centuries!) The museum houses antique dolls, tools, toys, portraits of sea captains, seashells from around the world, Sandwich glass, and other Chatham seafaring artifacts. The adjoining train barn features a three-panel mural by Alice Wright that depicts more than 130 townspeople with a "modern Christ." Adults $3, children 12–18 $1.

Mayo House (945-4084), 540 Main Street. Open 11–4 Tuesday through Thursday, June through September. Built in 1818 by Josiah Mayo (who served for 40 years as Chatham's first postmaster) and filled with period antiques, the Mayo House is the headquarters of the Chatham Conservation Foundation. The tiny, yellow three-quarter Cape isn't the "best this" or the "oldest that"; it's just a nice little old house. Donations.

SCENIC DRIVES

Chatham has a number of beautiful roads. Old Queen Anne Road is lovely; it starts on Route 137 and ends on the rotary at Route 28 and Main Street. Route 28 toward Orleans is quite scenic, with views of Pleasant Bay to the east. Shore Road passes handsome cedar-shingled houses.

The causeway to Morris Island affords harbor views as well as views of the open ocean beyond tall grasses and sandy shores.

TO DO

AIRPLANE RIDES

☞ **Cape Cod Flying Circus** (945-9000, 945-2363), Chatham Municipal Airport, George Ryder Road. Open year-round; reserve 1 day in advance in summer. To really appreciate Chatham's shoreline and the fragility of the Outer Cape landscape, head 900 feet above it in a three-seater Cessna. These wonderful sight-seeing rides are a bargain (20 minutes, $50). Most of Jim and Michelle McDevitt's customers, though, opt for a ride in Jim's two-seater biplane (one of five he's built). The 20-minute trip includes acrobatics, loops, and rolls ($85). Prices are per ride, not per person.

BICYCLING/RENTALS

With gentle inclines and quiet lanes that are easily accessible from any street in town, Chatham is a nice place for bicycling. **Monomoy Sail & Cycle** (945-0811), 275 Route 28, and **Bert & Carol's Lawnmower and Bicycle Shop** (945-0137), 347 Route 28, both in North Chatham, offer rentals. Bert & Carol's makes personalized routes and recommendations based on your level and needs, and carries a full line of accessories like roof racks, baby seats, and trail-a-bikes. Open from April through December, with parking on premises.

See also Bikes & Blades under *In-Line Skating*.

BOAT EXCURSIONS/RENTALS

Water Taxi (430-2346, 246-1325 cellular), Art Gould's Boat Livery, at the Fish Pier. John McGrath's grandfather started this business in 1944, and he'll take you anywhere you want to go: Monomoy Island, North Beach ($10 per adult, $2–6 per child, round-trip), South Beach, or another destination of your choice. He also offers harbor tours, sunset tours, fishing charters, and seal-sighting tours.

Chatham Harbor Tours (255-0619), at the Fish Pier. Mid-June through September. In addition to prearranged charters, Captain Bill Amaru offers a 90-minute narrated tour of North Beach, Pleasant Bay, and the Chatham Break four times a day during summer. Adults $15, children over 5 $10.

Outermost Harbor Marine (945-2030), Seagull Road, off Morris Island Road. Late June to mid-September. This outfit offers seal cruises and shuttles to South Beach between 10 AM and 4:30 PM. Adults $9, children under 12 $4.50. As for the seal trips, these hour-long excursions are by appointment only; minimum cost $60. Otherwise, $15 adults, $7.50 children under 12.

Monomoy Island Ferry (587-4540, 945-5450), Wikis Way, off Morris Island Road. Boats daily late June to early September, weekends in spring and fall; make reservations the night before. Park on the causeway.

From Chatham's fish pier

Launches run to Monomoy, South Beach, North Beach. Inquire about fly-fishing, bird-watching, surf-casting, and seal trips.

Cape Water Sports, at the Wequassett Inn (432-5400, ext. 530), Route 28, and at Ridgevale Beach (432-4339), Ridgevale Road. You can rent sailboats, Hobies, windsurfers, and Sunfish from the beachfront Wequassett Inn location (see *Lodging—Resorts*) from mid-April through October. It also gives lessons. Call for reservations. Ridgevale Beach has a more limited season.

Boats can be rented at **Oyster River Boatyard** (945-0736), Barn Hill Lane extension, off Route 28, West Chatham, and **Monomoy Sail & Cycle** (945-8011), 275 Route 28, North Chatham.

FISHING/SHELLFISHING

See the town clerk (945-5101) at 549 Main Street for a fishing license. Shellfishing licenses are required; contact the Town Hall Annex (945-5180) on George Ryder Road in West Chatham.

The Fishin' Bridge. Follow Stage Harbor Road to Bridge Street, where Mill Pond empties into Stage Harbor. You'll probably haul in several crabs, small flounders, eels, and perhaps even a bluefish. Locals will certainly be there with long rakes, harvesting shellfish.

North Beach is a good choice for surf casting for striped bass.

Schoolhouse Pond off Schoolhouse Road and **Goose Pond** off Fisherman's Landing offer freshwater fishing for rainbow trout.

For sportfishing charters, you have a few choices: try **Booby Hatch Sport Fishing** (430-2312), Captain Ron McVickar's *Banshee* (945-0403), and Captain Jim Mellors's *Tiger Too* (945-9215); all are out of Stage Harbor in West Chatham.

Captain John Wesley Randall (432-4630) leads guided charter fly-fishing trips. Call for reservations.

For more charters, see Water Taxi under *Boat Excursions*.

FOR FAMILIES

Play-a-Round Playground, on Depot Road behind Chatham Elementary School. This wonderful, multilevel, wooden structure includes an area for disabled children and a fenced-off area for toddlers.

GOLF

Chatham Seaside Links (945-4774), 209 Seaview Street, next to the Chatham Bars Inn (see *Lodging—Resorts*). Open late March to mid-November. A nine-hole, par-34 course.

IN-LINE SKATING

Bikes & Blades (945-7600), 195 Crowell Road. Rentals of just what the name implies: bicycles and in-line skates. Bikes are $12–15 daily; skates $20–23. Half-day, 3-day, and weekly rates, too.

SEAL CRUISES

About 500 gray seals summer off the shores of Chatham. For information on getting out to them, see *Boat Excursions:* Water Taxi, Monomoy Island Ferry, and Outermost Harbor Marine.

SPECIAL PROGRAMS

Creative Arts Center (945-3583), 154 Crowell Road. The center offers year-round classes in pottery, sculpture, photography, painting, metal-smithing, and other fine arts. Work is shown at the **Edward A. Bigelow Gallery.** Since 1971, the center has held an annual art festival in August, where you may meet the artists and purchase their works.

Baseball clinics (945-5109) are sponsored by the Chatham A's during July and August. There are weekly sessions for 6–8-year-olds, 9–12-year-olds, and 13–17-year-olds. Register on Monday mornings; $50-80 weekly.

TENNIS

Public courts are located on **Depot Road** by the Railroad Museum (see *To See*) and at **Chatham High School** on Crowell Road.

Chatham Bars Inn (945-0096), Shore Road. Mid-May to mid-October. Four all-weather, waterfront courts are rented to nonguests for $15 an hour. Lessons are $50 per hour.

WINDSURFING

Monomoy Sail & Cycle (945-0811), 275 Route 28, North Chatham, rents sailboards. Pleasant Bay enjoys easterly and northeasterly winds, while Forest Beach receives southwesterly winds.

GREEN SPACE

Monomoy National Wildlife Refuge. North and South Monomoy Islands, acquired by the federal government as a wildlife refuge in 1944, comprise a 2700-acre habitat for more than 285 species of birds. Birds and seaside animals rule the roost; there are no human residents, no paved roads, no vehicles, and no electricity. (Long ago the island did support a fishing community.) The lovely old lighthouse, built in 1823 and not used since 1923, was restored in 1988. It's a quiet, solitary place. Beaches are closed from April to mid-August to protect threatened nesting areas for piping plovers and terns. Monomoy, one of four remaining "wilderness" areas between Maine and New Jersey, is an important stop for shorebirds on the Atlantic Flyway—between breeding grounds in the Arctic and wintering grounds in South America. Conditions there may well determine whether the birds will survive the journey.

In the spring of 1996, the US Fish and Wildlife Service embarked on an unpopular course of action at Monomoy. In an effort to increase habitat for endangered piping plovers and roseate terns, the Fish and Wildlife Service poisoned thousands of seagulls that had "taken over" the island. It is their contention that once the gulls are gone, the plovers and terns will move in, many of them from mainland beaches. Protesters argued that the Fish and Wildlife Service took this action under pressure from off-road-vehicle drivers who were often banned from driving on mainland beaches because of nesting endangered birds.

Monomoy was attached to the mainland until a 1958 storm severed the connection; a storm in 1978 divided the island in two. The islands are only accessible by boat (see *To Do—Boat Excursions*), and only under favorable weather conditions. Guided tours are available from the Cape Cod Museum of Natural History (896-3867 for reservations), Route 6A, Brewster, and the Wellfleet Bay Wildlife Sanctuary (349-2615 for reservations). Groups of six or more must obtain a permit from the refuge headquarters on Morris Island (945-0594). The 40-acre, uninhabited Morris Island is accessible by car and foot: Take your first left beyond the Chatham Light, on Main Street between Bridge Street and Shore Road; then take your first right and follow Morris Island Road.

BEACHES

Weekly beach stickers for cottage renters are purchased at Hardings, Ridgevale, and Cockle Cove Beaches. Parking for day visitors is $7.

Hardings Beach, on Nantucket Sound. From Route 28, take Barn Hill Road to Hardings Beach Road. Small dunes. Rest rooms, lifeguard, and concession stand.

Ridgevale Beach, on Nantucket Sound. Take Ridgevale Road off Route 28. Rest rooms, lifeguard, and snack bar.

Cockle Cove Beach, protected from Nantucket Sound by Ridgevale Beach. Take Cockle Cove Road off Route 28. Gentle waves and soft sand make Cockle Cove a good choice for families with small children. Picturesque waterways and inlets line the way to the beach. Lifeguard.

North Beach, on the Atlantic Ocean. North Beach, which is actually the southern end of Nauset Beach, is only accessible by boat (see *To Do— Boat Excursions/Rentals* for water-taxi services).

South Beach, on the Atlantic Ocean. There is no parking, but you can bicycle or walk to the lane off Morris Island Road just beyond the lighthouse; a sign points the way to South Beach. The most desolate part of the beach requires quite a long walk, but the early sections are nice, too. Many ferries (see *To Do—Boat Excursions/Rentals*) take passengers to the farthest, most remote reaches of the beach. One of the best aspects of this beach is that you've got surf on the east side and calm bay waters on the west.

Chatham Light Beach, below the parking area for Chatham Break and Light. A nice place to walk.

PONDS

Oyster Pond Beach, off Stage Harbor Road, near the rotary. This inland saltwater pond is connected to Nantucket Sound by way of Oyster Creek and Stage Harbor. Good for families, its shores are calm and its waters are the warmest in town. Free parking; lifeguard.

Schoolhouse Pond, off Schoolhouse Road via Sam Ryders Road. Free parking; rest rooms.

WALKS

Conservation Foundation. More than 500 acres in Chatham have been donated by private citizens to the Conservation Foundation. Walking trails in four distinct areas have been developed; contact the town information booth on Main Street (see *Guidance*) for directions. Trails traverse marshes, wetlands, and meadows.

The Dog Runs, as it's known locally. Walk 10 minutes along Bridge Street from the lighthouse to find the entrance to this forested coastal trail that runs along Stage Harbor. Take a picnic along, to be enjoyed in the cattail marshes.

See also Monomoy National Wildlife Refuge.

LODGING

Many inns and bed & breakfasts require a 2-night minimum stay July 4 through Labor Day. Many of Chatham's most notable places are booked for July and August well before July 4. Chatham, by the way, is one of the most expensive places to stay on Cape Cod. Unless otherwise noted, all lodging is in Chatham 02633.

RESORTS

✎❋ **Chatham Bars Inn** (945-0096, 1-800-527-4884, e-mail: resrvb@chatham-barsinn.com), Shore Road. Open year-round. This quintessential, grand, historic seaside resort was built in 1914 as a hunting lodge. The grande dame's gracious elegance is rivaled by few places in New England. Scattered over 20 acres, the main inn and adjacent cottages have undergone extensive, multimillion-dollar renovations and now total 152 rooms. Grounds are lushly landscaped. Rooms and cottages, many with fireplaces, are comfortably decorated with wicker, hand-painted furniture, and understated florals. Some rooms have private balconies or decks with lovely ocean views. One and two-bedroom suites within lodge-style cottages share a living room and fireplace. The inn boasts a lot of extras: private beach, heated outdoor pool, four tennis courts, croquet, fitness room, nine-hole golf course, launch service across Pleasant Bay to the southern tip of Nauset Beach, and a full schedule of daytime activities and children's programs. In summer, legendary traditions include theme dinners every night in-season and a Sunday Grand Buffet. In addition, a lavish buffet is laid out every morning. The hotel also boasts an expansive veranda, comfortable living rooms, and renowned dining rooms (see *Dining Out* and *Eating Out*). It's a 10-minute walk from town. Early April to mid-June $110–355; mid-June to late September $170–480; November and December $80–265. Inquire about off-season packages and special event weekends.

Wequassett Inn (432-5400, 1-800-225-7125), Orleans Road. Open May through October. A 10-minute drive north of Chatham on picturesque Pleasant Bay, the Wequassett is a first-class resort. The complex consists of 18 buildings set on 23 beautifully landscaped acres, a fine restaurant (see *Dining Out*), four tennis courts, sailing, and a 68-foot outdoor pool bordered by a strip of private beach on Pleasant Cove. (There isn't a more perfectly situated pool on the Cape.) The inn is renowned for its attentive staff, knowledgeable concierge, and exceptional level of service. As for the rooms, most cottages have cathedral ceilings and their own decks, though not all have views of boat-studded Round Cove. Triple sheeting, morning delivery of the newspaper, and turn-down service are standard. The Early American–style and country-pine furnishings are lovely. Other resort amenities include a tennis shop, fitness center, complimentary transport to nearby golf courses, boat rentals, and baby-sitting. The inn also ferries guests across the bay to an uncrowded section of the Cape Cod National Seashore. Light lunches, snacks, and cocktails are served poolside. Late June to early September $230–270 for a non-water-view room, $330–340 for a water view, $480 for a suite; off-season 10–25 percent less.

INN

❋ **Chatham Wayside Inn** (945-5550), 512 Main Street. Open year-round. Welcoming visitors since 1860, this historic hostelry was expertly renovated from top to bottom in 1994. The inn's dignified presence on Main Street is fitting. The 56 guest rooms are furnished with flair and a decorator's sure touch. Triple sheeting, thick towels, and top-notch bathroom amenities are standard. Each room has a canopied or four-poster bed, private bath, air-conditioning, TV, and reproduction period furniture. Some rooms have a fireplace, whirlpool tub, or a private patio or balcony. Views are of the town green, golf course, or parking lot. Summer and winter, cocktails are served fireside in the pub and dining room (see *Dining Out*). Outdoor swimming pool and tennis courts. Late June to early September $145–310; otherwise $90–275.

BED & BREAKFASTS

❊ **Captain's House Inn of Chatham** (945-0127, 1-800-315-0728), 369–377 Old Harbor Road. Open year-round. On 2 acres of tended lawns are a traditional and elegant Greek Revival inn, a cottage, and a carriage house. Jan and Dave McMaster, innkeepers since 1993, preside over a British staff and 16 handsome rooms and suites, all with private baths and antique furnishings. Rooms vary considerably, but none will disappoint you; ask for a description when making a reservation. Late in the afternoon, after you've played croquet on the lawn, enjoy tea and scones at the inn. $130–250 May weekends through October, $112–165 November through May weekdays, full breakfast included.

❊ **Cyrus Kent House** (945-9104, 1-800-338-5368), 63 Cross Street. Open year-round. This exquisitely restored 19th-century sea captain's home is set back from the road and just a few minutes' walk from the bustle of Main Street. Innkeeper Sharon Swan regularly fills her 10 antiques-filled rooms with return visitors who appreciate fine Victorian architecture and furnishings. If you like a bit more privacy than B&Bs often afford, try the adjacent carriage house. Room 8, with a cathedral ceiling, large Palladian window, sleep sofa, fireplace, and canopy bed, is particularly desirable. In the main house, I like room 6 with a private entrance and deck. The quiet backyard is for all to share. Late June to early September $125–165; $95–145 late May to late June and early September to mid-October; $75–115 the rest of the year; includes continental breakfast.

☞ **The Moorings** (945-0848), 326 Main Street. Open April through December. Completely renovated in 1996 by Roberta and Frank Schultz, this centrally located B&B has five rooms in the main house, all with new, private baths. They're all lovely, but the yellow room is the best and brightest. The large and comfortable living room is equally soothing, with high wainscoting and Oriental carpets. Breakfast is served in the cheery, bright dining room. The Schultzes also have one-, two-, and three-bedroom efficiency units and motel rooms behind the main house. At press time they hadn't been upgraded yet, but you may wish to ask about them. The hideaway cottage is charming and completely renovated. Mid-June to early September $120–145 for rooms, $210 for suite, $155–225 for efficiencies, $120 for motel rooms. Cottage $1250 weekly.

Bow Roof House (945-1346), 59 Queen Anne Road. Open year-round. A 5-minute walk from town, Vera Mazulis's late-18th-century B&B is a real find. After seeing so many fancied-up inns, decorated with designer this and that, the Bow Roof House is a breath of fresh air. It feels authentic. Of the six guest rooms (all with private bath), I prefer the ones on the first floor. Room 1 features an old beehive oven, antiques, and two double beds. The comfy living room, with woodstove, leads to a deck. A continental breakfast is served at one table in the plant-filled dining room. Vera has owned this B&B since 1975 and allows children. May through October $65–70, off-season $60–65.

❀ **Carriage House Inn** (945-4688, 1-800-355-8868), 407 Old Harbor Road. Open year-round. Innkeepers Pam and Tom Patton run a friendly B&B on the edge of town. Of the six guest rooms, my favorites are the more private ones in the adjacent Carriage House. Each has a peaked ceiling, private deck, and fireplace. On my last visit the full breakfast buffet included a strawberry frappe and thick French toast topped with poached pears. $135-165 late June to early September, $95-145 in the spring and fall, $75-120 from November through April.

Rosewood Bed & Breakfast (945-5432), 188 Vineyard Avenue. Open year-round. Dex Smith's homey B&B is delightfully off the beaten path: 1 mile from the center of town, 1 mile from Harding Beach, and steps from Oyster Pond. Of the two rooms upstairs, one is much larger; both have private bath. Since there's no real common space (the living room is Dex's), he'll set out afternoon cheese and crackers in your room if he knows when you're coming back. Mid-May to mid-October $89, off-season $65, including expanded continental breakfast.

COTTAGES

J.B. Horne Cottages (945-0734, 1-803-837-7477 in winter), off Morris Island Road. Open mid-May to mid-October. These eight housekeeping cottages—nicely kept, weathered to a deep, silvery gray—are on the largest (and perhaps nicest) private beach in Chatham. Cottages range in size from a two-bedroom to a four-bed, two-bath house. Thankfully they are set apart from the summertime congestion in town. The owners of the cottages, the Hornes, belong to one of Chatham's oldest families. Call February 1 to get your pick of the litter. In-season $900–1800 weekly for as many as the cottage can comfortably handle; off-season $550 weekly for two (each additional person $25–40).

Metter's Cottages (432-3535), Cockle Cove Road, West Chatham 02669. Open late April through October. These four completely remodeled waterfront or waterview cottages are more like homes than cottages. Talk with George and Donna Metter about your needs when reserving; there's probably a cottage with your name on it. July to early September $875–975 weekly for a water-view three-bedroom, $1850 for a waterfront four-bedroom; off-season $550 and $1250, respectively. Reservations are taken after January 1 for the upcoming summer.

See also The Moorings under *Bed & Breakfasts*.

EFFICIENCIES AND MOTELS

Chatham Tides Waterfront Motel (432-0379), 394 Pleasant Street, South Chatham 02659. Open mid-May to mid-October. This beachfront complex is a delightful find: It's been in Elaine and Ed Handel's family since 1966 and is still maintained with impressive care. Children must be over 8. Rooms: $125–140 daily, $800–900 weekly. Townhouses and suites: $160–230 daily, $1050–1500 weekly.

❀ **The Dolphin of Chatham** (945-0070, 1-800-688-5900), 352 Main Street. Open year-round. Situated between the center of town and Shore Road and beaches, this neatly landscaped complex includes seven rather small but cheery inn rooms (dating to 1805) and 28 motel rooms behind the inn. Motel rooms, good for families, surround the heated pool and Jacuzzi. Cottages with kitchenettes are also available (call for rates). Late June to early September $129–194; $74–124 the rest of the year.

Hawthorne Motel (945-0372), 196 Shore Road. Open mid-May to mid-October. About a 10-minute walk to Chatham's main shopping district, this motel is popular because nothing stands between it and Pleasant Bay except green grass and a path down to the motel's private beach. The 16 rooms are 1960s-style, and the 10 efficiencies are "summer campish," but who cares—you're coming for the easy access to sunning, swimming, and lazing on the beach. There are four much larger corner rooms. Mid-June to mid-September $130 for a room with a view ($110 without); $225 for a two-bedroom cottage; $120 for an efficiency. See also The Moorings under *Bed & Breakfasts.*

RENTALS

Sylvan Realty (432-2344), 2469 Route 28, South Chatham, has listings ranging from basic beach cottages to luxury homes.

WHERE TO EAT

Dining in Chatham runs the gamut from elegant to child-friendly places. Reserve ahead on summer weekends or be prepared for a lengthy wait.

DINING OUT

Chatham Bars Inn (945-0096, 1-800-527-4884), Shore Road. Open for breakfast year-round, dinner late May to mid-November. The formal main dining room is a treat from start to finish, especially with its panoramic ocean views and romantic candlelit ambience. Chef Al Hynes creates early New England cuisine at its finest. Save room for a sweet treat at the end—this is the place to indulge in desserts you might normally forgo. Children's menu. Breakfast buffet $12 adults, $8 children, dinner entrées $17–28. Jacket and tie requested at dinner and reservations highly recommended.

Wequassett Inn's Eben Ryder House (432-5400), Orleans Road (Route 28). Open for lunch and dinner, mid-April to mid-November. Executive chef Frank McMullen has designed award-winning regional American menus, and you are served in an understated, elegant dining room. Specialties include lobster-clam enchiladas, duck and mushroom strudel, crab bisque, grilled duckling, escargots, and rich chocolate truffle cake. A jazz piano duo plays nightly in July and August. Reservations recommended. Entrées $19–22 ($32 for the grilled lobster).

✻ **Christian's** (945-3362), 443 Main Street. Open for dinner nightly, mid-May to mid-October and on weekends in winter. Creative Continental and American dishes featuring seafood from near and far. Recent menu highlights include "sea of love," sautéed shrimp, scallops, and lobster with artichoke hearts, mushrooms, and sun-dried tomatoes over penne pasta. The filet mignon and roast duck are always popular. The quiet, bistrolike atmosphere is comfortable, as is the terrace. (See also Upstairs at Christian's under *Eating Out*.) Reservations highly recommended. Entrées $8–26.

❈ **Impudent Oyster** (945-3545), 15 Chatham Bars Avenue. Open for lunch and dinner nightly year-round. Bring several friends along to this lively establishment with an extensive menu. By passing your plates around the table, you'll be able to eat your way around the world, sampling internationally inspired fish and shellfish specialties. Grilled veal piccata is one of the more popular choices. A cathedral ceiling with exposed beams, skylights, and hanging plants create a pleasant atmosphere. Children's menu. Reservations recommended. Lunch $6–11; dinner entrées $14–22.

❈ **Chatham Wayside Inn** (945-5550), 512 Main Street. Open for all three meals year-round; closed Mondays mid-October through March. The simple but lovely dining rooms, with shiny wooden tables and Windsor chairs, are hopping with visitors in summer. Locals return en masse after Labor Day and keep the place busy through winter. Salads and sandwiches dominate the lunch menu, while dinner is more ambitious: sautéed scallops with tomatoes and zucchini in an herbed crème fraîche served over pasta. Vegetarians will appreciate the risotto, and meat lovers have a choice of rack of lamb or filet mignon. Streetside dining under an awning is popular in-season. Lunch $5–12; dinner entrées $13–22.

❈ **Campari's** (945-9123), 352 Main Street, at the Dolphin of Chatham. Open for dinner daily, June to early September, and Wednesday through Sunday the rest of the year. Bob and Lisa Chiappetta have leased this homey space from the Dolphin motel since 1990. The small restaurant revolves around an open, homestyle kitchen and two-sided hearth. It feels like something you'd find in a tiny Tuscan town. The limited dinner menu features Italian-inspired seafood and vegetable dishes like shrimp scampi on capellini pasta and eggplant stuffed with ricotta and spinach. The wine list is short yet comprehensive. Campari's has such a good reputation that even on a Saturday in winter, you need to make reservations. Reservations suggested. Entrées $17–23.

Vining's Bistro (945-5033), 595 Main Street. Open for dinner April to early January (often closed Sunday and Monday in the off-season). On the second floor within the Gallery, the bistro, with high ceilings and exposed beams, serves a wide variety of dishes: spit-roasted pork, seafood stir fry over angelhair pasta, and a North African vegetable curry. The warm lobster taco is gaining renown. This is one of the more adventurous restaurants in town, thanks to the vision of owners Lynda and Steve Vining. Entrées $13–18.

EATING OUT

☞❈ **Chatham Squire** (945-0945 for the restaurant, 945-0942 for the tavern), 487 Main Street. Open for lunch and dinner daily year-round. Chatham's best family restaurant offers something for everyone—from burgers and moderately priced daily specials to a raw bar and excellent chowder. Plaid carpeting, low booths, captain's chairs at wooden tables, exposed beams, and pool tables add to the family-den feel of the place. Drop in for a drink in the busy and colorful tavern (a haven for twenty-somethings in summer until locals take it back off-season). Children's menu. Lunch $4.50–9.50, dinner entrées twice that.

❊ **Upstairs at Christian's** (945-3362), 443 Main Street. Open for lunch and dinner year-round. Upstairs is more boisterous and casual than downstairs at Christian's (see *Dining Out*). You still get the same menu, but you can also choose burgers or pizza. Old-time favorites include chicken and biscuits, meat loaf with mushroom gravy, and mashed potatoes. Dine in the traditional pub-style room with mahogany paneling or outside on the trellised deck. Don't be surprised by spontaneous piano sing-alongs in summer and on weekends in winter. Entrées $8–18.

Beach House Grill (945-0096, 1-800-527-4884), Shore Road. Open for breakfast and lunch, mid-June to early September. Across the street from its parent Chatham Bars Inn (see *Dining Out*), this is the only place in Chatham where you can eat oceanside. Dine alfresco on a deck anchored in the sand or, on windy days, in a dining room enclosed by wall-to-wall sliding glass doors. A stylish crowd orders from a limited menu of upscale seaside standards: burgers, summer salads, lobster rolls, and baby back ribs. The continental breakfast buffet features an omelet station. Dishes $7–15.

❊ **North Beach Tavern** (945-0096), Shore Road, at the Chatham Bars Inn. Open for lunch and dinner, daily year-round. The menu and atmosphere of the tavern is casual. Lunch $5–15, dinner entrées $8–18.

Samuel's Place (945-4959), 14 Chatham Bars Avenue. Open for lunch and dinner (various days), April through December. New in 1995, Samuel's fills a niche in Chatham—good food, reasonable prices, pleasant surroundings, and an in-town location. Fare is simple but good: pizza, calzones, grinders, and Italian specials like chicken Parmesan and linguine with clam sauce. $5.75–14 (more for pizzas large enough to feed a family).

☞✐❊ **Chatham Cookie Manor/Bob's Best Sandwiches** (945-1152), 499 Main Street. Open year-round for breakfast, lunch, and sweets. The most reasonable place to grab a bite in Chatham is also one of the best. Sandwiches are made with thick slices of homemade bread and thick slices of home-smoked turkey or roast beef. For breakfast, you have a choice of eggs or French toast; that's it. But what more could you want from this storefront eatery, except a few indoor and sidewalk tables (which they have). $4–5.50.

❊ **Carmine's** (945-5300), 595 Main Street. Open for lunch and dinner year-round. For quick and inexpensive eats, try Carmine's, which offers slices of pizza (and whole pies, for that matter).

Chatham Cookware (945-1550), 524 Main Street. Open year-round, ostensibly. Although this is primarily a kitchenware shop, in the rear of the store is served a different sandwich and soup selection every day. They're always good. Best of all, there are cheery indoor tables and a hidden outdoor deck.

✎ **Sea in the Rough** (956-1700), 1077 Route 28. Open for lunch and dinner April through October. Families appreciate the simple seafood and pasta dishes as well as the casual atmosphere and airy dining rooms. Children's menu. Dishes $4–14.

Pampered Palate (945-3663), 1287 Main Street, Cornfield Market Place. Open daily, year-round. A couple of miles west of town, this specialty food shop is a great source for picnic fixings, including a tempting array of sandwiches, cold salads, seafood entrées, soups, pâtés, and pastas.

Cafe CQX (945-9464) at Chatham Municipal Airport, George Ryder Road. Open for breakfast and lunch daily, late May to early September. You don't have to charter an airplane to eat here. But you'll enjoy sitting outside watching the planes take off at this tiny airstrip. If the quirky indoor decor doesn't hold your attention, the tasty omelets, eggs, and waffles will. Salads and sandwiches for lunch.

Marion's Pie Shop (432-9439), 2022 Main Street (Route 28). Open year-round. Savory pies from Marion's are a delicious alternative to prepared sandwiches or salads. You can't go wrong with the chicken pot pies or the breakfast baked goods.

See also Concerts (lobster suppers) under *Entertainment*.

DRINKS

Chatham Bars Inn (945-0096), Shore Road). Before you leave town, head up to the grand hotel for a late-afternoon drink on the front terrace. It overlooks the ocean, and the setting can't be beat.

FISH MARKET

Chatham Fish & Lobster Company (945-1178), Route 28, Cornfield Market Place). Open year-round. For all you with cooking facilities: They hook 'em, you cook 'em.

ENTERTAINMENT

Monomoy Theatre (945-1589), 776 Main Street. Performances from late June to late August. Operated by Ohio University, the Monomoy is among the Cape's better-known and oldest (1930) playhouses. A new production—anything from a Rodgers and Hammerstein musical to Shakespeare—is staged every week. There isn't a bad choice among the 255 seats. Evening curtain at 8:30, matinees at 2.

☞✎ **Band concerts** at Kate Gould Park (945-0342). Every Friday night at 8, early July to early September, this brass band concert is the place to be. As many as 6000 lighthearted visitors enjoy music and people-watching as they have for the past 60 years. Dance and swing to Sousa marches, big-band selections, and other standards. The bandstand, balloons tied to strollers, bags of popcorn, blankets on the grass, and the "Star-Spangled Banner" that closes the program—it hasn't changed a "whit" since it began. (Except that beloved Whit Tileston, who led the band for almost 50 years, passed away in 1995.)

Concerts, First United Methodist Church (945-0474), 16 Cross Street. On Sunday summer evenings at 8, the church sponsors free concerts: choral, jazz, big band, light classical, a cappella. Since the mid-1960s the church has held popular lobster-roll suppers at 5 PM before the band concerts in Kate Gould Park. Adults $8, children $3.50.

Baseball, Veterans Field. The Chatham Athletics (the A's), one of 10 teams in the Cape Cod Baseball League, usually play ball at 7 PM; the information booth has schedules.

SELECTIVE SHOPPING

ANTIQUES

Ivy Cottage Shop (945-1809), 416 Main Street. Open mid-March through December and on winter weekends. This shop carries English country pine and European antiques, as well as quality reproductions. This historic house, by the way, was a former Town Hall Annex; in the 1970s it was transported right down Main Street to its present location.

Mildred Georges Antiques (945-1939), 447 Main Street. Open May through October. You'll find funky treasures here, from a dressmaker's dummy to an antique Oreo cookie tin. Mildred has been here since 1956.

Spyglass (945-9686), 618 Main Street. Open year-round. Although the store is best known for its telescope collection, there are all sorts of nautical antiques like barometers, sextants, maps, charts, and even a few paintings and sea captain portraits.

ART GALLERIES

Munson Gallery (945-2888), 880 Main Street. Open June to mid-October. Munson's has been in business since 1955 as one of *the* Cape galleries for paintings, photographs, and sculpture by area artists.

Falconer's (945-2867), 492 Main Street. Open year-round. Get your limited-edition lithographs of the Friday-night band concerts here. Original oils and other Cape lithos are also available.

Creative Arts Center. See *To Do—Special Programs*.

ARTISANS

Odell's Studio and Gallery (945-3239), 423 Main Street. Open daily except Sunday year-round, and evenings by chance in summer. Tom and Carol Odell, metalsmith and painter, respectively, have lived and worked in their lovely old home since 1975. They've turned it into a bright and airy gallery space. Carol does colorful nonobjective, multimedia paintings. They complement Tom's jewelry and sculpture, which he fashions from precious metals and alloys. Recent work has taken on Japanese overtones.

Chatham Pottery (430-2191), 2058 Route 28, South Chatham. Open daily May through January; call first in February and March. Gill Willson and Margaret Willson-Grey's large production shop offers a wide array of functional, decorative stoneware for everyday use—hand-thrown pots, pitchers, sinks, plates, bowls, tiles, and tables. They also carry a few other things to "accessorize" their pottery, including wrought iron, rugs, and handcrafted glass. You can see the workshop from the display area.

Chatham Glass Company (945-5547), 756 Main Street. Open daily except Sunday year-round. James Holmes and Deborah Doane design and create unique, colorful glass items—candlesticks, goblets, bud vases, and marbles—which are sold in Barneys, Neiman-Marcus, and Gump's. Glassblowing demonstrations are given.

BOOKSTORES

Cabbages and Kings (945-1603), 628 Main Street. New titles, paperbacks, and many children's books and toys in an airy, sunny, light-filled shop. Open year-round.

Yellow Umbrella Books (945-0144), 501 Main Street. Open year-round. A selection of Cape Cod titles and some used books, too.

SPECIAL SHOPS

Cape Cod Cooperage (432-0788), 1150 Old Queen Anne Road. Open year-round. Located in a rambling barn, this cooperage has made containers to hold fish and cranberries for shipment to Boston and New York since the late 1800s. It's the only remaining cooperage in the state, and coopers here still use the 100-year-old methods.

Artful Hand Gallery (945-4933), 459 Main Street. Open year-round. You'll find functional and contemporary accessories for the home in the great tradition of the American Arts and Crafts movement.

Yankee Ingenuity (945-1288), 525 Main Street. Open year-round. This eclectic assortment of "cool things" extends from art glass and jewelry to clocks and lamps. Prices run $2–1500.

Amazing Lace (945-4023), 726 Main Street. Open April through December. This collection of clothing, linens, lace collars and cuffs, estate jewelry, and accessories dates from the 1900s to the 1950s.

The Mayflower (945-0065), 475 Main Street. Open year-round. "Newspapers from Boston and New York," reads the painted sign on this venerable, old-time general store.

Regatta Shop (945-4999), 582 Main Street. Open mid-April through December. Seaside motifs and sailing-oriented gifts for your favorite sailor (or sailor wannabe). Prints of ships, lighthouses, and beach scenes; sterling pendants and charms; foul-weather gear; and colorful blankets to ward off chills aboard your yacht or sofa.

Photo Works (945-5353), 458 Main Street. Open year-round. Reliable 1-hour photo processing.

SPECIAL EVENTS

Early May: **Spring Fling** opens the summer season. Bake sales, a crazy-hat contest, jugglers and clowns, and a treasure hunt for children.

May: **Lighthouse Tour** of Chatham Light. During the Cape's Maritime Celebration, most lighthouses, including Chatham Light, are open.

July 4: **Independence Day Parade** from Main Street to Veterans Field.

Mid-August: **Chatham Festival of the Arts,** Chase Park. On the third weekend in August, the Creative Arts Center sponsors more than 100 exhibitors, from painters to quilters to sculptors (see *To Do—Special Programs*).

October: **Seafest,** an annual tribute to Chatham's maritime industry. There are exhibits and demonstrations on net mending, casting techniques, quahog raking, the proper way to eat a lobster, fishing skills, boating, filleting fish, and rigging.

December: **Christmas by the Sea.** Throughout the month, events include a tree-lighting ceremony and mulled cider served at the Mayo House, hayrides, open houses, and a dinner dance at the Chatham Bars Inn.

New Year's Eve: **First Night Celebration.** Fireworks over Oyster Pond.

Orleans

Many could argue, with some success, that Orleans's biggest draw is Nauset Beach, an Atlantic Ocean barrier beach more than 9 miles long. It can accommodate hundreds of sun-seekers and sandcastle-builders in summer. But in the off-season, you'll be practically alone, walking in quiet reflection, observing shorebirds and natural rhythms. It's a beautifully haunting place to walk during a storm—so long as it's not a huge storm. Nauset Beach also has historical significance. It was explored by Gosnold in 1602 and Champlain in 1605. It was the location of the first recorded shipwreck on the eastern seaboard, in 1626, when the *Sparrow Hawk* ran aground near Pochet. It is the only place in the continental United States to be fired upon in the War of 1812 (by the British) or World War I (in 1918 it was shelled by a German submarine). Most recently, two Englishmen set off from nearby Nauset Harbor to row successfully across the Atlantic Ocean.

The real charm of Orleans, which has few historical sights, lies not in the sand but in the waters that surround the town. A large number of fingerlike inlets creep into the eastern shoreline from aptly named Pleasant Bay, dotted with tiny islands. And most of these quiet inlets are accessible via back roads and town landings. Excursion boats explore the rich habitat of Nauset Marsh to the north, while bayside, Rock Harbor is home to the Cape's most active charter fishing fleet.

Because Routes 6, 6A, and 28 converge in Orleans, traffic is heavy in summer; getting anywhere takes time. But Orleans straddles the two distinct worlds of the Outer and Lower Cape. On the one hand, Orleans serves as a year-round commercial and retail center for the area. It offers plenty of activities and a variety of dining and lodging options. On the other hand, Orleans has its share of exclusive residential areas and plenty of quiet, waterside spots.

Orleans is the only Cape town without a Native American or English name. Incorporated in 1797 after separating from Eastham, Orleans was named for Louis-Philippe de Bourbon, duke of Orleans (and later king of France), who visited Orleans in 1797 during his exile.

GUIDANCE
Orleans Chamber of Commerce Information Booth (240-2484 booth, 255-1386 administration office), PO Box 153, Orleans 02653.

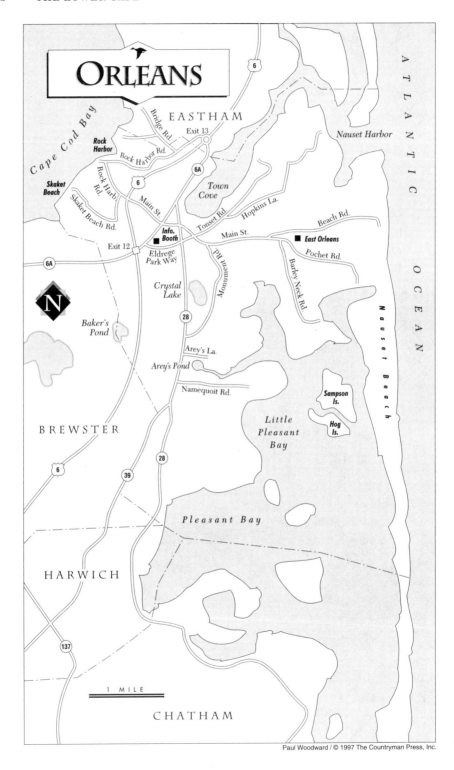

ORLEANS

EASTHAM

Cape Cod Bay

Bridge Rd.

Exit 13

Rock Harbor

Rock Harbor Rd.

6A

Nauset Harbor

Skaket Beach

Rock Harb. Rd.

6

Main St.

Town Cove

Skaket Beach Rd.

Info. Booth

Tonset Rd.

Hopkins La.

Beach Rd.

Main St.

East Orleans

Exit 12

6A

Eldrege Park Way

Monument Rd.

Pochet Rd.

Barley Neck Rd.

N

Crystal Lake

28

Baker's Pond

Arey's La.

Arey's Pond

Namequoit Rd.

Nauset Beach

Little Pleasant Bay

Sampson Is.

Hog Is.

BREWSTER

6

39

28

ATLANTIC OCEAN

Pleasant Bay

HARWICH

137

1 MILE

CHATHAM

Paul Woodward / © 1997 The Countryman Press, Inc.

Booth open 9–8 Monday through Saturday and 10–6 Sunday, late May
to mid-September; slightly shorter daily hours until mid-October; and
Friday through Sunday until Thanksgiving; administration open year-
round. The booth is on Eldredge Park Way (just off Route 6A), south of
the Orleans rotary. Like most Cape towns, Orleans publishes a helpful
townwide booklet (which you can pick up here), but the information
booth is also full of menus and lodging brochures.

PUBLIC REST ROOMS

Public rest rooms are located at the information booth, Town Hall Annex (also known as the Orleans Community Building) on Main Street,
and at Parrish Park.

GETTING THERE

By car: Take Route 6 east from either the Sagamore Bridge or the Bourne
Bridge for about 35 miles to exit 12. Route 6A east takes you directly
into town.

By bus: The **Plymouth & Brockton** bus line (775-5524) connects Orleans
with other Cape towns and with Boston's Logan Airport.

GETTING AROUND

East Orleans Village and Nauset Beach are 3 miles east of the center
of Orleans (which is located along Route 6A); Rock Harbor and Skaket
Beach are 1.5 miles west of the center. Parking isn't a problem in Orleans.

MEDICAL EMERGENCY

Orleans Medical Center (255-9577), Route 6A or exit 12 off Route 6,
Orleans. Walk-ins accepted.

TO SEE

Meeting House Museum (255-1386), at Main Street and River Road,
Orleans. Open 10–noon Tuesday and Wednesday, July through September. Built in 1833 as a Universalist meetinghouse, and now operated by the Orleans Historical Society, the museum contains artifacts
documenting Orleans's early history. Among the items are an assessor's
map of Orleans homes in 1858, photographs, Native American artifacts,
and a bicentennial quilt. The building is a fine example of Greek Revival Doric architecture. Free.

French Cable Station Museum (240-1735), Route 28 at Cove Road, Orleans. Open 2–4 Tuesday through Saturday in July and August only; by
special appointment otherwise. Before there was an "information su-
perhighway" and wireless communications, there was the French Cable
Station. Direct transmissions from Brest, France (via a 3000-mile underwater cable), were made from this station between 1890 and 1941,
when transmissions were automated. Among the relayed news items:
Charles Lindbergh's successful crossing of the Atlantic and landing in
Paris in 1927 and Germany's invasion of France. Much of the original
equipment and instruments is still set up and in working order. (Alas,

the cable is no longer operational.) The displays, put together with the help of the Smithsonian Institution, are a bit intimidating and confusing, but someone is on hand to unravel the mysteries. Free.

Jonathan Young Windmill, on Route 6A at Town Cove Park, Orleans; park at the old Orleans Inn. Open 11–4 daily in July and August. This circa-1720 gristmill was built in East Orleans, transported to the center of town in 1839, moved to Hyannisport in 1897, and returned to Orleans in 1983. Although it's no longer operational, the windmill is significant because of its intact milling machinery. Within the mill are interpretive exhibits, a display of a 19th-century miller's handiwork, and a resident miller—who explained the origins of "keep your nose to the grindstone": Since grain is highly combustible when it's ground, a miller who wasn't paying close attention to his grain might not live to see the end of the day. The setting, overlooking Town Cove, provides a nice backdrop for a picnic. Free.

Rock Harbor, on Cape Cod Bay, at the end of Rock Harbor Road from Main Street, Orleans. This protected harbor, the town's first commercial and maritime center, served as a packet landing for ships transporting goods to Plymouth, Boston, and Maine. When the harbor filled with silt, several old houses in the area were built from the lumber of dismantled saltworks. During the War of 1812, Orleans militiamen turned back Britain's H.M.S. *Newcastle* from Rock Harbor. In case you're wondering about the dead trees in the harbor entrance, they mark the channel that is dredged for the charter fishing fleet.

SCENIC DRIVES

Pleasant Bay, Little Pleasant Bay, Nauset Harbor, and Town Cove creep deep into the Orleans coastline at about a dozen named inlets, ponds, and coves. With the centerfold map from the Orleans Chamber of Commerce guide in hand, head down the side roads off Tonset Road, Hopkins Lane, Nauset Heights Road, and Barley Neck Road to the town landings. After passing beautifully landscaped residences, you'll be rewarded with serene, pastoral scenes of beach grass and sailboats. Directly off Route 28 heading toward Chatham there are two particularly lovely ponds with saltwater outlets: **Arey's Pond** (off Arey's Lane) and **Kescayo-Gansett Pond** (off Monument Road).

TO DO

BICYCLING/RENTALS

Cape Cod Rail Trail runs along the Old Colony Railway bed past Rock Harbor, on the other side of town from Nauset Beach. **Orleans Cycle** (255-9115), 26 Main Street, and **Goose Hummock Outdoor Center** (255-2620), off Route 6A on Town Cove, rent bicycles; both are open year-round. Expect to spend $10 per day for a BMX bike, $17 per day for a high-performance ATB Cross, $10 for a children's bike.

BOAT EXCURSIONS/RENTALS

Nauset Explorer (896-3867, 1-800-479-3867), behind the old Orleans Inn off the Orleans rotary. Trips late May to mid-October. Sponsored by the Cape Cod Museum of Natural History (see *To See* and *To Do* in "Brewster"), these 90-minute trips aboard a power catamaran can accommodate a maximum of 18 people. Gliding through Nauset Marsh and into the bay, you'll see hundreds of seabirds, and perhaps some harbor seals, and you'll experience this fragile, ever-changing ecosystem up close and personal. From below the waterline, you'll also haul six or eight different crab, eel, and worm traps. Adults $24, children half price.

Sea Gypsy Pirate Adventure (896-9616), Town Cove, behind the old Orleans Inn. Mid-June to early September. Particularly fun for kids 3–9, Captain Than Drake's trip begins with face painting on the dock. Then kids sign onto the pirate ship as crew, take a pirate oath, look for sunken treasure with a treasure map, and fire water cannons against the invading Spanish. The treasure is eventually found and hauled in. And on the return voyage, the booty is shared and pirates celebrate with song and dance. Also ask about Drake's straightforward daily excursion through Nauset Marsh, where all he hands out is a pair of binoculars. Rates unavailable at press time.

Seashore Park Boat Tours (240-3100), at Town Cove, behind the old Orleans Inn off Route 6A. Not affiliated with the National Seashore, the Seashore Park offers 90-minute tours three times daily July and August; at 10:30 and 1:30 in June and September to mid-October. This big, enclosed boat is best for off-season trips when it's less crowded. Adults $11, children $7.

BOWLING

Orleans Bowling Center (255-7077), 191 Route 6A. Open year-round. Okay, so you didn't come to the Cape to go bowling, but if it's raining and you've got a few kids in the car, it might be a great idea.

CANOEING/KAYAKING

The protected, calm waters of northern **Pleasant Bay** offer delightful canoeing opportunities. (Southern Pleasant Bay can be treacherous; talk with the folks at the outdoor center before setting off.) There is limited parking at each of the numerous town landings, but it's free.

Goose Hummock Outdoor Center (255-2620), off Route 6A on Town Cove. Open year-round. Pick up the Nauset Harbor tide chart and rent a canoe ($20 per half-day) or touring kayak. If you're new to kayaking, take the 2½-hour course ($40) to learn basic paddle strokes and skills. Otherwise, consider one of the center's organized half-day trips ($50.)

FISHING/SHELLFISHING

Freshwater fishing requires a state permit, obtainable at the town clerk's office (240-3700). Check Pilgrim Lake, off Kescauogansett Road and Monument Road, and Crystal Lake, off Monument Road (see *Green Space—Ponds*). There are at least a dozen fresh- and saltwater town landings in Orleans. Anglers looking for trout and perch will most likely find them in Crystal Lake. Contact the harbormaster (240-3755), Route 28, Orleans, about a shellfishing permit and regulations before you head out with your shovel, rake, and bucket.

Casey Scott (896-4048) offers an unusual service. If you've always wondered how people find clams and how they dig with those shovels and rakes, Casey will teach you how and where. Casey, who has a commercial permit, has been clamming all her life and says she grew tired of seeing people use rakes like hacksaws. This tide-dependent activity is not as easy as it looks, but after searching out littlenecks and cherrystones with Casey, you'll be a pro. $25 per person for a 2½-hour adventure, plus a $15 seasonal shellfish permit (per family).

Bruce Scott (896-4048) knows the ins and out of fishing Nauset Inlet. Yes, he'll help you catch striped bass, but he'll also teach you about finding your own bait and observing where the birds feed. This will increase your chances of landing stripers no matter where you go on the Cape. If you want to get away from the crowds, a quiet paddle through this fragile inlet will do it. Half day: $50 per person.

Goose Hummock Outdoor Center (255-2620), Route 6A on Town Cove, Orleans. Open year-round. This outfitter will fulfill all your fishing-related needs, including rod rentals, fishing trips, instruction, and wintertime fly-tying seminars. Staff offer lots of free advice and information.

Rock Harbor Charter Fleet (255-9757, 1-800-287-1771 within Massachusetts), Rock Harbor, Orleans. Trips mid-May to mid-October; harbor booth staffed from June through September. These 18 boats comprise the largest charter fleet on the Cape. US Coast Guard–licensed captains offer 4- and 8-hour trips for groups in search of bluefish, striped bass, and mackerel. Children welcome. $85 per person for a 4-hour trip, $95 per person for an 8-hour trip. If you round up six people, it costs $340 for a half day, $450 for a full day.

FITNESS CENTER

Willy's Gym and Fitness Center (255-6826), 130 Route 6A, Orleans Marketplace. Open year-round. In 1989 this former supermarket was converted to house the Cape's largest weight room. More than 60 different step-aerobics classes are held per week. $10 per day, $25 for a 3-day weekend, $35 per week.

IN-LINE SKATING

Nauset Sports (255-4742), Jeremiah Square, Route 6A at the Rotary. Open year-round. Not only do they rent in-line skates, but they also rent equipment for practically any other "action" sport you can think of.

MINI-GOLF

Apple Grove Mini Golf (255-6184), Main Street, behind Kadee's Lobster & Clam Bar (see *Eating Out*) in East Orleans. Open seasonally. The course isn't very interesting, but kids can play while you get takeout.

Cape Escape (240-1791), Canal Road, off Route 6A near the Orleans rotary, is more challenging.

SAILING

Arey's Pond Boat Yard (255-0994), Arey's Lane off Route 28, South Orleans. Mid-June through August. Arey's offers 10 hours of beginning and intermediate sailing instruction over the course of 5 days for $150. Private lessons by appointment.

SKATING

Charles Moore Arena (255-2971), O'Connor Way, near the town landfill; look for signs at the information booth. Open year-round. The 80-by-200-foot arena is reserved for ice skating most of the year. In-line skaters take their turn Tuesday through Thursday 7–9 PM, mid-June through July. On Friday evenings from late May through July, the strobe-lit rink is reserved for kids age 9–14.

SPECIAL PROGRAMS

Academy of Performing Arts (255-5510 for the school), 5 Giddiah Hill Road, Orleans. The academy offers year-round, Cape-wide instruction to more than 400 students of all ages, including dance classes in jazz, tap, and ballet; instruction in a wide variety of musical instruments; courses in drama and creative writing. Two-week sessions (concentrating on musical theater, ballet, and drama production) in July and August end with a public performance. Children's summer matinees at 10 every Friday.

Baseball clinics (255-0793). The Orleans Cardinals hold a 7-week baseball clinic for boys and girls 6–13 that begins in early June. There can be as many as 90–100 kids, but there is always a good ratio of player-instructors to kids. Contact the Cardinals Office, PO Box 504, Orleans 02653. The cost is $50 for the first week, $45 each additional week.

Recreational Department (240-3785) offers instructional tennis for adults and kids over 7, a playground program for kids 7–14, and swimming lessons. Call for schedule details and registration.

TENNIS

Public courts are located at **Eldredge Park,** off Route 28.

See also the Recreational Department under *Special Programs.*

WINDSURFING

Nauset Sports (255-4742), Jeremiah Square, Route 6A at the rotary. Open year-round. Board rentals for bodyboarding, windsurfing, surfing, and wakeboarding.

GREEN SPACE

BEACHES

Nauset Beach (240-3780), on the Atlantic Ocean, off Beach Road, beyond the center of East Orleans. It doesn't get much better than this: good bodysurfing waves and 9 miles of sandy Atlantic shoreline, backed by a low dune. (Only about a half-mile stretch is covered by lifeguards; much of the rest is deserted.) A gently sloping grade makes this a good beach for children. Four-wheel-drive vehicles are allowed onto Nauset Beach with

Nauset Beach, the 9-mile-long barrier beach on the Atlantic Ocean in Orleans

a permit (purchased at the beach from May to mid-October) except during certain bird-breeding and -nesting periods. Obtain permits in the off-season from the Parks and Beaches Department (240-3775), 18 Bay Ridge Lane. Facilities include an in-season lifeguard, rest rooms, changing rooms, a snack bar, chairs and umbrellas for rent, and plenty of parking (parking is never a problem). Parking is $8 daily ($25 weekly), late June to early September; $4 on June weekends.

Skaket Beach (255-0572), on Cape Cod Bay, off Skaket Beach Road. Amenities include an in-season lifeguard, rest rooms, changing rooms, and a snack bar. This beach is popular with families. The parking lot often fills up early, creating a 30-minute wait for a space. At low tide, you can walk a mile out into the bay; at high tide the beach grass is covered. Parking $8 daily from late June to early September. (The parking fee is transferable to Nauset Beach on the same day.)

Cabana Cape Cod (240-2436), 211 Beach Road. Open seasonally. For $10 daily (or $55 weekly) you can rent one of these colorful wind- and sun-screen huts. Cabanas can be delivered, too.

PONDS

Crystal Lake, off Monument Road, and **Pilgrim Lake,** off Kescauogansett Road and Monument Road, are good for swimming. Pilgrim Lake has an in-season lifeguard, rest rooms, changing rooms, picnic tables, a dock, and a small beach; parking is $8 daily. At Crystal Lake parking is free but limited.

WALKS

Paw Wah Point Conservation Area, off Namequoit Road from Eldredge Park Way, has one trail leading to a nice little beach with picnic tables.

Village green, Route 28 and Main Street. This rhododendron park is a nice place for a picnic.

LODGING

RESORT MOTOR INN

✏✳ **The Cove** (255-1203, 1-800-343-2233), 13 Route 28, Orleans 02653. Open year-round. As the name implies, this well-kept complex of 47 rooms is situated on 300 feet of shorefront along Town Cove. A gazebo, a dock for sunning and fishing, picnic tables, and grills are well situated to take full advantage of the view. There is also an outdoor heated pool. In summer the Cove offers a free boat tour of Town Cove and Nauset Beach. There are deluxe rooms with a sitting area and sofa bed; waterfront rooms with a shared deck overlooking the water; two-room suites with a kitchen (and some with a fireplace and private deck); and inn rooms with a bit more decor (some of these also have a fireplace and private deck). July to early September $96–167; "mid-season" $72–112; November through April $52–82. Children under 18 free in parent's room.

BED & BREAKFASTS

☞ **Nauset House Inn** (255-2195, e-mail: jvessell@capecod.net), Beach Road, East Orleans 02643. Open April through October. These 14 rooms (half with private bath) are the best in the area for many reasons. The inn has genuinely hospitable hosts; it's a half-mile from Nauset Beach; guest rooms are thoughtfully and tastefully appointed; a greenhouse conservatory is just one of the many quiet places to relax. You'll have Diane and Al Johnson, their daughter Cindy, and her husband, John, to thank; they've owned and constantly upgraded the 1810 farmhouse since 1982. Rooms in the carriage house are generally larger than inn rooms, while the cottage, with peaked ceiling, is quite private and cozy. $65–115; breakfast $3–5 extra. One single room rents for $55.

✳ **Parsonage Inn** (255-8217), 202 Main Street, East Orleans 02643. Open year-round. This very pleasant, rambling, late-18th-century house has eight guest rooms (all with private bath) comfortably furnished with country antiques. Wide pine floors, canopy beds, and newly redone bathrooms are common. The studio apartment Willow has a kitchenette and private entrance, while the roomy Barn, recently renovated with exposed beams and eaves, has a sitting area and sofa bed. English innkeepers Elizabeth and Ian Browne serve a full breakfast of apple crepes or lemon ricotta pancakes at individual tables or on the brick patio. June through September $80–105; October through May $65–95.

✳ **Morgan's Way** (255-0831, e-mail: morgnway@capecod.net), Nine Morgan's Way, Orleans 02653. Open year-round. Page McMahan and Will Joy opened their contemporary home, about a mile south of town, to guests in 1990. Lush landscaping extends across 5 acres and a multilevel deck wraps around a 20-by-40-foot heated pool. The interior is spacious; guests may use the open, second-floor living room, complete with TV and VCR, and wood-burning stove, and enjoy panoramic views beyond the pool. One of the two guest rooms has a small attached greenhouse. The delightful poolside guest house is bright and modern, with a full kitchen and private deck. A find. Rooms: $100 May through October, $85 November through April, including a full breakfast. Pool house: $700 weekly May through September; $500 otherwise. No credit cards.

✱ **Rive Gauche** (255-2676), 9 Herringbrook Way, Orleans 02653. Open year-round. Artist Ruth Hogan's light and airy studio is located in a carriage house in a residential neighborhood about a mile south of town. It's situated on a saltwater pond (just 100 feet from a freshwater lake), and guests are welcome to use the Hogans' dock and canoe. Ruth stocks the refrigerator with juice, milk, and cereal and drops off baked goods every morning. A deck overlooks the pond; it feels like a real hideaway. For convenience, there is also a microwave and coffeemaker. $110.

✐✱ **Arey's Pond Relais B&B** (240-0599, 1-800-541-6226, e-mail: orleansbnb-@capecod.net), 16 Arey's Lane, Orleans 02653. Open year-round. Innkeeper Susanne Strenz-Thibault, whose marvelous trompe l'oeil walls and furniture dominate the living room, rents two ground-floor rooms that share a bath. (Susanne doesn't rent them to people who aren't traveling together.) Guests enjoy a private entrance and use of the Strenz-Thibaults' hot tub and living room. A full breakfast is served on the private, landscaped patio. A mile and a half from town, the namesake Arey's Pond is just beyond the driveway. $60–70; children's rates on request. No credit cards.

MOTELS

✐✱ **Barley Neck Inn** (255-0212, 1-800-281-7505), Beach Road, East Orleans 02643. Open mid-April to mid-November. Joe and Kathi Lewis purchased this rambling, three-story captain's house and attached motel during a bankruptcy auction in mid-1994. Since then they've completely rehabbed the formerly neglected 18-room bi-level motel, much to the appreciation of area residents. Rooms are tastefully appointed, albeit with hotel/motel-style furnishings. Swimming pool. The Barley Neck is halfway between Orleans and Nauset Beach. Late June to mid-September $95–115; off-season $65–95.

Nauset Knoll Motor Lodge (255-2364), Nauset Beach, East Orleans 02643. Open mid-April to mid-October. Nauset Knoll, located a few steps from Nauset Beach, is often booked long before other places because of the expansive views of dune and ocean. You can watch the sun as it rises over the ocean from lawn chairs atop the lodge's namesake knoll. The 12 simply furnished rooms (à la 1950s) with large picture windows are in three separate units, distinctively modeled after a barn, shed, and Cape cottage. Mid-June to early September $125; off-season $75–85.

Early morning at Nauset Marsh

COTTAGES AND ROOMS

☞✐**Ridgewood Motel & Cottages** (255-0473), junction of Routes 28 and 39, South Orleans 02662. Cottages open May through October. These six tidy housekeeping cottages, constantly upgraded since 1980 by the Knowles family, are a couple of miles south of Orleans center. Units 12, 18, and 17 are all very comfortable. A large pool, grill and picnic area, and playground are set within the wooded compound. A Knowles daughter is available for baby-sitting. Weekly cottage rates, mid-June to early September, are $300–460 for two or three people, $380–580 for five to six people. Rates go as low as $240 and $290, respectively.

☞✳ **Hillbourne House** (255-0780), 654 Route 28, South Orleans 02662. Open year-round. Since 1984, hosts Barbara and Jack Hayes have offered a variety of accommodations atop a hill commanding views of Pleasant Bay. The carriage house, which sleeps five people in three bedrooms, has a full kitchen and a large living room. The cottage has a great view of Pleasant Bay. Each of the three motel-style rooms in the former paddock has two double beds. Request the room in front; it has the best view. An expanded continental breakfast is included for inn and "paddock" guests; all guests have use of the private beach and private dock. Mid-June to mid-September $60–85 for rooms, $500–550 weekly for cottage and carriage house for four people; otherwise, $50–70 for rooms, $450–500 for cottage and carriage house. No credit cards.

See also Nauset House Inn under *Bed & Breakfasts*.

EFFICIENCIES

✳ **Kadee's Gray Elephant** (255-7608), 216 Main Street, East Orleans 02643. Open year-round. In 1992 Kris Kavanagh opened these fanciful accommodations next to her wildly popular Kadee's Lobster & Clam Bar (see *Eating Out*). (The 200-year-old former sea captain's house had belonged to her grandmother.) Every surface of woodwork and furniture has been whimsically painted lavender, sea green, and bright pink. Each of the 10 efficiencies (some carpeted) has cable TV, phone, and air-conditioning. Kitchens are equipped with a coffeemaker, electric burners, a microwave, refrigerator, and portable cooler. Don't come here if you're looking for a warm B&B experience; these studios are for independent travelers who want to come and go without anyone noticing them. In summer $100 nightly, $650 weekly; September to late May $65.

See also Morgan's Way under *Bed & Breakfasts*.

RENTALS

Compass Real Estate (240-0022), 2 Academy Place, Orleans 02653. Listings $300–3000, from Harwich to Wellfleet, from cottages that sleep 2 to houses that sleep 10.

WHERE TO EAT

Orleans has an excellent variety of restaurants; many are open year-round.

DINING OUT

✳ **Nauset Beach Club** (255-8547), 222 East Main Street, East Orleans. Open for dinner year-round; closed Sunday and Monday mid-October through late May. Within this former duck-hunting cottage, peach walls and lovely tableware set the stage for an excellent meal. The sophisticated northern Italian entrées, cooked on a wood-fired grill or oven, are enormous. A select, well-priced wine list complements chef-owner Jack Salemi's ever-changing menu: veal chops, lobster pizzetti (that is, small pizza), nightly fish specials, and homemade pastas. No reservations are taken; get there early. You won't be disappointed. Entrées $12–19.

☞⊘✳ **Captain Linnell House** (255-3400), 137 Skaket Beach Road. Open for dinner and Sunday brunch; closed mid-February through March. Chef-owner Bill Conway's fine fare matches the graceful mansion setting. Dining is romantic, with candles, fine china, and linens. One dining room overlooks a small water garden; the salon overlooks the side garden. Start with oysters sautéed with julienne vegetables and champagne-ginger sauce and move to rack of lamb or scallops and shrimp sautéed in a tarragon lobster sauce. Conway will dish out small portions for children with refined palates. If you're seated by 6, you'll receive a complimentary lobster bisque or chowder and dessert. Bill and his wife, Shelly, have owned and been restoring this former diamond-in-the-rough since 1988. It now sparkles. Reservations suggested. Entrées $16–25.

✳ **Off-the-Bay Cafe** (255-5505), 28 Main Street. Open daily year-round for lunch and dinner; open for breakfast late June to late September; jazz brunch on Sunday. Although hearty game dishes are very popular, Off-the-Bay also makes gallant efforts with jazzed-up regional American dishes like tuna marinated in Caribbean spices, mango, and habanero relish. The handsome and casual dining room has high ceilings, brass fixtures, wainscoting, some wooden booths, tin ceilings, ceiling fans, and an evocative mural of the harbor and dunes. Service can be uneven, but overall this is one of the best places in town. Reservations accepted. Dinner entrées are $16–23.50. Lunch is more like $10.

❋ **Barley Neck Inn/Joe's Beach Road Bar & Grille** (255-0212), Beach Road, East Orleans. Main dining room open weekends, late April through December for dinner, nightly early May to mid-October. Joe's is open year-round. New in 1995, the Barley Neck offers two dining choices. A limited New American menu is served in four lovely and intimate dining rooms. When making a dinner reservation, ask for a description of the dining rooms, since each has a different feel. Popular dishes include grilled pork loin with garlic mashed potatoes and sautéed chicken tenderloins with Asian-style vegetables. Joe's is a more casual, barnlike space, with barn-board walls. It's quite relaxing. The fare is lighter: pizza, pasta, soup, and salads. In the off-season, the most popular dishes from the main dining room are also offered at Joe's. Main dining room entrées $16–23; Joe's $7–15.

❋ **The Arbor** (255-4847), 20 Route 28. Open for dinner Friday through Sunday year-round, nightly in-season. The eclectic antiques and decor at The Arbor, with five small dining rooms, are as varied as the menu. Seafood, lots of veal, pasta, prime meats—they're all here, both creative and classic versions. In addition, there are always lots of nightly specials. Dishes tend to be hearty; this is not the place for a light meal. Popular dishes include pasta Lindsay, seafood and mushrooms smothered with a sherry cream sauce, and lobster with julienne chicken in a Harvey's Bristol Cream sauce. Children's menu. Reservations recommended. Entrées $12–22.

EATING OUT

☞❋ **Old Jailhouse Tavern** (255-5245), 28 West Road. Open daily 11:30–3:30 PM and 5–1 AM year-round; no reservations. This casual tavern with good service is always crowded and boisterous. It's a great place to go when everyone in your party wants something different: nachos, soup and salad, fish-and-chips, or a broiled seafood sampler. Eat in one of the booths, on the atrium-like terrace overlooking the garden, at the long bar, or within the rock walls of the old jail. Dishes $6–16.

✐ **Kadee's Lobster & Clam Bar** (255-6184), 212 Main Street, East Orleans. Open 11:30–9:30 daily, late May to early September; no reservations. Kadee's has been a summer tradition since 1975 because of the location (on the way to Nauset Beach) and the accomplished kitchen that serves fresh seafood from local waters. The setting is casual: Sit at shellacked picnic tables under an open-air tent (enclosed in cool or inclement weather), in the casual dining room, or at umbrella-covered tables next to the crushed-seashell parking lot. Choose from oysters on the half shell, broiled, steamed, or fried seafood, kale soup, or a rich "seafood simmer" with lobster, shrimp,

Taking a harborside break for lobster

and scallops in a sherry wine sauce. This is what summer is all about. Children's menu. Lunch $5–10; dinner entrées $10–16.

☞✻ **Binnacle Tavern** (255-7901), 20 Route 28. Open nightly for dinner, April to mid-October; Thursday through Sunday the rest of the year. Barn-board walls, low lighting, "oldies" top-40 music, and a ubiquitous nautical motif pervade the interior of this cozy, popular tavern. The Binnacle is deservedly well known for its pizzas, but it also serves homemade pastas. This place is always full, even in the dead of winter. Entrées $3–11.

☞✐✻ **Land Ho!** (255-5165), Route 6A. Open daily year-round. John Murphy, owner since 1969, is responsible for this favorite local hangout. Don't miss it. It's very colorful (literally), from red-and-white-checked tablecloths, to old business signs hanging from the ceiling, to a large blackboard menu. Newspapers hang on a wire to separate the long bar from the dining area. Land Ho! serves club sandwiches, fried seafood dishes, and burgers and hot dogs. The chowder is great. You'll find lots of families, college students, and old-time locals here. Dishes $3–6.25.

Wheel Haus Café (240-1585), 2 Academy Place at Route 28. Open for lunch and dinner April through December. Deutschlander Uli Pruesse and his American-born wife, Aleta, opened this light and airy café in 1992. Salads and sandwiches dominate the lunch menu; the dinner menu features German specialties like roasted pork (an OctoberFest special), sauerbraten, and Wiener schnitzel, as well as a few pasta and seafood dishes. There's a patio, too. Lunch $5–6; dinner $11–15 (see also *Snacks*).

Cap't Cass Rock Harbor Seafood, 117 Rock Harbor Road. Open 11–2 and 5–9 daily in July and August; 11–2 and 4–8 on Friday and Saturday,

11–2 on Sunday, from April through June and September and October. This classic roadside lobster shack on the harbor, adorned with colorful buoys on the outside and checkered tables on the inside, is as good as they come. The food is a cut above: The lobster roll ($9.45) hasn't a shred of lettuce in it and the chowder and clam dinners are great, too. The menu is written on poster board, as it's been done since 1958. There really is a Captain Cass, by the way; George Cass, his wife, Betty, and their daughter Sue run the place. Lunch $5–10, dinner $9–20.

✎ **The Lobster Claw** (255-1800), Route 6A, near the Orleans rotary. Open 11:30–9 daily, April through October. The Berigs have served fresh seafood at this large, convenient, family-style restaurant since 1970. A few sandwiches and steaks have nudged their way onto the predominantly seafood menu. Other features include a second-floor raw bar, a children's menu, and early-bird specials from 4 to 5:30. Lunch $3.25–6.50, dinner entrées $9–16.

☞✎❊ **Hearth 'n Kettle** (240-0111), on West Road at Route 6A. Open daily year-round. This Early American–themed, family-style restaurant (one in a chain operated by the Catania family) offers reliable service, good food, and moderate prices. Breakfast is served until 4 and early-bird specials (like chicken teriyaki and broiled scrod) until 6. When you're in another neighborhood, there are also branches in Falmouth, South Yarmouth, Centerville (Barnstable), and Hyannis. Meals $4–14.

☞✎❊ **Hole-in-One Donut Shop & Deli** (255-3740), Route 6A. Open 5 AM–4 PM (until 3 on Sunday), year-round. This pleasant, airy place is a real local hangout. It's packed at breakfast time and friendly all day. $2–4.50.

☞✎❊ **Sir Cricket's Fish 'n Chips** (255-4453), Route 6A. Open daily year-round. This tidy hole-in-the-wall, next to the Bird Watcher's General Store (see *Special Shops*), dishes out plates and pints of fried seafood. There are chicken tenders and hot dogs for the kids. Plan on takeout since there are only a couple of tables.

See also Barley Neck Inn/Joe's Beach Road Bar & Grille under *Dining Out*.

SNACKS

❊ **Cottage St. Bakery** (255-2821), Cottage Street near Routes 6A and 28. Open 6:30 AM–10 PM; irregular hours January through March. JoAnna Keeley, who's been buttering up the community since 1984, has a number of oddly named specialties, including "dirt bombs," an old-fashioned French doughnut recipe that requires baking, not frying, and "fly cemeteries," a puff pastry square, knotted on top and filled with currants and nuts. Her breads—cinnamon butter bread, multigrain breads, and a garlic and herb oregano bread—are also great. Knead I say more? Okay, I will: You can get some homemade soup and a sandwich here, too. There are a few indoor tables.

❊ **The Hot Chocolate Sparrow** (240-2230), Route 6A. Open 7 AM–11 PM daily year-round. Located inauspiciously in the Lowell Square strip mall, this place makes the best cappuccino between Beantown and Provincetown.

Marjorie Sparrow also offers tasty no-fat muffins and a blackboard menu of drinks like iced or frozen "hot" chocolate. At lunchtime have a tasty grilled focaccia sandwich with mozzarella, pesto, and sun-dried tomatoes for just $3.75.

✳ **New York Bagels** (255-0255), 125 Route 6A. Open daily year-round. New York? They're not kidding: The bagels are shipped in daily from H&H in Manhattan. Add salmon, smoked whitefish, or kosher pastrami, or opt for potato pancakes, knishes, bialys, or challah.

Fancy's Farm (255-1949), 199 Main Street, East Orleans. Open daily mid-March through December. Fancy's is more than your average farm stand. You can assemble a gourmand's feast with cold pastas, Thai salads, roasted chicken, and sesame noodles. There's a salad bar, too.

Wheel Haus Café (240-1585), 2 Academy Place at Route 28. (See *Eating Out* for hours.) The Pruesses have created a place that's part Italian café, part French bistro, and part Bavarian sweet shop, à la Cape Cod. Come anytime for a strong coffee with a slice of hazelnut torte or raspberry chocolate cake. $5–6.

✳ **Phoenix Fruit & Vegetable** (255-5306), Orleans Marketplace, Route 6A. Open daily year-round. This tiny shop, tucked into the corner of a strip mall, is a delight for foodies. If you have cooking facilities, you'll appreciate organic greens, locally grown shiitake mushrooms, locally made clam pies, and hearty Pain d'Avignon bread from Hyannis.

Choose your ice cream parlor based on location, since both shops offer sublime flavors. **Emack & Bolio's** (255-5844) is on Route 6A, and the **Sundae School** (255-5473) is at 210 Main Street in East Orleans. (Tasters rave about the black raspberry and Grape-Nut ice cream.)

COFFEE

See The Hot Chocolate Sparrow under *Snacks*.

FISH MARKETS

Smoked Fish, Route 6A. Fisherman Jim Keneway smokes his own fish and puts together fish platters, appetizers, and creative spreads (like one made with rose hip powder). If you want your fish fresh, not smoked, all you have to do is ask.

Young's Fish Market (255-3366), Rock Harbor. Open 10–6 mid-June to mid-September. Call ahead and they'll cook a lobster to order for you; otherwise, the lobster rolls ($6) are always good. The market, by the way, has been in the Harrison family since 1962, when they bought it from the Youngs.

ENTERTAINMENT

Baseball. The Orleans Cardinals (255-0793) play ball at Eldredge Park Field mid-June to early August.

Academy Playhouse (255-1963 box office), 120 Main Street. The performance space for the Academy of Performing Arts, this 162-seat playhouse occupies the Old Town Hall, built in 1873. It holds a prominent position high above Main Street. Over the years the building has been host to local government, record hops, movies, and theater. The theater company (established in 1975) stages 10 to 12 dramas, comedies, and musicals throughout the year. Since 1986, the season has kicked off with a literary cabaret, *A Night of New Works.* The eagerly awaited March event ($8) brings established and unknown Cape writers (who have been working holed up all winter) together with audiences.

SELECTIVE SHOPPING

ANTIQUES
Pleasant Bay Antiques (255-0930), 540 Route 28 in South Orleans. Open year-round; closed on Sunday. Steve Tyng acquires most of his high-quality 18th- and 19th-century American antiques from area residents rather than auctions. They're displayed in a lovely old barn.
Continuum (255-8513), 7 Route 28. Open year-round; off-season days vary, but usually open on Saturday. Dan Johnson expertly restores antique lamps and fixtures from the Victorian to the art deco period. He also sells old advertising signs, folk art, and wooden decoys.
Countryside Antiques (240-0525), 6 Leis Road, behind the Box Lunch on Main Street, East Orleans. Open year-round except January. Deborah Rita, who opened her doors in 1986, has filled eight rooms with English, Irish, Scandinavian, and European antiques.
Yellow House (255-9686), 21 Route 28, South Orleans. Open late May to mid-November. In addition to French country antiques, there are Oriental carpets, garden ornaments, bric-a-brac, and modern paintings.

ART GALLERIES AND SHOWS
Tree's Place (255-1330), Route 6A at Route 28. Open daily year-round, except closed on Sunday early January to mid-April. With the opening of this shop in 1962, Elaine and Julian Baird were among the first to put the Lower Cape on the art map. Tree's offers a vast collection of unusual gifts (like Russian lacquerware) displayed throughout nine little rooms; perhaps the Lower Cape's best gallery of representational New England painters; and a tile shop. Meet-the-artist champagne receptions 5–7 Saturdays in summer.
Hogan Art Gallery (240-3655, e-mail: fhogan@capecod.net), 39 Main Street. Open Monday through Saturday in summer; hours vary the rest of the year. Ruth Hogan has amassed a fine body of work: primitive white-line woodblock prints, impressionistic landscape paintings, and lovely pastels. Husband Frank offers a collection of 20th-century regional paintings. The Hogans also feature Susanne Strenz-Thibault's trompe l'oeil and painted furniture (see Arey's Pond Relais B&B under *Lodging—Bed & Breakfasts*).

Artful Hand Gallery (255-2969), Main Street Square. Open daily year-round. Emerging and established artists, practicing in the tradition of the American Arts and Crafts movement, have created functional and aesthetic objects for the home.

Nauset Painters, sponsors of the Cape's oldest juried outdoor art shows, holds shows from mid-August to late September at various town locations and on various days; look for the current flyer. Painting demonstrations are often held on Sunday.

ARTISANS

Orleans Carpenters (255-2646), Commerce Drive. Open year-round. Orleans Carpenters makes magnificent reproduction Shaker nesting oval boxes, oval trays, oval carriers, and music boxes. Only fine cherry and bird's-eye maple are used. These traditional oval boxes are so expertly made and durable that you could put your full weight on one and it would feel more sturdy than a stepladder. Although Paul and Beth Dixon's business is primarily a wholesale shop with museum customers, the front of the unprepossessing shop has a small display of goods. The "seconds," which look perfect to all but the most expert eyes, go very quickly in summer. Everything is gone within an hour at their big yearly sale: Be there, at 10 AM on the Saturday of Memorial Day weekend (in late May). You can also send for a catalog. Orleans Carpenters can be hard to find; it's off Finlay Road (from Route 28), behind the Daniels Car Wash.

Nauset Lantern Shop (899-2660), 169 Route 6A. Open year-round. Just north of the bowling alley, Ken Alman expertly handcrafts copper and brass Colonial- and Early American–style lanterns. Most of the nautical and onion lanterns are for exterior use, but he also makes sconces and indoor accessories. You can watch him work.

Kemp Pottery (255-5853), Route 6A near the rotary. Open Monday through Saturday year-round. Steven Kemp creates unusual designs from this unassuming location. Utilizing Nauset Beach sand, Kemp makes crockery, stoneware, bird feeders, bathroom sinks, and less common items for the garden like pagodas, torsos, and moated castles.

BOOKSTORES

Compass Rose Book Shop (255-1545), 43–45 Main Street. Open year-round. Extensive selections about Cape Cod, nature and the environment, women's studies, biographies, and books by local authors. The basement is filled with even more books (at 40 percent off).

Booksmith/Musicsmith of Orleans (255-4590), Skaket Corners, Route 6A, Orleans. Paperbacks and best-sellers.

CLOTHING

Karol Richardson (255-3944), 47 Main Street, and **Hannah** (255-8324), 47 Main Street, both sell stylish women's clothing.

FARMER'S MARKET

Orleans Farmer's Market, Orleans Marketplace, Route 6A. Pick up local produce and shellfish 8–noon every Saturday in June, July, and August.

SPECIAL SHOPS

Bird Watcher's General Store (255-6974, 1-800-562-1512), Route 6A near the Orleans rotary. Open daily year-round. If it pertains to birds or watchers-of-birds, this store has it: bird feeders in every size and shape, birdseed in barrels (almost a ton of seed is sold every day), fountains, bird note cards, bird kitchen magnets, bird playing cards. As important as commerce is, though, this place is an invaluable resource for news of where and when birds have been sighted or will be sighted. (This place isn't just for the birds!)

Oceana (240-1414), 1 Main Street Square. Open year-round. True to her theme, proprietor Carol Wright stocks things from and about the sea and nature. (Sometimes the definition is stretched a bit when there's a really great gift or an "intelligent" toy she wants to carry.) A percentage of total sales from her Ocean Information Center is donated to the Center for Coastal Studies (see "Provincetown.")

Clambake Celebrations (255-3289, 1-800-423-4038), 9 West Road at Skaket Corners, Orleans. Open year-round. Lobsters and steamers (clams) are air-shipped (or delivered in the immediate area with notice) in a cooking pot layered with a bed of seaweed. Just add water and boil. Packages also include mussels, corn on the cob, new potatoes, and sweet Italian sausage, as well as claw crackers, bibs, forks, and moist towelettes. Lobsters for four people is $134; clambake for four $218; combinations priced accordingly.

Bel Vasaio (240-3996, 1-800-962-7061 for its colorful catalog), 56 Main Street. Open year-round. New in 1996, this shop imports fine Italian pottery, primarily Tuscan pieces. Although the shop carries traditionally designed pots, platters, mugs, tiles, and vases, it also has pieces with more unusual functions, sizes, and shapes.

Orleans Whole Food Store (255-6540), 46 Main Street, Orleans. Open daily year-round. Healthy foods, pizza on Tuesday and Thursday, vitamins, books, and lots of items that generally promote holistic living.

Wheel Haus Nautiques & Gifts (240-1585), 2 Academy Place at Route 28. Open April through October. The proprietor, a schooner captain from Hamburg, Germany, offers ship models, compasses, and myriad nautical items.

Baseball Shop (240-1063), 26 Main Street. Open year-round. The shop carries more than 1000 caps, as well as trading cards, clothing, and other paraphernalia.

Cape Cod Photo & Art Supply (255-0476), 38 Main Street. Open daily except Sunday, year-round. One-hour film processing, and painting supplies if you become inspired by the wonderful Cape Cod light.

SPECIAL EVENTS

July and August: **Art fairs and festivals,** Middle School. Most weekends.

Late August: **Pops in the Park.** The Cape Cod Symphony performs a concert in Eldredge Park.

Late August: **Old Home Week.** In celebration of Orleans's 200th birthday in 1997, this weeklong festival will include bathtub races, a fishing derby, and fireworks.

October: **Fall for Orleans Festival.** New in 1993, activities include a car show, line dancing at Rock Harbor, a progressive dinner, and a pancake breakfast.

IV. THE OUTER CAPE

Eastham
Wellfleet
Truro

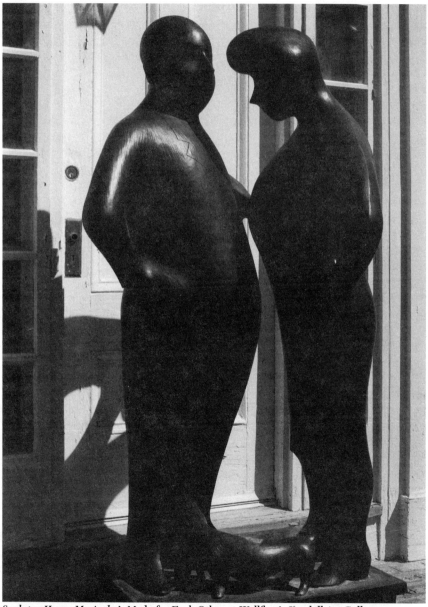

Sculptor Harry Marinsky's Made for Each Other *at Wellfleet's Kendall Art Gallery*

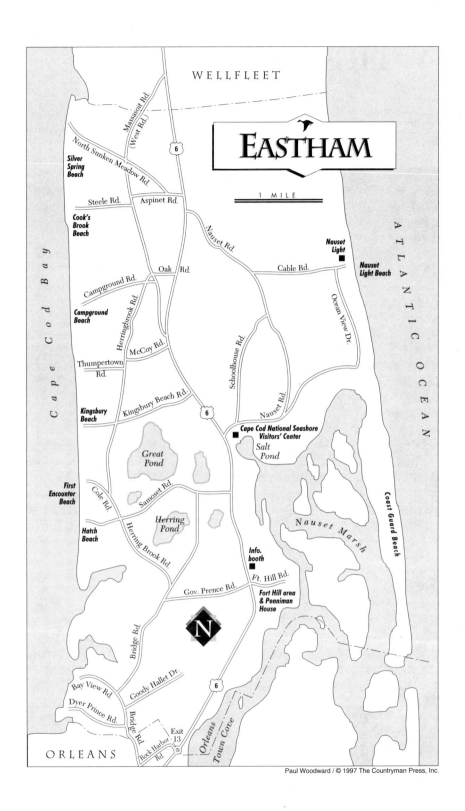

WELLFLEET

EASTHAM

1 MILE

Massasoit Rd. (West Rd.)

6

North Sunken Meadow Rd.

Silver Spring Beach

Steele Rd.

Aspinet Rd.

Cook's Brook Beach

Nauset Rd.

Nauset Light

Nauset Light Beach

Cable Rd.

Oak Rd.

Campground Rd.

Campground Beach

Herringbrook Rd.

McCoy Rd.

Thumpertown Rd.

Ocean View Dr.

Schoolhouse Rd.

Kingsbury Beach

Kingsbury Beach Rd.

6

Nauset Rd.

Cape Cod National Seashore Visitors' Center

Salt Pond

First Encounter Beach

Cole Rd.

Samoset Rd.

Great Pond

Hatch Beach

Herring Pond

Herring Brook Rd.

Nauset Marsh

Info. booth

Coast Guard Beach

Ft. Hill Rd.

Gov. Prence Rd.

Fort Hill area & Penniman House

N

Bridge Rd.

Bay View Rd.

Goody Hallet Dr.

Dyer Prince Rd.

Bridge Rd.

6

Exit 13

Rock Harbor Rd.

Orleans Town Cove

ORLEANS

Cape Cod Bay

ATLANTIC OCEAN

Paul Woodward / © 1997 The Countryman Press, Inc.

Eastham

Settled by the Pilgrims in 1644, Eastham is content to remain relatively undiscovered by late-20th-century tourists. In fact, year-round residents (fewer than 5000) seem downright pleased that any semblance of major tourism development has passed them by. There isn't even a Main Street or town center per se.

What Eastham does boast, as the gateway to the Cape Cod National Seashore (CCNS), is plenty of natural diversions. The Salt Pond Visitor Center, one of two headquarters of the CCNS, dispenses a wealth of information and offers ranger-guided activities and outstanding nature programs. Take an informative boat trip onto Nauset Marsh, a fragile ecosystem that typifies much of the Cape. A marvelous network of bicycle and walking trails traverses this part of the seashore, including the Fort Hill area. The Cape's famed, uninterrupted stretches of sandy beach, backed by high dunes, begin in earnest in Eastham and extend all the way up to Provincetown. One of them, Coast Guard Beach, is also where exalted naturalist Henry Beston spent 1928 living in a cottage observing nature's minute changes and recording his experiences in *The Outermost House*.

Eastham is best known as the site where the *Mayflower's* Myles Standish and a Pilgrim scouting party met the Nauset Indians in 1620 at First Encounter Beach. The "encounter," in which a few arrows were slung (without injury), served as sufficient warning to the Pilgrims: They left and didn't return for 24 years. When the Pilgrim settlers, then firmly entrenched at Plymouth, went looking for room to expand, they returned to Eastham. Led by Thomas Prence, they purchased most of the land from Native Americans for an unknown quantity of hatchets.

Although the history books cite these encounters as the beginning of Eastham's recorded history, the 1990 discovery of a 6,000-year-old settlement (see Coast Guard Beach under *Green Space—Beaches*) is keeping archaeologists and anthropologists busy.

GUIDANCE

Eastham Chamber of Commerce (255-3444, 240-7211 year-round), near the Fort Hill area on Route 6 (write to PO Box 1329, Eastham 02642). Open 9–7 daily, July to early September, and 10–5 late May through June and September.

❄ **Salt Pond Visitor Center** (255-3421), off Route 6, CCNS. Open daily 9–5 in summer and daily 9–4:30 the rest of the year, except open only on weekends in January and February. Encompassing more than 43,000 acres, the Cape Cod National Seashore is visited by over 5 million visitors each summer. The information center is an excellent resource for both first-time and repeat visitors. Short films on Thoreau's Cape Cod, Marconi, and the ever-changing natural landscape are shown in the auditorium throughout the day. Ranger-guided activities include sunset campfires on the beach, talks on Cape geology and tidal flats, and bird walks. There seems to be something going on every night of the week in summer. The fine museum includes displays on the salt and whaling industries and the diaries of Captain Penniman's wife, who accompanied him on several voyages. Free.

PUBLIC REST ROOMS
Public rest rooms are located in the Salt Pond Visitor Center.

GETTING THERE
By car: Eastham is 40 miles from the Sagamore Bridge via Route 6.
By bus: The **Plymouth & Brockton** bus line (775-5524) connects Eastham with other Cape towns and with Boston's Logan Airport.

GETTING AROUND
Eastham is only a few miles wide and 6 miles long. Beaches and places to stay and eat are all well marked along or off Route 6. The CCNS is to the east of Route 6.

MEDICAL EMERGENCY
Call **911**.

TO SEE

Edward Penniman House (255-3421), off Route 6 in the Fort Hill area, CCNS. Open intermittently; call for current schedule. At age 11, Penniman left Eastham for the open sea. When he returned as a sea captain 26 years later, he had this 1868 house built for him. Rumor has it that he used ships' carpenters because he didn't trust landlubber architects. Boasting indoor plumbing and a kerosene chandelier, this French Second Empire–style house has Corinthian columns, a mansard roof, and a cupola that once afforded views of the bay and ocean. Although the house is only partially restored and contains a few period furnishings, the ever-helpful National Park Service guides are on hand to dispense lots of historical information. Free.

Swift-Daley House and **Tool Museum** (240-1247), next to the post office on Route 6. Open 1–4 weekdays in July and August. This completely furnished Colonial house (1741) is a fine example of a full-Cape built by ships' carpenters in the mid-1700s. It has wide floorboards, pumpkin-pine woodwork, narrow stairways, and a fireplace in every room on the first floor. The Tool Museum behind the house displays hundreds of

The National Park Service's Edward Penniman House is graced by the jawbone of a whale.

tools for use in the home and in the field. Free.

Old Schoolhouse Museum (255-0788), off Route 6 across from the Salt Pond Visitor Center. Open 1–4 weekdays in July and August. Set off by an arched whale jawbone, this former one-room 1869 schoolhouse served the town until 1936. During that time there were separate entrances for boys and girls. Inside you'll learn about Henry Beston's year of living alone with nature on nearby Coast Guard Beach. Thanks to the Eastham Historical Society you can also learn about the town's farming history, daily domestic life, Native Americans, offshore shipwrecks, and the impressive Lifesaving Service. Free.

Oldest windmill, on Route 6 at Samoset Road. Across from Town Hall, the Cape's oldest working windmill was built in Plymouth in the 1680s and moved to Eastham in the early 1800s. Corn is sometimes ground here in summer, when someone is on hand explaining the gristmill's operation.

First Encounter Beach, off Samoset Road and Route 6. A bronze marker commemorates the place where the Pilgrims, led by Captain Myles Standish, first met the Native Americans. The exchange was not friendly. Although arrows flew, no one was injured. The site goes down in history as the place where the Native Americans first began their decline at the hands of the European settlers. On a more modern note of warfare history, a ship used by the US Navy for 25 years of target practice sits on a sandbar about a mile offshore. The beach, with its westward vista, is a great place to catch a sunset.

Doane Homestead Site, between the Salt Pond Visitor Center and Coast Guard Beach, CCNS. Only a marker remains to identify the spot where

Doane, one of Eastham's first English settlers, made his home.

Old Cove Cemetery, Route 6. Many graves date back to the 1700s, but look for the memorial to the three *Mayflower* Pilgrims who were buried here in the 1600s.

Nauset Light and **Three Sisters Lighthouses,** at the corner of Cable Road and Ocean View Drive, CCNS. In 1838 this coastal cliff was home to three brick lighthouses that provided beacons for sailors. They collapsed from erosion in 1892 and were replaced with three wooden ones. When erosion threatened these in 1918, two were moved away; the third was moved in 1923. Eventually the National Park Service acquired all three and moved them to their present location, nestled in the woods far back from today's coastline. The large red-and-white steel Nauset Light was recently moved away from the eroding shoreline like its predecesssors, the Three Sisters. To reach Three Sisters from Nauset Light, take the paved walkway from the parking lot.

TO DO

BICYCLING/RENTALS

Cape Cod Rail Trail. This scenic, well-maintained, 26-mile (one way) paved path winds from Dennis to Wellfleet.

Nauset Bike Trail, CCNS. This 1.6-mile (one-way) trail connects with the Cape Cod Rail Trail and runs from the Salt Pond Visitor Center, across Nauset Marsh via a boardwalk, to Coast Guard Beach. The trail passes large stands of thin, tall black locust trees not native to the area—they were introduced to return nitrogen to the soil after overfarming.

Rental prices are about the same at **Idle Times Bike Shop** (255-8281), on Route 6 north of the Salt Pond Visitor Center, open year-round, and **Little Capistrano Bike Shop** (255-6515), across from the Salt Pond Visitor Center, open April through December. Rentals run about $17 a day, $8 for 2 hours. Both shops do repairs.

FOR FAMILIES

Poit's Place (255-6321), Route 6. Open mid-May to mid-September. Families have stopped here since 1954 for mini-golf, ice cream, pizza slices, hot dogs, and fish-and-chips.

T-Time Family Sports Center (255-5697), Route 6, North Eastham. Open daily in summer, weekends only in autumn, mid-May to mid-October. If you're desperately in need of a bucket of balls to belt out, this will suffice. The mini-golf is a bit run down, but there are slim pickings on the Outer Cape.

FISHING/SHELLFISHING

Purchase your required freshwater fishing license at Town Hall (240-5900) on Route 6. Spring-fed **Herring Pond** is the best bet since it's stocked. Contact the Department of Public Works (Department of Natural Resources, 255-5972), Old Orchard Road, for shellfishing

When the snow falls, sledding on Fort Hill is the thing to do.

permits and regulations. Open 9–4 Monday through Saturday. Shellfishing is permitted at Salt Pond and Salt Pond River only on Sunday.

FITNESS CLUB

Norseman Athletic Club (255-6370), Route 6. Open daily year-round. Facilities include racquetball and squash courts, Nautilus and free weights, an Olympic-sized pool, saunas and steam rooms, a whirlpool, and six indoor tennis courts. Daily ($12), weekly, and weekend rates.

SPECIAL PROGRAMS

Recreational programs run 9–noon, late June to mid-August. Visitors and summer residents are encouraged to bring their children (ages 6–16) to the playground at Nauset Regional High School (on Cable Road, North Eastham) to participate in various programs including archery, arts and crafts, and soccer. Supervised swimming and instruction are offered at Wiley Park (on Great Pond) for children ages 3–16 on weekday mornings. Register any weekday at 9. Fees vary.

TENNIS

Nauset Regional High School, Cable Road, North Eastham. The public can use the courts after school gets out.

See also *Fitness Club.*

SPECIAL PROGRAMS

Cape Cod Photo Workshops (255-6808), PO Box 1619, North Eastham 02651. These hands-on workshops offer a chance to work closely with professional photographer/artists from the Cape and Boston. Location work, view camera use, portraiture, darkroom classes, critiques; weekend and weeklong; beginner and advanced.

GREEN SPACE

BEACHES

❊ **Coast Guard Beach,** CCNS, on the Atlantic Ocean. This long beach, backed by grasses and heathland, is perfect for walking and sunning. Facilities include excellent changing rooms, rest rooms, and in-season lifeguards. In summer a shuttle bus ferries visitors from a well-marked parking lot. Parking $5 per day (good all day on any CCNS beach); seasonal pass $15; walkers and bicyclists free.

Gray seals and small brown harbor seals (sometimes hundreds of them) congregate at the southern tip of Coast Guard Beach in winter. They feed on the ever-present sand eels. Take the walk at low tide and allow an hour to cover the 2 miles.

Henry Beston wrote his 1928 classic, *The Outermost House,* during the year he lived in a two-room bungalow on Coast Guard Beach. The book chronicles Beston's interaction with the natural environment and records seasonal changes. The cottage was designated a National Literary Landmark in 1964, but the blizzard of 1978 washed it into the ocean. Bundled up (tightly!) against the off-season winds, you'll get a glimpse of the haunting isolation Beston experienced.

After a brutal 1990 storm washed away a large chunk of beach, an amateur archaeologist discovered evidence of a prehistoric dwelling on Coast Guard Beach. (Watch the video at the Salt Pond Visitor Center.) It is one of the oldest undisturbed archaeological sites in New England, dating back 6000 years to the Early Archaic and Woodland cultures. Because Coast Guard Beach was then 5 miles inland, the site provided a safe encampment for hunters and gatherers.

The Coast Guard Station at the top of the cliff was decommissioned in 1958 and now serves as the Environmental Educational Center for CCNS. The US Coast Guard evolved from the Lifesaving Service established in 1872 in response to the thousands of ships that were wrecked off the treacherous coast. When the Cape Cod Canal was built in 1914, and ships could pass through instead of going around the Cape, fatalities decreased dramatically.

❊ **Nauset Light Beach,** CCNS, on the Atlantic Ocean. An idyllic, long, broad, dune-backed beach. Facilities include changing rooms, rest rooms, and a lifeguard in-season. Parking $5 per day (good at any CCNS beach).

First Encounter Beach, Campground Landing Beach, and **Cook's Brook Beach.** These are bayside town beaches, open 9–4 Monday through Saturday. All bayside beaches are well suited to kite flying and shelling. They are safe for children because of the shallow water and gradual slope. Parking is $5 daily. Get parking stickers for weekly stays from the Department of Public Works (Department of Natural Resources, 255-1965) on Old Orchard Road.

The Nauset Light Trail boardwalk crosses below the Coast Guard Station.

PONDS

Herring Pond and **Great Pond,** west of Eastham Center off Samoset, Great Pond, and Herring Brook Roads. Parking $5 per day in-season. Of the two, Great Pond has a larger beach area.

WALKS

❊ **Fort Hill area,** CCNS, trailhead and parking off Route 6. The trail is about 1½ miles round-trip with a partial boardwalk, some log steps, and some hills. It offers lovely views of Nauset Marsh, especially from Skiff Hill, but also winds through the dense Red Maple Swamp and past the Edward Penniman House (see *To See*). Birders enjoy this walk year-round but it is particularly beautiful in autumn when the maples turn color. Pastoral Fort Hill was farmed until the 1940s and rock walls still mark boundaries.

❊ **Nauset Marsh Trail,** CCNS, trailhead behind the Salt Pond Visitor Center. About 1 mile round-trip; some log steps. This trail runs along Salt Pond and yields expansive vistas of Nauset Marsh. Nauset Marsh was actually Nauset Bay when it was charted by Frenchman Samuel de Champlain in 1605. As the barrier beach developed, so did the marsh. In a similar vein, Salt Pond was a freshwater pond until the ocean broke through from Nauset Marsh. This complex ecosystem sustains all manner of ocean creatures and shorebirds.

Buttonbush Trail, CCNS, trailhead at the Salt Pond Visitor Center. The trail is ¼ mile, with some boardwalk, some log steps. It was specially designed with Braille markers for the blind or visually impaired.

Eastham Hiking Club (255-3021). From September through June, the club meets at 9 AM on Wednesday for a vigorous 2-hour walk somewhere between Yarmouth and Provincetown. Call for the week's location.

LODGING

HOTEL

✎❊ **Sheraton Four Points Hotel** (255-5000, 1-800-533-3986), Route 6, Eastham 02642. Open year-round. This bi-level Sheraton hotel has all the amenities you'd expect: an indoor and an outdoor pool, a whirlpool, health club facilities, and two tennis courts. The odd thing is, you just don't expect to see a Sheraton on the Outer Cape. About half of the 107 nicely appointed rooms and suites overlook the tasteful indoor pool area, which resembles an inverted ship's hull. The other rooms overlook woods; these are slightly larger and brighter and have small refrigerators. Restaurant on the premises. In-season $151, a little less if you book ahead with a "sure saver"; off-season rates go as low as $79, but if you head down without a reservation, you'll sometimes find that the marquee advertises rooms for less. Children under 17 free in parent's room.

BED & BREAKFASTS

Whalewalk Inn (255-0617), 220 Bridge Road, Eastham 02642. Open April through November and select winter weekends. Delightfully off the beaten path, this 19th-century whaling captain's home has been operated with flair and grace by Carolyn and Dick Smith since 1990. My favorite accommodations are the four suites in the outbuildings: They are large and afford great privacy; all have a kitchen and fireplace, one has a deck, and one has a cathedral ceiling. There is also a lovely, airy, romantic cottage. The 6 rooms in the inn are among the top 10 best rooms on the Outer Cape, decorated with country sophistication, a smattering of fine antiques, and breezy floral fabrics. (Unfortunately, the deluxe room is right next to the kitchen, which is bustling at times.) One of the nicest features is the quiet brick patio where a full breakfast is served and an afternoon drink and hors d'oeuvres can be had. The inn also has loaner bikes. Late May to mid-October $125–180.

❊ **Sylvanus Knowles House** (240-2870), 75 Fort Hill Road, Eastham 02642. Open year-round. Across from the Penniman House (see *To See*), Jean and Gordon Avery's two-room B&B has one of the best locations on all of Cape Cod. The 19th-century Greek Revival farmhouse is idyllically perched on a little knoll overlooking Nauset Marsh. As if that weren't enough, the hosts are friendly and the house elegantly appointed. The three-room Emma suite has a library and oversized tub; on the second floor, Lucille is charming with slanted eaves and wide pine floors. A full breakfast is included. This place is a charmer; book well in advance. $95–115, 3-night minimum in summer, 2 nights the rest of the year. No credit cards.

✎❊ **Over Look Inn** (255-1886, web site: http://www.capecod.com/overlook), 3085 Route 6, Eastham 02642. Open year-round. This big, yellow Victorian house is difficult to see even though it's right on Route 6, across from the Salt Pond Visitor Center. The common rooms are unusual: There's a billiards room with Nigerian art, a library dedicated to Winston Churchill, and a parlor with velveteen curtains. Afternoon tea is served amid a collection of Andrew Wyeth prints, while the hallways are lined with the hosts' son's large canvases. The 11 guest rooms, generally light and airy, all have private baths; some have cathedral ceilings and skylights; all have lace curtains and antique furnishings. There is also a cottage behind the inn that can accommodate a family (and the family pet). Nan and Ian Aitchison have been welcoming guests with their Scottish hospitality since 1983. Full breakfasts include such hearty dishes as kedgeree (smoked cod and rice, sautéed with onions). April through October $95–145; off-season $75–95.

❋ **Penny House Bed & Breakfast** (255-6632, 1-800-554-1751), 4885 Route 6, North Eastham 02651. Open year-round. From the street, this bow-roof Cape doesn't look nearly as old as it is; sections date back to the mid-1700s. The dining room (where a full breakfast is served) has wide floorboards, original beams, and barn-board walls. The rest of the house has a newer feel: Each of the 11 guest rooms (of varying sizes and styles) has a new bathroom and comfortable furnishings; most have air-conditioning. Penny Serenade, tucked under the eaves, features a private balcony and separate entrance. The mother-daughter team of Margaret and Rebecca Keith are particularly helpful innkeepers. Common space includes the great room with a working fireplace, and a brick patio in the back of the house. $105–165 July to early September; $80–145 off-season.

COTTAGES

Anchorage On-The-Cove (255-1442), Route 6, Eastham 02653. Open May through October. These neat and tidy cottages, some right at the water's edge on Town Cove, are an old-fashioned find. Foremast, Bell-Buoy, and Top Sail are two-bedroom cottages with private decks on the water. You can't get any closer to the water than this unless you're in one of the Reades' rowboats. Kitchens, pine paneling, 1970s-style furnishings, gas grills, cribs, and cable TV are the order of the day. Some cottages also have a fireplace. Pilot House and Top Deck—neither of which is on the water—have access to the dock. Joanna and Bill also rent three B&B rooms in an adjacent house. $650–800 a week in summer for up to four people; $450–525 off-season. No credit cards.

☞✍ **Gibson Cottages** (255-0882), off Samoset Road from Route 6. Open mid-April to mid-November. Down a little dirt road marked with the sign GIBSON, you'll find some of the best lakeside cottages on the Cape. Jerry and Mary Jane Gibson have owned the seven cottages since 1966 and take great pride in maintaining them. Each of the well-spaced one-, two-, and three-bedroom cottages has a screened porch or deck and fully equipped kitchen. They're very neat and tidy, painted fresh white. A swimming dock, sailboat, rowboats, and barbecue area are shared by all. There are also two bike trails on the other side of the clean lake, which boasts a private, sandy beach. "Quiet" pets are permitted. This is a gem. Call as soon as you can to get a cottage. $600–700 in-season, $400–500 off-season.

Nauset Lighthouse

⌂ **Midway Motel & Cottages** (255-3117, 1-800-755-3117), Route 6, North Eastham 02651. Open February through October. Pine and oak trees shield this reasonably priced complex of motel units and cottages from the road. Ron and Sally Knisely have presided over this tidy place since 1983. The grounds feature a nice children's play area, shuffleboard, badminton, horseshoes, picnic tables, and grills. Some motel units can accommodate additional people for an additional nominal charge. One of the two cottages has three bedrooms; bring your own linens and towels. In-season $74–100 for rooms, $560–695 per week for cottages; off-season $42–68 rooms, $310–460 per week cottages. Children under 16 free.

☞ **Saltaway Cottages** (255-2182, 644-1242 in winter), Aspinet Road, North Eastham 02651. Open mid-May to mid-October. The cottages are sited in a pine grove a half mile off the much traveled Mid-Cape Highway. Walter and Sally Morse purchased these seven cottages in 1988 and have been spiffing them up ever since. The shellacked knotty-pine walls give the one- and two-bedroom cottages an immaculate feel. Kitchens are fully equipped and furnishings tasteful. Brewster cottage has a fireplace. In-season $460–680 weekly for two to four people; off-season $310–400 weekly; 2–4-night minimums also available. No credit cards.

Salt Marsh Cottage (255-4139), 2170 Route 6, Eastham 02642. Open May through October. This two-story red barn commands a beautiful, distant view of Nauset Marsh and is owned by the Turcottes, who live next door. Two bedrooms upstairs have twin beds, while the first floor comprises a good-sized kitchen and separate living room. A screened-in porch with cement floor faces the marsh. Mid-June to early September: $560 per week; off-season $400 per week. No credit cards.

See also Whalewalk Inn and Over Look Inn under *Bed & Breakfasts.*

MOTEL

☞⌘ **Captain's Quarters** (255-5686, 1-800-327-7769, e-mail: cqmcc@aol.com), Route 6, North Eastham 02651. Open April through November. These above-average motel rooms have air-conditioning, a small refrigerator, and cable TV. Many of the 75 rooms have two double beds, and for an additional $16 four people can share one room, making it a good value. Children under 12 stay free. Other amenities include a pool, tennis courts, picnic area, basketball court, free use of bicycles (the Rail Trail runs right behind the motel), and a constant supply of popcorn in the coffee shop. July and August $80–101; off-season $50–72.

RENTALS

Anchor Real Estate (255-2258), Route 6, North Eastham. Talk to Mary Carey about summertime rentals.

HOSTEL

☞ **Hostelling International Mid-Cape** (255-2785), 75 Goody Hallet Drive, off Bridge Road, Eastham 02642. Open mid-May to mid-September. Located in a quiet residential neighborhood off the Orleans rotary, this nonprofit organization is open to people of all ages and promotes cross-cultural understanding through educational travel. The hostel sponsors programs on environmental topics, budget travel, bike repair, stargazing, and such. It's a warm, cooperative environment with 50 beds in eight cabins. Facilities include a common kitchen, a volleyball and basketball court, a game room, table tennis, a barbecue area, and a screened-in gazebo. It's about a mile to the nearest bay beach. Advance reservations are essential in July and August. $12 for AYH members, $15 for nonmembers; children under 14 are half-price. Lock-out 9:30 AM–5:30 PM.

WHERE TO EAT

❋ **Mitchel's Bistro** (255-4803), Main Street Mercantile, Route 6, North Eastham. Open for dinner Wednesday through Sunday year-round. Inquire about the breakfast and lunch menu, which was being revised. Chef-owner Mitch Rosenbaum and his partner, Laxmi Venkateshwaran, developed a following at Cielo Cafe in Wellfleet before moving here in 1995. Mitch is known for his curries, which top royal shrimp and scallops, lamb, and chicken. But he also has other popular dishes up his sleeve: nightly variations on grilled duck breast, and sole baked in ground cashews and served with black beans and plantains. There are always fancy and fresh pasta dishes. Mitchel's also has special "theme" nights featuring Indian and West Indian buffets. Dinner entrées $10–18.

Eastham Lobster Pool (255-9706, 255-3314 for takeout), 4360 Route 6, North Eastham. Open 11:30–9 daily, April through October. Although this place has the requisite fried fish and seafood platters, you can also order fish poached, broiled, or grilled ($14–18). Or just snack on peel-

and-eat shrimp (10 for $6.50) and a side of clam chowder ($2.50). The choices and combinations are practically endless. Weekly and daily specials (like a lobster shore dinner for $18) are usually a good bet. The indoor dining room is pleasant, with wooden tables and chairs. There's outdoor dining and less expensive takeout, too. Although the Pool offers burgers and steaks, stick to the fish.

Arnold's Lobster & Clam Bar (255-2575), 3580 Route 6. Open 11–10 daily, mid-May to early September. A raw bar complements the usual assortment of fish rolls and fried seafood baskets. Get a generous side order of fried shrimp or clam strips or a weekday lunch special for $3. Onion rings are excellent. Choose nondescript indoor dining, the open-air patio, or tables under pine trees. Dishes $7–16. No credit cards.

✳ **Box Lunch** (255-0799), Route 6, North Eastham. Open daily year-round, until 4 PM in the off-season. If you've got a hungry family or a hankering for a sandwich made with pita bread, stop at this inconspicuous strip mall. (In case you didn't know, they roll their sandwich meats in pita bread at this franchise.) Sandwiches $2–5.

SNACKS

Ben & Jerry's (255-2817), Route 6 at Brackett Road. Open March through November. The trademark black-and-white cows of Vermont have migrated to the warmer pastures of Cape Cod. The "bluesberry" frozen yogurt, with blueberries, strawberries, and raspberries, can't be beat; or choose from dozens of creamy, crunchy, and chunky ice cream offerings.

ENTERTAINMENT

First Encounter Coffee House (255-5438), Samoset Road. Open year-round except September and May. Performances on the first and third Saturday of each month; open mike every fourth Saturday. Acoustic and folk music reign here, attracting musicians with national reputations—including such notables as Wellfleet's very own Patty Larkin and Vineyarder Livingston Taylor. The coffeehouse has been home to the 1899 Unitarian-Universalist church (aka Chapel in the Pines) since 1974. The intimate venue has only 100 seats, beneath stained-glass windows. Tickets are usually $10; children free; open mike $3.

SELECTIVE SHOPPING

ARTISAN

Sunken Meadow Basketworks & Pottery (255-8962), North Sunken Meadow Road, North Eastham. Open year-round but call first in winter. Look for Hugh and Paulette Penney's handwoven baskets, wall sculptures, stoneware, and jewelry in a newly constructed barn.

ART SHOW

Eastham Painters' Guild, at the Schoolhouse Museum. Outdoor art shows are held here every Friday (and most Thursdays) in summer.

SPECIAL SHOPS

Collector's World (255-3616), Route 6. Open year-round. Since 1974, Chris Alex has been selling an eclectic lineup of antiques, gifts, and collectibles like Russian lacquer boxes, scrimshaw, pewter, and wooden nutcracker soldiers. It's one of the most eclectic collections on the Cape.

The Chocolate Sparrow (240-0606), 4205 Route 6. Open year-round. Marjorie Sparrow opened this shop in 1989 to sell her luscious hand-dipped chocolates and homemade fudge.

Exposure (255-6808), 135 Oak Leaf Road, North Eastham. Open year-round. One of the few Cape places that process black-and-white film.

SPECIAL EVENTS

Mid-July: **Arts and Crafts Show.** At Nauset Regional High School, off Route 6 near Nauset Light Beach. Over 150 artisans; since 1968.

Mid-September: **Windmill Weekend.** This community fair and festival features road races, band concerts, an arts and crafts show, square dancing, and a parade.

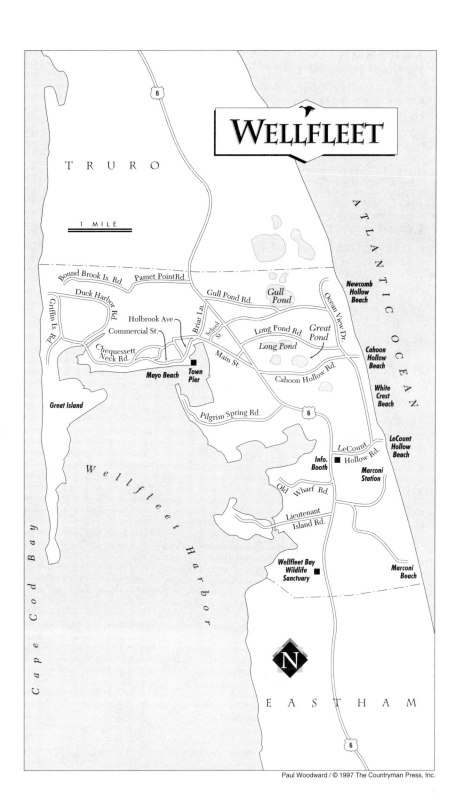

WELLFLEET

TRURO

1 MILE

Bound Brook Is. Rd. Pamet Point Rd.
Duck Harbor Rd.
Griffin Is. Rd.
Holbrook Ave.
Commercial St.
Chequessett Neck Rd.
Mayo Beach
Town Pier
Great Island

Gull Pond Rd.
Gull Pond
Briar Ln.
School St.
Main St.
Long Pond Rd.
Long Pond
Great Pond
Ocean View Dr.
Cahoon Hollow Rd.

Newcomb Hollow Beach
Cahoon Hollow Beach
White Crest Beach

ATLANTIC OCEAN

Pilgrim Spring Rd.

6

LeCount Hollow Rd.
LeCount Hollow Beach
Info. Booth
Marconi Station

Old Wharf Rd.

Lieutenant Island Rd.

Wellfleet Harbor

Cape Cod Bay

Wellfleet Bay Wildlife Sanctuary

Marconi Beach

N

EASTHAM

6

Wellfleet

Although a whopping 70 percent of Wellfleet is conservation land, the town is perhaps best known as an art stronghold. Wellfleet's two principal thoroughfares, Main Street and Commercial Street, are dotted with 20 or so galleries, some of them in little weathered cottages reminiscent of fishing shacks. The galleries represent a wide gamut of art: from souvenir works to images that transcend their media. Many of the artists and artisans who exhibit here call Wellfleet home, at least for a short time each year, gaining inspiration from pristine landscapes and an unrelenting ocean.

Wellfleet appeals to a distinct crowd, many of whom have returned year after year for decades. When shopkeepers and restaurateurs begin dusting off the shelves in early to mid-June, it feels like a real homecoming—old friends catching up over a coffee in a café, neighbors renewing relationships as they tend their gardens, and acquaintances greeting a faintly familiar face from the previous summer. Families rent houses here for the entire summer. And although Wellfleet is very popular with vacationing psychiatrists, there's a notable contingent of lawyers, professors, and writers. They've all come for the same purpose—to commune with their thoughts, recharge their batteries, and lead a simpler life (albeit a temporary one). But they also venture out of their cocoons to dine on wonderful food in laid-back settings, to square dance outdoors, and to engage in lively conversation. No enterprise in town is more fondly supported than the adventurous Wellfleet Harbor Actors Theater.

Even so, Wellfleeters are an independent bunch. Almost 30 percent of the 2500 year-rounders are self-employed, more than any other Cape town. Most of the town rolls up its shutters from mid-October to mid-May. In fact, even on a weekday in mid-June, Wellfleet may feel eerie, like a ghost town. The off-season has its own allures, however. If you visit midwinter, you'll find a few warm beds and a hot meal or two, and the frozen bay is a romantic sight on an overcast day.

In addition to art, Wellfleet's draw is the natural environment. The Audubon Society's outstanding Wellfleet Bay Wildlife Sanctuary offers practically unparalleled opportunities for observing marine and bird life through a variety of guided activities and self-guided walks. A mostly sandy, 8-mile-long trail on Great Island, part of the Cape Cod National Seashore (CCNS), yields solitude and commanding views of Wellfleet Bay. And like other towns along the Outer Cape, the entire Atlantic coastline of Wellfleet is CCNS land. The broad, uninterrupted beaches east of Route 6 are backed by dunes and cliffs. The meandering roads of Wellfleet are perfect for cycling, leading you past ponds, salt marshes, heathlands, and scrub pines.

Wellfleet was most likely named after a town in England, which, like "our" Wellfleet, was also renowned for its oyster beds. As early as the 17th century, when Wellfleet was still a part of Eastham known as Billingsgate, the primary industries revolved around oyster and cranberry harvesting. Whaling, fishing, and other related industries also flourished until the mid-1800s. And by the 1870s, commercial markets had really opened up for littlenecks, cherrystones, and clams for chowder. Today, with the depletion of natural fish and shellfish stocks, year-round fishermen have turned to aquaculture. Currently about 50 or so aquaculturists lease 120 acres of Wellfleet Harbor; you'll see them off Mayo Beach at low tide. Shellfish like quahogs and oysters are raised from "seed," put out in "protected racks," and tended for two to three years while they mature. Since as many as 2 million seeds can be put on an acre of land, this is big business. For those looking for fishing charters, though, the harbor and pier are still centers of activity.

In the name of "progress," houses and businesses were assigned street numbers in 1995. Although they're helpful to the fire department, they're of relatively little use to visitors, as many shops don't post the numbers and when they do, numbers are often not in consecutive order. Don't despair, Wellfleet's a small town; you won't have trouble finding what you're looking for.

GUIDANCE

Wellfleet Chamber of Commerce (349-2510), Route 6, PO Box 571, Wellfleet 02667. Open 10–4 Friday through Sunday, mid-May to mid-October, 9–6 daily in July and August. The information booth is well marked, right off Route 6 in South Wellfleet. The chamber publishes a rudimentary foldout map of Wellfleet bicycle routes.

PUBLIC REST ROOMS

Public rest rooms can be found in summer at Baker Field across from Mayo Beach, on the Town Pier and Marina. Throughout the year, during business hours, head to the basement of Town Hall on Main Street.

GETTING THERE

By car: Wellfleet is 50 miles beyond the Sagamore Bridge via Route 6.

By bus: The **Plymouth & Brockton** bus line (775-5524) connects Wellfleet with other Cape towns and with Boston's Logan Airport.

GETTING AROUND

From Route 6, take Main Street to the center of town or veer from Main to Commercial Street to the colorful harbor and marina. Park your car and stroll along Main and Commercial Streets. (The walk can be long if you mosey from one end of town to the other; furthermore, the eastern end of Commercial Street doesn't have any sidewalks.) There is free parking at the Town Pier at the end of Commercial Street and behind Town Hall on Main Street. As the seagull flies, the town is anywhere from 2 to 5 miles wide.

MEDICAL EMERGENCY

Outer Cape Health Services (349-3131), Route 6, Wellfleet. Open for walk-ins 8–5 weekdays, 8–8 on Thursday.

TO SEE

Marconi Wireless Station, CCNS, off Route 6 at the Marconi Area. Guglielmo Marconi began construction of the first wireless station on the US mainland in 1901. Two years later the first US wireless transatlantic message was transmitted between this station and England: President Roosevelt sent King Edward VII "most cordial greetings and good wishes." (Canada beat the United States in sending a wireless transatlantic message by one month.) The station was closed in 1917 for wartime security reasons and was dismantled and abandoned in 1920 because of erosion and the development of alternative technologies. There are few remains today, save the concrete foundation of the transmitter house (which required 25,000 volts to send a message) and sand anchors that held guy wires to the 210-foot towers. The Cape Cod peninsula is at its narrowest here. And from a well-positioned observation platform you can scan the width of it—from Cape Cod Bay, along Blackfish Creek, to the Atlantic Ocean.

Wellfleet Historical Society Museum (349-9157), 266 Main Street. Open 2–5 Tuesday through Saturday, late June to early September. The society has collected photographs, toys, salvage from shipwrecks, marine artifacts, displays on Marconi and oystering, and household items to illustrate and preserve Wellfleet's past. Adults $1, children under 12 free.

First Congregational Church of the United Church of Christ, 200 Main Street. The church was organized in 1721, but this meetinghouse dates to 1850. The interior is graced with a brass chandelier, pale blue walls, curved pews, and a Tiffany-style stained-glass window depicting a 17th-century clipper ship similar to the *Mayflower.* On Sunday evenings at 8 in July and August, concerts are given on the recently restored Hook and Hastings pipe organ. The church's architecture is Greek Revival, except for the bell-shaped cupola, which was added in 1879 after a storm destroyed the traditional one. (It was thought that a bell-shaped tower would be more sturdy—and perhaps it has been.) Sunday services at 9:30 in July and August.

Town clock, First Congregational Church, Main Street. According to the arbiter of superlatives, *Ripley's Believe It or Not,* this is the "only town clock in the world that strikes ship's time." Listen for the following chimes and figure out what time it is for yourself: Two bells distinguish 1, 5, and 9 o'clock; six bells signify 3, 7, and 11 o'clock; eight bells toll for 4, 8, and 12 o'clock. To make matters even more interesting, the half hours are signified by adding one chime to the corresponding even hours. (You might wish to double-check your digital wristwatch!)

Our Lady of Lourdes Church, Main Street. On the occasion of the country's 1976 bicentennial, two troubadours expressed their thanks to the town after a long celebration. Their handsome painted carvings are attached to the doors, thankfully kept open for all to see.

❉ **Uncle Tim's Bridge,** East Commercial Street. The often photographed wooden footbridge connects Commercial Street to a small wooded island, crossing a tidal creek (Duck Creek) and marshland. Short, sandy trails circle the island.

Samuel Rider House, Gull Pond Road. Although the house is not open to the public, it's a fine early-1700s Outer Cape farmstead.

Atwood Higgins House (255-3421), Bound Brook Island Road, off Pamet Point Road. Under the auspices of the National Seashore, this homestead can be toured by reservation only, at 1 PM on Wednesday mid-May to mid-October. The property owners created an authentic-looking replica of a little 18th-century town, complete with a small store and post office. Volunteers lead you around the 5-acre property and through the 18th-century full Cape. Free.

SCENIC DRIVES

Ocean View Drive. Take LeCount Hollow Road to Ocean View (despite its name, it has only limited ocean views) and head back to Route 6 via Gull Pond Road. You'll pass heathlands, cliffs, and scrub pines.

Chequessett Neck Road. Cross the dike at Herring River and head to the end of the road for magnificent sunset views. Although there is only room for a few cars at the very end of the road, you can park near the Great Island trailhead and walk down to the beach.

Pilgrim Spring Road. Not to be confused with the Pilgrim Spring Trail in Truro, where the Pilgrims got their first taste of fresh water, this quiet road offers lovely views of inlets and a cove; at the end of the road, look back to Wellfleet Harbor.

TO DO

BICYCLING/RENTALS

Cape Cod Rail Trail. Extended in 1994, the trail now ends in Wellfleet at LeCount Hollow Road, just east of Route 6.

Idle Times Bike Shop (349-9161), Route 6. Open mid-June to mid-September. A full line of bicycles for the whole family. 24-hour repairs.

BOAT EXCURSIONS/RENTALS

Jack's Boat Rentals (349-7553, 1-800-300-3787), Gull Pond. Open late May to early September. Jack's offers guided kayak and canoe tours on kettle ponds at sunset and along the Pamet and Herring Rivers. Jack's also rents canoes, boogie boards, kayaks (and double kayaks), Sunfish, pedal boats, and sailboards.

Wellfleet Marine Corp. (349-2233), Town Pier. From mid-June to mid-September you can rent Stur-Dee Cat sailboats, sloops, and fishing skiffs by the hour or by the day.

See also *Fishing/Shellfishing.*

FISHING/SHELLFISHING

Obtain a freshwater fishing permit at Town Hall (349-0301) on Main Street. Freshwater fishing holes include **Great Pond, Gull Pond,** and **Long Pond.** Shellfishing permits are required ($40 nonresident) for the taking of oysters, clams, and quahogs. Wellfleet's tidal flats are wondrous places at low tide. Contact the Beach Sticker Booth (349-9818) on the pier in July and August or Town Hall (349-0300) on Main Street the rest of the year. Try your luck surf casting early in the morning or at night at **Newcomb Hollow, White Crest Beach, LeCount Hollow** (all on the Atlantic), or at **Duck Harbor** on the bayside.

Black Duck Sports Shop (349-9801), off Route 6, South Wellfleet. Open April to mid-October. Get your tide chart, live eels, squid, worms, and sand eels here, along with outdoor maps and camping equipment.

Among the half- and full-day fishing charters that generally operate from mid-May to mid-October, contact *Snoop* (349-6113), *Jac's Mate* (255-2978, 240-8310), and *Altimate* (349-9576). All are docked at the Wellfleet Harbor Marina.

Naviator (349-6003), Wellfleet Harbor Marina. With more than 30 years of experience plying Cape Cod waters, Captain Rick Merrill offers a little bit of everything: morning and afternoon fishing trips, an hour-long harbor cruise on variable evenings in-season, and a marine-life cruise in conjunction with the Audubon Society. The boat holds 49 people.

GOLF

Chequessett Yacht & Country Club (349-3704), Chequessett Neck Road. Open April through November, weather permitting. This nine-hole, par-35 course offers beautiful views of Wellfleet Harbor. Non-members can reserve tee times up to 5 days in advance.

MINI-GOLF

At the Wellfleet Drive-In (349-2520), Route 6. Open mid-April to mid-October. The course is nothing special, but it's the only game in town and it's conveniently located next to the flea market and drive-in.

SAILING

Sailing lessons (349-0198), Chequessett Yacht & Country Club, Chequessett Neck Road. Junior and adult sailing programs that run from early July to late August. Group instruction is $45 per week and individual instruction (for one or two people) is $30 an hour.

SEAL CRUISES

Wellfleet Bay Wildlife Sanctuary (349-2615). Year-round trips offered on most weekends and some weekdays; call for the tide-dependent

A boardwalk crosses the dunes to the National Seashore.

schedule. Excursions are scheduled out of Wellfleet Harbor (2-hour trips in late fall), Chatham (90-minute trips off South Beach and Monomoy Island in summer), and Harwichport (3–4-hour trips in winter). Onboard naturalists will tell you all about the hundreds of harbor and gray seals you'll see sunning themselves or bobbing in the water. Tickets: $25–35 for nonmembers; $5 less for members.

SPECIAL PROGRAMS

- **Wellfleet Bay Wildlife Sanctuary Natural History Day Camp** (349-2615), PO Box 236, South Wellfleet 02663. July and August. Intended for children 4–14, these excellent weeklong, half-day, and daylong programs are designed to "expand curiosity about and respect for the environment through hands-on outdoor experiences . . . and to develop skill in discovering the natural world using the principles of scientific inquiry." $65 for nonmembers ($55 members) for a half day, $175–200 for nonmembers for a full day. (See *Green Space* for adult programs.)

- **Summer Recreation Programs** (349-0330), Bakers Field and Gull Pond. Weekdays 9–noon, July and August. Sports, arts and crafts, and swimming lessons for children over 6. Nonresidents $10 per week per child.

TENNIS

Town courts are on Mayo Beach, Kendrick Street.

Oliver's Clay Tennis Courts (349-3330), Route 6. Open daily May through October, weather permitting. You'll notice the Saabs parked in front of the courts before you notice the seven well-hidden clay courts or the one Truflex court. Matches can be arranged and racquets restrung.

Chequessett Yacht & Country Club (349-3704), Chequessett Neck Road. Open March through December, weather permitting. Five all-weather courts are available to the public for a fee.

GREEN SPACE

✳ **Wellfleet Bay Wildlife Sanctuary** (349-2615), off Route 6, South Wellfleet 02663. Trails open daily sunrise to sunset; center open daily 8:30–5, year-round, except closed Monday from November through April. The sanctuary encompasses almost 1000 acres of pine, moors, freshwater ponds, tidal creeks, salt marsh, and beach. This is one of the most active sanctuaries in New England and an excellent resource for Cape Cod naturalists. Even non-naturalists will appreciate the relative lack of human presence after a day of gallery hopping and sunbathing. In 1993 an environmentally friendly visitors center was built as a result of the efforts of director Bob Prescott; its composting toilets should save 100,000 gallons of water per season.

The sanctuary offers a continuous stream of activities throughout summer (and plenty all year round, for that matter): canoe trips, sunset walks, night hikes, night bat watches, birding expeditions for beginners and aficionados, cruises on Nauset Marsh, and trips to Monomoy Island (see *Green Space*, "Chatham"). Summertime evening bayside talks focus on the Cape's natural history. Wintertime seal cruises to Monomoy Island and South Beach are also popular. Advance reservations are required for some of the offerings, like the adult field schools and cruises. Fees range from $1 for Audubon members ($3 for nonmembers) for talks to $55 for excursions. Drop in or write for a detailed schedule. Trails free to members, $3 for adult nonmembers, $2 for children nonmembers. Members may tent in the wooded, natural setting.

BEACHES

Marconi Beach, CCNS, on the Atlantic. A boardwalk and steep staircase lead to the long, narrow beach backed by dramatic dunes. Amenities include lifeguards, outdoor showers, and superb changing facilities. Parking $5 (permit valid all day at any CCNS beach); seasonal pass $15. Free to enter on foot; bicyclists pay $3.

Cahoon Hollow Beach and **White Crest Beach,** town beaches on the Atlantic Ocean. Sandy shoals create shallow, warm pools of water. Although each beach is wide and sandy, local townsfolk favor the sea grass and dunes of White Crest, and hang gliders and surfers appreciate the surf. White Crest has more parking. Amenities include lifeguards and rest rooms. Parking $10 per day.

Mayo Beach, Kendrick Street. Parking is free, but the beach is nothing to write home about. From here you can see some of the offshore areas—marked by yellow buoys—where modern aquaculture thrives in the form of constructed shellfish farms. The Bayside Lobster Hutt restaurant (see *Eating Out*) is supplied by an 8-acre aquafarm similar to this.

The following beaches require a town sticker: **LeCount Hollow Beach** and **Newcomb Hollow Beach,** both off Ocean View Drive on the Atlantic Ocean; **Burton Baker Beach** (the only place in town where windsurfing is permitted) and **Indian Neck Beach,** both off Pilgrim

Spring Road on the bayside; **Powers Landing** and **Duck Harbor,** both off Chequessett Neck Road on the bayside. Cottage renters may purchase a sticker at the well-marked Beach Sticker Booth (349-9818) on the Town Pier in July and August. $25 per week, $75 per season.

PONDS

Great Pond, Long Pond, and **Gull Pond** offer freshwater swimming. Parking stickers are required (stickers may be purchased at the Beach Sticker Booth, 349-9818, on the Town Pier). All have lifeguards.

WALKS

❋ **Wellfleet Bay Wildlife Sanctuary** (see full listing above). The sanctuary offers three trails totaling more than 5 miles: Silver Spring Trail, a lovely, wooded walking trail alongside a long pond; Goose Pond Trail, past ponds, woodlands, a marsh, and heathland (a boardwalk leads to the bay from here); and Bay View Trail.

❋ **Great Island Trail,** CCNS, off Chequessett Neck Road. About 8 miles round-trip, this trail is relatively flat, but soft sand makes for a challenging trek. Walk at low tide when the sand is more firm. (Jeremy Point, the tip of land farthest out to sea, is covered at high tide.) You'll be rewarded with scant human presence and stunning scenery during the 4-hour round-trip hike. Bring plenty of water and sunscreen. The trail is best on a sunny spring day or a crisp autumn one. It's great for birders.

This area was once an island, hence its name. But over time Cape Cod Bay currents deposited sandbars that eventually connected it to the mainland. Long ago, Great Island was home to various commercial enterprises—oystering, cranberry harvesting, and shore whaling—and the land was dotted with lookout towers used to spot whales. There was even a local watering hole and overnight hostelry, Smith Tavern, which was built in 1690 and used until about 1740. But as shore whaling died, so did the community on Great Island. By 1800 the island was deserted and deforested. (Pines have been planted in an effort to keep erosion under control.)

Atlantic White Cedar Swamp Trail, CCNS, Marconi Area. The early and latter parts of this 1¼-mile round-trip trail traverse steep stairs and soft sand; the swamp is navigable via a boardwalk. The swamp has a primordial feel, and the dense overhead cover keeps the trail cool even on the most stifling of days. Because white cedar was prized by the settlers for its light weight and ease of handling, a century of overuse took its toll. Recently the swamp (in places, 24 feet deep with peat) has begun to recover. Nature has its own cycles, however, and the red maples will eventually choke the white cedars out of existence. For now, appreciate one of the few remaining stands of white cedar left on the Cape. In August wild trailside blueberries are ripe for the picking.

LODGING

Most summer visitors to Wellfleet stay in cottages and houses, rented by the week or longer, but there are places for short-term guests as well. The zip code is 02667.

INNS

✐ **Inn at Duck Creeke** (349-9333), 70 Main Street. Open mid-May to mid-October. A half-mile from the center of town is a rambling, old-fashioned inn. The 1800s inn is situated between an idyllic duck pond (rooms 26 and 27 overlook it) and a salt marsh (ask for rooms 21 and 30 for this view). My favorite guest rooms are in the two outbuildings. Try one of four rooms in the Saltworks Cottage—they share a lovely living room. The two rooms in the carriage house have a spiffed-up, romantic cabin feel. Rustic, air-conditioned rooms on the third floor of the main inn are well suited to large groups and families. Continental breakfast included. In-season $70–90 with private bath, $65–75 with shared bath; off-season $40–70.

☞ **Holden Inn** (349-3450), 140 Commercial Street. Open mid-April to mid-October. Letitia Fricker has operated this old-fashioned hostelry since 1969, but it's been in her family since 1924. Guest rooms are simple and sparsely decorated with a braided or shag rug. The 14 lodge rooms, all with shared baths, provide shelter from the elements and a view of the harbor. Of the country-style rooms in the main house (most with private baths, many with twin beds), the Fountain Room is the most private. One of the best features of the Holden Inn is the long screened-in porch with rockers. No credit cards; no breakfast. $60–70 double, $47 single.

BED & BREAKFASTS

☞✻ **Blue Gateways** (349-7530, 349-3528), 252 Main Street. Open year-round. In 1996, Bonnie and Richard Robicheau opened what Wellfleet had heretofore lacked: a comfortable, cheery, completely refurbished night's stay in the center of town. Since Richard is a builder, the house has been expertly renovated. The three guest rooms share an upstairs TV room and a downstairs living room, complete with one of the house's three working fireplaces. An expanded continental breakfast is served in the sun porch, overlooking the little reflecting pool. Late May to early September $80–90, $10 less off-season.

☞✻ **Cahoon Hollow Bed & Breakfast** (349-6372), 56 Cahoon Hollow Road. Open year-round. Host Bailey Ruckert has created an elegant and comfortable environment within this 1842 sea captain's house, tucked away on a wooded road (2 miles from the beach and town center). Common space is plentiful: two living rooms, a lush garden patio, a hammock on the lawn. The multicourse breakfast may include popovers with honey butter, homemade yogurt and granola, and a deep-dish custard French toast with beach plum jam. Guests can use Bailey's bicycles and store items in the refrigerator. Bailey and her husband live next door, so ostensibly the house is yours to enjoy. Of the two guest rooms (both with private baths), the one upstairs is more private and has its own sitting room. $85–90 year-round; children $15 additional.

☞ **Sea Cliff** (349-3753, 212-741-1832 off-season), 740 Ocean View Drive. Open mid-June to mid-October. Although Marla Perkel has only one guest accommodation, what a room it is! The guest house, which is separate from the main house, is perched 110 feet above the Atlantic on a 2200-square-foot deck. All you can see is the falling away of beach grass and the endless sky and ocean. That sense of scale has a way of easing life back into perspective. Room amenities include a microwave, refrigerator, TV, VCR, and outdoor shower (there's an indoor one, too). There is no direct beach access, but there are beaches 0.2 mile in either direction. $125 nightly (2-night minimum, 7-night maximum). No credit cards.

COTTAGES AND HOUSES

Surf Side Cottages (349-3959; e-mail: surfside@capecod.net; http://www.-virtualcapecod.com/market/surfside), Ocean View Drive, South Wellfleet 02663. Open April through October. Within the CCNS, the 1950s-style housekeeping cottages aren't much to look at. (The exteriors cannot be remodeled under National Park Service regulations.) But what's really important is that most are within a minute's walk of the dunes. Nothing separates them from the ocean except other Surf Side cottages and scrub pines. A few have ocean views. Most larger cottages have roof decks; each has a screened-in porch and wood-burning fireplace. Modern kitchens, knotty-pine paneling, and tasteful rattan furnishings are the norm. Bring sheets and towels and leave the cottage clean and ready for the next tenants. Reserve early. Weekly, from late June to early September, $700 for one bedroom, $1000–1275 for two or three bedrooms; $70–125 per day or $400–650 per week off-season.

The Colony (349-3761), 640 Chequessett Neck Road, Wellfleet 02667. Open late May to mid-September. This is not your average cottage colony. It was built as a private club in 1949 by Ned Saltonstall (one of the founders of Boston's Institute for Contemporary Arts), who decided that his art buyers needed a place to stay when they came to view his collection. These days guests flock to The Colony for a quiet, calm atmosphere and excellent service (including turn-down service and fresh flowers on arrival) provided by Eleanor Stefani, who purchased the place back in 1963. Each of the 10 cinder-block units has a different view and charm, but they all have daily maid service, working fireplaces, original artwork, and picture windows or sliding glass doors. Galley kitchens and screened-in porches are standard features of the one-, two-, and three-bedroom units. Each of the patios or decks has a view of the natural, preserved surroundings; many have water views. The 1949 low-slung duplexes were built in the Bauhaus style, which was intent on doing the most with the least. Hence, there is no separate living room and bedroom; sofas-by-day double as twin-beds-by-night.

There aren't any hard-and-fast rules about renting from Saturday to Saturday, just one of the refreshing changes about the low-key style of The Colony. $825–1750 per week or $150–300 daily.

✐❋ **The Even'tide** (349-3410, 1-800-368-0007 within Massachusetts; e-mail: eventide@capecod.net), Route 6, South Wellfleet 02663. Open year-round. Operated by the Fillimans and Audettes since 1965, these eight cottages are a cut above the rest. Set back from Route 6 in a wooded area, the complex has a nice children's play area and a 30-by-60-foot heated indoor pool. The Cape Cod Rail Trail runs along the back of the property, and a ¾-mile walking trail leads to Marconi Beach. All cottages have cable TV, telephone, fully tiled bathrooms, and full kitchens (except Tern). Bedrooms in the peak of the A-frame cottages get warm in summer. Also available are above-average motel rooms and suites that rent for $62–99 nightly in-season. Weekly, in July and August, $575 for two, $625 for four, $690–820 for six; $415–515 weekly for four to six people in the off-season (or $69–88 nightly).

❋ **Mill Hill House** (349-6372), off Route 6, Wellfleet 02667. Open year-round. Situated on a hill with Wellfleet Harbor in the distance, this newly constructed house has a 21-by-23-foot living room and a full kitchen. Upstairs, the master bedroom is just as large and also boasts a telescope and long outdoor deck. A second bedroom also has its own TV. Furnishings are a tasteful, eclectic mix of modern, antique, and reproduction. $900 weekly in July and August; $600 weekly in the off-season.

MOTEL

❋ **Wellfleet Motel & Lodge** (349-3535, 1-800-852-2900), Route 6, South Wellfleet 02663. Open year-round. The highly visible sign proclaiming "squeaky clean rooms" begs inspection and, fortunately, the 65 rooms live up to the boasting. Located across from the Wellfleet Bay Wildlife Sanctuary, the bi-level, 1960s-style motel units are typically appointed and air-conditioned. Rooms in the lodge, built in 1986, are generally more spacious than the motel rooms. Gas grill, a whirlpool, restaurant, and indoor and outdoor pools are on the premises. There is direct access to the rail trail. July and August $79–170 double, $10 each additional person; off-season $55–95 double.

CAMGROUNDS

Paine's Campground (349-3007, 1-800-479-3017), off Old Colony Road from Route 6, South Wellfleet 02663. Open mid-May to mid-October. At this tenters' haven there are designated areas for "quiet" campers, youth groups, and families, as well as sites to which you must lug your tent. Of the 150 sites, only 6 are reserved for RVs. You can walk from the campground to the National Seashore. Freshwater swimming is found in nearby kettle ponds. Sites $8.50–12 per person.

Maurice's Campground (349-2029), Route 6, Wellfleet 02667. Open mid-May to mid-October. 180 wooded sites for tents and trailers. There are also cottages that can sleep four and cabins that can sleep three with a cot. $20 for two; additional adults $4, additional children $2. Cottages $375 weekly for two, $395 for four. Cabins nightly $55.

See also Wellfleet Bay Wildlife Sanctuary under *Green Space.*

RENTALS

Compass Real Estate (349-1717), Main Street, Wellfleet 02667. Compass has more than 200 house and cottage listings. They start at $500 for a small 350-square-foot cottage and go up to $2500 per week for a four-bedroom house on the water. Most of the properties are booked in January, February, and March, but Compass also has last-minute listings.

WHERE TO EAT

Wellfleet oysters are renowned: Legend has it that England's Queen Victoria served Wellfleet oysters (no others would do) at her state dinners. According to aficionados, Wellfleet oysters taste better when harvested from the cooler waters off-season, but you'll have little choice if you vacation in July or August; order them anyway. Wellfleet is also known for its hard-shell quahog and steamer clams. In the early 1990s, these waters yielded more than $2 million worth of shellfish per year.

Although there are many restaurants listed here, look closely and you'll find that most are closed prior to mid-June and after early autumn. Most of the opening and closing dates are quite fluid, wholly dependent on the weather and amount of tourist traffic each season.

DINING OUT

Aesop's Table (349-6450), 316 Main Street, next to Town Hall. Open for lunch and dinner nightly, late June to early September, and dinner Thursday through Sunday, Mother's Day to late June and early September to mid-October. Lunch is often served on weekends in the off-season. The accolades over the years for Wellfleet's premier dining spot are well deserved: The New American menu is ambitious and well executed under the supervision of executive chef Peter Rennert, who has been at Aesop's since 1992. As a starter, Monet's Garden Salad leaves quite an impression. With pine nuts, goat cheese, and a bounteous variety of greens from the restaurant's garden, it is large enough for two. Pan-roasted lamb chops with grilled polenta are skillfully prepared. Of the six dining rooms decorated with local art, avoid the rear one next to the kitchen. Although the small tables and table settings undersell the quality of the food, you must remember: This befits low-key, understated Wellfleet. A tavern menu (see Upstairs Bar at Aesop's Table under *Eating Out*) is served at lunch on the brick terrace overlooking Main Street. There is a special children's menu 5:30–6:15. Reservations highly recommended. Lunch $5.50–10; dinner entrées $15.75–23.75.

☞ **Painter's** (349-3003), 50 Main Street. Open for dinner mid-April through October (nightly except Tuesday in-season; off-season schedule varies.) Kate Painter—who apprenticed at both Biba's and Hammersley's in

Boston and Stars in San Francisco before graduating from college—has been serving remarkable New American cuisine to Wellfleet audiences since 1992. She moved from an offbeat waterfront joint to this more "adult" space in 1995. It's friendly, elegantly casual, and still a bit funky. I've never tasted a dish from her ambitious menu that I didn't enjoy. A few renowned modern classics, like the "rockin' lobster roll," still reflect her former moderate pricing structure. The upstairs bar features a lighter menu and local musicians. Entrées $12–20.

✳ **Finely JP's** (349-7500), Route 6, South Wellfleet. Open year-round for dinner: nightly in July and August; Wednesday through Sunday in May, June, September, and October; Thursday through Sunday, November through April. Don't let appearances fool you; you'd probably drive by this nondescript roadside place if someone didn't recommend it to you. But chef-owner John Pontius has been serving large portions of tasty New American cuisine here since 1991. The pine paneling and decor are simple, but candlelight and linens make it more special. The menu may include a warm spinach and scallop salad to start, followed by oven-poached salmon with ginger and soy sauce. A good alternative is the tasty vegetarian lasagna with pesto, ricotta, grilled tomatoes, and zucchini. Loyal Cape vacationers have been known to return many nights during a 2-week vacation. No reservations taken. Entrées $12–16.

✐ **Sweet Seasons Restaurant & Cafe** (349-6535), 70 Main Street. Open for dinner nightly, late June to mid- September. Executive chef Judy Pihl has owned this place since 1974 and serves cuisine that bridges the traditional and creative. Dishes like seared tuna and oysters Rockefeller vie for attention with lobster bisque and seafood tarts. The spacious candlelit dining room of the 19th-century house has wood floors and is decorated with plants and local art. Sweet Seasons also offers early specials, prix fixe options, and a lighter café menu, too. Menu accommodations for children are happily made. Entrées $12–18.

EATING OUT

All establishments are in Wellfleet unless otherwise noted.

☞ **Flying Fish Cafe** (349-3100), 29 Briar Lane, between Route 6 and Main Street. Open early April to mid-October. Generally, all three meals are served daily in July and August; in the off-season breakfast and lunch are served Wednesday through Sunday, dinner on the weekends. The food is more creative than the simple decor suggests: modest tables, local art, a natural-wood counter, and a partially visible kitchen. Very little on the vegetarian and ethnic menu is ordinary. For breakfast, try scrambled tofu with veggies or green eggs and ham (even if you can't proclaim "Sam I am"). For lunch, sample Brazilian black beans with rice or a smoked salmon plate with assorted condiments. Keep dinner simple with a vegetable stir fry or spice it up with jerk chicken Caribe. Don't pass up appetizers such as baked Brie and Eastham mussels. The quality of the in-house bakery parallels the mealtime dishes. Breakfast $4–6, lunch $5–7, dinner $10–18.

Upstairs Bar at Aesop's Table (349-6450), 316 Main Street. Open nightly, late June to mid-September, and Thursday through Sunday, Mother's Day to late June and then again mid-September to mid-October. Low lighting, plush chairs, and velvety divans make this converted attic space a comfortable place to end an evening. Sip an apéritif or special coffee with your Death by Chocolate, a dense chocolate mousse with a brownie crust. There's no better way to go. (A substantial tavern menu including salads, barbecued ribs, and steak sandwiches is also available.) Local musicians entertain on Thursday night in summer.

Bayside Lobster Hutt (349- 6333), 91 Commercial Street. Open nightly for dinner, late May to mid-September. Owned by longtime Wellfleet resident David Francis since 1974, the deliberately low-brow Lobster Hutt serves seafood every way you like it: baked, broiled, in chowder (an excellent version), and in sandwich rolls. Or order an old-fashioned clambake with lobster and steamed clams and corn on the cob. Dine inside at communal picnic tables. This is the kind of place where you have unspoken permission to use your hands and get messy (there's a wash basin for after you've finished). Fries, burgers, and hot dogs are available for those kids who won't eat anything else. BYOB. No credit cards. Entrées $10–16.

Duck Creeke Tavern Room (349-7369), 70 Main Street. Open for dinner and late-night appetizers Thursday through Sunday, May to mid-October; nightly in summer. This is a cozy place offering less-formal dishes like steak and ale, burgers, pizzas, seafood stew, and—in a nod to "bistro fare"—roasted eggplant on basil focaccia. A fireplace, beamed ceilings, greenery, and a bar fashioned from old doors set the tone for live entertainment throughout the season. Thursday and Friday nights are usually reserved for jazz, but you'll also hear folk, piano, pop, and country some nights. Judy Pihl of Sweet Seasons (see *Dining Out*) oversees the kitchen here, too. Entrées $11–17.

✍❊ **The Lighthouse** (349-3681), Main Street. Open for breakfast, lunch, and dinner daily year-round. A fixture in the center of town since 1930 (although the present owners have had it "just" since 1978), this is the only restaurant in town that's open all year. Get a no-nonsense omelet for $4.75, waffles, or two eggs any style for a mere $2.45 (until noon). The lunch menu is primarily sandwiches, nothing fancy, for $4–9; dinner will run you $9–16. Between the front door and the kitchen, the small dining room bustles at a high pitch. Try to get a table in the quieter, glassed-in dining room on the side. Other features include a children's menu, homemade desserts, and Guinness on tap.

On the Creek Cafe, 55 Commercial Street. Open for breakfast and lunch (until 5 PM in summer) mid-April to mid-October. This casual café has perhaps the most tranquil location in town: Tables on the back lawn almost touch the edge of Duck Creek. Inside the old depot-style building, Jeanne Woodes's place is simple and cheery. Offerings are simple,

Wellfleet's winter "skyline" from across Duck Creek at low tide

too: eggs, bagels, and French toast for breakfast; sandwiches, cold salads, and PB&J or fluffernutter for the kids at lunch. Blackboard specials might include a tasty ginger carrot soup. Dishes $3–6.

Captain Higgins Seafood Restaurant (349-6027), next to the Town Pier. Open noon–9 daily, mid-June to mid-September. The thing here is to sit outside on the large deck surrounded by tall grasses and enjoy the boats moored across the street at the town dock. Well-prepared native bluefish, Wellfleet sea scallops, lobsters, and oysters and littlenecks from the raw bar are a few menu specialties. Seafood rolls are served on French rolls rather than flimsy hot-dog buns. Children have their own menu, coloring books, and crayons for the paper tablecloths. Dave Balch and Jeanne Coser have run this family business since 1968. Lunch $6–12, dinner $11–17.

So. Wellfleet Clam Shack (349-2265), at the corner of Route 6 and LeCount Hollow Road, South Wellfleet. Open mid-May to mid-October. Bill Millett has owned this classic New England–style fast-food eatery for years. Every town has a clam shack, but this one is significantly better than most: oysters and littleneck clams on the half shell, chowder, calamari rolls ($6.25), and broiled scallops ($9.50). The Clam Shack also offers fruit and vegetable salads. Eat at cheery indoor tables or at outdoor picnic tables. Dishes $5–10.

Serena's (349-9370), Route 6, South Wellfleet. Open nightly June through September; Wednesday through Sunday, April, May, October, November. It may seem odd to recommend a restaurant on Route 6 in South Wellfleet when there are so many choices in the center of Wellfleet, but Serena's has offered very good seafood and Italian fare at moderate prices in pleasant surroundings since 1978. Entrées $9.25–16.50.

✐ **Moby Dick's** (349-9795), Route 6. Open 11:30–10 daily, mid-May to early October. Order from the big blackboard over the counter and take a seat at tables surrounded by the weathered nautical paraphernalia or on the spacious, open upper level. The waitstaff bring your order. Fried seafood dinners, lobsters, burgers, clambakes, and seafood rolls are the fare here; BYOB. Children's menu. Entrées $4–15.

✳ **Box Lunch** (349-2178), 50 Briar Lane. Open daily year-round. The "roll-wiches" are perfect for the beach or a hike out on Great Island. Roast beef, ham, tuna salad, seafood salad, or a vegetarian alternative is rolled up tight in a piece of pita bread for $4–5. This particular branch of the ever-expanding chain is also open for breakfast.

See also Beachcomber under *Entertainment*.

DESSERT

Just Dessert, 91 Commercial Street, in the rear of the parking lot of the Bayside Lobster Hutt. Open 5–10:30 nightly, late June to early September. This place offers what its name promises: just dessert. David Francis opened this oversized screened-in porch in 1980 as a way to satisfy his own sweet tooth. Confections include cakes, ice cream, frozen yogurt, and coffee and tea. Prices are on the high side, but you're paying for the chance to enjoy a classic summer outing without the bother of mosquitoes. The old railroad tracks leading from Just Desserts used to be lined with oyster shacks in the late 1800s.

See also Upstairs Bar at Aesop's Table under *Eating Out*.

COFFEE

Beanstock Coffee Roasters (349-7008), 70 Main Street. Open 6:30–11:30 for morning coffee April through November and 3:30–6:30 for afternoon coffee in summer. Polli-jo and Kyle learned to roast beans in Costa Rica and their espresso is rich and flavorful. It's served with a small selection of homemade scones, bagels, biscotti, and the like. There are two tiny rooms in the coffeehouse, plus outdoor seating along a curvy brick walkway in the rear. Beanstock was planning evening entertainment in the off-season; stop in to see if it got it off the ground.

ENTERTAINMENT

Wellfleet Harbor Actors Theater (349-6835), 1 Kendrick Avenue, PO Box 1118, Wellfleet. Performances mid-May to mid-October (nightly except Monday in summer, Thursday through Sunday in the off-season); 90 seats. Known locally as WHAT, this highly regarded theater company puts on experimental, new-wave, and sometimes misunderstood shows. WHAT produces plays by new writers and directors as well as established folks like David Mamet and David Wheeler of the American Repertory Theater in Cambridge, Massachusetts. A fixture in the community since 1985, WHAT can always be counted on to be provocative. Founder Gip Hoppe (a marvelous actor) writes some of the plays himself. Tickets $12.50–14.

✐ **Wellfleet Drive-In** (349-7176, 1-800-696-3532), Route 6. One of the last holdouts of a vanishing American pastime, this drive-in has lured patrons since 1957, when the number of US drive-ins peaked at 4000. Today there are fewer than 800 left, only a handful in New England, no others on the Cape. Hence, it remains a treasured local institution. Owner John Jentz, a former engineering professor at MIT, designed the screen with friends of his from MIT; perhaps that's why it's withstood hurricanes with winds up to 135 mph. Double features are shown nightly at dusk (about 8 in summer), May through September, come rain or shine (well, come rain or stars is more appropriate). Movies change three times a week, and there's a play area behind the reasonably priced concession stand. The box office opens at 7. Most films are family-oriented. Tickets: $6 adults, $3.50 kids.

Square dancing, Town Pier. On Wednesday evenings in July and August, the pier takes on a different tone. Dancing begins at 7 or 7:30, and the steps get progressively more difficult until 10 or so.

Beachcomber (349-6055), off Ocean View Drive on Cahoon Hollow Beach. Open daily noon–1 AM, late June to early September. In its former incarnation, this 1850 structure was one of the Outer Cape's nine lifesaving stations. Today, this 300-person-capacity club, perched on a bluff above the beach, is better known as a bar/club, but it also serves food. There's nothing else like it on the Cape; a *Boston Globe* review once remarked that the atmosphere feels like "you've entered the Twilight Zone." Be careful about wandering out onto the beach after a couple of drinks; the first step is a doozy! Cool, hip Boston bands perform in the evenings, but the club is perhaps best known for its Sunday-afternoon concerts and reggae-filled happy hours (frozen mudslides are very popular). By day, shuffle from the beach to hang out with a twenty-something crowd on the outdoor deck, complete with a 40-foot-long raw bar. Burgers, boneless buffalo wings, and a full children's menu are also offered. Inside is dark, with wooden booths. Only appetizers and pizza are available after 9 PM. Dishes $5–11.

See also the Upstairs Bar at Aesop's Table, Duck Creeke Tavern Room, Painter's, and Beanstock Coffee Roasters under *Where to Eat.*

SELECTIVE SHOPPING

Arts and crafts shows are held on many Mondays and Tuesdays in July and August next to the Wellfleet Drive-In (see *Entertainment*) on Route 6. This is generally high-quality stuff, from oils and watercolors to pottery, jewelry, and objets de wood or glass.

Wellfleet Flea Market (349-2520, 1-800-696-3532), at the Wellfleet Drive-In, Route 6. Open Saturday and Sunday mid-April to mid-October, as well as Wednesday and Thursday in July and August. With more than 300 stalls, there's more junk than treasure, but you never know what you'll find: name-brand clothing, a hat to ward off the summer sun, used and antique furniture and trinkets, tea sets, colored glasses. Wander in with the intention of spending a few minutes and a few dollars and you'll probably find that hours have passed and you've bought more than you bargained for! It's the Cape's biggest and best.

ART GALLERIES

Wellfleet is an art town; pick up the Art Gallery Association map for a complete list of current galleries. Some galleries are excellent; others cater to souvenir art. In July and August, many galleries host wine-and-cheese openings on Saturday evenings.

Cherry Stone Gallery (349-3026), 70 East Commercial Street. Open Tuesday through Sunday, late May to late September. Sally Nerber has collected and sold works by Abbott and Atget, Motherwell and Rauschenberg (and emerging artists) since 1972. Unpretentious and friendly, this small place is for the serious collector. A top Cape gallery.

Swansborough Gallery (349-1883), 230 Main Street. Open late May to mid-October. Dick and Annie Hall's large, contemporary, light-filled building showcases a wide variety of contemporary, semiabstract, and representational photography, painting, and prints. You can't miss the sculpture garden out back.

Left Bank Gallery (349-9451), 25 Commercial Street. Open daily mid-May to mid-October; weekends the rest of the year. Audrey and Gerald Parent converted the former American Legion Hall in 1972; head past the paintings to the craft-filled potter's room.

Left Bank Print Gallery (349-7939), 3 West Main Street. Open daily from late May to mid-October, weekends January through March, and daily except Tuesday and Wednesday the rest of the year. Works on paper and contemporary jewelry are highlighted.

Blue Heron Gallery (349-6724), Bank Street. Open daily mid-May to mid-October. Del Filardi and Harriet Rubin have managed to pack a lot of art and crafts (Cape scenes, jewelry, and pottery) into a seemingly endless series of small rooms. More than 30 representational contemporary artists and artisans are shown.

Kendall Art Gallery (349-2482), Main Street. Open daily mid-May to mid-October. Walter and Myra Dorrell sell not only Walter's paintings but also work by more than 40 other artists and craftspeople. There are a few buildings behind the 1840s Greek Revival house filled with even more paintings and ceramics. The sculpture garden is tranquil.

Cove Gallery & Custom Frame Shop (349-2530), 15 Commercial Street. Open daily early May to mid-October. Larry Biron and Liane Schneider-Biron feature oils and pastels in this airy gallery and also have a lively sculpture garden overlooking Duck Creek.

Karol B. Wyckoff Gallery (349-1443), 25 Bank Street. Open daily mid-May to mid-October. The namesake artist shows original watercolors and limited editions of idyllic and naturalistic Cape and island scenes.

ARTISANS

Salt Marsh Pottery (349-3342), 115 Main Street. Open year-round. Katherine Stillman was attracted to Wellfleet because of its reputation as a community of tolerant eccentrics. Now she's one of them, living and shaping her clay beside a salt marsh. Her lead-free vessels gracefully combine simple lines with utilitarian purposes. Fellow potter Maria Juster makes blue-green stoneware pottery, tiles, mirrors, and tables.

Wellfleet Pottery (349-6679), Commercial Street. Open June through September. Trevor and Kathleen Glucksman have been making pottery in Wellfleet since 1970. He designs and crafts the small-scale china, employing all methods of casting, throwing, and pressing to achieve the desired results. Kathleen glazes and hand-paints them with simple depictions of wildflowers and grasses. The umber country china (a very strong china good for daily use) is displayed as sparingly as it's "decorated." You'll also find watercolorist Kathleen Hill's work here.

Narrow Land Pottery (349-6308), 3 West Main Street. Open April through December. Joe McCaffery, who studied at the School of the Museum of Fine Arts, throws pots, vases, mugs, lamp bases, and plates. His glazes, porcelain, and stoneware come in a variety of colors.

BOOKSTORE

Herridge Books (349-1323), Main Street. Open mid-April through December, and perhaps on weekends throughout winter. This is the place to go for used books covering a wide range of subject matter.

CLOTHING

Women in search of interesting, style-conscious clothes have lucked out in Wellfleet. The predominant style is of loose-fitting designs in cotton, linen, and rayon; earth tones reign. Try **Hannah** (349-9884), 234 Main Street; **Eccentricity** (349-7554), 361 Main Street; **Eccentricity's Off Center** (349-3634), across the street; and **Karol Richardson** (349-6378), nearby at 11 West Main Street. Eccentricity offers kimonos.

FARM STAND

Hatch's Fish Market/Hatch's Produce (349-2810), behind Town Hall on Main Street. Open late May to late September. Although you'll probably find better prices at the local supermarket, the fish and produce here are fresh and beautifully displayed; and the location can't be beat. Hatch's smokes its own fish, pâté, and mussels.

SPECIAL SHOPS

Chocolate Sparrow (349-1333), Main Street. Open daily late June to early September, weekends until mid-October. As long as anyone can remember, Wellfleet has had a penny-candy store. The Chocolate Sparrow opened in 1990 to continue the tradition, and added rich, hand-dipped chocolates.

The Wellfleet Collection (349-0900), Main Street. Open mid-April to mid-October and for a week before Christmas. A fine assortment of things for the home, including art in various media, folk art, limited-edition prints, turned wood, pottery, table linens, country antiques, and a little of this and that.

Abiyoyo (349-3422), 313 Main Street. Open late May through October. Creative, educationally oriented toys, as well as stuffed animals and artsy sweatshirts and T-shirts. The ground-floor shop, **Down to Earth Crafts,** displays a varied selection of crafts.

The Secret Garden (349-1444), Main Street. Open April through December. Decorative accessories, folk art, jewelry, and garden items.

Truro

Considered by many to be the last vestige of "Old Cape Cod," Truro has no stoplights, no fast-food outlets, no supermarket, no automatic teller machine; there's no motorboat gasoline sold at Pamet Harbor. It does have the last working farm on the Outer Cape, though. Truro "center" consists of a tiny strip mall and a nearby gourmet food shop. That's it. And local folks and summer people (vacationing writers and urban professionals who have built large houses in the rolling hills and dunes) are determined to keep it that way.

North Truro is also tiny but has blue-collar ties to Provincetown. Compare Dutra's Market (an old institution) to Jams (a relatively new gourmet shop) and the differences are readily apparent. As you head toward Provincetown, the only real development—in a nod to the tourist industry—consists of hundreds of tiny cottages, motels, and houses lining a narrow strip of shore wedged between Cape Cod Bay and the dramatic Parabolic Dunes on Pilgrim Lake. It's an odd juxtaposition, but one that you'll come to look forward to.

There aren't many human-made sites to explore, except for Highland Light and the Truro Historical Museum, but there are plenty of natural ones. Almost 70 percent of Truro's 42 square miles (one of the largest towns on the Cape, in acreage) falls within the boundaries of the Cape Cod National Seashore (CCNS). There are hiking and biking trails as well as long expanses of beach. Rolling moors and little valleys characterize the tranquil back roads east and west of Route 6. Windswept dunes, lighthouses, beach grass, and austere shoreline scenes will inspire you, as they did Edward Hopper. The painter built a summer house in Truro in the 1930s and worked there until 1967.

Truro, established in 1697, has endured many name changes. Originally it was called Payomet or Pamet, after the Native American tribe that inhabited the area before the Pilgrims. In 1705 it was known as Dangerfield because of the large number of offshore sailing disasters. Eventually it was named Truro, after a Cornish coastal town in England.

Although today Truro is sleepy and rural, it has been, at times during the last few centuries, a hotbed of activity. The *Mayflower's* Myles Standish spent his second night ashore in Truro. His band of 16 fellow Pilgrims found their first fresh water in Truro, as well as a stash of corn

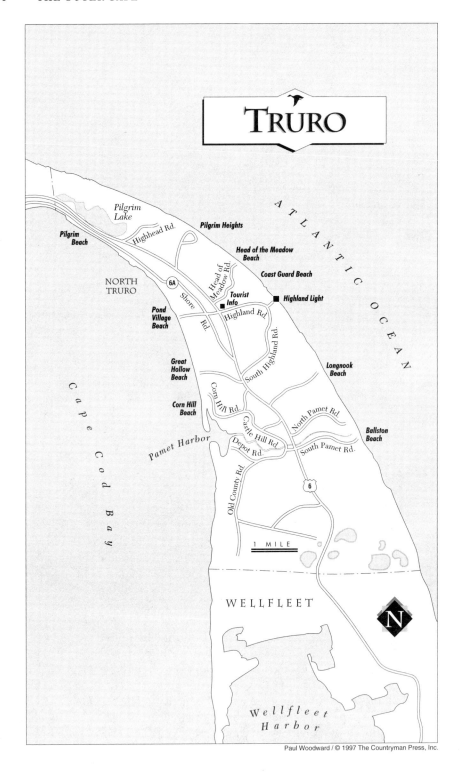

TRURO

Pilgrim
Lake

Pilgrim Heights

ATLANTIC OCEAN

Pilgrim
Beach

Highhead Rd.

Head of the Meadow
Beach

NORTH
TRURO

6A

Head of Meadow Rd.

Shore Rd.

Coast Guard Beach

Tourist Info

Highland Rd.

Highland Light

Pond
Village
Beach

Great
Hollow
Beach

South Highland Rd.

Longnook
Beach

Corn Hill
Beach

Corn Hill Rd.

Castle Hill Rd.

North Pamet Rd.

Ballston
Beach

Cape Cod Bay

Pamet Harbor

Depot Rd.

South Pamet Rd.

Old County Rd.

6

1 MILE

WELLFLEET

N

Wellfleet
Harbor

Paul Woodward / © 1997 The Countryman Press, Inc.

(which belonged to the Native Americans) from which they harvested their first crop. Although you wouldn't know it today, since the Pamet Harbor choked up with sand in the mid-1850s, Truro's harbor once rivaled neighboring Provincetown as a whaling and codfishing center. By the late 1700s, shipbuilding was thriving and the harbor bustling. Vessels bound for the Grand Banks were built here, and a packet boat sailed from Truro to Boston. The whaling industry also owes a debt to early Truro residents, one of whom (Ichabod Paddock) taught Nantucketers how to catch whales from shore.

In 1851 the population soared to a rousing 2000 souls. But in 1860 the Union Company of Truro went bankrupt due to the declining harbor conditions, and townspeople's fortunes and livelihoods sank with it. Commercially, Truro never rebounded. Today, the year-round population is 1500; the summer influx raises that number tenfold.

GUIDANCE

Chamber of Commerce (487-1288), Route 6, PO Box 26, North Truro 02652. Open 10–5 daily, late June to early September; 10–5 Friday and Saturday, noon–4 Sunday, late May to late June and early September to mid-October.

PUBLIC REST ROOMS

Public rest rooms are at the Pilgrim Heights area in summer.

GETTING THERE

By car: The center of Truro is about 60 miles from the Sagamore Bridge via Route 6. Route 6A and Shore Road are synonymous.

By bus: The **Plymouth & Brockton** bus line (775-5524) connects Truro with other Cape towns and with Boston's Logan Airport.

GETTING AROUND

Beaches, sites, and roads are well marked off Route 6. Generally, the CCNS is east of Route 6. The Shore Road exit in North Truro takes you into North Truro and eventually to Beach Point, choked with motels as it approaches Provincetown. At its narrowest, Truro is only a mile wide; it's 10 miles long.

North Truro Shuttle System (487-6870). If you're going into Provincetown from the campgrounds, North Truro center, Beach Point, or anywhere in between, this bus might make sense for you. Buses run daily from late May to mid-October. In-season (late June to early September), they run every 20 minutes from 7 AM to 1 AM; off-season they run hourly. Adults: $2 one way, $7 weekly pass; children $1.

MEDICAL EMERGENCY

Outer Cape Health Services (487-9395, Harry Kemp Way, Provincetown, and 349-3131, Route 6, Wellfleet) is open for walk-ins weekdays, year-round.

Golfers play on the Cape's oldest course in the shadow of Highland Light.

TO SEE

Cape Cod Light or **Highland Light,** CCNS, Lighthouse Road, off South
Highland Road, North Truro. The original lighthouse that guarded
these treacherous shores was erected in 1798, the first lighthouse on
Cape Cod. It was rebuilt in 1853, the year when 1200 ships were recorded to have passed by within a 10-day period. Henry David Thoreau
stayed in the lighthouse during one of his famous walks along the Outer
Cape. The spot where Thoreau said he could stand "and put all America
behind him" is thought now to be 150 feet offshore, thanks to erosion.
One of only four working lighthouses on the Outer Cape, it was the last
to become automated, in 1986. The original light shone with whale oil
from 24 lamps, while later lamps were fueled with lard and kerosene.
The modern light has a 1000-watt bulb. Visible 30 miles out to sea, it's
the brightest lighthouse on the New England coast. At 120 feet above
sea level, the lighthouse is aptly named Highland.

In July 1996 the National Park Service, Coast Guard, and state joined
forces to avert a looming disaster. If the lighthouse was not moved soon,
engineers cautioned, it would crumble into the ocean. Erosion, at the
rate of 3–4 feet per year, had chewed away the cliff upon which the lighthouse was built. (Thanks to ferocious storms in 1990, 40 feet were lost in
one year alone!) And when the cliffs erode to within 100 feet of a lighthouse, it is too dangerous to bring in the heavy equipment needed to
move it. So at a cost of $1.5 million, the 420-ton historic lighthouse was
jacked up onto steel beams and pushed along steel tracks by hydraulic
rams. The project took 18 days (that's about 25 feet a day), including
moving the lightkeeper's house. It was moved 450 feet west and 12 feet

south (i.e., inland), to a spot on the golf course. It should be safe for another 150 years, unless we get a lot of bad winters.

Truro Historical Museum (487-3397), Lighthouse Road, North Truro. Open 10–5 daily mid-June to mid-September. Operated expertly by the Truro Historical Society and housed in the old Highland House, the large building is wholly dedicated to preserving Truro's maritime and agricultural past. Items on display include a pirate's chest, fishing and whaling gear, 17th-century firearms, photos of Truro residents and places, toys, and scrimshaw. One room is dedicated to Courtney Allen, the Truro Historical Society founder, artist, model maker, and wood-carver. The old Highland House is a fine example of the fashionable turn-of-the-century summer hotels that were once prominent. Adults $3, children 12 and under free.

Jenny Lind Tower, CCNS, off Lighthouse Road, North Truro. Between the Highland Golf Links (see *To Do—Golf*) and the former **North Truro Air Force Base** is a 55-foot tower of granite that seems a bit out of place. In fact, it is. In 1850, P.T. Barnum brought Swedish singing legend Jenny Lind to America. He oversold tickets to a Boston concert, and when Lind heard the crowds were going to riot, she performed a free concert from the roof tower for the people in the street. When the building was to be destroyed in 1927, a Boston attorney purchased the tower and brought it here (he owned the land at that time). The CCNS owns the property now and the entrance is blocked, but the granite tower still stands 150 feet above sea level, visible to passing ships.

Congregational Church and **cemetery,** Meetinghouse Road (off Castle Road), Truro. A marble shaft commemorates the terrible tragedy of the October Gale, when seven ships were destroyed and 57 crew members died. Renowned glassmakers of Sandwich made the church windows and Paul Revere cast the bell hanging in the steeple.

SCENIC DRIVES

It's difficult to find an unpicturesque road in Truro. North and South Pamet Roads used to be connected before the breach at Pamet Beach; both roads wind past bayberry, beach plums, and groves of locust trees. From Truro center, Castle Road is lovely out to Corn Hill Beach. From North Truro, Priest Road to the bay and to Bay View Road offer great bay views.

TO DO

BICYCLING

High Head Road, CCNS, off Route 6, North Truro. Just south of Pilgrim Lake, this 4-mile bikeway runs from High Head Road, past salt marshes and dunes, to Head of the Meadow Beach. Four-wheel-drive vehicles with proper stickers can enter the dunes here.

BOATING

Pamet Harbor, off Depot Road, Truro. You can only get a boat in here for 2–3 hours before or after high tide. There are no boats to rent, but you can contact the harbormaster (349-2555) for information.

FISHING/SHELLFISHING

Permits for freshwater fishing and shellfishing are available from Town Hall (349-3635) on Town Hall Road, off Castle Road, Truro.

Kids will love fishing from the grassy shores off **Pond Road;** it's tranquil for a picnic or watching as the sun sets. Surf-fishing is good all along the Atlantic coastline. For freshwater fishing, try **Great Pond,** off Savage Road from Route 6 in southern Truro.

GOLF

Highland Golf Links (487-9201), Lighthouse Road, off South Highland Road, North Truro. Open year-round. Perched high on a windswept bluff, this is the oldest course on the Cape (founded in 1892) and one of the oldest in the country. At the turn of the century the course was part of the Highland House resort (see the Truro Historical Museum under *To See*), which drew visitors by train from Boston. Today, the museum sits between the eighth and ninth holes and the course is the only public one between Orleans and Provincetown. The course exemplifies the Scottish tradition, with deep natural roughs, Scotch broom, heath, unirrigated open fairways, occasional fog, and spectacular ocean views. That's why golfers come to this nine-hole, par-35 course. That, and dime-sized greens, whale sightings from the sixth tee in summer, and the view of Highland Light adjacent to the seventh hole. Avoid the crowds by playing on Sunday. $6 for nine holes.

SPECIAL PROGRAMS

Truro Center for the Arts at Castle Hill (349-7511), Castle and Meetinghouse Roads, PO Box 756, Truro 02666. Open early July to early September. A nonprofit educational institute, Castle Hill was founded in 1972 and has evolved into an important cultural voice in the Outer Cape art scene. Classes and workshops are offered in a converted 1880s barn to people of all ages in painting, drawing, printmaking, photography, clay, metal, fiber, and sculpture. Castle Hill also sponsors events like a mid-August open house, lectures, concerts, and artist receptions. Renowned artists and writers lead classes that can last for 1, 5, or 18 sessions. Register by mail prior to June 1 or by phone after June 1.

GREEN SPACE

BEACHES

Head of the Meadow Beach, on the Atlantic Ocean. Half of this beach is maintained by the town, the other half by the CCNS. The only difference is that the latter has changing rooms and rest rooms; otherwise it's the same wide, dune-backed beach. Parking $5.

Cottages surrounded by beach grass overlook Cape Cod Bay in Truro.

Corn Hill Beach, off Corn Hill Road, on Cape Cod Bay. This is the only other town-managed beach where nonresidents can pay a daily fee to park ($5). Facilities include Porta-potties and a large parking area. Backed by a long, low dune, the width of Corn Hill Beach decreases measurably as the tide comes in. There's good windsurfing, too.

Long Nook Beach, off Long Nook Road, on the Atlantic Ocean. Although this wonderful beach requires a town parking sticker, in the off-season anyone can park here.

Coast Guard Beach, off Highland Road, and **Ballston Beach,** off South Pamet Road; both on the Atlantic Ocean. Each is town-owned and requires a resident sticker, but anyone can bicycle in for free. (This Coast Guard Beach is not to be confused with Henry Beston's Coast Guard Beach in Eastham, which is under the auspices of CCNS.) No lifeguard; Porta-potties. Cottage renters can get their "residential" parking sticker behind the post office at the Beach Commission in Truro Center; $30 for 2 weeks. Use caution because of the treacherous undertow.

WALKS

Pilgrim Heights Area (349-3785), CCNS, off Route 6, North Truro. This area's two short walks yield open vistas of distant dunes, ocean, and salt marsh. As the name implies, the easy ¾-mile round-trip Pilgrim Spring Trail leads to the spot where the Pilgrims reportedly tasted their first New England water. One subsequently penned: "We . . . sat us downe and drunke our first New England water with as much delight as ever we drunke in all our lives." A small plaque marks the spot. Small Swamp Trail (about the same distance) was not named for the size of the swamp or trail but rather after the farmer (Mr. Small) who grew asparagus and corn on this former 200-acre farm. By August, blueberries are ripe for the picking. Wooded picnic area. In spring, look for migrating hawks.

Cranberry Bog Trail, North Pamet Road, Truro. You won't want to pick this tangy/sour fruit come late September, but take the lovely walk—part over a boardwalk—around the bog. The trailhead is located at the parking lot below the youth hostel (see *Lodging—Hostel*).

LODGING

BED & BREAKFAST

❋ **South Hollow Vineyards** (487-6200), Route 6A, North Truro 02652. Open year-round. Judy Wimer and Kathy Gregrow opened this 19th-century Federal-style farmhouse in 1994 after renovating it from top to bottom. The first floor of the large house is kind of dark and sparsely furnished, with a slate floor, large hearth, heavy beams, and a burgundy and deep green color scheme. (It's very cool in summer.) The five guest rooms, all with private bath, have four-poster beds. A full breakfast—perhaps a tomato and basil frittata—is served in the flagstone dining room or on the brick patio. The 5-acre property was planted with vinifera grapes in 1993, and three years later wine was bottled. Mid-May to mid-September $79–119; off-season $69–99.

COTTAGES AND EFFICIENCIES

Kalmar Village (487-0585; 617-247-0211 in winter), Route 6A, North Truro 02652. Open mid-May to mid-October. On a strip chock-full of cottage colonies, Kalmar stands out. The Prelacks have owned the place since 1968, and you can spot their care and attention in the details: well-tended, trim lawns around the pool, black-and-white chimneys atop the shingled cottages, and six new waterfront cottages. All cottages are delightfully roomy inside, with modern kitchens. Other perks include daily housekeeping and private outdoor space. There are also small, large, and two-room efficiencies and three motel rooms. This is a great place for families, since Kalmar sits on 400 feet of private ocean-front beach. The 45 cottages are rented by the week in July and August, $725–985 for one- or two-bedroom cottages; $1150–1495 for the new two-bedroom units. In the off-season they rent for $400–615 weekly or $66.50–89 nightly ($115–162.50 for the new units). Efficiencies rent for $320–600 weekly or $55–100 nightly in July and August.

✐ **East Harbour** (487-0505), 618 Route 6A (Shore Road), North Truro 02652. Open mid-April to late October. Although there are dozens of small cottage communities, this one rises to the top. These tidy two-bedroom beachfront cottages (some are mere water-view units) enjoy daily maid service. Seven cottages, nine motel rooms. Late June to early September $725–825 weekly; $100 per additional child, $200 per additional adult; cottages rent by the night in the off-season, when they are available. Make reservations in February if you can.

White Village (487-3014), Route 6A (Shore Road), North Truro (the mailing address is PO Box 191, Provincetown 02657). Open May to late

Truro's First Congregational Parish Church and cemetery

October. The Bento family has owned this distinctive row of 46 little white cottages since 1976, but some guests have been summering here since 1950. The firmness of the mattresses varies, but don't be shy about requesting one to your liking. Most of the one- and two-bedroom cottages have full kitchens; none has TV or telephone; there are only a few three-bedroom units. Most are oceanfront on Cape Cod Bay; a long cement "boardwalk," dotted with red Adirondack chairs, is all that separates the units from the beach. Late June to early September $430–640 weekly; off-season $280–480 weekly, $45–80 per night. No credit cards.

MOTEL

Top Mast (487-1189), Route 6A, North Truro 02652. Open May to mid-October. This nicely maintained two-story motel flanks Route 6A. Beachfront units are built right on sandy Cape Cod Bay, and each opens onto a long porch with lawn chairs. Nonbeachfront rooms rent by the night, even in high season. There are 33 rooms and two 2-bedroom apartments. Swimming pool. Mid-June to early September: $600 weekly for beachfront rooms, $650 weekly for beachfront efficiencies, $825 weekly for apartment, $65 nightly for nonbeachfront room; in the shoulder seasons all rooms are $55–60 nightly or $350–400 weekly.

RENTALS

Duarte/Downey Real Estate (349-7588), 12 Truro Center Road, is one of the big names in Truro.

CAMPGROUNDS

North of Highland Camping Area (487-1191), Head of the Meadow Road, North Truro 02652. Open mid-May to mid-September. The Currier family operates this campground within the CCNS on 60 acres of scrub pine. The 237 sites are suitable for tents and tent trailers only and are a 10-minute walk from Head of the Meadow Beach. There are strict quiet hours. From mid-July to mid-August, reservations must begin and end on a Saturday or Sunday night. $18 for one or two people with one car; $2 each additional child; $8 additional adult.

❋ **North Truro Camping Area** (487-1847), Highland Road, North Truro 02652. Open year-round. Within the CCNS, these 15 acres of wooded sites can accommodate 350 tents and RVs. It's less than a mile to Coast Guard Beach. $15 per day for two, plus $5 for hook-ups; $7.50 each additional person.

HOSTEL

☞ **Hostelling International, Truro** (349-3889), North Pamet Road, Truro 02666. Open late June to early September. Originally a US Coast Guard station, the hostel commands a dramatic location—amid dunes, marshes, and a cranberry bog. The hostel is within the CCNS and just a 7-minute walk to Ballston Beach. National Park Service interpreters host special programs each week; they're free to all and not to be missed. Each of 42 dormitory beds rents for $12 per night to members, $15 to nonmembers.

WHERE TO EAT

EATING OUT

☞ **Adrian's** (487-4360), Route 6, North Truro. Open for breakfast and dinner daily, mid-June to mid- September; open for breakfast on weekends and dinner nightly, mid-May to mid-June and mid-September to mid-October. Chef Adrian Cyr and his wife, Annette, have wooed and won a decidedly loyal and ever-growing following since they opened their first area restaurant in 1985. In 1993, when Adrian's moved to this more visible location atop a bluff on Route 6, the Provincetown regulars didn't miss a beat. Dine on the outdoor deck or in the dining room with candlelight, large picture windows, and well-spaced tables. There are many reasons to dine here: creative brick-oven pizzas, inspired pasta dishes, a good selection of antipasti and insalate, rich *tira mi su,* and for breakfast, huevos rancheros, specialty omelets, and cranberry pancakes. You can also come just for dessert or coffee. The waitstaff are perfectly accommodating. Breakfast $3–7; dinner entrées $7–15.

☞ **Terra Luna** (487-1019), Route 6A, North Truro. Open for breakfast 8–1 and dinner 5:30–10, mid-May to mid-October. High ceilings, large canvases, assorted objets d'art, shellacked wooden tables, and candlelight transform this otherwise unassuming roadside eatery with barn-board walls into a hip space. Deftly executed New American and Italian cuisine includes spinach tortellini with crab, tofu strudel, and thin-crust sourdough pizzas. Terra Luna also has unusual breakfasts. Dinner $8–17.

❋ **Blacksmith Shop** (349-6554), off Route 6A, Truro. Open for dinner year-round. Traditional fare like jumbo slice of prime rib or marinated pork

⌣ chops is offered at this charming local favorite along with kale soup, sautéed seafood, and pasta dishes. Shrimp dishes rule on Wednesdays in the off-season; order shrimp cooked one of seven ways, and add soup and salad for $14. Entrées $9–20. Early-bird specials 4:30–6.

✽ **Montano's** (487-2026), Route 6, North Truro. Open nightly year-round. This slightly upscale family restaurant serves dependable Italian favorites, with unlimited refills on the garden salads, a full children's menu, and early-bird specials (4:30–6) for $10. Entrées $9–15.

Village Cafe (487-5800), 4 Highland Road, North Truro center. Open daily 7 AM–10 PM in-season, 7–5 off-season, mid-May through September. New in 1996, this pleasant sandwich place has a big brick patio where you can take your bagel with smoked mozzarella and sun-dried tomato. Turkey sandwiches, hearty soups, muffins, espresso and desserts too.

SEAFOOD MARKETS

Pamet Seafood (349-1818), behind the post office in Truro center; **Nana Molly's** (487-2164), on Route 6 next to the Hillside Farm Stand. Both open mid-May to mid-October. Fish, lobsters, and clambakes-to-go.

SNACKS & COFFEE

Jams (349-1616), off Route 6 in downtown Truro. Open 7:30 AM–"closing" daily, late May to early September. Jams caters to sophisticated palates who need their *Times* and tonic water as well as their truffles and pesto pizzas. Coffee aficionados take note: Jams serves rich espresso and lattes. Basic groceries share the stage with sun-dried tomatoes, rotisserie-roasted chicken, and Port Salut cheese. Carry your picnic fixings to the small field across the street, perfect for bicyclists and the car-weary. Jams makes a PB&J or bologna sandwich for the kids. Sandwiches $4–7.50; salads by the pound.

SELECTIVE SHOPPING

Susan Baker Memorial Museum (487-1063 for the main store in Provincetown), 46 Route 6A, North Truro. Open almost year-round; weekends only in the dead of winter. Whimsical, satirical, and lyrical three-dimensional pieces will either tickle your funny bone or make you scratch your head. By the way, Susan Baker is very much alive; she decided that she didn't want to wait until she died to have a "memorial museum." Look for the new series of Cape and Italian landscapes.

Atlantic Spice Co. (487-6100, 1-800-316-7965), Route 6 and 6A, North Truro. Open 9–5 weekdays, 10–2 Saturdays, year-round. Culinary herbs and spices, botanicals, make-your-own potpourri, teas, spice blends, nuts and seeds; they're all here, they're all fresh, and they're in a cavernous warehouse. Although this is primarily a wholesaler, you can purchase small quantities (less than the usual 1-pound increments) of most products. At the very least, send for the mail-order form.

Secrest Studio (349-6688), 54 Old King's Highway, Truro. Take Longnook Road, turn right on Higgins' Hollow Road, and watch for signs. Open in the summer and by appointment. Philip and Rosamond Secrest make functional and decorative clay and steel pieces.

Trifles and Treasures (349-9509), Truro center. Open May to mid-October, and nice-weather weekends in the off-season. A little bit of art, a few quilts, some pine furniture, and a few collectibles.

Truro Crafters (487-3239), South Highland Road, North Truro. Open June to mid-October. Jobi pottery, scrimshaw, wood carvings.

Whitman House Quilt Shop (487-3204), Route 6, North Truro. Open mid-May to mid-October, daily in summer and weekends off-season. This former schoolhouse is packed with Amish quilts.

SPECIAL EVENTS

Mid-September: **Truro's Treasures.** Since 1992, this folksy 3-day weekend features a craft fair, parade, beach bash, road race, pancake breakfast, and parade. The highlight, with more than 300 townsfolk in attendance, is the dump dance—held at the recycling center (aka town dump).

V. PROVINCETOWN

The Lobster Pot Restaurant, an old-time favorite overlooking the harbor

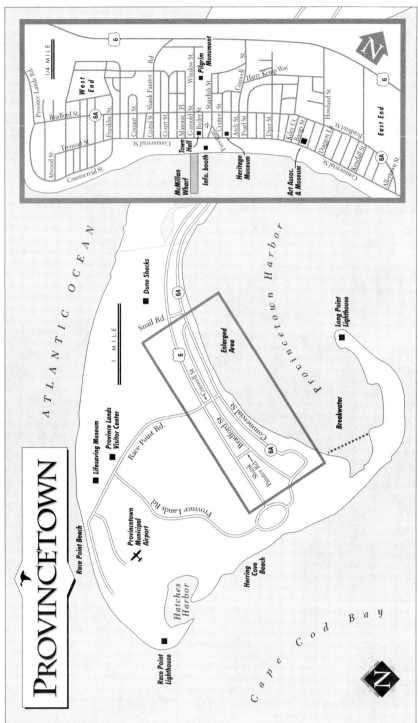

PROVINCETOWN

Provincetown

As you cross the town line into Provincetown, where high dunes drift onto Route 6, you begin to sense this is a different place. This outpost on the tip of the Cape, where glaciers deposited their last grains of sand millions of years ago, attracts a varied population. Whether seeking solitude or freedom of expression in the company of like-minded souls, visitors relish Provincetown's fringe status. P-town, as it's affectionately called by nonlocals, is perhaps best known as a community of tolerant individuals—gay men and lesbians, artists, Portuguese fishermen, and families all call it home and welcome equally tolerant visitors.

Visitors parade up and down Commercial Street, the main drag, ducking in and out of hundreds of shops and galleries. The town has a carnival-like atmosphere, especially in July and August, with visitors testing the limits of acceptability. As you might imagine, people-watching is a prime activity. On any given Saturday, the cast of characters might include cross-dressers, leather-clad motorcyclists, barely clad in-line skaters, children eating saltwater taffy, and tourists from "Anytown, USA," who can't quite figure out what they've stumbled into.

Provincetown's history began long before the *Mayflower* arrived. It's said that Leif Eriksson's brother, Thorvald, stopped here in 1004 to repair the keel of his boat. Wampanoag Indians fished and summered here—the tiny strip of land was too vulnerable to sustain a year-round settlement. In 1620 the Pilgrims first set foot on American soil in Provincetown. They anchored in the harbor for 5 weeks, making forays down-Cape hoping to find an agreeable spot to settle. By the late 1600s and early 1700s, only 200 fishermen lived here.

But from the mid-18th to the mid-19th century, Provincetown was a bustling whaling community and seaport. After the industry peaked, Portuguese sailors from the Azores and Cape Verde islands, who had signed on with whaling and fishing ships, settled here to fish the local waters. The Old Colony Railroad was extended to Provincetown in 1873, transporting iced fish to New York and Boston. Upwards of four trains a day departed from the two-room station, located where Duarte Motors parking lot is today, two blocks from MacMillan Wharf. But by the early 1900s, Provincetown's sea-driven economy had slowed. Trains stopped running in 1950. Today, although a small fishing industry still exists, tourism is the steam that drives the economy's train.

In 1899 painter Charles W. Hawthorne founded the Cape Cod School of Art. He encouraged his Greenwich Village peers to come north and take advantage of the Mediterranean-like light. By 1916 there were six art schools in town. By the 1920s, Provincetown had become as distinguished an art colony as Taos, East Hampton, and Carmel. Hawthorne advised his students to get out of the studio and set up their easels on the beach, incorporating the ever-changing light into their work. By the time Hawthorne died in 1930, the art scene had a life of its own, and it continues to thrive today.

Artistic expression in Provincetown wasn't limited to painting, though. In 1915 the Provincetown Players, a group of playwrights and actors, staged their plays in a small waterfront fish house. In their second season they premiered Eugene O'Neill's *Bound East for Cardiff* before moving to New York, where they are still based.

Provincetown's natural beauty isn't overshadowed by its colorful population. Province Lands, the name given to the Cape Cod National Seashore (CCNS) within Provincetown's borders, offers bike trails, horseback riding trails, and three remote beaches, where, if you walk far enough, you can find real isolation. Most summertime visitors venture onto the water—to whale-watch or sail and windsurf in the protected harbor. A different perspective comes with a dune or aerial tour.

Provincetown is a delight in the late spring and again in fall, when the 40,000 summer visitors return home. Commercial Street is navigable once again, and most shops and restaurants remain open. Tiny gardens still bloom profusely, well into October. From January to March, though, the town is given back to the 3500 hardy year-rounders—almost half of whom are unemployed during this time. Although it's said that 80 percent of the businesses close for January and February, there are still enough guest houses (and a handful of restaurants, especially on the weekends) open all winter, luring intrepid visitors with great prices and stark natural beauty. Steel yourself against the wind and take a walk on the beach, attend a reading at the Fine Arts Work Center, or curl up with a good book.

GUIDANCE

Chamber of Commerce (487-3424, http://www.capecodaccess.com/provincetownchamber/), 307 Commercial Street at MacMillan Wharf, PO Box 1017, Provincetown 02657. Open 10–4 daily except Sunday in the off-season, March through December; 9–5 daily in summer. Pick up a good general information brochure as well as a winter guide detailing which establishments are open year-round.

Provincetown Business Guild (487-2313, 1-800-637-8696), 115 Bradford Street, PO Box 421-94, Provincetown 02657. Open 9–2:30 weekdays. The guild, established in 1978 to support gay tourism, promotes about 250 gay-owned businesses.

Province Lands Visitor Center (487-1256), Race Point Road, Cape Cod National Seashore (CCNS). Open daily, mid-April through November. First things first: Climb atop the observation deck for a 360-degree view of the outermost dunes and ocean. The center offers informative exhibits on Cape history, local flora and fauna, and dune ecology, along with frequent short films. Organized activities include sunset campfires and storytelling, birding trips, dune tours, and a junior ranger hour for children ages 8–12.

☞ **Provincetown Historical Association** publishes three walking pamphlets — for the East End, Center, and West End—full of historical anecdotes. Purchase them ($.50 each) at the Province Lands Visitor Center and the Provincetown Heritage Museum (see *To See*).

PUBLIC REST ROOMS

Public rest rooms are located behind the Chamber of Commerce on MacMillan Wharf (in-season), at the Shank Painter Road parking lot (in-season), at the Grace Hall parking lot (in-season), and in the Provincetown Town Hall at 260 Commercial Street (open year-round).

GETTING THERE

By car: Provincetown is the eastern terminus of Cape Cod, 63 miles via Route 6 from the Bourne Bridge and 128 miles from Boston and Providence. It takes almost 2½ hours to drive from Boston.

By boat: **Bay State Cruise Company, Inc.** (487-9284 seasonally, or 617-723-7800 on Boston's Commonwealth Pier, Northern Avenue). Weekend departures late May to late June and early September to mid-October; daily departures late June to early September. Boats leave Boston at 9:30 AM and return at 3:30 for the 3-hour voyage. One-way tickets are $16 adults, $13 children, $5 bicycles. Discounts for same-day return trip, with a 3-hour layover in Provincetown. The schedule doesn't permit a day trip to Boston, but you can spend the night in Boston and take the morning boat back to Provincetown.

Cape Cod Cruises (Capt. John's Boats) (747-2400, 1-800-242-2469), State Pier (next to the *Mayflower*) in Plymouth and MacMillan Wharf in Provincetown. The ferry schedule is designed so that you leave Plymouth at 10 AM, spend about 5 hours in Provincetown, and are back in Plymouth by 6 PM. You even get a narrated history of Plymouth Harbor as the boat pulls away from shore. Weekends late May to late September; daily in summer. Round-trip tickets: $22 adults, $14 children under 12, $2 bicycles. Free parking on the waterfront.

By bus: The **Plymouth & Brockton** bus line (775-5524) connects Provincetown with other Cape towns and Boston's Logan Airport. The bus stops at the Chamber of Commerce; purchase tickets on-board. There are four buses a day; travel time is 3½ hours; $20 one way.

By air: **Cape Air** (487-0241, 771-6944, 1-800-352-0714) provides daily year-round service from Boston to Provincetown Municipal Airport. The flight takes 25 minutes, and the airport is 4 miles from town. Summer fares $132–162 round-trip; off-peak fares, too.

GETTING AROUND

By car: The first exit off Route 6 (Snail Road) leads to the East End. (Street numbers in the East End are higher than in the West End.) Take the second exit for MacMillan Wharf and Town Hall, where street numbers are in the 300s. Shank Painter Road, the third exit, leads to the West End. Follow Route 6 to its end for Herring Cove Beach. A right off Route 6 takes you to the Province Lands section of the CCNS.

Provincetown's principal thoroughfare, Commercial Street, is narrow, one way, and 3 miles long. When you want to drive from one end of town to another quickly, use Bradford Street, parallel to Commercial. There are no sidewalks on Bradford, known as Back Street in the days when Provincetown only had a front and a back street. About 40 narrow cross-streets connect Commercial and Bradford.

Parking is a problem in Provincetown. Municipal lots are next to Pilgrim Monument and the high school off Bradford Street; on Mac-Millan Wharf; and toward the eastern end of Commercial Street. There are also a few lots off Commercial Street on the waterfront.

By bus: **Summer Shuttle** (487-3353, 240-0050) operates daily mid-June to early September. One route travels Bradford Street, with a detour at MacMillan Wharf; flag down the bus anywhere along the route. Buses run once each hour 8:15 AM–midnight. The other route runs to Herring Cove Beach on the hour 10–6. Fare is $1.25 one way.

Flyer's Shuttle (487-0898), 131A Commercial Street. From mid-June to mid-September, an hourly shuttle takes bathers and picnickers to and from remote, unspoiled Long Point (see *Green Space—Beaches*). Fare is $7 one way, $10 round-trip; children under 7 free.

☞ *Sight-seeing tours:* **Art's Dune Tours** (487-1950), at Commercial and Standish Streets, offers daily trips mid-April to mid-October. Art Costa has led tourists on these narrated, 75-minute trips through the CCNS dunes since 1946. The GMC Suburbans stop twice (on the beach and atop a high dune) for photos, so you can take in the panoramic view. Rates $9–10 per person. Highly recommended. Reservations necessary for sunset trips.

Provincetown Trolley, Inc. (487-9483), on Commercial Street in front of Town Hall offers a 40-minute, narrated sight-seeing trip that departs approximately every half hour from 10 to 4 and on the hour from 5 to 8 daily, May through October. You can get on and off at the Provincetown Art Association & Museum (see *To See*), the Provincetown Inn next to the breakwater (see *Green Space—Walks*) the western end of Commercial Street, and the Province Lands Visitor Center (see *Guidance*). Adults $7, children 12 and under $5.

Rambling Rose Carriage Co. (487-4246), on Commercial Street in front of Town Hall, offers daily tours May to mid-October and on weekends before and after that in good weather. Prices vary according to the number of people and the distance traveled; generally, horse-and-buggy rides with Chris Lorenz start at $15 for two people.

MEDICAL EMERGENCY

Outer Cape Health Services (487-9395), Harry Kemp Way. Open 8–5 weekdays, until 8 PM on Tuesday and Thursday, and 9–noon on Saturday year-round.

TO SEE

Listings are from east to west.

Commercial Street. Until Commercial Street was laid out in 1835, the shoreline served as the town's main thoroughfare. Since houses had been oriented toward the harbor, many had to be turned around or the "front" door had to be reconstructed to face the new street. Some houses, however, still remain oriented toward the shore.

❉ **Provincetown Art Association & Museum** (487-1750), 460 Commercial Street. Open noon–5 daily and 8 PM–10 PM on Friday and Saturday, late June through early September; noon–5 on Saturday and Sunday the rest of the year. Organized in 1914 by a few artists to "promote education of the public in the arts, and social intercourse between artists and laymen," members have included Ambrose Webster, Milton Avery, and Marsden Hartley. One of the country's foremost small museums, the four galleries feature established and emerging artists. Selections from the permanent collection of 1700-plus works change frequently. Special exhibitions, juried shows, and other events are sponsored throughout the year. The bookstore specializes in the local art colony. Admission $3.

Provincetown Heritage Museum (487- 7098), Commercial and Center Streets. Open 10–6 daily, late May to mid-October. This former 1861 Methodist church is topped with a 162-foot-high steeple that serves as a landmark for fishermen sailing into the harbor. From 1958 to 1974, when Walter Chrysler (of automobile fame) owned the building, it was a fine-arts museum. Today, the emphasis is on the nautical: The museum contains the world's largest indoor model (66 feet long) of a fishing schooner. *Rose Dorothea* was built from scratch in Francis Santos's workshop at Flyer's Boatyard (see *Boat Excursions/Rentals*) and assembled upstairs in the museum. Impressive as it is, the museum has more to offer: local artwork, an offshore whaling boat, 19th-century fishing artifacts, and a trap fishing boat. Adults and children 12 and over $3.

MacMillan Wharf. By 1800 Provincetown was one of the country's busiest seaports; 50 years later it was the second largest whaling port. MacMillan Wharf (1873), originally called Old Colony Wharf after the railroad that met Boston packets, was ultimately named for native son Admiral Donald MacMillan, who explored the North Pole with Peary. By the 1880s, at the peak of cod fishing when Provincetown had the Cape's largest population, the wharf was just one of 56 jutting into the harbor. The town bustled

Parabolic dunes on the National Seashore

with herring canning, cod curing, whaling, and fishing. Although only a few wharves remain, MacMillan Wharf remains true to its original purpose: About 16 fishing boats dock here, unloading their daily catch late in the afternoon. (The fishing industry has suffered recently because of overfishing; no one knows how long fishermen can eke out a living from these waters.) Instead of whaling ships, the wharf today is lined with whale-watching boats. Don't miss the view from the end of the pier.

Expedition *Whydah* (487-7955), 16 MacMillan Wharf. Open daily 10 to 5 April to mid-October, weekends through January. This museum, new in 1996, is solely devoted to chronicling the story of the *Whydah,* the only pirate ship ever salvaged. It sank 1500 feet offshore from Wellfleet's Marconi Beach on April 26, 1717, and it was raised in 1984 by Cape Codder Barry Clifford. Adults $5, children 3–12 $3.50.

Provincetown Town Hall (487-7000), 260 Commercial Street. Built in 1878, the building serves as the seat of local government and community agencies. The auditorium is also used for concerts. Look for the Works Project Administration (WPA)–era murals of farmers and fishermen by Ross Moffett and the portrait by Charles Hawthorne.

Pilgrim bas-relief, Bradford Street, behind Town Hall. Sculptor Cyrus Dalin's memorial commemorates the Mayflower Compact, which has been called the "first American act in our history." After traveling from England for almost 2 months, the *Mayflower* sat in the harbor until the compact was drawn up. No one was allowed to go ashore until he signed the document, attesting to his willingness to abide by laws. One relief memorializes the five Pilgrims who died before reaching Plymouth. (Three Pilgrims are buried near the center of town.) The other relief contains the text of the compact and the names of the 41 people who signed it.

✍❋ **Pilgrim Monument & Provincetown Museum** (487-1310, 1-800-247-1620), High Pole Road, off Winslow Street from Bradford Street. Open 9–7 daily in July and August; 9–5 daily April through June and September through November. The 252-foot monument (the tallest all-granite monument in the United States) commemorates the Pilgrims' landing in Provincetown on November 11, 1620, and their 5-week stay in the harbor while searching for a good place to settle. President Theodore Roosevelt laid the cornerstone in 1907, and President Taft presided over the dedication in 1910. Climb the 116 stairs of the monument—modeled after the Torre del Mangia in Siena, Italy—for a panoramic view of the Outer Cape. On a clear day you can see 30 miles to Boston.

One wing of the museum is devoted to early Pilgrim travails: The *Mayflower*'s first landing, finding corn and fresh water, the unsuccessful search for a place to settle. The other wing contains dioramas and changing exhibits dedicated to a whaling captain's life ashore, shipwrecks, dolls and toys, the Lower and Outer Cape, and local art. Free parking for 2 hours; but beware—your car will be towed if you linger or park illegally. Adults $5, children 4–12 $3.

Universalist Meetinghouse (487-9344), 236 Commercial Street. This 1847 Greek Revival church contains trompe l'oeil murals (by Carl Wendt, who did similar murals for Nantucket's Unitarian Universalist Church), a Sandwich glass chandelier, and pews made with Provincetown pine (the pews are decorated with medallions carved from whales' teeth).

Pilgrim plaque, at the western end of Commercial Street. Provincetown's version of Plymouth's Rock—a plaque in the middle of the traffic circle—commemorates the Pilgrims' landing.

On the outskirts of town

Old Harbor Lifesaving Museum (487-1256), Race Point Beach. Open 10–4 daily in July and August, 10–4 on Saturday and Sunday in June and September. This 1872 structure, one of nine original Lifesaving Service stations on the Outer Cape, was floated by barge from Chatham to its present location in 1977. The Lifesaving Service, precursor to the Coast Guard, rescued crews from ships wrecked by shallow sandbars and brutal nor'easters. The museum contains the original equipment, but on Thursdays at 10 AM, demonstrations are given using the old-fashioned techniques. "Surfmen" launch a rescue line to the wrecked ship and haul the distressed sailors in one at a time. Plaques lining the boardwalk to the museum explain how the service worked. Donations.

❋ **Dune shacks,** beyond the end of Snail Road. In the dunes between Race Point and High Head in North Truro, on 2 miles of ridges and valleys, stand about 17 weather-beaten dune shacks. Made of driftwood and scavenged materials between 1935 and 1950, they are the subject of local legend. Over the years, notable writers and artists have called them home for weeks, months, even years: Among the tenants have been Jack

Kerouac, e.e. cummings, Norman Mailer, Jackson Pollack, poet Harry Kemp, and Eugene O'Neill. When the CCNS was created in 1961, the federal government set up 25-year or lifelong leases with squatters who were living in the shacks. (Only one of the inhabitants held a clear title to the land.) Some shacks are still occupied. In 1985, Joyce Johnson, a dune-dweller since the early 1970s, founded the Peaked Hill Trust to oversee three shacks. Members of the trust win stays at the shacks through the lottery system; write to PO Box 1705, Provincetown 02657, for member-ship information. Since Province Lands was added to the National Register of Historic Places in 1989, the maintenance and fate of most of the historic shacks have fallen to the National Park Service. In 1996 the park service opened two shacks to artists-in-residence.

There are only a few off-road parking spots at the end of Snail Road. To get a view of the shacks, walk through the short woodland trail and hike up the first steep dune then over the next two crests; the shacks will appear in the distance. You can also reach the shacks by walking east from Race Point Beach. Remember, however, that some shacks are still occupied, and one reason people live out there is privacy, to pursue the creative process uninhibited, to contemplate in isolation.

TO DO

AIRPLANE RIDES
☞ **Willie Air Tours** (487-0240), Provincetown Municipal Airport, Race Point Road, offers rides late May to early September. These 15-minute trips in a 1930 Stinson Detroiter help you grasp how narrow and vulnerable this strip of land is. A flight costs $45, whether you go up by yourself or bring three friends along; either way, it's a bargain. Purchase tickets at the Last Flight Out shop (487-1311) in the Aquarium Mall, 205 Commercial Street.

BICYCLING/RENTALS
Province Lands. Seven miles of paved trails—around ponds, cranberry bogs, and dunes—wind through Province Lands' 4000 acres. Spur trails lead to Herring Cove and Race Point Beaches. Access: Race Point Road near Route 6 and parking areas at the Beech Forest Trail, Province Lands Visitor Center, and Race Point and Herring Cove Beaches.

Arnold's (487-0844), 329 Commercial Street, since 1937, enjoys a prime location right in the middle of town. Beach umbrellas and chairs for rent, too; open mid-April to mid-October. **Galeforce Bicycle Rent-als, Inc.** (487-4849), 144 Bradford Street Extension, is located on the western edge of town. Open seasonally; free parking. **Nelson's Bike Shop** (487-8849), 43 Race Point Road, is located about 100 yards from the bike trails and you can park your car there for free; open April through October. Bike rentals cost about $2–4 hourly, $8–16 daily, $35–65, depending on what kind of bike you get.

BOAT EXCURSIONS/RENTALS

Provincetown Harbor Cruises (487-4330, 487-2353), MacMillan Wharf. Forty-minute trips every hour from 11 to 7 mid-May to mid-October, daily in summer, weekends in shoulder seasons. Adults $5, children $3.

Tiger Shark (487-4275, 1-800-923-8773), MacMillan Wharf. Mid-June through October, four trips daily. Captain Mike offers educational and hands-on trips collecting sea creatures. It's a great experience for young kids, teens, and their parents. Adults $15, children 4–12 $10.

Bay Lady II (487-9308) and *Schooner Hindu* (487-0659, 1-800-296-4544), both on MacMillan Wharf. Mid-May to mid-October. These 2-hour harbor sails into Cape Cod Bay are aboard traditionally gaff-rigged schooners. Four trips a day in-season (two off-season), including a sunset trip. Adults $11–13, children under 12 $5.

Flyer's Boat Rentals (487-0898, 1-800-750-0898), 131A Commercial Street. Daily 8–6, May through October. Flyer's, in business since 1965, has a rental boat to suit your needs: Sunfish, catamaran, sloop, powerboat, rowboat. Rates are $60–125 per day or $14–25 per hour (less for rowboats). Flyer's also offers its equivalent to early-bird dinners—early bird fishing specials: for 4 hours (8 AM–noon), you get a boat, bait, and two rods for $40. Two-hour sailing instruction is also offered for $60 per person; the price for additional people is negotiable.

FISHING

Surf casting is great on Race Point Beach in the early morning or after sunset. There is no shellfishing allowed by nonresidents.

Cee Jay (487-4330, 1-800-675-6723), MacMillan Wharf. There are three daily departures in July and August and four per week in June and September to mid-October. Four-hour bluefishing and fluke excursions: adults $20, children 12 and under $15. The third-generation crew will fillet your fish if you have a place to cook it.

Nelson's Bait & Tackle (487-0034), 43 Race Point Road. Open mid-April to mid-October. If you're not hiring a charter boat (which supplies the necessary equipment), Nelson's is the source for rod rentals, live and frozen bait, and fresh- and saltwater tackle.

See also Flyer's Boat Rentals under *Boat Excursions/Rentals.*

FITNESS CLUBS

Mussel Beach Health Club (487-0001), 35 Bradford Street. Open daily year-round, the club has state-of-the-art equipment, free weights, and cardiovascular equipment. Day-use fee: $12.

Provincetown Gym (487-2776), 170 Commercial Street. Open year-round. Cardiovascular machines and free weights; perhaps less intimidating for women. Day-use fee: $10 or six visits for $45.

FOR FAMILIES

Bayberry Hollow Farm (487-6584), West Vine Street Extension, offers pony rides May through October and by appointment off-season. From the owners of Rambling Rose Carriage, rides are $5 and up.

✐ Playgrounds are located at both ends of town: at Bradford and Howland Streets (East End) and at Bradford and Nickerson Streets (West End).

HORSEBACK RIDING

Nelson's Riding Stables (487-1112), 43 Race Point Road. Rides daily April through October; off-season, weather permitting. Guided western-style trail rides (for 1 hour) through dunes and woods on three CCNS trails. Experienced riders can take a spectacular 2-hour sunset trip, galloping on the beach. Hour rides $25 per person, sunset rides $50 per person (sunset trips are not available in July and August; it's too hot for the horses). Children 12 and under not permitted to ride.

IN-LINE SKATES

Cape Tip Sports (487-3736), 224 Commercial Street. Open year-round, but rentals from April to mid-October only. Skate rentals by the day, weekend, or week include protective equipment.

SPECIAL PROGRAMS

Fine Arts Work Center (487-9960), 24 Pearl Street. The center was founded in 1968 by a group of writers, artists, and patrons, including Robert Motherwell, Hudson Walker, Stanley Kunitz, and Myron Stout. The intent was to provide a place for emerging artists to pursue independent work within a sympathetic community of their peers. In 1972 the center purchased Days Lumber Yard, where artists have worked in small studios since 1914. (Frank Days Jr., who had been concerned about the plight of artists, built 10 studios over his lumberyard. Charles Hawthorne was one of the first tenants in 1914.) Writing and visual-arts residencies, which include a small monthly stipend and materials allowance, run October through April; the deadline for applications is February 1. Twenty candidates are chosen from a pool of about 1000. Readings, seminars, workshops, and exhibits year-round are open to the public.

✐ **Provincetown Museum School** (487-1750), 460 Commercial Street. Open early July to late August. Printmaking, painting, etching, monotypes, and watercolor are some of the classes taught by notable artists at the Provincetown Art Association and Museum (PAAM). Children's painting and drawing classes are held Tuesday and Thursday, 9:30–noon.

Cape Cod School of Art (487-0101), 48 Pearl Street. Workshops June through September. This excellent program carries on Provincetown's impressionist tradition established by Charles Hawthorne in 1899. Workshops in a variety of media, mostly held outdoors, are available for practically all ages and levels. Director Lois Griffel was a longtime student of Henry Hensche, Hawthorne's successor.

Center for Coastal Studies (487-3622; http://www.provincetown.com/coastalstudies/index.html), 59 Commercial Street. Library open to members year-round. (See also the center's Whale & Dolphin Shop, under *Selective Shopping—Special Shops.*) This independent, nonprofit, membership-supported institution is dedicated to research, public education, and conservation programs for the coastal and marine envi-

Early morning surf fishing at Race Point

ronments. Summer field walks for children and adults are scheduled and educational programs also include trips and lectures for school groups and Elderhostel. The center supplies naturalists for the Dolphin Fleet whale-watch trips (see *Whale-Watching*). Among other things, researchers study endangered right whales (there are only about 300 in the world) and have raised important environmental questions about Boston's Outfall Pipe, which will discharge treated sewage just 16 miles from Stellwagen Bank and 36 miles from Provincetown. Center scientists are always on the scene when pods of pilot whales strand themselves on area beaches. (With the possible exception of a place or two in New Zealand and Australia, Cape Cod has more whale strandings than any other place in the world. It happens primarily on the bayside beaches between Brewster and Provincetown in November and December. Scientists are at a loss to explain these mysterious mass suicides.)

Provincetown Community Center (487-7097), 44 Bradford Street. Open year-round. In addition to a host of classes sponsored by the Provincetown Recreation Department and held here, the center has a weight room, karate classes for adults and children, and aerobics classes. Call for current schedule, offerings, and fees.

SWIMMING POOL

Provincetown Inn (487-9500), 1 Commercial Street. May to mid-October. You can use this indoor, heated, Olympic-sized pool for a fee.

TENNIS

Town courts are located at **Motta Field** off Winslow Street.

Provincetown Tennis Club (487-9574), 286 Bradford Street. Open 8 AM–7 PM daily, late May to mid-October. Five clay and two hard courts are available for non–club members. $12 singles, $14 doubles, plus daily membership dues of $3 per person. Tournaments in July and August.

Bissell's Tennis Courts (487-9512), Bradford Street Extension behind The Moors restaurant (see *Dining Out*). Five clay courts and lessons are offered late May to late October.

WHALE-WATCHING

Located just 8 miles from Provincetown, the fertile feeding grounds of Stellwagen Bank attract migrating finback and humpback whales. Although it was designated the country's first National Marine Sanctuary in 1992, the government's attempts to control the ocean's intricate eco-system don't always work out as planned. For instance, whales feed on sand lance, which thrive when herring populations are small. (Herring eat sand lance larvae.) But since the government began protecting dwindling stocks of herring, the number of sand lance larvae has dwindled. Some naturalists theorize that humpbacks are heading elsewhere in search of more abundant food supplies. Fear not, though; a whale-watching trip without a whale sighting is rare.

Most whale-watch cruises last about 3½ hours and have an on-board naturalist. Bring a sweater (even in summer) and sea sickness pills if you think you'll need them.

Dolphin Fleet Whale Watch (349-1900, 1-800-826-9300), MacMillan Wharf. Mid-April through October. Scientists aboard the Dolphin Fleet, the best outfit in town, hail from the Center for Coastal Studies. Adults $17.50, children 7–12 $15.50, children under 7 free.

***Portuguese Princess* Whale Watch** (487-2651, 1-800-442-3188), MacMillan Wharf (tickets at 309 Commercial Street). Mid-April to mid-October. Adults $12–18.50, children 12 and under $10–16.50; early-bird rates $3 less. Free off-season parking at 70 Shank Painter Road; in-season parking is $5.

Provincetown Whale Watch Inc.'s *Ranger V* (487-3322, 1-800-992-9333), MacMillan Wharf. May through October. Adults $16–18, children over 10 $10–12, children under 10 free. Look for the ubiquitous discount coupons saving you $4.

GREEN SPACE

BEACHES

After you look at a map or go on an airplane tour—to see the long spit of sand arching around the harbor—you won't doubt that there are about 30 miles of beach within the CCNS in Provincetown.

Race Point Beach, CCNS, off Route 6. Race Point faces north, and, as such, it gets sun all day; it also has long breaking waves coming in off the Atlantic Ocean. Surrounded by dunes as far as the eye can see, Race Point feels as remote as it is. In spring, with the help of binoculars, you might see whales spouting and breaching offshore. Amenities include lifeguards, showers, and rest rooms. Parking from mid-June to early September is $5 daily (good all day on any CCNS beach); bikes and walk-ins are $2; a yearly pass is $15.

Herring Cove Beach, CCNS, at the end of Route 6. The water here is calmer and "warmer" (it's all relative) than at Race Point. Since the beach faces due west, you'll often find large groups gathering here to watch spectacular sunsets. Lifeguards, showers, rest rooms, and a snack bar. Parking is the same as at Race Point. Both lots fill up by 11 AM in summer; usually there is no charge to park after 5:30 PM.

Harbor Beach is about 3½ miles long and parallels Commercial Street. Although there is very little beach at high tide, and few public access points, it's great to walk the flats at low tide.

Long Point. Long Point is easily accessible by boat in summer (see Flyer's Shuttle under *Getting Around*), although few people make the effort. You'll be rewarded if you do, but don't forget to pack a picnic and plenty of water. You can walk atop the Breakwater (see *Walks*), but it takes about 2 hours. Long Point Lighthouse, at the tip of the spit, was built in 1816, two years before a community of fishermen began to build homes out there. By 1846 there were 61 families on Long Point, all of whom returned to town during the Civil War. (Two Civil War forts were built on Long Point.) As you walk around, notice which old houses sport a blue enamel plaque in the shape of a barge. This plaque identifies Long Point houses that were floated across the harbor on barges.

WALKS

Beech Forest Trail, CCNS, off Race Point Road from Route 6. This sandy, 1-mile trail circles a freshwater pond before steep stairs cut through a forest of beech trees. Warblers migrating from South America pack the area from mid- to late May, but the trail is also beautiful in autumn.

Breakwater, at the western end of Commercial Street (at the Provincetown Inn) and Bradford Street Extension, is a jetty that doubles as a wide footpath to the secluded Long Point beach. But even if you only walk out partway, it's a great place to sit and watch the tide roll in. **Wood End Lighthouse** (1872) is to the north.

Hatches Harbor. From Herring Cove Beach, at the end of Route 6, walk about 10 minutes toward Race Point Light to the entrance of Hatches Harbor. There's a dike along the back of the salt marsh and tidal estuary that you can walk across.

See also Dune shacks under *To See* and Province Lands Trail under *To Do— Bicycling/Rentals.*

LODGING

I don't advise going to Provincetown in summer without reservations. If you can, it's wise to reserve an apartment in January for the following summer. Although there are more than 100 places to stay, good ones fill up fast. Innkeepers recently informed me that they have vacancies mid-week in July. Most places have lengthy minimum-night stays during special events and holiday weekends—again, reserve early. Rates for holiday weekends are always higher than I've posted. Last, Provincetown has a limited water supply; try to conserve.

The zip code for Provincetown is 02657.

GUEST HOUSES

✳ **Watermark Inn** (487-0165, 1-800-734-0165 within Massachusetts), 603 Commercial Street (East End). Open year-round. These 10 contemporary and stylish suites are on the water's edge. They have triangular gabled windows, skylights, Scandinavian-style furniture, modern bathrooms, spacious living areas, cable TV, and either a full kitchen or kitchenette (two rooms have a fireplace). Sliding glass doors open onto decks, many of which are private; at high tide the water laps at the deck. A 20-minute walk from town; parking. July to early September $125–290; November through May $65–145 (7th night free). Weekly minimum in-season; rates are for two people; each additional person is $20–40 per night.

✳ **Land's End Inn** (487-0706, 1-800-276-7088), 22 Commercial Street (West End). Open year-round. As you walk up the hidden path, catching glimpses of turrets and decks, you'll quickly realize this is the most unusual place to stay in Provincetown. (No amount of describing it can prepare you for it.) At the end of the West End, perched atop Gull Hill, many rooms have wonderful ocean views. The interior is a visual feast, chock-full of Victoriana, wood carvings, stained glass, and Oriental rugs atop floral carpets. The inn offers 16 rooms (all with private baths) and three apartments; the tower rooms and loft suite are spectacularly situated. Some rooms can sleep four. There are lots of common spaces to relax. Continental breakfast; on-site parking. Summer $120–190 for rooms, $140–150 for apartments, $285 for suite; off-season $87–165 for rooms, $97–110 for apartments, $185 for suite; rates are for two people; each additional person $25 per day.

☞✳ **White Horse Inn** (487-1790), 500 Commercial Street (East End). Open year-round. Frank Schaefer has presided over this low-key, artsy hostelry since 1963, intent on providing clean, comfortable rooms at good prices. Six studio apartments are individually decorated with an eclectic, bohemian flair. Some are light and airy, some are dark and cozy. All defy description; even Frank has a hard time describing them to people over the phone. (On my last visit, though, he did describe one bathroom aptly as postmodern nautical.) Suffice it to say, each is a work of art in progress. Although the 12 rooms are basic (most with a shared bath), they are filled with local art from the last 30 years. They're a real find; in fact, as many Europeans find their way here as Americans. Mid-June to early September $70–75 ($35–40 single) for rooms, $125 for studio apartments with a 3-night minimum. Off-season $50 for rooms ($50 single) and $90 for studios. Weekly studio rates. No credit cards.

Windamar House (487-0599), 568 Commercial Street (East End). Open April through December. This circa-1840 sea captain's house has six rooms (two of which have private baths) and two apartments. Bette Adams, innkeeper since 1980, has filled them with antiques, local art, and coordinated fabrics and wallpapers. The small common room, where a continental breakfast is set out, has a refrigerator and TV. The most spectacular guest room overlooks the garden and grape arbor. One large and airy apartment has cathedral ceilings and a view of the harbor. The well-manicured lawns and gardens in the backyard are an oasis. On-site parking. Although all are welcome, the clientele is mostly female. Late May to mid-September $60–110 for rooms; off-season $45–95. In-season $750–850 weekly for apartments; mid-September to mid-October $650–750 weekly; off-season $85–95 nightly. No credit cards.

❋ **Bradford Gardens Inn** (487-1616, 1-800-432-2334, e-mail: BradGardnn@ aol.com), 178 Bradford Street. Open year-round. This appealing knoll-top inn is a 10-minute walk from the center. Inside you'll find hardwood floors covered by braided rugs, as well as lovely antiques and local artwork. All but two rooms in the main house have fireplaces. A full breakfast is included with the inn rooms. Six tastefully decorated town houses, each with two bedrooms, a full kitchen, and hardwood floors, were built in the early 1990s. The four cottages are less uniform but no less nicely decorated and furnished. A new penthouse has a private deck with unobstructed view of the bay, two bedrooms, fireplace, and full kitchen. Outside, there are plenty of places to sit within the lush gardens. On-site parking. The clientele here is predominantly female, but all are welcome. Late May to early September $116–138 for rooms, $115–225 for cottages and town houses; off-season $65–118 for rooms, $75–195 for cottages and town houses. Rates are for two people; each additional person is $20. Pets accepted off-season with advance permission.

❋ **Six Webster Place** (487-2266, 1-800-693-2783, e-mail: sixwebster@ aol.com), 6 Webster Place. Open year-round. This 18th-century guest house sits at the end of a quiet lane behind Provincetown Town Hall. It was handsomely and authentically restored in 1985 to reflect its colonial origins. Most of the six rooms have working fireplaces and private bath; all have cable TV. Common areas include a small living room, a sunny reading nook, gardens, and decks or patios. Studios and one- and two-bedroom apartments are contemporary and sophisticated. In-season, the clientele is predominantly gay; in the off-season, it's more mixed. Host Gary Reinhardt offers an expanded continental breakfast. On-site parking; Jacuzzi and tanning area. Mid-June to mid-September $85 for a shared bath, $95–140 for a private bath, $850 weekly for the studio, $950–1300 weekly for apartments; off-season $55–110 for rooms, $95–150 for the studio and apartments. Pets permitted in studios.

Captain Lysander Inn (487-2253), 96 Commercial Street (West End). Open February through December. Set back from the road, this whaling captain's house has 13 largish, traditional rooms; half have private bath. Room 13 is particularly pleasant, with exposed brick, a fireplace, and hardwood floors. A continental breakfast is set out in the wicker sun room. Next door, the newly constructed, tasteful carriage house has two bedrooms upstairs and a full living room and separate kitchen/dining room downstairs. On-site parking. Late May to mid-September $85–95; off-season $45–55. Carriage house: $1200 weekly in-season, $900 weekly off-season, $150 nightly off-season.

❋ **The Viewpoint** (487-4526, 487-1939 off-season), 63 Commercial Street (West End). Open year-round. These two newly renovated guest rooms, with modern bathrooms, have summertime access to the owner's roof deck and living room. July and August $1300 weekly; off-season $65 nightly. No credit cards.

❋ **Three Peaks** (487-1717, 1-800-286-1715), 210 Bradford Street. Open year-round. This 1870s Victorian house set back from the road, with rocking chairs on the front porch, has five well-appointed rooms (each with a private bath) and two apartments, all with wall-to-wall carpeting. In-season the clientele is 99 percent gay; off-season it's about 50/50. On-site parking. Late May to mid-September $80–85 for rooms, $105 for apartments; off-season $50–65 for rooms, $65–85 for apartments.

APARTMENTS, COTTAGES, AND STUDIOS

✐❋ **The Masthead** (487-0523, 1-800-395-5095), 31–41 Commercial Street (West End). Open year-round. At the far end of the West End, about a 20-minute walk to the center of town, The Masthead offers a superb variety of well-maintained apartments, cottages, and rooms. The neatly landscaped complex, operated by the Ciluzzi family since 1959, has a boardwalk with lounge chairs and access to the 450-foot private beach below. Each cottage has a large picture window facing the water. Units, in buildings more than 100 years old, have fully equipped kitchens, low ceilings, pine paneling, and Early American furnishings that are a bit dated but nonetheless charming and comfortable. Although most units can accommodate four people, one sleeps seven. The brochure contains a very accurate and detailed description of each room. Great for families; children under 12 stay free. Limited on-site parking. July to early September $150–253 ($73–166 for rooms); off-season $83–110 ($57–85 for rooms). Rates are for two people; each additional person is $20 per night. In-season weekly and off-season weekend rates available.

❋ **Hargood House** (487-9133), 493 Commercial Street (East End). Open year-round. Three of these five buildings are waterside, clustered around landscaped grounds, lounge chairs, and a beach. (Two-bedroom units are across the street, but have access to the lawn and beach.) Most of the 19 units have private decks or patios and large picture windows facing east; all have well-equipped kitchens; a few have fireplaces. The shingled, traditional exteriors belie individually and newly decorated interiors. When former guests Ann Maguire and Harriet Gordon purchased the complex in 1994, they set about updating the decor. The rate sheet details each unit's special features. About a 15-minute walk from the center of town. Late June to early September $900–1300 weekly for one and two bedrooms (studio $670–700 weekly); off-season $72–142 nightly. Rates are for two people; each additional person is $10. Pets accepted.

🖎 **Ship's Bell Inn and Motel** (487-1674), 586 Commercial Street. (East End.) Open mid- May to mid-November. Most of these seven apartments and seven studios have decks with water views across Commercial Street. A few units sleep five or six people; all have modern, fully equipped kitchens. Ship's Bell also rents 10 motel rooms off a cozy fireplaced living room, but they're less impressive than the other accommodations. Nancy and Bill McNulty have owned Ship's Bell since 1971, and their staff provide hospitable service. On-site parking; private beach across the street. July and August $500–525 weekly for rooms, $60–1150 weekly for apartments; nightly rentals in the off-season. Rates are for two people; each additional person is $12 per night.

Capt. Jack's Wharf (487-1450, 487-1673 in winter), 73A Commercial Street (West End). Open late May to late September. On a rustic old wharf, these 10 colorfully painted bohemian apartments transport you back to Provincetown's early days as an emerging art colony. Many units have whitewashed interiors, with skylights and lots of windows looking onto the harbor. Some first-floor units have narrow cracks between the planked floorboards—you can see the water beneath you! Some specifics: Australis is a two-story unit with a spiral staircase and more than 1000 square feet of space; Hesperus has a cathedral ceiling and loft; Spindrift is at the end of the wharf with wraparound views; Bridge has a private deck. The wharf is strewn with bistro tables, pots of flowers, and Adirondack chairs. In-season $600–875 weekly; off-season $480–700 weekly or $69–100 nightly (3-night minimum). No credit cards.

✳ **Bull Ring Wharf** (487-3100), 381 Commercial Street (East End). Open year-round. These 16 comfortable units are just far enough from the center of town to avoid most of the noise but close enough to be convenient. Apartments, occupying the length of the old wharf, share two large waterfront decks. (Some units have a private deck.) Many have fireplaces, all have fully equipped kitchens and cable TV. On-site parking. Mid-June to mid-September $100–175 nightly; off-season $70–140 nightly; November through March $50–100. Rates are for up to four people where they can be accommodated. No credit cards.

See also *Guest Houses.*

MOTELS

Best Western Tides (487-1045, 1-800-528-1234), 837 Commercial Street (East End). Open early May to mid-October. This 6-acre complex on the Provincetown-Truro line sits right on Cape Cod Bay. Most of these pleasant motel rooms are waterfront, within shuffle of the motel's 600-foot private beach. Ground-floor rooms open onto the beach. All rooms

Provincetown's Pilgrim Monument and Town Hall

have a king-sized bed or two doubles. On-site parking. July and August $119–169; off-season $59–99. Children under 18 free in parent's room.

Surfside Inn (487-1726), 543 Commercial Street (East End). Open late April to mid-October. At four stories, this is the tallest commercial building in Provincetown. Rooms are nothing to write home about, but there are 84 of them—with balconies—and they're clean. One building fronts the private beach; the other overlooks the pool. Waterfront rooms have two double beds and cost only $10–20 more than other rooms. Parking. Late June to early September $95–125; off-season $65–95.

CAMPGROUNDS

Dune's Edge Campground (487-9815), off Route 6. Open May through September. One hundred wooded lots, mostly for tents, on the edge of the dunes; $20–22 for two people.

Coastal Acres Camping Court, Inc. (487-1700), West Vine Street Extension. Open April through October. Wooded sites on the western edge of town; $21 for two in a tent, $28 with hook-ups.

HOSTEL

Outermost Hostel (487-4378), 28 Winslow Street (for registration). Open mid-May to late October. Not affiliated with the American Youth Hostel (AYH) system, this private hostel offers 30 bunks in 5 cabins. Common space includes a small kitchen and living room; the yard has barbecues and picnic tables. $14 per person nightly.

RENTALS

Roslyn Garfield Associates (487-1308), 115 Bradford Street. Listings for 2-week rentals and seasonal rentals in Truro and Wellfleet as well as

Provincetown. Prices start at $900 for 2 weeks, $3200 for the entire season from late May to early September. They have properties available year-round.

All Provincetown Real Estate (487-9000, 1-800-786-9699) deals with in-season weekly apartment, condo, and cottage rentals, and listings for long weekends in the off-season.

RSVPtown (487-1883, 1-800-677-8696, e-mail: rsvptown@aol.com), 4 Standish Street, is similar to All Provincetown. Rentals are Saturday to Saturday and start at $700 for a one-bedroom, $1000 for a two-bedroom, and $1500 for a three-bedroom.

WHERE TO EAT

Provincetown has dozens of restaurants, so you'll have plenty of choices to suit your budget and taste buds. Instead of listing places in order of preference (as I usually do), listings are from east to west. The opening and closing months listed here are only a guideline, and many places are closed certain days of the week. If you have your heart set on a particular place, call ahead in the off-season, and make reservations when you can, especially in summer.

DINING OUT

Flagship Restaurant (487-4200; http://www.ptownlib.com/users/ptown/flagship.html), 463 Commercial Street. Open for breakfast on weekends and dinner almost nightly, May through October. Built on an old wharf, the dark-paneled, candlelit dining room has harbor views on three sides. Provincetown's oldest fish house (open since 1933), the Flagship has been invigorated by chef-owner Polly Hemstock, who took over in 1995. She serves creative twists on traditional dishes like fish tacos, Thai marinated duck, and pignoli-crusted cod. Grilled fish and lobster dishes are a good bet. Children's menu. The **Dory Bar,** built from an authentic Grand Banks fishing schooner, is a fun place to have a drink; there is live acoustic music on weekends in summer. Reservations recommended. Breakfast (including omelets, eggs Benedict, and avocado scramble) $3–7; dinner entrées $11–24.

✐❋ **Ciro & Sal's** (487-0049), 4 Kiley Court. Open for dinner nightly in-season and on weekends off-season. What began as a coffeehouse and sandwich shop for artists in the early 1950s has become a very popular northern Italian restaurant. Upstairs, Ciro & Sal's has a nice bar, candlelight dining, and opera music playing in the background. The ground-floor "cellar" is cozy, with brick and plaster walls and Chianti bottles hanging from the rafters. Reservations recommended. Children's menu. Entrées $15–20; pasta dishes about $11.

❋ **The Mews** and **Cafe Mews** (487-1500), 429 Commercial Street. Open for lunch and dinner daily in-season and on weekends in the off-season, mid-February through December. The downstairs beachfront restaurant is elegant, awash in peach tones and bleached woods. Longtime chef Laurence deFreitas features a popular mixed-seafood grill and dishes like baked lobster stuffed with crab and scallops, and blackened scallops with tequila lime butter. Sauces are rich and delicious. The upstairs café also has great views but is more casual; the "American Fusion" menu features all the same imaginative entrées as downstairs, with the addition of fancy burgers, appetizers, salads, and pasta. It's a great place for a before-dinner drink or after-dinner dessert and coffee; there's entertainment in summer. Reservations recommended. Lunch $6–12; dinner entrées $14–21.

Pepe's (487-0670), 371 Commercial Street. Open for lunch and dinner, late May through October. Pepe's **Top Deck,** an enclosed bar with great views of the harbor, serves sandwiches and raw-bar delicacies. Downstairs is elegant and romantic, with an international menu of gourmet seafood dishes prepared by chef-owner Astrid Berg. Specialties include bouillabaisse, pan-roasted lobster, filet mignon, and rack of lamb. Children's menu; early specials. Reservations recommended. Lunch $5–15, dinner entrées $15–25; about $11 in the bistro.

Cafe Edwige (487-2008), 333 Commercial Street. Open for dinner mid-May to late October. With sophisticated cuisine that surpasses the lovely atmosphere, the Edwige is one of Provincetown's top two or three places to dine. Although Edwige is a hopping breakfast place (see *Eating Out*), by night it's romantic, with subdued lighting and solicitous service. Dishes might include Thai spiced chicken on a skewer or something off the mix-and-match menu: Have a fish of your choice grilled, pan-roasted, or blackened and pair it with your choice of a side dish (like roasted potatoes) and a sauce (like charred tomato salsa). You can't go wrong here; kudos to proprietor Nancyann and chef Steven Frappolli, who came on board in 1994. Entrées $15–21.

✏❋ **Napi's** (487-1145), 7 Freeman Street. Open for lunch October through April, and dinner, year-round. Chef-owners Helen and Napi Van Dereck built this unusual restaurant in 1973 and have filled it chockablock with local art, plants, stained glass, and lively objects to stir your imagination. The eclectic menu has an international flair: dishes made with Portuguese sausage (linguica), organic salads, a large selection of vegetarian dishes, fresh fish, pasta dishes, and stir fry. Health-conscious Napi's also accommodates no-fat and low-salt diets. A favorite of local artists and townsfolk, Napi's is even more lively in the off-season. For a quick bite, you can always get cold snacks and appetizers at the bar. Reservations recommended, essential in summer. Parking on the premises; children's menu; early specials. Dinner entrées $12–20.

Dancing Lobster Cafe (487-0900), Ryder Street Extension, Fisherman's Wharf. Open for dinner mid-May through October. Chef-owner Nils "Pepe" Berg honed his considerable skills at his family's restaurant Pepe's. But there's a big difference in execution: Whereas Pepe's uses lots of butter and cream, the Dancing Lobster uses olive oil to bring out delicate Tuscan flavors. It's a wonderfully successful place favored by locals and visitors. Located in a red, low-slung building on the wharf, this upbeat café has the feel of an urbane trattoria, albeit one with windows looking onto the water. Tables are dressed in white paper tablecloths and "decorated" with bottles of olive oil and sparkling water. The exposed kitchen puts out simple, flavorful Italian specialties: rigatoni, ravioli pomodoro, grilled squid on bruschetta with roma tomatoes, scaloppine of veal. No credit cards; no reservations. Get there when it opens and watch the sun set or expect to wait at least an hour, no kidding. Entrées $8–16.

Mario's Mediterraneo (487-0002, 487-0003), 265 Commercial Street. Open for lunch and dinner, mid-May to mid-September. Mario's is a casually stylish place, in a California sort of way: splashes of color, striped canvas chairs, rag-woven place mats, painted tables. An open layout makes indoor tables feel close to the outdoor deck on the beach. Lunch revolves around fancy salads, sandwiches, pastas, and burgers ($7.50–16). Reservations necessary to ensure an outdoor table. Dinner entrées $11.50–22.

Front Street (487-9715), 230 Commercial Street. Open for dinner May through December; closed Tuesday in the off-season. This romantic but convivial restaurant is located in the cozy cellar of a Victorian house. The bistro-style dining room is outfitted with low lighting, small tables placed close together, local artwork, and brick walls. Service is unobtrusive. Donna Aliperti, chef-owner since 1988, reigns over a kitchen serving much-lauded dishes as varied as rack of lamb, tea-smoked duck, and softshell crabs. The creative repertoire of Italian and Continental dishes changes weekly; the wine list is excellent. A full Italian-only menu is served in the off-season. The small, popular bar is open until 1 AM. Reservations recommended. Entrées $12–24.

❉ **Martin House** (487-1327), 157 Commercial Street. Open for dinner year-round. Siblings Glen, Gary, and Wendy Martin have created one of my favorite Cape Cod restaurants. The circa-1750 whaling captain's house is Colonial through and through: exposed beams, wall sconces, stenciling, fireplaces, wainscoting, and low ceilings. The cuisine lives up to its surroundings and is complemented by courteous, well-paced service. Internationally influenced dishes might include roast duck or vegetable lasagna on a spinach purée with mushroom demiglaze. Reservations recommended. Entrées $11–20.

❉ **Gallerani's Cafe** (487-4433), 133 Commercial Street. Open for dinner year-round; closed Monday and Tuesday in the off-season. David Gallerani's candlelit café opened in 1986 to rave reviews and continues to be packed by loyal and sophisticated patrons. With three walls of small-paned windows, the bistro-style dining room has always had a warm, neighborhood feel to it. It's a fun place with a friendly staff; you never know what's going to happen—perhaps it will be a spur-of-the-moment dress-up night, i.e., pajama night. The menu encourages you to mix and match half-orders of grilled meats, seafood, and pasta dishes. Specialties include chicken stuffed with roasted red peppers, mozzarella, and pear chutney, and almost anything off the grill. Sauces tend to be simple but very tasty. Reservations for parties of five or more. Full entrées $13–21.

☞⌀**Sal's Place** (487-1279), 99 Commercial Street. Open for dinner early May through October. Reserve a waterside table on the deck covered in grapevines, and enjoy southern Italian dishes as you listen to the waves lapping at the deck pilings. There's no better to way to spend a summer evening. One of the two indoor dining rooms is classic trattoria: Chianti bottles hang from the ceilings and red-and-white-checked cloths cover the tables. Two or three nightly specials like scampi Adriatico (grilled shrimp with squid in pesto) supplement classics like melanzane alla Parmigiana or a 28-ounce bistecca pizzaiola. Service is very friendly, portions large, and the *tira mi su* heavenly. Children's portions; reservations suggested. Entrées $9–20.

The Moors (487-0840), Bradford Street Extension. Open for dinner April through October. The Moors has been serving classic Portuguese dishes since 1940 (chef Ryan Roderick has been at the helm since 1975), and people love it. This is the place to try Portuguese kale soup, *lagosta Viera a moda de Peniche* (lobster and scallop casserole with an herb tomato sauce and wine and brandy), or their version of an old favorite: scampi Moors (with a cheese, garlic, and mustard flavor). For the less adventurous, there are lobsters and standard seafood entrées. The Moors is lively and rustic, with low ceilings, nautical flotsam and jetsam, and barn-board and driftwood walls. The candlelit dining room is so dark that the friendly waitstaff regularly offer flashlights to patrons reading the menu. The wine list is reasonably priced. Reservations suggested. Children's menu; early specials. Entertainment downstairs in the bar. Lunch $3.50–12; dinner entrées $12.75–18.

EATING OUT

☞ **Dodie's Diner** (487-3868), 401 Commercial Street. Open for all three meals mid-April to mid-October. Dodie Silano opened the tiny diner in 1993 to serve "comfort food" like blueberry muffins, corned beef hash, fried chicken, BLTs, seafood baskets, and pies and cakes baked by Dodie's sister. Decorated with family photos, old toys, and 1950s odds and ends, Dodie's is a fun place for kids. There's limited outdoor, streetside seating. Lunch and dinner $5–10.

❊ **Fat Jack's** (487-4822), 335 Commercial Street. Open for breakfast, lunch, and dinner year-round, except closed in December. This popular, tavernlike, storefront eatery has a casual ambience. Fat Jack's serves burgers, fish-and-chips, sandwiches, and grazing foods like guacamole and potato skins. Dishes $5–13.

Cafe Edwige (487-2008), 333 Commercial Street. Open for breakfast from mid-May to late October; dinner also served (see *Dining Out*). If you don't get here in the morning by 8:30 or 8:45, expect to wait; loyal locals know a good thing when they find it. Frittatas, a wide selection of omelets, fruit pancakes, broiled flounder and eggs, a tofu casserole—they're all on the menu. High-backed booths and small tables fill the lofty second-floor space, bright with skylights, and local art. Dishes $3.50–7.

☞∅✳ **Lobster Pot** (487-0842), 321 Commercial Street. Open daily for lunch and dinner year-round except January. This venerable institution has been under the same ownership—Joy McNulty's—since 1979. (It has operated as a bar since 1866.) Over the years, the Lobster Pot's neon red lobster sign has been a symbol of Provincetown. But there's a contingent who think the Lobster Pot has recently become like an assembly-line factory. With that caveat, the menu features a wide selection of fresh seafood, including great clam chowder. Look for the red neon and the first-floor bakery, then head down the long corridor, past the kitchens and up the stairs. Lunch $7–13, dinner $13–19, children's dinner specials $8.

☞✳ **Post Office Café** (487-3892), 303 Commercial Street. Open daily for breakfast, lunch, and dinner year-round except mid-January to mid-February. This casual and popular eatery serves sandwiches, salads, seafood platters, and lots of fried appetizers. But you can also get full-fledged dinners like chicken parmigiana and barbecued ribs. Dishes $4–14.

Mario's Mediterraneo (487-0002, 487-0003), 265 Commercial Street. Open for all three meals, mid-April to mid-October. The front of Mario's serves as a fast-food emporium, dishing out slices of tasty thin-crust pizza, fancy sandwiches ($5) like grilled chicken with mozzarella and avocado and cold pasta salads. Order at the counter for takeout or wait for a table (turnover is high). Skip the coffee drinks.

Euro Island Grill (487-2505), 258 Commercial Street. Open for lunch and dinner May to mid-October, and breakfast on summer weekends. This grill–cum–dance club and tiki bar has outdoor tables and umbrellas on a second-floor deck overlooking the street parade. (Patrons move indoors when it rains.) By the looks of the bar—a veritable shrine to Jamaica and reggae music—you'd be hard-pressed to believe Euro Island served anything besides tropical drinks. But it does. Grilled fish is a good bet, whether it's served with a spicy Caribbean sauce or with a salad. Seafood pastas, a full line of appetizers, and a raw bar are also popular. Satisfy late-night munchies with a limited menu served until 1 AM. Lunch $7–12; dinner entrées $14–20.

☞ **Cafe Heaven** (487-9639), 199 Commercial Street. Open daily for all three meals in summer and on Friday, Saturday, and Sunday in the off-season, May through October. This pleasant storefront eatery with high ceilings is usually lively, but sometimes it just feels noisy and cramped. (Look in the window and see for yourself what it's like at the moment.) There is an extensive lunchtime selection of cold salads, sandwiches, and "hamburger-heaven" creations at dinner—all moderately priced.

Breakfast specialties include omelets and homemade granola. Friendly service. Breakfast $3.50–8; lunch $5.25–8.50.

Bubala's By The Bay (487-0773), 183 Commercial Street. Open for breakfast, lunch, and dinner, April through October. Bubala's large dining room is replete with ocher walls, diner-style booths, large vases of gladiola, and windows on three sides. As stylish as the indoor seating is, simple outdoor tables on Commercial Street are just as popular. As for the food, lunch dishes include focaccia sandwiches, burgers, fajitas, and salads like lobster tarragon. Dinnertime dishes include oven-roasted penne, baked Cuban cod, and grilled chicken Santa Fe. Generous portions. Lunch $6–10.50; dinner $15–22.

☞ **Sebastian's Waterfront Restaurant** (487-3286), 177 Commercial Street. Open for lunch and dinner April through October (daily in summer, generally Thursday through Sunday in the off-season). This casual waterfront eatery is pleasant and serves competitively priced dishes. The glass-enclosed restaurant serves generous portions of American fare like the popular prime rib, baked chicken, and seafood scampi with sautéed lobster, scallops, and shrimp over linguine. Lunch tends toward sandwiches and fried fish specials for $5–8; dinner entrées $9–13.

✐ **Tip For Tops'n Restaurant** (487-1811), 31 Bradford Street. Open for all three meals, mid-March to early November. Owned by the Carreiros since 1967, this family-style restaurant offers good, simple food at good prices, away from the madding Commercial Street crowds. The name, by the way, is shorthand for "the tip of the Cape for tops in service." Breakfast specials ($3.75) are served until 3 PM. There are plenty of seafood and Portuguese specialties for lunch and dinner, as well as a few sandwiches and a children's menu. Early-bird specials from 4:30 to 6. Parking on the premises; no credit cards. Dishes $8–15.

Silva's Seafood Connection (487-1574), 175 Bradford Street. Open for daily lunch and dinner (11:30–10 in summer, 11:30–7:30 in the off-season) May to mid-October. Housed in a former Dairy Queen, this informal fry house serves up barely floured and lightly fried seafood platters ($10), lobster rolls, and scallop dinners ($9.)

TAKEOUT

Express Deliveries (487-4300). Open noon–midnight daily in summer, nightly at dinnertime in spring and fall; closed January and February. For all you house renters who don't want to leave the comfort of your home, for a charge of $3–5, these folks deliver meals from local restaurants. Look for their menu book, which has 25 or so restaurants to choose from—many of the above restaurants participate.

☞ **Mojo's** (487-3140), Ryder Street, next to the MacMillan Wharf parking lot. Open for lunch mid-May to mid-October and dinner in summer. Locals and visitors love this clam shack/fry joint with good reason. There are two important distinctions between it and others of its genre: The selection of dishes is extensive and the fried foods are light and fresh. Try almost anything and you'll not be disappointed: fried mushrooms, baskets of fried shrimp or fish, chicken tenders, subs, burgers, Mexican dishes, salads, and vegetarian sandwiches. Take your enormous portions to the beach, pier, or, if you're lucky, to one of a few outdoor tables. $2–10.

☞ **Café Crudité** (487-6237), 336 Commercial Street. Open for lunch and dinner, May through October. Large portions of macrobiotic and vegan vegetarian dishes are the order of the day at this new (as of 1995), predominantly take-out place. The veggie burger, which boasts 28 ingredients, is served in a tortilla at lunch and with rice and veggies at dinner. If you've been longing for grilled tempeh or tofu eggless salad like you make at home, this is the place for you. There are a few tables above Commercial Street offering a bird's-eye view of the street scene. Lunch $4–5.50, dinner $5–10.

Clem + Joe's Rotisserie Chicken + Ribs (487-8303), 338 Commercial Street. Open for lunch and dinner mid-April to mid-October. Clem Silva, a fourth-generation Provincetown native, dishes up authentic southern-style pulled and shredded pork, barbecued ribs, and roasted chicken. Perhaps unique to all of Provincetown, you won't find any seafood on the menu here. Order a "family-style" serving of rotisserie chicken with corn bread, slaw, pasta salad, and potato salad for $15.50. (It should feed four people.) A similar platter of ribs goes for $29.50. From the moment it opened in 1995, Clem's has been a hit. Takeout only. If you're by yourself, $5 will get you a lot of food.

See also Mario's Mediterraneo and Mojo's under *Eating Out*.

CAFÉS AND COFFEE

Spiritus (487-2808), 190 Commercial Street. Open daily noon–2 AM, April to early November (from 8 AM in summer). Most patrons come for great thin-crust pizza, munching it down while socializing out front. But Spiritus also has excellent coffee, espresso shakes, freshly squeezed orange juice, baked goods on summer mornings, and ice cream all day long. There are wooden booths inside for rainy days. Take your coffee across the street to the picnic tables overlooking the bay.

Flying Cups & Saucers (487- 3780), 205–209 Commercial Street. Open 7:30 AM–5 or 6 PM daily (until 11 PM in summer), mid-April to early November. This take-out coffee and pastry bar serves some of the best cappuccino in town. It also has protein powder drinks, ginseng, and fruit drinks as well as a few baked goods. Take your coffee to the deck overlooking the harbor—preferably in the early morning when the town is still quiet.

❋ **Café Express** (487-3382), 214 Commercial Street, next to the New Art Cinema. Open daily 9 AM–2 AM, May through September, and daily 9 AM– 6 PM, October through April. Provincetown has very few outdoor cafés. Although this one only has a few outdoor tables (and limited indoor seating), it has good coffee. The menu is light: salad plates, soups, sandwiches on pita bread, and omelets for breakfast.

✐ **Café Blasé** (487-9465), 328 Commercial Street. Open daily 9 AM–11 PM, May through September. There's no better location for people-watching. Blue and pink umbrellas and large paper lanterns, all enclosed by a white picket fence and window boxes, set this place apart. Get a drink, a streetside table, and stay for a while. The food is OK: two specialties from the full menu are raspberry marinated chicken and fish tacos with grilled marinated swordfish, cabbage, jalapeño peppers, and white salsa. Children's menu. Lunch $6.50–13; dinner entrées $9–14.

SNACKS

Provincetown Portuguese Bakery (487-1803), 299 Commercial Street. Open daily April through October. If you haven't tried Portuguese pastries, this is the place to come (short of hopping on a plane to Lisbon): *pasteis de coco,* meat pies, *pasteis de nata* (a custard tart), and *tarte de Amendoa* (almond tart). In summer the ovens are baking 24 hours a day and the fried dough flies out as fast as they can make it.

Pucci's Harborside (487-1964), 539 Commercial Street. Open for Sunday brunch and dinner, mid-April to mid-October. If you find yourself in the East End suffering from hunger pangs or lusting for a water view, stop in here. The atmosphere is informal, bright, and simple, with an enclosed deck over the water and a harborfront bar. I really only recommend drinks (they make a good margarita) and snacks like chicken wings, spare ribs, and buffalo wings.

Georgie Porgie's Bagel Factory (487-1610), 100 Shank Painter Road, off Route 6. Open until 5 PM daily in summer; 6 AM–noon daily from mid-March to mid-December. Porgie's makes its own New York–style, kettle-boiled bagels daily. Stop on your way in or out of town (by bike or car, because it's not on the beaten path) for a bagel sandwich.

Adams' Pharmacy (487-0069), 25 Commercial Street. Open daily year-round. Provincetown's oldest business in continual operation was opened in 1875 by Dr. John Crocker, who was also the first publisher of *The Advocate* newspaper. Adams' still has an old-fashioned soda fountain dispensing coffee and soda.

The deli market is cornered in Provincetown. The East End has **Martin's Market** (487-4858), 467 Commercial Street, open May through October. The town center is served by **Provincetown Cheese Market & Deli** (487-3032), 225 Commercial Street, open year-round. The West End is catered to, royally, by **Scherer's Deli** (487-3303), 93 Commercial Street, open early May to mid-September. Scherer's is the fanciest, with items like peppers stuffed with prosciutto, red potato salad with dill, and penne with tomatoes.

ENTERTAINMENT

Provincetown Reservation System (487-6400), 293 Commercial Street. Open daily, year-round. A stone's throw from MacMillan Wharf, this bustling place gives out information and makes reservations for most of

Provincetown's dazzling entertainment scene. What's playing when and where is just a phone call away. Be prepared for theatrical experimentation, innovation, and an occasional over-the-top show. Town Hall is the biggest venue, but there are lots of shows at the Post Office Cabaret (a long, narrow room with too many seats).

Provincetown Playhouse Mews Series (487-0955, 487-6400), Town Hall, on Commercial Street. Since 1982 this renowned series has brought chamber music, folk, and jazz to audiences in July and August.

Provincetown Theatre Company (487-9500), 1 Commercial Street at the Provincetown Inn. New local playwrights and classic drama are featured year-round by this group, which was founded in 1963 to carry on the goals of the early-20th-century Provincetown Players.

Provincetown Repertory Theater (487-0060). Directed by Ken Hoyt, this group was founded in 1995 and has performed to enthusiastic audiences in Town Hall and at Pilgrim Monument (see *To See*).

Chamber music concerts (487-6400). About four concerts are given from mid-July through August. Tickets: $10.

New Art Cinema (487-9222), 214 Commercial Street. Open mid-June to mid-September. New releases in two theaters.

Movies at the Holiday Inn (487-1711), Route 6A at Snail Road. Year-round except for a couple of weeks in January. Every night an ever-changing group of about 40 locals get together to watch a free movie and eat unlimited popcorn in the Whaler Lounge. Movies aren't first run, but they haven't made it to video yet, either.

NIGHTLIFE

Provincetown's after-dark scene can get rather spicy. There's something for everyone: gay, straight, and in between. When the bars, clubs, and shows close at 1 AM, it seems like everybody ends up at the Provincetown Town Hall or Spiritus (see *Where To Eat—Cafés and Coffee*).

Club Euro (487-2505, 487-2501), 258 Commercial Street, features world-beat music—African, blues, zydeco, jazz, and reggae. Although it's known primarily for live music, the club also shows classic dance videos inside the 1843 former Congregational church, now embellished with a deep-sea mural and a three-dimensional mermaid emerging from the wall. Open May through October.

The Moors (487-0840), Bradford Street Extension, draws a sing-along crowd that comes to hear pianist Lenny Grandchamp, who has played nightly in-season since the late 1970s. Free. (Also see *Dining Out*.)

The Boatslip (487-1669), 161 Commercial Street, which offers Two-Steppin' on Friday nights, is best known for its gay summertime Tea Dances (3:30–6:30 daily) on the poolside, waterfront deck. Open late May to late October.

Atlantic House (487-3821), 4 Masonic Place, more commonly referred to as the A-House, is the home of the so-called Macho Bar, a nationally known men's bar upstairs. Downstairs at the nautically decorated Dance Bar and the Little Bar, the clientele is more mixed. Open year-round.

Pied Piper (487-1527), 193A Commercial Street. The Pied is Provincetown's waterfront women's bar; open year-round. In 1996, for the first time in Provincetown's collective memory, year-round women outnumbered year-round men.

Vixen (487-6424), 336 Commercial Street. Open seasonally. This women's bar and dance club opened in 1995 in the newly rebuilt Pilgrim House.

Crown & Anchor (487-1430), 247 Commercial Street, is many things to many people: leather bar, disco, popular drag show, and cabaret venue. Shows through winter on weekends.

Lizard Lounge (487-8800), 135 Bradford Street. Open May through "who knows when." Above the Iguana Grill, this bar and club has live entertainment in the form of drag shows, as well as videos.

Governor Bradford (487-9618), 312 Commercial Street. Open year-round. To get a different but equally "real" flavor of Provincetown, stop into this tavern for a game of chess or backgammon. From the game tables, you can watch people on the streets watching each other.

See also Flagship Restaurant and Cafe Mews under *Where to Eat.*

SELECTIVE SHOPPING

Most shops are open mid-April to mid-October, although some galleries keep a shorter season (mid-June to mid-September). Most shops stay open until 11 PM in July and August, and many offer sales in mid-October. Shops designated as "open year-round" are usually open in winter on weekends only. Other shops that aren't "supposed" to be open year-round open without notice in winter, depending on the weather.

Listings are from east to west.

ANTIQUES

Remembrances of Things Past (487-9443), 376 Commercial Street. Open daily mid-April through October and weekends the rest of the year. Nostalgic pieces from the turn of the century to the 1960s, including celebrity memorabilia, phones, neon items, and costume jewelry.

West End Antiques (487-6723), 146 Commercial Street. Open daily mid-May to mid-September, and weekends mid-March through December. This small shop, which opened in 1994, sells a bit of this and that: glass, toys, paper, books, tools, and ephemera.

ART GALLERIES

"Provincetown Gallery Guide," with more than 20 listings, is produced yearly by the Provincetown Gallery Guild, PO Box 242, Provincetown 02657.

Provincetown Arts (487-3167), PO Box 35, Provincetown 02567, a 150-page annual published early in summer, is Provincetown's bible of visual arts, literature, and theater (send $10 and you'll receive a copy).

Galleries hold Friday openings staggered between 5 and 10 PM, so patrons may stroll the street, catching most of the receptions. Artists are on hand to meet patrons. Most galleries change exhibits every 2 weeks.

One of more than 20 art galleries in Provincetown

DNA Gallery (487-7700), 288 Bradford Street, above the Provincetown Tennis Club. Open 11 AM–10 PM daily, late May through September. DNA, or Definitive New Art, opened its spacious gallery in 1994 with innovative work emphasizing biological and environmental themes. Various media, and artists from Boston, New York, and Provincetown, are shown. In addition, DNA holds video screenings, poetry jams, and on Sunday evenings, a reading series.

Rising Tide Gallery (487-4037), 494 Commercial Street. Open daily, mid-June to mid-September, and on weekends for a month prior to and after that. Located in a mid-1800s schoolhouse, this cooperative opened in 1989. All 16 members have connections to the Lower or Outer Cape. Minimalists and impressionists, oil paintings and small pastels, monoprint landscapes and abstracts—Rising Tide has something for everyone. Group shows begin and end each season.

Long Point Gallery (487-1795), 492 Commercial Street. Open daily late June to mid-September, and by appointment. Featuring works by Provincetown notables such as Robert Beauchamp, Paul Bowen, Robert Motherwell, Paul Resika, and Judith Rothschild, this prestigious "blue-chip" cooperative has been central to Provincetown's gallery scene since 1977.

❋ **Berta Walker** (487-6411), 208 Bradford Street. Open daily June through September and on weekends off-season; otherwise, "often by chance and always by appointment." Walker represents Provincetown-affiliated artists of the past, present, and future. An excellent gallery that would be at home in uptown Manhattan.

William Scott Gallery (487-4040), 439 Commercial Street. Open mid-May to early September. Housed in the former Poor Richard's Landing and new to the gallery scene in 1995, this small venue showcases contemporary work that draws viewers into specific times and places.

✳ **Harvey Dodd Gallery** (487-3329), 437 Commercial Street. Open daily in summer and on weekends the rest of the year. Dodd has exhibited his watercolors, pastels, and oils of Provincetown and other Cape Cod scenes since 1960.

Cortland Jessup Gallery (487-4479), 432 Commercial Street. Open daily except Tuesday June to early September, and on weekends May through December. Established and emerging artists are given a venue for cutting-edge painting, photographs, and sculpture. And more recently, this gallery has showcased contemporary Japanese artists, too. Always interesting.

Rice/Polak Gallery (487-1052), 430 Commercial Street. Open May through December. Rice/Polak represents more than 100 contemporary artists working in painting, photography, assemblages, graphics, and sculpture. Biweekly exhibitions featuring the work of four artists; art consulting, too.

UFO Gallery (487-4424), 424 Commercial Street. Open late May to early September. Fine contemporary art, always worth dropping in.

Packard Gallery (487-4690), 418 Commercial Street. Open late May to mid-October. Gallery director Leslie Packard showcases the work of her sister Cynthia and her mother, Anne, both painters. In fact there are five generations of Packards who have painted in Provincetown. Anne's grandfather was Max Bohm, an early member of the Provincetown Art Association. The gallery is housed in a former Christian Science church, which Anne's grandmother used to attend.

✳ **Ellen Harris Gallery** (487-1414), 355 Commercial Street. Open daily April through October, and on weekends the rest of the year. In addition to serious paintings and sculpture, Harris has offered choice arts and crafts (and some whimsical ones too) since 1969. A fine place to shop.

Gallery 349 (487-1200), 349 Commercial Street. Open May through October. New to the scene in 1995, this gallery opened with a splash and features contemporary Provincetown-made art.

East End Gallery (487-4745), 349 Commercial Street. Open late April through November. Director Bunny Pearlman has an eye for art; come view what she thinks is worth a look-see.

✳ **Julie Heller Gallery** (487-2169), 2 Gosnold Street. Open daily June through October, and on weekends April through December; call ahead in winter. In a little building on the harbor, Heller offers work by luminaries who established this art colony: Milton Avery, Ross Moffet, and Charles Hawthorne. But the gallery doesn't slight contemporary artists who represent Provincetown's traditions; it also sells newer prints, photographs, and lithos. Don't miss it.

Walker's Wonders (487-8794), 153 Commercial Street. Open daily June through September and on weekends off-season; otherwise, "often by chance and always by appointment." Folk art, functional art, imaginative "special delights," sculpture, and jewelry assembled by Berta Walker.

See also Provincetown Art Association & Museum under *To See* and Fine Arts Work Center under *To Do—Special Programs.*

ARTISANS

Tiffany Lamp Studio (487-1101), 432 Commercial Street. Open year-round. Stephen Donnelly designs and makes genuine Tiffany lamps.

Halcyon Gallery (487-9415), 371 Commercial Street. Open daily April through December and on weekends in winter. Suzanne Larsen's gallery specializes in wearable art, crafts, and hand-blown glass.

Impulse (487-1154), 188 Commercial Street. Open daily, April through December, and on weekends, January to March. This contemporary American crafts shop offers a large selection of kaleidoscopes, wind chimes, wood objets d'art, fragile and colorful glass creations, jewelry, and signed celebrity photos and letters.

BOOKSTORE

Provincetown Bookshop (487-0964), 246 Commercial Street. Open year-round. A good selection of children's books, Cape titles, and cookbooks.

SPECIAL SHOPS

Giardelli/Antonelli Studio Showroom (487-3016), 417 Commercial Street. Open daily late April through December and weekends the rest of the year. Sassy women's clothing and eye-catching silver jewelry.

Llama (487-2921), 382 Commercial Street. Open daily mid-April to mid-October, and on weekends mid-October through December and in March. Two floors of international folk art, Oriental rugs and kilims, and tapestries and ceremonial baskets from major African tribes.

Kidstuff (487-0714), 381 Commercial Street. Open April through November. Clothing for babies, toddlers, and preteens. The owners have another kids' shop, **Littlebits** (487-3860), at 214 Commercial Street.

Womencrafts (487-2501), 376 Commercial Street. Open daily April through December, and on weekends in winter. In addition to books and music, this store features handcrafted items made by and for women.

Susan Baker Memorial Museum Franchise (487-1063), 379A Commercial Street. Open daily June through September and on weekends throughout the year, depending on the weather. Baker opened this "franchise" in 1990 (see *Selective Shopping* in "Truro"), but she's been in Provincetown since 1969, when she received a Fine Arts Work Center fellowship. Her colorful and whimsical objects take the shape of artists' books, papier-mâché items, clocks, and mirrors. She also has a series of Cape Cod and Italian landscapes.

Northern Lights Leather (487-9376, 487-0506), 361 Commercial Street. Open year-round. There are many leather shops in Provincetown but Northern Lights scores the most points for quality and style: hats, wallets, coats, shoes, and everything else made of silky-smooth leather.

Northern Lights Hammock Shop (487-9376), 361 Commercial Street. Open daily, March through December. Tired from traipsing up and down the strip? Sample a hammock—in rope, wood, and cotton.

Mad Hatter (487-4063), 360 Commercial Street. Open daily May through October and on weekends year-round. If it fits on your head, it's here.

Small Pleasures (487-3712), 359 Commercial Street. Open daily May through October and on weekends the rest of the year. Every shop has its niche: Here it's antique jewelry and vintage accessories for men.

Shop Therapy (487-9387), 346 Commercial Street. Open year-round. It's hard to miss this landmark, psychedelic-swathed building; note the head-line atop the building: "Monsters attack P-town. Shop Therapy blamed." Whether you want to venture inside is up to you—merchandise revolves around current alternative lifestyles and the retro look.

Puzzle Me This (487-1059), 336 Commercial Street. Open April through December. If you're stuck with nothing to do on a rainy day, this shop's brainteasers and mind-bogglers should help.

Fragrance Shop (487-8266), 309 Commercial Street. Open May to late October. This tiny shop custom blends scents from a supply of over 400 "designer" oil essences. Looking for something different? If you're not careful they'll sell you a supply of oil of "new car." (It really does smell like new vinyl!) A colorful collection of perfume bottles lines the windows. Expect ¼ ounce, about a year's supply, to run you $25.

Cape Cod Photo & Art Supply (487-9689), 301 Commercial Street. Open year-round. Overnight processing.

Cabot's Candy (487-3550), 276 Commercial Street. Open daily March through November, and on weekends in December. The Cicero family has made its own saltwater taffy here since 1969—it's the only shop on the Lower or Outer Cape to do so.

Outer Cape Kites (487-6133). Ryder Street Extension. Open mid-May through October. There's no better place to fly a kite than the National Seashore dunes—no pesky telephone wires or tall trees here.

Whale & Dolphin Shop (487-6115), 307 Commercial Street. Open mid-April through October. All profits from these educational and souvenir items go toward funding the educational programs at the Center for Coastal Studies (see *To Do—Special Programs.*)

☞ **Marine Specialties** (487-1730), 235 Commercial Street. Open daily mid-February through December and weekends the rest of the year. One of the Cape's most popular and unusual shops sells an odd assortment of army-navy items in a warehouselike space: parachutes, wool blankets, candles, camel saddles, sand dollars, camping supplies, ships' salvage, and other random military surplus items. You'll undoubtedly walk out with some strange gewgaw you hadn't even thought of buying but you just couldn't pass up for the price.

Norma Glamp's Rubber Stamps (487-1870), 212 Commercial Street. Open year-round. The name says it all—this shop has thousands of wacky (and not-so-wacky) rubber stamps.

No Place Like Home (487-6283), 150 Commercial Street. Open May through December. Woody Shimki opened this shop selling environmentally friendly products in 1992. If it's "green," it's here: natural soaps, recycled paper, cotton clothing, and cleaning products.

SPECIAL EVENTS

More and more it seems like there's a special event going on every weekend in the off-season, whether it's geared toward single gay men, cross-dressers, lesbians, or whomever. If you want to be assured of a quieter off-season retreat, call the Chamber of Commerce (see *Guidance*) for an up-to-the-minute listing of events.

February: **Year-rounders Festival,** Provincetown Town Hall. It's not what you know but who you know at this party: dinner, talent show, dancing.

Early May: **Spring Fling.** A women's weekend to kick off the season.

June: **O'Neill-By-The-Sea Festival.** Staged readings of some of Eugene O'Neill's early plays.

Late June: **Blessing of the Fleet,** MacMillan Wharf. On the last Sunday of the month, the bishop blesses a parade of fishing boats, each decked out with flags and families aboard. As the fishing fleet has thinned, so (unfortunately) has the attendance. Nonetheless, traditional.

Late June: **Portuguese Festival.** A 3-day celebration, coinciding with the Blessing of the Fleet, that includes special historic and art exhibits, Portuguese menus at various restaurants, a food court and bazaar on Fisherman's Wharf, parade, competitions like "lobster pot pulls" and "cod fish relays," and fireworks.

July 4: **Independence Day.** Parade and spectacular fireworks display.

Early August: **Fine Arts Work Center Annual Benefit Silent Auction** (487-9960). Benefit for the nationally recognized fellowship program for artists and writers; since 1969.

Mid- to late August: **Carnival Week** (487-2313). A weeklong gala sponsored by the Provincetown Business Guild, capped by a New Orleans Mardi Gras–style parade.

Early September: **AIDS Support Group Auction** (487-9445), at the Universalist Meeting House. It seems as if every artist in Provincetown donates a work to this auction.

Mid-September: **Art Festival,** a 10-day gala featuring gallery openings with artists and craftspeople, open studios, and an ever-growing consignment auction of early Provincetown artists sponsored by the Provincetown Art Association and Museum (PAAM). **Swim For Life,** an amateur swim from Long Point to the Boatslip to raise money for AIDS research.

Late September through October: **O'Neill-By-The-Sea Festival.** Staged readings of more of Eugene O'Neill's plays. If you recall, it was O'Neill's *Bound East for Cardiff,* which premiered in Provincetown in 1916, that heralded the beginnings of modern American theater. Look for O'Neill's · birthday to be celebrated on October 15.

Mid-October: **Women's Week,** featuring women artists and entertainers.

Mid- to late October: **Fantasia Fair,** a 10-day event for transvestites.

Late October: **Halloween,** costume balls and contests.

Early November: **Men's Single Weekend** (487-1800), workshops, parties, and lots of other organized activities for single gay men.

Late November: **Lighting the Pilgrim Monument** (487-3424). Nearly 5000 white lights (4 miles' worth) illuminate the monument on Thanksgiving Eve and remain lit until early January.)

Early December: **Arts and Crafts Fair,** sponsored by the Provincetown Art Association and Museum.

December 31: **First Night,** ringing in the New Year.

VI. MARTHA'S VINEYARD

Cliffs at Gay Head

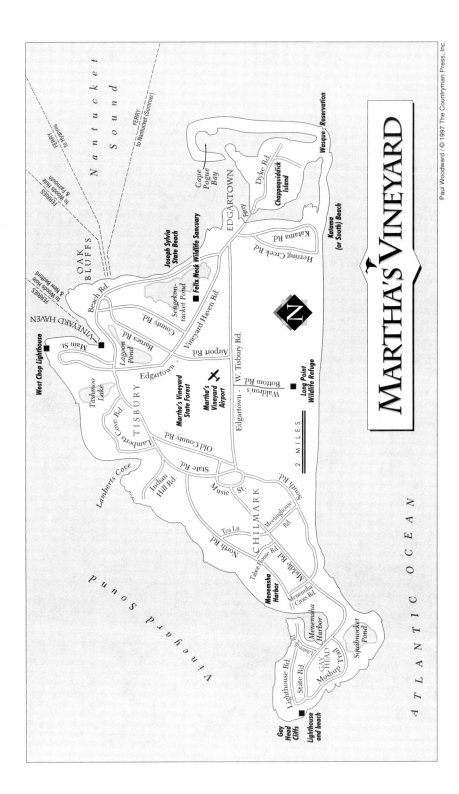

MARTHA'S VINEYARD

Martha's Vineyard

Intrepid explorer Bartholomew Gosnold was the first European known to have visited Martha's Vineyard (in 1602), although Leif Eriksson may have done so earlier. Gosnold named the island for its bounty of wild grapes. Martha's identity, however, remains a mystery; she may have been his daughter. The island was formally colonized in 1640, when a shipload of English settlers bound for Virginia ran short of supplies. They docked in Edgartown, found the native Wampanoags friendly, and decided to stay.

The settlers converted the Wampanoags to Christianity with startling success, perhaps aided by the fact that imported diseases were killing Wampanoags by the thousands. A century after Edgartown was founded, the island's Native population had dropped from 3000 to about 300. During that time, Vineyarders learned (from the surviving Wampanoags) how to catch whales; they farmed in Chilmark and fished from Edgartown and Vineyard Haven.

During the American Revolution, islanders suffered extreme deprivation after British soldiers sailed into Vineyard Haven Harbor and looted homes and ships. Among their plunder were some 10,000 head of sheep and cattle from island farms. The island didn't fully recover until the 1820s, when the whaling industry took off. The Vineyard enjoyed a heyday from 1820 until the Civil War, with hundreds of whaling vessels sailing in and out of Edgartown. Whaling captains took their enormous profits from whale oil and built large Federal and Greek Revival homes all over the island. Many still stand today as gracious inns, renowned restaurants, and private homes.

After the Civil War, with the whaling industry in decline, tourism became the Vineyard's principal source of income. By 1878 the Methodist Campground of Oak Bluffs had become a popular summer resort, with 12,000 people attending the annual meetings. Over the next 30 years, other travelers discovered the island and returned summer after summer to enjoy its pleasant weather, relatively warm water, excellent fishing, and comfortable yet genteel lifestyle. By the turn of the century, there were 2000 hotels rooms in Oak Bluffs alone—there aren't that many rooms on the entire island today! Summertime traffic was so high that it warranted building a rail line from the Oak Bluffs ferry terminal to Katama, as well as daily ferry service from the New York Yacht Club to Gay Head.

Although the whaling industry rapidly declined, other sea-related businesses continued to reap healthy profits. In 1900, Vineyard Sound was the second busiest sea lane in the world, second only to the English Channel. Heavy sea traffic continued until the Cape Cod Canal was completed in 1914. Tourism picked up again in the early 1970s. When President Clinton, Hillary, and Chelsea spent their 1994 and 1995 summer vacations here, they created a tidal wave of interest in the island.

Today, the year-round population of 11,000 mushrooms in July and August to about 89,000. Grumpy year-round Vineyarders are fond of saying that the island sinks 3 inches when ferries unload their passengers.

The terms "up-island" and "down-island" are holdovers from the days when the island was populated by seafarers—as you travel west, you move up the scale of longitude. Up-island refers to the less developed, hilly western end, which includes West Tisbury, Chilmark, Menemsha, and Gay Head. Edgartown, Oak Bluffs, and Vineyard Haven, which are the biggest and most touristy towns, are all down-island.

Elegant Edgartown, called "Uncle Edgar" by some of the old-timers, is chock-full of grand white Greek Revival ship captains' houses, with fanlights and widow's walks. Many of these private homes are clustered on North Water Street, while elsewhere downtown you'll find chic boutiques and shops, galleries, and restaurants.

Although it's less showy than Edgartown, Vineyard Haven maintains a year-round level of activity that Edgartown doesn't. It's the commercial center of the island, where "real" people live and work. The harbor is home to more wooden boats than any other harbor of its size in New England. For an experience straight out of the 19th century, stop in at Gannon and Benjamin Boatbuilders on Beach Road; it's one of the few remaining wooden-boat rebuilding shops in the country.

In Oak Bluffs, Wesleyan Grove began in 1835 as the site of the Methodist congregation's annual summer camp meetings. The campers' small tents became family tents; then primitive, wooden tentlike cottages; and finally, brightly painted cottages ornamented with fanciful trim. Cupolas, domes, spires, turrets, and gingerbread cutouts make for an architectural fantasyland. The whimsical, precious, and offbeat cottages are worlds away from Edgartown's traditional white houses.

West Tisbury is often called the Athens of the Vineyard because of its fine New England Congregational church, town hall, and Agricultural Hall. Music Street, where descendants of the island's 19th-century ship captains still live in large houses, was so named because many of these families used whaling profits to purchase pianos.

Chilmark is a peaceful place of rolling hills and old stone fences that outline 200-year-old farms. You'll find dozens of working farms up-island, some still run by descendants of the island's original European settlers. Travel down North Road to Menemsha, a small (truly pictur-esque) village and working harbor that you may recognize as the loca-tion of the movie *Jaws*. The surrounding area is crisscrossed by miles and miles of unmarked, interconnected dirt roads, great for exploring.

The Wampanoag Indians own the brilliantly colored bluffs and the face of Gay Head cliffs. Of the 700 members listed on the tribal rolls, approximately 300 reside on the Vineyard, half in Gay Head (Aquinnah). Tribal legend holds that the giant Moshup created the Vineyard, taught the Wampanoags how to fish and catch whales, and still protects them.

Martha's Vineyard has always attracted celebrity summer visitors. But in recent years many who visited decided they needed to own a piece of it. In the late 1980s, a tremendous building boom changed the face of the Vineyard. Although residents are generally unaffected by their celebrity neighbors—movie stars, authors, television journalists, musicians, financial moguls, and even presidents—many locals and longtime visitors agree that the Vineyard is no longer the quaint, tran-quil island it was prior to the mid-1980s.

Martha's Vineyard is unlike most of the rest of America; people tend to get along pretty well with one another. They work hard to main-tain a sense of tolerance and community spirit. Most lengthy debates center on land use and preservation rather than race or religion. Every-one relies, to some extent, on the hectic summer season that brings in most of the island's annual income, though they do breathe a sign of relief when the crowds thin each autumn. From January to March, the Vineyard is a more sobering place; unemployment can be as high as 16 percent in the off-season. The island is swarming with visitors in July and August. To experience the Vineyard at its best, visit from May to mid-June or mid-September to mid-October.

GUIDANCE

Chamber of Commerce (693-0085, e-mail: mvcc@vineyard.net, http:// www.mvy.com), Beach Road, PO Box 1698, Vineyard Haven 02568. Open 9–5 weekdays year-round and Saturdays in summer. Here you'll find booklets, brochures, maps, and other valuable information.

Information booth (693-4266), Circuit Avenue at Lake Avenue in Oak Bluffs. Open 9–5 daily, mid-May to mid-October. Behind the Flying Horses Carousel (see *To See*).

Edgartown Visitors Center, Church Street, Edgartown. Open 9–5 daily, June to early September. Around the corner from the Old Whal-ing Church (see *To See* in "Edgartown"), the center has brochures, souvenirs, rest rooms, postcards, and a post office, and also serves as a shuttle-bus stop (see *Getting Around*).

PUBLIC REST ROOMS

Public rest rooms in Vineyard Haven are located at the top of the A&P parking lot and within the Steamship Authority terminal off Water Street. In Oak Bluffs they are next to the Steamship Authority terminal on Seaview Avenue; on Kennebec Avenue, one block from Circuit Avenue; and next to Our Market on Oak Bluffs Harbor. In Edgartown, they're at the visitors center on Church Street. Facilities are located near the parking lot for Gay Head cliffs, and at Dutcher's Dock in Menemsha Harbor. In West Tisbury, rest rooms are in the old Agricultural Hall next to the town hall.

GETTING THERE

By boat from Woods Hole: The **Steamship Authority** (477-8600 for advance auto reservations, 771-4000 for day-of-sailing information), Railroad Avenue, Woods Hole. Provides daily, year-round transport—for people and autos—to Vineyard Haven and Oak Bluffs. The Vineyard is 7 miles from Woods Hole, and the trip takes about 45 minutes. About 15 boats ply the waters daily year-round.

The Steamship Authority begins taking auto reservations on or about February 12; call or write. (For reservation information, write: Reservation Bureau, 509 Falmouth Road, Suite 1C, Mashpee 02649.) If you write, include payment and make sure to post your request by mid- to late January. During that time, they receive up to 8000 pieces of mail per week requesting reservations. Auto reservations are necessary on weekends between May 13 and September 5, and are needed every day between June 27 and July 8. At other times, you can travel standby: If you arrive without an auto reservation and queue up in the standby line by 2 PM, the Steamship Authority guarantees you and your car passage sometime that day.

There are lockers at the steamship terminal for storing luggage.

Round-trip tickets from mid-May to mid-October are adults $9.50, children 5–12 $4.80, bicycles $6, autos $76. In the shoulder season, auto prices drop to $48; from January to mid-March they are $36. If you are not taking your car, the Steamship Authority provides free, frequent transportation between the parking lots and the ferry dock. Parking is $7.50 per calendar day.

By boat from Falmouth: **Island Queen** (548-4800), Falmouth Heights Road, Falmouth. Operates late May to mid-October; departures from Falmouth Inner Harbor to Oak Bluffs. This ferry service does not take automobiles. The *Island Queen* is smaller and more comfortable than the Steamship Authority, which also handles freight and delivery trucks. There is plenty of parking near the *Island Queen*'s dock (approximately $8 per calendar day). Round-trip fares are adults $10, children under 13 $5, bicycles $6.

Falmouth-Edgartown Ferry (548-9400), 278 Scranton Avenue, Falmouth. From late May to mid-October, this service plies the waters three times a day between Falmouth and Edgartown. Round-trip: adults $22, children 5–12 $16, bicycles $6; parking is $8 per calendar day.

By boat from Hyannis: **Hy-Line Cruises** (778-2602, 693-0112 in Oak Bluffs), Ocean Street Dock, Hyannis, runs boats to and from Oak Bluffs

The ferry, On-Time, *makes the 100-yard-dash between Chappaquiddick and Edgartown harbor.*

from early May through October. The trip is approximately 1¾ hours. In May there is one morning boat per day on weekends. From late May to early June, there are three round-trips a day; from early June to mid-September, there are four. If you haven't purchased advance tickets, it's wise to arrive an hour early in July and August. From mid-September through October, the schedule drops back to one trip per day. Round-trip tickets: adults $22, children $11, and bicycles $9.

By boat from New Bedford: **Martha's Vineyard Ferry Schamonchi** (997-1688) operates passenger boats to and from Vineyard Haven, mid-May to mid-October; the trip takes about an hour. From mid-May through mid-June and early September to mid-October, there is only one boat per day. But on weekends during these periods, they run two or three boats. During high season, mid-June to early September, there are three or four. Round-trip fares are adults $18 ($16 same day), children $9 ($7.50 same day), and bicycles $5. Parking is $6 per calendar day. For visitors coming from the south, New Bedford is a more convenient departure point than Woods Hole. Even those driving from points north may wish consider taking the New Bedford ferry to avoid traffic tie-ups at the bridges. From I-195, take exit 15 (Route 18 south) to the third set of lights, turn left, and follow signs to ferry parking.

By boat from Nantucket: **Hy-Line Cruises** (778-2600, 693-0112 in Oak Bluffs, 228-3949 on Nantucket) offers interisland service between Oak Bluffs and Nantucket from early June to mid-September. The trip takes 2½ hours; three boats make the trip daily. The round-trip fare is adults $22, children $11, and bicycles $9. No credit cards.

By bus: **Bonanza Bus Lines** (1-800-556-3815) provides daily year-round service to Woods Hole from Boston, New York, and Providence. Buses are scheduled to meet ferries, but ferries won't wait for a late bus.

By plane: **Cape Air** (1-800-352-0714) flies to Martha's Vineyard from Boston, Hyannis, Nantucket, and New Bedford. Cape Air has joint ticketing and baggage handling between its flights and Continental, Delta, Northwest, TWA, United, USAir, and other airlines. It also offers charter services. **Air New England** (693-8899) offers charter services to Martha's Vineyard from airports in the Northeast.

GETTING AROUND

By car and moped: The infamous Five Corners is the trickiest and most dangerous intersection on the island. It's also the first thing you'll encounter as you disembark from the Vineyard Haven ferry terminal. If you're going to Oak Bluffs, Katama, Edgartown, and Chappaquiddick, take the left lane. For West Tisbury, North Tisbury, Lambert's Cove, Menemsha, Chilmark, and Gay Head, enter the right lane and turn right. A few sample distances: Vineyard Haven to Oak Bluffs, 3 miles; Vineyard Haven to Edgartown, 8 miles; Oak Bluffs to Edgartown, 6 miles; Vineyard Haven to Gay Head, 18 miles.

Unfortunately, summertime traffic jams are commonplace in down-island towns. Try to park outside of town and take shuttles into town (see below).

In-season, expect to pay $50–70 daily for the least expensive rental car; $100–150 for a van, convertible, or 4-wheel drive; and $50–60 for a moped. In the off-season, don't be afraid to bargain; rental companies will go as low as $40 daily for a car. Although mopeds are a convenient mode of transportation, if most Vineyarders had their way, they would be banned. Visitors are always having accidents with them, and they're noisy. Ride with a great deal of caution; roads are winding, narrow, and busy in summer.

Car rental companies include **Budget Rent-a-Car** (693-1911, 1-800-527-0700 within Massachusetts, 1-800-527-0700 out-of-state), 95 Beach Road, Vineyard Haven; Circuit Avenue Extension (at the ferry dock), Oak Bluffs; 257 Edgartown Road, Edgartown; and Martha's Vineyard Airport. Budget has cars, convertibles, Explorers, and Jeeps. Prices include free customer pickup. Budget generally has the lowest prices. **Adventure & Thrifty** (693-1959), 7 Beach Road, and **Atlantic Rent-a-Car** (693-0480), 15 Beach Road, are both in Vineyard Haven near the ferry. **All-Island Rent-a-Car** (693-6868) is located at the airport. **Vineyard Classic Cars** (693-5551), Lake Avenue in Oak Bluffs, rents fun cars like a '64 Mustang convertible, '57 Chevy Bel Air, or a '64 Falcon convertible. Expect to pay $100–150 daily for specialty cars.

As for mopeds, many rental agencies are located near the ferry terminals in Oak Bluffs and Vineyard Haven. **Adventure Rentals** (693-1959), 7 Beach Road in Vineyard Haven, and **Sun 'n Fun** (693-5457),

Lake Avenue in Oak Bluffs, both have mopeds. Sun 'n Fun won't quote prices over the phone, but it will match any competitor's price once you get to the shop. (It's a cutthroat market; you have lots of leverage, in the off-season especially.)

By bus: **Gay Head Sightseeing** (693-1555), **Island Transport** (693-0058), and **M.V. Sightseeing** (627-8687) all operate early May to late October. Buses are clearly marked, and they meet the ferries in Vineyard Haven and Oak Bluffs daily 9–4. The tours are approximately 2½ hours long. Tour buses make one stop—at the Gay Head cliffs—where there are small food stands, souvenir shops, public rest rooms, and a wonderful view of the cliffs and the ocean. Adults $11.50, children $3.

By van: **Adam Cab** (627-4462), Edgartown. Tours daily at 1 PM, year-round ostensibly. This 2-hour tour heads up-island to West Tisbury, Chilmark, Menemsha, and Gay Head for $15 per person. If you'd prefer to arrange your own itinerary, hire a driver through Adam Cab for $30–50 per hour.

By shuttle: **Martha's Vineyard Transportation Services** (693-1589, 693-0058) operates buses traveling among Vineyard Haven, Oak Bluffs, and Edgartown. May through October. Buses run every 30 minutes 8 or 9 AM–5 or 6 PM in spring and fall, and every 15 minutes until 11 PM in summer. Tickets $1.75 one way or $2.25 round-trip. A three-town pass, which allows you to ride from Vineyard Haven to Oak Bluffs to Edgartown and back to Vineyard Haven again, costs $3. The up-island shuttle (which operates from late June to early September) runs out to the airport, West Tisbury, Chilmark, and Gay Head. $8.25 round-trip from any down-island town. The shuttle buses stop across from the Steamship Authority and Pier 44 on Beach Road in Vineyard Haven; near the Civil War statue in Ocean Park in Oak Bluffs; and across from the Old Whaling Church, Church Street in Edgartown.

Edgartown Trolley (627-9663). Late May to mid-October. Martha's Vineyard Transit Authority has an alternative to wrangling for a parking place in Edgartown's car-choked streets. Leave your car at Four Flags shopping mall (corner of Edgartown–Vineyard Haven Road and Oak Bluffs Road) or across from the Edgartown Elementary School (corner of West Tisbury Road and Robinson Road), and ride the shuttle. From mid-May to mid-September, trolleys run every 10 minutes 7:30 AM–7 PM (until 11:30 PM in July and August). The fare is $.50 one way; parking is free.

Vineyard Haven Park 'n Ride (627-7448), State Road. Late May to mid-October. Avoid the parking nightmare and let the shuttle drop you off downtown or at the Steamship Authority. Trolleys run every 15 minutes and cost $.50 per person, children under 12 free. Parking is free.

South Beach Trolley (627-7448). Mid-June to early September. Service from Church Street in Edgartown and South Beach (Katama) runs 9–5:30 daily. The trolley ($1.50) runs every 15 minutes on fair-weather days and hourly in inclement weather. Wait for the bus at the information building, near the corner of Main and Church Streets; there are three drop-off and pickup points at South Beach.

By foot: **Vineyard History Tours** (627-8619); meet at the Vincent House Museum behind the Old Whaling Church, 89 Main Street. From late May to mid-October, various walking tours are given for $7 at 3 PM. On Wednesday, Friday, and Saturday, the walk is called "Ghosts, Gossip, and Downright Scandals," on Saturday you'll learn about Edgartown's whaling days, and on Thursday "Martha's Daughters" centers on Edgartown's women.

MEDICAL EMERGENCY

Martha's Vineyard Hospital (693-0410), off Vineyard Haven–Oak Bluffs Road, Oak Bluffs.

Vineyard Walk-In Medical Center (693-6399), State Road, Vineyard Haven. Open weekdays 9–noon in June, 9–1 in July and August.

TO SEE

In Vineyard Haven

Compass Bank (696-4400), 91 Main Street. Open 8:30–3 weekdays year-round. This distinctive 1905 fieldstone building has lovely stained glass and great acoustics inside. On this site, incidentally, stood the harness shop where the Great Fire of 1883 started. The conflagration destroyed 60 buildings.

William Street. The only street in town that survived the devastating 1883 fire boasts some fine examples of Greek Revival architecture. Carefully preserved sea captains' homes include the **Richard G. Luce House** near the corner of William Street and Spring Street. Captain Luce never lost a whaling ship or crew member during his 30-year career, and apparently his good fortune at sea extended to life on land.

Seaman's Bethel (693-9317), 15 Beach Street. Open 9–1 weekdays in summer. For over 100 years this bethel has served its seafaring community, and in return it has received some interesting gifts from those it assisted. The bethel's maritime collection includes "sailor souvenirs," tusk carvings, schooner models in bottles, and early photographs of Vineyard Haven. Free.

West Chop Lighthouse, at the western end of Main Street. Built in 1817 with wood and replaced with the current brick in 1838, the lighthouse has been moved back from the shore twice, first in 1848 and again in 1891. Today the lighthouse is inhabited by a family from the Menemsha Coast Guard base.

In Oak Bluffs

East Chop Lighthouse. The circa-1850 lighthouse was built by Captain Silas Daggett with the financial help of prosperous fellow seafarers who wanted a better system of relaying signals from the Vineyard to Nantucket and the mainland. Up to that point, they'd used a complex system of raising arms, legs, flags, and lanterns to signal which ships were coming in. In 1875 the government purchased the lighthouse from the consortium of sea captains for $6000, then constructed the metal structure that stands today.

Trinity Park Tabernacle, behind Lake, Circuit, and Dukes County Avenues. The enormous, tentlike tabernacle was built in 1879 to replace the original meeting tent used by the Methodists who met here. It is among the largest wrought-iron structures in the country. **Wesleyan Grove** surrounds the tabernacle, which, in turn, is encircled by rows of colorful "gingerbread" cottages, built during the late 19th century to replace true tents. Owners painted the tiny houses with bright colors and pastels to accentuate the Carpenter's Gothic architecture and woodwork. Visitors are free to wander around the community as residents visit with one another and sometimes strike up a conversation with tourists. Note that no bicycles are allowed in Wesleyan Grove, and quiet time is strictly observed after dark.

Cottage Museum (693-0525), 1 Trinity Park. Open 10:30–4 Monday through Saturday, mid-June to mid-September. The interior and exterior of this 1867 cottage are typical of the more than 300 tiny cottages in Wesleyan Grove. Admission fee.

Flying Horses Carousel (693-9481), Circuit Avenue at Lake Avenue. Open daily, mid-April to mid-October (10–10 in high season). The oldest operating carousel in the country, carved in New York City in 1876, is marvelously well preserved and lovingly maintained. Adults visit this National Historic Landmark even without a child in tow to grab for the brass ring. Rides $1.

Arcade, Circuit Avenue. This three-story wood-frame structure, which houses several stores and small businesses, was added to the National Register of Historic Places in 1994. It is one of only two remaining major works by architect and inventor Samuel Pratt. An open arcade runs through the center of the building and a three-tier porch dominates the facade. The Victorian Gothic architecture preserves all the major elements from its original design.

Ocean Park, along Ocean Avenue. Fringed with some of Oak Bluffs's best-preserved gingerbread cottages, the park's centerpiece is a large white gazebo that serves as a bandstand for summer-evening concerts.

In Edgartown

Vineyard Museum and Dukes County Historical Society (627-4441), 8 Cooke Street at School Street. Open 10–5 Tuesday through Saturday, mid-June through August; 1–4 Wednesday through Friday and 10–4 Saturday the rest of the year. Operated by the Dukes County Historical Society, this excellent collection is spread throughout several buildings. Perhaps the most interesting exhibit is the Oral History Center, which preserves the island's history through more than 250 recorded testaments

Rolling, open farmland typifies the up-island landscape.

from the island's older citizens. (The project was begun in 1993.) Other facilities include a fine pre–Revolutionary War house, which has undergone little renovation since the mid-19th century. It contains relics of the Vineyard's whaling days, including some scrimshaw and other artifacts. Other features are a maritime gallery, a tryworks replica, a carriage shed that houses boats and vehicles, and a historic herb garden. The enormous original Fresnel lens from the Gay Head Lighthouse is here, too, and it's illuminated for a few hours each night. Adults $5, children ages 6–15 $3, children under 6 free.

Dr. Daniel Fisher House (627-8017), 99 Main Street. The island's best example of Federal-period architecture, the 1840 house has an enclosed cupola, roof and porch balustrades, a shallow hipped roof, large windowpanes, and a portico, all exquisitely preserved. Dr. Fisher was a Renaissance man: doctor, whaling magnate, banker (he founded the Martha's Vineyard National Bank), merchant, and miller. He insisted that his house be constructed with the finest materials: Maine pine timbers soaked in lime for two years and brass and copper nails, for instance. The house is headquarters for the Martha's Vineyard Preservation Trust, which is charged with saving, restoring, and making self-sufficient any important island buildings that might otherwise be sold for commercial purposes or radically remodeled. Tours of this house (627-8619) as well as the Vincent House and Old Whaling Church are offered late May to mid-October at 11, noon, 1, and 2. The cost is $5.

Vincent House Museum (627-8619), behind the Old Whaling Church. Open noon–3 daily, late May to mid-October (10:30–3 in summer). Dating to 1672, this is the Vineyard's oldest residence. It was in the same family until 1977, when it was given to the Preservation Trust. The house has three rooms filled with reproduction furniture depicting how the residence looked in the 17th, 18th, and 19th centuries. Admission $3; with tour of Dr. Fisher House and Old Whaling Church, $5.

Old Whaling Church (627-4442 for events, 627-8619 for tour), 89 Main Street, at the corner of Church Street. Tours late May to mid-October. Built in 1843, the church now functions as a performing arts center, hosting plays, lectures, concerts, and films. The building, now owned by Martha's Vineyard Preservation Trust, originally housed the Edgartown Methodist Church and was constructed with the same techniques used to build whaling ships. $5 for tours, including visits to the Dr. Fisher House and Vincent House.

North Water Street. Some of these fine Colonial, Federal, and Greek Revival houses may look familiar because many clothing companies, including Talbot's, send crews of models and photographers here to shoot their catalogs. Architectural detailing on these white houses trimmed in black is superb, but there are more whimsical touches too: riotous flower gardens and, in the widow's walk of one house, a costumed mannequin.

Vineyard Gazette (627-4311), 34 South Summer Street, Edgartown. Open daily 9–5 year-round. It's best to make an appointment if you want a tour of the newspaper building. The newspaper that first rolled off the press on May 14, 1846, is a beloved island institution. As the masthead declares, it's "A family newspaper—neutral in politics, devoted to general news, literature, morality, agriculture and amusement." Although its year-round circulation is only 14,000, the paper is mailed to island devotees in all 50 states. Richard Reston is the publisher.

Edgartown Lighthouse, at the end of North Water Street. The first lighthouse to direct boats into and around Edgartown Harbor was built in 1828 on a small island. The island became connected to the "mainland" of the Vineyard by a spit of sand soon after a new lighthouse was placed (in 1938) on the site of the old one. Today, the lighthouse is accessible by foot.

Chappaquiddick Island, accessible via the "Chappy Ferry," *On Time III* (627-9427), at the corner of Dock and Daggett Streets. The entire journey between the main island and Chappy lasts about 5 minutes. The ferry doesn't really have a schedule; it just goes when it's needed, and thus it's always on time. Since it's the only method of transportation between the two islands, and a surprising number of people live on Chappy year-round, the ferry runs daily year-round. $4.50 round-trip for car and driver; $2.50 for passenger and bike.

Chappaquiddick contains several lovely beaches and wildlife refuges, including the 500-acre Cape Pogue Wildlife Refuge, the 14-acre Mytoi, and the 200-acre Wasque Reservation (see *Green Space*). Unfortunately, the beautiful island is perhaps best known for Dike Bridge, the scene of the drowning incident involving Senator Edward Kennedy in July 1969. To reach Dike Bridge, stay on Chappaquiddick Road after you get off the ferry until the road turns into Dike Road. When the road takes a sharp turn to the right (about a mile), continue straight on the dirt road until you reach the bridge.

The bridge was rebuilt in 1995 and pedestrians once again have direct access to Cape Pogue, a thin ribbon of sand that stretches along the east side of Chappaquiddick. Four-wheel-drive vehicles can use the bridge when endangered shorebirds are not nesting. Cape Pogue is also accessible by foot or four-wheel-drive vehicle, over the sand of Wasque Point, several miles south of the beach.

Up-island

Mayhew Chapel and **Indian Burial Ground,** Christiantown Road, off Indian Hill Road, West Tisbury. This tiny chapel, burial ground, and memorial to the Praying Indians (who were converted to Christianity by the Reverend Mayhew Jr. in the mid-1600s) is a quiet place, owned by the Wampanoag tribe of Gay Head.

Alley's General Store (693-0888), State Road, West Tisbury. Open year-round. Alley's is a beloved Vineyard landmark. "Dealers in almost everything" since 1858, Alley's has a wide front porch where locals have gathered over the decades to discuss current events and exchange friendly gossip. But in the early 1990s, economic conditions almost forced Alley's to close. In true island spirit, the Martha's Vineyard Preservation Trust stepped in to renovate the building and ensure its survival. Alley's continues to feel like a country store, selling everything useful: utilitarian housewares, mismatched saucers, Pendleton blankets, and locally grown produce.

Beetlebung Corner, at the intersection of Middle, South, State, and Menemsha Cross Roads; the center of Chilmark. The intersection was named for the grove of beetlebung trees, the New England name for tupelos, which are unusual in this region. Tupelo wood is very hard and was an excellent material for making mallets (also called beetles) and the plugs (or bungs) that filled the holes in wooden casks and barrels during whale-oil days.

Menemsha Creek and **Dutcher's Dock,** at Menemsha Cross Road near Beetlebung Corner. This working fishing village has simple, weathered, gray-shingled boathouses and small, sturdy docks that line the narrow channel. Islanders still eke out a living on the large and small boats of Menemsha's fishing fleet. It's a great location from which to watch the setting sun. In the past few years, little shacks (shops and fast-food eateries) have sprung up on the road to Dutcher's Dock.

Quitsa Overlook, off State Road. At Beetlebung Corner, bear left onto State Road, heading toward Gay Head. After a mile or so, you'll pass over a bridge; Nashaquitsa Pond (also known as Quitsa) is on your right and Stonewall Pond is on your left. Just beyond, a spot overlooks Quitsa and Menemsha Ponds. About half a mile farther locals fill pitchers with water from a fresh, sweet stream that's been siphoned off to run out of a pipe. Local lore attributes various cures to the water—from stress relief, to a flu antidote, to a hangover remedy.

Baptist church (693-1539), Gay Head. Turn left at the small red schoolhouse (now the town library) across the street from the Gay Head Town Hall, Fire Station, and Police Department. The lovely church is the oldest Indian Baptist church in the country. It may have the prettiest location, too, overlooking windswept grassy dunes, stone walls, and the Atlantic Ocean.

Gay Head cliffs. The brilliantly colored clay cliffs, a designated National Landmark, rise 150 feet above the shore and were formed 100 million years ago by glaciers. For a fine view of the full magnitude of this geological oddity, walk beyond the souvenir shops. In the distance you can see Noman's Land Island and the Elizabeth Islands. A wooden boardwalk leads to the beach, where you can see the towering clay cliffs from water level. The Wampanoags have lived here for more than 5000 years and own most of this land (although most of the beach is public); only they may remove clay from the eroding cliffs.

Gay Head Lighthouse. The redbrick lighthouse was built in 1844 to replace a wooden lighthouse that had stood there since 1799. In 1856 a powerful Fresnel lens was mounted atop the lighthouse, where it warned ships from the perilous Gay Head coast; it was used for almost 100 years. From July to mid-September, on Friday and Saturday evenings, you can ascend the lighthouse to enjoy the sunset. Fee $20.

TO DO

BERRY PICKING

Thimble Farm (693-6396), Stoney Hill Road (off State Road), West Tisbury. Open mid-June through September, the farm allows you to pick your own strawberries or raspberries and offers other farm-stand goodies as well—homegrown melons, tomatoes, flowers, and other in-season produce. Children are welcome for strawberry picking, but should be over age 12 for raspberry picking.

BICYCLING/RENTALS

Several excellent bicycle paths connect the main towns: Vineyard Haven to Oak Bluffs, Oak Bluffs to Edgartown, Edgartown to West Tisbury, and Edgartown to South Beach via Katama Road. A hilly but beautiful up-island circular trail begins at the Gay Head Lighthouse: Take Lighthouse Road to Lobsterville Road and backtrack up Lobsterville Road to State Road to Moshup Trail. The Manuel E. Correllus State Forest, off the Edgartown–West Tisbury Road, also has several bicycle paths.

Bike Ferry. Daily, June to early September; weekends until mid-October. Some riding out to Menemsha and Gay Head will be thrilled to know that Hugh Taylor's little ferry takes cyclists across Menemsha Creek, which separates the picturesque harbor from Lobsterville Beach and Gay Head beyond. This 150-yard ferry ride saves cyclists a 7-mile bike ride. $7 round-trip, $4 one way.

Bikes are rented at: **Scooter & Bike** (693-0782) on Union Street in Vineyard Haven (open mid-March to early November); **Anderson Bike Rentals** (693-9346) on Circuit Avenue Extension in Oak Bluffs (open year-round—call ahead in winter); **R.W. Cutler Bikes** (627-4052) at 1 Main Street, in Edgartown, and **Wheel Happy** (627-5928), 8 South Water Street and 204 Upper Main Street in Edgartown (open winter weekends by calling ahead). In general, expect to pay $10 daily for a three-speed and $15 for an all-terrain or hybrid bike.

Cycle Works (693-6966), at 105 State Road in Vineyard Haven, repairs bicycles. John Stevenson and his enthusiastic and helpful crew have the largest selection of cycling equipment, accessories, and parts on island.

Quawk Cycle (693-1188, 694-1188), 73 Lagoon Pond Road, Vineyard Haven. Open year-round. In addition to manufacturing custom steel frames and selling bikes, this shop is perhaps the most knowledgeable on-island about off-road cycling. There are over 200 miles of double- and singletrack dirt roads on the Vineyard; you just have to know where to find the trailheads. These folks can help.

BOAT EXCURSIONS/RENTALS

Laissez Faire (693-1646), Owen Park, Vineyard Haven. Expert and personable sailors John and Mary Clarke, who run the Lothrop Merry House (see *Lodging*), spend as much time as possible on their handsome 54-foot Alden ketch, which they sail in the Bahamas during winter months. Since the mid-1970s they have offered half-day trips ($60 per person, beverages included) and full-day trips ($100 per person, beverages included, $10 extra for lunch) along the coast.

Gosnold Cruises/*Andy Rosse* (693-8900), Pier 44, Vineyard Haven. Various cruises are offered mid-June to late September: lobstering (especially fun for kids); a half-day excursion to Cuttyhunk (with a 2-hour layover at this lovely island); sunset trips to Menemsha (with dinner at the Home Port restaurant for an additional $20 per person; see *Eating Out*); and voyages to the Gay Head cliffs. Tickets: lobstering $15 adults, $10 children; Gay Head and Menemsha $20 adults, $15 children; Cuttyhunk $40 adults, $25 children. Purchase tickets at the Gosnold Maritime Center in the Tisbury Market Place across the street.

Arabella (627-0243, 645-3511), Menemsha Harbor. Captain Hugh Taylor's 50-foot catamaran sails to Cuttyhunk daily at 11 AM in summer. The 6-hour sail includes a 2-hour layover on Cuttyhunk, the only public island in the chain of Elizabeth Islands, and a swim at a remote beach (tide permitting). At 6 PM he offers a sunset excursion with stunning views of the Gay Head cliffs. Taylor, a long-time Gay Head resident, has sailed these waters since 1970. $60 to Cuttyhunk; $35 for sunset cruise.

Vineyard Haven's protected harbor

Edgartown Harbor Tours (627-4388), Main Street near the Edgartown Yacht Club. These narrated tours, which depart hourly 11–7 in summer, cost $9 adults, $4 children.

Mad Max (627-7500), Dock Street, Edgartown Harbor. This 60-foot catamaran sets sail twice daily (in the afternoon and at sunset) from late May to mid-October. Tickets are $40 adults, $30 children under 10.

Vineyard Boat Rentals (693-8476, http:www.boatrentals.com), Dockside Marina, Oak Bluffs Harbor. Open mid-May to mid-October. One-hour, morning, 4-hour, and daily rentals of Boston Whalers that seat up to five or six people.

Wind's Up! (693-4252, 693-4340), 199 Beach Road, Vineyard Haven. Rentals and instruction open mid-May to late September; retail open March through December. You can rent Sunfish and small catamarans or get beginning, intermediate, and advanced instruction from this full-service outfit. It's been on-island since 1962.

BOWLING

Spinnaker Lanes (693-9691), State Road, Tisbury. Open year-round for candlepin bowling and billiards.

CANOEING

Wind's Up! (693-4252, 693-4340), 199 Beach Road, Vineyard Haven. Rentals and instruction open mid-May to late September; retail open March through December. Canoe rentals run $40 for a half day, $60 for a day.

Poucha Pond and **Cape Pogue Bay** (693-7662), Dike Bridge, Chappaquiddick. Mid-June to mid-September. Take a self-guided tour of this tidal estuary with a map that comes with the canoe rental: $25 for a half day, $35 daily. Boats are available 9–5 daily. Or take a 2-hour guided natural history trip offered by the Trustees of Reservations. Call for trip registration. This rich ecosystem will delight birdwatchers.

See also Cape Pogue Wildlife Refuge under *Green Space—Walks.*

FISHING

Fishing is excellent at most of the Vineyard's beaches and bridges; the bridge between Oak Bluffs and Edgartown is perfect for anglers. There's a wide area that hangs over the swiftly running channel between Nantucket Sound and Sengekontacket Pond. You're most likely to catch striped bass and bluefish before sunrise. Surf casting is best from south-facing beaches and the beaches at Gay Head.

The following shops rent fishing rods, tackle, and other equipment: **Dick's Bait & Tackle** (693-7669), on New York Avenue in Oak Bluffs; **Larry's Tackle Shop** (627-5088), on 258 Upper Main Street; and **Captain Porky's** (627-7117), on Dock Street, both in Edgartown.

Capella (627-3122, 627-2128), Edgartown Harbor. May to late October. Sportfishing with light tackle, flies, and conventional means.

Slapshot II (627-8087), Edgartown Harbor. Rob Coab offers charters.

Hi-Line Sport Fishing (696-8859), Oak Bluffs. Mid-April to mid-October. (No relation to the ferry.) Captain Fred Ferreira leads half-day charters for bass and blues ($350 for up to six people) and full-day trips in search of shark and tuna ($750–800 for up to six). But he specializes in fly-fishing by boat ($50 per person per hour).

North Shore Charters (645-2993), Menemsha. May through October. Captain Scott McDowell takes anglers in search of bass and blues.

Fly Fishing (696-7551), Vineyard Haven. June to mid-November. Ken and Lori VanDerlaske specialize in shoreline, saltwater fly-fishing for stripers. Typically they take out one ($145) or two ($205) people for a 6–7-hour trip that includes lunch or dinner.

FITNESS CLUBS

Muscle Discipline (693-5096), Kennebec Avenue, Oak Bluffs. Open year-round. A full-service facility; $10 per visit.

Triangle Fitness (627-9393), Post Office Square, at Beach and Vineyard Haven Roads, Edgartown. Open year-round. Daily ($10), weekly ($25), and 10-visit ($60) passes available.

FOR FAMILIES

Takemmy Farm (693-2486), State Road, West Tisbury. Open 1–5 Monday through Saturday, May to mid-November. Frank and Mary Bailey open their llama farm to introduce the public to these low-maintenance animals. Kids love visiting these gentle, large-eyed creatures, as well as miniature donkeys and horses, goats, sheep, and roosters. There's also a large jungle gym, a sandbox, and a swing set. $3 donation per car.

The Game Room (693-5163), across from the Flying Horses Carousel (see *To See*). Open 10 AM–11 PM daily, late June to mid-September. This noisy, chaotic arcade is just the way kids like it.

GOLF

Farm Neck Golf Course (693-2504 clubhouse, 693-3057 reservations), off County Road, Oak Bluffs. Open April through December. Reservations are strongly suggested at this 18-hole course, but they're taken no earlier than 2 days in advance. $35–73 for 18 holes.

Mink Meadows (693-0600), Franklin Street, Vineyard Haven. Open April through October. According to the *Vineyard Gazette*, President Bill Clinton preferred this nine-hole course to stately Farm Neck because "it has shorter holes and fewer people staring at him. Clinton said Farm Neck is beautiful and all that, but it's more for a pro—and he's not a pro." $18–25 for 9 holes, $25–42 for 18 holes.

HORSEBACK RIDING

The MV Horse Council (693-9246) provides current information on which farms and stables are offering riding instruction and trail rides. It serves as a kind of central clearinghouse.

ICE SKATING

Martha's Vineyard Ice Arena (693-5329), Edgartown–Vineyard Haven Road, Oak Bluffs. Open for public skating July through April.

IN-LINE SKATING

MV Blade Runners (693-8852), Circuit Avenue Extension, Oak Bluffs. Open May to mid-October. A free lesson is offered with every rental. Inquire about 2-hour tours of the state forest, which include a guide and equipment. Rentals: $10 hourly, $25 daily, including safety equipment.

KAYAKING

Martha's Vineyard Kayak (627-0151), Vineyard Haven. Late May to mid-October. Eric Carlsen will pick the right pond or protected waterway depending on your skill level, although there really is no experience necessary for paddling on protected, shallow ponds. He delivers kayaks to five locations around the island, including Edgartown Harbor ($20 for 2 hours), which affords unobstructed views of fine summer homes; Edgartown Great Pond ($30 for 3 hours), which features an outer beach and a hidden sanctuary; and Squibnocket and Quista Ponds ($40 for 3 hours), with pristine views. Inquire about sunrise and sunset paddles and scheduled tours. Tandem kayaks have child seats, so you can bring a youngster along, too. All rates are per person.

Wind's Up! (693-4252, 693-4340), 199 Beach Road, Vineyard Haven. Rentals and instruction mid-May to late September; retail open March through December. Wind's Up! offers kayak rentals ($40 for a half day, $50 for a tandem) and introductory group instruction ($25 per person.)

MINI-GOLF

✐ **Dockside Miniature Golf** (696-7646), on the roof of Dockside Marketplace, Oak Bluffs Harbor. Open daily mid-May to mid-September.

✐ **Island Cove** (693-2611), State Road, Vineyard Haven. Open weekends mid-April to mid-October, daily in summer.

SPECIAL PROGRAMS

❋ **Vineyard Conservation Society** (693-9588), Lambert's Cove Road, Tisbury. Since it was established in 1965, this nonprofit group has protected thousands of acres from commercial development. The society also sponsors a wide range of public activities, most of them free, including the Winter Walks program, a summer environmental lecture series, educational seminars and workshops on such topics as alternative wastewater treatment and solar building technology, and the annual Earth Day all-island cleanup.

Sketch (696-8255, 693-6450), PO Box 2676, Vineyard Haven. July to late August. This art and theater camp, appropriate for children 7–12, is sponsored by the Vineyard Playhouse (see *Entertainment*) and Etherington Fine Art. Children work together to explore a different theme every week—impressionism, Japan, medieval life, for instance—and the art and theater teachers help them write a play, design a set, and perform on Friday. Sketch welcomes children for 1 week, 1 month, or the entire 8 weeks. $85–100 weekly, 9–1 weekdays.

For art classes, see Luce House Gallery under *Selective Shopping—Art Galleries.*

For weekend cooking classes, see Tuscany Inn, Edgartown, under *Lodging—Bed & Breakfasts.*

TENNIS

Public courts are located at the following places: **Church Street** near the corner of Franklin Street in Vineyard Haven; **Niantic Avenue** in Oak Bluffs; **Robinson Road** near Pease's Point Way in Edgartown; **Chilmark Community Center** on South Road at Beetlebung Corner in Chilmark; **Old County Road** in West Tisbury. Courts are also available for a fee at the **Island Country Club Tennis Courts** (693-6574) on Beach Road in Oak Bluffs. Open mid-April to mid-October.

WATER-SKIING

MV Ski and **MV Parasailing** (693-2838), Owen Park Dock, Vineyard Haven. Open seasonally. If you're over 4 years old, Mark Clarke can teach you how to waterski and parasail. If you've always wanted to learn but thought you were too klutzy, Mark is the one to teach you. He runs a very safe outfit. Waterskiing $100/hour for up to six people; parasailing $50 per flight ($85 tandem); jet skis $65/hour.

WINDSURFING

Wind's Up! (693-4252, 693-4340), 199 Beach Road, Vineyard Haven. Rentals and instruction mid-May to late September; retail open March through December. Sheltered Lagoon Pond, where Wind's Up! has a facility, is a great place for beginners to learn windsurfing and sailing. The water is shallow and the instructors patient. Those more experienced can rent equipment, consult the shop's map, and head out on their own. Windsurfing is excellent all over the island, but experienced surfers should head to Menemsha, Gay Head, and South Beach.

WINERY

❋ **Chicama Vineyards** (693-0309), Stoney Hill Road, West Tisbury. Tastings and tours 11–5 Monday through Saturday and 1–5 Sunday, late May to mid-October (1–4 Saturday from mid-October to late May). Follow State Road out of Vineyard Haven for 2.5 miles and look for the sign on your left. Opened in 1971, Chicama Vineyards was the first commercial winery licensed in Massachusetts since colonial days. Today, it annually sells well over 90,000 bottles of Chardonnay, Cabernet, Merlot, and other varieties. Chicama produces an excellent line of herb vinegars, as well as jams, jellies, mustards, and salad dressings.

GREEN SPACE

❋ **Felix Neck Wildlife Sanctuary** (627-4850), off Edgartown–Vineyard Haven Road, Edgartown. Trails open dawn–7 PM. Visitors center open 8–4 daily June through October, and 8–4 Tuesday through Sunday, November to May. The Vineyard is populated by many species of birds that flock to the island's forests and wildlife sanctuaries. This 350-acre preserve, affiliated with the Audubon Society, has 6 miles of easy trails that traverse thick woods, open meadows of wildflowers, beaches, and salt marshes. The interpretive exhibit center has turtles, aquariums, a gift shop, and a library. There are year-round activities for children and adults, including guided nature walks (almost every day during summer) and bird-watching trips for novices and experts alike. Adults $3, children $2, free to Audubon Society members.

Cedar Tree Neck Sanctuary (693-5207), off Indian Hill Road, West Tisbury. The 300-acre sanctuary, managed by the Sheriff's Meadow Foundation, has trails through bogs, fields, and forests to the bluffs overlooking Vineyard Sound.

❋ **Cape Pogue Wildlife Refuge** and **Wasque Reservation** (693-7662), Chappaquiddick. These adjoining tracts of land on the southeastern corner of Chappaquiddick are relatively isolated, so even on the busiest summer weekend you can escape the crowds. This seaside wilderness contains huge tracts of dunes, cedars, salt marshes, ponds, tidal flats, and scrub brush. Overseen by the Massachusetts Trustees of Reservations, Cape Pogue (489 acres) and Wasque (200 acres) are the group's oldest holdings. Half of the state's scallops are harvested each autumn off the coast near the Cape Pogue Lighthouse (on the northern tip of the cape). The lighthouse was built in 1893 and automated in 1964. Parking fee.

Three-hour **natural history tours** (627-3599) of remote Cape Pogue are offered twice daily in summer (8:30 and 4). The naturalist-led tours, in an open-air four-wheel-drive vehicle, cost $30 for adults, $15 for children under 15. Bring binoculars and water. **Lighthouse tours** (75 minutes) of remote Cape Pogue Lighthouse depart daily at 10 and 2 from Dike Bridge. Adults $12, children under 15 $6.

Long Point Wildlife Refuge (693-7662), off Edgartown–West Tisbury Road, West Tisbury. Open 10–6 daily, mid-June to mid-September. A long, bumpy, dirt road leads to a couple of mile-long trails, Long Cove Pond, and a deserted stretch of South Beach. Parking is limited at this 586-acre preserve, maintained by the Massachusetts Trustees of Reservations, so get there early. Parking $5, plus $2 per person over age 15.

Mytoi (693-7662), off Dyke Road, Chappaquiddick. Open daily sunrise to sunset, year-round. This 14-acre Japanese garden, built by Hugh Jones in 1958, has azaleas, irises, a goldfish pond, and a picturesque little bridge. It is under the auspices of the Trustees of Reservations. Free.

Manuel E. Correllus State Forest (693-2540), off Edgartown–West Tisbury Road or Barnes Road. Comprising 4400 acres of woodland and meadows in the center of the island, the forest's trails are used regularly by bikers, joggers, picnickers, and hikers. There's also an exercise trail just north of the headquarters on Barnes Road. Parking near the Barnes Road entrance. Free.

Fulling Mill Brook, off South Road, about 2 miles beyond the Chilmark Cemetery, Chilmark. Hiking trails pass through 46 acres of forests, fields, and streams.

BEACHES

Unlike Nantucket, many Vineyard beaches are private, open only to homeowners or cottage renters. Many innkeepers, especially those in the up-island establishments, provide resident parking passes to their guests. (A much-coveted Chilmark pass will get you access to **Lucy Vincent Beach** off South Road, the island's prettiest.) If you can't bicycle to a beach, you can take an island shuttle or a taxi—many beaches have pay phones for just this purpose. The following are public beaches.

Lake Tashmoo Beach (or **Herring Creek Beach**), at the end of Herring Creek Road, Vineyard Haven. This small beach offers good swimming, surf-fishing, and shellfishing. No facilities or lifeguards.

Oak Bluffs Town Beach, on both sides of the ferry wharf, Oak Bluffs. This calm beach is popular with Oak Bluffs families and seasonal visitors with small children. No lifeguards or facilities, although there are public rest rooms next to the ferry dock.

Fuller Street Beach, at the end of Fuller Street near Lighthouse Beach, Edgartown. A favorite among college students, the beach is a short bike ride from town and generally quiet. No facilities or lifeguards.

Lighthouse Beach, on Starbuck's Neck off North Water Street, Edgartown. From here you can watch boats going in and out of the harbor. No facilities or lifeguards.

Katama Beach (or **South Beach**), off Katama Road, Edgartown. A shuttle runs from Edgartown to this popular, 3-mile-long barrier beach with medium to heavy surf and high dunes. No facilities, but there are lifeguards, although not along the entire beach.

Joseph Sylvia State Beach, along Beach Road between Edgartown and

Oak Bluffs. The Edgartown end of this 2-mile-long beach is also called Bend-in-the-Road Beach; this part of the gentle beach has lifeguards but no facilities.

Menemsha Beach, Menemsha Harbor. This calm, gentle beach is also pebbly. No lifeguard, but nearby rest rooms.

Gay Head Beach, just south of the Gay Head cliffs. Take the boardwalk and path through cranberry and beach plum bushes down to the beach, about a 10-minute walk. Resist the temptation to cover yourself with mud from the cliff's clay baths; the cliffs have eroded irreparably over the past century. Instead, walk along this 5-mile beach (called, from north to south, **Gay Head, Moshup, Philbin,** and **Zack's Cliffs Beaches**). The cliffs are to the north, but the beaches are wider to the south. Philbin and Zack's Cliffs Beaches are reserved for residents, but if you stick close to the waterline, you won't have a problem. The farther south you walk, the fewer people you'll see. But those people you do see, you'll see more of—people come here specifically to sunbathe nude. It's not legal, but generally the authorities look the other way. Swimming is very good here; the surf is usually light to moderate, and the shore doesn't drop off as abruptly as it does along the island's south shore. Facilities include rest rooms and a few small sandwich and chowder shops at the head of the cliff. Parking is plentiful; $10–15 per day, depending on the time of the summer; $5 for 2 hours.

Lobsterville Beach, off State and Lobsterville Roads, Gay Head. This beach is popular with families because of shallow, warm water and gentle surf.

PICNICS

Owen Park, off Main Street, north of the ferry dock, Vineyard Haven. This thin strip of grass runs from Main Street down to the harbor beach. You can usually get a parking space; there are swings for the kids, and it's a great vantage point for watching boats sail in and out of the harbor.

Mill Pond, West Tisbury. This wonderful place to feed ducks and swans is next to the simple, shingled West Tisbury Police Department.

LODGING

Reservations, made well in advance of your visit, are imperative during July and August and on weekends from September to mid-October. The height of high season runs, of course, from late June to early September, but many innkeepers define high season from mid-May to mid-October. In addition, many up-island inns are booked months in advance by bridal parties who want meadows, stone walls, and spectacular ocean views as the backdrop for their wedding photographs. Most inns require a 2- or 3-night minimum stay in summer and 2 nights on weekends in autumn. Although there are quite a few year-round lodging choices, the island is incredibly quiet from January through March.

Gingerbread-style houses in Wesleyan Grove, Oak Bluffs

INNS
In Vineyard Haven 02568
✳ **Thorncroft Inn** (693-3333, e-mail: kgb@tiac.net), 278 Main Street. Open year-round. Under the care of Lynn and Karl Buder since 1980, this elegant Craftsman-style bungalow on a 3½-acre wooded estate (about a mile out of town) is perhaps the island's best-run inn. It's perfect for special getaways. All 14 guest rooms are decorated with Victorian-period antiques and have thick carpeting and private baths. Amenities include plush robes, cable TV, air-conditioning, two telephone lines, and the morning paper delivered to your door. Some rooms have hot tubs or Jacuzzis-for-two; many have working fireplaces. A complimentary full breakfast is served in the inn's two small dining areas, or you may opt for a continental breakfast in bed. Finally, there's afternoon tea and pastries and evening turn-down service. Mid-June to early September $200–400; otherwise $150–350.

In West Tisbury
✳ **Lambert's Cove Country Inn** (693-2298), Lambert's Cove Road, West Tisbury. Open year-round. This idyllic country inn, a few miles from Vineyard Haven, has one of the Vineyard's most popular restaurants (see *Dining Out*). The estate once belonged to an ardent horticulturist, and the impressive formal gardens are well preserved. A tennis court, a lush wisteria arbor surrounded by thick lilacs, an apple orchard, and ancient rock walls also grace the property. Guest rooms are scattered throughout the inn, carriage house, and converted barn. They vary considerably; ask for a full description. Some of the 15 rooms (all with private bath) open onto sun decks; one especially comfortable room has a private green-

house sitting room. Guests receive parking passes to nearby Lambert's Cove, one of the island's prettiest beaches. Full breakfast included. Late May to mid-October $135–175; mid-October through November and mid-March to late May $95–135; December to mid-March $75–120.

In Edgartown 02539

Tuscany Inn (627-5999, e-mail: 70632.3363@compuserve.com), 22 North Water Street. Open April through December. When Laura and Rusty Scheuer took over this 1893 house in the year of its centennial, it was in dreadful condition. Now it's one of the island's top places to stay. Laura, a native of Florence (hence, the inn's name), is a designer. Her flair for balancing color and space with magnificent antiques, fabrics, and unusual decorative pieces creates an elegant feel. The eight guest rooms with fine linens have private baths (one is detached), and many have whirlpool baths. Common space includes a library, a plush living room, and a flagstone terrace. Laura is a marvelous cook and her breakfasts are served in a tiled dining room with exposed kitchen. (You'll swear you're in Italy.) Inquire about Laura's Tuscan-style cooking school offered on off-season weekends. Mid-June to early September $200–325; May to mid-June and early September through October $150–245; November, December, and April $100–150. (The least expensive rooms are quite small, but cozy).

❊ **Charlotte Inn** (627-4751), South Summer Street. Open year-round. Innkeepers Gery and Paula Conover preside over the Vineyard's grande dame. They aren't resting on their laurels, however; they restore and refurbish each room every five years. Ardent Anglophiles, they make frequent trips to the UK to purchase antiques. Of the inn's 21 rooms and three suites, many have fireplaces and most have TV and telephone. Equestrian prints, elegant armchairs, and collections of beautifully bound classic novels makes each room a luxuriously inhabitable museum. The Conovers' taste for all things English reveals itself in the inn's grounds, too: ivy-edged brick sidewalks, small croquet-quality lawns, impeccable flower beds. Continental breakfast. June through October $250–550; May $165–450; November through April $95–450.

☞ **Edgartown Inn** (627-4794), 56 North Water Street. Open April through October. A hostelry since the early 1800s, the inn has hosted such notables as Daniel Webster, Nathaniel Hawthorne, and then Senator John F. Kennedy. Longtime managers Susanne and Sandi have worked hard at maintaining and upgrading the inn's 20 rooms with firm mattresses and homey antiques. The rooms are simply but nicely decorated and represent perhaps the best value in town. Bathrooms are newly retiled. Two more modern, light and airy rooms in the Garden House have private entrances. A full breakfast is included and served in the charming dining room or on the back patio. Late May through October $75–80 for a shared bath, $95–175 for a private bath; off-season $45–60 and $75–115 respectively. No credit cards.

✳ **Daggett House** (627-4600, 1-800-946-3400), 59 North Water Street. Open year-round. This is Edgartown's only waterfront B&B. The original building served as the Vineyard's first tavern in 1660, and since then has been a store, a boardinghouse for sailors, a countinghouse, and a private home. The 20 guest rooms and three suites (each with private bath and phone) are furnished with antiques and reproductions, lace-canopied beds, and comfortable armchairs. Rooms in the main house are generally preferable to those across the street. The Secret Staircase guest room (one of the inn's best) has a "private" entrance through one of the bookcases in the dining room. Rooms in the cottage, closest to the harbor, have private entrances. A full breakfast is available (for a fee) in the authentically Colonial dining room. Children are welcome. Mid-May to mid-October $145–185; mid-October to mid-May $75–95.

Shiretown Inn (627-3353, 1-800-541-0090), 21 North Water Street. Open mid-May to mid-October. Centrally located, the Shiretown offers a variety of rooms (all with private bath). Some guest rooms are furnished with period furniture and have private entrances; other rooms, especially those in the carriage house out back, are plain and serviceable rather than quaint. A breakfast voucher good at four in-town restaurants is included. Late June to mid-September $75–259 nightly; off-season $59–199.

Up-island

Inn at Blueberry Hill (645-3322, 1-800-356-3322), North Road, Chilmark 02535. Open May through Thanksgiving. Lunch and dinner served daily in-season; Thursday through Sunday off-season. This secluded 56-acre retreat has an intentionally exclusive feel to it. Miles from anything but conservation land and stone walls, it's the kind of place you won't want to leave. Completely renovated in 1995, the 25 soothing rooms are scattered throughout six elegantly simple buildings. Privacy is paramount here: Most rooms have a private deck or balcony. A wide array of spa treatments are available by advance request. An expanded continental breakfast and use of fitness facilities (lap pool, tennis court, aerobic and weight equipment) is included. Lunch is available. Fine dinners are also served. In-season $210 for a room, $250 or $370 for suites; off-season $147–179 for rooms, $150–315 for suites. (There is one petite room available in-season for $150.)

Outermost Inn (645-3511), Lighthouse Road, Gay Head (mailing address: RR 1, Box 171, Gay Head 02535). Open April through November. Hugh and Jeanne Taylor's 20-acre parcel of land has the island's second best ocean view. (The best view is just up the hill from the Gay Head Lighthouse, where Jeanne's great-great-grandfather was born.) The inn's six rooms and one suite (one with whirlpool) boast natural fabrics, wool rugs, and down duvets. Subdued colors and unpainted furniture emphasize the seaside light. Rooms are named after the wood used in each: beech, ash, hickory, and cherry. All rooms have TV and telephone.

In keeping with the family's musical tradition, guitars, pianos, and other instruments are placed in the common areas. (You might get lucky and wander into an impromptu living room concert given by brother James.) The inn's restaurant (see *Dining Out*) is popular. Full breakfast included. May through October $250–285; off-season $190–210.

Beach Plum Inn (645-9454), Beach Plum Lane (off North Road), Menemsha 02552. Open May to mid-October. Secluded amid 8 acres of woods overlooking Menemsha Harbor, the Beach Plum is a first-rate inn with exceptional food (see *Dining Out*). Longtime innkeepers Paul and Janie Darrow have decorated the rooms with a simple style and grace that attract a monied clientele who want a private place to unwind. Facilities include beach access, a croquet court, and a tennis court. Mid-June to mid-September $175–300 with breakfast, $285–410 with breakfast, afternoon cocktails and hors d'oeuvres, and dinner; off-season $100–225 with no meals.

BED & BREAKFASTS
In Vineyard Haven 02658

☞✱ **The Farmhouse** (693-5354), State Road. Open year-round. Drive 10 minutes from the ferry to this unpretentious B&B, and you'll be in another world. Dating to 1810, this warm house and its longtime innkeepers—Kathleen and Volker Kaempfert—are a delight. The five guest rooms (four share two baths) are furnished with country antiques and down comforters. The living and dining rooms, where a continental breakfast is served, feature exposed beams and wide floorboards. Additional common space includes a quiet back patio. $85–110 in-season; 15 percent less off-season.

Crocker House Inn (693-1151, 1-800-772-0206), 12 Crocker Avenue. Open April through October. Innkeeper Darlene Stavens's B&B is on a quiet side street, just a few minutes' walk from town. It's a turn-of-the-century house, with a wraparound porch set with rockers. Each of the eight guest rooms (all with private bath) are cozy and charming. The third-floor loft room is tucked under the eaves and can accommodate three people. Room 5 feels spacious, with a cathedral ceiling. Ask for a complete description of what's available. Continental breakfast included. Mid-June to mid-September $85–160; off-season $10–25 less.

✱ **Lothrop Merry House** (693-1646), Owen Park. Open year-round. The sea is very much a part of the 1790 Lothrop Merry House. The lawn stretches down to a small beach; continental breakfast is served on a terrace overlooking the harbor; and the owners, John and Mary Clarke, split their time between the inn and their boat, the *Laissez Faire* (see *To Do—Boat Excursions*). Each of the seven guest rooms has its own charms—some have harbor views, some have private baths, some have fireplaces. This is a historic house, so be prepared for uneven floors, latch doors, and imperfect plaster walls. Children are welcome. Mid-June to mid-October $119–185; mid-April to mid-June and mid-October through

November $88–165; December to mid-April $68–125.

Captain Dexter House (693-6564), 100 Main Street. Open April through December. This centrally located 1843 B&B has everything you'd expect from a sea captain's house—large rooms, wide-plank wood floors, fireplaces, and dormer windows. Seven guest rooms and one suite all have private bathrooms; two have fireplaces, great for those stormy fall and winter days. Despite the Victorian–cum–New England charm, the decor is in need of spiffing up. Continental breakfast included. Mid-June through September $115–175; off-season $85–150.

☞❋ **Nancy's Auberge** (693-4434), 102 Main Street. Open year-round. Nancy Hurd's unpretentious mid-19th-century home has three guest rooms (one with private bath) that share two comfortable living rooms. One room is well suited to a family or two couples traveling together. An expanded continental breakfast is served in the back patio. If you're one of those who think the Vineyard has gotten too commercial or that too many inns are run by managers, this place is for you. Mid-May to mid-September $88–108.

❋ **Pierside** (693-5562), off State Road (PO Box 1951, Vineyard Haven 02568). Open year-round. Far from the madding crowds, down a dirt road through the woods, Pierside offers rooms just 100 yards from Lake Tashmoo. Innkeepers Ilse and Philip Fleischman built the house, which features a large room with kitchenette, cathedral ceilings, and a private deck. One of the two other rooms doesn't have a kitchenette, but the Fleischmans will prepare almost anything you want for breakfast. Swim from their pier or rent a little boat and sail around the saltwater lake. Mid-June to mid-September $95–165, off-season $75–125, $15 additional person.

In West Tisbury 02575

❋☞✐**The House at New Lane** (696-7331), New Lane. Open year-round. Off the beaten path, this house is appealing to "real B&Bers," according to owners Ann and William Fiedler. By that they mean guests who are happy to cut through the kitchen to get to the sun room/breakfast room; guests who are happy to see family photos above the mantel. Surrounded by acres of woods and gardens, these five rooms (three of which are quite large) share two baths. One room has a private deck and entrance. Children are welcome; futons available for an additional $20 nightly. May through October $85, off-season $65, full breakfast included.

In Oak Bluffs 02557

Oak House (693-4187), at Seaview and Pequot Avenues. Open mid-May to mid-October. The shingled, gingerbread Oak House is appropriately named—there's oak everywhere, from the walls to the ceilings. Innkeeper Betsi Convery-Luce's 1872 inn is itself a finely preserved antique, and she's added a lot of Victoriana. Most of the 10 rooms (2 of which are suites) have water views; all have private bath and air-conditioning. Even if your room has a private balcony, you may find yourself spending time in the rocking chairs and swings on the large wraparound veranda. Home-baked continental breakfasts and afternoon teas are delectable. Mid-May to mid-June $100–175; mid-June to early September $140–250; mid-September to mid-October $115–190.

✎ **Oak Bluffs Inn** (693-7171, 1-800-955-6235), Circuit Avenue at Pequot Avenue. Open May through October. You can't miss the inn—it's the pink building with an enormous cupola atop the third story. Innkeepers Maryann and Glen Mattera encourage guests to climb up to the cupola for a view of Oak Bluffs rooftops. All nine guest rooms have a private bath (small but newly redone), air-conditioning, cottage-style bedroom sets, and views of colorful neighboring cottages from every window. A continental buffet breakfast is included; guests may eat on the wraparound porch. Children are welcome. Mid-June to early September $120–145 for rooms, $165–190 for suites (the higher end of the range is charged on weekends; off-season $110–120 for rooms, $150 for suites.

❋ **Brady's Bed & Breakfast** (693-9137), 10 Canonicus Avenue. Open year-round. On the edge of town, this house has been in Brady Aikens's family since 1929; he summered here in the 1940s and opened it as a B&B in 1991. Choose your shared-bath guest room according to direction: north, south, east, or west. The summery, whitewashed rooms have wood-slat walls and are decorated in soothing colors and designer linens. West (with sunset views) is the largest and nicest room. All rooms but one have a private balcony. Start your day with a continental breakfast (homemade bagels and mixed fruit juices) on the wraparound porch, and end up back here as the sun sets. The comfortable living room, decorated with southwestern influences, has a large video and CD collection. May through October $88–98, off-season $55–65.

☞ **Attleboro House** (693-4346), 11 Lake Avenue. Open mid-May through September. This authentic gingerbread cottage faces Oak Bluffs Harbor and sits on the outer perimeter of the Methodist Camp Meeting Association. It's been taking in seaside guests since 1874, and it hasn't changed much since then. In Estelle Reagan's family since the 1940s, the guest house has 11 simple but tidy guest rooms that share five bathrooms. (Some rooms have a sink in them.) Most rooms have a porch, but if yours doesn't, there's a wraparound porch on the first floor. One suite on the third floor can accommodate six people. $45–75 for rooms, $95–175 for the suite.

Narragansett House (693-3627), Narragansett Avenue. Open mid-April to mid-October. This 1860s gingerbread cottage was originally built as an inn to house visiting Methodist "campers." It's surrounded by colorful, whimsical cottages just like it, most of which are private houses. Each of 13 simple guest rooms has a private bath. I like room 9, with a separate entrance and new bath. Surrounded by a picket fence, perhaps the B&B's best attribute is its front yard and porch. It's set with rockers and potted plants and teeming with birds and squirrels. At press time innkeepers Jane and Paul Lofgren had begun renovating seven more rooms in a period house across the street. They also rent two apartments. Late May to mid-September $110, off-season $50–95.

In Edgartown 02539

❋ **Victorian Inn** (627-4784), 24 South Water Street. Open year-round. This centrally located B&B has been steadily improving since Stephen and Karyn Caliri took over in 1993. There are 14 luxurious guest rooms, some with four-poster canopy beds; all have private baths. Rooms are furnished with substantial, comfortable armchairs, sofas, loveseats, and desks. Third-floor rooms have harbor views. A three-course breakfast is served on the flower-bordered back patio or indoors at tables for two in the formal breakfast room. This is one of the few B&Bs that accept children; dogs are permitted in the off-season. Mid-June to early September $125–265; November through March $70–145.

❋ **Shiverick Inn** (627-3797, 1-800-723-4292), at Pent Lane and Pease's Point Way. Open year-round. Built in 1840 by Edgartown's leading physician, this Greek Revival building with a cupola is grand and elegant. Denny and Marty Turmelle's 10 guest rooms, all with private baths, polished wood floors, and central air-conditioning, are decorated with lush wallpapers, thick throw rugs, and fine antiques. Most guest rooms have fireplaces. Room 10 has a private porch. All are welcome to use the library porch, from which you can see the Old Whaling Church (see *To See*). The postage-stamp-sized backyard is tranquil, with a flagstone terrace and flower garden. An expanded continental breakfast is included. Mid-June to mid-October $185–265; off-season $120–175.

Summer House (627-4857), 96 South Summer Street. Open mid-May to mid-October. Three blocks from Main Street and a block from Edgartown Harbor, this homey and charming B&B is a welcome relief from many overdone inns. Innkeeper Chloe Nolan offers three rooms (one with private bath), quiet nights, a deep front yard, and a secret garden. Guests enjoy a continental breakfast served at a long teak dining table or on the brick terrace, both overlooking the yard. $110–140 shared bath, $155 private bath. No credit cards.

✐☞**Meeting House Inn** (627-6220, 1-800-627-2858), 40 Meeting House Way. Open May to mid-October. A few miles from town and set on 58 acres, this lovely B&B has two living rooms and four large corner guest rooms that share two baths. A delightful place and a fine choice for families. $85–95.

Up-island

Captain Flanders' House (645-3123), North Road, between Menemsha Cross and Tabor House Roads, Chilmark (mailing address: PO Box 384, Chilmark 02535). Open April to mid-November. Location, location, location. The 17th-century Captain Flanders' House sits on the crest of a hill overlooking a pond and meadows crisscrossed by stone walls. There's no real innkeeper presence here, but no matter. This is the kind of place where you want to be left alone to savor the peace and quiet that envelop the place. The main house has six guest rooms (one with a pond view), only two of which have private baths. Two adjacent buildings have been converted into cottage-style suites, one with working fireplace. All rooms are comfortably furnished with unfussy country antiques. A continental breakfast is served on the sun porch. The inn provides parking passes to Lucy Vincent Beach. Late May to mid-October $60 single, $105–170 double; otherwise $40 single, $65–75 double.

Up Island Country Inn (645-2720), 2 Lobsterville Road, Gay Head 02535. Open mid-April to mid-November. This beautifully crafted contemporary home, and much of the furniture in it, was built by the owners. It's quite impressive. The inn, within walking distance of a nice beach, offers luxury and privacy in three spacious suites. Innkeepers John Walsh and Lynne Aune take requests at breakfast. $175 in the summer; $125–150 off-season.

COTTAGES, EFFICIENCIES, AND APARTMENTS
In Vineyard Haven 02568
✐❋ **Causeway Harborview** (693-1606, 1-800-253-8684), Skiff Avenue. Open year-round. These 24 individually owned apartments and cottages sleep from one to six people. Manager Jean Ellis is good about renting the best units first. Each has a small but fully equipped kitchen, TV, and linens. Some have harbor views. There are barbecue grills and a swimming pool on the shaded grounds. A 5-minute walk from the center of town, the small complex feels just far enough away from the crowds. Late June to late September $630–755 weekly for one bedroom, $925–960 weekly for two bedrooms, $1050 weekly for three bedrooms. Rates are cut by about 50 percent in spring and fall. No credit cards.

In Oak Bluffs 02557
✐ **East Chop Harborfront Apartments** (696-0009), 21–23 East Chop Drive. Open May through October. These five very well-maintained apartments are right on the harbor, a 5-minute walk from the center of town. The one- and two-bedroom units, with full kitchens, are great for families. Units open onto private, waterfront decks. Call as early as you can; these modern apartments are very nice indeed. July and August $1200–1400 weekly Sunday to Sunday, $600–800 off-season.

In Edgartown 02539
☞✐ **Edgartown Commons** (627-4671; 1-800-439-4671 within Massachusetts), Pease's Point Way. Open May to late October. These 35 efficiencies— from studios to one- and two-bedroom apartments—are near the center of town. It's a great place for families. Three-quarters of the units are in very good condition; these are rented first. Units in the main building have high ceilings and thus feel more spacious. Many units surround the pool. All are comfortably furnished and most feature new kitchens. Outside, there are grills, picnic tables, and an enclosed play area. Late June to early September $135–205; off-season $75–115.

Up-island
✐ **Menemsha Inn and Cottages** (645-2521), North Road, between Menemsha Cross Road and Menemsha Harbor, Menemsha (mailing address: PO Box 38C, Menemsha 02552). Open May to early November.

In 1984 Richard and Nancy Steves purchased this 10½-acre parcel of forest that boasts lovely views of Vineyard Sound. They've been fixing up the rooms and cottages ever since. An emphasis on peace and quiet, rather than fussy interior decorating, prevails. The complex has six luxurious suites in the carriage house, nine smaller but bright and lovely rooms in the main building, and 12 tidy housekeeping cottages. Each cottage has a screened-in porch, fully equipped kitchen, outdoor shower, barbecue, and wood-burning fireplace. All rooms and cottages have decks. Beach passes to residents-only Lucy Vincent and Squibnocket Beaches are provided. Reserve well in advance; this place has a loyal, repeat clientele. Mid-June to mid-September: $115–130 for rooms (including breakfast), $170 for suites, $1075–1475 weekly for cottages; off-season: $85 for rooms, $100 for suites, $750–850 weekly or $120 nightly for cottages, with a 2-night minimum. No credit cards.

HOTELS

In Oak Bluffs 02557

✐ **Wesley Hotel** (693-6611, 1-800-638-9027), 1 Lake Avenue. Open May to mid-October. Even before its restoration in the early 1990s, this four-story hotel was the only place in honky-tonk Oak Bluffs that could be called gracious. It's now the last of seven turn-of-the-century oceanfront hotels in Oak Bluffs. A wide veranda (with rocking chairs) wraps around the Carpenter Gothic–style building, across the street from the marina. Try to reserve a harbor-view room. The main hotel has 82 rooms that are fairly large and modestly furnished. The Wesley caters to groups, and it stages popular Mystery Weekends in June and September. Rooms in the adjacent **Wesley Arms** are primitive, with thin walls, better left to college students accustomed to dorm rooms. They haven't been touched in 100 years. (They're worth a peek if only to see how things used to be.) Children under 12 free in parent's room; otherwise $15–25 each additional person. Mid-June to mid-September $65 shared bath, $165 private bath; off-season $45 shared, $105 private.

✐ **Island Inn** (693-2002, 1-800-462-0269), Beach Road. Situated between Oak Bluffs and Edgartown, this 7-acre resort is within walking distance of two beaches and adjacent to Farm Neck Golf Course (see *To Do—Golf*). In all there are 51 units (studios, one- and two-bedroom suites) in several low-slung buildings. Facilities include tennis courts and a swimming pool. Open March to mid-December. Mid-June to early September $130–215; spring and fall $85–130; $20 each additional person. Inquire about the larger town house and cottage; each sleeps six.

In Edgartown 02539

✐❄ **Harbor View Hotel** (627-7000, 1-800-225-6005), 131 North Water Street. Open year-round. Overlooking a lighthouse, grass-swept beach, and Chappaquiddick, the 1891 Harbor View is Edgartown's grand and luxurious waterfront resort. It has 124 rooms and one- and two-bedroom suites with kitchens or kitchenettes. There are tranquil harbor

A wildlife refuge and beaches draw visitors to Chappaquiddick.

views from the hotel's spacious veranda and some guest rooms. Other guest rooms have porches overlooking the pool. Rooms are generally large, appointed with wicker chairs, pecan-washed armoires, antique prints, and watercolor landscapes by local artists. Facilities include tennis, room service, a private beach, swimming pool, and concierge. The hotel has two restaurants (see Starbuck's under *Dining Out* and Breezes under *Eating Out*). Mid-June to late September $225–385 for rooms, $400–565 for one- and two-bedroom suites; fall and spring $155–265 for rooms, $265–415 for suites; winter $90–100 for rooms, $185–225 for suites.

✎❋ **Harborside Inn** (627-4321, 1-800-627-4009), 3 South Water Street. Open year-round. This four-building time-share condominium is one of the few waterfront (harborfront no less!) accommodations on the island. Practically all rooms have some sort of water view. Rooms are well appointed with standard hotel-issue furnishings. Facilities include a heated pool overlooking harbor boat slips. Summer: $120 for a few small rooms, $190–200 for "regular" rooms, $250–260 for water-view rooms with porches or patios, $260–280 for two-bedroom suites; $25 each additional person. Children under 12 stay free in parent's room. Rates are about 40 percent less in spring and fall and less than half price in winter.

RENTALS

Up-Island Real Estate (645-2632), State Road, Chilmark. David Flanders and his daughter Julie (as well as the rest of the staff) know up-island like it was their own backyard—because it is. They manage properties for homeowners all around up-island. Rental prices suit nearly every budget, starting at $750 per week for a small cottage.

CAMPGROUND

Webb's Camping Area (693-0233), Barnes Road (mailing address: RR 3, Box 100, Vineyard Haven 02568). Open mid-May to mid-September. Eighty acres of pine groves overlook Lagoon Pond in Oak Bluffs with 150 sites, including a separate area for backpackers and cyclists. Facilities are well maintained. $29 for a lagoon or private site, plus $1 for each child over 5; $203 weekly per family. Other sites $27 nightly, $189 weekly.

✐ **Martha's Vineyard Family Campground** (693-3772), 569 Edgartown Road, Vineyard Haven 02568. Open mid-May to mid-October. In addition to tent and trailer sites, the campground also has rustic one- and two-room cabins that sleep five or six people ($75–85). Tents $26; additional adults $9, children under 18 $2.

YOUTH HOSTEL

Manter Memorial AYH Hostel (693-2665), Edgartown–West Tisbury Road, West Tisbury (mailing address: Box 158, West Tisbury 02575). Open April to mid-November. This saltbox opened in 1955, and it remains an ideal lodging choice for cycling-oriented visitors. The hostel is at the edge of the Manuel E. Correllus State Forest (full of bike paths) and next to the path that runs from Edgartown to West Tisbury. Bring your own linens or rent them for the single-sex, dormitory-style bunk beds. The large kitchen is fully equipped and the common room has a fireplace. Reservations strongly recommended, especially from June to September, when large groups frequent the hostel. Reserve by phone or mail at least 2 weeks in advance. $12 for AYH members, $15 for nonmembers, half price for children.

WHERE TO EAT

Most restaurants are open May to mid-October; some are open through Christmas. A few Vineyard Haven restaurants are open year-round. Generally, chef-owned places provide the most reliable food. Many Oak Bluffs establishments are family-oriented and casual, though there are a few trendy options. The dress code in Edgartown is a bit more conservative, but most places don't warrant a jacket and tie. Dining options are more scarce up-island, and require reservations well ahead of time. Vineyard Haven, Tisbury, and up-island towns are "dry," so BYOB; some restaurants charge a nominal fee to uncork your wine.

DINING OUT

In Vineyard Haven

Le Grenier (693-4906), 96 Main Street (above La Patisserie Française; see *Eating Out*). Open for dinner mid-March through December. Chef-owner Jean Dupon's place is consistently great. Lyons-born, his traditional French offerings include bouillabaisse, escargots, frogs' legs provençale, and calf's brains grenobloise. The menu is extensive, but each item is expertly prepared. Save room for desserts like crème caramel or banana flambé. The decor is light, with green-and-white accents and hand-painted florals. Reservations recommended. BYOB. Entrées $18–28.

✿ **Black Dog Tavern** (693-9223), Beach Street Extension. Open for breakfast, lunch, and dinner daily, as well as Sunday brunch, year-round. Longtime Vineyarder Bob Douglas became frustrated when he couldn't find good chowder within walking distance of the harbor, so he opened this place in 1971, naming it for his dog. Now, the Black Dog—and the ubiquitous Black Dog T-shirt—is synonymous with Vineyard life. It's a pretty good place to eat, too, although you usually have to wait at least an hour, since they don't take reservations. Interior decor is simple, with pine floors, old beams, and plain wooden tables packed close together. Best of all, the shingled saltbox sits right on the harbor. Fresh island fish and locally grown vegetables dominate the menu; toothsome desserts are made in the Black Dog Bakery (see *Snacks*). Although the staff are often eager to hustle you out the door, don't be shy about finishing your coffee. BYOB. Breakfast $3–6, lunch $3–11; dinner entrées $20–23.

Dry Town Cafe (693-0033), 70 Main Street. Open for dinner April through December. This handsome and hip neighborhood bistro, which would fit quite nicely in SoHo, serves an eclectic menu. Dishes lean heavily toward seafood; try some locally caught striped bass, marinated in sake-ginger and served with baby carrots and wilted pea greens. Reservations suggested. BYOB. Entrées $19–28.

Stripers (693-8383), 26 Beach Road. Open for dinner Thursday through Monday, May through October, nightly in summer; Sunday brunch. New in 1995, Culinary Institute of America chef Louis Valentine offers harborfront tables—an island rarity. French and Italian dishes are spiced up with Thai and Japanese accents. Lobster stuffed with crabcakes is popular, as is swordfish with grilled pineapple salsa. There's a raw bar and sushi, too. Entrées are usually dressed with five or six vegetables. Tables glow with hurricane lamps. Make reservations for a waterfront table. BYOB. Entrées $17–24.

In West Tisbury

✿ **Lambert's Cove Country Inn** (693-2298), Lambert's Cove Road, West Tisbury. Open for dinner nightly, June to mid-September; weekends from mid-September through May. This traditional country inn serves a limited New American and Continental menu that changes nightly. On my last visit it leaned heavily toward meat (with one salmon offering): steak, duck, chicken, pork, and veal. Reservations recommended. BYOB. Entrées $19–24.

In Oak Bluffs

Oyster Bar (693-3300), 162 Circuit Avenue. Open for dinner Wednesday through Sunday early May to mid-October, nightly in summer. This is perhaps the most see-and-be-seen place on-island. High tin ceilings, an exposed kitchen, and a single strip of red neon conspire to create a lively and boisterous bistrolike scene. The 40-foot oak-and-granite bar is also quite popular. Chef-owner Ray Schilcher's food is creative and well executed. Three popular selections include "pan-roasted soup" made with lobster or shrimp; seafood risotto; and a lobster and tenderloin dish with garlic mashed potatoes and béarnaise sauce. Reservations suggested. Entrées $26–36.

In Edgartown

Savoir Fare (627-9864), 14 Church Street. Open for dinner Thursday through Sunday April through October, nightly in July and August. Rising to the top of everyone's not-to-miss list, this American bistro with Italian-influenced dishes is an unpretentious, gourmand's haven. Although the menu changes monthly, signature dishes include the house salad with fried baby artichoke croutons and chèvre, an untraditional osso buco and fettuccine, and grilled and sautéed calamari with squid ink pasta. Entrées $24–28.50.

L'Étoile (627-5187), South Summer Street, at the Charlotte Inn. Open nightly in summer; off-season schedule varies; closed January to mid-February. Brunch is served on holidays. Dine in an elegant garden setting: Brick walls and a glass roof surround the conservatory–dining area, filled with plants and flowers. The cuisine, meticulously prepared and artistically presented by chef-owner Michael Brisson, is nothing short of spectacular. On my last visit the roasted pheasant breast with sweet potato, jicama, and celery root gratin exceeded already high expectations. Reservations required. Prix fixe dinner $58; prix fixe brunch $26.

❊ **Starbuck's** (627-7000), 131 North Water Street, at the Harbor View Hotel. Open daily for breakfast, lunch, and dinner, as well as Sunday brunch. The decor and pace of this restaurant are about as formal as it gets on the Vineyard. (Still, attire is "smart casual.") It's a nice choice for lunch: salads, bisque, and sandwiches (like the spicy swordfish steak sandwich) hover around $7–10. At dinnertime, try the mixed seafood grill and 2-pound lobsters. Reservations recommended at dinner. Breakfast $6–9, lunch $7–29, dinner entrées $19.50–32.

☞ **Chesca's** (627-1234), 38 North Water Street. Open for breakfast, lunch, and dinner, mid-April through October; call for nightly off-season schedule. Chesca's offers a reliable selection of Italian-inspired seafood and pasta specials. For dinner, mix and match a pasta and sauce of your choice and perhaps add a side of eggplant parmigiana. Or get a scampi-style dish with your choice of chicken, shrimp, veal, or scallops. Lunches are limited to creative salads and sandwiches like roasted chicken salad, burgers, and warm goat cheese. For breakfast try the egg bowl—seasoned scrambled eggs baked in a hollowed bread round. No reservations taken at dinner; expect to wait. Breakfast $6–7.50, lunch $5–8.50, dinner entrées $9–23.

O'Brien's Serious Seafood & Grill (627-5850), 137 Upper Main Street. Open for dinner Thursday through Monday, May through December; nightly from late June to mid-October. Continental veal and meat dishes share the stage with traditional seafood. But on my last visit one of the most popular dishes was steamed fish (perhaps salmon and halibut) served in a Japanese bamboo steamer, lined with bok choy, julienne vegetables, and Japanese white rice. Chef-owner John O'Brien and his wife, Carolyn, offer dining on the candlelit veranda, in the patio rose garden, or at one of many small rooms in the 19th-century house. **Sadie's Pub,** downstairs, offers lighter fare. Entrées $19–29.

Up-island

Beach Plum Inn (645-9454), Beach Plum Lane (off North Road), Menemsha. Open for breakfast and dinner, mid-May to mid-October. Although you may be drawn to the Beach Plum Inn for its panoramic view of Menemsha Harbor (spectacular at sunset), the crowning glory of Janie and Paul Darrow's place is the superb food. The menu features creatively prepared seafood and locally grown produce. Call for the menu, which changes nightly. BYOB. Reservations only; prix fixe $55.

Outermost Inn (645-3511), Lighthouse Road, Gay Head. Open for dinner nightly except Wednesday, late May to mid-October. Even the dramatic sunset over the ocean won't distract you from the classic New American dishes prepared by Culinary Institute of America–trained chef Barbara Fenner. A typical meal might include crabcakes, a seafood brochette, and a scrumptious cheesecake. BYOB. Reservations only; two seatings for the three-course, prix fixe dinners, $39–50.

Feast of Chilmark (645-3553), State Road at Beetlebung Corner, Chilmark. Open for dinner nightly except Monday in May, June, September, and October; open nightly in July and August. Owner-chefs David Dubiel and Tony Saccoccia offer sophisticated New American selections, which might include a warm pecan-crusted goat cheese salad followed by seafood marinara with lobster, shrimp, scallops, and clams over linguine. This casually upscale restaurant doubles as a gallery for local photographer Peter Simon's Vineyard scenes and landscapes. (Peter is Carly's brother.) Reservations suggested. Entrées $17–24.

The Red Cat (693-9599), State Road, North Tisbury. Open for dinner April through December; call for nightly shoulder-season schedule. Loyal followers of chef Ben DeForest know him from his early days at the Dry Town Cafe and Oyster Bar; assuredly he won't be going anywhere now that he has his own place. The exterior of this unpretentious roadside joint belies the creative goings-on in the kitchen. On my last visit, we were impressed with the seared yellowfin tuna served with organic greens, grilled polenta, and blackberry syrup. Adventurous (and hungry) diners might want to indulge in a tasting menu for $42 per person. Desserts are best on weekends when the pastry chef is there. BYOB. Reservations recommended in summer. Entrées $18–28.

EATING OUT

In Vineyard Haven

☞✐❊ **Louis'** (693-3255), 102 State Road, a bit out of town. Open for lunch and dinner daily, year-round. At lunchtime, the take-out counter features an array of cold pastas and appetizers sold by the pound. On my last visit, there wasn't one that wasn't excellent: baked orange ginger chicken, sesame teriyaki noodles, French green beans, and the like. Subs and pasta dishes are available too. It's also a vegetarian's delight. At the pleasant restaurant, there are excellent pasta dishes, as well as rotisserie-roasted chicken, lasagna, and a salad bar. Louis Giordano's place is also known for its rolls and carrot soup—even kids love the carrot soup! As if that weren't enough, islanders swear by Louis' pizza, also available for takeout. Children's menu. BYOB. Entrées $10–23.

✳ **La Patisserie Française** (693-8087), 96 Main Street. Open for lunch and Sunday brunch year-round. Below Le Grenier (see *Dining Out*), the lighter fare includes quiche, salads, soups, and grilled chicken sandwiches. Don't miss the homemade croissants and pastries. $5–15.

☞✳ **90 Main Street Deli** (693-0041), 90 Main Street. Open daily, year-round. Great salads, thick sandwiches prepared to order, homemade soups, baked goods, and delicious coffee, all at reasonable prices.

✳ **Vineyard Gourmet** (693-5181), Main Street. Open year-round. This mouthwatering specialty food store carries picnic baskets and boxed lunches filled with items like smoked salmon and spiced asparagus spears. Who says picnics can't be tasty *and* easy? Those with cooking facilities will find even more of interest.

In Oak Bluffs

☞✐ **Jimmy Sea's Pan Pasta** (696-8550), 32 Kennebec Avenue. Open daily for dinner, May until mid-October; Wednesday through Sunday, mid-October to late December. Locals, who pack the place, know a good thing when they find it. Head to this small, casual place when you're in the mood for enormous portions of delicious pastas, all cooked to order and served in the pan. Chef-owner Jimmy Cipolla's garlic-infused place is an even better value if you have facilities to heat up your leftovers; it's virtually impossible to eat everything you're served. No reservations. Get there early or be prepared to wait. Children's portions. Dishes $13–20.

☞✐✳ **Linda Jean's** (693-4093), 128 Circuit Avenue. Open daily 6 AM–8 PM year-round. Established in 1979, this pleasant storefront eatery serves old-fashioned meals at old-fashioned prices. Pancakes are thick but light; the fish sandwich is quick and good; and onion rings are crispy. Kids are happy with burgers and PB&J. And the waitstaff are friendly. What more could you ask for? If you haven't tried that famed New England "delicacy" Grape-Nut custard, this is the place to do it. Dishes $3–15.

☞✐ **Giordano's** (693-0184), 107 Circuit Avenue, at the corner of Lake Avenue. Open 11:30–10:30 daily, May to mid-September. This classic, family-style restaurant is run by fourth-generation Giordanos, who pride themselves on serving value-packed portions. Giordano's serves some of the best fried clams on-island, along with large portions of chicken cacciatore with spaghetti, veal Parmesan, pizza, sandwiches, and fried seafood. The cocktails are also big and the salad bar is fresh. Children's menu $6; lunch $6.50–14, complete dinners $10.50–14.50.

☞✐**Dee's Harbor Cafe** (693-6506), Lake Avenue. Open 6:30–3 daily, early May to mid-October. New in 1995, Dee Smith-Geiger's tiny café is known for cheese-fried grits and cream of wheat pancakes, topped with fresh fruit and maple syrup. Breakfast is available all day—everything from two eggs (any way you like them), to a bagel with lox, to fancy omelets. At lunchtime, get a burger, sandwich, or pasta of the day. Seating is limited, but you can get everything to go. Dishes $2.75–8.

✐ **Zapotec Cafe** (693-6800), 10 Kennebec Avenue. Open for dinner March through December and lunch in summer. This small, festive place with twinkling lights serves Mexican and southwestern dishes like grilled chicken with mole sauce, swordfish fajitas, and Mexican-style paella, as well as old standbys like burritos and enchiladas. Children's menu $4–6; crayons too. Dinner $11–18.

☞✐✷ **Papa's Pizza** (693-1400), 158 Circuit Avenue. Open daily year-round for lunch and dinner. Papa's serves excellent deep-dish and whole-wheat pizza from this storefront eatery. Despite its central location, it's not loud, expensive, or particularly crowded, even though the food is good and the atmosphere friendly. The pleasant interior has lots of long, rustic wooden tables, a tin ceiling, and brass lighting. Takeout, too.

☞✐✷ **Stand By Cafe** (696-0220), Lake and Oak Bluffs Avenues. Open for all three meals, March through January. This casual, diner-style restaurant opened in 1995 and offers no-nonsense breakfasts and lunches, fancier dinners. Seating is limited, prices reasonable, and the interior bright thanks to dozens of tiny windows. Omelets and frittatas ($5.25) rule in the morning, burgers and sandwiches ($5–7.50) at lunch. For dinner, try the popular specials rather than ordering off the menu ($7.50–18.)

In Edgartown

☞✐ **Among the Flowers** (627-3233), Mayhew Lane, off North Water Street. Open for breakfast and lunch, May through October, and dinner in July and August. This small café has been under the same ownership since 1981 and much of the staff has been here for years. Perhaps that's why this is one of the friendliest places on-island. And if that weren't enough, prices are the most reasonable in Edgartown ($4–10 for lunch, $7–12 for dinner). There aren't many indoor tables, but there is an outdoor patio, enclosed during inclement weather. A variety of light meals are offered, from excellent omelets and corn chowder, to peanut butter and jelly for the young, crêpes, salads, quiches, and ice cream. Even the cappuccino is good.

☞ **Truly Scrumptious** (627-3990), 11 South Summer Street. Open for lunch and dinner until 8, early May to mid-October. This small, countryish, storefront café makes "truly scrumptious" dishes. Light fare might include quiche with spinach and goat cheese, Thai chicken salad, or couscous with shrimp, eggplant, zucchini, and squash. Dinner is more substantial: poached salmon fillets or fish kabobs. Dishes are served on paper plates and with plastic utensils because of zoning issues, but that doesn't diminish the savory flavors. $5–10.

Menemsha Harbor remains an active fishing village.

☞❋ **The Newes from America** (627-4397), 23 Kelley Street. Open 11–11 daily for lunch and dinner year-round. The food is good for pub grub— renowned burritos, as well as burgers and sandwiches. The Newes's motto, printed on the menu, sums up the clientele: "You can never be too tan or have too many blue blazers." About $8 per person.

❋   **Breezes** (627-7000), 131 North Water Street, at the Harbor View Hotel. Open 11–10 daily, year-round. This casual pub serves light fare like crab and Asiago crostini, a turkey and Swiss sandwich, swordfish steak with lime and banana chips, and clams from the raw bar. Order takeout so you can eat on the veranda overlooking the bluff and lighthouse. $7–12.

Carolina's (627-8857), Upper Main Street. Open for dinner Thursday through Sunday, May to late October, and lunch and dinner daily in-season. A southern barbecue on the Vineyard? You bet, and with all the trimmings. The menu features hearty sandwiches, as well as grilled smoked chicken, chicken and ribs combo plates, brisket, and pulled pork. There's plenty of parking, since Carolina's is on the edge of town. Carolina's smokes meat every day in-season, but not as often once the crowds start thinning out. $3–18.

☞✐❋ **Main Street Diner** (627-9337), 65 Main Street, Old Post Office Square. Open for all three meals daily, year-round (closed Sunday at 2 in the off-season.) New in 1995, Nancy and Wayne Talley's nostalgic 1950s-style diner is a fun place for kids because there's plenty to look at—from old signs to a jukebox. As for the actual dining, you've got your basic eggs, pancakes, grilled cheese, meat loaf, PB&J, and burgers. Parents won't mind the prices either: Most dishes are $3–5.

Up-island

Home Port (645-2679), North Road, Menemsha. Open for dinner, mid-April to mid-October. Views of Menemsha Creek are the big attraction at this local institution. It's a surf-and-turf kind of place, with lots of lobster, thick swordfish, steaks, and a raw bar. Frankly, some prefer to get takeout from the back door and enjoy a harbor view *from* the harbor. Reservations required. BYOB. Prix fixe $16–32.

✐ **The Aquinnah** (645-9654) on the cliffs, Gay Head. Open for breakfast, lunch, and dinner, mid-May to mid-October. Cantilevered over the cliffs of Gay Head, this restaurant's reason for being is simple: breathtaking views of the cliffs, ocean, and Elizabeth Islands. The food ranges from chowder and fish sandwiches to fried platters and lobster. BYOB. Lunch averages $10, dinner $17.

☞✐❈ **Back Alley's** (693-7366), West Tisbury. Open daily, year-round. Behind Alley's General Store (see *To See—Up-Island*), Back Alley's has sandwiches, salads, soups, and baked goods—perfect for bicyclists.

☞✐ **Menemsha Deli** (645-9902), Basin Road, Menemsha. Open for all three meals daily in summer. You needn't go hungry if you forgot to eat before heading up-island to explore. This place has dozens of sandwiches and specials from which to choose, all for about $5.

See also Larsen's Fish Market, below.

SNACKS

In Vineyard Haven

❈ **Black Dog Bakery** (693-4786), Water Street. Open daily year-round. At the Five Corners intersection near the Steamship Authority parking lot, the Black Dog is well positioned to accommodate the hungry hordes that arrive each day. Indeed, it is many visitors' first stop—for a cup of strong coffee and a sweet pastry, muffin, or other goodie.

❈ **Scottish Bakehouse** (693-1873), State Road (between Old County Road and Lambert's Cove Road); also at 3 Union Street Mall (693-5582), just off Main Street. Open year-round. Since 1963, Isabella Maxwell White's bakery has served some of the best shortbread west of the Highlands. The bakehouse also supplies the island with great sandwich breads, especially sourdough and Scottish Crusty loaves. Blueberry pies, scones, spinach quiche, meat pies, steak and kidney pies, too.

In Edgartown

Soigné (627-8489), 190 Upper Main Street. Open daily April through December. A connoisseur's deli just outside Edgartown, Soigné has all the makings for a gourmet picnic: the island's best take-out sandwiches, cold salads, and soups. Soigné also sells "designer" pastas, dried fruits, sauces, teas, and wines. It's a bit pricey, but worth it.

Mrs. Miller's Muffins (627-9608), 3 Dock Street. Open April to late November. Enormous muffins that aren't just for breakfast—they make a great treat when you can't face another ice cream cone. Mrs. Miller also offers soups, salads, and fresh-squeezed OJ.

Around the island

Mad Martha's has irresistible homemade ice cream and many locations: Union Street (693-5883), near the ferry, Vineyard Haven; North Water Street (627-8761) in Edgartown; and three parlors in Oak Bluffs: 117 Circuit Avenue (693-9151), Lake Avenue (693-5428) at the Coffee Shop, and Dockside Marketplace (no phone). Open late May to mid-October.

Up-island

☞ **Chilmark Store** (645-3739), State Road, near Beetlebung Corner, Chilmark. Open May to mid-October. This general store offers great pizzas and baked goods (especially the pies) in addition to conventional general-store items. (Rockers on the front porch are coveted.)

COFFEE

Espresso Love (627-9211), South Water Street. Open daily March through December. This tiny place makes the strongest cappuccino in town. Their pastries are among the sweetest.

❋ **Mocha Mott's Good Coffee** (696-1922), Circuit Avenue, Oak Bluffs. Open year-round. This tiny, aromatic basement café is where college students meet on their day off. The espresso is strong and flavorful.

FISH MARKETS

Larsen's Fish Market (645-2680), Dutcher's Dock, Menemsha. Open mid-April to late October. Swallow some oysters and cherrystones at the raw bar while you wait for your lobsters to be boiled. Then grab one of the picnic tables overlooking the fishing boats or head to the beach.

❋ **Poole's Fish** (645-2282), Dutcher's Dock, off Basin Road, Menemsha. Open year-round (daily April through November). Everett Poole has been selling fish since 1946. He also smokes his own fish and provides a small raw bar while you wait for your fish to go.

John's Fish Market (693-1220), 39 State Road, Tisbury. Open mid-April through mid-October.

TAKEOUT

Island Indulgence (693-4130). Open for dinner deliveries nightly year-round, lunch late May to early September. For all you house renters who don't want to leave the comfort of your home, these folks deliver meals from many local restaurants in Vineyard Haven, Oak Bluffs, and Edgartown. The charge is $4. Look for their menu book, which has 25 or so restaurants to choose from—many above restaurants participate.

See also Louis', Dee's Harbor Cafe, Papa's Pizza, Breezes, and Home Port under *Eating Out*.

ENTERTAINMENT

ARTS & MUSIC

Vineyard Playhouse (693-6450, 696-6300 box office), 24 Church Street, Vineyard Haven. This small, community-based group of professional actors, dancers, and musicians performs plays and musicals year-round.

The main stage is within a former Methodist meetinghouse. Tickets $25; preview tickets on first 2 nights of each show $12.50; rush tickets (remaining unsold tickets, 10 minutes prior to curtain) $15. Look for the varied lineup (Shakespeare or theater for younger folks) at the troupe's Tisbury Amphitheater.

The Yard (645-9662), Middle Road, near Beetlebung Corner, Chilmark. Late May to late September. Founded in 1973, this colony of performing artists is always engaging and appreciated. Choreography and dance are spirited. The Yard also holds community dance classes.

Chamber Music Society (645-9446). Year-round performances have been given since 1972. Look for the 10-concert summer series.

Band concerts. The location alternates between Ocean Park in Oak Bluffs and Owen Park in Vineyard Haven, but the time remains constant: Sunday evenings at 8 in July and August.

NIGHTLIFE

Wintertide Coffeehouse (693-8830), Five Corners, Vineyard Haven. Open daily except Monday, year-round. *Billboard* magazine rates Wintertide as "easily one of the top 10 coffeehouses in the country." This smoke-free and alcohol-free oasis is a classic venue for the singer-songwriter crowd, including Tom Paxton, Patty Larkin, and Robin Batteau. You never know who might pop in. Founded in 1978, this volunteer-run, nonprofit coffeehouse (sparingly decorated) also puts on an occasional poetry reading and authors' discussion. It's also a model of community service; over 250 programs are offered annually. The lunch and dinner menu extends to sandwiches, soups, and salads.

The Newes from America (627-4397), 23 Kelley Street, Edgartown. Open daily year-round. This colonial-era basement tavern is atmospheric and cozy, with hand-hewn beams. The Newes features micro-brews; try the specialty Rack of Beers, a sampler of five brews from the outstanding and unusual beer menu (see *Eating Out*).

Hot Tin Roof (693-1137), Martha's Vineyard Airport, Edgartown. Open May through October. When Carly Simon co-owned this club years ago, it was the coolest nightspot on the island. Then its popularity dipped. Now that she's affiliated with it again, it's back on the map. There are live bands and DJs, depending on the night.

David's Island House (693-4516), 120 Circuit Avenue, Oak Bluffs. May to mid-October. Stop in for a frozen mudslide at the renowned piano bar; the musical oeuvre varies nightly.

Atlantic Connection (693-7129), 124 Circuit Avenue, Oak Bluffs. Open year-round. The AC is the hottest nightclub on the island. Live bands, DJs, comedy, and reggae alternate nights.

Lampost/Rare Duck (696-9352), 111 Circuit Avenue. Open April through November. Live music or a DJ spinning tunes; either way, it's loud.

Ritz Cafe (693-9851), 1 Circuit Avenue. Open daily year-round. Locals hang out at this funky blues bar.

The Wharf (627-9966), Dock Street, Edgartown. Open year-round. Nightly in-season, there's live music at this popular pub by the wharf.

Boathouse Bar (627-4320), Lower Main Street, within the Navigator, Edgartown. Open May to mid-October. Sailing types stop here for cocktails when they dock—it's just a few boat-lengths from the harbor. Live entertainment nightly in summer.

SELECTIVE SHOPPING

ANTIQUES SHOP

C.W. Morgan Marine Antiques (693-3622), Beach Road. Open Thursday through Saturday April through December (also open Monday and Tuesday in summer). Frank Rapoza carries museum-quality marine paintings, instruments, prints, scrimshaw, porcelain, sea chests, lanterns, and other nautically inspired items.

ART GALLERIES

The Martha's Vineyard Center for the Visual Arts (645-9671; PO Box 4377, Vineyard Haven 02568) publishes an annual guide to artisans and art galleries. Serious collectors should pick one up.

Shaw Cramer Gallery (696-7323), 76 Main Street, Vineyard Haven. Open year-round. This fine contemporary crafts gallery carries an eclectic assortment: candlesticks, teapots, handmade paper, and tapestries.

Luce House Gallery (693-5353), Beach Road, Vineyard Haven. Gallery open May through December; classes year-round. Built in 1804, this house is one of the few that survived the Great Fire. It now houses a contemporary art gallery and holds summer art classes for children and year-round classes in a variety of media for all ages. All proceeds from the gallery fund the Dukes County Historical Society.

Vineyard Studio/Gallery (693-1338), 860 State Road (opposite Lambert's Cove Road), Vineyard Haven. Open mid-June to mid-September. Within this 18th-century barn, you'll find modern paintings, photographs, and sculpture. The shows change every 2 weeks and because this is a cooperative, artists are on hand to discuss their work.

Old Sculpin Gallery (627-4881), corner of Dock and Daggett Streets, Edgartown. Open late June to early September. Now operated by the nonprofit Martha's Vineyard Art Association, the building was originally Dr. Daniel Fisher's granary, then a boatbuilder's workshop. Look for the long, wide depression in the main room where boatbuilder Manuel Swartz Roberts's feet wore down the floor as he moved along his workbench during the early 20th century. Paintings and photographs of varying degrees of quality are exhibited.

Gardner-Colby Gallery (627-6002), 27 North Water Street, Edgartown. Open May through December. This large gallery represents local and national artists who depict Vineyard landscapes in various media.

Granary Gallery at the Red Barn Emporium (693-0455, 1-800-472-6279), Old County Road, West Tisbury. Open daily, late May to mid-October, year-round by appointment. In addition to folk art and landscape paintings, this gallery carries old and new photography. There are classic photos by the venerable *Life* magazine photographer Alfred Eisenstadt (who came to the island on assignment for *Life* in 1937 and vacationed here until his death in 1995) as well as photographer Alison Shaw's island scenes.

Field Gallery (693-5595), State Road, West Tisbury. Open mid-June to mid-September. This field of dancing white figures has become an icon of the Vineyard's cultural life. Tom Maley's joyful figures seem to be celebrating the beauty that surrounds them. Works of other Vineyard artists are exhibited during summer months; open-invitation artists receptions are held 5–7 on Sundays in July and August.

Gay Head Gallery (645-3634), State Road (between Lobsterville Road and the Gay Head Town Hall), Gay Head. Open late May to mid-October. In the mid-1980s, Bill Sargent and Megan Ottens converted their spacious old home into a stylish gallery featuring Vineyard landscapes, contemporary paintings, photography, jewelry, furniture, and sculpture. An engaging couple, Bill and Megan enjoy discussing the artists they represent. Even when a specific artist is featured, there is still a wide range of art displayed.

See also the Feast of Chilmark under *Dining Out*.

ARTISANS

Chilmark Pottery (693-6476), Field View Lane off State Road, West Tisbury. Open year-round. A few miles from Vineyard Haven, potter Geoffrey Borr's studio (in a big rustic barn) has doubled as a showroom since 1982. He and his apprentices are constantly busy throwing pots: functional mugs and goblets as well as fish-carved vases and hand-painted octopus plates. (The shop at 170 Circuit Avenue, Oak Bluffs, is open June to mid-October.)

Martha's Vineyard Glass Works (693-6026), State Road, West Tisbury. Open mid-May through October. Three designers share this dynamic studio, where you can watch the artists and apprentices working. The shop is a visual feast.

M.E. Pratt Bookbinder (645-3035), Moshup Trail, Gay Head. Open year-round, by appointment only. Using traditional 19th-century bookbinding materials, these folks create handbound journals, photo albums, and sketchbooks using a variety of materials—decorated paper, linen, leather, bark, wasps' nests. Stop in for a wonderfully tactile visit.

Hataraku Te (645-3517), PO Box 2245, Vineyard Haven 02568. Ethan Fierro crafts traditional Japanese furniture, builds meditation huts, balances rocks, cuts stones for elemental sculptures, and makes bamboo fencing. He doesn't have a shop per se; his "office" is a mobile meditation hut. *Hataraku Te,* by the way, means "hands in motion." His work is quietly expressive.

BOOKSTORES

Bickerton and Ripley (627-8463), Main Street at South Summer Street, Edgartown. Open April through December. A charming bookshop.

Bunch of Grapes Bookstore (693-2263), 68 Main Street, Vineyard Haven. Open year-round. A larger general bookstore.

CLOTHING

Black Dog General Store (696-8182), Water Street, Vineyard Haven. Open 10–6 daily, year-round. Buy your Black Dog T-shirt here. Then wash it repeatedly, but don't wear it for several years if you want to be *really* cool—regular Vineyard visitors consider it gauche to wear a Black Dog T-shirt in public before it has aged four or five years. Also sweatshirts, towels, caps, and so on.

The Great Put-On (627-5495), Mayhew Lane, Edgartown. Open May through October. The most fashionable clothing store on the island stocks an impressive selection of dressy clothing for women, more shoes for men than women, and unisex accessories like leather backpacks, loose jackets, and sweaters.

Pandora's Box (645-9696), Basin Road (off North Road), Menemsha. Open May to mid-October. The emphasis is on comfortable style— sweaters, jackets, and lounging clothes.

SPECIAL SHOPS

Allen Farm (645-9064), South Road (near Beetlebung Corner), Chilmark. Open late May to mid-November. This sheep farm is located on one of the most beautiful spots on the island, overlooking sloping meadows crisscrossed with stone walls, with the Atlantic Ocean as a backdrop. A diet of fresh sea air and dense grass makes for thick wool, which the Allens and their friends knit and weave into beautiful clothing.

Parton's Parcels (627-3307), West Tisbury. Open year-round; call to arrange a time to stop in, or drop by their booth at the West Tisbury Farmer's Market (see *Special Events*). At their small sheep and goat farm, Teena and Charlie Parton raise the animals for their fleece and spin the yarn themselves. If you want to purchase their fiber or yarn, they'll be happy to share knitting and weaving ideas. The Partons ran Alley's General Store for several years, so they're good sources of information about the island's history and people.

Chilmark Chocolates (645-3013), State Road, near Beetlebung Corner, Chilmark. Open irregular hours, days, and months. Rich and creamy truffles, lollipops, and other assorted sweets.

Vineyard Photo (627-9537), Dock Street, Edgartown, and **Mosher Photo** (693-9430), 25 Main Street, Vineyard Haven are both open year-round for quickie film processing.

SPECIAL EVENTS

Throughout the year: **Mountain Bike Rides** (693-4905), Old Agricultural Hall, West Tisbury, every Sunday sponsored by the Vineyard Off Road Bicycle Association. **West Tisbury Farmer's Market,** at the West Tisbury Agricultural Hall, 9–noon Saturday, mid-June to mid-October, and 3–6 Wednesday late June to late August. **Chilmark Flea Market** (693-0085), Chilmark Community Church Grounds, every Saturday and Wednesday 8:30–3 from late June to late August. **Community Sings** (693-0525), Tabernacle, Methodist Campground, Oak Bluffs, every Wednesday at 8 PM in July and August.

Mid-July: **Edgartown Regatta.** Fifteen different classes of boats race.

Early August: **Edgartown House Tour.** This competitive event is limited to six houses each year, and the rivalries are fierce. Tea is served in the final house on the tour.

Early August: **Possible Dreams Auction,** Harborside Inn, Edgartown. Given the celebrity involvement, it's not surprising that national publicity usually surrounds this event. Celebrities offer "dreams" that vary from predictable to unusual. If you're the high bidder, you might win a tour of the *60 Minutes* studios with Mike Wallace; a sail with Walter Cronkite on his yacht; a seat at a Knicks game with Spike Lee; a song and a peanut butter sandwich from Carly Simon; or a lesson in chutzpah at the Five Corners intersection in Vineyard Haven with Alan Dershowitz. Longtime island celebrities see the auction as their chance to give back to the Vineyard—the auction raises money for Martha's Vineyard Community Services.

Mid-August: **Illumination Night.** The actual date is kept secret and varies each year, but the evening begins when a selected Oak Bluffs resident (usually the oldest) lights a single Japanese lantern after all the electric lights in town are turned off. Following this signal, the rest of the Oak Bluffs townspeople illuminate their cottages with lanterns and candles.

September: **Striped Bass and Bluefish Derby.** When dozens of surf casters begin furiously fishing from your favorite beach, you'll know it's Derby time. Prizes are awarded for the largest fish caught each day, with a grand prize for the largest fish caught during the monthlong tournament. Weighing is done in Edgartown Harbor.

Mid-September: **Tivoli Day.** The big event is a 62-mile bike race, the Tour of Martha's Vineyard (part of the Pro-Am tour), but there's also a lively street fair on Circuit Avenue in Oak Bluffs.

Late October: **Haunted Playhouse** (696-6300). A 4-day treat for kids at the Vineyard Playhouse.

VII. NANTUCKET

Thomas Macy II House on Main Street

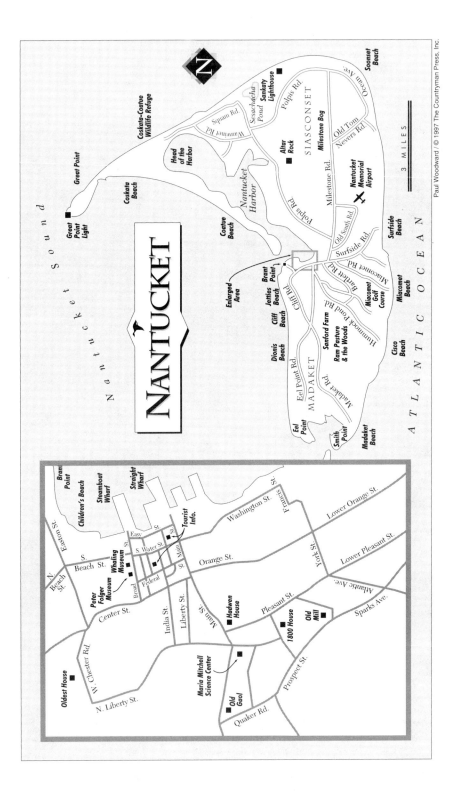

NANTUCKET

Nantucket

Thirty miles out to sea, Nantucket was called "that far away island" by Native Americans. Only 14 by 3½ miles long, Nantucket is simultaneously an island, a county, and a town. In 1659 Thomas Mayhew, who purchased Nantucket sight unseen (he was more interested in Martha's Vineyard), sold it to Tristram Coffin and eight of his friends for £30 and "two Beaver Hatts." These "original purchasers" quickly sold half-shares to craftsmen whose skills they would require to build a community. When Mayhew arrived, there were more than 3000 Native American residents, who taught the settlers about the crops to farm, how to raise sheep, and how to spear whales from shore. By the early 1700s, the number of settlers had grown to more than 300, and the number of Natives had shrunk to less than 800, primarily because of disease. (The last Native descendant died on-island in 1854.)

In 1712, when Captain Christopher Hussey's ship was blown out to sea, he inadvertently harpooned a sperm whale. For the next 150 years, whaling dominated the island's economy. The ensuing prosperity allowed the island's population to climb to 10,000. In comparison, there are 7000 year-rounders today.

Nantucket sea captains traveled the world to catch whales and to trade, and they brought back fortunes. By the late 1700s, trade was booming with England, and in 1791 the Beaver, owned by islander William Rotch, rounded Cape Horn and forged an American trade route to the Pacific Ocean. Fortunes were also made in the Indian Ocean—hence, Nantucket's India Street.

In its heyday, Nantucket Harbor overflowed with smoke and smells from blacksmith shops, cooperages, shipyards, and candle factories. More than 100 whaling ships sailed in and out of Nantucket. But when ships grew larger, to allow for their longer voyages at sea, they couldn't get across the shallow shoals and into Nantucket Harbor. The industry began moving to Martha's Vineyard and New Bedford. In 1846, at the height of the whaling industry, the Great Fire began in a hat shop on Main Street and ignited whale oil at the harbor. The catastrophic blaze wiped out the harbor and one-third of the town. Although the citizens began to rebuild immediately, other adventurous and energetic souls were enticed to go West in search of gold in 1849. And in the 1850s, kerosene replaced whale oil as a less expensive fuel, leveling the final blow to the island's maritime economy. By 1861 there were only 2000 people on-island.

Although tourism began soon after the Civil War and picked up with the advent of the railroad to 'Sconset, the island more or less lay in undisturbed isolation until the early 1970s. But perhaps it was the sleepiness of those 100 years that ultimately preserved the island's architectural integrity and community spirit, paving the way for its resurrection. In the late 1950s and early 1960s, islander Walter Beinecke Jr. organized a revitalization of the waterfront area, replacing decrepit wharf buildings with cottages. He also declared the premise that guides tourism to this day: It is preferable to attract one tourist with $100 than 100 tourists with $1 each. In accordance with the maxim, strict zoning laws were adopted, land conservation groups were launched, and Nantucket's upscale tourism industry began in earnest.

In 1966 Nantucket was declared a National Historic Landmark: It boasts more than 800 buildings built before 1850—the largest concentration of such buildings in the United States. The historic district is "picture perfect": paved cobblestone streets, brick sidewalks, electrified "gas" street lamps. Gray-shingled houses are nestled close together on narrow lanes, which wind as you amble beyond the downtown grid of streets. Sturdy white residences are trimmed with English boxwood hedges, white picket fences, and flower gardens.

With a summer population that swells to 40,000, today's tourist industry is about as well oiled as the whale industry was. It's difficult to find a grain of sand or a seashell that hasn't been discovered. Most sites in Nantucket are within a mile of the historic center—you'll probably walk a lot more than you're accustomed to. Although there are little pockets of settlements around the island, the only real "destination" is 'Sconset, an utterly quaint village with rose-covered cottages. But with more than one-third of the island's 10,000 acres held by conservation trusts, you'll be able to explore places where most tourists don't venture. In addition to outstanding historic houses (many of which have been turned into bed & breakfasts) and museums, the island boasts excellent bicycle paths and almost limitless public beaches. Nor is it an exaggeration to say that Nantucket prides itself on world-class dining.

Nantucket is a year-round destination. Millions of daffodils blanket the island in yellow as the earth reawakens each April. Where once there were whaling ships, yachts now fill the harbor in summer. Warm ocean water and beach barbecues beckon, wild roses trail along picket fences, and hundreds of special events are staged. Come September (my favorite month on-island), the crowds recede. You can swim in the still-temperate ocean by day and not have to wait for a table at your favorite restaurant at night. Skies turn crisp blue, and cranberry bogs, heathlands, and the moors blaze red, russet, and maroon. Before the monochrome days of winter set in, there is one last burst of activity: the monthlong Nantucket Noel and Christmas Stroll (see *Special Events*). In January, February, and March you'll discover why whaling captains called the island the "little grey lady"—she is often shrouded in fog. It's a time of reflection and renewal for year-rounders and visitors alike.

GUIDANCE

Nantucket Visitor Services & Information Bureau (228-0925), 25 Federal Street. Open 9–6 daily, year-round, until 9 PM Monday through Saturday in-season. Seasonal special events are posted and there is a rack of brochures, but best of all is the very helpful staff. The bureau also maintains seasonal kiosks at Steamboat Wharf, Straight Wharf, and Nantucket Memorial Airport. The bureau has information on daily vacancies at guest houses, but I don't recommend you wait until you're on-island to locate a place to stay.

Nantucket Island Chamber of Commerce (228-1700), 48 Main Street. On the second floor, the chamber is open year-round 9–5 weekdays. It produces a glossy, free book, *The Official Guide: Nantucket.*

Nantucket Historical Association (NHA) (228-1894), 2 Whaler's Lane. The NHA, which celebrated its centennial in 1994 and owns 14 historic properties, is a great source of historical information. NHA properties represent island life from its farming beginnings to its prosperous whaling days. As you walk around Nantucket, notice the small, round plaques—made of different materials—that date the houses: 17th century (silver), 1700–1775 (bronze), 1776–1812 (brass), 1813–1846 (green), and 1847–1900 (black). Generally, the NHA properties are open 10–5 daily, mid-June to early September, with shorter hours from late May to mid-June and from early September to mid-October. Since the hours change from year to year, it's best to stop in or call ahead. Combination ticket valid for admission to all properties, all seasons: adults $10, children 5–14 $5. Purchase combination tickets at the Nantucket Whaling Museum on Broad Street.

Island Web Site: http://www.nantucket.net.

PUBLIC REST ROOMS

Rest rooms are located at the Information Bureau on Federal Street (open year-round), and at Children's Beach and Straight Wharf (both open seasonally).

GETTING THERE

By boat from Hyannis: **The Steamship Authority** (477-8600 for advance auto reservations; 771-4000 for day-of-sailing information in Hyannis; 228-0262 for information on Nantucket), South Street Dock, Hyannis. The Steamship Authority, established in 1948, carries autos, people, and bikes to Nantucket's Steamship Wharf from Hyannis year-round. Make car reservations in spring for summer if you can; no advance reservations are needed for passengers. In the high season there are six sailings per day, in the off-season three. Parking in Hyannis is $6–7.50

per calendar day. The voyage takes 2¼ hours. Round-trip fares: adults $20, children 5–12 $10, free under age 5; bicycles $10; automobiles $180 mid-May to mid-October, $140 mid-March to mid-May and mid-October through December.

There are lockers at the Steamship terminal for storing luggage.

Hy-Line Cruises (778-2600 in Hyannis; 228-3949 on Nantucket), Ocean Street Dock, Hyannis, transports passengers and bicycles to Nantucket's Straight Wharf, early May through October. In summer there are six boats daily, one to three daily in the off-season. There is a first-class lounge aboard the M/V *Great Point* if you don't mind paying $42 round-trip. Otherwise, round-trip fares are adults $22, children 4–12 $11, bicycles $9. Parking in Hyannis is $6–9 per calendar day.

Hy-Line's *Grey Lady* (778-0404, 1-800-492-8082 within Massachusetts), Ocean Street Dock. This high-speed catamaran makes year-round trips to Nantucket in 1 hour, but for a price: $52 adults, $39 children 12 and under.

By boat from Harwich: **Freedom Cruise Line** (432-8999), Saquatucket Harbor in Harwichport provides daily passenger service to Nantucket, mid-May to mid-October and during the Christmas Stroll (see *Special Events*). Two of the three trips are scheduled so you can explore Nantucket for about 6 hours and return the same day. Advance reservations are highly recommended. Round-trip prices: adults $29, children 4–12 $18; bicycles $10. Free parking for the first 24 hours; $8 per day thereafter.

By boat from Martha's Vineyard: **Hy-Line Cruises** (778-2600 in Hyannis; 228-3949 on Nantucket; 693-0112 in Oak Bluffs, Martha's Vineyard) offers one daily, interisland departure from early June to mid-September. (There is no interisland car ferry. From the Vineyard, you must take the ferry back to Falmouth or Woods Hole and drive your car to Hyannis—30 to 45 minutes—if you want to take your car to Nantucket.) Adults $22, children 5–12 $11, bicycles $9.

By air: **Cape Air** (228-7695, 1-800-352-0714) offers more than 100 daily flights direct from Boston, Hyannis, New Bedford, and Martha's Vineyard. Frequent-flyer coupon books for 10 one-way trips are available. Cape Air merged with **Nantucket Airlines** (790-0300, 1-800-635-8787 within Massachusetts) to provide even more year-round flights from Hyannis. Round-trip summer fares $99–119 from New Bedford, $62 from Hyannis, $169–199 from Boston, and $68 from Martha's Vineyard. **Island Air** (228-7575, 1-800-248-7779) offers daily, year-round flights from Hyannis. Flight time is 20 minutes and fares are competitive. **Colgan Air** (325-5100, 1-800-272-5488) offers year-round service from Nantucket to Hyannis ($60 round-trip) and Newark, New Jersey ($220–315 round-trip). **Business Express/Delta Connection** (1-800-345-3400) flies from Boston year-round and from La Guardia seasonally. **Northwest Airlink** (1-800-225-2525) flies through Boston seasonally. **Continental Express** (1-800-525-0280) flies from Newark,

New Jersey, in-season. **Ocean Wings** (325-5548, 1-800-253-5039) and **Coastal Air** (228-3350, 1-800-262-7858) offer charter flights.

GETTING AROUND

By shuttle: **NRTA Shuttle** (228-7025), Salem and Broad Streets. June through September. This is an economical and reliable way to travel; the buses run daily 7 AM–11:30 PM. The 'Sconset bus runs every hour on the hour and the Madaket route runs every 30 minutes on the quarter hour. Fares are $1 each way. The Miacomet route is traveled every 15 minutes and the short South Loop every 10 minutes. These fares are $.50 each way. Many shuttles have a bike rack, so you can take the bus out to 'Sconset, for instance, and ride back.

By car: There isn't a single traffic light in Nantucket, and Nantucketers intend to keep it that way. You really don't need a car unless you're here for at least a week or unless you plan to spend most of your time in conservation areas or on outlying beaches. Even then, a four-wheel-drive vehicle is the most useful, since many of the stunning natural areas are off sandy paths. Parking is definitely limited in the historic center. Rent from **Nantucket Windmill Auto Rental** (228-1227, 1-800-228-1227), based at the airport and offering free pickup and delivery of vehicles; **Nantucket Jeep Rental** (228-1618, 1-800-228-1227), which also delivers; **Affordable Rentals** (228-3501), South Beach Street; and **Young's** (228-1151), Steamboat Wharf. **Budget** (228-5666) and **Hertz** (228-9421) are based at the airport. Rental cars ($45–60 a day in summer, $40 in the off-season) disappear quickly in summer, but four-wheel-drives ($125–150 per day in-season, $80–100 off-season) go even faster. Reserve four-wheel-drives at least a month in advance of summer. Renting a car for a couple of days is still cheaper than bringing your own over on the ferry.

Contact the **Police Department** (228-1212), South Water Street, for overland permits, which are required for all four-wheel, over-sand driving: $20 for private vehicles per year. Purchase them on weekdays only. The Coatue–Coskata–Great Point nature area (see *Green Space*) requires a separate permit, available from the **Nantucket Conservation Foundation** (228-2884 for information; 228-0006 for the refuge gatehouse, where permits are purchased daily, mid-May through October): $20 per day for rental vehicles; $75 per year. At other times during the year, pay the rangers who may patrol the area. Most beaches are open to four-wheel-drive traffic, except when terns are nesting.

By taxi: Taxi fares can add up, but cabs are a useful way to get to the airport or to an outlying restaurant. Taxis usually line up on lower Main Street and at Steamboat Wharf. Flat rates are based on the destination: $11 to 'Sconset, $7 to the airport, and $3 within town, for instance. Rates are for one person; add $1 for each additional person.

By bicycle: Bicycling is the best way to get around the island (see *To Do—Bicycling/Rentals*).

Nantucket, often called the "little grey lady," is shrouded in fog.

Van or bus tours: **Gail's Tours** (257-6557), run by seventh-generation Nantucketer Gail Nickerson Johnson, offers year-round, 90-minute narrated van tours for up to 13 people. Tours leave at 10 AM, 1 PM, and 3 PM from the Information Bureau on Federal Street (see *Guidance*). Gail's tour is the best offered; she gives tidbits of trivia, both historic and contemporary, that will bring the island alive. You can even jump out for photo opportunities. Hers is a unique perspective; her mother began giving tours in the mid-1950s. $10 per person; reservations advised.

Bob Pitman Grimes (228-9382), Lower Main Street, also offers a good van tour for up to eight people, departing at the same times as Gail's Tours. $10 per person, tours year-round.

Ara's Tours (228-1951), early April to early January. These late-afternoon, 3-hour barrier beach tours of Great Point seem to attract a lot of photographers and outdoors types. $40 per person.

Barrett's Tours (228-0174, 1-800-773-0174 in eastern Massachusetts), 20 Federal Street, and **Nantucket Island Tours** (228-0334), Straight Wharf, offer 90-minute narrated minibus tours April to early December. Cost: $10 adults, half-price for children. Barrett's also operates the regularly scheduled Surfside Beach bus that departs from 20 Federal Street every hour on the quarter hour, late June to early September. Round-trip fare is $3; children half-price.

By foot: **Walking Tours of Nantucket** (228-1062) is run by longtime islander and former municipal officeholder Roger Young. The most entertaining tour of the historic district, his is a leisurely 2-hour stroll, with anecdotes you wouldn't possibly read in a guidebook (even this one). Daily at 9:30 or 1:30, mid-May through September: $10 adults, children negotiable.

By carriage: **Carried Away** (228-0218), 15 Broad Street, offers horse-drawn carriage rides, with Sarah Tomkins, through the historic center and out to the moors during summer. $50 per hour for one to four people. Tomkins also offers Victorian Outings, an old-fashioned picnic with wholesome foods, linens, and the like, for about $200—2 hours, two people, food included.

MEDICAL EMERGENCY

Nantucket Cottage Hospital (228-1200), South Prospect Street. Open 24 hours.

TO SEE

On the harbor

The wharves (from north to south). The Steamship Authority is based at Steamboat Wharf; but from 1881 to 1917, steam trains (they met the early steam-powered ferries and transported passengers to Surfside and 'Sconset) originated here. **Old North Wharf** is home to privately owned summer cottages. **Straight Wharf**, originally built in 1723 by Richard Macy, is a center of activity. It was completely rebuilt in the 1960s (except for the Thomas Macy Warehouse) as part of an effort to preserve the town. The wharf is home to Hy-Line, a few T-shirt and touristy shops, restaurants, a gallery, a museum, a nice pavilion area, and charter boats and sailboats. Straight Wharf was so-named because one could cart things from here "straight" up Main Street. **Old South Wharf** houses art galleries, crafts shops, and clothing shops in quaint little one-room "shacks" (see *Selective Shopping*). **Commercial Wharf**, also known as Swain's Wharf, was built in the early 1800s by Zenas Coffin.

Thomas Macy Warehouse (228-3899), Straight Wharf. Built after the Great Fire of 1846, when the wharves were completely destroyed and more than 400 houses burned, the warehouse stored supplies to outfit ships. Today, the second floor serves as a visitors center, and provides an orientation to the NHA's historic properties and an introduction to the island's history. Free.

Main Street

Main Street. The lower three blocks of Main Street were paved in 1837 with cobblestones brought to Nantucket as ballast from England. Cobblestones proved quite useful—they kept carts laden with whale oil from sinking into the sand and dirt as they were rolled from the wharves to the factories. After the Great Fire swept through town, Main Street was widened considerably to prevent another fire from jumping from house to house so rapidly. In the mid-1850s Henry and Charles Coffin planted dozens of elm trees along the street, but only a few have survived disease over the years. The former drinking fountain for horses, which today spills over with flowers, has been a landmark on Lower Main since it was moved here in the early 1900s.

Pacific Club, Main Street at South Water Street. This three-story, Georgian brick building was built as a warehouse and countinghouse for shipowner William Rotch, owner of the *Beaver* and *Dartmouth,* two ships that took part in the Boston Tea Party. In 1789 it served as a U.S. Customs House. In 1861 a group of retired whaling captains purchased the building for use as a private social club, where they swapped stories and played cribbage. Descendants of these original founders carry on the tradition of the elite club.

Pacific National Bank (228-1917), 61 Main Street at Fair Street. Anchoring the other end of this section of Main Street is this two-story, 1818 Federal-style building, one of only four brick buildings to survive the Great Fire. This bank almost single-handedly financed the wealthy whaling industry. Step inside to see the handsome main room, original teller cages, and murals of the port and street scenes. It's no coincidence that the two important buildings anchoring Main Street are named Pacific for the fortunes reaped from the Pacific Ocean.

Thomas Macy II House, 99 Main Street. Many think this is Nantucket's most attractive doorway, with its silver doorplate, porch railing that curves outward, and wooden fan work above the doorway.

"Three Bricks," 93, 95, and 97 Main Street. These identical Georgian mansions were built in 1836 for the three sons (all under the age of 27) of whaling-ship magnate Joseph Starbuck. Joseph retained the titles to the houses to ensure that his sons continue the family business. When the sons approached age 40 (firmly entrenched in the business), Joseph deeded the houses to them. One house remains in the Starbuck family; none is open to the public.

Hadwen House (228-1894), 96 Main Street. Taken together, 94 Main (privately owned) and 96 Main are referred to architecturally as the "Two Greeks." Candle merchant William Hadwen married one of Joseph Starbuck's daughters and built this Greek Revival house (#96). (Starbuck's two other daughters also ended up living across the street from their brothers—at 92 and 100 Main Street—creating a virtual Starbuck compound.) Docents point out gas chandeliers, a circular staircase, Italian marble fireplaces, silver doorknobs, and period furnishings. Don't overlook the lovely historic garden in back. The "other" Greek (#94) was built in the mid-19th century for Mary G. Swain, Starbuck's niece; note the Corinthian capitals supposedly designed after the Temple of the Winds in Athens. NHA property (see *Guidance* for hours); $3 adults, $2 children.

Henry Coffin House and **Charles Coffin House,** 75 and 78 Main Street. The Coffin brothers inherited their fortunes from their father's candle-making and whaling enterprises and general mercantile business. They built their houses across the street from each other, using the same carpenters and masons. Charles was a Quaker, and his Greek Revival house (#78) has a simple roof walk and modest brown trim. Henry's late Federal-style house (#75) has fancy marble trim around the front door and a cupola.

John Wendell Barrett House, 72 Main Street. This elegant Greek Revival house features a front porch with Ionic columns and a raised basement. Barrett was the president of the Pacific National Bank and a wealthy whale-oil merchant, but the house is best known for another reason. During the Great Fire, Barrett's wife, Lydia, refused to leave the front porch. Firefighters wanted to blow up the house in order to deprive the fire of fuel. Luckily for her, the winds shifted and further confrontation was averted.

North of Main Street

✳☞✎**Atheneum** (228-1110), Lower India Street. Open year-round. This fine Greek Revival building with Ionic columns was designed by Frederick Coleman, who designed the "Two Greeks" (see Hadwen House). When the library and all its contents were lost in the Great Fire, a new building replaced it within 6 months; donations poured in from around the country. The Great Hall on the second floor hosted such distinguished orators as Frederick Douglass, Daniel Webster, Horace Greeley, Henry David Thoreau, Ralph Waldo Emerson (who gave the inaugural address), and John James Audubon. (The hall seats about 100 people; there are numerous free readings and lectures here.) Maria Mitchell (see Maria Mitchell Association) was the first librarian. Since then there have only been five other librarians in the course of its long history. In addition to comfortable reading rooms on both floors, the Atheneum has an excellent children's wing and a nice garden out back. Some of the more than 40,000 volumes include town newspapers dating back to 1816, early New England genealogy, and ships' logs. Portraits of whaling captains grace the space, while display cases are filled with scrimshaw and other historical artifacts. This is one of the island's most special places. It's a quiet refuge from the masses in the height of summer, as well as a delightful place to spend a rainy day. Call for hours and for information about special events and story hours (see *To Do—For Families*).

Nantucket Whaling Museum (228-1736), Broad Street. Open late April through October. This 1846 brick building began as Richard Mitchell's spermaceti candle factory. (Spermaceti, by the way, is a substance found in the cavity of a sperm whale's head; it was a great source of lamp and machine oil.) Now the building houses an outstanding museum preserving Nantucket's whaling history. It's a must-see on even the shortest itinerary. Exhibits include the lens from the Sankaty Lighthouse, a 43-foot skeleton of a finback whale (beached in the 1960s), lightship basket and scrimshaw collections, an around-the-world map tracing the voyages of the whaling ship *Alpha,* and a reproduction tryworks, which was used to boil down whale oil onboard ships. You'll also see a fully rigged whale boat, which will help you envision the treacherous "Nantucket sleigh ride": When the small boat harpooned a mammoth whale and remained connected by a rope, the boat was dragged through the waves until the whale tired. Daily lectures are offered by museum staff. NHA property (see *Guidance* for hours); adults $5, children $3.

Edouard A. Stackpole Library and Research Center (228-1655), 15 Broad Street. The museum displays an outstanding collection of manuscripts, photographs, ships' logs, and other items from the research center's archives, located on the second floor. The center is open only to researchers; $5 per day. NHA property (see *Guidance* for hours).

Peter Foulger Museum (228-1894), 15 Broad Street. Peter Foulger, not so incidentally, was one of the island's first settlers; he acted as an interpreter when the first settlers were purchasing the island from the Natives in 1659. His daughter Abiah was Ben Franklin's mother. The NHA displays its extensive collections in the exhibit "Away Off Shore," which covers the island's major historical periods. NHA property (see *Guidance* for hours); adults $3, children $2.

Centre Street. Centre Street was referred to as Petticoat Row during the whaling era, when men were out to sea and women were left to run the shops and businesses. It's still chock-full of fine shops.

☞ **First Congregational Church** (228-0950), 62 Centre Street. Open 10–4 Monday through Saturday, mid-June through September; 6–8 PM Wednesdays in July and August. This church is known for its 120-foot steeple, from which there are stunning 360-degree panoramic views of the island and ocean. On a clear day you can see from Eel Point to Great Point, and the moors in between. The present steeple was built in 1968; the previous one was dismantled in 1849 when it was deemed too shaky to withstand storms. The church was built with whaling money in 1834, at the height of the industry, and before you leave, note two of the things money could buy: a 600-pound brass chandelier and trompe l'oeil walls. The rear wing of the church contains the simple vestry, the oldest church building on the island (circa 1720). Since the late 1970s a special concert has been given in early July on Rose Sunday, when the church interior and island are full of blooming wild roses. Donation of $1.50 suggested to climb to the top of the steeple.

Oldest House (228-1894), Sunset Hill Road. Also known as the Jethro Coffin House, this 1686 house was built as a wedding present for Jethro Coffin and Mary Gardner Coffin by their parents. The marriage joined two prominent island families—the Coffins were "original purchasers" while the Gardners were "half-share men." When lightning struck the house in 1987, the NHA decided it was time to restore it. Features include small, diamond-shaped, leaded windows, sparse period furnishings, and a huge central chimney decorated with an upside-down horseshoe. Peter Coffin cut and shipped timbers from his land in Exeter,

New Hampshire, for the house. NHA property (see *Guidance* for hours); adults $3, children $2.

Brant Point Lighthouse, off Easton Street. In 1746 the island's first "lighthouse" (and the country's second oldest after Boston Light) guarded the harbor's northern entrance. It was rather primitive, consisting of a lantern hung on rope between two poles. The lighthouse standing today is small in size but large in symbolism. Folklore and tradition suggest that throwing two pennies overboard as you round the point at the lighthouse ensures your return. Many do, and many do.

Near or Off Upper Main Street

Quaker Meeting House (228-0136), 11 Fair Street. Open mid-June to mid-September. This small, simple building with wooden benches and 12-over-12 windows began as a Friends school in 1838. NHA property (see *Guidance* for hours); free.

Fair Street Museum (228-0722), 11 Fair Street. This concrete building looks out of place on Nantucket, but the museum houses changing exhibits from the NHA's permanent collection of paintings (including works by John Singleton Copley and Gilbert Stuart) and other artwork. NHA property (see *Guidance* for hours); adults $3, children $2.

St. Paul's Episcopal Church (228-0916), 20 Fair Street. Open 9–6 daily, year-round. Stop in to admire this granite church's Tiffany windows.

Unitarian Universalist Church (228-5466), 11 Orange Street. Open July to mid-September. Orange Street was once home to more than 100 whaling captains. This 1809 church, also called South Church, is known for its tall spire (quite visible at sea and a distinct part of the Nantucket "skyline"); a wonderfully illusory trompe l'oeil golden dome; and a mahogany and ivory 1831 Goodrich organ. For years, a town crier watched for ships and fires from the tower. Free.

Macy-Christian House (228-1894), 12 Liberty Street. This circa-1740 two-story lean-to was built by Thomas Macy, and it stayed in the family until 1827. The upstairs bedrooms remain the most Colonial part of the house. When the Reverend Mr. Christian purchased the house in 1934, he renovated much of the house in Colonial Revival style. Docents help you sort out what belongs to which period. NHA property (see *Guidance* for hours); adults $3, children $2.

The Coffin School (228-2505), Winter Street. Open daily from late May to mid-October. The school was founded in 1827 by Admiral Sir Isaac Coffin, English Baronet and descendant of Tristram Coffin, one of the island's first settlers. It was established to provide a "good English education" to Coffin descendants. (In the early 19th century, more than half of Nantucket's children were Coffin descendants. At the time, there was no public schooling, only "cent schools," where parents would pay a penny a day for schooling.) The impressive brick Greek Revival building now serves as home for the Egan Institute of Maritime Studies. Featured is a fine collection of 19th-century paintings, including works by Elizabeth R. Coffin, a student of Thomas Eakin. Admission $1.

Beyond Upper Main Street

Fire Hose Cart House (228-1894), 8 Gardner Street. This small 1886 neighborhood fire station is the only one of its kind remaining. As you can imagine, lots of stations were built after the Great Fire. On display are leather buckets and an old hand pumper from 'Sconset, used more than 100 years ago. NHA property (see *Guidance* for hours); free.

Old Gaol (228-1894), 15R Vestal Street. This 1805 penal institution, built of logs bolted together with iron, was used until 1933. It had only four cells. The first incarcerated felon escaped, but others weren't so lucky. Well, perhaps, they were—it's said that most of the prisoners got to sleep at home rather than on the planks that served as beds. NHA property (see *Guidance* for hours); free.

Maria Mitchell Association (228-9198), 2 Vestal Street. Founded in 1902, the association owns the following five properties that celebrate the life and continue the work of Maria (pronounced Mar-EYE-a) Mitchell, born on-island August 1, 1818. At age 13 Maria helped whaling captains set their navigational devices, with the aid of astronomical projections. At 18 she became the librarian at the Atheneum, where she served for the next 20 years. At 29, Mitchell was the first woman to discover a comet (which was dubbed Mitchell's comet)—from atop the Pacific National Bank, where her father (bank president and amateur astronomer) had set up an observatory. Maria was also the first woman to be admitted to the American Academy of Arts and Sciences and the first woman college professor of astronomy (she taught at Vassar from 1865 until she died in 1888). The association hosts a number of children's programs, which foster an appreciation of the connection between science and "beauty and poetry." A combination ticket for the properties (available at any of the properties) costs $5 for adults and $2 for children, but tickets may also be purchased separately.

Maria Mitchell Birthplace (228-2896), 1 Vestal Street. Open 10–4 Tuesday through Saturday, mid-June through August. Built in 1790, Mitchell's birthplace contains family memorabilia and the telescope she used to spot her comet. Tour the house and check out the island's only public roof walk. Adults $3, children $1.

❋ **Maria Mitchell Science Library** (228-9219), 2 Vestal Street. Open 10–4 Tuesday through Saturday, mid-June to mid-September, and 2–5 Wednesday through Friday and 9–noon on Saturday, mid-September to mid-June. The library, which has a children's section, houses 19th-century science books, current scientific periodicals, Maria's own papers, and natural-history and astronomy books. Maria's father taught sailors how to navigate by the stars in this former schoolhouse. Free.

✎ **Hinchman House** (228-0898), 7 Milk Street. Open 10–4 Tuesday through Saturday, mid-June through August. This natural-science museum has live reptiles and preserved plant and bird specimens from the island.

Inquire about excellent nature programs and field trips for children. Adults $3, children $1.

Loines Observatory (228-8690), Milk Street Extension. The observatory is closed to the public except on clear Monday through Wednesday evenings in summer, when lectures and telescope viewings are held.

Aquarium (228-5387), 28 Washington Street. Open 10–4 Tuesday through Saturday, mid-June through August. Near the town pier, the small Aquarium has fresh- and saltwater tanks; science interns are on hand to answer questions you may have. Admission $1. Popular marine-life collecting trips are offered Tuesday through Thursday and Saturday; reservations recommended.

Old Mill (228-1894), South Mill and Prospect Streets. Reputed to be made with salvaged wood, this 1746 Dutch-style windmill has canvas sails and a granite stone that is still used to grind corn in summer. A reminder of the days when the island's principal activity was farming, this windmill is the only one of four that remains. (It's in its original location, too.) It's also one of the oldest in the country. NHA property (see *Guidance* for hours); adults $3, children $2.

African Meeting House (no telephone), York and Pleasant Streets. Built as a schoolhouse in the 1820s when black children were barred from public school, this house is thought to be the second oldest such building in the country. Currently undergoing restoration, it will be open in the near future as an educational center with interpretive exhibits on the island's African American and Cape Verdean communities. Nantucket Visitor Services publishes a pamphlet with a walking tour of the island's black heritage sites.

Moor's End, 19 Pleasant Street. This large 1830s Georgian house, the first on-island to be built of brick, belonged to Jared Coffin. Although it is today considered to be among the island's finest, Mrs. Coffin was not satisfied with its location. She wanted to be closer to town and so Jared built another at 29 Broad Street (see Jared Coffin House under *Lodging—Inns*). A beautiful garden lies behind the tall brick wall, but unfortunately for us, like the house, it's private.

Around the island

Siasconset. More commonly referred to as 'Sconset, this charming village on the eastern shore is the island's only real "destination," 7 miles from town. (Well, for the adventuresome, Great Point is the other "destination.")The village is renowned for its tiny rose-covered cottages, all quite close to one another. Some of the oldest are clustered on Broadway, Center, and Shell Streets. You won't have any problem finding them since the town only consists of a post office, a liquor store, a market, and three restaurants (see *Dining Out*). Of course, 'Sconset has its share of grand summer homes— along Ocean Avenue and Sankaty and Baxter Roads (on the way to Sankaty Lighthouse). Recently, the combination of severe winter storms and the absence of offshore shoals (to break the incoming waves) has

Nantucket Lifesaving Museum

created extreme beach erosion. A couple of homes had to be moved; many more are in danger.

Siasconset, which means "land of many bones," was probably named after a right whale was found ashore. The 17th-century village was settled by and used as a base for fishermen in search of cod and whales. When wives began to join their husbands here in summer, the one-room shanties were expanded with additions called warts. (Perhaps the early summer visitors wanted to escape the burning oil refineries in town, too.) When the narrow-gauge railway was built in 1884, among the new summer visitors it brought were actors from New York City, who established a thriving actors colony. It's hard to imagine that today there are 150 hardy souls who live here year-round.

A few "sites" in 'Sconset include the 'Sconset Pump, an old wooden water pump dug in 1776, and the 'Sconset Union Chapel, the only place of worship in town. Despite its name, the Siasconset Casino, built in 1899 as a private tennis club, has never been used for gambling. Actors who flocked here at the turn of the century used it for summer theater; movies are now shown in summer (see *Entertainment—Theater/Film*).

Sankaty Light, 'Sconset. Partially solar powered, this red-and-white-striped light stands on a 90-foot-high bluff at the edge of a rapidly encroaching shoreline. Its light is visible 30 miles out to sea.

Great Point Light, Great Point, is accessible by four-wheel-drive vehicle or a difficult 5-mile (one-way) trek through soft sand. A 70-foot stone structure guarded the northeastern tip of the island from 1818 until a ferocious storm destroyed it in 1984. This new one was built to withstand 20-foot waves and 240-mph winds.

Madaket. When Thomas Macy landed here in 1659, he found sandy, poor soil and didn't stay long. Today there is a large summer community, with many houses available for rent. On the western coast, Madaket is a great place to enjoy the sunset, do some bluefishing, or get a boat repaired in the boatyard. The picturesque creek is best viewed from the little bridge to the right of the main road.

Nantucket Lifesaving Museum (228-1885), Polpis Road on Folger's Marsh. Open 10–5 daily, mid-June to mid-October. This 1874 building is a re-creation of the original Surfside Lifesaving Service station. Instead of being at water's edge, however, this station is scenically situated at the edge of a pond—a nice place for a picnic. Dedicated to the drama of man's efforts against the relentless sea, this museum houses two lifesaving surfboats, buoys, photographs, accounts of rescues, artifacts from the *Andrea Doria,* which sank off Nantucket 40 years ago, and equipment used in the daring rescues of sailors stranded in their boats, sinking offshore. Note the Coast Guard beach cart still used to demonstrate the beach apparatus drill. Admission $3 adults, $2 children over 5.

TO DO

BICYCLING/RENTALS

Excellent paved, two-way bicycle paths lead to most major "destinations."

Madaket Bike Path begins on Upper Main Street. This 6-mile (one-way) road takes you to the western end of the island in about 45 minutes. Although the route is a bit hilly and winding, it's beautiful. There are rest areas along the way and a water fountain at the halfway point. Picnic tables at Long Pond, and usually elegant swans, too.

'Sconset (or **Milestone**) **Bike Path** begins at the rotary east of the historic district. This 7-mile (one-way) route with slight inclines runs parallel to Milestone Road, forests, bogs, and moors; it takes about an hour to get to 'Sconset. There's a water fountain at the rotary.

Surfside Bike Path. Take Main Street to Pleasant Street and turn right on Atlantic Avenue to Surfside Road. There are benches and water fountains along the 3-mile (one-way) route. This flat route is very popular in summer; it takes about 20 minutes to get to the beach.

Polpis Road. There has been talk for years about a bike path for this road, lined with thousands of daffodils in springtime. The loop from the 'Sconset Bike Path to Polpis Road and back to town is about 16.5 miles. Construction on a Polpis bike path should be completed by late 1997.

Cliff Road Bike Path begins on Cliff Road from North Water Street. This 2.5-mile, slightly hilly road passes large summer houses.

With more than 3000 rental bikes on-island, companies offer competitive rates. Average prices: $16–20 per day for adult bikes (less in the off-season), $75 per week; $10–15 for children's bikes; $35–40 per day for tandems. Inquire about discounts for family rentals. The following shops rent bicycles: **Young's Bicycle Shop** (228-1151), Steamboat

Wharf, open year-round; **Nantucket Bike Shop** on Steamboat Wharf (228-1999), and on Straight Wharf (325-5898), open seasonally; **Cook's Cycles** (228-0800), 6 South Beach Street, open seasonally.

Nantucket Cycling Club (228-1164) sponsors races May through October; anyone can participate.

BIRD-WATCHING

Maria Mitchell Association (228-9198, 228-0898), on Vestal Street, offers birding walks all over the island, mid-June to mid-September. Adults $7, children $4.

Birding Adventures (228-2703) was founded in 1987 by John Simons, a writer and adventure guide, who takes up to six people per tour. A 2-hour trip costs $50 for two people; $20 per person for three or more people; custom trips are arranged year-round.

BOAT EXCURSIONS/RENTALS

Endeavor (228-5585), Slip 15, Straight Wharf. May through October. Captain Jim Genthner's 31-foot Friendship sloop offers three daily harbor tours, a sunset cruise, and trips to Coatue. Adults $20–30 for a 90-minute sail; $15 for a 60-minute sail. There's also a replica of a 19th-century whaleboat, which passengers are expected to row and sail.

Harbor Cruises *Anna W. II* (228-1444), Slip 12, Straight Wharf. June to mid-October. Lobstering demonstrations (only until mid-September), shoreline sight-seeing, sunset, and moonlight cruises aboard a former lobster boat. Inquire about wintertime seal cruises on weekends November through April. Sight-seeing $15 adults, $10 children; lobstering $22.50 adults, $17.50 children 4–12.

Sparrow Yacht Charters (228-6029), Slip 18, Straight Wharf. Early June to mid-September. Offers 90-minute group sails, trips to Monomoy, and private charters to Coatue on a 40-foot sailboat.

Nantucket Boat Rentals (325-1001), Slip 1, Straight Wharf. Rents powerboats by the day or week in-season.

Force 5 Watersports (228-5358) on Jetties Beach (also at 37 Main Street, 228-0700). Open daily mid-June through August; hours are variable the rest of the year. Rents kayaks and Sunfish; also offers lessons, clinics, and guides. A 3-hour sailing lesson or kayak clinic costs $100; a kayak rents for $15–20 an hour or $60 a day.

COOKOUTS

Permits are required for cookouts and fires on the beach. Contact the Fire Department (228-2324) on Pleasant Street.

FISHING/SHELLFISHING

Permits for digging clams, mussels, and quahogs are obtained from the Marine Department and shellfish warden (228-7260), 38 Washington Street. Scalloping season opens October 1, after which you'll see fishermen in the harbor and off nearby shoals of Tuckernuck Island; bay scallops harvested from November through March are delicious.

Try your luck at freshwater fishing at Long Pond (see *Green Space—Ponds*). Nantucket blues can be caught from the southern shore; they run in schools from May through October. Fishing isn't as good there in July and August when the waters are warmer, but if that's the only time you're here, toss out a line anyway.

Whitney Mitchell (228-2331) has taken surf-fishers to locations accessible only by four-wheel-drives since 1983. Mid-June to mid-October, $45 per person.

Paul Doyle Fishing Excursions (228-7660) are geared toward fly-fishing from the shore. These 5-hour trips are best taken at night, but Doyle also takes customers at dawn and dusk, early May to late October. $300. He also operates a surf-fishing charter service; $50 per person including equipment.

Mike Monte (228-0529, 325-1676), a year-round island resident, takes people surf-fishing and fly-fishing from May through October. He also provides all the equipment necessary. Fly-fishing for about 4 hours runs $100 per person.

Bill Fisher Tackle (228-2261), 14 New Lane, rents a full line of equipment, supplies daily fishing reports, and provides guide service.

Two charters that go in search of the island's principal catch (bass and bluefish) are **Herbert T** (228-6655), Slip 14, Straight Wharf, and **Albacore** (288-5074), Slip 17, Straight Wharf.

FITNESS CLUB

Club N.E.W. (228-4750), 10 Young's Way. Open daily year-round. Offers a full array of machines, free weights, and classes, in addition to baby-sitting services and individualized programs. $12 day-use fee.

FOR FAMILIES

✐✳ **Nantucket Babysitting Service** (228-4970) provides parents a respite from the responsibilities of toddlers and youngsters. Services are available year-round, and after assessing your needs, they'll match a sitter with your kids and send him or her over to your place.

✐ **Dial-a-Story** (228-6050), 62 Centre Street, at the First Congregational Church. Call anytime and listen to the recording, which may be an educational, historical anecdote.

✐ **Story Hour** (228-1110), Lower India Street. Sponsored by the Atheneum year-round. In July and August, stories are told in the Atheneum garden (weather permitting) on Tuesday at 7 PM for children 5 and older, and Wednesday and Friday at 10 AM for children 4–6. In the off-season, there are slightly different hours, and stories are told in the new children's wing of the Atheneum. No sign-up necessary; free.

GOLF

Siasconset Golf Club (257-6596), Milestone Road. Open mid-May to mid-October. This nine-hole public course, encircled by conservation land, dates to 1894.

Miacomet Golf Club (325-0333), off Somerset Road. Open year-round. This flat, nine-hole course, owned by the Nantucket Land Bank, has views of Miacomet Pond, heathland, and the coastline.

Sankaty Head Golf Club (257-6391), Sankaty Road, 'Sconset. Although this links-style, 18-hole course is private, it's open to the public from October to mid-May. Magnificent views of the lighthouse.

IN-LINE SKATING

Sports Locker on Wheels (228-6610), 14 Cambridge Street, is the island's only source. $25 for a full day, $18 for a half day in-season; $18 for a full day in the off-season.

KAYAKING

Sea Nantucket (228-7499), at Francis Street Beach, Washington Street Extension. Open seasonally. Conducts tours for children and adults and rents roll-proof kayaks for half days ($25 single, $45 double) and full days ($35 single, $55 double). It's usually calm paddling along the 8 miles of scalloped bays at Coatue. When the harbor is choppy, you can have a kayak delivered to an inland pond.

See also Force 5 Watersports, under *Boat Excursions/Rentals.*

MINI-GOLF

J.J. Clammp's (228-8977), Nobadeer Farm and Sun Island Roads, off Milestone Road and the 'Sconset Bike Path. Open daily June to mid-September, until 11 PM in July and August. Families are lured to the island's only mini-golf establishment by the course itself, to be sure: Adults appreciate the lovely gardens, while kids enjoy the golf and remote-control boats on two ponds. But there's also an on-site restaurant, a convenient NRTA bus stop nearby, and it's just off the 'Sconset Bike Path. Adults $6, children $5.

SCUBA DIVING

The Sunken Ship (228-9226), Broad and South Water Streets. Open year-round. A full-service dive shop that offers charters, lessons, and rentals. There are lobstering trips in summer and scalloping in autumn.

SPECIAL PROGRAMS

Nantucket Island School of Design and the Arts (228-9248), Wauwinet Road. Holds an extraordinary range of classes and lectures for adults and children, year-round. Affiliated with the Massachusetts College of Art in Boston, the school offers college graduate and undergraduate summer sessions in the Sea View Farm Barn, a converted dairy barn.

Nantucket Community School (228-7257), 10 Surfside Road. Offers adult-education classes, and programs and camps for kids, year-round.

Artists Association of Nantucket (228-0722), Gardner Perry Lane. Offers workshops and demonstrations in a variety of disciplines for adults and children, year-round. Groups attending classes may rent studios and one-bedroom cottages on the harbor (call 228-9248 about rentals).

Murray Camp (325-4600), 25½ Bartlett Road. Late June through August. Send your child to day camp while you explore the island. Children 5 to

Brant Point Lighthouse guards the entrance to Nantucket harbor.

14 can enroll by the week; activities include swimming, sailing, ecology, "fun French," kayaking, biking, and more. $200–325 weekly.

Lightship Shop (228-4164), 20 Miacomet Avenue. Offers kits and materials, or year-round classes ($200), so you can make your own basket (see *Selective Shopping—Special Shops*). Four-day classes including accommodations (228-4625) are offered from late March to mid-June for $410 per person. It's a long walk to the shop; take the South Loop shuttle.

SWIMMING POOLS

Nantucket Community Pool (228-7262), Atlantic and Sparks Avenues. An Olympic-sized pool at the Nantucket High School. Open daily for swimming; inquire about lessons (for a fee).

TENNIS

Public courts are located at Jetties Beach. Sign up at the Parks and Recreation Building (325-5334), North Beach Street, for one of six courts. Clinics and lessons are offered for adults and children.

Brant Point Racquet Club (228-3700), 48 North Beach Street. Open May to mid-October. A full-service place, with nine clay courts, a pro shop, round robins (in summer), and rentals.

Tristram's Landing Tennis Center (228-4588), 440 Arkansas Avenue, Madaket.

WHALE-WATCHING

Nantucket Whalewatch (283-0313, 1-800-942-5464 within Massachusetts), Straight Wharf at the Hy-Line dock. Daylong trips depart Tuesdays at 9:30, mid-July to mid-September. The on-board naturalist simultaneously conducts ongoing whale research. $65 adults, $35 children under 12. Reservations recommended.

WINDSURFING

Force 5 Watersports (228-5358) on Jetties Beach (also at 37 Main Street, 228-0700) and Indian Summer Sports (228-3632), 6 Steamboat Wharf, rent boogie boards and windsurfers seasonally. Surfing is best on the southern beaches.

WINERY AND BREWERY

Nantucket Vineyard (228-9235), 3 Bartlett Farm Road, about 2.5 miles south of town off Hummock Pond Road. Open noon–5 daily May through December (longer hours in summer). Dean and Melissa Long have cultivated vinifera grapes on-island since 1981, but they use other grapes as well. Tours and tastings are offered, as are bottles of evocatively named vintages like Nantucket Sleighride and 'Sconset Rose.

Cisco Brewers (325-5929), 5 Bartlett Farm Road. Open 10–6 daily except Sunday in summer, weekends the rest of the year. Although Randy and Wendy Hudson don't have a license to serve beer, you can still have a taste of their fresh, traditionally made ales, porters, and stouts. No tours at press time. Look for Cisco beer at island restaurants.

GREEN SPACE

Nantucket is renowned for the amount of open, protected land on the island. In fact, thanks to the efforts of various conservation groups, more than one-third of the island is protected from development. Two organizations deserve much of the credit: **Nantucket Conservation Foundation** (228-2884), 118 Cliff Road, open 8–4 weekdays; and the **Nantucket Land Bank** (228-7240), 22 Broad Street. Established in 1963 to manage open land—wetlands, moors, and grasslands—the Nantucket Conservation Foundation has since purchased or been given more than 8400 acres on the island. Since the foundation is constantly acquiring land, call for a map of its current properties, published yearly; $4 by mail, $3 in person. The Nantucket Land Bank was formed in the mid-1980s, when a tax was enacted that assessed a 4 percent fee on all real estate and land transactions. The tax receipts are used to purchase property to be kept as conservation land.

Coatue–Coskata–Great Point, off Wauwinet Road, accessible only by four-wheel-drive vehicle or by foot. These three adjacent wildlife areas are owned by different organizations, but that doesn't matter to visitors. The world's oldest land trust, the Trustees of Reservations, manages part of this 1110-acre preserve. Ara's Tours offers the only tour of Great Point; see *Getting Around.*

The strip of land leading to Great Point is about 5 miles long, over very soft sand. You'll pass the "haulover," which separates the head of the harbor from the Atlantic Ocean. This stretch of sand is so narrow that fishermen would haul their boats across it instead of going all the way around the tip of Great Point. During severe storms, the ocean breaks through the haulover, effectively creating an island of the refuge. (Sand is eventually redeposited by the currents.) The spit of sand known as Coatue is a series of concave bays that reach all the way to the mouth of Nantucket Harbor. The foundation owns both Coatue and the haulover.

There's a wealth of things to do in this pristine preserve: bird-watching, surf casting, shellfishing, sunbathing, picnicking, and walking. Since the riptides are dangerous, especially near the Great Point lighthouse (see *To See*), swimming is not recommended. For information about four-wheel-drive permits, see *Getting Around.*

Eel Point, off Eel Point Road from the Madaket Bike Path, about 6 miles from town. Leave your car or bicycle at the sign that reads 40TH POLE BEACH. Walk the last half mile to the beach. There aren't any facilities, just unspoiled nature, good birding, surf-fishing, and a shallow sandbar. Portions of this beach are often closed to protect nesting shorebirds. For in-depth information, pick up a map and self-guided tour for $4.50 from the Maria Mitchell Association (228-9198), 2 Vestal Street, or from the Nantucket Conservation Foundation (228-2884), 118 Cliff Road, Box 13, Nantucket 02554 ($4 in person, $5 by mail).

Sanford Farm, Ram Pasture, and **the Woods,** off Madaket Road. These 900-plus acres of wetlands, grasslands, and forest are owned and managed by the Nantucket Conservation Foundation and the Nantucket Land Bank. The Sanford Farm was purchased for $4.4 million in 1985 from the estate of Mrs. Anne Sanford. There is 6½-mile (round-trip) walking and biking trail that goes past Hummock Pond to the ocean, affording great views of heathlands along the way. Ram Pasture and the Woods comprised one of the foundation's first purchases in 1971, for $625,000. Interpretive markers identify natural and historic sites. There is a popular 45-minute (1.7-mile) loop trail as well as a Barn Trail (1½ hours, 3 miles) that affords beautiful expansive views of the island's southern coastline.

Milestone Bog, off Milestone Road on a dirt road to the north, about 5 miles from town. When cranberries were first harvested here in 1857, there were 330 acres of bogs. Today only about 220 acres are cultivated by Northland Cranberries, a company that leases the land from the Nantucket Conservation Foundation (the land was donated to the foundation in 1968). Berries are shipped off-island for processing, but honey made by the bees that pollinate the flowering fruit is sold on-island.

Windswept Cranberry Bog, off Polpis Road to the south. This 40-acre working bog is also part-owned by the Nantucket Conservation Foundation. The autumnal harvest is a visual feast. First bogs are flooded with water; then a machine shakes and loosens the ripe red berries from the plant. They float to the top of the water, and are corralled with netlike booms and scooped from the water into waiting trucks. Harvest season generally runs from late September through October, during which time people work in the bogs from dawn to dusk, 7 days a week (see Cranberry Harvest Weekend under *Special Events*).

BEACHES

Nantucket is ringed by 50 miles of beaches, most privately owned but all open to the public. In general, beaches on the south and east have rough surf and undertow; western and northern beaches have warmer, calmer waters. There is limited parking at some of the beaches; **Barrett's Tours** (228-0174) provides transportation to Surfside and the **NRTA** (228-7025) provides it to other beaches (see *Getting Around*).

Northern beaches

Children's Beach, off South Beach Street on the harbor. A few minutes' walk from Steamboat Wharf, this is a great place for children (hence its name). Amenities include a lifeguard, rest rooms, a bathhouse, a playground, food (see Downy Flake under *Where to Eat—Light Fare*), picnic tables, games tables, a bandstand, a horseshoe pit, and a grassy play area. Tie-dying is held Friday at noon during July and August.

Brant Point, off Easton Street. A 15-minute walk from town, and overlooking the entrance to the harbor, this scenic stretch of sand is great for boat-watching and surf-fishing. A strong current and a beach that drops off suddenly don't create ideal swimming conditions.

Jetties, off Bathing Beach Road from North Beach Road. Shuttle buses run to this popular beach—otherwise it's a 20-minute walk. (There is also a fairly large parking lot.) A great place for families because of the amenities (rest rooms, lifeguards, showers, changing rooms, snack bar, chairs for rent), and activities (volleyball, tennis, swings, a playground, an assortment of sailboats and kayaks). The July 4 fireworks celebration is held here. Also a good beach for walking. Look for the new skateboarding park; helmets and pads are required and can be rented at the Parks and Recreation Building tennis office (325-5334).

Francis Street Beach, a 5-minute walk from Main Street, at Washington and Francis Streets. This harbor beach is calm. There are kayak rentals, rest rooms, and a small playground.

Dionis, off Eel Point Road from the Madaket Bike Path. Nantucket's only beach with dunes, Dionis is about 3 miles from town. The beach starts out narrow but becomes more expansive (and less populated) as you walk farther east or west. Amenities include lifeguards and a new bathhouse.

Southern beaches

Surfside, off Surfside Road; large parking lot. Three miles from town and accessible by shuttle bus, this wide beach is popular with college students and families with older kids because of its proximity to town and its moderate-to-heavy surf. Rest rooms, lifeguards, showers, and a snack bar. Kite flying, surf-casting, and picnicking are popular.

Nobadeer, east of Surfside, near the airport and about 4 miles from town. There are no facilities at Nobadeer, but there is plenty of surf.

Madaket, at the end of the scenic Madaket Bike Path. About 5 miles west of town (served by shuttle bus), Madaket is perhaps the most popular place to watch sunsets. This long beach has heavy surf and strong currents; there are lifeguards and portable rest rooms.

Cisco, off Hummock Pond Road from Milk Street. About 4 miles from town, this long beach is popular with surfers. Lifeguards.

Eastern beaches

'Sconset (aka Codfish Park), at the end of the 'Sconset Bike Path, turn right at the rotary. About 7 miles from town, accessible by shuttle bus, this narrow, long beach takes a pounding by heavy surf. Lifeguards and a playground. (See Claudette's under *Where to Eat—Light Fare* for informal box lunches.) Seaweed clutters the beach when the surf whips up.

PONDS

Long Pond. Take Madaket Road from town; when you reach the Hither Creek sign, turn left onto a dirt road. This 64-acre Nantucket Land Bank property is great for birding. A mile-long path around the pond passes meadows and a cranberry bog.

Miacomet Pond, Miacomet Avenue (which turns into a dirt road), off Surfside Road. This long, narrow, freshwater pond next to the ocean has a sandy shore and is surrounded by grasses and heath. This Nantucket Land Bank property is a pleasant place for a picnic, and the swans and ducks make it more so.

Sesachacha Pond. Take Polpis Road to Quidnet Road. A narrow barrier beach separates the pond and ocean. There is a nice view of the Sankaty lighthouse from here.

WALKS

The Moors and **Altar Rock,** off Polpis Road, to the south, on an unmarked dirt road. When you want to get away from the summertime masses, head to the Moors (preferably at dawn or dusk, when they're most magical). The Moors are crisscrossed with trails and bumpy and deeply rutted dirt roads. From Altar Rock, the highest point on the island at 90 feet above sea level, there are expansive views of lowland heath, bogs, and moors. It's stunning in autumn.

Lily Pond Park, North Liberty Street. This 5-acre Nantucket Land Bank property supports lots of wildlife and plant life, but the trail is often muddy. You may find wild raspberries, grapes, or blueberries.

LODGING

Although there are more than 1200 rooms to rent on Nantucket, January is not too early to make reservations for July and August. The historic district, while convenient, has its share of foot traffic (and boisterous socializers) late into the evening; houses are also very close together. A 10-minute walk from Straight Wharf will put you in more quiet surroundings. Most lodgings require a 2- or 3-night minimum stay in-season; I have only indicated minimum-night-stay policies that are extraordinary. Most places also have slightly higher rates on special holiday weekends like Christmas Stroll and Daffodil Festival (see *Special Events*). Most places are not appropriate for small children.

Unless otherwise noted, all lodging is Nantucket 02554.

RESORTS

Around the island

The Wauwinet (228-0145, 1-800-426-8718), Wauwinet Road, Nantucket 02584. Open mid-May to late October. When price is no object and extraordinary service is, the Wauwinet is the place to stay. A lodging place since the mid-1800s, the hotel was magnificently restored in 1986. It occupies an unparalleled location between low dunes on the Atlantic Ocean and a beach-rimmed stretch of Nantucket Harbor. Public rooms are awash in chintz, trompe l'oeil, fresh flowers, and bleached woods. The 25 guest rooms and five cottages have luxurious bed linens and toiletries, pine armoires, Audubon prints, and soothing and sophisticated decorating touches. Cottages have fireplaces and kitchens and can accommodate between four and eight guests. Although the inn is 8 miles from town, there's practically no reason to leave the property. Facilities include clay tennis courts, a pro shop, boating and lessons, mountain bicycles, croquet, a videocassette library, and four-wheel-drive nature trips out to Great Point. The staff ensure that practically any request is met. Topper's (see *Dining Out*) offers outstanding dining; a full breakfast is included with the rates. Mid-June to mid-September $210–690 for rooms, $540–1400 for cottages (4 nights may be required in July and August).

In town

Cliffside Beach Club (228-0618, 1-800-932-9645), Jefferson Avenue. Open late May to mid-October. Stylish simplicity, understated elegance, and breezy beachside living are the watchwords here. You can't get a bed closer to the beach than this: Front doors and decks sit right on the beach and a boardwalk over the sand connects the low-slung, weathered-shingle buildings. Once a private club, which opened in 1924, it's been in Robert Currie's family since 1958. The reception area is large, light, and airy, decorated with white wicker furniture, local art, and quilts hanging from the rafters. A continental breakfast is set out here. The 22 contemporary guest rooms (most with ocean views) feature outstanding woodwork, all crafted by islanders. Many have a sofa bed, fine for a young child or two. Four newer suites, with outstanding views of dunes and sunsets, offer the most privacy. There are also a few luxuriously simple three-bedroom apartments. Exercise facilities and a restaurant on the premises. Cliffside is a 15-minute walk from the center of town. Late June to early September $270–425 for rooms and studios, $525–695 for suites, apartments, and cottages; off-season $175–315 and $395–490, respectively.

✐ **The Beachside** (228-2241, 1-800-322-4433), 30 North Beach Street. Open late April to late October. Although neither on the beach (as its name suggests) nor offering the resort amenities of the other establishments in this category, The Beachside is appealing for different reasons. Five minutes from Jetties Beach, this tasteful bi-level motel offers 92 rooms surrounding a heated pool. Rooms—some with two double beds—are freshly decorated with floral wallpapers, fine bedding, and white wicker. The nicest rooms feature French doors opening onto a small private patio; all rooms have a TV/VCR. Children 16 and under stay free in parents' room. Shoulder-season packages. Late June to mid-September $185–225; off-season $95–225. Rates include a continental breakfast.

✐ **White Elephant Hotel & The Breakers** (228-2500, 1-800-475-2637), Easton Street. Open mid-May to late October. Hardly a white elephant, this first-class resort is renowned for its service and harborfront location. The 22 rooms in the main hotel are comfortably furnished and brightly decorated. Common rooms are large and airy, furnished with wicker and overstuffed sofas. The 26 elegant rooms in the exclusive Breakers each have a private deck, minibar, and fresh flowers, and complimentary wine on arrival. There are also 34 luxury cottages with separate living rooms and kitchens. Facilities include a concierge, harborside pool and hot tub, putting green, clay tennis courts, and croquet. Elegant dinners and casual luncheons are served (see The Regatta under *Dining Out*). It's a 10-minute walk to the center of town. Late June to mid-September $240–315 in the hotel, $335–475 at The Breakers, $285–690 for cottages.

✐ **Harbor House** (228-1500, 1-800-475-2637), South Beach Street. Open mid-April through mid-December. A few blocks from the center of town on a quiet lane, these traditional Nantucket town houses surround a renovated, late-19th-century summer hotel. Gas lanterns and brick walkways connect a total of 112 rooms. The spacious townhouse guest rooms are nestled among small gardens or near the heated pool. Some have a private patio or deck, cathedral ceiling, and whirlpool tub. All rooms have a TV and VCR and are generally decorated with canopy beds, upscale country-style furnishings, and floral fabrics. The hotel offers a concierge, room service, and a full-service restaurant (see The Hearth under *Dining Out*). Inquire about off-season packages. Late May to mid-October $225 for hotel rooms, $265 for townhouse rooms.

INNS

In town

Woodbox Inn (228-0587), 29 Fair Street. Open mid-June to mid-October. Innkeeper Dexter Tutein's atmospheric inn and restaurant (see *Dining Out*) is located in one of the island's oldest houses, which dates to 1709. On a quiet street just beyond the densest concentration of activity and shops, the Woodbox has three rooms and five larger suites, some with working fireplace and all with period antiques and private baths. The two-bedroom suites are a good value at $220 since they can comfortably accommodate four people; they also have a living room. A rollaway cot can be added to the one-bedroom suites ($160) for an additional $10. The renowned breakfasts include wonderful popovers and egg creations. No credit cards. $130–220; 10 percent service charge added.

Ship's Inn (228-0040), 13 Fair Street. Open May through October. Beyond the bustle of Main Street, a 10-minute walk from Straight Wharf, the Ship's Inn is a very comfortable choice for lodging as well as dining (see *Dining Out*). The three-story 1831 whaling captain's house was completely restored in 1991. Its 10 large guest rooms, named after Captain Obed Starbuck's ships, all have private baths and televisions. Like the living room, they're large and airy, sparely furnished to create a summery feel. $125–150 double, $75 single with shared bath. Rates include continental breakfast.

❋ **Jared Coffin House** (228-2400, 1-800-248-2405, e-mail: jchouse@nantucket. net; http://www.nantucket.net/lodging/jchouse), 29 Broad Street. Open year-round. The brick mansion, topped with a cupola and slate roof, was built in 1845 by a wealthy shipowner for his wife. In fact, it was the island's first three-story house. It was also one of the few buildings to survive the Great Fire of 1846; it's been an inn since 1847. Guest rooms are located in six adjacent buildings, most with their own common areas. All 60 rooms have private telephone and TV. Rooms outside the main inn are larger, featuring Colonial reproduction four-poster canopy beds and in-room refrigerators. (Harrison Grey House rooms are the nicest, although guests usually are drawn to the Jared Coffin for its history.) More like a small hotel than an inn, the Jared Coffin employs a concierge and has two restaurants (see Jared's under *Dining Out* and the Tap Room under *Eating Out*). July through September $150–200 ($85 single); late October to early April $95–190 ($55–60 single).

Quaker House Inn (228-0400), 5 Chestnut Street. Open mid-May to mid-October. The Quaker House offers eight guest rooms in the heart of the historic district. Many of the rooms have wide floorboards and newly retiled baths. Corner rooms are the nicest; rooms on the third floor are small, tucked beneath the dormer. Caroline and Bob Taylor, innkeepers since 1982, head back to New Zealand in the off-season. Rates include an $8 voucher for breakfast in their restaurant, which features vegetable omelets, blueberry waffles, or the house specialty: baked apple pancakes. $125–160 in the high season, $90–130 otherwise.

BED & BREAKFASTS

In town

❋ **Corner House** (228-1530), 49 Centre Street. Open year-round. The Corner House's period restoration is true to its 1723 origins. Refined without being pretentious and comfortable without being casual, this B&B rises to the top of a places-to-stay list. Sandy and John Knox-Johnston, innkeepers since 1981, offer a variety of rooms to suit a variety of budgets. Seventeen rooms and suites, all with private bath, are scattered throughout three buildings. The main house—with two living rooms, a brick terrace, and an enclosed screened porch where a luscious afternoon tea is served—is filled with period English and American antiques. Even the least-expensive rooms on the third floor are charming, with rough plaster walls and exposed beams. There is also a lovely apartment. Late June to mid-September $100–175; mid-October to mid-May $65–110.

☞✴ **Martin House Inn** (228-0678), 61 Centre Street. Open year-round. Ceci and Channing Moore, a gracious innkeeping duo, have created an elegantly comfortable space within this 1803 mariner's house. It's definitely one of the best values on-island. The side porch is decked with white wicker and a hammock; on cooler days you can curl up in front of the fire or in a window seat in the large living room. Many of the 13 guest rooms (4 with shared baths) have canopy beds, period antiques, fireplaces; all have a welcoming decanter of sherry. Some bright singles are tucked under the eaves on the third floor. An expanded continental buffet breakfast is served at one long table, or you can take a tray table to the porch or your room. Mid-June to mid-October, $85–155 private bath, $80–95 shared bath, $55 single; off-season $65–125 private bath, $55–80 shared bath, $40–45 single.

✴ **Cliff Lodge** (228-9480), 9 Cliff Road. Open year-round. On a little hill in a quiet residential neighborhood, a 10- to 15-minute walk from Straight Wharf, Cliff Lodge is another of the island's beautifully converted sea captains' houses. Dating to 1771, this B&B has 11 English-country-style guest rooms. Glossy, paint-spattered floors and floral wallpapers are offset by white bedding, quilts, and white furniture. Guest rooms have a fresh, light, and airy feel to them. They're also outfitted with telephones and TVs. Guests have access to a refrigerator, garden patio, wicker-furnished sun porch, and a roof walk with great views of the town and Nantucket Sound. There is also an apartment. Islander John Bennett and his wife, Debby, purchased the house in 1996 and are bringing an innkeeper presence back. Mid-June through September $125–165 ($85 single); off-season $65–125. Rates include a continental breakfast.

Ten Lyon Street (228-5040), 10 Lyon Street. Open late April to early December. Ann Marie and Barry Foster completely rebuilt and renovated this old house in 1986. Its seven romantic and antiques-filled guest rooms (all with private and modernized baths) are spacious and airy with white walls and light woods. The house is on a quiet street, about a 10-minute walk from Straight Wharf. Although there is little common space, except for the check-in area and a little nook where a continental breakfast is served, guests can relax outside in the front garden. Mid-June to mid-September $135–195; off-season $70–125.

✴ **Anchor Inn** (228-0072), 66 Centre Street. Open year-round. Of the 11 guest rooms in this 1806 house, the more spacious ones are corner rooms with a canopy bed. All have private bathrooms and comfortable period furnishings. One room has a private porch. The less expensive rooms are snug but inviting, under the eaves in the back of the house. An expanded continental breakfast is served on the enclosed porch or carried to the side garden. Charles and Ann Balas's inn is adjacent to the Old North Church, from which there is a great view of town. Mid-June to mid-September $115–155 for rooms; $55–95 prior to late May and after mid-October.

Nantucket Landfall (228-0500), 4 Harbor View Way. Open mid-April to late October. Overlooking Children's Beach, the Landfall is just a few minutes' walk to downtown, yet far enough to be delightfully quiet. All the whitewashed rooms have a breezy summer feel to them, thanks to billowing curtains and colorful quilts. A few have panoramic views of the harbor; one has a screened-in porch with daybed. The nautically inspired living room has a fireplace and library, but you'll probably end up spending most of your time on a front porch rocker. Inquire about the two-story cottage, complete with brick patio, that rents for $1500 weekly. Mid-June through September $110–225; off-season $85–150.

Centerboard Guest House (228-9696), 8 Chester Street. Open April through December. A 10-minute walk from Straight Wharf, on the edge of the historic district, Centerboard was renovated in 1986 with a refreshingly light Victorian sensibility. The six guest rooms are romantic, with feather beds, quilts, fresh flowers, luxurious linens, and stripped woodwork. Modern amenities like a refrigerator, TV/VCR, and private bath haven't been sacrificed, though. One room has a working fireplace; another has a private entrance and sleeps four; yet another has two brass beds. Mid-June to mid-October $165 ($285 for the two-room suite); off-season $110 ($185 for the two-room suite). Additional person $25. Rates include a continental breakfast.

Fair Winds Guest House (228-1998; 617-244-3953 off-season), 29 Cliff Road. Open late April to late October. On the outskirts of town, a 15-minute walk from Straight Wharf, Kathy Hughes has been innkeeping here since 1978. Four of her seven lovely rooms (all with private baths) have a great view of Nantucket Sound. Comfortable common space includes a long back deck (with the same great view) and two living rooms. The house has a breezy, summery, cottage feel with stripped wainscoting and doors. Mid-June to early-September $145–185. Rates include a continental breakfast.

🖉✳ **Accommodations et al.** (228-9267, 1-800-673-4559, 1-800-837-2921, e-mail: rhinn@aol.com). Open year-round. Sara and Michael O'Reilly own a consortium of guest houses—including the Manor House, Roberts House, Meeting House, and Linden House around Centre Street and the Periwinkle Guest House and Cottage at 7 North Water Street. Rates, room styles, and furnishings vary; tell them what's important to you and they'll find something that meets your needs, including family suites or a two-room cottage. There are a total of 60 rooms available; all have phones, some have TV or air-conditioning. Among the plethora of options, rooms 10, 11, and 12 at Periwinkle, the first property Sara purchased in 1971, are favorites. They're quaint, with barn-board wainscoting under the eaves. Mid-June to late September $165–300 for standard rooms, larger rooms, and family suites ($95–135 for rooms with shared baths); November to mid-May $65–140 for private baths, $50 for shared baths.

Four Chimneys (228-1912), 38 Orange Street. Open mid-May through October. This elegant and refined 1835 sea captain's house, on a quiet street 10 minutes from Straight Wharf, features 10 large guest rooms with canopy beds and down comforters. The formal but comfortable living room has two fireplaces, while half the guest rooms have a fireplace. Read on the quiet back porch or seek more complete refuge in the secluded Japanese garden. Late May to mid-October $150–250. Rates include a continental breakfast and afternoon hors d'oeuvres.

Westmoor Inn (228-0877), Cliff Road. Open mid-April to early December. About a mile from town, this large yellow 1917 Colonial Revival mansion with a widow's walk was built as a wedding gift for Alice Vanderbilt. Innkeeper Nancy Holdgate has decorated with a light touch the spacious living room, graced with a baby grand piano, game table, and fireplace. (Afternoon wine and hors d'oeuvres are served here.) The 14 guest rooms, all with private bath and telephone, vary greatly in size and view, but all are airy and bright. Carpeted third-floor rooms are generally smaller, tucked under the eaves, but they're still summery white. An expanded continental breakfast is served on a flagstone sun porch overlooking a garden patio. Nancy rents two rustic, antiques-appointed cottages that sleep four or five people for $800 weekly in-season. Mid-June to mid-September $135–255 rooms; off-season $100–185 rooms.

☞✐**Nesbitt Inn** (228-0156, 228-2446), 21 Broad Street. Open February through December. One block from Steamboat Wharf, the Nesbitt Inn exemplifies Nantucket's simpler lodging roots. Built in 1872 as an inn, the house has been in the same family since 1914. The inn, with in-room sinks and shared showers, is a favorite among Europeans. Eleven double and two single rooms (which share only three baths) are Victorian in style; many of the furnishings are original to the house. The living room has a fireplace, games, and a television. Guests can people-watch from the front porch, relax on the back deck, and make use of the outdoor grill, refrigerator, and beach towels. Children are welcome and there's a swing set in the backyard. The inn is located next to the boisterous Brotherhood of Thieves restaurant (see *Eating Out*). Late May to mid-October $70–80 double, $50 single. Rates include a continental breakfast.

COTTAGES AND APARTMENTS
In town
Wharf Cottages (228-4620, 1-800-475-2637), New Whale Street. Open late May to late September. These cottages occupy a unique location—in the midst of harbor activity. Cottages are popular with landlubber

A typically weathered 18th-century cottage in 'Sconset

families as well as boaters who wish to spend the night on firmer ground. The 25 charming cottages offer private decks, small gardens, water views, fully equipped kitchens, TVs/VCRs, and daily maid service. Although the cottages are small, they're efficiently designed and crisply decorated in whites and blues. Late June to mid-September $240 studio, $355 one bedroom, $425 two bedrooms, $525 three bedrooms; off-season $200, $250, $295, and $395, respectively.

✳ **Nantucket Settlements** (228-6597, 1-800-462-6882). Open year-round. Nantucket Settlements' seven cottages and three 19th-century houses, which vary considerably, are scattered around town. Perhaps their most popular attribute is the galley kitchens. Orange Suites are about a 10-minute walk from the center of town; the best of these four units is a duplex with a fireplace and roof walk. Cottages are about a 15-minute walk from the center of town; the most modern and tasteful are Bayberry Upper, Bayberry Lower, and Honeysuckle. Mid-June to mid-September $1505–1750 weekly for cottages and two-bedroom units; $140–165 nightly for studios and one-bedrooms. Mid-April to mid-June and mid-September through October $105–180 nightly for all units.

See also Nantucket Landfall, White Elephant Hotel, Anchor Inn, and Cliff Lodge under *Bed & Breakfasts*.

Around the island

The Summer House (257-4577), 'Sconset 02564. Open late April to late October. The brochure's photograph is almost too idyllic to believe: Honeysuckle vines and roses cover a shingled cottage with small-paned windows; the double Dutch door opens to a white, skylighted interior that's cozy, charming, and luxuriously simple. But it's true! Dating to the 1840s, the eight enchanting cottages surround a colorful garden set with Adirondack chairs. Cottages have been updated with marble Jacuzzi bathtubs and English country antiques; some have a fireplace and kitchen. Shuffle across the street to the beach or the inn's pool in the dunes, just below the bluff. Drinks and lunch are served at the pool. In addition to a piano bar, the inn (a few minutes' walk from the "center" of 'Sconset) has a lovely restaurant; an expanded continental breakfast is included in the rates. Mid-June to mid-September $350–500; off-season $225–400.

Wade Cottages (257-6308; 212-989-6423 off-season), 'Sconset 02564. Open late May to mid-October. A portion of this private estate is still used by Wade family members. Its great appeal lies in the fact that there's nothing between the property and the ocean except a broad lawn and an ocean bluff. Some guest rooms are in the main house, where the only common space doubles as a small breakfast room. These rooms are furnished modestly, and they're a bit worn. The multibedroom suites, apartments, and cottages are well equipped for the required minimum stays. Ocean views are de rigueur. The best of the three cottages (all with large living room) is the newest one closest to the ocean. Mid-July through August $975 weekly for a room with private bath, $585 weekly for a room with shared bath, $1550–2200 weekly for a one- to four-bedroom apartment or suite. Rates up to 50 percent lower in the off-season. (Call for room rates for 3-night periods.)

See also Wauwinet and Cliffside Beach Club under *Resorts*.

RENTALS

Congdon & Coleman (325-5000), 57 Main Street. At the start of the season, the agency has in its rental pool of perhaps 1000 one- to seven-bedroom houses all over the island. In-season weekly rates begin at $1000 and go way up. You tell them your requirements; they'll fax you a listing sheet.

Lucille Jordan Associates (228-4449), 8 Federal Street, and **Nantucket Real Estate Co.** (228-3131), 6 Ash Lane, behind the Jared Coffin House, have similar listings.

CAMPGROUNDS

No camping is permitted on Nantucket.

HOSTEL

Nantucket Hostel, of Hostelling International (228-0433), 31 Western Avenue (off-season reservations: 1020 Commonwealth Avenue, Boston 02215; 1-617-739-3017). Open mid-April to mid-October. Originally built in 1873 as the island's first lifesaving station, and on the National Register of Historic Places, the hostel is 3 miles from the center of town on Surfside Beach. Facilities include a kitchen, barbecue and picnic area, and volleyball. Dormitory-style, gender-separated rooms accommodate about 50 people. Daily chores are meant to foster a communal spirit as well as to keep the place clean. Advance reservations are essential in July and August and on all weekends; maximum stay of 5 nights. $12 for IH members; $15 nonmembers.

WHERE TO EAT

Nantucket has one of the densest concentrations of fine dining establishments anywhere in the country. Many of these restaurants would hold their own quite well in New York or San Francisco. And repeat visitors know it: It's not unheard of for visitors to make dinner reservations for an entire stay when they book their lodging. Although dining can be extremely expensive, many restaurants now offer lighter, less expensive, bistro-style fare in addition to their regular menu. Although it's rare to be served a "bad meal" in Nantucket, some restaurants offer better value than others. Reservations are highly recommended at the finer establishments; many offer only two seatings. There are perhaps 10 restaurants (not all are reviewed here) that serve the year-round community. I have not included shoulder-season hours of operation because they are so variable; they depend on weather, number of tourists, and the whim of the owners. Generally, you can assume places are open daily late June to early September.

DINING OUT
In town

❋ **Boarding House** (228-9622), 12 Federal Street. Open for lunch and dinner mid-June to mid-September and for dinner year-round; closed Tuesday. One of the most consistently superior restaurants on-island, its chef Seth Raynor prepares innovative, contemporary cuisine. With brick and plaster arched walls, the main subterranean dining room is cozy. Upstairs there's a lively bar favored by locals and visitors alike; it's a real scene. A less expensive, lighter bistro menu is served here. But in good weather, the patio on Federal Street, surrounded by flowers and a white picket fence, is the place you'll want to be. An award-winning all-American wine list accompanies such dishes as grilled lobster tails with mashed potatoes and chive beurre blanc or pan-roasted salmon with Thai curry cream and crispy rice noodles. Reservations recommended. Entrées $23–32.

Company of the Cauldron (228-4016), 7 India Street. Open for dinner late May through October; closed Monday. Peer through ivy-covered, small-paned windows, and you'll see what looks like an intimate dinner party. With low-beamed ceilings and plaster walls illuminated by lanterns and wall sconces, it's a romantic place (made more so by the harpist who plays a few nights a week). The New American prix fixe menu changes nightly and is set a week in advance. It might go something like this: roasted red and yellow pepper soup; Nantucket greens; baked stuffed jumbo shrimp with Maine crabmeat, fava beans, orzo, and asparagus; and a "very chocolate" tart to top it off. Reservations requested. $44 per person. No credit cards.

21 Federal (228-2121), 21 Federal Street. Open for lunch Wednesday through Saturday and dinner nightly (closed Sunday in the off-season, January through March). *The* place to see and be seen since it burst onto the scene in 1985 (decor is elegant and reserved), loyal patrons return for sophisticated New and traditional American cuisine. Although the menu highlights seafood, you might also try spit-roasted chicken or a country grill dish served with a creamy potato and leek gratin. In good weather, lunch is served in the courtyard terrace. A convivial, dark-paneled bar opens at 4:30; there is also a lighter bistro menu. Reservations recommended. Lunch $10–14, dinner entrées $18–28.

India House Restaurant (228-9043), 37 India Street. Open for Sunday brunch and dinner April through December. The eclectic New American and Continental menu features dishes as varied as lobster-artichoke crêpes and Danish-style bouillabaisse, but it also has Asian influences, as seen in the 12-spice salmon sashimi. The restaurant's signature dishes are a pecan-and-cashew-glazed swordfish roasted on a cedar plank, and lamb rolled in bread crumbs, honey, and Dijon mustard served with a béarnaise sauce. Dine in one of the three romantic Colonial rooms with fireplaces and candlelight, or in the garden café behind the house. Brunch ($10) is very popular, but reservations are not accepted; reservations are recommended for dinner, however. Entrées $16–28.

❋ **Second Story** (228-3471), 1 South Beach Street. Open for dinner year-round, but call for off-season schedule. Practically unknown to non-islanders, this intimate restaurant is inconspicuously located over an antiques shop near the waterfront. Chef-owner David Toole (his wife, Barbara, is pastry chef and manager) changes his menu almost daily to keep his loyal clientele coming back—and that they do! The eclectic menu is influenced by southwestern, European, and Asian culinary traditions and features spicy, savory dishes for the adventurous. Reservations recommended; service is often politely referred to by locals as "relaxed." Entrées $19–30.

Straight Wharf Restaurant (228-4499), Harbor Square. Open for dinner nightly except Monday, June to late September; bar open until mid-October. The renowned seafood-only menu, served at two or three seatings, changes weekly. It is always extremely well prepared and elegantly presented. New American dishes might include grilled tuna with wasabe lime butter or poached halibut and scallops with sage shiitake beurre rouge. Desserts are decidedly rich. In addition to the patio and main dining room, a lofty space with exposed rafters, there is a pleasant bar featuring a less expensive grill menu. Reservations recommended. Entrées $28–33.

Club Car (228-1101), 1 Main Street. Open for lunch and dinner mid-May to early December; closed Tuesday and Wednesday in the off-season. Chef Michael Shannon has been preparing technically perfect, really fabulous Continental cuisine here since 1979. (He grows his herbs on the roof.) Feast on roasted California squab, Wisconsin veal, or Maryland soft-shell crabs. The elegant and somewhat haughty dining room is set with linen and silver; the lighting is subdued. Or have a simple lunch of soup and salad in the only remaining club car from the narrow-gauge train that used to run between Steamboat Wharf and 'Sconset. Lighter dishes are served in the bar/club car to the accompaniment of a nightly pianist. Reservations recommended. Entrées $28–37.

Le Languedoc Restaurant (228-2552), 24 Broad Street. Open for dinner in summer, lunch and dinner mid-May to mid-December. If you're intimidated by some of the restaurants in town, you should know that this is one of the friendlier places. The food is quite good, too. Specialties include soft-shell crabs provençale, steamed sea bass, and rack of lamb. Upstairs dining rooms are intimate, country-French style, while downstairs is less formal, more bistrolike; both are popular. (A lighter, less expensive menu is available downstairs.) The garden patio is a delightful option in warm weather. Jacket and reservations recommended for upstairs dining. Lunch $9.50–18, dinner entrées $18–26.

DeMarco (228-1836), 9 India Street. Open for dinner May through October; closed Tuesday. Delightfully light northern Italian haute cuisine is offered in this old restored sea captain's home. Downstairs has a taverny feel (which doesn't quite jibe with the cuisine) with wood, brick, and curtains, while upstairs is more airy with white walls. Start with an antipasto of risotto, foie gras, asparagus, and porcini mushrooms, followed by i secondi of fricassee of lobster, vegetables, and rock shrimp ravioli in a broth of lobster and saffron. Fresh pasta and grilled seafood are house specialties. Don DeMarco, who has owned his namesake restaurant since 1979, has put together an outstanding wine list. Children's menu. Reservations recommended. Entrées $20–30.

American Seasons (228-7111), 80 Centre Street. Open for dinner mid-April through December. With a nod to the four corners of the United States, you'll find dishes influenced by the Wild West (like trout with sweet corn and chili), Pacific Coast (angelhair pasta with artichokes and sun-dried tomatoes), Down South (BBQ duck with black-eyed peas, bacon, and yams), and New England (grilled salmon on a bed of arugula and apples). The dining room features folk art murals and tables painted with game boards, while the cuisine is artfully presented on oversized plates. Reservations recommended. Entrées $16.50–21.50.

Woodbox Inn Restaurant (228-0587), 29 Fair Street. Open for breakfast, Sunday brunch, and dinner, June to mid-October; closed Monday. This 1709 house has three intimate, candlelit dining rooms with low ceilings, dark wainscoting and paneling, and wide floorboards. (If the rear room feels and looks like a colonial kitchen, that's because it was.) Just off the beaten path, the Woodbox is known for its old-fashioned, classical Continental cuisine: beef Wellington, roast duck, and rack of lamb. Popovers, which accompany all entrées, are delicious, too. Chef Joseph

Keller has presided over the kitchen since 1990. If you can't get one of the two dinner seatings, come for an outstanding breakfast in order to enjoy the authentic atmosphere. Reservations highly recommended. Look for the wine-tasting dinners before mid-July and after Labor Day. Breakfast $9–10; dinner entrées $17–24. No credit cards.

Cioppino's (228-4622), 20 Broad Street. Open 11:30 AM–1 AM for lunch, Sunday brunch, and dinner, mid-May to mid-October. This newcomer opened in 1992 and serves Continental and New American cuisine like hazelnut-crusted salmon or twin fillet of beef topped with lobster and hollandaise. The dining room is lovely, but in good weather the garden patio is even more tempting. Cioppino's offers a "twilight dining" special and boasts a good wine list. Reservations recommended. Lunches $7–10, dinners $17–26, $34 prix fixe.

Ship's Inn Restaurant (228-0040), 13 Fair Street. Open for dinner June through October; closed Tuesday and Wednesday. Chef-owner Mark Gottwald serves California-French cuisine in a well-lighted, slightly subterranean space. Many of the dishes are healthful (that is, sans butter or cream) without sacrificing taste or creativity: grilled monkfish with polenta and lemon-thyme vinaigrette, for instance. Otherwise there's the ever-popular medallions of lobster with leeks and sauterne. Reservations recommended. Entrées $17–25.

West Creek Cafe (228-4943), 11 West Creek Road (between Pleasant and Orange Streets). Open for dinner year-round. A 10-minute bicycle ride from the center of town (near the bike path to 'Sconset), this charming and casual place is a real treat. It's a small space, decorated with a New American flair that complements the eclectic menu. There are three distinct dining rooms, one with a fireplace that brings patrons in throughout winter. Owner Pat Tyler, who has been on-island for years (at the Boarding House and Second Story), opened the café in 1995. Try the pan-seared tuna with roasted veggies and sour cream mashed potatoes. Reservations. Entrées $17–24.

☞ **Quaker House Restaurant** (228-9156), 5 Chestnut Street. Open for breakfast and dinner, mid-May to mid-October. The Quaker House is known for bountiful breakfasts and value-conscious, three-course regional American dinners. A typical meal might go something like this: clam chowder followed by beef tournedos (in a port jus over garlic mashed potatoes) or shrimp scampi, and topped off with chocolate mousse or fruit tarte. The owners have a commitment to healthful agricultural practices and will only purchase free-range chicken and nitrate-free bacon, for instance. The two modest dining rooms are countryish, with lacy curtains and candlelight. Dine before 6:30 and get an additional 15 percent off. Since there are only 11 tables, reservations are essential. Prix fixe dinners $20–26; breakfast $5.50–8.50.

The Galley Restaurant (228-9641), Jefferson Avenue, off Spring Street. Open for lunch and dinner, mid-June to early October. At the Cliffside

Beach Club beyond the center of town, you'll dine beachside, taking in the sunset views. But this isn't a sand-in-your-shoes kind of place—it's elegant, bistro-style, candlelit dining under an awning facing the Sound. The "world-influenced" menu features Nantucket mussels steamed in white wine; grilled swordfish marinated with basil and served with sweet pepper ragout; and grilled duck with pancetta and Swiss chard. Dinner entrées $29–34.

✐ **Ropewalk** (228-8886), 1 Straight Wharf. Open for lunch and dinner, mid-May to mid-October. Night or day, try to get an outdoor patio table at Nantucket's only harborside (yachtside might be more appropriate) restaurant. If you can't, don't worry; the interior is open to sea breezes. Although the casual ambience might suggest standard seafood fare, the cuisine is really quite innovative and the menu extensive. Ropewalk also has an excellent raw bar. Children's menu. No reservations taken. Lunch $5–11, dinner entrées $9–24.

✐ **The Regatta** (228-2500), Easton Street. Open for breakfast, lunch, and dinner, June through September. At White Elephant Hotel, the Regatta is perfect for a harborside luncheon. The main dining room serves contemporary American fare that's always very good but rarely overly creative. Specialties include shrimp and lobster cakes, coconut-encrusted halibut, and braised lamb shank. There is nightly entertainment (except Monday) in the lounge. Reservations recommended. Children's menu. Lunch $5–12, dinner entrées $19–29.

✐❋ **Jared's** (228-2400), 29 Broad Street at Centre Street. Open for breakfast year-round, dinner April through October. One of Nantucket's most elegant, traditional candlelit dining rooms, Jared's has salmon-colored walls, murals of Nantucket in the 1800s, heavy silver table settings, and linen cloths. The traditional American cuisine is well prepared and occasionally inspired. The all-you-can-eat seafood buffet ($25) is a bargain on Wednesday and Sunday evenings from May to mid-October. Children's menu. Jackets and reservations preferred. Entrées $18-32.

☞✐❋ **The Hearth** (228-1500), 7 South Beach Street, at the Harbor House hotel (see *Lodging—Resorts*). Open for breakfast, Sunday brunch, and dinner, year-round. The Hearth has a lot of things going for it. It offers a three-course "sunset dinner" for $16. Children under 13 dine free when accompanied by an adult. The Sunday brunch (with a raw bar, large dessert selection, and complimentary champagne) is renowned. As for the food, stick to traditionally prepared fare like chowder, chicken pot pie, fresh local shellfish, or New England boiled dinner. The large, barnlike lounge is dominated by a weather-vane chandelier, beams, a fireplace, and live entertainment, while the formal dining room has comfortable upholstered chairs. This is a cozy place to come in the off-season. Children's menu. Dinner entrées $14–25; brunch $20 for adults, $10 for children.

Around the island

The Chanticleer (257-6231), 9 New Street, 'Sconset. Open for lunch and dinner, mid-May to mid-October; closed Monday. The Chanticleer has won endless accolades since it opened in 1970: Nantucket's premier dining spot; one of the world's top 10 romantic places to dine; one of the finest wine lists in the world, with more than 1000 bottles in the cellar. Chef Jean-Charles Berruet's exquisite classical French cuisine is served in the courtyard of a rose-covered cottage, in small dining rooms overlooking the courtyard through small-paned windows, or in the more formal main dining room with low ceilings. Highlighting local fish, local produce, and game birds, a meal might go something like this: an assortment of smoked fish with a horseradish mousse, followed by sautéed Tuckernut lobster and Nantucket bay scallops served with summer truffles and Madeira wine sauce, garnished with a risotto. Dessert is equally sublime: fresh figs and raspberries poached in a sweet white wine with spices and herbs, served with a raspberry sauce. Dining here will live on in your memory for years. Reservations and jacket required. Lunch entrées $15–25; prix fixe dinner $65 ($25–35 à la carte).

Topper's (228-8768), 120 Wauwinet Road, Wauwinet. Open for lunch, Sunday brunch, and dinner, mid-May through October. "Luxurious," "sophisticated," and "relaxed" are words that come to mind when reflecting on a dining experience at Topper's. So are "worth every penny" and "lovely service." An outstanding French and California wine list complements the regional New American cuisine, which might include grilled arctic char with matchstick potatoes, lemon, and fried capers; or braised and grilled Long Island duckling. Save room for rich desserts, perfectly paired with an after-dinner cordial. A bar menu offers lighter fare. The lunch concept is decidedly different: Choose three, four, or five selections to create your own sampler plate. Tempting options may include sautéed tenderloin tips, smoked-seafood chowder, or grilled flatbread with salsa and cheddar cheese. Lunch can be served on the bayside porch, which is also a lovely spot for a sunset drink. Because of its remote location, Topper's offers complimentary van service from town, as well as transportation aboard the Wauwinet Lady, which takes guests from Straight Wharf to the restaurant's private dock (mid-June to mid-September). Reservations recommended, jacket requested at dinner. Lunch $19–23.50, dinner $26–34.

'Sconset Cafe (257-4008), Post Office Square at Main Street, 'Sconset. Open for breakfast, lunch, and dinner, mid-May to mid-September. Inexpensive and creative salads and sandwiches are featured at lunch, but dinner tends toward sophisticated New American dishes like local shellfish bouillabaisse with roasted saffron broth and focaccia. Chocolate volcano cake is a dessert specialty. No credit cards; BYOB; reservations accepted for 6 PM seating only. Lunch $4.50–8; dinner entrées $16–26.

The Summer House (257-9976), 17 Ocean Boulevard, 'Sconset. Open for lunch June through September; dinner mid-April to mid-October. The summery, comfortable dining room is filled with plants and flowers, white wicker and painted furniture, and paintings depicting idyllic Nantucket scenes. "New World" dishes might include fettuccine and poached lobster with a mustard, cognac, and tomato glaze or grilled sirloin with a roast tomato sauce and sautéed potato in phyllo. Gershwin and Porter piano melodies waft through the bar (where you can get a light menu) and lounge. Light lunches of grilled fish, salads, and sandwiches are served poolside. Lunch $9–19, dinner entrées $25–35.

EATING OUT

In town

☞✐✳ **Arno's** (228-7001), 41 Main Street. Open for breakfast, lunch, Sunday brunch, and dinner year-round. This two-story storefront eatery is atmospheric, with hurricane lamps on the tables, high ceilings, and large canvas artwork on brick walls. Although it's been around since the early 1960s, Arno's has gained a following recently. Bountiful breakfasts feature frittatas, "bananza" pancakes, and eggs Benedict. Moderately priced lunch and dinner fare includes sandwiches, Thai peanut noodles, lobster bisque, fish-and-chips, and a few vegetarian dishes. Children's menu; takeout. Lunch $6–12; dinner $13–19.

☞ **Black Eyed Susans** (228-3459), 10 India Street. Open daily for breakfast, daily except Thursday for dinner, April through October. New in 1993, this small, pine-paneled place is part bistro, part diner. The downscale decor, with captain's chairs and a counter, belies the stylishly presented plates. One of the nicest elements at Susans is that you can mix and match selected half-orders. Or try full entrées such as sourdough-crusted cod on a bed of roasted vegetables. Breakfasts run the gamut from bagels and grits to Pennsylvania Dutch pancakes or a veggie scramble with pesto (made with eggs or tofu). Breakfast averages $8, dinner entrées $13–18. No credit cards; BYOB.

✳ **Sea Grille** (325-5700), 45 Sparks Avenue. Open for lunch and dinner year-round. Located on the edge of town, this attractive restaurant is often overlooked by nonlocals. Seafood and fish are prepared practically every way: grilled, blackened, steamed, fried. Light meals at the bar are a good alternative; there is also outside seating. For those in your party who may be tired of seafood, chef-owners E.J. and Robin Harvey also offer a few pasta, steak, and lamb dishes. Lunch $8–15, dinner $16–35.

Café on Old South Wharf (228-2212), 15 Old South Wharf. Open for breakfast and lunch, late May to mid-October; open for dinner late May to mid-September. Located on a quaint, crushed-seashell lane lined with art galleries, this eatery is known for its wood-fired grill, New American cuisine, and outdoor seating. For breakfast try a blue corn tortilla with red chile and eggs or spiced sweet bread French toast. Lunchtime bistro fare might include a smoked salmon and watercress salad or a fancy "short stack club" sandwich with crisp bacon and balsamic tomatoes. Dinner is more elaborate and equally creative. Reservations for the first seating only. Breakfast and lunch $5–9.25, dinner $18–25.

☞✳ **Brotherhood of Thieves,** 23 Broad Street. Open for lunch and dinner year-round. The 1840s former whaling tavern feels like an English pub; it's

These identical Georgian mansions, the "Three Bricks," were built side by side in 1836 for three sons of a whaling magnate.

dark, with brick walls, beamed ceilings, and no windows. It's a convivial place—helped along by an extensive coffee and drink menu—frequented by locals who chow down on chowder, burgers, shoestring fries (long and curly), and sandwiches. Open until late at night, there is live folk music on most nights in-season; otherwise the music is limited to weekends. No credit cards; no reservations; expect a long line in summer. Dishes $7–13.

☞✐❋ **Espresso Cafe** (228-6930), 40 Main Street. Open 7:30–5:30 daily, year-round, until 11 PM in summer. This spacious European-style café with small marble tables is a popular meeting place—everyone ends up here sooner or later. (Do yourself a favor and make it sooner.) Come early for a bracing morning cappuccino (the best in town) and a breakfast pastry. Come back for black bean chili, hearty soups, quiche, and vegetarian dishes. Or come for a rich dessert any time of day. Linger as long as you like in the large garden patio out back. Takeout, too. Dishes $4–8. The shop at 117 Orange Street, **Fast Forward,** is open for takeout only.

☞ **Off Centre Cafe** (228-8470), 29 Centre Street. Open for breakfast mid-April to mid-December, lunch in the off-season, and dinner June to mid-September. There are only a few tables inside this artsy space, but that's fine since most people prefer to people-watch and eat on the sidewalk patio. Many think this café has the island's best breakfast; I'd have to agree. Among the offerings are homefries loaded with veggies, fresh fruit pancakes, breakfast burritos, or huevos rancheros with black beans and corn bread. Liz Holland's dinner menu is internationally influenced: Vietnamese spring rolls, warm chèvre salad with jalapeño cucumbers, fresh cod in parchment paper. There are always a couple of pasta and seafood specials nightly. Reservations at the first dinner seating only. Breakfast $4.75–7.25, dinner $13–17.25. No credit cards.

☞ **Moona** (325-4301), 122 Pleasant Street. Open for dinner year-round. Long-time island restaurateurs Everett and Linda Reid opened Moona in 1995 with the intent that it provide moderate alternatives to skyrocketing island dining prices. The New American dishes roam the four corners of the country, and are organized according to fishing, farming, hunting, and grazing. Particularly popular dishes include lamb shanks and pan-roasted sea scallops. It's quite comfortable, designed in the style of an 18th-century home. Although it's on the edge of town, the shuttle stops a few doors from Moona. Takeout, too. Dishes $10.75–17.50.

☞⊘✳ **Tap Room** (228-2400), 29 Broad Street at Centre Street, in the basement of the Jared Coffin House (see *Inns*). Open for lunch and dinner, year-round. This casual gathering spot has a cozy, publike atmosphere with dark paneling, a fireplace, and beamed ceilings. It's best enjoyed with a group of people, as many of the tables for two are quite close together. The Tap Room serves traditional New England fare like prime rib, fried clams, and baked sea scallops. You can also do some between-meal grazing on fried mozzarella sticks or chicken teriyaki skewers. (The garden patio ringed with flower boxes is lovely in warm weather.) Children's menu. Lunch $5.25–10; dinner $14.25–18.75.

☞ **Vincent's Restaurant** (228-0189), 21 South Water Street. Open for all three meals, mid-April to mid-December. Chianti wine bottles hang from the ceiling of this traditional, casual Italian-American restaurant, with classic red-and-white-checked tablecloths. Moderately priced, it's a great choice for families, with plain and fancy pasta dishes, grilled seafood, and pizza. Children's menu; takeout. Breakfast $6–10; lunch specials $7–12; dinner entrées $10–18. No credit cards.

☞⊘✳ **Atlantic Cafe** (228-0570), 15 South Water Street. Open for lunch and dinner year-round. This casual place gets boisterous later in the evening (there's a full bar), but before that, families enjoy the relaxing atmosphere, large portions, and good prices. You can munch on nachos, zucchini sticks, and wings, or go for clam chowder (many say the island's best), burgers, sandwiches, and fish. Children's menu $4. Dishes $5–18.

☞⊘ **Rose & Crown** (228-2595), 23 South Water Street. Open for lunch and dinner until late at night, mid-April to mid-December. This hopping place with live entertainment serves American fare like sandwiches, pastas, chicken wings, and seafood in a traditional pub atmosphere. Formerly a carriage livery, the large, barnlike room is decorated with signs from old Nantucket businesses. Early specials, children's menu, and kids can draw on the paper-covered tabletops, too. Lunch $5–10, dinner $9–18.

Lobster Trap (228-4041), 23 Washington Street, across from the electric plant. Open for dinner mid-April to mid-October. If you've got a hankering for lobster, plain and simple, head to this casual eatery with barn-board walls and booths. (I only recommend the lobster here.) Early specials at 5:30. The restaurant also delivers clambakes and cooked lobsters to your guest house garden or cottage (call between 3 and 6.)

☞ **Patio J** (228-0363), 12 Nobadeer Farm Road. Open for lunch and dinner mid-May to mid-October. New in 1996 from the owners of Black Eyed Susans, Patio J serves inexpensive Mexican and Latin American dishes like burritos, empanadas, chili rellenos, handmade tamales, and tortas with grilled fish, chicken, or steak. Enjoy your meal under an awning in a garden setting or get takeout on the way to the beach. Play a game of mini-golf (next door) on the way home. Dishes $2.75–12.50.

✐ **The Tavern** (228-1266), Straight Wharf at Harbor Square. Open for lunch and dinner until late at night, late May to mid-October. On the edge of the marina, the outdoor tables are well positioned for people-watching, and the American food is above average. If you want a Caesar salad, a plate of fried calamari, or a drink before hopping on the ferry, this place fits the bill, too. Children's menu. Lunch $7–10, dinner $7–19.

☞✐**Chin's Restaurant** (228-0200), Chin's Way, off Lower Pleasant Street, near the rotary heading toward 'Sconset. Open for lunch and dinner, March through December. Chin Manasmontri has created wonderful Thai and classic Chinese dishes here since the late 1970s. You can't go wrong with anything from chicken satay to moo goo gai pan. Takeout, too. Dinner dishes $10–15.

Sushi by Yoshi (228-1801), 2 East Chestnut Street. Open 11:30 AM–10 PM daily, mid-April to mid-December. Opened in 1994, this small place serves fresh sushi and sashimi, Tekkamaki rolls with Nantucket tuna, smoked Japanese creations, dumplings, and miso soup. Sushi $5–6; nori rolls $6–11; dinners $13.50–19.

Around the island

☞✐❋ **Hutch's** (228-5550), Nantucket Memorial Airport. Open 6 AM–8 or 9 PM daily year-round. Counter, table, and take-out service is available at this better-than-serviceable place. Children's menu. Breakfast and lunch $2–8; dinner dishes run $6–11.

The Westender (228-5100), 326 Madaket Road, Madaket. Open for lunch and dinner late May to mid-October. Conveniently located at the end of the bike path, you have three options at the Westender. Head to the general store, purveyors of roasted chicken, sandwiches, and pasta salads. Head to the basement bar (the drink of note is the Madaket Mystery rum drink) and a light café menu. Or head upstairs for fine dining. Of course, the restaurant is popular at sunset, when the place glows. Café and lunch $7–10; dinner $19–29.

See also Carried Away under *Getting Around.*

LIGHT FARE

In town

❋ **Provisions** (228-3258), Straight Wharf at Harbor Square. Open 8–6 in summer, 9–4 the rest of the year. Excellent sandwiches (including one with mildly smoked turkey, stuffing, and cranberries), hearty chowders and soups, and pizza. An island institution, since 1978. Hot and cold vegetarian dishes, too.

Something Natural (228-0504), 50 Cliff Road. Open for breakfast, lunch, and dinner, mid-April to mid-October. As you head out of town toward Madaket, stop here for perhaps the island's best breads and sandwiches (big enough for two to share), as well as salads and other healthful foods.

Chanticleer-To-Go (325-5625), 15 South Beach Street. Open mid-May to mid-October. Brioches and croissants for the morning; rotisserie chicken, country paté, and sandwiches in the $6–8 range for fancy picnic fixings to take to the beach. They also have a good selection of wine. There are a few indoor tables.

Foood for Here and There (228-4291), 149 Lower Orange Street. Open for lunch and dinner April through October. Mark Arnold has offered great value in casual surroundings since 1979. On the way to 'Sconset and Surfside Beach, Foood offers sandwiches made with fresh rolls, specialty pizzas, quiches, and salads. After 5 PM delivery within a 2-mile radius of the shop is available. As the name implies, eat in or take out.

Downy Flake (228-3127), 6 Harbor View Way. Open 7–2 or 2:30 daily, mid-May to mid-September. On Children's Beach, this one-room beachfront place has been a favorite since the mid-1960s. Order coffee and the famous doughnuts (the pancakes are almost as famous) while the kids run and play on the small, protected beach. Light lunches, too; $2–7. The newer location at 18 Sparks Avenue (228-4533) is open year-round.

The Juice Bar (228-5799), 12 Broad Street, one block from the Steamship. Open mid-April to late October. Once you find this place, you'll probably stop in a few times before catching your ferry home. Yes, they offer fresh juices like carrot, lemonade, and orange, but they also make their own lowfat ice cream and nonfat yogurts, watermelon creams, and breakfast baked goods. In fact, they make everything from scratch.

Nantucket Bake Shop (228-2797), 79 Orange Street. Open daily except Sunday, April through December. Its advertisement claims more than 100 different items baked daily, including Portuguese breads, desserts, muffins, croissants, quiches, cakes, and pastries. You can take Jay and Magee Detmer's word for it; they've baked the goodies since 1976.

Steamboat Pizza (228-1131), Steamboat Wharf. Open May through October. Pizza by the slice when you're running for the boat.

Dave's Soda Fountain (228-0020), inside Congdon's Pharmacy at 47 Main Street, and **Nantucket Pharmacy** (228-0180) next door at 45 Main Street. Both open year-round. These old-fashioned drugstore soda fountains, complete with swivel stools at Formica counters, offer inexpensive soups, sandwiches (PB&J, tuna salad), ice cream, sodas, and coffee.

Light Generation Market (228-4554), 95 Washington Street Extension. Open year-round. A natural grocer with a juice bar.

See also Espresso Cafe under *Eating Out.*

Around the island

Claudette's (257-6622), Post Office Square at Main Street, 'Sconset. Open 9–4 daily, mid-May to mid-October. Box lunches, clambakes to go, and lemon cake are the raison d'être. There are a few indoor tables, but most people take their sandwiches to the beach or their ice cream to a bistro table on the front deck.

INTERNET CAFE

InterNet Cafe (228-6777, http://www.nantucket.net), 2 Union Street. Open year-round. If you can't leave the modern world behind, if you want to send or receive e-mail, if you need to check in with the office (or the world, for that matter), this upstairs café with eight computers is the place. $10 per hour for computer use.

ENTERTAINMENT

The **Nantucket Arts Alliance** sponsors many events across a spectrum of artistic media. The weekly Nantucket Map & Legend, which bills itself as an events and arts paper, has complete listings, but the island's other free weekly, Yesterday's Island, http://www.yesterdaysisland.com, is also useful. The island's "regular" newspapers, *The Inquirer* and *Mirror* (published on Thursdays since 1821) and *The Nantucket Beacon* (published on Wednesdays), also have current listings.

Box Office Nantucket (228-8118), Thomas Macy Warehouse, Straight Wharf. Open 10–4 daily, mid-June to early September. Advance and same-day ticket purchase for island events and performances.

MUSIC

Band concerts (228-1700) are held at a new bandstand at Children's Beach on Thursday and Sunday evenings at 6:15 in July and August.

Noonday concerts (228-5466), 11 Orange Street at the Unitarian Universalist Church, are held on Thursdays in July and August. Concerts feature ensembles, soloists, and an 1831 Goodrich pipe organ. Free.

Nantucket Musical Arts Society (228-1287), 62 Centre Street at the First Congregational Church, sponsors concerts with world-renowned musicians on Tuesday evenings at 8:30 in July and August. On the night before the concert, there is a "meet-the-artist" event hosted at various locations. Ticket prices vary.

THEATER/FILMS

Actors Theatre of Nantucket (228-6325), Centre and Main Streets at the Methodist church, has staged comedies and plays from late May to mid-October since 1985.

Theatre Workshop of Nantucket (228-4305), Bennett Hall, 62 Centre Street. In existence since 1956, this year-round, community-based group stages a variety of plays and musicals.

Nantucket Filmworks (228-3783), Centre and Main Streets at the Methodist church, produces island photographer Cary Hazlegrove's "On Island:

Nantucket's Main Street is paved with cobblestones brought over as ballast in ships.

The Small Town Life on Nantucket." Each year the show is produced with different images culled from her extensive collection. The program is shown Monday through Saturday at 7 and 8 PM, mid-June to mid-September. Adults $4.50, children $2.50.

Dreamland Theatre (228-5356), 19 South Water Street, which shows first-run movies (June through September), looks like an old warehouse from the outside. This building began as a Quaker meetinghouse, was converted to the Atlantic Straw Company, and was moved to Brant Point to serve as part of a hotel before it was floated back across the harbor in 1905 on a barge. On rainy days they sometimes have matinees.

Gaslight Theatre (228-4435), 1 North Union Street, shows art films and is connected with the **White Dog Cafe,** where you can have a drink before or after the program. The theater is open seasonally. Call about rainy-day matinees.

Siasconset Casino (257-6661), New Street, 'Sconset, shows first-run movies in July and August.

NIGHTLIFE

See The Hearth (live music and dancing), The Regatta (live piano), and The Summer House (live piano in 'Sconset) under *Dining Out;* see Brotherhood of Thieves (live folk), Tap Room (live piano or guitar), and Rose & Crown (dancing or live bands) under *Eating Out.*

SELECTIVE SHOPPING

The principal shopping district is bordered by Main, Broad, and Centre Streets. About 90 percent of the shops stay open year-round, although many are open only on weekends in winter. A dense cluster of shops is located at Old South Wharf, lined with small galleries, clothing stores, artisans, and a marine chandlery. Straight Wharf shops cater more toward the middle-brow tourist market. Look for the free brochures: "Nantucket Guide to Antique Shops" and the "Guideline to Buying a Nantucket Lightship Basket." Nantucket Arts, a glossy annual with paid advertisements, is useful in that it profiles artists, artisans, and craftspeople. You can find it in galleries and studios. Below is just a sampling to get you started.

ANTIQUES

There are more than 25 antiques shops on the island. In July and August, three large annual antiques shows benefit the Nantucket Historical Association and the Nantucket schools.

Rafael Osona (228-3942), 21 Washington Street at the American Legion Hall, holds auctions from late May to early December. Osona auctions 18th-, 19th-, and 20th-century antiques from England, the Continent, and the United States.

Tonkin of Nantucket (228-9697), 33 Main Street. Open mid-March to mid-February. Purveyors of English and French antiques (both country and formal), brass and silver items, and marine objects.

Nina Hellman Antiques (228-4677), 48 Centre Street. Open April through December and by appointment in the off-season. Offers nautical items, scrimshaw, folk art, and Nantucket memorabilia.

Antiques Depot (228-1287), 14 Easy Street. Open late April to mid-December. An interesting collection of furniture and fine decorative arts.

Forager House Collection (228-5977), 20 Centre Street. Open year-round. Carries folk art, botanical prints, and whirligigs.

ART GALLERIES

Web Site: http://www.ArtsNetNantucket.org. This web site has pages devoted to independent artists, galleries, a calendar of exhibits, and an interdisciplinary journal on the arts.

Main Street Gallery (228-2252), 2 South Water Street. Open year-round. Carries serious traditional and contemporary art.

(X) Gallery (325-4858), 12 Orange Street. Open mid-May to mid-October and by appointment. Displays more unusual and imaginative art.

Artists Association Little Gallery (228-0294), Straight Wharf. Open May to mid-October. This cooperative of 200 artists was founded in 1945 to showcase juried members' work. At press time the gallery expected to be moving to 19 Washington Street.

William Welch Gallery (228-0687), 14 Easy Street. Open late April to late December. Displays the artist's renderings of idyllic island scenes in watercolors, pastels, and oils.

Sailor's Valentine Gallery (228-2011), Lower Main Street at the Thomas Macy Warehouse. Open mid-April to mid-December. Carries folk art and, as the name suggests, beautiful valentines made by sailors.

BOOKSTORES

Mitchell's Book Corner (228-1080), 54 Main Street. Open year-round. Carries a great selection of maritime, whaling, and naturalist books. There's also a quiet corner, dubbed the Nantucket Room, where you can sit and browse through titles that cover all things Nantucket.

Nantucket Bookworks (228-4000), 25 Broad Street. Open daily, year-round. Selective travel, literature, children's books, and biographies.

CRAFTS SHOPS

Four Winds Craft Guild (228-9623), 6 Straight Wharf. Open year-round. Carries baskets, lightship purses, scrimshaw, and marine items.

The Spectrum (228-4606), 26 Main Street. Open April through December. Offers distinctive contemporary objects made from a wide spectrum of materials.

Nantucket Looms (228-1908), 16 Main Street. Open year-round. Features weavers at work on their looms and their creations.

Erica Wilson Needle Works (228-9881), 25 Main Street. Open mid-April through December. Features the designs of its namesake, an islander since 1958. Wilson also has a boutique in Manhattan and has penned many a title on needlepoint.

Claire Murray (228-1913), 11 South Water Street. Open year-round. Claire Murray came to Nantucket in the late 1970s as an innkeeper and began hooking rugs during the long winter months. She's long given up the B&B business to concentrate on designing and opening more stores; her staff make the rugs now. She sells finished pieces as well as kits.

FARM PRODUCE

Main Street. Local produce is sold from the backs of trucks daily except Sunday, May through October.

Bartlett's Ocean View Farm & Greenhouse (228-9403), off Hummock Pond Road. Open year-round. Bartlett's boasts a 100-acre spread run by an eighth-generation islander family; pick-your-own strawberries in June.

SPECIAL SHOPS

There are perhaps 20 stores and studios that sell the famed lightship baskets, which, since they go for hundreds to thousands of dollars, have become quite a status symbol! It is thought that the first baskets were made in the 1820s, but they didn't get their name until a bit later. When the first lightship was anchored off the coast of Nantucket to aid navigation around the treacherous shallow shoals, crew members were stationed on board for months at a time. In their spare time they would spend hours weaving these rattan baskets with wooden bottoms. Among the shops that make them and take custom orders: **Michael Kane Lightship Baskets** (228-1548), 18A Sparks Avenue; **Bill and Judy Sayles** (228-9876), 112 Washington Street Extension; and **The Lightship Shop** (228-4164), Miacomet Avenue.

The Hub (228-3868), 31 Main Street. Open daily, year-round. Carries newspapers and magazines from all over. Lines form on summer Sunday mornings for *The New York Times*.

The Toy Boat (228-4552), Straight Wharf. Open year-round. This old-fashioned children's toy store sells things like a wooden ferryboat and dock system, rocking boats as cradles, handmade toys and puzzles, marbles, and great children's books.

Stephen Swift (228-0255), 34 Main Street. Open daily April through October and weekends the rest of the year. Beautifully handcrafted chairs, benches, beds, and dressers, among other furnishings.

The Fragrance Bar (325-4740), 5 Centre Street. Open year-round. This shop, a treat for the senses, deals in essential oils and perfumes and looks like an old apothecary.

Nantucket Kiteman (228-7089), 7 Cambridge Street. Open April to late December. Although the "kite man" sells kites, you can also rent them in summer.

Museum Shop (228-5785), Broad Street next to the Whaling Museum (see *To See*). Open mid-April to mid-December. This classy stop sells island books, spermaceti candles, toys, and reproduction furniture; all items are somehow island-related.

Goldsmith Diana Kim England (228-3766), 56 Main Street. Open year-round. Elegant and unusual designs and gold lightship baskets.

The Golden Basket (228-4344), 44 Main Street. Open year-round. Sells miniature gold versions of the renowned rattan lightship baskets.

Murray's Toggery Shop (228-0437, 1-800-368-2134), 62 Main Street. Open year-round. This shop "invented" and practically owns the rights to Nantucket Reds, all-cotton pants that fade to pink after numerous washings—almost as "Nantucket" as lightship baskets. This is the only shop (which, by the way, is featured in *The Preppy Handbook*) that sells them and has since 1920.

Zero Main (228-4401), 0 Main Street. Open year-round, ostensibly. This is a women's store for classic as well as contemporary clothes and shoes.

The Camera Shop (228-0101), 32 Main Street. Open year-round. Film and same-day processing.

SPECIAL EVENTS

Late April: **Daffodil Festival** (228-1700). In 1974 an islander donated more than a million daffodil bulbs to be spread along the island's main roads. It is estimated that after years of naturalization there are now over 3 million bulbs. The official kickoff weekend to celebrate spring includes a vintage-car parade to 'Sconset, a tailgate picnic in 'Sconset, house tours, and a garden-club show. This is a very popular weekend.

Late May: **Figawi Boat Race** (778-1691), from Nantucket to Hyannis; since 1972.

Mid-June: **Harborfest** (228-0925). These festivities, which kick off the summer season, include a chowder festival, Blessing of the Fleet, kids' pirate and mermaid parade, and kayak clinics.

July: **Independence Day** (228-1135). Festivities include fireworks from Jetties Beach. Main Street is closed off for pie- and watermelon-eating contests, parades, face painting, and more.

Mid-July: **The Homestead Fair** (228-1700), 115 Main Street, since 1931.

Early August: **Billfish Tournament** (228-2299), Straight Wharf, since 1969.

Mid-August: **Nantucket Garden Club House Tour** (228-0452), since 1955. **Sandcastle and Sculpture Day** (228-1700), on Jetties Beach since 1974.

Mid-September: **County Fair,** at the Tom Nevers Recreation Area.

Mid-October: **Cranberry Harvest Weekend** (228-1700), at the Milestone Bog. Includes bog tours, demonstrations and displays, a food festival, an inn tour, and all sorts of crafts celebrating the tart little red berry (more than 900 tons of which are harvested on-island). A very popular event; make lodging reservations early.

Late November: **Nantucket Noel** (228-1700), starts on the day after Thanksgiving and runs through December. Live Christmas trees, which have been decorated by island schoolchildren, line Main Street.

December: **Christmas Stroll** (228-1700). On the first Saturday of December; since 1973. The stroll is a very popular event, with vintage-costumed carolers, festive store-window decorations, wreath exhibits, open houses, and a historic house tour.

General Index

Lodging Index